ULTIMATE
SUPERFOODS

A Complete Guide to Cooking with Kale, Coconut, Chia, and Super Seeds

STEPHANIE PEDERSEN • WAYNE COATES, PHD • KIM LUTZ

STERLING
New York

STERLING
New York

An Imprint of Sterling Publishing
1166 Avenue of the Americas
New York, NY 10036

Ultimate Superfoods published in 2015

This material originally published as
Kale © 2013 by Stephanie Pedersen
Coconut © 2015 by Stephanie Pedersen
Chia © 2012 by Wayne Coates, PhD
Super Seeds © 2014 by Kim Lutz

Color photography by Bill Milne, © Sterling Publishing, Inc.;
Monochromatic photography by Getty Images, © Ian O'Leary: 527, © Maximillian
Stock Ltd: 553; © Corbis: 312; © Grafe & Unzer Verlag/Stockfood: 510; Additional
monochromatic photography by Shutterstock, iStock, and Wikimedia Commons

ISBN 978-1-4549-1805-9

For information about custom editions, special sales, and premium and corporate purchases,
please contact Sterling Special Sales at 800-805-5489 or specialsales@sterlingpublishing.com.

This special edition was created exclusively for BTMS.

Manufactured in China

2 4 6 8 10 9 7 5 3 1

www.sterlingpublishing.com

CONTENTS

KALE

STEPHANIE PEDERSEN, MS, CHHC

CONTENTS

I came late to kale. My Danish cousins ate it in Aunt Jensen's grønkålssuppe. My friends from Scotland and Wales and Ireland and Sweden and Germany and Poland and Russia grew up eating it. Thousands of generations of European peasants, soldiers, artisans, royalty, merchants, men, women, and children were nourished by it.

But me? I was an adult before I even laid eyes on the leafy stuff. That may be because I spent my early years in Australia and California, surrounded by non-leafy vegetables. Or, it could be that, like many children of the 1970s and '80s, the only vegetables I ate came from a can and were usually green beans, peas, peas 'n carrots, tomato sauce, or beetroots, with the occasional fresh cob of corn or head of iceberg lettuce.

My first hands-on experience with kale came when I was in my 20s and working in New York City as a kitchen assistant at the Natural Gourmet Institute, the renowned whole foods cooking school where revolutionary natural foods chefs such as Peter Brearley, Myra Kornfield, Elliot Praag, and Dianne Carlson taught.

Kitchen assistants are the people who help cooking instructors get ready for a class by prepping the ingredients and doing the backstage work during a cooking class. That particular day, a note was waiting for me and two others: "Wash and dry all bunches of kale." Despite a childhood spent tending my parents' berry patch and fruit trees, I couldn't identify which of the gorgeous leafy bundles in front of me was kale.

I turned to another assistant, who shrugged. The third assistant, also unsure, shook his head. Finally, the chef wandered in, saw our confusion, and gave us a quick lesson in kale. The dark, nubbly leaves were Lacinto kale from northern Italy. The tightly ruffled leaves were everyday curly kale. The kale with the magenta rib, was red kale.

Over the course of the next four hours, the three of us eagerly learned how to clean kale, prep it, cook it, and use it. We learned it was one of the most nutrient-dense veggies around and that it was just as good in soups as it was sautéed in coconut or olive oil.

We also learned the subtle differences of the different types. That it tasted sweeter after a frost. That it grew in the Northern Hemisphere.

That it was an ancient member of the cabbage family, more ancient than cabbage itself and the vegetable most other brassica family offispring (such as broccoli and kohlrabi) had descended from. That hippos in the Washington, D.C. zoo ate more than 10 pounds of kale each per day. That the Irish made something called colcannon out of it.

Wanting to get every drop of wisdom we could on this new-to-us veggie, we assigned one of us to take frantic notes while the other two of us worked the kitchen.

After that class, I headed for the farmer's market to stock up, then to the library to check out every cookbook I could find that contained kale recipes. I tried a different kale recipe nearly every day, all the while thanking my luck for having a husband who likes kale! After two months, I got bored. Attempting to shake things up, I began writing some of my own kale recipes.

I adored the way this mighty brassica tasted—bitter and smoky, pungent and slightly sour. Deeply earthy and nourishing. I loved its meaty texture. I was in awe of the omega-3 fatty acids, fiber, phytonutrients, vitamins, minerals, and all of the other good things this leafy green contains. The vegetable felt substantial and fortifying.

What all this experimentation showed me is that kale is gloriously versatile. I began using kale as the basis of vegan, vegetarian, and non-vegetarian main dishes. I started to garnish with kale. I use it today as a salad, as a side veggie, as a snack, and in drinks and soups and sauces. I have even been known to use it in a floral arrangement, as a centerpiece, and as packing material (the curly leaf is best for this!).

Along the way, I learned a few wonderful things firsthand:

• Kale can make your skin look phenomenal, due to its high content of skin-beautifying omega-3 fatty acids, antioxidants, and vitamins A, C, and E. I was no longer experiencing monthly breakouts, my crow's feet softened, and some of the sunspots on my face faded or disappeared.
• Kale provides a sustained energy and increased physical stamina, due to the omega-3 fatty acids.

- Kale helps joints feel better and promotes faster healing between sessions of heavy exercise, thanks to vitamin K, omega-3 fatty acids, and an outstanding number of anti-inflammatory flavonoids. For me, this meant I could go running four days a week without pain.
- Kale's generous fiber content fills the tummy, which left me feeling so satisfied I wasn't interested in after-meal snacking.
- The high beta-carotene content has been linked with improved eyesight. My own fuzzy low-light sight improved after two weeks of eating kale on a daily basis.
- Improved immune system function. Before adding kale to my diet, I caught one cold every four to six weeks. After eating a serving of kale each day, I caught two colds during an entire year. The veggie's antioxidant content is the reason.
- While I don't have personal experience with the following conditions, my kale research uncovered mountains of studies on kale's numerous nutrients and how they help prevent and heal heart conditions, high cholesterol, cancer, and diseases of the gall bladder and liver.

And, perhaps most important to my personal life, kale also helps your body powerfully and quickly get rid of toxins and old wastes.

Pregnant during the 9/11 World Trade Center attacks, I was exposed to a massive amount of toxins. I passed these on to my son, who was born with off-the-charts levels of heavy metal poisoning.

It took me a few years to learn that heavy metal poisoning was behind my child's perplexing symptoms (a complex mix of skin, digestive, sensory, sleep, and mood disorders). Once I got to the bottom of his health crisis, I began working hard to rebuild his immune system and naturally and gently detox his small body. Kale puree was one of our mainstays. I hid it in smoothies and marinara sauce. I made green eggs and mashed potatoes. I minced kale leaves into soup and meatballs and pots of brown rice, millet, and quinoa.

I increased my own kale intake to help rid myself of the metals I'd acquired while pregnant. Today, we're both clean and healthy, in large part due to this ancient food's super healing abilities.

Kale is indeed a "superfood," and a popular one at that. While it hasn't yet surpassed potatoes as America's favorite vegetable, you can check out any raw food blog, vegan restaurant, vegetarian magazine, or alternative health Web site and find "unofficial proof" that kale is the darling of the health set.

I have my own unofficial proof that kale is the health world's most popular vegetable: At one point in my career I worked as a writer for the Institute of Integrative Nutrition in New York City. One of my duties was to compose alumni bios for the school's Web site. I would send each IIN graduate a questionnaire, read through their answers, edit them, and post the answers online for other people to see. When asked "What is your favorite health food?", 195 out of about 200 people said "kale."

Just to make my proof a little more official: I began quizzing my nutritionist and natural chef friends. My alternative healer friends. My acupuncturist, massage therapist, chiropractor, Reiki healer, and several personal trainers. Yoginis. Raw foodists. Feng shui masters. Vitamin supplement peddlers. People standing behind me in the Whole Foods' checkout line.

Every single one of them had the same favorite vegetable: Kale.

I suppose I could have found more people to ask, but the above was enough for me. In my opinion, kale is the country's favorite superfood. For so many reasons.

Keep reading to learn what these reasons are!

Love and kale chips to you all,
Stephanie Pedersen, MS, CHHC AADP
Holistic Nutritionist

CHAPTER 1

GETTING FRIENDLY WITH KALE

Hello kale lovers! I am so excited to share my favorite veggie with like-minded foodies. And welcome, also, to you healthy folks who have heard that kale is a great way to uplevel your health. And lastly, friendly greetings to those of you out there who cannot stand kale, but are here because you love someone who loves kale, or your doctor or nutritionist told you that you need to be eating more green veggies, or you want to make sure your family gets the greens they need to be their best.

Kale comes in several colors, sizes, and leaf styles, including the popular curly (also known as ruffled or frilled); the shiny, smooth leaves (such as Lacinto kale); and the red-hued, lobed leaves (such as red Russian kale). By all means experiment with the different types. You may be like me and love all varieties equally. Or, you may find you prize one type above the rest. All have near-identical nutritional profiles and that green, earthy taste you expect from kale. All can be used interchangeably in kale recipes. And all should be chosen and stored following the same guidelines.

For those of you who prefer tender, mild-tasting kale, opt for bunches with smaller-sized leaves, which are younger and less fibrous than their larger, more mature siblings. Note that although kale is now available throughout the year, the sweetest, mildest greens are available during the plant's peak, which is from winter through the beginning of spring.

KALE'S ILLUSTRIOUS HISTORY

Wild kale was first found growing in cool, sandy soil in the Eastern Mediterranean (though some researchers say Asia Minor was kale's first home). Early kale was a scraggly, leggy plant. As humans became aware of its deliciousness and its ability to create and maintain health, they began seeking the plant out, gathering its seeds and planting their own stash of kale. They also began trading the seeds with people of other regions and carrying the plant through other lands in the rations of soldiers and explorers, spreading the plant up into Europe and the British Isles, over to Russia, and even across the sea to North America.

Regardless of the size of leaves or varieties you choose, however, one of the best, most foolproof ways to be sure your loved ones (you included!) eat their weekly servings of kale is to start with the best quality kale you can. The first step in doing that is to "eat fresh."

Curly leaves or smooth leaves, green leaves or red leaves, whether you're in the supermarket or farmer's market, look for kale with spry, bouncy leaves. Yes, I did just say "spry." I know it sounds strange, but you'll know what I mean when you see a bunch of kale. Avoid kale with any slimy spots, a yellow tinge (or bright yellowing of the leaves), or greens with dried-out stem ends. Further, you do not want wilted or dehydrated or shriveled-looking kale. Here's why:

Kale and other veggies wilt when they lose moisture. For those science aficionados out there, this happens because as moisture evaporates from the veggie, its cell walls lose rigidity. The vegetables become soft and flexible. As unappetizing as a wilted veggie is, there is an even bigger issue at hand: As moisture leaves the plant, it takes nutrients with it. Moisture loss not only reduces vitamin C and A levels, it also contributes to yellowing and bitterness. This means that the more flabby and dehydrated a kale leaf is, the less nutrients and taste it contains. And that's a problem.

KALE THEN AND NOW

The kale we grow today is almost identical to the kale that tribes foraged thousands of years ago. The prime difference is that now the leaves are bigger. The change in leaf size happened over many seasons as people who cultivated kale saved leaves from the plant that had the largest leaves. Meet the seed for next year's crop! Repeat this process over hundreds of years, maybe longer, and you will end up with large-leafed kale.

If you grow your own kale (see Chapter 10 if you'd like to try this yourself), allow kale to stay in the garden until you plan to use it. Otherwise, place kale in the fridge as soon as you get it home. Several studies have shown that kale loses up to 89 percent of its vitamin C when left at 70°F (the typical temperature in a transport truck or even a vase of water on the kitchen counter, something many chefs unfortunately suggest) for two days after picking, compared to 5 percent for kale stored at just above freezing for that same period.

As for washing beforehand, don't: Washing kale before storage encourages spoilage *and* it hastens nutrient loss. So wrap it or bag it and place it in the fridge. Although you can store kale for up to five days if it was super-fresh when purchased, I'd personally use it sooner. Not only will it lose important nutrients the longer it hangs out in your fridge, the more bitter its flavor will become. This is not a good thing for kids, or other veggiephobes. If you notice the leaves yellowing, toss it: Not only will the flavor be too strong, the nutrients will be almost nil.

Brassica oleracea is the Latin name for kale. Brassica, the genus name, meaning *cabbage family*, and olacerea, the species name, meaning *without a head*. Soon, variations cropped up; some seeds sprouted into kale with large smooth leaves, or that bunched together or flowered at the top, or had engorged roots or swollen nodes at its base or stalk. Soon, people were saving seeds of these variants, which came to be known, respectively, as collards, cabbage, broccoli, rutabaga, turnip, kohlrabi, and Brussels' sprouts—all grandchildren of wild kale.

Another nutrient no-no: Pre-prepping your kale, then stashing it in the fridge until you have time to cook with it. Cooking magazines, mommy blogs, and television chefs champion the practice of prepping veggies in the fridge to encourage healthy nibbling and easier weeknight cooking. In theory, the idea is awesome: Open the fridge, grab whatever prepped bit of produce you need, and voila:

A healthy, convenient, economical snack. If, after you read what I have to say on the subject, you still want to pre-prep your kale, go ahead. Eating pre-prepped kale is so much better than eating no kale at all! But do hear me out: Pre-cut fruits and veggies lose between 10 to 25 percent of their vitamin C and carotenoids. That's because oxygen destroys antioxidants. When kale (or any produce) is cut, the cut area is instantly exposed to oxygen, starting the breakdown of nutrients. Precooking kale (or other veggies and fruit) to use at a later time also saps nutrients.

So, how to store your kale so you get the most nutrient dense veggie possible? Again, don't wash it, for starters! Remove any wilted or yellowed or spotty bits, then place your kale in a storage bag, first removing as much air from the bag as possible before tightly fastening shut. Store the bag in the vegetable crisper section of the refrigerator for no more than five days.

KALE BY ANY OTHER NAME...

Kale is often called "borecole" in some English-speaking countries. "Kale" is a Scottish word derived from *coles* or *caulis*, terms used by the Greeks and Romans in referring to the whole cabbage-like group of plants. The German word *kohl* has the same origin.

If you are nearing day four and you still haven't used your kale, you are in the perfect place! Simply check out one of the recipes in this book and head to the kitchen!

No time to cook? Go ahead and wash the kale, then de-rib it by folding the leaf together and pulling out the center rib. No need for a knife! This can be done entirely by hand. Next, place a large pot of water on the stove. When the water is boiling, blanch the de-ribbed kale by submerging it in the boiling water for two to three minutes. Immediately place the kale in a bowl or colander and run very cold water over it until the kale is cool to the touch. Tuck it into an airtight container and place in the fridge to use within two or three days or freeze it immediately for up to a month. You can defrost the kale and add it to soups, pasta, casseroles, and other dishes.

DID YOU KNOW…?

You may hear kale being labeled as a member of the cruciferous family. What is this family and how is it different than the brassica family everyone lumps kale into? Well, actually they're the same family. At one point, botanists referred to the group as *Cruciferous*, a Latin word meaning "cross-bearing." This described the four petals of mustard flowers—one of kale's cousins—which are reminiscent of a cross.

THE TALE OF TWO KALES

When you shop for kale, you will notice that the veggie sports various types of leaf shapes. That's because there are two kinds of kale, Brassica napus and Brassica oleraceae. Brassica napus is the curly or ruffled-leaf kale, and includes the Pabularia group known as Siberian kale or red Russian kale.

Brassica oleraceae is the smoother-leaved family, including the Acephala group, which features collards and dinosaur kale. Dinosaur kale is a much more recent variety. It was discovered in Italy in the late 19th century.

KALE'S ENORMOUS PLANT FAMILY

Kale is a member of the brassica family, an insanely diverse family with thousands of relatives. The *Cambridge World History of Food* cites 400 types of one relative, the cabbage, alone. It is estimated that there are more than 78,000 samples of the major brassicas and their wild relatives (inelegantly called "weeds") in more than 130 countries throughout the world. Here is just a sampling of kale's many cousins:

- Horseradish
- Land cress
- Ethiopian mustard
- Collard greens
- Chinese broccoli (Gai-Lan)
- Cabbage
- Brussels sprout
- Kohlrabi
- Broccoli
- Broccoflower
- Broccoli romanesco
- Cauliflower brassica
- Wild broccoli
- Bok choy
- Komatsuna
- Mizuna
- Rapini (Broccoli rabe)
- Flowering cabbage brassica
- Chinese cabbage (Napa cabbage)
- Turnip root / turnip greens
- Rutabaga
- Siberian kale
- Canola / rapeseed
- Wrapped heart mustard cabbage
- Mustard greens
- Mustard seed, brown
- Mustard seeds, white
- Mustard seeds, black
- Tatsoi
- Arugula / rocket / roquette
- Field pepperweed
- Maca
- Garden cress
- Watercress
- Radish
- Daikon
- Wasabi

CHAPTER 2

KALE: THE NUTRIENT POWERHOUSE

Kale tastes great. It's versatile, straight-forward to cook, and easy to find. But it's kale's nutrient profile that makes it the darling of the healthy-living set. With dozens of vitamins and as many minerals, plus fiber, antioxidants, fatty acids, amino acids, and protein, kale is the veggie world's most-valuable-player.

For maximum health benefits, plan to eat kale at least three times a week (more often is even better!), enjoying anywhere from one cup to two cups at a time. Because different nutrients become available for the body to use in different concentrations when kale is eaten raw, lightly cooked or long-simmered, try to enjoy your greens in a variety of ways so that your body gets a hefty dose of everything.

For a deeper look at the nutrients kale offers—and what it can do for your health— keep reading. I think you'll be very impressed.

VITAMIN A

Kale is loaded with the plant-source form of vitamin A, called beta carotene (the form of vitamin A from animal-source food is called a retinoid). One cup of cooked kale contains an outrageous 17707.30 IU of vitamin A, which equals 354.1 percent of an adult's daily recommended allowance of the nutrient. This means enjoying kale a few times a week is a super way to ensure your body gets the vitamin A it needs.

VITAMIN A: WHAT HAPPENS WHEN THERE IS NOT ENOUGH

While most of us get plenty of vitamin A, deficiencies in this important vitamin are not uncommon. This is especially true for chronic dieters, those living on processed food, and individuals suffering from food scarcity. Here's what a lack of vitamin A can cause:

- Night blindness. This is one of the first signs of vitamin A deficiency
- Dry eyes, also known as Xerophthalmia
- Complete blindness
- Maternal mortality in pregnant women
- Miscarriage
- Inability to breast feed
- Increased risk of catching infection diseases
- Retarded or decreased childhood growth
- Slow bone development in children

Why this is important: Vitamin A has been shown to protect the body against cancer and it is a potent anti-inflammatory ingredient. It softens premature aging (including wrinkles, sun spots, and slack skin), wards off asthma, helps knock out pneumonia, and fights candida, heart disease, and inflammatory conditions such as arthritis and heart disease. It strengthens the immune system by helping the body fend off virus, bacterial attacks, and other illnesses. It improves photosensitivity and fertility, and fights macular degeneration. It even helps improve the bio-availability of iron and zinc in the body and prevent low birth-weight babies. How's that for a wide range of benefits?

VITAMIN B1

Vitamin B1, also known as thiamin, was the first of the B vitamins to be discovered. (The B vitamins—known collectively as B-complex vitamins—are a group of eight related water soluble nutrients.) Its discovery was a bit of an accident. Dutch doctor and medical researcher Christiaan Eijkman was studying beriberi patients in Jakarta when he realized that people who ate brown rice (which still has its bran coating intact) didn't get the disease. Upon closer study and after conducting several research trials, Eijkman was able to identify a nutrient contained in brown rice that he later named Vitamin B. This substance seemed to protect people from beriberi.

The vitamin works wonders in maintaining nervous system and muscle health, as well as helping the body convert sugar to usable energy.

Brown rice, seeds, and legumes (such as lentils and beans) are terrific sources of vitamin B1. With each serving containing .07 mg of vitamin B1, 4.9 percent of an adult's daily recommended allowance, kale does not contain as much vitamin B1 as these sources, but it is a good, easy way to add thiamin to your daily diet.

STUTTERING BE GONE!

Did you know there are approximately 68 million people worldwide who stutter, most of them males? (Males are 4 times as likely to stutter as females.) Fortunately, there is help. One is vitamin B1, a vitamin also known as thiamine that is found in kale. Numerous studies have found the B-vitamin helpful in lessening or even eradicating adult stuttering. One of the most recent, completed by the National Center for Stuttering in 2011, followed 38 male stutterers, ages 21 to 37, for two weeks. One group received 300 mg of vitamin B1 daily, while the other group received a placebo. The placebo group showed no improvement through the course of the trial, while in the vitamin B1 group, something curious happened: Everybody in the vitamin group showed some improvement, and one-third of them were completely cured. Even after a seven-month follow-up, the stutter-free men still had not returned to stuttering.

VITAMIN B2: DID YOU KNOW...?

- Riboflavin has been shown to lessen the severity of and decrease the number of migraine headaches a person has.
- Drinking caffeinated beverages can deplete vitamin B2 (as well as other important nutrients such as magnesium and vitamins A, B1, B3, and B5).
- Ariboflavinosis is the official term for vitamin B2 deficiency.
- A deficiency of vitamin B2 can cause cracked skin in the corners of the mouth, chapped lips, and soreness and inflammation of the mouth and tongue.
- Vitamin B2 deficiency can lead to cataracts.
- Children who do not get enough vitamin B2 may experience retarded growth.
- Sugar depletes the body's store of vitamin B2, as well as all other B-complex vitamins.
- People who are often fatigued and lethargic are frequently also low in vitamin B2.
- Riboflavin helps the body metabolize iron, making the vitamin an important nutrient for those suffering from iron-deficiency anemia.
- Hypersensitivity to light can be a sign of a vitamin B2 deficiency.

VITAMIN B2

Known alternately as riboflavin and vitamin B2, this special nutrient plays several roles, including helping the body to maintain its supply of other B-complex vitamins, protecting the cells from oxygen damage and supporting cellular energy production. It also helps to prevent and treat anemia, carpal tunnel syndrome, cataracts, dry eyes, eye conditions including sensitivity to light and blurry vision, recurring headaches (including migraines), rosacea, and skin rashes.

Kale is a good source of this important vitamin. I've got to be completely honest: kale does not contain the extreme riboflavin levels that cremini mushrooms, spinach, and venison do, but one cup of our favorite brassica provides .09 mg, or 5.3 percent of an adult's daily recommended allowance for vitamin B2. Kale is an easy, yummy way to get more of this essential B-complex vitamin into your diet.

VITAMIN B3

You may know vitamin B3 by its other name: Niacin. Like its B-complex cousins, niacin helps the body with energy production at a cellular level. It is also necessary to sustain healthy levels of cholesterol, stabilize blood sugar, help the body process fats, and help the cells create new DNA.

VITAMIN B3: DID YOU KNOW…?

- Niacin was first discovered by chemist Hugo Weidel in 1873 in his studies of nicotine.
- Vitamin B3's original name, nicotinic acid, was changed to niacin (*nicotinic acid* + *vitamin*) to disassociate it from nicotine.
- Symptoms of vitamin B3 deficiency include: aggression, dermatitis, diarrhea, insomnia, intolerance of cold, mental confusion, and physical weakness. Late-stage conditions associated with vitamin B3 deficiency include pellagra.
- In the 1930s, vitamin B3 was also called Pellagra-Preventing Factor, as it was essential in preventing and curing pellagra.
- Foods rich in vitamin B3 include: brewer's yeast, broccoli, carrots, cheese, dandelion greens, dates, eggs, fish, kale, milk, peanuts, potatoes, tomatoes, tuna, veal, beef liver, and chicken breast.
- Niacin was named vitamin B3 because it was the third of the B vitamins to be discovered.
- Another name for vitamin B3 is vitamin PP.
- Vegemite, the Australian spread made of barley-based brewer's yeast extract, is one of the highest sources of niacin. A 5-gram serving contains 25 percent of an adult's daily recommended intake of the vitamin.

That's a lot of important jobs for one nutrient! Don't get enough vitamin B3 and you may feel tired and lethargic—you may even experience muscle weakness, digestive upset, or skin rashes.

Kale contains moderate amounts of most B-complex vitamins, including vitamin B3. One cup of cooked kale contains .65 mg of niacin, which is 3.2 percent of an adult's daily recommended allowance. Every little bit counts!

VITAMIN B6

When vitamin B6 was first discovered in 1934, it was called Antidermatitis Factor for its role in preventing and healing skin conditions, such as general inflammation, dermatitis, psoriasis, and eczema. It also helps the body heal cardiovascular disease, carpal tunnel syndrome, depression, diabetic neuropathy—it has even been shown to improve autism and epilepsy conditions, as well as alleviate the effects of alcoholism, adrenal gland dysfunction, asthma, HIV/AIDS, kidney stones, PMS, and vaginitis. Vitamin B6 has also been used to reduce pregnancy-related nausea, prevent brain shrinkage in Alzheimer's patients, lower the risk of lung cancer, and even to help break up kidney stones. With all that, it's no wonder that vitamin B6 is the most thoroughly studied of the B-complex vitamins.

Luckily for you, every time you eat kale, you are getting a good amount of this wonder nutrient. One cup of cooked kale gives you .18 mg of B6, which equals 9 percent of an adult's daily recommended allowance. As if you needed another reason to eat kale!

SWEETER DREAMS WITH B6

A 2002 study at the City College of New York suggests that 250 mg of vitamin B6 a day increases one's dream vividness and the ability to recall dreams. The explanation for this phenomena is that vitamin B6 increases sleeptime arousal during periods of rapid eye movement (REM) sleep.

VITAMIN B9

If you are a woman of childbearing age, have been a woman of childbearing age, or know a woman of childbearing age, you may know vitamin B9 by its other names: Folate, or folic acid. This is the nutrient obstetricians and midwifes urge their patients to take starting the moment they are considering having a baby.

Here's why: Folate gets a lot of attention for helping to prevent birth defects, specifically those involving the neural tube (the body part that later forms the brain and spinal column) and the cleft palate. It has also been found to reduce the risk of nervous system disorders in infants, help ward off Alzheimer's disease and dementia, prevent osteoporosis, and lower the risk of cancers of the esophagus and lung, uterus, cervix, and intestine. Folate also keeps skin dermatitis-free.

Vitamin B9 is another B-complex vitamin that is available in moderate amounts in kale. One cup of the cooked greens contains 16.90 mcg, or 3.6 percent of an adult's daily allowance for the nutrient.

VITAMIN C

Vitamin C was the first-discovered—and remains one of the best known—of antioxidant vitamins, meaning it fights oxidation in the body. You probably already know what oxidation is: Think of a cut apple. What happens when its flesh is exposed to air; It gets brown, right? That's oxidation.

A small bit of oxidation happens naturally in the body during regular cell function. But unsafe levels of oxidation can occur when you are exposed to steady amounts of pollution, chemicals, processed food, excess sugar, alcohol, cigarette smoke, and even stress. The result is cell damage and even death. Oxidation makes our skin look older, our immunity weaker, and our bodies more prone to fatigue and illness.

Vitamin C, also known as ascorbic acid, can help the body ward off oxidation by a complex chemical reaction that kills oxidized cells. It also helps with wound healing, maintains healthy tissue (from skin tissue to gum tissue to the tissue that makes up our blood vessels), and boosts the immune system. Fortunately, kale is packed with this hardworking nutrient. One cup of our favorite veggie packs 53.30 mg of the vitamin, providing 88.8 percent of an adult's recommended daily allowance.

VITAMIN E

Vitamin E, known in nutritionist circles as tocopherol, is a powerful antioxidant. Actually, it's a powerful *family* of antioxidants—vitamin E is a generic term for a cluster of eight structurally-similar, related molecules that work together to protect the body from oxidative stress, strengthen the immune system, and protect the nervous and cardiovascular systems.

A 1-cup serving of kale can give you 1.11 mg of vitamin E. That's 5.6 percent of an adult's recommended daily allowance. True, that's not a huge amount, but it is a respectable quantity, in a delicious, easily digestible form. And because vitamin E is fat soluble—meaning that it is stored in your body's fat tissue until needed—most people don't need as much vitamin E as they would a water-soluble vitamin in which any extra amount is immediately excreted from the system.

VITAMIN K

There are many people in the world who have never heard of vitamin K. Identified in 1929 by Danish scientist Henrik Dam, the nutrient was named vitamin K after its discovery was mentioned in a German medical journal, which referred to it as *Koagulationsvitamin.*

Vitamin K is perhaps best known for its role in helping blood to clot normally. Many people who are deficient in the vitamin notice that they bruise easily, or experience heavy nose bleeding, excessive bleeding from everyday cuts, overly-heavy menstrual bleeding, and even rectal bleeding. But the nutrient also assists with strengthening healthy bones, helping to protect against bone loss and fractures.

Kale is one of the richest dietary sources of vitamin K around—just one cup of the greens contains 1,062.10 mcg of the vitamin, or 1,327.6 percent of an adult's recommended daily allowance of vitamin K.

CAROTENOIDS

Carotenoids are chemicals that exist in plant and animal pigments. In other words, they help give living things their color. While science is still studying carotenoids, as of now 600 different carotenoids have been identified including, beta-carotene, alpha-carotene, gamma-carotene, lycopene, lutein, beta-cryptoxanthin, zeaxanthin, and astaxanthin. Carotenoids happen to be powerful anti-oxidants that protect and strengthen human cells—each carotenoid provides slightly different benefits, but overall, they work to increase immune system function and fight off the damages of free radicals in the body.

Long-term low intake of carotenoids—which is not uncommon among people who don't eat several servings of veggies a day—can make you susceptible to infertility, lowered immunity against infectious diseases, and an increased risk of cardiovascular diseases and cancers. It can also diminish the quality of your skin, hair, and nails.

No current recommended dietary intake levels have been established for carotenoids. However, in order to get adequate carotenoid levels, the United Sates National Academy of Sciences recommends that individuals consume five or more servings of fruits and vegetable (such as kale!) every day.

KALE KEEPS EYES YOUNG

Age-related macular degeneration (known as ARMD) is the world's leading cause of blindness for people 65 and older. It occurs when cells (called macular cells) in the center of the eye's retina begin to deteriorate. Fortunately, kale can help prevent ARMD, as well as slow its progress. The specific nutrients in kale responsible for this feat? Two carotenoids called lutein and zeaxanthin.

As antioxidants, lutein and zeaxanthin help in three ways: By defending the retina against cell-damaging free radicals, by maintaining blood vessels in the macula (so oxygen and other nutrients thus ensuring a constant supply of healing oxygen and nutrients), and by filtering out UV light, which has been found to be damaging to eyesight.

Consider recent evidence: Two separate studies show that eating foods rich in lutein can increase macular pigment. In 1995, The Eye Disease Case-Control Study, conducted at the Massachusetts Eye and Ear Infirmary in Boston, found that individuals with the highest blood levels of lutein and zeaxanthin were 70 percent less likely to develop ARMD than those with the lowest levels. The study also found that people who ate lutein- and zeaxanthin-rich greens (such as kale and spinach) five or more times a week (averaging 6 mg of lutein a day) were 43 percent less likely to suffer from ARMD than those who consumed the greens less than once a month. Moreover, the Harvard Nurses' Health Study, in which nurses (71,494 women and 41,564 men ages 50 years and older) were followed for 18 years through the 1980s and into the '90s, found that eating spinach more than five days a week lowered ARMD risk by 47 percent.

FLAVONOIDS

Flavonoids are plant-based pigments that boast powerful antioxidant benefits. Over 4,000 have been identified and it is believed there may ultimately be between 5,000 to 10,000 flavonoids in existence. Like carotenoids, flavonoids help protect the body's cells from degeneration and damage. In a 2010 research study in the Netherlands, it was found that individuals with the greatest flavonoid intake (30 to 50 mg) had a 20 percent lower risk of stroke than those in the study who had the lowest flavonoid intake. While no dietary recommendations have been set for flavonoids, and few foods have been measured for exact flavonoid amounts, you can easily get 30 to 50 mg of flavonoids in your diet by eating between three to five servings of veggies a day, including kale, which is rich in the nutrient.

FINDING FLAVONOIDS

Originally known only for their roles as plant pigments, no one realized that flavonoids were beneficial until 1938 when a Hungarian scientist named Albert Szent-Gyorgyi—the same researcher who won a Nobel Prize in 1936 for isolating and identifying vitamin C—realized that flavonoids did so much more than create pretty colors.

TOO STINKY FOR BUGS

We humans consider them cancer-fighters, but kale and other brassica-family plants manufacture strong-smelling glucosinolate to repel bugs.

GLUCOSINOLATES

Glucosinolates are phytonutrients. More precisely, they are sulfur-containing compounds that have been shown to have a powerful effect on cancer—both lowering your risk and helping cancer patients beat their illnesses. Glucosinolates also have strong detoxifying effects, helping the body rid itself of potentially dangerous toxins, which can contribute to a number of diseases and brain differences. Lastly, glucosinolates have been shown to have anti-inflammatory abilities, helping the body reduce the cellular inflammation that is tied to a range of illnesses, from heart disease to rheumatoid arthritis.

There is no current recommended daily allowance of glucosinolate, but kale is rich in the nutrient. Eating three or more servings of kale per week is all you need to get the glucosinolate that can help you stay your healthiest.

FIBER

Fiber gives structure to food. In animal protein, it is typically the muscle fiber. In plant food, such as kale, it provides the tell-tale shape of the leaf (or stalk, root, tuber, bulb, flower, pod, or seed). There are a few reasons why fiber is a good thing for humans to eat: First, fiber binds to things—bad things—and helps escort them from the body. Cholesterol is one of these things. Fiber surrounds cholesterol in the blood, basically absorbing it, so it never has to be sent to the liver to be broken down. This helps lower blood cholesterol levels and the amount of cholesterol in the liver

Secondly—and you probably already know about this one—fiber helps promote bowel regularity. Yep, it helps make digestion easier, by surrounding waste in the large intestine and helping carry it out of the body. This prevents constipation and lessens the time intestinal tissue is in contact with waste that may contain carcinogens, thus lessening one's risk of cancer. Another digestive benefit of fiber: Fiber feeds the "friendly" flora in the large intestine, helping keep flora populations strong and healthy so they can break down any poorly digested food that makes its way into the colon.

Fiber also helps keep blood sugar levels low, which is important for diabetics, people with hypoglycemia, and anyone who suffers from food cravings. Fiber does this by slowing the rate at which food (and blood sugar) leaves the stomach after eating. Why this is good: It means a big rush of blood sugar isn't dumped into the blood all at once, which in

THE TWO TYPES OF FIBER

Fiber is what gives food structure. It comes in two varieties, insoluble and soluble. Insoluble fiber, the type found in kale and brassica-family veggies, does not change, break down or dissolve in the presence of liquids. Soluble fiber (which I call "swellable fiber") is found in things like oats. It softens and swells when it gets wet. You need both for good health.

turn creates dangerous spikes in blood sugar, weakness, moodiness, irritability, and cravings.

Those trying to lose weight find diminished cravings helpful in warding off overeating. Plus, fiber creates a feeling of supreme satiety in the stomach, making you feel so full that you don't want to put unneeded food in your system. Voila! Less calories!

Kale contains a good amount of fiber. A 1-cup serving of the cooked green provides 2.60 grams and 10.4 percent of an adult's daily recommended allowance of fiber.

INDIGESTION AID?

It is said that Julius Caesar ate a generous serving of collards as an indigestion preventive after attending royal banquets—a testimony to the green's detoxifying properties! Does this make collards nature's all-natural antacid?

OMEGA-3 FATTY ACIDS

Omega-3 fatty acids are essential in helping a large number of body systems to function efficiently; quickly improve the look and health of skin, hair, and nails; enhance attention and mental acuity; and boost the immune system. They've been found to help the body lose weight and keep it off, guarding against a wide range of health conditions, such as cardiovascular disease, stroke, cancer, inflammatory bowel disease, and immune system diseases such as lupus and rheumatoid arthritis.

Because the body does not produce omega-3 fatty acid molecules on its own, it must get the nutrient through food. Kale can help! One cup of the cooked green contains .13 g, which equals 5.4 percent of an adult's daily recommended allowance for omega-3 fatty acids.

NON-KALE SOURCES OF OMEGA-3 FATTY ACIDS

A serving of these foods provides the following USDA's recommended daily allowance of omega-3 fatty acids:
- Chia seed, 2 tablespoons: 150%
- Flax seed, 2 tablespoons: 132.9%
- Walnuts, ¼ cup: 94.5%
- Salmon, 4 ounces: 61.2%
- Sardines, 4 ounces: 55.8%
- Soybeans, 1 cup: 42.9%
- Halibut, 4 ounces: 25.8%
- Scallops, 4 ounces: 17%
- Shrimp, 4 ounces: 15.4%
- Tuna, 4 ounces: 13.7%

PROTEIN

Protein is one of the most important, and most misunderstood, nutrients in the modern diet. Taken from the Greek word *proteos*, which means "primary" or "taking first place," protein was the first substance to be recognized as a vital part of living tissue. Accounting for 20 percent of our body weight, proteins perform a wide variety of functions throughout the body as vital components of body tissues, enzymes, and immune cells, including production of structural tissue such as muscle, tendons, and skin; production of antibodies, which are used by the immune system to ward off infections; production of enzymes and hormones; and maintenance of the body's proper fluid balance.

Individuals who are pregnant, recovering from physical or emotional illness or trauma, chronic illness sufferers, endurance athletes, physical laborers, and children need more protein than the general population. That said, protein deficiency is rare in the western world—most North Americans and Europeans get more protein than they can use. However, about 300 million children in the developing world are believed to be protein-deficient; 40 percent of them die from increased susceptibility of infections. Deficiency symptoms include muscle weakness, fatigue, hair loss, brain fog, water retention, frequent infections, lowered immune system function, enlarged fatty liver, and muscle wasting.

While most people don't think of leafy greens having much protein, kale has a moderate amount. One cup of cooked greens contains 2.47 grams, or 4.9 percent of an adult's daily recommended allowance of easy-to-digest protein.

COMPLETE VS. INCOMPLETE

When it comes to protein, there are two kinds: complete and incomplete. Complete protein contains all nine essential amino acids. Animal food sources such as meat, fish, poultry, eggs, milk, and cheese that fall in this category are always complete proteins. Other complete proteins are a few plant foods, such as chia, quinoa, buckwheat, amaranth, chlorella, and spirulina. In most cases, however, plant foods are deficient in one or more essential amino acid, making them incomplete proteins. This isn't such a big deal—just eat two of them within the same day (or same meal, such as beans and brown rice, or a millet-kale-nut pilaf), and you'll get the full complement of essential amino acids necessary to create complete protein.

HOW OUR DIETS HAVE CHANGED

Back before electricity, plumbing, and perhaps even before the wheel, humans ate much differently than they do today. One of the most dramatic changes to the human diet has been the ratio between omega-3 and omega-6 essential fatty acids (EFA). Our bodies require both of these essential fatty acids. However modern diets consist of much more omega-6 fatty acids, the fatty acid found in grain-fed poultry and meat, and industrially produced cooking oils, such as safflower and canola oils.

Historically, during the hunter-and-gatherer era, this balance was 1:1 or even 1:2 in favor of omega-3 fatty acids, the fatty acids that protect the nervous and cardiovascular systems, and which come from plant food and animals that eat wild plant food.

Today, this balance has shifted to 10:1 or even 20:1! What this means is that we consume 10 (or 20) times more omega-6s than omega-3s.

Why this is a problem: Research has shown that too high of a ratio of omega-6 to omega-3s, can cause heart disease, along with a whole host of other illnesses. This is most likely because omega-6 has inflammatory properties, while omega-3 is anti-inflammatory. With the high dose of omega-6 that we consume, it is likely that most of us experience some sort of inflammation, the root of many health issues.

CALCIUM

Most people, no matter how nutritionally savvy, know that calcium helps builds strong bones and teeth. Calcium has other functions as well, such as maintaining healthy muscle tissue and supporting the healthy function of nerves and muscles—it even helps your blood to clot. Without enough calcium in your diet, your bones can grow brittle and you may experience frequent breaks and fractures; you may experience muscle aches, muscle spasms, and even that prickly tingly sensation in your hands or feet. In children, a deficiency of calcium can cause retarded growth or deformed skeletal formation.

Something else that everyone may not know: Plant foods, such as kale, can be terrific sources of well-digested, easily-absorbed calcium. (Yes, we're so used to seeing milk mustaches that it is hard to think of calcium coming from any source other than a cow!) One cup of cooked kale 93.60 mg of calcium, which is 9.4 percent of an adult's daily recommended amount.

CALCIUM: THE NAME

The word calcium is a geological one, coming from the Latin word *calx*, meaning limestone, a sedimentary rock formed of calcite and aragonite, two forms of calcium carbonate crystals.

COPPER

Copper is the third most abundant trace mineral in the body; it's also responsible for helping enzymes function properly in our bodies. It also helps the body utilize iron, eliminate free radicals, create bone and connective tissue and produce the hair and skin pigment known as melanin.

Because it is found in most plant food and seafood, deficiency is rare, though lack of copper can lead to elevated LDL cholesterol levels, skin sores, anemia, susceptibility to infection, weakness, fatigue, osteoporosis, joint aches, shortness of breath, ruptured blood vessels, irregular heartbeat, and poor thyroid function. (An interesting bit of trivia: Many vegetables and whole grains grown today are lower in copper than they were during the mid-1900s and earlier, thanks to depletion of copper from the soil.) One cup of kale provides a respectable .20 mg of copper, which is 10 percent of an adult's daily recommended allowance of the mineral.

IRON

Iron is found in every cell of the body. One of its most high-profile functions is serving as the core of the hemoglobin molecule. This is the part of the red blood cell responsible for transporting life-sustaining oxygen throughout the body. Iron also helps the body utilize energy, utilize fat, and aids immune system function.

ABOUT COPPER POTS

Your body needs some copper to perform most body functions. Fortunately it's an easy mineral to get your fill of, as it's in a wide range of animal and plant foods, including grains and legumes. That said, there is such thing as too much copper, especially for those who use unlined copper cookware. The mineral leaches into food when copper pans are heated or come in contact with acidic ingredients, such as tomatoes or citrus. Signs of too much copper include vomiting, diarrhea, and nausea. If you're going to use copper cooking vessels, be safe and make sure they're lined with tin or another metal.

Dietary iron comes in two forms, heme iron (the kind in animal flesh) and non-heme iron (the type found in kale and other plant foods). A lot of attention is given to the two types of iron—which one is better? Which one does the body absorb more thoroughly? Which one does this, that, or the other? Here's the scoop: The body uses heme iron (again, the type from animal products) most efficiently, absorbing it at a rate of 7 to 35 percent depending upon the person. Non-heme iron (the kind from plant sources), normally gets absorbed at a rate of 2 to 20 percent. What this means is just because you eat a certain amount of iron—regardless of the source—doesn't mean your body is going to metabolize all of it.

Fortunately for your body—and your taste buds—kale contains iron! A one-cup serving of cooked kale contains 1.17 mg of iron, providing 6.5 percent of an adult's daily recommended amount of the mineral.

ARE YOU IRON DEFICIENT? JOIN THE CLUB.

The word anemia means "without blood." This refers to a deficiency in iron-rich red blood cells. Symptoms include fatigue, brain fog, memory loss, irritability, shortness of breath, dizziness, sallow skin, and blurry vision. Unfortunately, the disease is common, affecting an estimated 400 million women worldwide. In the United States alone, 20 percent of all women of childbearing age have iron deficiency anemia. Only 2 percent of men the same age experience anemia. Why the gender difference? Women menstruate, which means a regular and heavy loss of iron.

MANGANESE

Manganese is a trace mineral, which means the body needs it in very small amounts. It was first recognized as a nutrient in 1931 by researchers who were studying deficiency diseases in laboratory animals. It was found that animals with low levels of what we now call manganese suffered from weakness, retarded growth and infertility.

Manganese works as an enzyme activator. What this means is it activates the enzymes that are responsible for body functions. Without enough manganese, the body can exhibit a very large range of deficiency symptoms, including high blood sugar levels, diabetes, rashes, bone loss, abnormally low cholesterol levels, allergies, asthma, dizziness, hearing loss, learning disabilities, multiple sclerosis, premenstrual syndrome, rheumatoid arthritis, schizophrenia, infertility, nausea, vomiting, muscle weakness, vertigo, convulsions, recurring sprained muscles, paralysis, and/or blindness.

Fortunately, getting enough manganese isn't difficult. Kale is an excellent source of the mineral. One cup of the cooked greens contains .54 mcg, which is 27 percent of an adult's daily recommended allowance of manganese.

MANGANESE: DID YOU KNOW....?

The mineral manganese was found in a black mineral from the ancient Greek kingdom of Magnesia called *magnes*.

SIGNS OF MAGNESIUM DEFICIENCY

- Headaches
- Fatigue
- Sleep disturbances, insomnia
- Muscle weakness, tremors, or spasms
- Imbalanced blood sugar levels
- Elevated blood pressure
- Heart arrhythmia, irregular contraction, or increased heart rate
- Softening and weakening of bones

MAGNESIUM

Did you know that magnesium is the second most abundant mineral in your body? It's true! Human bodies contain about 25 grams of it, mostly in the skeleton. Furthermore, the mineral plays a role not only in the skeleton, but in every living cell in the human body. In fact, magnesium is involved in over 300 biochemical reactions in the body. Its presence is crucial to glucose and fat breakdown; reduction of proteins, enzymes and antioxidants such as glutathione; creation of DNA and RNA; and regulation of cholesterol production.

Magnesium is known as a macromineral, one that our food must provide. Kale, containing moderate amounts of this nutrient, can help you get the daily magnesium you need. One cup of the cooked greens provides 23.40 mg and 5.8 percent of an adult's daily recommended allowance of the mineral.

PHOSPHOROUS

Phosphorus is found in every cell in the body, concentrated most heavily in bones and teeth—perhaps it's not surprising that the mineral's primary function is in the formation of bone and teeth? Phosphorous also works with the B vitamins in nerve conduction and contraction of muscles; in addition, it helps maintain your heart's regular beat and healthy kidney function.

Because phosphorous is found in so many foods, deficiency is extremely rare. Animal products are the richest source of the mineral, but kale contains a moderate amount as well. One cup of cooked kale provides 36.40 mg and 3.6 percent of an adult's daily recommended allowance of phosphorous.

PHOSPHORUS: TOO MUCH OF A GOOD THING

Americans drink more soda—regular and diet—than any other people in the world. In fact, the average American drinks 170 liters of soda per year. To put things in perspective, the average citizen of France consumes 43 liters of soda per year, Italians drink 46 liters. Why this is a problem? Soda contributes to everything from obesity to diabetes to tooth decay. Soda is also high in phosphorus, which can lead to reduced bone density, osteoporosis, and cardiovascular disease. If you are drinking more than three servings of soda a week, cut down. For your health's sake.

TRYPTOPHAN: DID YOU KNOW…?

Tryptophan is an essential amino acid but also the least abundant, generally found in smaller quantities and in fewer number of foods than other amino acids.

TRYPTOPHAN

Tryptophan is one of the ten essential amino acids that the body uses to synthesize protein. But you may know the ingredient not for what it is, but what it does: No doubt you've heard the bit about Thanksgiving meals causing sleepiness because of the tryptophan in the turkey? Because of its calming effect on the nervous system and its role in helping the body fall asleep, tryptophan is often referred to as "the sleepy nutrient." Indeed, tryptophan is a precursor for serotonin, a neurotransmitter that helps the body regulate sleep, mood, and even appetite. Other tasks tryptophan attends to include helping treat headaches, easing premenstrual syndrome, and regulating weight by reducing those tough carb cravings.

One cup of kale contains .03 grams of tryptophan, which is 9.4 percent of an adult's daily allowance. This is enough of the mineral to contribute toward your body's requirement, but not enough to send you to sleep!

CHAPTER 3

DRINK YOUR KALE!

People come to kale in different ways. For many people, it's kale chips. Others are lured in by a raw kale salad. Still others grow up eating sautéed kale or kale soup. But a large portion of people in the "health set" first stumble upon kale as the secret ingredient in their health club's green drink or the neighborhood raw food joint's superfood smoothie.

This is a perfect way to be introduced to this easygoing, high-nutrient powerhouse. Blending kale into a drink makes it easy to create your own health bar-style beverages at home. But before you start, let's talk blenders. If you've got a turbocharged VitaMix or BlendTec (the gold standards of the health food world), go ahead and use any type of kale you'd like. Your blender is so powerful, you could even use the leaf's rib.

Everyone else will want to stick to the more tender baby kale leaves. They break down more easily and thoroughly than their mature counterparts, which is important when using a mainstream kitchen blender.

If you've got a juicer, you'll find plenty of recipes here to get you started. And yes, you can use whatever type of kale you'd like—with the rib.

Lastly, a health warning: If you have suffered from a kidney stone or have been told to take it easy on foods with oxalic acid, ask your health care professional about drinking smoothies and juices containing raw kale. As you learned in Chapter Two, raw kale contains oxalic acid, which can contribute to kidney stone formation in some people.

If you're told to hold off on raw kale recipes, we've got you covered. There are plenty of cooked kale recipes throughout this book to enjoy. If you've got your heart set on a kale drink, however, here's something to try: Follow any of the blender recipes below (this trick won't work for juicer drinks) and where raw kale is listed, simply swap in ¼ to ⅓ cup of cooked unseasoned kale. Easy! Start your blenders!

SHAKES

CHOCO-KALE HEALTH SHAKE

MAKES 1 TO 2 SERVINGS

This yummy shake combines chocolate, coconut, and kale to create a sweet source of nutrients and healthy fats. If you're giving it to kids or picky adults, leave out the spirulina and chlorophyll, which can give a subtle yet decidedly "green" taste to the drink.

1   tablespoon chia seed

2   or 3 tablespoons raw cacao powder or ¼ cup carob or cacao nibs

2   cups coconut milk

2   cups raw baby kale (mature kale is just too "kaley" for this)

½   avocado

1   teaspoon cinnamon

8   ice cubes

   Stevia to taste

CACAO VS. COCOA

Cacao (pronounced cah-COW) is made of the solids left behind after the liquid (called "liquor" or "liqueur") and butter have been removed from the cacao beans. There is loud, frequent debate among foodies about the difference between cacao and cocoa powders. In truth, there is no difference, other than spelling. If you come across the word "raw" tacked onto cacao powder, it simply means that the product has not been heated above 110°F.

Optional: 1 or 2 tablespoons virgin organic coconut oil

Optional: 1 scoop chocolate or vanilla flavor protein powder (rice, hemp, legume, whey, etc.)

Optional: ¼ to ½ teaspoon spirulina or chlorophyll powder

1. Add all ingredients to a blender and liquefy using the most powerful setting. Blend until smooth.

2. Drink immediately.

MINT DESSERT SHAKE

MAKES 2 SERVINGS

Sometimes you want something creamy, sweet, and treat-like. But for whatever reason you also want this sweet thing to have some nutritional value. In my house, this is the recipe for

AVOCADOS—THE SEXIEST SUPERFOOD

Smooth and lush, with a rich texture, avocados are the darlings of the culinary world. But did you know that they are also bursting with a wide range of health-boosting benefits? Here are just a few of the reasons you should make avocados part of your weekly diet:

- Avocados are a powerful anti-inflammatory food, boasting a range of phytosterols, carotenoids, antioxidants, omega-3 fatty acids, and polyhydrozylated fatty acids, all of which help prevent or lessen arthritis joint afflictions, cardiovascular disease, and auto-immune disease.
- Avocados help the body absorb other nutrients. For instance, one cup of fresh avocado, when eaten with a salad or other food, can increase the body's absorption of carotenoids from that food between 200 to 400 percent.
- One cup of avocado supplies 30 percent of the daily recommendation of fiber.
- Avocado has been found to help prevent the occurrence of cancers of the mouth, skin, and prostate gland, probably due to its antioxidant boosting ability and its high content of anti-inflammatory nutrients.
- One cup of avocado has over 35 percent of one's daily allowance for vitamin K, a vitamin associated with bone formation and proper blood clotting, as well as the transport of calcium through the body.
- Individuals with latex allergies should eat limit their avocado consumption or avoid it completely. Unfortunately, the fruit contains high amounts of something called chitinase enzymes, which are associated with latex allergies. Cooking the food lightly does slightly deactivate these enzymes.

those times. It's our birthday go-to, celebrating a straight-A report card go-to, and even where we turn when we need to drown our sorrows. We use coconut-based ice cream and milk, but you can use whatever milk you love, including rice, hemp, hazelnut, oat, almond, goat, or cow.

2   *to 3 cups milk (depending on how thick you like your shake) of your choice (we use coconut)*

2   *cups vanilla or mint-chocolate chip ice cream (we use coconut)*

1   *cup baby kale leaves*

¼   *to ½ avocado*

2   *drops peppermint extract*

1. Put all ingredients into a blender and blend until kale has been liquidized and all ingredients have been blended.

NUTTY CHOCO-KALE SHAKE

MAKES 1 TO 2 SERVINGS

If you tolerate nuts well, they make a high-protein, high-fiber, high-nutrient addition to the smoothies. You can make it easy on yourself and throw a handful of nuts into any smoothie you are making or spoon in a dollop of nut butter. Or, you can try this yummy recipe. It is super satisfying and one of my kids' favorite after-homework treats.

2   *cups non-dairy milk of choice*
1   *cup baby kale leaves*
¼   *cup nut butter of choice*
2   *tablespoons honey, agave or maple syrup*
2   *tablespoons cocoa*
Optional: 1 banana

1. Put all ingredients into a blender and blend until kale has been liquidized and all ingredients have been blended.

SMOOTHIES

KALE BERRY BLAST

MAKES 1 SERVING

Kale, strawberries, and blueberries—three potent superfoods, all brimming with vitamins and antioxidants. To keep natural sugar intake at a minimum, I prefer to use water to make this.

1½ *cup water, coconut water, or fruit juice of choice*
½   *cup fresh or frozen blueberries*
½   *cup fresh or frozen strawberries*
1   *cup baby kale leaves*

1. Put all ingredients into a blender and blend until kale has been liquidized and all ingredients have been blended.

CREAMY KALE SMOOTHIE

MAKES 1 SERVING

This mild-tasting, creamy smoothie is a great introduction to green drinks. It's one of my kids' absolute favorites. For more sweetness, blend in a peeled banana or pear.

1½ cup unsweetened almond, hazelnut, coconut, rice, or hemp milk

1 cup baby kale

¼ cup raw cashews (you can also use almonds or walnuts)

½ avocado

Optional: A splash of vanilla or almond extract

1. Put all ingredients into a blender and blend until kale has been liquidized and all ingredients have been blended.

CASHEW TRIVIA

Lower in fat than other nuts, high in protein, and addictively delicious, cashews are the darlings of the snack world. You know you love them, but did you know this about them?

- Cashews are native to the coastal regions of Brazil.
- The cashew nut is actually the kidney-shaped seed that sits at the bottom of the cashew apple, a delicacy in Brazil and the Caribbean, where the fruit grows prolifically.
- Cashews are always sold shelled. Why? Because the interior of the cashew shell contains a caustic resin known as cashew balm, which is carefully removed before nuts are packaged for human consumption. This resin is used to make insecticides and varnishes.
- Cashew's scientific name is Anacardium occidentale.
- Cashews belong to the same family as the pistachio and mango.
- In the 16th century, Portuguese explorers took cashew trees from Brazil and introduced them to other tropical countries, including India and Africa.
- Currently, the leading commercial providers of cashews are Brazil, Mozambique, Tanzania, and Nigeria.
- Cashew wood is a precious, much-prized resource in Brazil.

THE BEST SMOOTHIES

A smoothie is a blended drink containing healthy ingredients (think milkshake without the dairy and ice cream!). Really, you can blend any fruit or veggie together and get a smoothie—the recipes in this section are simply some of our favorites. Before you begin, however, these tips can make your smoothie-making adventures to be even more successful:

- If your smoothie is too thick, add more water or juice or other liquid.
- Process your smoothie for as long as you need to in order to get a smooth, silky drink. No one wants to be drinking bits of pulp.
- If you're using a weaker blender, you may find it necessary to pour the liquid through a colander or strainer to remove large bits of fiber.
- Kale and other greens can often create a green foam when whirred in a blender or when juiced. This foam is edible and healthy—however (total honesty here!) most people loathe the stuff. My own kids call it pond scum. That's why we always take a spatula and scrape it off into the sink or into a compost pile.

KALE LIME SLUSHY

MAKES 4 SERVINGS

This icy cold treat is a summer staple in our house. It is refreshing, fun, tangy, and (yep!) healthy! Everything you could want from a slushy!

1 *cup baby kale leaves*
½ *cup applesauce or pearsauce*
2 *cups water or coconut water*
1 *can limeade (or lemonade) concentrate, preferably organic*
8 *to 10 ice cubes*

1. Put all ingredients except ice into a blender and blend until kale has been liquidized.
2. Add limeade concentrate and ice to blender and pulse until drink is icy and well-blended.

BANANA KALE SMOOTHIE

MAKES 1 SERVING

If you've ever picked up one of those bottled green drinks, you know how sweet and thick they are. Banana is the reason why. It provides intense sweetness and a thick creamy quality to non-dairy smoothies, like this one. For a creamier smoothie, use coconut milk for the liquid.

1 *medium banana, ripe*
1 *cup baby leaf kale*
1½ *cup water, coconut water, or fruit juice of choice*
    Squirt lemon juice
Optional: 1 slice fresh ginger

1. Put all ingredients into a blender and blend until kale has been liquidized and all ingredients have been blended.

GO BANANAS

Ah, the banana! This ubiquitous yellow fruit is strongly associated in the U.S. with breakfast, but how well do you really know this tropical treat? Read on:

- A banana plant grows between 10 to 26 feet.
- Banana plants belong to the same family as the lily and the orchid.
- Bananas grow in clusters of 50–150 fruits known as "hands."
- A medium-size banana contains 467 mg of potassium and only 1 mg of sodium.
- Most of today's bananas are grown in tropical and subtropical countries, most commonly Costa Rica and Ecuador, but also Mexico and Brazil.
- In addition to its cardiovascular benefits, the potassium found in bananas may also help to promote bone health. Potassium may counteract the increased urinary calcium loss caused by the high-salt diets typical of most Americans, thus helping to prevent bones from thinning out at a fast rate.
- Bananas have long been recognized for their antacid effects that protect against stomach ulcers and ulcer damage. In an animal study, researchers found that fresh bananas protected the animals' stomachs from wounds.
- Because they are high in electrolytes, bananas are a traditional cure for diarrhea.
- Bananas contain high levels of a compound called fructooligosaccharide. This probiotic nourishes beneficial bacteria in the colon, improving the body's ability to absorb nutrients. This, in turn, decreases the body's risk of colon cancer.
- It's not known exactly where bananas originated, though many experts believe the fruit was first grown in Malaysia around 4,000 years ago. From there, they spread throughout the Philippines and then India, where they were first encountered by Alexander the Great's soldiers in 3227 BCE.
- Bananas spread first to the Middle East, then Africa, where they were discovered by Portuguese explorers on their way to the New World. They were widely planted in what is now South and Central America.
- Bananas were not brought to the United States until late in the 19th century. Because they were so fragile, bananas were at first only available in the sea towns where they were unloaded.

STEPHANIE'S BUILD-YOUR-OWN KALE SMOOTHIE BLUEPRINT

MAKES 1 TO 2 SERVINGS

This is the blueprint I give to my private clients, my detox clients, and my weight loss clients. It's a fun mix-and-match blueprint that allows you to make a different smoothie every day if you'd like, depending upon what you have available in our kitchen and what you feel like. You can even tailor it to suit specific health needs.

2   cups liquid of choice (I use a mixture of water
      and coconut water or just regular water.) Add
      more water if you want the drink more "liquidy"
1   cucumber, peeled and cut into large chunks
      so your blender can process it better
1   to 2 cups baby kale, spinach or salad greens
3   or 4 sprigs parsley or mint
Optional: Squirt of lemon or lime—fantastic
      for helping to flush toxins from the body
Optional: 1 tablespoon coconut oil and/or
      ½ of an avocado and/or 2 tablespoons nut
      butter and/or ¼ cup nuts of choice. (These
      are all fantastic sources of brain-nourishing,
      cardiovascular-helping fats)
Optional: 1 teaspoon spirulina powder and/or
      1 teaspoon greens powder, and/or 1 to
      2 tablespoons chia seed, and/or 1 table-
      spoon rice or legume-based protein powder.
Optional: 1 or 2 tablespoons maple syrup,
      honey, or agave

1. Fill your blender with your chosen liquid and ingredients. Process as long as necessary to create a smooth drink.

THE MARVELS OF MAPLE

Maple syrup is the sweet sap of the sugar, black, and red maple trees, and it's a terrific sweetener to add to the health-supportive kitchen. That's because, ounce for ounce, maple contains less calories and more minerals than honey or sugar. Look for grade B or Dark Amber grade maple—it's darker and richer in taste than the lighter, less complex Grade A or Light Amber. All shades, however, are high in manganese and zinc, two minerals essential for health immune system function.

SUPERFOOD PROTEIN SMOOTHIE

MAKES 1 TO 2 SERVINGS

This fun smoothie is packed with all kinds of superfoods. It's as perfect for someone training for a marathon as it is for anyone convalescing from an illness. It's tasty, too!

1½ cups coconut water
1   cup baby kale leaf
2   tablespoons coconut oil
1   tablespoon maple, honey, or agave
¼   cup raw walnuts
¼   cup raw cashews
2   tablespoons chia
2   tablespoons goji berries
1   slice ginger (as big or small as you'd like)

1. Put all ingredients into a blender and blend until kale has been liquidized and all ingredients have been blended.

EASY ENERGY

Chia has been used for energy since BCE times. Aztec warriors and athletes were thought to have performed on as little as one tablespoon of chia per day. The seeds are about 20 percent protein per weight and offer about 2 grams of protein per tablespoon. This makes chia ideal for increasing the protein content in any low-protein food. In fact, Aztec warriors and runners are believed to have sustained themselves for an entire day on just a tablespoon of chia, making it one of the original "breakfasts of champions." Further, chia also helps the body maintain sustained hydration, which can come in handy for anyone engaged in heavy, prolonged activity.

TROPICAL SMOOTHIE
MAKES 1 SERVING

Sweet and soothing, this fruity smoothie is loved by everyone. Kids love it when it's made with pineapple juice. Thanks to the mango, the drink is especially high in vitamin A, which is important for healthy eyesight and skin, and immune system function.

1½ cup water, coconut water, or pineapple juice (you can use a combination of these)
1 cup frozen mango chunks
½ cup baby kale
Squirt or two of lemon or lime juice

1. Put all ingredients into a blender and blend until kale has been liquidized and all ingredients have been blended.

MANGO MADNESS!

Sweet, soft, and sensual, mangos are one of my favorite tropical fruits. Just as wonderful as their full-bodied flavor? Mangos are also loaded with health benefits:

- One average size mango contains 105 calories and provides 76 percent of an adult's daily requirement of vitamin C, 25 percent vitamin A, and 11 percent vitamin B6.
- Mangos provide insoluble fiber, which helps promote digestive health.
- Research has shown that the antioxidant compounds in mango help protect against colon, breast, leukemia, and prostate cancers. These compounds include quercetin, isoquercitrin, astragalin, fisetin, gallic acid, and methylgallat.
- The high levels of fiber, pectin and vitamin C help to lower serum cholesterol levels.
- Vitamins C and vitamin A in mangos, plus 25 different kinds of carotenoids, keep the immune system healthy and strong.

SMOOTHIES ON THE ROAD

Smoothies are a fantastic way to give your-self a concentrated dose of super-nutrients in one sitting. They can even be made on the road—in fact, they are ideal for busy types who like to start their days off in a powerful way. To ensure you are set-up for success while you're on the road, follow these easy tips.

- Carry a small portable blender—such as a Magic Bullet—in your handbag or luggage, while you're traveling.
- Opt for pre-washed baby kale, baby spinach, or baby salad greens—they break down much easier in a small, portable blender. Save the heavy greens for a hardcore blender.
- For liquid, use water from the tap, or pack a few aseptic single-serving size containers of coconut water or other beverages.

JUICE

KALE JUICE STRAIGHT UP

Kale juice is one of the most nutritious juices around. It boasts extremely power-ful antioxidant, anti-inflammatory, and anti-cancer properties. It strengthens the immune system and is loaded with beta carotene, vitamin C, vitamin K, lutein, zeaxanthin, and calcium. It's also pretty hard to stomach on its own. Of course you can try, but you may find it to be so "green-tasting" (as one of my sons says), that you just cannot stand it. (I'm just be-ing honest!) That's why I've collected a few blended juice recipes, which will al-low you to enjoy the enormous benefits kale juice has to offer, in a more palatable format. Enjoy!

TO DILUTE OR NOT TO DILUTE? THAT IS THE QUESTION!

Many people dilute their fresh-pressed juice with pure water. This is an easy way to lighten up heavy juices (think those made solely of root veggies) or give strong-tasting juices a milder taste. Where do I fall on the dilution question? Nowhere, really. If I make a juice with lots of beets or carrots (or other root vegetables), I almost always add a half cup to two cups of water. I'll also add one or two cups of water if it looks like the juice I made isn't going to stretch far enough to serve four people (myself, Leif, Anders, and Axel—my poor husband won't go near juice!). I typically do not dilute juice when it contains a lot of watery fruits and vegetables, such as cucumber or citrus. In other words, there is no hard-and-fast dilution rule. It's all good.

LOSE THE BLOAT KALE DRINK

MAKES 1 SERVING

This is the juice I sip when I wake up retaining water or have a black-tie event and for some reason, can't comfortably fit into my dress. It is a diuretic and helps safely (yet quickly!) flush excess water from the body. (Just a warning: The dandelion gives this drink a bitter flavor, a flavor I happen to like. Feel free to add a cup of pineapple to the mix if you'd like.)

5   *kale leaves*
1   *medium to large cucumber, cut into slices*
    small enough to fit in your juicer's feed tube
2   *celery stalks*
10 *dandelion leaves*
10 *sprigs parsley*
    1-inch ginger
1   *lemon*

1. Run all ingredients through the juicer's feed tube. Strain finished liquid if necessary.

PARSLEY POWER

If you haven't yet juiced or blended parsley into one of your drinks, I have one question: What are you waiting for? This refreshing herb is more nutrient-dense than many vegetables.

- Parsley's volatile oils have been shown to inhibit tumor formation in animal studies, and particularly, tumor formation in the lungs.
- Two tablespoons of parsley provide 155.8% of the body's requirement of vitamin K, 16.8% of vitamin C, and 12.8% of vitamin A.
- Parsley is native to Mediterranean Europe.
- Parsley, which has been grown domestically for more than 2,000 years, was originally used not as a food, but as a medicine.
- The Greeks considered parsley to be sacred and used it for decorating tombs and celebrating winning athletes.
- Parsley contains strong antioxidants called flavonoids, which strengthen the body's immune system.

RED KALE JUICE

MAKES 2 OR MORE SERVINGS

For this drink I specify red kale. Yes, you can use other varieties, but the juice's color won't be as pretty. It'll still taste great and be full of antioxidants. I begin making this drink around Thanksgiving when cranberries appear in stores.

5   *leaves red kale*
1   *cup fresh cranberries*
2   *medium beets, cut into slices small enough to fit in your juicer's feed tube*
    ½-inch piece of ginger
1   *blood orange, peeled and sectioned*

1. Run all ingredients through the juicer's feed tube. Strain finished liquid if necessary.

REFRESHING KALE COOLER

MAKES 4 OR MORE SERVINGS

This fun recipe requires you to add something to the juice after pressing it. It's a great warm-weather drink, beloved by even the most ardent kale haters.

1   *medium to large cucumber, cut into sections small enough to fit in your juicer's feed tube*
1   *bunch kale*
3   *apples, cut into slices small enough to fit in our juicer's feed tube*
1   *lemon or lime, cut into slices small enough to fit in your juicer's feed tube*
    1-inch section of ginger
1   *to 2 cups coconut water*

1. Run all ingredients through the juicer's feed tube. Strain finished liquid if necessary.
2. Add 1 to 2 cups of coconut water to the pressed juice. Stir to combine. Drink immediately.

STAY-WELL KALE JUICE

MAKES 2 OR MORE SERVINGS

This is the juice I make for my kids when a cold is going through their school. It is rich in enzymes and antioxidants. It also tastes good.

1   *cup pineapple, cut into sections small enough to fit in your juicer's feed tube*
1   *bunch kale*
2   *large cucumbers, cut into sections small enough to fit in your juicer's feed tube*
1   *lemon, cut into sections small enough to fit in your juicer's feed tube*
¼   *cup mint*
    ½-inch slice ginger

1. Run all ingredients through the juicer's feed tube. Strain finished liquid if necessary.

WHY YOU NEED PINEAPPLE

When I was growing up, one of the moms on our street would always juice a pineapple for me anytime I caught a cold. "It's the enzymes," she'd say knowingly. "They eat away the virus." And it did seem as though the cold would lessen after downing that sweet, tangy juice. Time passed and I grew up. Without even questioning, I also juice a pineapple anytime one of my children, my husband, or I come down with a cold. After studying nutrition, I learned that the pineapple's enzymes are anti-inflammatory and certainly work to keep you healthy, but it was probably the fruit's high vitamin C content (75 percent of the daily recommended allowance) at work in wiping out offending viruses.

MUCH TO-DO ABOUT JUICERS

There's a lot of debate in the juicing world around juicer types, and which type makes the best, healthiest juice. Twin-gear or triturating juicers flatten produce between two rollers. They work excruciatingly slow, but because they do not generate any heat, it's believed that the juice's nutrient profile stays most intact. Masticating juicers (I've got one of these) "chew" the produce sending the juice down one tube and the pulp down another. These do warm up produce slightly, but are considered the most healthful and effective juicers for home use. Centrifugal juicers are the fastest and easiest to clean of the bunch, and are also the most economical. They work by grating the fruit or vegetable into a pulp, and then use centrifugal force to push the pulp against a strainer screen by spinning it at a very high RPM. The juice is forced from the screen and down a juice shoot. While centrifugal juicers do cause the most "damage" to nutrients, fresh-pressed juice made with them is still a deeply nourishing food. My take: Use whatever juicer you like enough to operate on a daily basis! Fresh kale juice does the most good when consumed daily.

SUNSHINE JUICE

MAKES 2 OR MORE SERVINGS

Give my second son, Anders, a collection of grapefruits, oranges, lemons, limes, oranges, pomelos, and tangerines and he is in heaven. He is definitely my citrus kid. Not surprisingly, this juice is his favorite. If, like Anders and me, you love bitter flavors, add a grapefruit to the mix.

5   *kale leaves*
1   *apple, cut into slices small enough to fit in your juicer's feed tube*
1   *orange, peeled and sectioned*
1   *tangerine or Clementine, peeled and sectioned*
½   *lemon*
½   *lime*

1. Run all ingredients through the juicer's feed tube. Strain finished liquid if necessary.

SUGAR? CHECK THE INDEX!

If you're health conscious, you've probably heard the term "glycemic index." This list of common foods shows which ingredients are best at creating stable blood sugar and which wreck havoc, creating dramatic spikes then falls in blood glucose levels (leaving you feeling tired, irritable, with insatiable cravings). For ideal health, you want to choose foods that are low on the glycemic index—closer to a "1"—and avoid those foods which are rated higher (the highest of them rate around 100). Here's a list of popular smoothie and juice ingredients and where they stand on the glycemic index, from highest to lowest:

Watermelon	72	Grapefruit	25
Cherries	63	Raspberries	2
Banana, ripe	62	Broccoli	0
Grapes	59	Celery	0
Blueberries	53	Cucumber	0
Apple juice, unsweetened	44	Ginger	0
Dates, dried	42	Green beans	0
Peach	42	Kale	0
Carrots	41	Lemons	0
Orange	40	Lettuce	0
Strawberries	40	Limes	0
Apple	39	Spinach	0
Pear	38	Tomatoes	0
Prunes	29	Zucchini	0

V8-STYLE JUICE

MAKES 4 OR MORE SERVINGS

My four-year-old son, Axel, is crazy for commercial tomato and V8-style juices. Up until recently I always bought several cans and bottles of the stuff each week. However, when a client gave me a shopping bag of tomatoes, I decided to make my own tomato-veggie blend. Axel loves it just as much as the stuff from a can! (I do, too.)

3   *large tomatoes, cut into slices small enough*
    to fit in your juicer's feed tube (feel free to
    use more tomatoes if you're lucky enough
    to have a surplus)
½   *bunch kale, washed and dried*
1   *celery stalk*
1   *small to medium cucumber*
1   *carrot*
2   *to 4 sprigs of parsley, stem included*
½   *red or green bell pepper*
1   *half lemon*
1   *small garlic clove*
Optional: 1 sliver fresh jalapeño pepper
    or a radish
Optional: A shake of Tabasco sauce for
    finished juice

1. Run all ingredients through the juicer's feed tube. Strain finished liquid if necessary. Season with Tabasco sauce if desired.

SERIOUSLY? GARLIC JUICE?

I know you've already heard what a powerful ingredient garlic is. It supercharges the immune system to fight off marauding viruses, fungi and bacteria. It helps with high blood pressure and cholesterol. Garlic has also been shown to help the body heal faster and more thoroughly. But juicing it? Adding it to smoothies?

Yes, I am serious. I really am. You may not want to add a clove of garlic to your sweet berry supreme smoothie, but it's the perfect addition to any tomato-based drinks or veggie-heavy green juices. Just one clove is all you need in order to get all those juicy benefits. Just one clove. Try it! (I dare you.)

TOMATO TALES

In many parts of the world—think North America and Europe—nothing says summer like "tomato." This sunny vegetable (botanically a fruit) is as loved for its addictive taste as its powerful nutrient profile: vitamins A, B-complex, and C, antioxidants, potassium, and phosphorous. But in some dietary systems (such as macrobiotics), tomatoes are forbidden as a weakening food that ruins the gastrointestinal tract. Other healing systems, such as Ayurveda, applaud tomatoes when cooked with a generous amount of warming cumin and turmeric. My advice: If raw tomatoes bother you, try them cooked. If you can eat tomatoes with impunity, toss one into the juicer to make your own yummy V8-style drink.

WARMING AUTUMN KALE JUICE

MAKES 2 OR MORE SERVINGS

I generally try not to mix green veggies with orange or red veggies when I juice. This has nothing to do with health and everything to do with aesthetics: In my house we enjoy our juice out of glass tumblers and when I mix green and orange and red, what I get is an unattractive gray-brown color, which my junior high school art teacher called "taupe." Not something the kids want to consume. This recipe is an exception. I love the sweet, deep flavor that comes when I juice carrots and beets. Plus, this recipe is a powerful one, great for detoxing, fantastic for the skin, and superb for the immune system.

1   *bunch kale*
2   *large beets or medium sweet potatoes, cut into slices small enough to fit in your juicer's feed tube*
4   *large carrots, cut into slices small enough to fit in your juicer's feed tube*
2   *large apple or 3 pears, cut into slices small enough to fit in your juicer's feed tube*
½   *to 1 lemon, cut into slices small enough to fit in your juicer's feed tube*

1. Run all ingredients through the juicer's feed tube. Strain finished liquid if necessary.

WHAT IS AN ANTIOXIDANT?

To understand antioxidants, it's important to first understand oxidants. Oxidation is a chemical reaction that transfers electrons or hydrogen from a substance to an oxidizing agent. Oxidation reactions can produce free radicals, or oxidants. In turn, these radicals can start chain reactions. When the chain reaction occurs in a cell, it can cause damage or death to the cell. An antioxidant is a molecule capable of inhibiting the oxidation of other molecules.

The easiest place to get these protective molecules is from food. Namely, plant food. Brightly and darkly colored fruits and vegetables are some of the best sources of these powerful nutrients. Eating numerous servings of antioxidant-heavy food daily is one of the most effective ways to maintain wellness.

DRINK IMMEDIATELY!

You may have heard that fresh-pressed juice is most healthful if you can drink it immediately. Here's why: Immediately after being made, fruit and vegetable juice contains the highest levels of enzymes. The longer juice sits, the greater its exposure to oxygen. The longer it's exposed to oxygen, the more of its enzymes are affected by oxidation. After 20 minutes of exposure, the majority of enzymes in juice have been destroyed.

CHAPTER 4

BREAKFAST:
START YOUR DAY WITH KALE

Kale for breakfast? I guess it does sound a bit strange, especially for those of you who grew up eating white-flour-and-dairy for breakfast. But consider this: In many parts of the world, veggies for breakfast are the norm. In places like India, China, Japan, Israel, Australia (with their ever-present broiled tomatoes), and Europe, people enjoy soup, raw veggies, veggie rice dishes, and more as their first meal of the day.

The trend is catching on in North America, especially with "health foodies" who wouldn't dream of starting their day without a green juice or smoothie. (If you're intrigued, turn to Chapter 3 for some of our favorite green drinks—all of which are awesome for breakfast.) But kale is so much more versatile than just beverages.

Kale pairs beautifully with a number of the foods you're already eating for breakfast. Check out these recipes to see what I mean.

EGGS

BREAKFAST CASSEROLE

MAKES 6 TO 8 SERVINGS

This is one of those simple, fast, filling, delicious dishes you see on brunch tables. In Australia, these are called "bakes." In the States, they're known as breakfast casseroles. Not that your guests care what you call this slightly exotic taste dish—they'll just want to dig in!

3   *tablespoons extra virgin olive oil*
¼   *teaspoon minced fresh ginger*
3   *large onions, chopped*
3   *cloves garlic, minced*
1   *teaspoon ground turmeric*
1½ *cup cooked, steamed or blanched kale, squeezed dry and coarsely chopped*
    Salt and pepper to taste
4   *tablespoons all-purpose flour or all-purpose gluten-free flour*
½   *teaspoon baking soda*
7   *eggs, beaten*
Optional: 2 tablespoons chopped parsley
Optional: paprika for garnish

1. Heat oven to 400°F.

2. Heat 2 tablespoons of the olive oil in a large skillet over medium-high heat. Add the ginger, onions, and garlic. Cook until soft, about 6 to 8 minutes.

3. Add turmeric and kale to the skillet, seasoning with salt and pepper as desired. Cook until tender, about 10 minutes.

4. Turn off the heat and stir in 3 tablespoons flour and the baking soda.

5. Stir eggs into kale mixture.

6. Prepare a 9- by 13-inch casserole dish by greasing with remaining tablespoon of olive oil and dusting with remaining two tablespoons of flour.

7. Pour egg-kale mixture into prepared pan and place in oven. Bake until set, about 25 to 30 minutes. (You do not want to overcook; the dish will be a bit wobbly in the middle.)

8. Optional: Garnish with chopped parsley and/or paprika.

ONIONS: NOTHING TO CRY OVER

Onions make everything taste better. A quick sauté in butter or oil does wonders for fried foods, a few slices of crisp onion makes any sandwich or burger taste better, and what is a soup, stew, braise or piece or roasted meat without onion? In addition to being de rigueur in any food-lover's kitchen, onions are also incredibly healthy. Consider:

- Onions have just 40 calories per 100 grams.
- Onions are rich in soluble dietary fiber.
- The compound allicin found in onions give them cancer-fighting properties. Allicin has also been found to have anti-bacterial, anti-viral, and antifungal activities.
- Onions help decrease the risk of coronary artery disease, stroke, and peripheral vascular diseases. Again, it's the allicin, which decreases blood vessel stiffness and reduces total blood pressure. It also blocks the formation of blood clots.
- Onions contain chromium, a trace mineral that helps insulin act on and control sugar levels in diabetes.
- They are also a good source of the antioxidant flavonoid quercetin, which is found to have anti-carcinogenic, anti-inflammatory, and anti-diabetic functions.
- Onions help strengthen and protect the immune system, thanks to high levels of the antioxidant, vitamin C.
- Manganese is found in onions. This mineral is required for normal growth and health. It helps your body break down fats, carbohydrates, and proteins.
- Onions are also rich in the B-complex group of vitamins, which help to maintain healthy skin and muscle and nervous system function.

KALE-BACON QUICHE CUPS

MAKES 6 SERVINGS

Kids love these, adults love these, frou-frou types like these! Easy to make, freezable, and fun to eat—you'll love them, too. Oh, and they contain kale!

8   eggs
2   tablespoons half and half or non-dairy cream
2   strips thick-cut bacon
1   cup chopped red bell pepper
¼   cup cooked, steamed, or blanched kale, coarsely chopped
2 to 3 green onions, chopped
⅛ to ¼ teaspoon sea salt
    Pinch red pepper flakes
    Pinch sweet paprika

1. Preheat oven to 350°F.

2. Grease the cups of a standard muffin tin

3. Heat a medium skillet over medium high heat and add the chopped bacon. Sauté for 5 to 10 minutes until brown and crispy. Remove from pan and pat dry of grease.

4. Drain the bacon grease from the skillet to a heat-proof bowl. Reserve.

5. Add 1 tablespoon reserved bacon grease to the skillet. Sauté bell pepper and onion for 3 to 5 minutes, until soft.

6. Turn off heat and stir cooked kale into red pepper mixture.

7. In a medium bowl whisk together the eggs, salt, and half and half.

8. To the egg mixture, add the bacon and vegetable mixture, stirring until combined.

9. Pour the egg mixture into the muffin wells/sauté pan. (You may want to pour egg mixture from a large liquid measuring cup with a spout.) Top with Parmesan cheese and bake for 20 minutes or until just firm with browned edges.

BELLS OF THE VEGGIE BALL

Bell peppers—so named because of their blocky shape—are a veggie garden favorite. What you may not know, however, is that bell peppers aren't actually veggies. They're fruits, which boast over 195 percent of a body's daily requirement for vitamin C, 57 percent of vitamin A, and dozens of different carotenes and flavonoids, two families of antioxidants that help ward off cancers, viruses, bacteria, and fungi, as well as strengthen the immune system. Also known as capsicums (especially in England and Australia), these range in color from green to red in varying stages of ripeness. There are also brown, purple, yellow, orange, and black varieties.

KALE-MUSHROOM-POBLANO FRITTATA

MAKES 4 SERVINGS

If you're like me, you adore anything with a bit of bite to it, hence this delicious and hearty frittata. Use any type of mushrooms you'd like and when you're ready to branch out, experiment with other types of chili peppers. Notice the refreshing addition of cilantro. If you're a cilantro-hater, feel free to substitute chives or parsley. You'll need an ovenproof skillet for this one.

3   tablespoons extra-virgin olive oil

8   ounces assorted mushrooms (such as button, baby bella, crimini, oyster, and stemmed shiitake), thinly sliced

1   large fresh poblano chili, stemmed, seeded, thinly sliced into strips

1   cup chopped scallions

1   cup cooked, steamed, or blanched kale, squeezed dry and coarsely chopped
    Salt and freshly ground black pepper, to taste

6   large eggs

2   tablespoons chopped fresh cilantro

½   teaspoon ground cumin

Optional: Salsa for garnish

GOURMET SUPER VEGGIE!

In the current stampede to get more and more colorful veggies into our diets, it's easy to overlook the humble (and very uncolorful) mushroom. This is a darn shame, when you consider that mushrooms are not only exquisite-tasting, but antioxidant superpowers. They contain:

- B-complex vitamins, which play an important role in nervous system function.
- Riboflavin, to help maintain healthy red blood cells.
- Niacin, which ensures the digestive and nervous systems function properly.
- Selenium, a mineral that works as an antioxidant to protect body cells from damage that might lead to heart disease, some cancers, and other diseases of aging.
- Ergothioneine, a naturally occurring antioxidant that helps protect the body's cells.
- Copper, which helps make red blood cells, which in turn carry oxygen throughout the body. Copper also helps keep bones and nerves healthy.
- Potassium, an important mineral that helps maintain normal fluid and mineral balance, which helps control blood pressure. Potassium also plays a role in making sure nerves and muscles (the heart included!) function properly.
- Beta-glucans, which are antioxidants that help the body resist allergens and strengthen the immune system.

1. Preheat oven to 400°F.

2. Heat oil in a medium ovenproof skillet over medium-high heat. Add mushrooms, stirring occasionally, until just soft, about 5 minutes.

3. Add poblano and cook, stirring occasionally, until mushrooms and poblano are lightly browned, about 5 minutes more. Add kale and scallions, season with salt and pepper, and remove pan from heat.

4. Whisk eggs, cilantro, and cumin in a medium bowl. Season to taste with salt and pepper.

5. Lower heat to medium and pour eggs evenly over mushroom-poblano-kale mixture, using a heatproof spatula to evenly disperse ingredients. Cook until bottom is set, about 2 minutes.

6. Transfer skillet to oven and cook until eggs are just set, about 9 minutes. Remove from oven and let sit 2 minutes.

7. If you don't want to serve the frittata from the pan, you can run a heatproof spatula around the edge of the pan to release frittata. Slide frittata onto a warmed plate and cut into wedges to serve.

KALE, POTATO, AND ONION FRITTATA

MAKES 4 SERVINGS

A frittata is like an open-faced omelet filled with yummy things—in this case, hearty potatoes, savory onions, and delicious kale. You'll need an ovenproof skillet for this one.

1 tablespoon olive oil
1 onion, chopped
1 to 2 cups steamed, cooked, or blanched kale, squeezed dry and chopped
2 cloves garlic, chopped
2 cups boiled diced potatoes
4 whole eggs
Salt to taste
½ teaspoon paprika

DID YOU KNOW...?

- There are now 200 breeds of chickens.
- Europe has had domesticated hens since 600 BCE.
- An average hen lays 300 to 325 eggs a year. A hen starts laying eggs at 19 weeks of age.
- Chickens came to the New World with Columbus on his second trip in 1493.
- Because eggs are a sign of fertility, French brides break an egg on the threshold of their new home before stepping in.
- In the United States there are approximately 240 million hens, which produce roughly 50 billion eggs each year. That's about one hen for every man, woman, and child in the country.
- White-shelled eggs are produced by hens with white feathers and ear lobes. Brown-shelled eggs are produced by hens with red feathers and red ear lobes.
- There is no difference in nutrition between white and brown eggs.
- To produce one egg, it takes a hen 24–26 hours, and to do so, she requires 5 oz. of food and 10 oz. of water. 30 minutes later she starts all over again.
- Not all eggs have one yolk. Once in awhile, a hen will lay a double-yoked egg. And in rare circumstances, some young hens may produce a yolkless egg.
- Yolk color depends on the diet of the hen. Feed containing yellow corn or alfalfa produces medium yellow yolks, while feed containing wheat or barley produces lighter color yolks.
- As a hen grows older she produces larger eggs.
- A mother hen turns over her egg about fifty times per day (so the yolk won't stick to the sides of the shell).

1. Heat oven to 400°F.

2. In a cast iron or other oven-proof skillet over medium heat, add the olive oil and onion, cooking until onion becomes translucent, about 5 minutes.

3. Add kale and garlic; stir 5 minutes. Add potatoes.

4. In a medium bowl, whisk eggs, egg whites, 2 tablespoons water, salt, and paprika until well mixed.

5. Pour egg mixture over vegetables in skillet. Reduce heat to low and cook for 1 minute just to set the eggs.

POACHED EGGS WITH KALE-CHORIZO HASH

MAKES 2 SERVINGS

This dressy recipe is always a favorite, thanks to flavorful dry-cured chorizo. This is the Spanish type sausage, not the uncured Mexican-style (which is equally delicious!).

2   tablespoons extra virgin olive oil
1½ cups cooked, steamed or blanched kale, squeezed dry and coarsely chopped
8   ounces dried Spanish chorizo, halved lengthwise, and then sliced crosswise ¼-inch thick
2   eggs
2   tablespoons white vinegar
    Salt and pepper, to taste

1. Add the olive oil to a large skillet over medium heat. Add the chorizo and cook until it has rendered some of its fat, about 3 to 4 minutes.

2. Add the kale, seasoning mixture with salt and pepper and turning kale to coat in chorizo drippings.

3. Make the poached eggs: Pour water into a medium-sized saucepan, filling 3 or 4 inches of water. Bring to a gentle simmer. Once you see tiny bubbles rising from the saucepan, add the vinegar.

4. For the prettiest eggs, crack each egg into its own separate shallow dish. One at a time, gently slide each egg into the gently simmering water, being careful not to break the yolk. (You can use a spoon to coax any migrating egg white back toward the yolk.)

5. As the eggs are cooking (you'll be working quickly, here!), divide the kale-chorizo mixture between two plates.

6. Cook the eggs until the whites have completely set, usually from 2 to 4 minutes.

7. Using a slotted spoon, gently remove, placing each egg on a plate atop the arranged kale-chorizo mixture. Season with salt and pepper as desired. Eat immediately.

EGG NUTRITION

Versatile, inexpensive, and convenient, eggs are one of the nutrient dense foods around. With 75 calories and only 5 grams of fat, eggs are one of the few foods that contain vitamin D, essential for almost all body functions.

A LOOK AT LEEKS

Leeks, the national vegetable of Wales, are also an important part of French, German, Swiss, Austrian, Scottish, Irish, and English cuisines. This is a good thing. Not only do these onion-family favorites lend a rich, satisfying taste to foods, they have proven health benefits, thanks to the following nutrients:

- Soluble and insoluble fiber helps digestive health and cardiovascular health and protects against some cancers.
- Allicin, which laboratory studies show reduces cholesterol while simultaneously having have anti-bacterial, anti-viral, and antifungal benefits.
- B-complex vitamins, such as pyridoxine, folic acid, niacin, riboflavin, and thiamin, all of which assist with healthy nervous system function.
- Vitamin A for healthy eyesight and skin and immune system function.
- Flavonoid anti-oxidants, including carotenes, xanthin, and lutein, which help strengthen the immune system and protect against cancer.
- Vitamin C helps the body develop resistance against infectious agents.
- Vitamin K is essential for cell growth and helps the body maintain healthy blood clotting.
- Vitamin E helps protect the body from invading bacteria and viruses while also strengthening the immune system.
- Small amounts of important minerals such as potassium, iron, calcium, magnesium, manganese, zinc, and selenium.

QUICHE WITH KALE

MAKES 6 TO 8 SERVINGS

This classic-style quiche is a fun way to celebrate morning! It's also a great light supper and travels beautifully to a brunch or lunch potluck. In other words, this quiche is always right!

Your favorite pie or tart dough, fitted into a 9-inch tart pan and blind-baked

1 *cup whole dairy or unsweetened non-dairy milk (or if you have it, ½ cup dairy or non-dairy milk and ½ cup cream or non-dairy cream)*
2 *large eggs plus 1 large egg yolk, room temperature*
  Pinch of freshly grated nutmeg
  Kosher salt and freshly ground pepper to taste
1 *leek, cleaned, chopped and sautéed*
1 *cup cooked, steamed, or blanched kale, squeezed dry and coarsely chopped*
1 *cup grated Gruyère cheese*

1. Heat oven to 375°F.

2. In a medium bowl, stir together the kale and leeks.

3. In another medium bowl, whisk together the milk, eggs, and yolk until combined. Then whisk in the nutmeg and season with salt and pepper.

4. Place the tart pan on a rimmed baking sheet. Sprinkle the bottom of the tart with half of the Gruyère cheese, then with the chopped kale-leek mixture, and then with the remaining half of Gruyère.

5. Carefully pour the custard over the cheese and kale-leek mixture.

6. Bake for about 30 to 35 minutes, until the center is just set.

7. Cool for at least 10 minutes before serving. Serve warm or at room temperature.

IN SEARCH OF A FLUFFY OMELET

As you may already know, an omelet (also spelled omelette) is a dish made from beaten eggs quickly cooked with butter or oil in a frying pan, sometimes folded around a filling such as cheese, vegetables, meat, or some combination of the above. For many cooks, the mark of a good omelet is fluffiness. But how to get this elusive quality? Some cooks beat the eggs to incorporate air bubbles into the eggs. Others add a splash of water, which evaporates (leaving behind bubbles within the omelet's structure). Still others add baking powder to create rise.

QUICHE: THE REAL HISTORY

The word "quiche" is derived from the German word for cake, *kuchen*. Although typically attributed to the French, quiches are actually German in origin. They come from the medieval German kingdom, Lothringen, which was renamed Lorraine when overtaken by the French.

EGGCELLENT!

You've probably seen those omega-enriched eggs at the supermarket. Ever wonder how they got to be so high in these essential fatty acids? It all starts with chicken feed. In other words, whatever the chicken eats a lot of, ends up in her eggs. Thus, many farmers are feeding their chickens flax or chia to increase the amount of both omega-3 and omega-6 fatty acid in eggs.

ROASTED RED PEPPER-KALE STRATA

MAKES 6 TO 8 SERVINGS

A strata is a kind of savory bread putting, a terrific way to use stale bread and make eggs stretch further. It's also a terrific make-ahead-and-finish-right-before-serving-brunch kind of dish, one that is so elegant people will think you spent hours on it.

6   large eggs
2   cups half and half or unsweetened non-dairy
    creamer (such as coconut)
3   tablespoons butter or extra virgin olive oil
1   cup chopped onion
½   cup chopped celery
1   cup chopped drained roasted red peppers from jar
1   garlic clove, minced
2   scallions, chopped
2   tablespoons chopped fresh parsley
1   teaspoon chopped fresh thyme
1   cup cooked, steamed or blanched kale,
    squeezed dry and coarsely chopped
8   cups 1-inch bread cubes from crustless French
    bread or gluten-free sandwich bread
1   teaspoon salt
¾   teaspoon ground black pepper
½   cup freshly grated Parmesan cheese

1. Butter 10-inch-diameter cake pan with 2-inch-high sides.
2. Whisk together eggs and half and half in medium bowl to blend.
3. Add olive oil or melt butter in heavy large skillet over medium-high heat. Add onion and celery and sauté until soft, about 5 minutes.
4. Add peppers, garlic, and kale and sauté about 2 minutes.
5. Remove from heat and stir in scallions, parsley, and thyme.
6. Transfer vegetable mixture to large bowl. Add bread cubes and toss to combine.
7. Add whisked egg mixture to vegetable-bread mixture. Season with salt and pepper, mixing well to combine.
8. Transfer mixture to the prepared cake pan. Let stand 30 minutes or cover and refrigerate overnight.
9. When you're ready to cook the strata, preheat oven to 350°F. Sprinkle strata with cheese.
10. Bake until brown and puffed, about 1 hour.
11. Cool on rack 30 minutes. The center will fall, this is normal. Using sharp knife, cut around edge to loosen. Cut into wedges and serve.

SCRAMBLED KALE EGGS

MAKES 2 SERVINGS

This is an easy one, perfect for a fast breakfast on days where you want something healthy. It's a great way to get protein and veggies into your morning. Feel free to increase the kale by a half-cup if you'd like.

1   tablespoon butter or extra virgin olive oil
2   large, fresh eggs
1   cup cooked, steamed, or blanched kale,
    squeezed dry and chopped shredded kale
Optional: 1 tablespoon milk (dairy or unsweetened
    non-dairy milk of choice)
    Salt and pepper to taste

1. In a small bowl, whisk together eggs, optional milk, and salt and pepper.

2. Add butter or oil to a small skillet over medium heat.

3. Add kale to butter and oil and allow to cook until kale is thoroughly warmed through.

4. Add eggs, stirring and scrambling as they set.

5. Cook until eggs reach your desired state of doneness.

EGG SAFETY AND HANDLING

Want to know how to keep eggs healthy, safe, and delicious to eat? These tips can help:

- An egg can absorb flavors and odors through tiny pores (up to 17,000 of them!) on its surface. Storing eggs in cartons helps keep them fresh.
- As an egg gets older the air space in the egg increases, causing it to float in a bowl of water. Just-laid eggs will always sink in water.
- Eggs are placed in their cartons large end up to keep the air cell in place and the yolk centered.
- Eggs age more in one day at room temperature than in one week in the refrigerator.
- Keep eggs in the main section of the refrigerator at a temperature between 33 and 40°F—eggs accidentally left at room temperature should be discarded after two hours, or one hour in warm weather.
- If kept in a cool refrigerator, eggs can be kept refrigerated in their carton for at least 4 to 5 weeks beyond the pack date.
- A hard-cooked egg will peel more easily if it is a week old before it is cooked.
- To tell if an egg is raw or hard-cooked, spin it! If the egg spins easily, it is hard-cooked, if it wobbles, it is raw.
- A greenish ring around a hard-cooked (boiled) egg yolk can be caused by overcooking or high iron content in the cooking water.
- Eggs are used in recipes to bind, leaven, thicken, emulsify, add protein, and create tenderness.
- Egg whites will beat to a better volume if they're allowed to stand at room temperature for 20 to 30 minutes before beating.

BREAKFAST SANDWICHES

BACON, KALE, AND SWEET POTATO BREAKFAST BURRITOS

MAKES 6 SERVINGS

Breakfast burritos are a fun, delicious, and super-versatile way to get your breakfast greens! Use this recipe as a guide—you can make these without the eggs or meat. You can change up the veggies. You can switch regular potatoes for the sweet potatoes. Try different toppings. Be creative!

3   slices bacon, chopped
2½ cups peeled, cooked sweet potatoes, cubed
½   cups red bell pepper, diced
½   cups onion, chopped
1   cup cooked, steamed, or blanched kale,
     squeezed dry and coarsely chopped
4   eggs
½   cups salsa, homemade or purchased
6   whole soft flour tortillas
Optional: ½ cups shredded Jack or mild
     cheddar cheese
Optional; 1 cup shredded lettuce
Optional: sour cream, cilantro, diced avocado,
     pepitas, and/or guacamole

1. In a medium bowl, whisk eggs. Set aside

2. Cook bacon in a large skillet over medium heat for about 8 to 10 minutes or until crispy. Remove with a slotted spoon and set aside. Drain bacon fat and reserve.

3. Add one tablespoon reserved bacon fat and cook eggs over medium heat, scrambling until done. Remove eggs and set aside.

4. Add two tablespoons of the reserved bacon fat. Add the bell pepper and onion. Add a couple pinches of salt and pepper over the top and cook, stirring occasionally, for about 5 minutes until the onions begin to soften.

5. Stir in the sweet potatoes and kale. Continue to cook until vegetables are warmed another 5 minutes or so.

6. Remove vegetables to a bowl and get ready salsa, cilantro, tortillas, and optional ingredients.

7. To make breakfast burritos, add about ¼ vegetable filling, a few tablespoons of egg, a few tablespoons of salsa, and desired optional ingredients to the bottom third of a tortilla. Roll or fold tortillas around filling, as desired.

DID YOU KNOW...?

Cilantro is one of the most powerful detoxifying herbs in use today. Health benefits provided by this culinary favorite include:

- Powerful anti-inflammatory capacities that may help symptoms of arthritis
- Protects against bacterial infection from Salmonella in food products
- Has been shown to increase HDL cholesterol (the good kind), and reduces LDL cholesterol (the bad kind)
- Helps relieve stomach gas, prevent flatulence, and works as an overall digestive aid
- Wards off urinary tract infections
- Helps reduce feelings of nausea
- Eases hormonal mood swings associated with menstruation
- Gives relief for diarrhea, especially if caused by microbial or fungal infections
- Helps promote healthy liver function.
- Reduces minor swelling
- Strong general antioxidant properties
- Disinfects and helps detoxify the body
- Stimulates the endocrine glands
- Helps with insulin secretion and lowers blood sugar
- Acts as a natural antiseptic and antifungal agent for skin disorders like fungal infections

EVERYTHING KALE BREAKFAST SANDWICH

MAKES 1 SERVING

This is a yummy, healthy, easy-to-put-together sandwich that is perfect for every day.

1   tablespoon butter or extra virgin olive oil
½   cup cooked, steamed, or blanched kale,
squeezed dry and coarsely chopped
¼   teaspoon paprika
1   egg
1   egg white

2   slices of buttered wheat toast
Optional: 1 to 2 slices cheddar or other cheese

1. Add butter or oil to a medium skillet over medium heat. Add kale and paprika and cook together for 1 or 2 minutes.
2. In a small bowl, whisk together egg and egg white.
3. Pour egg mixture over the kale, allowing eggs to set. Add cheese if using.
4. Flip set eggs if desired.
5. Tuck egg-kale mixture between slices of toast.

KALE TARTINE

MAKES 1 OR 2 SERVINGS

This elegant sandwich is a black tie way to enjoy kale. It's perfect with a mimosa and a side of fresh strawberries.

2   *thick slices of good bread*
2   *tablespoon butter*
½   *cup cooked or steamed kale, squeezed dry and coarsely chopped*
    Salt and pepper to taste
2   *tablespoons chopped chives or mixed herbs of choice*
1   *egg*
    Salt and pepper

1. Toast the bread and scrape on up to one tablespoon of butter.

2. Melt remaining butter in a medium skillet over medium heat.

3. Sautee the kale, herbs, and salt and pepper for a minute, until thoroughly warmed.

4. Add egg and quickly cook until barely scrambled around the kale.

5. Remove from the heat. Season with salt and pepper, pile on the toasted bread, and eat immediately.

WHAT'S A TARTINE?

A tartine is a "dressy" open-faced sandwich with a spread on top. In France, a tartine is usually served with some kind of fancy bread and a complex spread, perhaps topped with a flourish of veggies.

MUFFINS

APPLE AND KALE SPICE MUFFINS

MAKES 12 MUFFINS

This muffin always reminds me of fall. I think it's the apples and the warm cinnamon-nutmeg flavor. This will become a fast favorite. Trust me.

1½ cup whole wheat pastry flour or all-purpose flour (you can use a blend)
1   teaspoon each baking soda and baking powder
½   teaspoon salt
1   teaspoon cinnamon
¼   teaspoon nutmeg
1   teaspoon vanilla extract
⅓   cup honey
1   egg
½   cup sour milk or plain unflavored dairy or coconut-based yogurt
⅓   cup virgin coconut oil
1½ cup grated apples (you can chop them fine in a food processor)
1   cup blanched kale, squeezed dry and finely hopped (you can do this in a food processor)
Optional: ½ cup raisins or chopped dried apple
Optional: 1 cup chopped walnuts or pecans

1. Preheat oven to 375°F.
2. Line 12-cup muffin pan with muffin liners.

3. In a large bowl, whisk together flour, baking soda, baking powder, salt, and spices.
4. In another bowl, whisk together honey, egg, yogurt, oil, vanilla, apples, kale, and optional dried fruit and nuts.
5. Add wet ingredients to dry ingredients, stirring just until combined.
6. Fill 12 standard muffin cups ⅔ full. Bake for 18 to 20 minutes, or until muffins are springy to the touch. Allow to cool for 20 minutes before removing.

VEGAN "BUTTERMILK"

If you don't use dairy products, you don't have to forgo recipes with buttermilk. Simply make your own vegan buttermilk by adding two tablespoons lemon juice or vinegar to a cup of soy, almond, rice, or other none-dairy milk. Allow milk to sit for 15 minutes and give it a quick whisk before using.

MORNING GLORY KALE MUFFINS

MAKES 12 MUFFINS

Lots of people love those apple and carrot-enriched whole grain muffins called Morning Glory muffins (I know I do!). This is just such a muffin, with the addition of (shhh!!!) kale. You'll love it, as will everyone else. Though you may want to keep the kale on the low-down, if you know what I mean.

¼ cup orange juice

¼ cup virgin coconut oil

½ cup agave syrup

1 egg

½ cup milk or unsweetened non-dairy milk (I like almond milk in this recipe)

1 teaspoon vanilla or almond extract

½ cup shredded carrots

½ cup kale, cooked, steamed, or blanched 'til tender then pureed with 2 tablespoons almond milk in food processor

1½ cup whole wheat pastry flour

½ teaspoon nutmeg or cinnamon

1 teaspoon baking soda

1 teaspoon baking powder

Optional: ½ cup chopped walnuts or other nuts

Optional: ½ cup raisins or dried cranberries or dried blueberries or fresh blueberries

1. Preheat oven to 375°F.

2. Prepare 12 standard muffin tins by fitting with cupcake liners.

3. In a food processor, puree kale with two tablespoons or so of the milk.

4. In a large bowl, sift together flour, nutmeg, baking soda, baking powder, and salt.

5. In the bowl of the food processor, add juice, coconut oil, syrup, egg, milk, and vanilla extract, pulsing ingredients until smooth.

6. Add liquid ingredients to dry ingredients, mixing only until combined.

7. Fold carrots and any optional ingredients to batter, being careful not to overmix.

8. Fill prepared muffin cups ⅔ full with batter. Bake for 17 to 22 minutes, or until muffins are springy to the touch. Allow finished muffins to cool 20 minutes or so before removing.

SAVORY CARROT AND KALE MUFFINS (grain-free/gluten-free)

MAKES 12 MUFFINS

I like this recipe because it's not sweet. Sometimes I think I am one of the only people in North America who doesn't like to have sweet foods for breakfast! It's also great tasting, healthy, and doesn't contain gluten, a real plus for my gluten-free sons.

2   cups blanched almond flour
½   cup coconut flour
1¼   teaspoons baking powder
1   teaspoon baking soda
1   teaspoon salt
1   or 2 teaspoons dried thyme
1   or 2 teaspoons dried basil
1   cup carrot, finely grated
1   cup blanched kale, squeezed dry and finely chopped
4   eggs
¼   cup honey
1   cup virgin coconut oil
½   cup dairy or non-dairy yogurt (I like plain coconut yogurt in this recipe)

1. Preheat oven to 350°F.

2. Line two 12-cup muffin pans with muffin liners.

3. In a large bowl, whisk together almond and coconut flours, baking powder, baking soda and salt, thyme, and basil.

4. Add carrots and kale to dry ingredients and mix together until everything is thoroughly combined.

5. In a food processor or high-speed blender (such as a VitaMix), add eggs and honey. Process for 20 seconds.

6. Add coconut oil and yogurt to the food processor or blender and process an additional 20 seconds until all ingredients are combined and the mixture is smooth.

7. Pour wet ingredients into dry ingredients, mixing until thoroughly combined.

8. Fill muffin cups ⅔ full and bake for 18 to 20 minutes, or until muffins are springy to the touch. Cool for 20 minutes before removing muffins from pan.

BAKING WITHOUT GLUTEN

Gluten, the protein in wheat, gives baked goods structure and a soft, springy texture. If you've been told you have to give up gluten, you have options, one of them being chia. Just keep in mind that baked goods made without wheat may have either a heavier moisture, or a drier texture, depending upon the non-gluten flour you bake with.

CINNAMON'S SWEET BENEFITS

- Cinnamon has a lot of fans, most recently among researchers who have been diligently studying its health-supportive properties. Some of the most impressive of these, include: ½ teaspoon of cinnamon per day can lower your bad cholesterol (LDL).
- Cinnamon may help treat Type 2 Diabetes by lowering blood sugar levels and increasing the amount of insulin production in the body.
- Cinnamon has an anti-clotting effect on the blood.
- Cinnamon has antifungal properties, and it's been said that Candida cannot live in the presence of cinnamon. Candida, known more formally as Candida albicans, is a yeast organism found in low levels in healthy bodies. In some individuals, it can "over-grow," leading to thrush, vaginitis, digestive upset or severe rectal itching.
- Cinnamon can reduce the proliferation of leukemia and lymphoma cancer cells.
- When added to food, cinnamon inhibits bacterial growth and food spoilage, making it a natural food preservative.
- Studies have found that the act of smelling cinnamon boosts cognitive function and memory.
- Cinnamon has been found to be an effective natural remedy for eliminating headaches and migraine relief.

SUMMER SQUASH-KALE MUFFINS

MAKES 12 MUFFINS

This yummy recipe is reminiscent of zucchini bread, that summertime staple in gardening homes. It's an easy, fun, portable breakfast on the go and makes a delicious mid-morning snack.

1½ cups grated fresh zucchini or yellow squash
1   *cup cooked or steamed kale, coarsely chopped*
2   *eggs*
1   *cup sugar*
1   *teaspoon vanilla*
¼   *cup virgin coconut oil*
¼   *cup applesauce, pearsauce or pumpkin puree*
2   *teaspoons baking soda*
1   *pinch salt*
3   *cups whole wheat pastry or all-purpose flour (you can use a mix)*
1   *to 2 teaspoons cinnamon (or a mixture of cinnamon, ginger, nutmeg, cloves, and/or allspice)*
Optional: 1 cup chopped walnuts, pecans, or other nuts

1. Preheat oven to 350°F.
2. Prepare a 12-cup standard muffin tin or 24-cup mini muffin tin with cupcake liners.
3. In a large bowl, whisk eggs.
4. Add sugar, vanilla, oil, and applesauce,

mixing until combined and beat until sugar is dissolved and mixture is light in color.

5. Fold in zucchini and kale, thoroughly combining.

6. In a large bowl, whisk together all remaining ingredients but nuts.

7. Add dry ingredients to wet ingredients, mixing just until combined. Gently fold in optional nuts, being careful not to overmix.

8. Fill muffin cups ⅔ full with batter and bake for 15 to 20 minutes for mini muffins, 25 to 30 minutes for standard muffins, or until muffins are springy to the touch. Let cool for 20 minutes before removing from pan.

EASY LEMON ZEST

I love the bright zing that fresh lemon zest brings food. But zesting lemons is not fun—unless you have a plane grater. These hand-held, wand-like graters make fast work of lemon zest. Try one and you'll wonder how you survived without one.

SUPER AWESOME HEALTH MUFFINS
MAKE 9 LARGE MUFFINS

These gorgeous muffins have all kinds of healthy things in them, including blueberries! My hubby loves one of these with his afternoon coffee.

1   cup whole wheat pastry flour or all-purpose flour
¾   cup golden flaxseed meal
½   cup brown sugar
1   tablespoon baking powder
1   teaspoon cinnamon or lemon zest
½   teaspoon salt
1   cup plain yogurt (can use coconut or other non-dairy yogurt)
2   tablespoons virgin coconut oil
1   egg, lightly beaten
1   cup cooked, steamed, or blanched kale, squeezed dry and finely chopped
1   cup fresh or frozen blueberries

1. Preheat oven to 375°F.

2. Prepare 9 muffin cups by lining muffin tin with cupcake liners

3. In a medium bowl, whisk together four, flaxseed meal, brown sugar, baking powder, and cinnamon.

4. In another bowl, whisk together the yogurt, coconut oil, and egg.

5. Pour the wet ingredients into the dry ingredients, stirring only to combine.

6. Add blueberries and kale, gently folding them into the batter. Be careful not to overmix.

7. Fill muffin cups ⅔ full and bake for 20 to 25 minutes or until muffins are springy to the touch. Allow them to cool for 20 minutes before removing them.

VEGAN BANANA-KALE MUFFINS

MAKES 6 MUFFINS

This easy eggless recipe is super versatile. Add chocolate chips, chopped nuts, even diced dried fruit. If you don't have whole wheat pastry flour, use regular unbleached all-purpose flour.

3   *medium ripe bananas*
4   *raw kale leaves, deribbed*
¼   *cup virgin coconut oil*
1   *cup sugar*
2   *cups whole wheat pastry flour*
½   *teaspoon cinnamon*
½   *teaspoons sea salt*
1   *teaspoon baking soda*

1. Fit a 6-cup standard muffin tin or 12-cup mini-muffin tin with cupcake liners.
2. Preheat oven to 350°F.
3. In the bowl of a food processor or high-speed blender, place the bananas and kale leaves. Pulse a few times until kale has been pulverized.
4. Add the oil and sugar and blend until smooth.
5. In large bowl, whisk together the whole wheat pastry flour, cinnamon, salt, and baking soda.
6. Pour the wet ingredients into the dry ingredients and mix just to combine, being careful not to overmix the batter.
7. Fill prepared muffin cups ⅔ full and bake for 15 minutes or until they are springy to the touch and a toothpick comes out clean.

ABOUT THE WORD "MUFFIN"

The name "muffin" is thought to come from the French word *moufflet*, meaning soft bread.

CEREAL

IRISH OATS
MAKES 2 SERVINGS

This recipe makes one bowl of very (very) green porridge. My kids will happily eat this on St. Paddy's Day, but avoid it on other, less Irish days of the year. Go figure.

½   *cups water*
    Dash of salt
1   *cup steel cut oats*
1   *cup blanched kale*
½   *cup almond milk*
¼   *cup unsweetened applesauce*
¼   *cup unsweetened coconut flakes*
3   *tablespoons maple syrup*
Optional: Chopped walnuts

1. In a medium pot, bring water to boil. Add a dash of salt.
2. Add oats to the boiling water. Lower heat and cook for 20 to 30 minutes.
3. While the oats are cooking, add kale, almond milk, applesauce, coconut, and maple syrup to a high-speed blender, such as a Vita-Mix. Process until completely liquefied.
4. Bring the heat up to medium-high on the oats. Pour in the green mixture and add the coconut flakes. Continue cooking until thick.
5. To serve, spoon into a bowl and sprinkle chopped walnuts on top.

YAY, OATMEAL

Oatmeal comes from the grain of the oat plant. After harvesting, oats are minimally processed—the manufacturer removes the hull of the oat grain and grinds the grain into coarse flakes. A one-cup serving of oatmeal contains 311 calories and the following percentages of the recommended daily value of these nutrients:

- 32% of dietary fiber
- 26% of protein
- 39% of thiamin
- 38% of phosphorus

- 30% of magnesium
- 19% of iron
- 14% of copper

HOTCAKES

DINER-STYLE KALE PANCAKES

MAKES ABOUT 8 MEDIUM-SIZED PANCAKES

This is a natural for St. Paddy's Day, is the perfect accompaniment to Green Eggs and Ham, and is fun for any kid who likes green. Plus, they taste good!

2   cups of whole wheat pastry flour or gluten-free all-purpose flour blend
1   tablespoon of ground chia
1   teaspoon of salt
2   tablespoons of sugar
1¾   tablespoons of baking powder
Optional: 1 teaspoon cinnamon or a mix of cinnamon, ginger, nutmeg, cloves, and allspice
4   tablespoons virgin coconut oil
8   tablespoons of applesauce or pumpkin puree
2   eggs

TENDER PANCAKES EVERY TIME

For tender pancakes, go easy on the blending. Whisk together the dry ingredients and the wet ingredients separately, then combine them. Mixing only until just barely incorporated. Stop immediately once that happens!

1½ cup of dairy or nondairy milk
½   cup cooked, steamed or blanched kale, pureed
½   teaspoon vanilla

1. In a large bowl, whisk together flour, chia, salt, sugar, baking powder, and optional spices.
2. In a separate bowl, whisk together oil, applesauce, eggs, milk, kale puree, and vanilla.
3. Add the liquid ingredients to the flour mixture, stirring only until combined and being careful not to overmix.
4. Cook on a nonstick griddle placed over medium-high heat.

PANCAKE FUN

- Some countries celebrate Mardi Gras (aka Shrove Tuesday) as Pancake Day. What better excuse to enjoy some buttery, super sweet, rich food before Lent?
- Pancakes begin appearing in written recipes and cookbooks in the very early 1400s.
- Once upon a time there was no such thing as pancake mix. Then, in 1889, the world's first ready-made mix was sold commercially. Its name? Aunt Jemima Pancake Flour, invented in St. Joseph, Missouri.
- Pancake breakfasts are a favorite fundraising activity. The world's largest of these happened in 1999 in Springfield, Massachusetts, with more than 71,233 servings of pancakes being served to over 40,000 people. If you stacked up all those pancakes, they'd be more than 2 miles high!

KALE WAFFLES

MAKES ABOUT 8 MEDIUM WAFFLES

Most of us have fond memories of our mothers or grandmothers making us waffles—or even ordering waffles in a diner or pancake house. Nowadays, however, we're so busy that most of us rely on prepackaged frozen waffles. I'm here to tell you that if you have a waffle iron, waffles are fast and easy to make. Plus, you can freeze a few for another day, creating your own stash of frozen breakfast treats!

1¾ cup almond, hemp or coconut milk

3   eggs

1   cup chopped raw kale leaves

¼   cup virgin coconut oil

1   teaspoon vanilla extract

1   teaspoon salt

1   teaspoon cinnamon

2   cups whole wheat pastry flour or gluten-free all-purpose flour blend

2   teaspoons baking powder

1. Plug in your waffle iron and set it to medium heat.
2. Place milk, kale, oil, vanilla, and salt in a high-speed blender, such as a VitaMix. Blend until liquefied.
3. Add cinnamon, flour, and baking powder to the VitaMix and pulse just until blended (being careful to not overmix).
4. To prevent deflated waffles, let batter sit 5 to 10 minutes before pouring in waffle iron.
5. Use waffle batter to make waffles per your waffle maker's instructions.

WAFFLE STACK

Looking for something different for breakfast? Take a frozen or homemade waffle, top it with a serving of scrambled egg, a thin red onion slice, ¼ cup of kale, an optional flourish of grated cheese, and pop into a toaster oven set on broil. Remove when cheese has melted. Serve as-is or with a splash of hot sauce or tablespoon of salsa. Yum!

SAVORY WAFFLES

MAKES ABOUT 4 MEDIUM WAFFLES

Sometimes you want something hearty and savory for breakfast. For those times, try these delicious waffles.

¾   cup whole wheat pastry flour or gluten-free all-purpose flour blend

¼   cup cornmeal

¼   teaspoon salt

1½   baking powder

¾   cup dairy or unsweetened nondairy milk

1   egg

½   cup cheddar cheese, shredded

½   cup cooked kale, squeezed dry and coarsely chopped

4   slices ham or other meat, chopped
     Ketchup, salsa, or other condiments for serving

1. Plug in your waffle iron and set it to medium heat.

2. In a large bowl, whisk together flour, cornmeal, salt, and baking powder.

3. In a separate bowl, whisk milk and egg until incorporated.

4. Stir liquid ingredients into dry ingredients, mixing only until combined.

5. Gently fold in meat, cheese, and kale, being careful not to over mix.

6. Use waffle batter to make waffles per your waffle maker's instruction.

A LOOK BACK

Waffles have a long and glorious history. The ancient Greeks used to cook a waffle-like something called *oblelios*, a type of flat cake cooked between two metal plates. By the Middle Ages, the Europeans were making *oblelios*, sometimes in their original flat form and sometimes rolled into cones. It wasn't until the 13th century, however, that decorated waffle plates appeared, changing the look of waffles as we know them!

LYCO-WHAT?

If you're a tomato lover, you may know about lycopene, an antioxidant in the carotenoid family that is present in tomatoes. This red, fat-soluble pigment helps neutralize harmful free radicals, which are implicated in cancer, heart disease, macular degeneration, and other age-related illnesses. It also helps protect the body against cancer.

Lycopene is especially high in cooked tomato products. Why? Cooking processed tomatoes breaks down cell walls, releasing and concentrating carotenoids. Ketchup, canned tomato soup, tomato juice, pasta sauce, and pizza sauce, are the richest sources of lycopene.

MORNING POTATOES

CHORIZO KALE HASH BROWNS

MAKES 4 TO 6 SERVINGS

I love potatoes, especially during the cold weather months when a body craves something filling. That said, I don't eat a lot of them—I'm one of those sensitive types whose blood sugar goes crazy after just one serving of the starchy tubers. However, I've found that by combining potatoes with protein and greens, sensitive people like me are much better able to enjoy the comforting veggie.

1   medium onion, finely chopped
1   or 2 garlic cloves, minced
2   tablespoons extra-virgin olive oil, divided
2   pounds russet (baking) potatoes (about 3), peeled
2   ounces Spanish chorizo (cured spiced pork sausage), finely chopped (about ½ cup)
½   cup cooked or steamed kale, squeezed dry and finely chopped
¼   cup chopped flat-leaf parsley
    Dash of paprika
½   teaspoon salt
    Dash black pepper
1   tablespoon unsalted butter

1. Add 1 tablespoon oil to a nonstick skillet and, over medium heat, sauté onion, and garlic until softened, about 3 to 5 minutes.

2. Using a box grater or the grating attachment of a food processor, coarsely grate potatoes. Squeeze out any excess water.

3. In a large bowl, mix together cooked onion mixture, grated potatoes, chorizo, kale, parsley, paprika, salt, and pepper until thoroughly combined.

4. Wipe out the skillet and heat butter and remaining tablespoon of oil over medium heat until butter is melted.

5. Add mixture, spreading it evenly in skillet and pressing gently to flatten. Cook over medium heat until crisp and golden, 8 to 10 minutes.

6. To turn the hash brown, invert a large plate over skillet. Holding plate and skillet tightly together, invert hash browns onto plate. Slide the hash browns back into skillet and press gently to flatten. Cook until golden and cooked through, 8 to 10 minutes more. Cut into wedges and serve.

HASH WHAT POTATOES?

While some people say hash browns originated from the Swiss potato dish rösti, hash brown potatoes are as American as apple pie, showing up in the American food lexicon in 1888, when food author Maria Parloa mentions "hashed browned potatoes." The name was gradually shortened to "hash brown potatoes." By the late 1960s, people were merely saying "hash browns."

OVEN HASH KALE CAKES

MAKES 4 SERVINGS

This oven recipe is a glorified potato pan-cake—as yummy and satisfying as any you've ever had, with the healthy addition of kale.

Butter for greasing pan
1½ cups paper-thin onion slices, preferably from a sweet onion such as Vidalia
1 pound Yukon Gold potatoes, peeled
¼ cup cooked or steamed kale, squeezed dry and chopped finely
1 teaspoon salt, divided
2 tablespoons unsalted butter, melted

1. Preheat oven to 425°F.

2. Grease a large rimmed nonstick baking sheet with butter.

3. Using a box grater or the grating attachment of a food processor, coarsely grate potatoes.

4. Toss potatoes with ½ teaspoon salt in medium bowl. Let stand 5 minutes. Using hands, squeeze out excess liquid from potatoes.

5. Place onion in large bowl. Add potatoes, kale, ½ teaspoon salt, and melted butter. Toss to coat.

6. Divide mixture into 4 mounds on prepared baking sheet, allowing space between mounds.

7. Roast 15 minutes, then turn mounds over with spatula, pressing down to flatten to 4-inch-diameter rounds (cakes will still be soft).

8. Reduce oven temperature to 350°F and bake until cakes are golden and crisp around edges, about 45 minutes longer.

POTATOES YOUR WAY

- Home fries are a basic potato preparation featured cubed potatoes cooked in oil or fat.
- Rösti is a Swiss shredded potato dish, traditionally eaten as a "farmer's breakfast."
- Potato pancakes feature shredded potato and egg, cooked in the shape of a griddle cake.
- Corned beef hash contains cubed or shredded potatoes fried with onions and corned beef.
- Potatoes O'Brien are hash browns cooked with green bell peppers.
- Tater Tots is a trademark name for a form of small shredded potato puffs.
- Potato waffles are waffle-shaped frozen potato cakes sold in the UK and Ireland.
- Hash is a dish made of fried potato and bits of leftover meat and veggies.
- Bubble and squeak potato contains potatoes, fried together with leftovers.
- Rappie pie is a French-North American casserole made with shredded potatoes.
- Boxty is a popular Irish potato dish.
- Croquettes are small fried items bound with mashed potatoes.
- Aloo tikki is a North Indian potato snack.

POTATO AND KALE GALETTE

MAKES 8 SERVINGS

I don't have superlatives enough for this elegant dish. All I can say is you must try it. Very soon. In order to slice the potatoes super-thin, you'll need a mandoline, or a food processor fitted with a slicing blade. You'll also need a super heavy large skillet, such as a cast iron pan, to use as a weight.

4   garlic cloves, finely chopped
2   cups cooked or steamed kale, squeezed dry
     and coarsely chopped.
1   stick (½ cup) butter, 6 tablespoons melted
     and cooled
2   pounds russet (baking) potatoes (4 medium),
     peeled
¾   teaspoon salt
¾   teaspoon black pepper
     Paprika

1. Heat 2 tablespoons of the unmelted butter in a large nonstick skillet over medium-high heat. Add garlic and cook, stirring occasionally, until golden, about one minute.

2. To the skillet add kale, ¼ teaspoon salt, and ¼ teaspoon pepper. Sauté until kale is warmed through, about 2 to 4 minutes.

3. Transfer kale mixture to a bowl and wipe out skillet.

4. Using a mandoline or a food processor outfitted with a slicing blade, slice potatoes crosswise no more than $\frac{1}{16}$ of an inch thick.

5. Working quickly to prevent potatoes from discoloring, generously brush bottom of skillet with some of melted butter and cover with $\frac{1}{3}$ of the potato slices, overlapping slightly. Dab potatoes with some of melted butter.

6. Spread half of kale over potatoes and sprinkle with ⅛ teaspoon salt and ⅛ teaspoon pepper.

BLACK PEPPER: NOTHING TO SNEEZE AT

Black pepper has a reputation as a sneeze-maker, thanks to the way small bits of the spice can enter and irritate the nasal cavity. Fortunately, this is more annoying than harmful, for black pepper has so many health benefits, you'll want to use it often:

- A two-teaspoon dose of black pepper contains 12% of your daily requirement of manganese, 8.6% of vitamin K, 6.7% of iron, 4.4.% of fiber, and 2.5% of copper.
- Black pepper is a carminative, a substance that helps prevent the formation of intestinal gas.
- Black pepper has diaphoretic properties, meaning it promotes sweating.
- It also is a diuretic, helping the body flush excess water through urination.
- It has powerful antibacterial effects, making it an important ingredient to help stay healthy.

7. Cover with half of remaining potato slices and dab with butter, then top with remaining kale. Sprinkle with ⅛ teaspoon salt and ⅛ teaspoon pepper. Top with remaining potatoes and sprinkle with remaining ¼ teaspoon salt and ¼ teaspoon pepper. Finish, if desired, with a dusting of paprika.

8. Brush a sheet of foil with melted butter, then brush galette with any remaining butter and place foil, buttered side down, on top. Place a 10-inch heavy skillet on top of foil to weight galette.

9. Cook galette over moderate heat until underside is golden brown, about 12 to 15 minutes. Remove top skillet and foil. Wearing oven mitts, carefully slide galette onto a baking sheet and invert skillet over it. Holding them together, invert galette, browned side up, back into skillet. Cook, uncovered, over moderate heat until underside is golden brown and potatoes are tender, 12 to 15 minutes. Slide onto a serving plate.

10. If you'd like, you can make the galette 4 or 5 hours ahead. Cool the cooked galette. Once it's cool, you can place it on a baking sheet covered with foil, allowing it to sit out at room temperature. To reheat, remove foil, then warm the galette in a 400°F oven until heated through and crisp, about 20 minutes.

CHAPTER 5

KALE FOR LUNCH

You know that old saying about breakfast being the most important meal of the day? For me, the most important meal of the day is lunch. Without a doubt. Midday is when your body is busiest, needing the most calories to fuel it through a marathon of mental and physical (even emotional) activities.

One wrong turn, and you can choose a meal that will make you sluggish, or put you on a cycle of cravings, or upset your tummy, or leave you spacey, or make you irritable, or create some other kind of outcome that will hamper your ability to be productive and creative.

Done right, lunch can energize you and leave you feeling satisfied, happy, intellectually sharp, happy, and powerful. Kale can help with that. Really. Sometimes when I am feeling sluggish and mentally slow, I add a green juice made with kale to my lunch menu. Or, I'll juice a soup or salad featuring kale. Afterward, I feel focused and clearheaded, ready to tackle anything that makes its way across my desk.

Try it for yourself. I dare you: Today (or tomorrow), have kale for lunch and see how great you feel afterward!

SOUPS, STEWS, AND CHILIS

BARLEY-KALE STEW
MAKES 6 SERVINGS

This hearty, meatless stew is satisfying as well as deeply healing thanks to the bountiful antioxidants found in barley, kale, leeks, tomatoes, garlic, and tomato—all ingredients in this yummy recipe.

1   *tablespoon olive oil, divided*
2   *small leeks, chopped (white and pale green parts only)*
1½ *cups thinly sliced button or cremini mushrooms (you can use a mix)*
2   *garlic cloves, minced*
2¼ *teaspoons minced fresh rosemary*
1   *(14.5-ounce) can diced tomatoes in juice*
1   *cup pearl barley*
4   *cups (or more) chicken or vegetable broth*
1   *bunch kale, deribbed and coarsely chopped*

1. Heat oil in heavy large pot over medium heat. Add leeks; sprinkle with salt and pepper and sauté until leeks begin to soften, stirring often, about 5 minutes.

2. Add mushrooms, garlic, and rosemary; increase heat to medium-high and sauté until mushrooms soften and begin to brown, stirring often, about 7 minutes.

3. Add tomatoes with their juice; stir 1 minute.

4. Add barley and 4 cups broth. Bring to boil.

5. Reduce heat to low, cover, and simmer until barley is almost tender, about 20 to 30 minutes.

6. Add kale. Cover and simmer until kale and barley are tender, about 15 minutes. Note: if you desire a more liquid consistency, add ¼ cup or more broth as desired.

GETTING TO KNOW BARLEY

Barley is a nourishing cereal grain rich in fiber, protein, and B-complex vitamins. Cultivated since ancient times, it is enjoyed in many different forms:

- **Hulled barley:** Chewy and dense, hulled barley is a whole grain that has only its outermost husk removed.
- **Scotch barley:** Also called pot barley, grains are polished to remove the outer hull. Not as dense, chewy, or nutritious as hulled barley, Scotch barley is still a high-nutrient food. Its name comes from Scotland, where it was and is a popular soup pot ingredient.
- **Pearl barley:** By polishing, or "pearling" grains of barley, the outermost hull, the grain's brain layer and even part of its inner endosperm layer, are all removed. Quicker cooking and lighter in texture than hulled barley, pearl barley is markedly lower in nutrients.
- **Barley flakes:** Think rolled oats—only with barley. Eaten as a hot cereal or added to baked goods.
- **Barley grits:** Hulled, Scotch, or even pearl barley can be toasted and cracked, creating what is known as barley grits. These can be cooked and eaten as a breakfast cereal or a side dish with meats and veggies.

CANNELINI-BUTTERNUT-KALE STEW

MAKES 6 SERVINGS

For me, butternut squash means autumn. I love roasted the squash and pureeing it into smoothies, sauces, and soups, or cutting into chunks and tossing with oil and herbs before roasting. In this warming recipe, this well-loved squash is joined by kale and white beans.

¼   cup olive oil
3   large onions, chopped
6   garlic cloves, minced
1   2- to 3-pound butternut squash, peeled, seeded, cut into 1½-inch cubes
3   red or orange bell peppers, seeded, cut into 1½-inch pieces
1½ cups chicken broth
1½ large bunches kale, deribbed and coarsely chopped
½   tablespoon dried rubbed sage
¼   teaspoon red pepper flakes
5   (15-ounce) cans cannellini (white kidney beans), rinsed, drained

Optional: Grated parmesan cheese, chopped parsley

1. Heat oil in heavy large Dutch oven over medium-high heat. Add onions and garlic; sauté until tender, about 10 minutes.

2. Add squash; sauté.

3. Add bell peppers and stir to coat with onion mixture. Add broth. Cover and simmer until squash is just tender, about 10 minutes.

4. Mix kale, sage, and red pepper flakes into stew. Cover and cook until kale wilts, stirring occasionally, about 8 minutes.

5. Add beans and stir until heated through. Season to taste with salt and pepper.

6. Serve with optional toppings.

HEALING WITH OLIVES

For years health advocates have been talking about the benefits olive oil—how it lowers cholesterol, helps with blood pressure, and even strengthens the immune system. Whole olives are just as healing. In fact, herbalists have long used preparations from olives and olive leaves to treat inflammatory conditions and allergies.

How do they work? Olive extracts function as antihistamines at a cellular level. Histamines are molecules that create inflammation. Thus, olives—your favorite cured olives!—are a wonderful addition to anyone's diet, especially those of you who suffer from environmental, food, or contact allergies.

CANNELLINI BEANS

Popular in Tuscany, cannellini beans are large white beans, with a firm texture and skin and a nut-like flavor. I love their versatility—they hold their shape well, making them great for salads. They are delicious in soup. And they are outstanding pureed with roasted garlic as a sandwich spread or dip. Want to get to know the cannellini better? Here's some fun facts about the bean:

- Cannellini are related to kidney beans, great northern, navy, and green beans, among others.
- Like other beans, cannellinies are low in fat and high in protein, fiber, minerals, and B vitamins.
- The Tuscans so love cannellini beans that the people are referred to as "bean eaters," or "mangiafagioli" in Italian.
- Some people call cannellini beans "white kidney beans."
- Cannellinies are a traditional ingredient in minestrone.
- One cup of the beans contain 20 grams of protein, 12 grams of fiber, 20 percent of an adult's daily requirement of iron and 8 percent of an adult's daily requirement of calcium.

KALE AND CANNELLINI SOUP

MAKES 6 SERVINGS

If you're a recipe collector—and there are a lot of us in the world—I know you've come across several recipes that feature the classic combo of kale and cannellini beans. It's a delicious, nutritious, hearty combination that is as beautiful to look at as it is wonderful to eat. Here, kale and cannellini find their way into the same soup pot with pancetta, chestnut, and parmesan!

½ *pound dried cannellini beans (about 1¼ cups), picked over and rinsed*
¼ *pound thinly sliced pancetta, chopped*
1 *large onion, chopped*
3 *garlic cloves, minced*
3 *tablespoons extra-virgin olive oil*
1 *(14-ounce) can diced tomatoes, juice reserved*
3½ *cups chicken broth*
2 *cups water*
1 *piece Parmigiano-Reggiano rind (roughly 3- by 3-inch)*
  Salt and pepper to taste
1½ *cups bottled peeled cooked whole chestnuts (8 ounces), halved*
½ *pound kale (preferably Lacinto), deribbed and roughly chopped*
2 *teaspoons chopped fresh thyme*
Optional garnish: Parmigiano-Reggiano shavings, black pepper

1. Soak beans in cold water to cover by 2 inches in a bowl at room temperature at least 8 hours. Drain well in a colander.

2. In a large, heavy pot over moderate heat, sauté pancetta, onion, and garlic in olive oil. Stir occasionally, cooking until browned, about 8 minutes.

3. Add tomatoes with juice, beans, broth, water, cheese rind, salt, and pepper and simmer, uncovered, until beans are tender, 45 minutes to 1 hour. Remove cheese rind.

4. Stir in chestnuts.

5. Transfer 2½ cups soup to a blender and purée until smooth. Return to the pot.

6. Stir in kale and simmer, uncovered, stirring occasionally, until leaves are tender, 10 to 15 minutes.

7. Stir in thyme.

HEALTH BENEFITS OF CHESTNUT

Chestnuts aren't like all those other nuts. They're starchier. Higher in vitamins. (In fact, their nutrition composition is very similar to sweet potatoes!) And they are loaded with minerals and phytonutrients. Want to know more? Here you go:

- Chestnuts are a good source of dietary fiber, providing 21% of daily recommended value per 100-gram serving. As you may know, fiber helps with digestion and lowers blood cholesterol levels by limiting excess cholesterol absorption in the intestines.
- Chestnuts are rich in vitamin C, with 72% of daily recommended value per 100-gram serving. Vitamin C strengthens the immune system and, as an antioxidant, it offers protection from harmful free radicals.
- Unlike other nuts and seeds, chestnuts are rich in folic acid. A 100-gram serving provides 15.5% of the daily recommended value. Folic acid is required for the formation of red blood cells and DNA synthesis, making it an essential during pregnancy.
- Chestnuts are rich source of mono-unsaturated fatty like oleic acid and palmitoleic acids. Studies suggest that monounsaturated fats in the diet help lower LDL (bad cholesterol) and increase HDL (good cholesterol) levels within the blood.
- Further, they are also rich in many important B-complex groups of vitamins, helpful for healthy nervous system function. A 100-gram serving of chestnuts provide 11% of niacin, 29% of pyridoxine (vitamin B-6), 100% of thiamin, and 12% of riboflavin.
- The nut is also an excellent source of minerals such as iron, calcium, magnesium, manganese, phosphorus, potassium, and zinc.

GARBANZO KALE SOUP

MAKES 6 TO 8 SERVINGS

This warming soup features one of my favorite flavor duos: chickpea and kale. One is mellow and nutty-tasting, while the other is a bit brassy and astringent. Both have a meaty bite and are outrageously healthy!

2   tablespoons extra-virgin olive oil
1   medium onion, chopped
2   garlic cloves, minced
    Salt and pepper to taste
1   bay leaf
2   medium red-skinned (boiling) potatoes, peeled and cut into ½-inch cubes
¾   pound kale, deribbed, leaves finely chopped
5½ cups chicken broth
1   (14-ounce) can chickpeas, rinsed and drained
¼   pound Spanish chorizo (cured spiced pork sausage), casing removed and sausage cut into ¼-inch dice (about 1 cup)

1. In a large, heavy pot over medium heat, sauté onion, garlic, salt, and pepper in oil, stirring frequently, until onion and garlic are softened and beginning to brown, about 5 to 7 minutes.

2. Add bay leaf, potato, kale, broth, and water and cook, partially covered, until potatoes are tender, 15 to 20 minutes.

3. Reduce heat to low, then add chickpeas and chorizo and gently simmer, uncovered, for about 3 to 5 minutes.

4. Remove bay leaf and season with salt and pepper.

GO GO GARBANZOS!

Garbanzos, also known as chickpeas, contain about 12.5 grams of fiber per cup. That's 50% of the daily recommended value. This explains why participants in a recent study reported more satisfaction with their diet when garbanzo beans were included, consuming fewer processed food snacks and less food overall. Bring on the hummus!

LENTIL AND VEGETABLE STEW WITH KALE

MAKES 8 SERVINGS

We use a lot of lentils in my house. They are inexpensive (important when feeding three boys, a couple who need costly special food), fast to cook, mild-tasting and incredibly versatile. Oh, and they are also nutritional, filled with protein and fiber. This soup is simple way to get more of this little legume into your daily diet.

2   tablespoons olive oil
1   large onion, chopped
2   large carrots, peeled and cut into large dice
1   to 2 large celery stalks, chopped
    Salt and pepper to taste
1   medium rutabaga, peeled and cut into large dice
1   to 2 garlic cloves, minced

1   pound brown lentils, rinsed
1   tablespoon herbes de Provence
8   cups (or more) chicken or vegetable broth
1   large bunch kale (about 9 ounces), deribbed
    and coarsely chopped

1. Heat oil in large pot over high heat. Add onion, garlic, carrots, celery and rutabaga; sprinkle with salt and pepper and sauté until beginning to soften and brown, about 10 to 11 minutes.

2. Stir in garlic, lentils, and herbes de Provence.

3. Add broth and kale. Bring to boil, stirring to incorporate kale.

4. Reduce heat to medium-low, cover with lid slightly ajar, and simmer until lentils are tender, stirring occasionally, about 20 minutes.

5. Add more broth to thin, if desired. Season with additional salt and pepper, if desired.

THE LENTIL: SMALL BUT MIGHTY!

This small legume—the tiniest of the legume family—packs a powerful nutritional punch.
1 one-cup serving contains:
- Molybdenum—198% of the daily recommended value
- Folate—89.5% of the daily recommended value
- Fiber—62.5% of the daily recommended value
- Tryptophan—50% of the daily recommended value
- Manganese—49% of the daily recommended value
- Iron—36.6% of the daily recommended value
- Protein—35.7% of the daily recommended value
- Phosphorus—35.6% of the daily recommended value
- Copper—25% of the daily recommended value
- Vitamin B12—2% of the daily recommended value
- Potassium—20.8% of the daily recommended value

POTATO SOUP WITH KALE AND CHORIZO

MAKES 6 SERVINGS

I love any kind of potato soup. I find them so warming and comforting. And I love kale! And though my family doesn't eat a lot of animal protein, I do love chorizo used as a flavoring agent, which it is here in this scrumptious recipe. Try this. You'll love it! If you don't have Spanish chorizo, try Portuguese choricua or Calabrese spicy salami. If you want to try a vegan sausage analog here, go right ahead, adding it at the very end of cooking.

5 tablespoons olive oil, divided

1 large onion, chopped (about 2 cups)

8 ounces fully cooked smoked Spanish chorizo or hot Calabrese salami, casing removed and cut into medium dice

2 teaspoons smoked (sweet) paprika

1½ pounds russet potatoes, peeled, cut into large cubes

8 cups low-salt chicken broth

1½ pounds kale, stemmed, torn into small pieces (about 16 cups lightly packed)

Optional garnish: 3 cups croutons (you can use gluten-free croutons if you'd like)

Optional garnish: 2 tablespoons fresh parsley, minced

1. Heat 3 tablespoons oil in large pot over medium heat. Add onion and cook until translucent, about 8 minutes.

2. Add chorizo and paprika, stirring for 1 to 2 minutes.

3. Add potatoes and broth. Increase heat and bring to boil.

4. Add kale and stir until barely softened and soup returns to boil.

5. Reduce heat to low, cover, and simmer for one hour, stirring occasionally.

6. Garnish with optional croutons and/or minced parsley.

WHAT IS CHORIZO?

Chorizo is a cured sausage made from coarsely chopped pork and pork fat, seasoned with smoked pimentón (paprika) and salt. (The Mexican version is uncured and instead of paprika, features dried ground chiles.) Highly flavored, a little bit goes a long way, making it an outstanding flavoring agent and condiment for veggie, bean, or grain dishes.

SAUSAGE: PUTTING IT TO GOOD USE

There are more than 200 types of sausages worldwide—nearly every country has some type of sausage, typically made of chopped animal protein (red meat, poultry, seafood, reptile, or other animal, even soy, grain, legumes, and nuts) and a blend of strong spices. Most of these countries have a range of ways to use these full-flavored foods—I've included a few of these recipes here. I love the idea of using meat as a flavoring agent. What this means: Instead of a big slab of meat, a smaller amount of flavorful animal protein is used to flavor soups, stews, stir-fry, grain dishes—or anything else, really.

KALED-UP SPLIT PEA SOUP

MAKES 4 SERVINGS

As the child of a Dane, I adore split pea soup. It is my absolute favorite, so I've eaten a lot of the stuff in my lifetime. I love it with curry, I love it with fennel, I love it with dill, with caraway, even with nettles and a splash of aquavit. This version surprised me (and yes, I also love it!) with its deep, smoky flavor. It's the sausage (yep, another sausage soup) that gives the soup its deep flavor, though you are welcome to leave the meat out for a vegetarian version.

1   (16-ounce) bag dried green split peas, picked over and rinsed

12 *ounces fully cooked smoked pork linguiça or andouille sausages, sliced into ½-inch rounds or cut into a large dice*
8   *cups (or more) chicken broth*
5   *Turkish bay leaves*
3   *to 4 cups coarsely chopped kale*
    Salt and pepper to taste

1. In a large pot over medium heat, combine split peas, sausages, eight cups broth, and bay leaves in heavy large pot.
2. Bring to boil over medium-high heat.
3. Add kale, cover, reduce heat to low, and simmer until peas are tender, stirring occasionally, about 25 to 40 minutes.
4. Season to taste with salt and pepper.

LEGUME POINTERS

- Uncooked dry beans can be stored for a year or longer in the unopened plastic bag in which they are sold.
- Once opened, store legumes in an airtight container in a cool, dry place.
- Before preparing, inspect and remove any debris or dirt.
- Dry beans and whole peas need to soak before cooking. Soak in a big pot of cold water overnight, or in hot water for 1 to 4 hours.
- To reduce gas-producing substances, soak longer, then discard the soaking water and use fresh water for cooking.
- Use beans in stews, soups, casseroles, combined with whole grains, in salads, and pureed for dips.
- Stretch meat in meatballs, meatloaf, shepherd's pie, and other dishes by mixing in a cup or two of mashed legumes.
- Lentils and split peas are the "fast foods" in the legume family; they need only about 30 to 40 minutes to cook, no pre-soaking required.
- One cup of dry beans and peas equals about 2½ to 3 cups cooked.
- When drained, a 15-ounce can equals about 1½ cups of beans.

PINTO-BEAN MOLE CHILI

MAKES 6 SERVINGS

I am a chili fanatic. I like it Texas-style. I like it Cincinnati-style and Utah-style and California-style. I like vegetarian and white and black bean and con carne styles. This rich-tasting recipe features a sophisticated mix of spices, for a deeply-flavored, super healthy (spices are rich in antioxidants) dish. Yum, yum, yum!

2   teaspoons chili powder
1   teaspoon chipotle powder
1   teaspoon cumin
1   teaspoon dried oregano
½   teaspoon dried coriander
Optional: 1 teaspoon epazote
⅛   to ¼ teaspoon cinnamon
2   medium onions, chopped
2   tablespoons olive oil
5   garlic cloves, minced
2   cups butternut or other winter squash, cut into a large dice (you can also use summer squash or sweet potatoes)
¾   pound kale, stems, and center ribs discarded and leaves coarsely chopped
1   teaspoon agave syrup
1   ounce unsweetened chocolate, finely chopped (3 tablespoons)
1   (14 ½-ounce) can whole tomatoes in juice
1¼   chicken broth
1   to 2 tablespoon lime juice
3   (15-ounce) cans pinto beans, drained and rinsed
    Salt to taste
Optional garnishes: salsa, diced avocado, guacamole, chopped scallion or red onion, sliced radishes, jalapeno slices, rice; chopped cilantro, and/or sour cream

1. In a large pot over medium-high heat, sauté onions, stirring occasionally, until softened. Add garlic and cook, stirring, about one minute.
2. Stir in chili powder, chipotle powder, cumin, oregano, coriander, epazote, and coriander.
3. Stir in squash and kale and cook, covered, 7 to 10 minutes, until squash begins to soften.
4. Stir in agave, chocolate, tomatoes with their juice, broth, and lime juice and simmer, covered, stirring occasionally, until vegetables are tender, about 20 minutes.
5. Stir in beans and simmer another 5 minutes to blend flavors. Season with salt to taste.

PORK PUMPKIN STEW

SERVES 6 TO 8

Pork and pumpkin are a gorgeous taste treat. Add the slightly astringent, green taste of kale and you have a beautiful balance of tastes and textures. You also have a high-nutrient dish, perfecto for a nippy autumn or winter (or even early spring) day. You'll love this!

¼   cup extra virgin olive oil
2   pounds boneless pork shoulder, cut into 1½-inch pieces and patted dry
2   onions, chopped
3   garlic cloves, minced
1   14-ounce can diced tomatoes, including the juice (I love using Muir Glen's fire-roasted diced tomatoes in this recipe)
1½   cups chicken broth

1 pound red-skinned (boiling) potatoes, cut into 1-inch pieces

4 cups kale, deribbed and coarsely chopped

1 2-pound sugar pumpkin or other winter squash, de-seeded (reserve the seeds for toasting if desired), peeled, and cut into 1-inch pieces

Salt and pepper to taste

1. Preheat oven to 350°F.

2. Add oil to a large heavy, ovenproof pot and set on the stove over medium-high heat. Add pork pieces, a few at a time, browning all sides then transferring pieces with a slotted spoon to a plate or bowl. Continue until all pork pieces are browned. Set pork aside

3. Add chopped onions to the pot and sauté until golden.

4. Add the garlic and sauté for a minute.

5. Add the tomatoes with their juice, the broth, the pork, and any accumulated juices. Bring to a boil and immediately remove from heat.

6. Place pot in oven for one hour.

7. Add potatoes, give the stew a stir, cover and cook for 20 more minutes

8. Add the greens and the pumpkin, give the stew another stir, cover the pot and cook for an additional 20 to 30 minutes, until pumpkin and kale are tender.

9. Season stew with salt and pepper.

PUMPKIN SEEDS: THE ULTIMATE SNACK

My kids' favorite autumn activity is making pumpkin seeds. In the weeks between Halloween and American Thanksgiving, we must roast 10 pumpkins' worth of seeds. It's something I am happy to do with them because not only is it fun to be in the kitchen together, the seeds are deeply nourishing, with vitamins, minerals, antioxidants, omega-3 fatty acids, protein, and fiber. We use the seeds from sugar and other baking-style pumpkins (we like their flavor best), cheese pumpkins, Australian blue Hubbard squash, and kabocha squash. All winter squash seeds can be roasted, but some are tougher to eat than others. Experiment to find your favorite.

If not making a Jack O' Lantern, we simply cut the squash into quarters and throw the in-nards—goop and all—into a large bowl of cold water. The water softens the bonds between fiber and seeds. We reach into the water and manually separate those seeds that haven't sepa-rated naturally. We then place seeds in a single layer on a clean dishtowel to dry. I like to let them dry overnight, but a couple of hours is fine. Some people skip this step and go straight to the roasting, though I find the seeds tougher to chew if you don't first let them air-dry.

To roast seeds, preheat oven to low, about 175°F. In a large bowl, toss seeds with a small splash of tamari and a dash of roasted sesame oil. (You can also try extra virgin olive oil and a dash of salt, virgin coconut oil, and a dash of curry and salt, or any other oil and seasoning combo you can think of.) Lay seeds in a single layer on as many baking sheets as necessary and roast for 15 to 20 minutes, until golden and fragrant.

SALADS

BASIC KALE SALAD

MAKES 6 SERVINGS

This is your basic, build-a-salad recipe. Enjoy it as-is, or throw in a handful of chopped nuts, seeds, or dried fruit. Play around with the oils. Try vinegar (you chose which kind) instead of lemon juice. Vary the spices. Add some minced herbs or your favorite veggie. And so on. Make this every single time your friends come over and soon, you'll be known as of those "I don't need a recipe" kinds of geniuses.

2   *tablespoons extra-virgin olive oil (I like toasted walnut oil in this recipe)*
2   *tablespoons lemon juice*
1   *teaspoon chili powder*
    Salt to taste
2   *bunches kale, deribbed, chopped very, very finely*

1. In a large bowl, whisk together oil, lemon juice, chili powder, and salt.
2. Add kale, toss to combine.
3. Allow to sit for 20 minutes before serving to allow flavors to blend.

BRASSICA SALAD

MAKES 4 SERVINGS

Before I tell you how fun and delicious this healthy recipe is, I want to clear something up: Brassica and Cruciferous are two words

A BETTER KALE SALAD

The key to a great kale salad—in my opinion at least—is to cut the leaves very thin. I like to chiffonade leaves. To do this, derib leaves, stack five to ten of them on top of each other, roll them up into a tube, and cut the tube of leaves into super-thin slices. They are easy to make, pretty, and ready to use in salads, or to sauté or steam.

for the same fabulous family, that large, talented clan that includes kale, collards, cabbage, kohlrabi, Brussels sprouts, and so on. Okay, now for the recipe. This contains two cousins: Kale and Brussels sprouts. (You could use cabbage instead, if you'd like.) It tickles me to use two members of the same family in one dish, especially a dish as tasty as this one. Lacinto kale does well in this recipe.

2   *tablespoons lemon juice*
1   *tablespoon Dijon mustard*
1   *tablespoon minced shallot*
1   *small garlic clove, minced*
    Salt and pepper to taste
    Freshly ground black pepper
1   *large bunch of kale (I prefer Lacinto), deribbed and leaves cut in a chiffonade*
6   *ounces Brussels sprouts (or cabbage), finely sliced*
1   *cup walnuts, toasted and coarsely chopped*
¼   *cup walnut oil (you can also use extra-virgin olive oil), divided*

Optional: ¼ cup finely grated Pecorino

1. In a medium bowl, whisk together lemon juice, mustard, shallot, garlic, a pinch of salt and pepper in a small bowl. Stir to blend. Set aside.

2. Combine kale and Brussels sprouts in a large bowl.

3. Whisk walnut oil into the lemon juice mixture, thoroughly combining. Season with salt and/or pepper, as desired.

4. Drizzle dressing over kale mixture and toss leaves to coat.

5. Add walnuts and pecorino, if using, and combine. Adjust seasonings with salt and/or pepper, as desired.

NUTTY KALE SLAW

MAKES 6 SERVINGS

This may be my favorite kale recipe. I first tasted kale salad at my brother and sister-in-law's house and fell in love with it instantly! Not only does this taste great, it makes me feel wonderful and strong after eating it. This is one of those recipes that people will ask for.

2   large bunches kale, about 2 pounds, deribbed and cut in a chiffonade

2   orange or red bell peppers, cleaned and cut into very fine strips

1   large carrot, peeled and shredded (you can use a box grater or a food processor with grater attachment)

WHY SPROUTS ARE NAMED BRUSSELS

Brussels sprouts and kale are cousins. While it isn't known exactly where these cabbage-like sprouts were first grown, they are believed to have originated in Belgium—they were first mentioned in Brussels in the late 16th century, where they became an important agricultural crop. It was during World War I that this local delicacy caught the attention of European and American soldiers, who named the vegetable after the Belgian city and carried them back to their homelands. And the rest, as they say, is veggie history. As proof of just how far these gorgeous sprouts have wandered from their original home: Today, almost all Brussels sprouts consumed in North America are grown in California.

1   cup roasted, salted almonds, pecans, or
     peanuts, divided
Optional: 2 tablespoons cilantro leaves
⅓ cup virgin coconut oil
3   tablespoons apple cider vinegar (you can also
     use lemon juice)
1   tablespoon agave syrup or honey
     Salt and pepper to taste
Optional: Couple shakes of Tabasco or other
     hot sauce

1. In a food processor, pulse together ¼ cup of the nuts, cilantro, oil, vinegar, agave, salt, pepper, and hot sauce. Pulse until nuts are half-way pureed. Set aside

2. In a large bowl, toss together kale, bell pepper, carrots, and nuts.

3. Using a spatula to get every last drop, scrape dressing over kale mixture. Toss with dressing to coat all leaves.

4. Allow dressing to sit for 20 minutes before serving to blend flavors.

BUTTERNUT SQUASH AND KALE SALAD

MAKES 4 TO 6 SERVINGS

Here it is again—that gorgeous winter squash and kale combo. It looks beautiful, tastes wonderful, and is outrageously healthy thanks to a range of antioxidants, vitamins, minerals, and fiber. You'll love this cooked salad.

2   bunches kale, deribbed, leaves finely chopped
1   cup chicken broth, divided
1   2-pound butternut squash or other winter
     squash, peeled, deseeded and cut into
     ½-inch cubes

PEANUT POWER

Peanuts have become mired in controversy. For the growing numbers of people allergic to them, even a small amount of dust or oil can mean anaphylactic shock, a situation where airways begin to close, cutting off oxygen to an individual. For others, the aflatoxin mold (a type of fungus) that grows on peanuts can contribute to conditions such as candida, eczema, and mold allergies. It has also been linked to cancer in laboratory rats, and has been studied as one cause of stunted growth in African populations relying heavily on peanut protein.

Despite all of this, peanuts are a part of American culture, showing up in sandwiches, cookies, smoothies, spread on apples and celery, mixed into ice cream and eaten straight for the jar. Interestingly, however, peanuts are not originally from North America: They were brought from South America by Spanish explorers and made popular centuries later by Union and Confederate soldiers in the American Civil War who needed cheap, portable protein. Also interesting: Peanuts aren't nuts at all: They are a legume, related to other members of the legume family.

1   red onion, coarsely chopped
4   pitted prunes, dates or ¼ cup raisins, very
    finely chopped
2   tablespoons sherry vinegar

1. In a large pot over medium heat, heat ½ cup of broth and kale. Cook, covered, stirring frequently, until kale is wilted, about 3 to 5 minutes.

2. Add squash and continue cooking, stirring occasionally, until kale and squash are barely fork-tender, about 10 minutes. Remove from heat and allow to cool to room temperature.

3. Meanwhile, in a small saucepan, combine the remaining ½ cup broth, onion, dried fruit, and vinegar in a small saucepan.

4. Bring liquid to a boil, then lower heat and simmer, uncovered, until onion is very tender and liquid is reduced by half, about 7 or 8 minutes.

5. Allow dressing to cool to barely-warm or room temperature. Drizzle over kale-squash mixture and serve room temperature.

DID YOU KNOW...?

Butternut squash is one of the most popular winter squash varieties. This large, pear-shaped squash has a sweet, slightly nutty taste and a smooth, just moist-enough texture. Here are a few reasons to get to know butternuts better:

- Every part of the butternut squash is edible: Its vines, leaves, flowers, flesh, and seeds. In many regions, such as Africa, all parts of the squash are eaten.
- Butternuts belong to the Cucurbitaceae family of field pumpkins, which are believed to have originated in the Central American region
- Butternuts are the most commonly grown winter squash in the Western Hemisphere.
- The butternut plant is monoecious as in pumpkins, and features different male and female flowers that require honeybees for effective pollination.
- Butternuts range in size from less than a pound to over 33 pounds. Most, however, are in the 2- to 5-pound range.
- In Argentina, butternuts are used as livestock food.
- Butternut squash seeds are used as nutritious snack food since they contain 35% to 40% oil and 30% protein. In Argentina, the fruit is also used to feed livestock.
- One cup of cooked butternut squash contains 82 calories and 2 grams of protein.
- It has more vitamin A than pumpkins, providing about 354% of recommended daily allowance.
- It contains plenty of amino acids, antioxidants, B-complex vitamins, iron, zinc, copper, calcium, potassium, phosphorous, and fiber.

KALE QUINOA SALAD

MAKES 4 SERVINGS

Adding grain to this kale salad makes it hearty and rich in protein. If you'd like, substitute the same amount of cooked brown or black or red rice, bulgur, millet, farro, or other favorite grain. You can even add a chopped avocado to the mix.

1 *bunch kale, deribbed and finely chopped*
1 *cup cooked quinoa*
3 *tablespoons prepared vinaigrette or salad dressing*
Optional: 2 tablespoons sunflower seeds, pepitas, or chopped nuts

1. In a large bowl, thoroughly combine all ingredients. Allow to sit for 20 minutes before serving.

FARRO: WHAT IT IS

Those of you who love regional Italian food have probably encountered Farro, popular in Italian soups and risotto-like dishes, it is a chewy, dense, nourishing grain that is grown in central and northern Italy. An ancient parent to wheat, farro was one of the most popular cereal grains in the ancient world. Wild plants were found at an archaeological site carbon dated around 17,000 BCE, in modern-day Israel. References to the plant appear in early Hebrew, Greek, and Latin documents. Today, it remains popular in central and northern Italy, where it is considered a health food of sorts, celebrated for its high protein and fiber content.

BULGUR: WHAT IT IS

Bulgur. Sounds exotic, doesn't it? This Middle Eastern staple is actually made up of wheat kernels that have been steamed, dried, and crushed. It is high in fiber (twice that of brown rice) and protein, low in fat and calories, making it another food that offers bulk and nutrients to fill you up without adding pounds. One thing to keep in mind, however, is because bulgur is made of wheat, it does contain gluten. Celiacs and those on gluten-free diets, you have been warned!

ALL HALLOWS KALE

Among Celtic people, kale is traditionally associated with Halloween, and it is one of the ingredients of colcannon, a dish customarily eaten in Ireland on that day.

Deeply nourishing, delicious Lacinto kale is also known as Tuscan kale or dinosaur kale.

Kale and Bean Bruschetta is the ideal appetizer: Delicious, healthy, easy, and very sophisticated.
Page 124

Top: Siberian kale is extremely cold hardy with a rich, almost sweet taste.

Bottom: Beautiful red Russian kale lends a lovely rosey hue to dishes.

Kale Chips are the ultimate nonguilty pleasure. Crispy, salty, and addictive. Page 116

Kale Mini Pizzas are easy, fast, nutritious, and delicious—the perfect afterschool snack! Page 124

Top: Potato Kale Cakes are a dressy addition to any appetizer tray. Page 150
Bottom: Bell peppers stuffed with Chicken with Kale Lentil Pilaf. Page 132

Health in a glass! Superfood Protein Smoothie is ideal as a meal replacement or a quick pick-me-up. Page 42

Garlicky Kale and Spinach Dip is a grown-up dip perfect for elegant cocktail parties. Page 129

NUTS-AND-SEED KALE SALAD

MAKES 4 SERVINGS

This is a nutrient-dense salad: Quinoa and the nuts have protein, kale is loaded with iron, avocado boasts brain-boosting fats, and the sesame is rich in calcium.

3 cups cooked quinoa
6 kale leaves, deribbed and finely chopped
½ red or orange pepper, finely chopped
Optional: ½ cup pine nuts
Optional: ¼ cup finely chopped
   almonds

1 avocado, diced
2 tablespoons lemon juice
2 tablespoons rice vinegar
4 tablespoons roasted sesame oil
1 tablespoon sesame seeds

1. In a large bowl, gently combine quinoa, kale, red pepper, pine nuts, almonds, and avocado.

2. In a small bowl, whisk together lemon juice, rice vinegar, roasted sesame oil, and sesame seeds.

3. Drizzle dressing over kale mixture, gently tossing to combine.

HEALTH BENEFITS OF PINE NUTS

A favorite of gourmet-types, pine nuts—aka pignoli or piñon—add a distinctive flavor and delicate bite to salads, soups, baked goods, grain dishes, and even sauce (pesto anyone?) But foodies aren't the only ones who love pine nuts! Nutritionists, do, too! That's because the small seeds (yes, they are actually pine tree seeds, which nestle in the crevices of pine cones) are rich in vitamins, antioxidants, and minerals and packed with numerous health promoting phyto-chemicals.

Pine nuts are an excellent source of vitamin E, with about 9.33 mg—or about 62 percent of the recommended daily allowance—per 100-gram serving. Vitamin E is a powerful antioxidant. Pine nuts are an excellent source of the B-complex group of vitamins such as thiamin, riboflavin, niacin, pantothenic acid, vitamin B-6 (pyridoxine), and folates. These vitamins help maintain a healthy nervous system. Pine nuts also boast essential minerals like potassium, calcium, iron, magnesium, zinc, and selenium. Plus: they are one of the richest sources of the mineral manganese around, boasting 8.802 mg of manganese—about 383 percent of the daily recommended intake—per 100-gram serving. Manganese happens to be essential in helping the body develop resistance against infectious agents and in obliterating harmful oxygen free radicals.

SESAME FACTS

- Sesame seeds have been grown in tropical regions throughout the world since prehistoric times.
- "Open sesame"—the famous phrase from the *Arabian Nights*—reflects the distinguishing feature of the sesame seed pod, which bursts open when it reaches maturity.
- The scientific name for sesame seeds is *Sesamun indicum*.
- Sesame seeds were one of the first crops processed for oil as well as one of the earliest condiments.
- Foods made with sesame seeds include tahini, halvah, hummus, and baba ganous.
- The seeds were thought to have first originated in India, where they symbolized immortality. From India, sesame seeds were introduced throughout the Middle East.
- Most of the sesame seeds we eat are grown in India, China, and Mexico, the three largest commercial producers of the seeds.
- Sesame seeds are a very good source of manganese, copper, calcium, magnesium, iron, phosphorus, vitamin B1, zinc, and dietary fiber.
- Sesame seeds contain two special lingnans called *sesamin* and *sesamolin*, both of which have been shown to have a cholesterol-lowering effect in humans.

KALE WALDORF SALAD

MAKES 4 SERVINGS

This yummy salad is a revved up version of the well-loved classic. Though it uses most of the same ingredients as the original, I've got to admit it tastes nothing like it. (Not to disparage the first Waldorf salad, but this version is also way more nutritious, thanks to nutrient-packed kale.) Enjoy!

4 cups Lacinto kale, deribbed and finely chopped
1 large tangy, hard apple, (such as Fuji or Honey-crisp), cut into a medium dice and divided
1 cup thinly sliced celery
¾ cup plus ¼ cup toasted walnuts, chopped
¼ cup plus 2 tablespoons raisins, divided
2 tablespoons Dijon mustard
1 tablespoon walnut oil
2 tablespoons water
1 tablespoon red wine vinegar
   Salt and pepper to taste

1. In a large bowl, combine kale, half the apple, celery, ¾ cup of the walnuts, and ¼ cup of the raisins. Toss to combine.

2. In the bowl of a food processor or in a high-power blender, add ¼ cup walnuts, 2 tablespoons raisins, mustard, walnut oil, water, vinegar, salt, and pepper. Purée until well combined and slightly thick, adding additional water if necessary to keep a "dressing-like" consistency.

3. Drizzle dressing over kale mixture, tossing gently to combine.

SANDWICHES

SPICY KALE-CHEESE SANDWICH

MAKES 4 SERVINGS

This yummy sandwich adds a fresh (and healthy) twist on the everyday grilled cheese. I love this with a bowl of soup!

1 *cup grated mild cheese, such as Monterey Jack*
1 *cup finely chopped kale*
1 *garlic clove, minced*
¼ *to ½ teaspoon Tabasco or other hot sauce*
   Salt and pepper to taste
8 *slices whole grain bread*
3 *tablespoons or more Dijon or other spicy mustard*
2 *tablespoons or more softened butter, divided*

1. In a large bowl, mix together cheese, kale, garlic, hot sauce and salt and pepper. Set aside.
2. Spread the inside of each piece of bread with mustard.
3. Create four sandwiches by topping four slices of bread with ¼ cup filling, then topping with remaining bread slices.
4. Butter the outsides of all bread.
5. Place a large skillet over medium-high heat. Place sandwiches in skillet and cook until one side is brown.
6. Turn sandwiches. Cook until second side is brown and cheese has melted.

GOOD KARMA KALE SANDWICH

MAKES 1 SERVING

It seems almost wrong to me to give you recipes for sandwiches. In my world, sandwiches are ad hoc things, stacked together with whatever sounds good at the moment, coupled with whatever we have in the fridge. It's from that creative yet practical place, that this Good Karma Sandwich comes from! Feel free to change it up in any way that appeals to you!

2 *tablespoons hummus or refried beans or white bean dip*
2 *pieces whole grain bread*
1 *thin slice red onion*
¼ *cup leftover kale salad or cooked kale dressed with 2 teaspoons of your favorite dressing*

1. Toast bread until golden.
2. Spread toasted bread with hummus.
3. Cover one slice of bread with leftover kale salad and red onion. Top with remaining piece of toasted bread.

KALE IN SCOTLAND

Kale was grown as a staple crop in the Scottish Islands due to its extreme hardiness, and was given protection from the elements in purpose-built kale yards. Indeed, almost every house had a kale yard and preserved kale in barrels of salt, similar to sauerkraut in Germany. They also fed it to livestock through the winter. Kale continued to be extremely important until potatoes came to the Islands towards the end of the 18th century.

VINEGAR ON GREENS?

When I was growing up, any time we had kale or spinach with dinner, my mom would plunk down a bottle of vinegar next to the serving dish. For us, the vinegar was a liter of store brand apple cider vinegar. But from what I now know, my family wasn't the only one who served their greens with vinegar; this is common practice the world over.

But why? Taste, for one. Vinegar adds spark and tang to bitter greens. But perhaps a more important reason, one my own mother did not know about, is that vinegar makes the calcium in dark leafy greens more bioavailable. Let me explain: While these greens are naturally high in calcium, they contain a compound that inhibits the body's ability to absorb the mineral. Vinegar deactivates these compounds, allowing the body to benefit from every drop of this bone-building mineral.

CARAMELIZED SHALLOT-KALE-PROSCIUTTO SANDWICH

MAKES 2 SERVINGS

Can a sandwich be elegant? (Particularly a sandwich that contains kale?) I say yes! Try this recipe and see for yourself.

1   *tablespoon extra virgin olive oil*
2   *shallots, sliced thin*
1   *garlic clove, coarsely chopped*
½   *cup fresh kale, cut into 1- to 2-inch pieces*
4   *slices prosciutto*
4   *ounces goat cheese*
4   *slices sourdough sandwich bread*
    Salt and pepper to taste

1. Heat olive oil in a medium skillet over medium-low heat. Add the shallot and garlic to the pan and sauté, stirring often, until brown, soft and buttery in texture, about 12 minutes. (Add more oil or a teaspoon or more of water if shallots begin to stick.)
2. Add the kale to the pan and sauté until wilted and softened. Season with salt and pepper.
3. Toast bread.
4. Spread the inside of each piece of toasted bread with goat cheese.
5. Divide the prosciutto between the sandwiches, then place shallot-kale mixture atop prosciutto.
6. Top with remaining slices of bread.

TURKEY ORCHARD SANDWICH

MAKES 1 SERVING

This is a fun, sweet-savory sandwich that's a bit different than your everyday lunch. It reminds me of Thanksgiving.

2   *slices whole grain bread*
½   *tablespoon Dijon mustard*
Optional: 2 tablespoons cranberry sauce
3   *to 4 ounces sliced turkey breast (sliced turkey deli meat is fine)*
1   *slightly firm Bosc pear or Asian pear, sliced into very thin slices*
2   *raw kale leaves*

1. Spread inside of bread with mustard.

2. If using, spread cranberry sauce over the mustard.

3. Layer turkey, pear slices, and kale leaves on top of one slice of bread.

4. Top with remaining bread slice.

KALE FOR VICTORY!

During World War II, citizens of the UK were encouraged by their government to grow kale as part of the country's Dig for Victory campaign. Why kale? It is easy to grow and provides important nutrients missing during the wartime diet because of rationing.

PEARS: DID YOU KNOW...?

- One pear contains 22% of your daily recommended allowance of fiber, 12.4% of vitamin C, and 10% of vitamin K.
- The gritty fiber in pears has been found to bind to cancer-causing toxins and chemicals in the colon, protecting it from contact with these poisons.
- Pears are rich in antioxidant carotenoids such as lutein, and zeaxanthins and flavonols such as querticin and kaempferol, all of which have been shown to have antioxidant as well as anti-inflammatory benefits.
- Pears have been associated with lowered risk of several common chronic diseases caused by chronic inflammation and excessive oxidative stress, including cardiovascular disease and diabetes.
- Pears contain some copper, iron, potassium, manganese, and magnesium, as well as B-complex vitamins.
- Herbalists suggest using pears to treat colitis, chronic gallbladder disorders, arthritis, and gout.

CHICKPEA AND KALE SANDWICH SPREAD OR SALAD

MAKES 4 SERVINGS

I love the idea of stuffing pita bread with a hearty, delicious filling—it's my favorite type of grab-and-go sandwich! You must try this delicious recipe—it just may replace your current hummus sandwich. I like to add slices of cucumber and a shredded carrot for a bright, fresh taste.

4   *medium kale leaves, deribbed*
1   *tablespoon yellow mustard*
2   *tablespoons extra virgin olive oil*
1   *to 2 tablespoons fresh dill leaves*
1   *scallions, white and light green portion*
1   *to 2 tablespoons lemon juice or rice vinegar, to taste*
½   *teaspoon curry powder*
½   *teaspoon ground cumin*
    Freshly ground pepper to taste
1   *(15- to 16-ounce) can chickpeas, drained and rinsed (you can also use cannellini beans)*

1. In a food processor, add all ingredients except chickpea and avocado. Pulse until mixture is smooth and thoroughly blended.
2. Add chickpeas and optional avocado and pulse just to chop and slightly blend. You want this mixture chunky.
3. Serve in a pita, on crackers, between slices of bread or as a salad.

WHAT IS DILL?

Part of the Umbellifarae family, which includes carrots and parsley, dill is a popular culinary plant. Both its leaves and seeds are used. The herb is popular in Scandinavian, northern Russian, and Polish cooking. The Scandinavians use so much of the stuff that they gave the plant the name we now use: "Dill" comes from the old Norse word *dilla* which means "to lull." This name reflects dill's traditional uses as both a carminative stomach soother and an insomnia reliever.

WHEN IN ROME...

The chickpea held a place of honor in food-loving ancient Rome. In fact, the legume was so valued, that the leader Cicero proudly claimed his name derived from *cicer*, the Latin term for chickpea. One of Cicero's ancestors was named Cicero because he had a wart on his nose that looked like a chickpea.

A BEAN BY ANY OTHER NAME...

A chickpea by any other name would be—yep, a chickpea! This member of the pea family is called *garbanzo* in Spanish-speaking countries, *ceci* in Italy, *chiche* in French.

Whatever you call them, they are the world's most widely-consumed legume. Probably because they taste so great, are easy to cook, and are terrifically versatile. They are also incredibly nutrient-dense, boasting protein, calcium, iron, and phosphorous.

CHAPTER 6

SMALL BITES: KALE APPETIZERS AND SNACKS

Sometimes you just want a little something. A snack. Or something fancy before a dinner party so you can show off your ingenious culinary skills. Then there are the times your kids come home from school or soccer practice absolutely famished and you want something yummy and healthy to offer them.

Instead of something out of a bag, think kale. Yes, kale! Kale is so versatile that it lends itself to a wide variety of appetizers, sandwiches, dips, and more. Get creative. Try the recipes in this section and then get improvising. I'm sure you'll come up with all kinds of yummy kale munchies.

KALE CHIPS AND CRACKERS

KALE CRACKERS

MAKES 2 TO 4 SERVINGS

Once you've mastered kale chips, you may want to try your hand at something a bit more substantial, like these fun and very healthy crackers! We love them with a bit of hummus.

6   leaves of Lacinto kale, deribbed
⅔   cup ground almonds or mixture of walnuts, pecans, and almonds
¼   cup sesame seeds
2   tablespoons chia seed
¼   cup nutritional yeast
½   teaspoon salt
    Dash pepper
1   teaspoon curry powder, chili powder, chipotle powder, or other favorite spice

1. Preheat oven to 250°F.
2. Line a baking sheet with parchment or aluminum foil.
3. Add kale to the bowl of a food processor. Pulse until ground into a paste.
4. Add remaining ingredients and pulse until combined.
5. Using a silicone spatula, spread mixture onto prepared baking sheet. Score into crackers (make them on the small size; the crackers break easily when too large).
6. Bake for 40 to 45 minutes.

BAKED KALE CHIPS

SERVES 4

These are a low calorie nutritious snack. Like potato chips, you cannot stop at just eating one. They are great for parties and a good conversation topic. They're also loaded with vitamins, minerals, phytonutrients, and fiber.

1 *bunch kale*
1 *tablespoon olive oil*
1 *teaspoon seasoned salt*

1. Preheat an oven to 350° F.
2. Line a non-insulated cookie sheet with parchment paper.
3. With a knife or kitchen shears carefully remove the leaves from the thick stems and tear into bite size pieces. Wash and thoroughly dry kale with a salad spinner. Drizzle the kale with olive oil and sprinkle with seasoning salt.
4. Bake until the edges brown but are not burnt, 10 to 15 minutes.

SALT AND VINEGAR KALE CHIPS

MAKES 4 SERVINGS

Crispy baked kale is seasoned with vinegar and salt in this snack recipe. It's a great healthy replacement to salt and vinegar chips.

1 *bunch kale*
1 *tablespoon extra-virgin olive oil, divided*
1 *tablespoon sherry vinegar*
1 *pinch sea salt, to taste*

1. Preheat an oven to 300°F (150°C).
2. Cut away inner ribs from each kale leaf and discard; tear the leaves into pieces of uniform size. (I made my pieces about the size of a small potato chip.) Wash torn kale pieces and spin dry in a salad spinner or dry with paper towels until they're very dry.
3. Put the kale pieces into a large resealable bag (or use a bowl if you don't mind getting your hands oily). Add about half the olive oil; seal and squeeze the bag so the oil gets distributed evenly on the kale pieces. Add the remaining oil and squeeze the bag more, until all kale pieces are evenly coated with oil and slightly "massaged."
4. Sprinkle the vinegar over the kale leaves, reseal the bag, and shake to spread the vinegar evenly over the leaves. Spread the leaves evenly onto a baking sheet.
5. Roast in the preheated oven until mostly crisp, about 35 minutes. Season with salt and serve immediately.

KALE AND FRUIT SNACKS

KALE CACAO ENERGY TRUFFLES

MAKES 16 TO 18 TRUFFLES

Sometimes you want something rich, chewy. This chocolate-based recipe is a great, healthy, yummy way to take care of yourself and indulge in the sweetness you crave.

1 *cup cashews*
¼ *cup rice or hemp or legume-based protein powder, vanilla flavored or unflavored*
¼ *cup finely chopped kale leaves*
½ *cup pitted dates, packed*
½ *cup pitted prunes, packed (or you can omit the prunes and use 1 cup of dates)*
2 *tablespoons agave nectar*
 Splash vanilla
 Dash salt
 Dash cinnamon
¼ *cup cacao nibs*

1. In the bowl of a food processor, add cashews and hemp protein. Pulse until mixture is coarse.
2. Add the kale, dates, and prunes and pulse until uniformly ground and it sticks together easily.
3. Add the agave, vanilla, salt, and cinnamon and pulse a few more times, until combined.

4. Add the cacao nibs and pulse until mixture is combined.

5. Refrigerate mixture for an hour or more.

6. Shape mixture into 1-inch balls, storing in the refrigerator.

HEALTH BENEFITS OF DATES

- Dates contain high amounts of dietary fiber, which can help with everything from cholesterol levels to digestion.
- The fruit contains flavonoid antioxidants that boast anti-inflammatory properties, while simultaneously strengthening the immune system and helping with healthy blood clotting.
- Dates contain vitamins A, B-complex, and K.
- The fruit is rich in the minerals iron, potassium, calcium, manganese, copper, and magnesium.

KALE CHEESE DATES

MAKES 6 TO SERVINGS

This simple appetizer needs only dates, kale, and almonds (and toothpicks) to prepare—and is sure to be a crowd-pleaser with a lovely mixture of sweet and savory.

¼   *cup cooked, steamed, or blanched kale, squeezed dry*

1   *(8-ounce) brick or tub of cream cheese (can be non-dairy cream cheese)*

1   *pound whole pitted dates*

1. Place kale and cheese in the bowl of a food processor. Pulse or mix until just blended. You want flecks of kale spread throughout the cream cheese.

2. Split the dates in half lengthwise.

3. Spoon a bit of kale-cream cheese mixture into the cavity of each date.

4. Refrigerate finished dates for 20 minutes or more before serving.

KALE GRANOLA BARS

MAKES ABOUT 18 BARS

Who doesn't love granola bars? They are crunchy, sweet, hearty, filling—and in this recipe, they also contain nutrient-dense kale!

2   *cups old-fashioned oats*

¼   *cooked or steamed kale, squeezed dry and finely chopped*

½   *cup raisins or other dried fruit (coarsely chopped)*

½   *cup toasted walnuts or pecans, toasted*

1   *teaspoon ground cinnamon*

½   *teaspoon ground ginger or fresh grated ginger*

6   *tablespoons virgin coconut oil*

⅓   *cup packed dark brown sugar*

3   *tablespoons honey*

1. Preheat oven to 350°F.

2. Line 9-inch square baking pan with foil, allowing foil to extend over sides. Grease foil.

3. In a large bowl, stir together oats, kale, raisins, walnuts, cinnamon, and ginger.

DATES: DID YOU KNOW...?

- Dates originated around the Persian Gulf.
- There is archaeological evidence of date cultivation in the area that is now western Pakistan from around 7,000 BCE.
- Ancient Egyptians made dates into wine.
- In later times, traders from the Middle East and Africa introduced dates to Spain. It was the Spaniards who, in turn, introduced dates to Mexico and California in 1765.
- Dates are naturally pollinated by the wind, but in many modern commercial orchards, farmers pollinate the trees manually. This is done by skilled "pollinators" standing on ladders.
- In the Sahara, dried dates are often fed to camels, horses, and dogs.
- Young date leaves are cooked and eaten as a vegetable, as is the terminal bud or heart, though its removal kills the palm.
- In times of famine, date seeds are often ground into a meal and mixed with flour that is used to make daily bread.
- The date tree has male and female flowers. The female blooms are edible and often used in salads or ground with dried fish to make a condiment.
- In India and Pakistan, North Africa, Ghana, and Côte d'Ivoire, date palms are tapped for the sweet sap, which is converted into palm sugar called jaggery or gur. This sap is also used as a molasses-like syrup or brewed into alcoholic beverages.
- To reduce the potency of their hand-crafted beer, Nigerians often mix in dates (and peppers).
- In North Africa, mature date leaves are used to make huts. They are also used in many cultures to create mats, screens, baskets, and fans.
- The wood from date palm trees is light and durable and is used for construction or burned as fuel.
- When Muslims break fast in the evening meal of Ramadan, it is traditional to eat a date first.
- Ground date seeds are also used as an additive to coffee.
- Another use for ground date seeds: As animal feed.

4. In a medium saucepan over medium heat, combine coconut oil, sugar, and honey. Stir until mixture is smooth and begins to boil.

5. Pour oil mixture over oat mixture. Stir until oat mixture is well coated.

6. Using a silicone spatula, transfer batter to prepared pan. Press down firmly on mixture.

7. Bake until top is golden, about 30 minutes.

8. Allow to cool before using the foil as a handle and removing the bars out of the pan.

9. Place the granola bar onto a flat surface. Using a very sharp knife, cut into 18 bars. (If they crumble as you cut them, you may need to allow them to cool further.)

YUMMY THINGS TO DO WITH GINGER

- Spiced-up grains: Grate a bit of ginger into your next pot of millet, rice, quinoa, or other grain. Great served with curries and stir-fries.
- Ginger lemonade: Simply combine freshly grated ginger, lemon juice, and either cane juice or honey and water.
- Perk up bottled salad dressing or a simple homemade vinaigrette with grated ginger.
- Add dry powdered or grated fresh ginger to pureed sweet potatoes. A squirt of lemon juice is a yummy addition.
- Add zing to your next fruit salad with by adding some grated ginger.
- Dress up sautéed veggies by tossing in a half-teaspoon of minced fresh ginger.

SAVORIES

KALE AND GORGONZOLA SWIRLS

MAKES 24 SERVINGS

Serve these scrumptious savory bites at a party and watch them disappear. They have a grown-up, sophisticated flavor—and yet their cheesiness will appeal to the child in each of us.

1   *piece frozen puff pastry, thawed*
1   *bunch blanched kale, deribbed, squeezed dry and finely chopped*
2   *cloves garlic, minced*
2   *tablespoons butter*
1   *egg, beaten in a small bowl with one tablespoon water*
⅓   *cups Gorgonzola cheese, crumbled*
¼   *cups grated Parmesan cheese*

1. Preheat oven to 400°F.
2. Prepare a baking sheet with parchment paper or aluminum foil.
3. Thaw puff pastry according to package directions.
4. Melt butter in a large pot over medium-high heat. Add garlic and sauté for 1 minute.
5. Add kale and sauté tender, about 2 to 3 minutes. Transfer to a bowl to cool.
6. Roll out thawed puff pastry on a floured surface to create a 13-inch square.
7. Brush puff pastry with half of egg-water mixture.

8. Spread kale mixture over entire surface of puff pastry.
9. Sprinkle cheeses evenly over the kale mixture.
10. Roll the puff pastry along the longest side, rolling tightly. When finished, pinch the roll together.
11. Using a sharp, serrated knife, slice the roll into ½-inch slices. (For you bakers out there, use the same process you'd use to make cinnamon rolls.)
12. Place slices at a time onto baking sheet lined with parchment paper. Bake for 15 minutes or until edges are golden. Serve immediately.

DOES KALE HAVE AN IDEAL COOKING TIME?

The noted herbalist, Susun Weed, maintains that kale offers the most nutrition when cooked for 40 minutes—though scientists have yet to study this.

KALE AS INSULT

Early in the 20th century, Kailyard (kale field) was a disparaging term used to describe a school of Scottish writers, including *Peter Pan* author J. M. Barrie, whose writing featured sentimental nostalgia for rural Scottish life.

CHICKEN AND KALE HAND PIES

MAKES 6 SERVINGS

These pies would also be delicious with spinach or Swiss chard in place of the kale. Or, make a vegetarian version with sautéed mushrooms instead of the chicken. You could even change things up further by using ground beef or pork or sausage in place of the poultry. Get creative!

2   *discs pie dough, either homemade or purchased*
2   *tablespoons all-purpose flour, plus, if needed, more for rolling*
1   *tablespoon unsalted butter*
1   *leek (white and light-green parts only), halved lengthwise, cut crosswise ¼-inch thick, and rinsed well*
1   *small bunch Lacinto kale, deribbed and coarsely chopped*
1   *teaspoon fresh thyme leaves*
¼   *teaspoon dried sage*
    Salt, to taste
    Pepper, to taste
1   *cup chicken broth*
1   *cup cooked chicken or turkey, shredded into bite-size pieces (about 5 ounces)*
1   *large egg, lightly beaten*

1. Preheat oven to 425°F.
2. Prepare two baking sheets with parchment or aluminum foil.
3. On a cool surface, roll out one disc of pie dough to a 14-inch round. Dust with flour first if needed to prevent sticking. With a knife or biscuit cutter, cut out six 4¼-inch circles, re-rolling dough just once if necessary. Note: These are the smaller rounds.
4. Transfer cut dough and transfer, on parchment, to a baking sheet. Repeat with remaining dough, cutting out six larger, 4½-inch rounds.
5. Place sheet in the refrigerator until ready to use.
6. In a large skillet over medium-high heat, melt butter. Add leek and sauté until soft, about 3 minutes.
7. Add kale, thyme, salt, and pepper, to the skillet and sauté until kale wilts, about 3 to 5 minutes.
8. Sprinkle flour over mixture. Stir to combine. Add broth and bring to a boil. Cook, stirring often, until mixture thickens, about 2 minutes.
9. Transfer to a medium bowl, season with more salt and pepper if desired, and stir in chicken. Let cool slightly.
10. Remove rounds from refrigerator.
11. Place a rounded ¼ cup chicken mixture on each of the smaller dough rounds, leaving a ½-inch border. Brush edges with egg and top with larger dough rounds; using fingers, press edges firmly to seal.
12. Cut a small vent in each pie. Bake until browned and crisp, 30 minutes, rotating sheet halfway through.

13. Let cool slightly on sheets that have been set on a wire rack. Serve warm or at room temperature.

BAKED FETA WITH KALE PESTO ON BAGUETTE

MAKES 8 SERVINGS

A little of this flavorful combo goes a long way, making it a true crowd-pleaser. For a gluten-free option, serve on gluten-free toasts or crackers.

1   *8-ounce piece of mild feta cheese, drained and patted dry*
2   *tablespoons extra-virgin olive oil*
½   *teaspoons dried rosemary*
½   *teaspoon dried basil*
½   *teaspoon dried parsley*
¼   *teaspoon black pepper*
1   *bunch kale, deribbed*
⅓   *cup toasted walnuts*
1   *or 2 garlic cloves*
2   *tablespoons lemon juice*
1   *sourdough or other baguette, thinly sliced*

1. Preheat oven to 400°F.
2. Place feta in a small oiled casserole dish with oil on top. Bake until warm throughout, about 20 minutes.
3. Meanwhile, pulse kale, rosemary, basil, parsley, pepper, walnuts, and garlic in a food processor until finely chopped.
4. With motor running, drizzle in oil and lemon juice to make a pesto. Spoon pesto around feta and bake 5 minutes more.
5. Serve with baguette slices.

KALE MINI PIZZAS

MAKES 4 SERVINGS

Kale is blended into sauce and used to top these yummy treats. Use whatever base you have on hand, from English muffins to pita breads. As you've probably already guessed, kids love these!

1 cups cooked or steamed kale, squeezed dry and coarsely chopped

2 cup marinara or prepared pasta sauce

¼ teaspoon freshly ground black pepper

4 whole-grain English muffins, split (you can also use tortillas, pitas breads, or individual pizza crusts)

½ cup or more shredded part-skim mozzarella cheese

Optional toppings: sliced olives, mushrooms, peppers, onions, pepperoni, or anything else that sounds appealing

1. Preheat oven to 425°F.

2. Place kale and marinara sauce in a food processor. Pulse until blended. You can leave the kale visible or, for picky eaters, you can puree the sauce until the kale is smooth.

3. Arrange muffin halves on a large baking sheet. Spread sauce on muffins.

4. Top muffins with cheese and optional toppings.

5. Bake until muffins are crisp and cheese is melted, 20 to 25 minutes.

KALE AND BEAN BRUSCHETTA

MAKES 12 SERVINGS

This easy bruschetta is fun, fast, and insanely delicious. It's a terrific option for the vegetarians in your midst. Make it vegan by omitting the cheese. You can even make it gluten-free by serving this on gluten-free toast or on rice crackers.

1 garlic clove, cut in half

1 cups cooked cannellini beans

½ cups cooked or steamed kale, squeezed dry and finely chopped

   Salt, to taste

   Pepper, to taste

Optional: Parmesan cheese shavings

1 long baguette, sliced into 12 half-inch-thick slices and toasted

1. In a large bowl, mix beans and kale. Season with salt and pepper.

2. Rub cut side of garlic on toasts.

3. Spoon bean-kale mixture onto toasts. Top with Parmesan shavings if desired.

PIZZA TRIVIA

- In 1987, October was named National Pizza Month.
- Americans eat approximately 350 slices of pizza per second.
- Each man, woman, and child in America eats an average of 46 slices (23 pounds) of pizza a year.
- Approximately 3 billion pizzas are sold in the U.S. each year.
- According to a recent Gallup Poll, kids between the ages of 3 to 11 prefer pizza to all other food groups for lunch and dinner.
- Basic pizza most likely began in prehistoric times, with bread cooked on flat, hot stones.
- Pizza as we know it could not have evolved until the late 1600s when Old World Europeans overcame their fear of tomatoes. Native to Peru and Ecuador, tomatoes came to Europe in the 1500s, carried back by Conquistadors to Spain; tomatoes were believed to be poisonous. It wasn't until the late 1600s that Europeans began to eat the tomato.
- Modern pizza was born in 1889 when Queen Margherita Teresa Giovanni, the consort of Umberto I, king of Italy, visited Naples. Don Raffaele Esposito, who owned a tavern-like place called Pietro Il Pizzaiolo, was asked to prepare a special dish in honor of the Queen's visit. Esposito developed a pizza featuring tomatoes, mozzarella cheese and basil, which mimicked the colors of the Italian flag. He named it the Margherita Pizza, after the guest of honor.
- In 1905, Gennaro Lombardi opened Lombardi's Pizzeria Napoletana, at 53½ Spring Street in New York City. This was the first licensed pizzeria in the United States.
- Pizza became an international food when World War II servicemen returned from Italy, abuzz about "that delicious Italian pizza."
- Pepperoni is America's favorite topping (36 percent of all pizza orders); we eat approximately 251,770,000 pounds per year.
- Anchovies are American's least favorite pizza topping.
- Women are twice as likely as men to order vegetable toppings on their pizza.
- Three of the top 10 weeks of pizza consumption occur in January. More pizza is consumed during Super Bowl week than any other week of the year.

SPINACH AND KALE TURNOVERS

MAKES 8 SERVINGS

In addition to being tasty, kale is a good source of lutein, benefiting eye health, and immunity-boosting vitamins A and C. Serve this as a snack, or enjoy two turnovers as a meatless entrée. They are great made ahead and brown-bagged; reheat in a microwave or toaster oven.

2   teaspoons extra virgin olive oil
1   cup chopped onion
1   garlic clove, chopped
1   bunch kale, blanched, squeezed dry and
    finely chopped
1   (8-ounce) package sliced mushrooms (button,
    cremini, or a blend)
¼   teaspoon salt
½   teaspoon freshly ground black pepper
¾   cup (3 ounces) crumbled feta cheese
1   (11.3-ounce) can refrigerated dinner roll
    dough (such as Pillsbury or Whole Foods Brand)
    Extra olive oil for brushing
Optional: 2½ tablespoons grated fresh Parmesan
    cheese

1. Preheat oven to 375°F.
2. Prepare a baking sheet by greasing very lightly with olive oil.
3. Heat olive oil in a large skillet over medium-high heat. Add onion; sauté 10 minutes or until tender and lightly browned. Add garlic; sauté 2 minutes.
4. Add kale and mushrooms; sauté 8 minutes or until kale is tender. Stir in salt and pepper.
5. Remove from heat; cool slightly. Stir in feta.
6. Separate dough into 8 pieces. Roll each dough piece into a 5-inch circle.
7. Spoon about ⅓ cup kale mixture on half of each circle, leaving a ½-inch border. Fold dough over kale mixture until edges almost meet. Bring bottom edge of dough over top edge; crimp edges of dough with fingers to form a rim.
8. Place turnovers on baking sheet. Lightly coat turnovers with olive oil; sprinkle each turnover with about 1 teaspoon optional Parmesan.
9. Bake at 375°F for 18 minutes or until golden brown. Let stand at least 5 minutes before serving; serve warm or at room temperature.

SQUASH-AND-KALE TOASTS

MAKES 8 SERVINGS

No one will be able to resist the kale when it's combined with sweet roasted squash. You can use any kale for this recipe, but I love the way Lacinto kale (also known as Tuscan or dinosaur kale) works here.

2   small delicata squash (2 pounds)—peeled,
    halved lengthwise, seeded and sliced crosswise
    ½-inch thick; you can also use butternut or
    another winter squash

½ cup extra-virgin olive oil, plus more for
   brushing
Salt, to taste
Pepper, to taste
Tabasco or other hot sauce, to taste
1 bunch kale, deribbed, coarsely chopped
4 garlic cloves, minced
1 teaspoon (squirt of) lemon juice
8 ½-inch-thick slices of toasted sourdough,
   multi-grain, peasant, or gluten-free bread
Optional: 4 ounces shaved Parmigiano-Reggiano
   cheese (1½ loose cups)

1. Preheat the oven to 350°F.
2. In a medium bowl, toss the squash with 2 tablespoons of the olive oil and season with salt and pepper.
3. Spread the squash on a baking sheet and roast for about 30 minutes, turning once, until tender and lightly browned.
4. In a large skillet over medium heat, add the remaining ¼ cup plus 2 tablespoons of olive oil. Add the kale, salt to taste, and hot sauce. Sauté until kale grows soft, about 8 minutes.
5. Add the garlic to the kale and continue to sauté until kale is tender, about 3 minutes longer. Adjust seasonings as desired.
6. Add the squash to the skillet, squirt with lemon juice, and toss gently to combine.
7. Spoon the squash-kale mixture on the toasts, top with the optional shaved cheese, and serve.

LEMON LOVE

Lemon juice is a favorite culinary ingredient thanks to the bright, sunny flavor it gives savory and sweet food. But did you know that lemon juice also has health benefits? It's a digestive aid, helps flush toxins from the body, and is a diuretic that helps the body release stores of trapped water.

PICKLED KALE—THE PERFECT CONDIMENT

Pickled kale is yummy, savory, and puckery—a great accompaniment to sandwiches, but it's also fantastic on an appetizer plate. Be warned: You will be asked for the recipe.

1 tablespoon sesame oil
1 bunch Tuscan or regular kale, stemmed,
   leaves torn
2 tablespoons fish sauce (such as nam pla
   or nuoc nam)
¼ cup unseasoned rice vinegar

1. Heat oil in a large saucepan. Add kale; sauté until wilted, about 5 minutes.
2. Stir in fish sauce, then rice vinegar.
3. Allow to sit for 15 minutes before servings, for flavors to meld.

DIPS

LEMON-RICOTTA KALE DIP

MAKES ABOUT 2 CUPS

Here's a quick and easy dip that's bound to win nutrient-packed kale a few new fans. Serve with vegetable dippers or whole-grain crackers.

1   *bunch green kale, deribbed and finely chopped*
1   *large shallot, minced*
1   *garlic clove, minced*
¼   *cup water*
¾   *cup part-skim ricotta cheese*
1   *teaspoon sugar or honey*
     Juice and zest of 1 lemon
     Salt and pepper, to taste
     A splash of Tabasco or other hot sauce

1. In a large saucepan over medium heat, combine kale, shallot, garlic, and water. Cover. Cook, stirring occasionally, until vegetables are very tender, about 12 minutes. Add more water if the vegetables begin drying out.

2. Transfer vegetables and any liquid in the pan to a food processor and let cool a few minutes.

3. Add ricotta, sugar, lemon juice and zest, salt, pepper, and hot sauce. Pulse until mixture is smooth. Transfer to a bowl and serve.

GARLICKY KALE AND SPINACH DIP

MAKES ABOUT 2 CUPS

This glorious dip is vegan, low-cal, and filled with antioxidants and powerful phytonutrients. Make this often—it's as delicious as it is virtuous.

1   cup cooked or steamed chopped kale, squeezed dry
1   cup cooked or steamed spinach, squeezed dry
2   medium garlic cloves, peeled
3   tablespoons toasted pine nuts
4   teaspoons balsamic vinegar
½   cup olive oil
    Salt and pepper to taste

1. Add kale and spinach to the bowl of a food processor. Pulse until pureed.
2. Add garlic, pine nuts, and vinegar. Pulse to puree, slowly adding in the olive oil.
3. Scrape down the bowl, add salt and pepper, and pulse to blend.

GREEN SURPRISE DIP

MAKES 2½ CUPS

A delicious dip perfect for crudités, chips, or other dippers. It is also great as a sandwich spread or binder for chicken or tuna salad!

1   cup cooked or steamed kale, squeezed dry
1   cup plain yogurt (non-dairy yogurt is fine)
1   cup canned chickpeas, rinsed and drained
¼   cup mayonnaise
2   cloves garlic
½   onion, minced
1   tablespoon lemon juice or to taste
    Salt to taste

1. Place all ingredients in a food processor or blender and puree until smooth.

CHOOSE YOUR PART

Almost all parts of some brassica species or other have been developed for food, including the root (rutabaga, turnips), stems (kohlrabi), leaves (cabbage, kale), flowers (cauliflower, broccoli, Brussels sprouts), and seeds (mustard seed, and oil-producing rapeseed).

CHAPTER 7

KALE FOR DINNER

In many countries—including ours less than a century ago—the last meal of the day was light and nourishing and casual. A bowl of soup or a salad or a sandwich eaten a few hours before bedtime and you were ready to relax and unwind from a long day of farm or factory work.

Today we do things a bit differently—dinner is a big deal, and for most people, it's also the largest meal of the day. It's a time to gather with friends or family to create a shared experience. It's also much less casual than it used to be, meaning many people feel pressured to "create a meal," something yummy and spectacular (or at least a bit showy). The drawback to this fancier way of eating? Health considerations often fly out the window.

Fortunately, you can keep dinner the entertaining meal you enjoy and look out for your health simply by adding nutritious ingredients, such as kale, to your menu. Plus, when kale is for dinner, you can be sure that you and those you are feeding, are getting the best nutrition on the planet, including omega-3s, vitamins, minerals, fiber, plant protein, antioxidants, amino acids, and more.

ENTREES

CHICKEN KALE BRAISE
MAKES 4 SERVINGS

Braising is a moist, covered way of cooking vegetables and meats that creates a tender, succulent finish. Feel free to use different chicken parts or even remove the skin if you'd like. You can even swap the olive oil for coconut oil and add a ½ tablespoon or more of your favorite curry powder. Serve with your favorite grain.

3 tablespoons extra virgin olive oil, divided
4 chicken leg quarters, skinned
½ teaspoon freshly ground black pepper
¼ teaspoon salt
¼ cup all-purpose flour
5 garlic cloves, minced
2 cups coarsely chopped kale
1 (14.5-ounce) can diced tomatoes, undrained (I like Muir Glen's Diced Tomato with Basil or Fire Roasted Tomatoes)
1 (14.5-ounce) can chicken broth
1 tablespoon red wine vinegar

1. Preheat oven to 325°F.

2. In a shallow baking dish, mix together pepper, salt, and flour.

3. Dredge chicken in flour mixture, making sure chicken is completely covered.

4. Heat a Dutch oven pan over medium-high heat. Add 1 tablespoon oil. Place 2 leg quarters in pan, and cook for 1½ minutes on each side, just to brown. Remove from pan. Add another tablespoon of oil and remaining 2 chicken pieces, cooking each 1 to 1½ minutes on each side to brown. Set chicken aside.

5. Do not clean pan. Add another tablespoon of oil, then add garlic, cooking for a minute.

6. Add kale to the pan, cooking until just wilted, about 5 minutes.

7. Add tomatoes with their juice, and broth. Bring to a boil, stirring frequently

8. Remove pan from heat, add chicken, cover with lid, and place in oven.

9. Bake for about 65 to 75 minutes, until chicken loses its pinkness and juices run clear.

10. Stir in vinegar. Serve chicken over kale.

CHICKEN WITH KALE LENTIL PILAF

MAKES 4 SERVINGS

This healthy, nourishing dish is so comforting. It's also easy. It's great for a family meal. If you'd like to take it to a potluck or buffet, chop the chicken into a medium dice and stir into the grain-kale mixture.

ARSENIC AND WHAT ELSE IN OUR CHICKEN?

My first encounter with arsenic-tainted chicken came after one of my son's blood tests came back showing dangerously high levels of arsenic. The doctor quizzed us a bit on my son's habits and his favorite foods. When I said "chicken," the doctor said, "Aha! That's where the arsenic is coming from." It turns out that in the United States, arsenic is routinely been fed to poultry (and sometimes hogs) because it reduces infections and gives the flesh an appetizing shade of pinkness. If you want your poultry without toxic heavy metals, go organic.

VINAIGRETTE

1   to 2 teaspoons cumin powder
¼   cup sherry vinegar
1   garlic clove, minced
¼   cup extra-virgin olive oil
1   tablespoon finely chopped raisins
1   teaspoon whole grain mustard
1   teaspoon fresh lemon juice
    Salt to taste

PILAF AND CHICKEN

4   tablespoons extra virgin olive oil, divided
1½ pounds skinless, boneless chicken breast cutlets
    Salt to taste
1   tablespoon unsalted butter
1   garlic clove, minced
1   bunch kale, deribbed and finely chopped

2 cups cooked grain (quinoa, millet, brown rice, etc.)
1 cup cooked lentils

1. Add cumin, vinegar, garlic, oil, raisins, mustard, lemon juice, and salt to a blender. Whir to puree. Set aside.
2. Season chicken with salt.
3. Heat 2 tablespoons oil in a large heavy nonstick skillet over medium heat. Working in two batches and adding 1 tablespoon oil between batches, cook chicken in single layers until browned on both sides and just cooked through, 2 to 3 minutes per side. Transfer to a plate and cover loosely with foil to keep warm.
4. Remove pan from heat; add ¼ cup water. Stir, scraping up browned bits. Whisk in ¼ cup vinaigrette. Scrape sauce into a bowl.
5. Melt butter with 1 tablespoon oil in same skillet over medium-low heat. Add garlic and cook until just beginning to soften, about 1 minute.
6. Working in 3 batches and adding more oil as needed, add kale to skillet and toss until wilted, about 2 minutes. Transfer kale to a large bowl, season lightly with salt and cover with foil to keep warm.
7. Do not clean out pan. Instead, add grain and lentils to the same skillet, turn the heat to medium-high, and sauté for 2 minutes, or until warmed through.
8. Add rice-lentil mixture to kale, stir to combine.
9. To serve, spoon pilaf onto plates. Top with chicken. Drizzle dressing over chicken and pilaf.

CUMIN: DID YOU KNOW….?

- Cumin seed's scientific name is *Cuminum cyminum*.
- The seed is a rich source of iron, a mineral that plays many vital roles in the body.
- In many cultures, including the West Indies, India, Pakistan, and Mexico, cumin is used as a digestive aid. Recent research has indeed found that cumin stimulates the secretion of pancreatic enzymes, which help with digestion and nutrient assimilation.
- Cumin boasts anti-carcinogenic properties. In one study, cumin was shown to protect laboratory animals from developing stomach or liver tumors.
- High in antioxidants, cumin enhances the body's immune system function.

KALE MUSHROOM POLENTA

MAKES 6 SERVINGS

Polenta is another comfort food, this one from Italy. If you've never eaten polenta before, it's basically savory porridge, made nowadays with corn meal. Adding kale and mushroom makes this a meal. Note: There is quite a lot of dairy in this recipe. Feel free to use non-dairy (unsweetened) milk, butter, and cheese.

1¼ pounds cooked, steamed or blanched kale, deribbed, coarsely chopped
4   cups milk
3½ cups water
2   cups stone ground corn meal
½   teaspoon salt
¾   teaspoon ground black pepper
4   ounces pancetta (Italian bacon) or no-nitrite bacon, coarsely chopped
4   ounces mushrooms (such as button crimini, oyster, and stemmed shiitake), sliced
4   tablespoons extra-virgin olive oil, divided
1   garlic clove, minced
½   cup chicken broth
1   tablespoon chopped fresh thyme or parsley or basil
4   tablespoons unsalted butter
⅔   cup freshly grated Parmesan cheese

1. In a large, heavy saucepan over medium heat, bring milk, water, polenta, salt, and pepper to boil, whisking constantly. Once the mixture hits a rolling boil, reduce heat

MORE ON MUSHROOMS

- A mushroom is the fleshy, spore-bearing fruiting body of a fungus, typically produced above ground on soil or on its food source.
- Mushrooms are the only natural fresh vegetable or fruit that contains Vitamin D.
- There are about 300 species of edible mushrooms.
- One serving of mushrooms is equivalent to 5 white button mushrooms.
- One serving of mushrooms contains only 20 calories.
- Mushrooms boast high levels of antioxidants, making them a popular healing food in herbal medicine and other alternative nutrition therapies.
- Pennsylvania produces 65% of the mushrooms grown in the U.S.
- September is National Mushroom Month.
- The average American eats almost 4 pounds of mushrooms per year.
- White, or button, mushrooms are the most popular mushroom followed by criminis.
- Almost 90% of all consumers use mushrooms as an ingredient in recipes.

immediately to low and simmer until mixture is thickened, about 20 minutes, stirring occasionally (you may need to switch to a spoon). Remove from heat.

2. Meanwhile, in heavy large skillet over medium-high heat, cook pancetta until golden brown, about 3 minutes. Using slotted spoon, transfer pancetta to paper towels. Do not wipe out pan.

3. Add mushrooms and 2 tablespoons oil to drippings in skillet. Sauté until mushrooms are tender, about 5 minutes. Stir in kale and pancetta. Add garlic and broth; simmer for about 5 or 6 minutes.

4. Stir in thyme, salt, and pepper.

5. Whisk butter and Parmesan into polenta until smooth. Spoon polenta attractively on plates and top with kale mixture.

NONA'S PASTA
MAKES 6 SERVINGS

Though it has grandma in the name, my husband is the one who first made this for me, back in our early rock-n-roll days we ate a lot of lentils and other legumes, as well as pasta. He learned this dish from his Sicilian grandmother. I find it faster to use already-cooked lentils and blanched kale, but you can start from scratch.

2   cups (you can use up to 4 cups if desired) cooked lentils (make sure they are a bit firm; you don't want mushy lentils in this dish)
     Salt, to taste
     Pepper, to taste
6   tablespoons extra-virgin olive oil
1   large onion, finely chopped
1   or 2 garlic cloves, minced
1   bunch kale, deribbed, blanched, squeezed dry and coarsely chopped.
½   cup chicken broth (or salted water)
1   pound dried elbow or ditalini or other short tubular pasta, cooked to al dente
Optional: Parmegiano-Reggiano cheese to grate over the top

1. In a large heavy skillet over medium-high heat, warm ¼ cup oil until hot but not smoking. Sauté onion and garlic with pepper and salt, stirring, for about 1 minute. Reduce heat to low and cook, covered, stirring occasionally, until onions are soft and golden (stir more frequently toward end of cooking), about 20 minutes. Remove lid and increase heat to moderate, then cook, stirring frequently, until onion is golden brown, 5 to 10 minutes more.

2. Add all remaining ingredients, stir, and increase heat to high. Cover pan and allow to cook for about 1 minute.

3. Adjust seasoning with salt and pepper before serving.

KALE-PORK GRATIN

MAKES 4 SERVINGS

I adore gratins! They are toasty, tasty, easy, and versatile. And, every single time I make one, everyone smiles, there is no complaining, and everyone (my four-year-old included) finishes their dinner. (Even if it contains kale.)

5   to 6 cups cooked, steamed or blanched kale, squeezed dry, deribbed, and finely chopped
      Salt to taste
3   tablespoons extra-virgin olive oil
¼   pound pancetta, ham, bacon, chopped into ½-inch pieces
1   cup cream
2   to 3 cloves garlic, minced
      Black pepper to taste
½   cup breadcrumbs (you can use gluten-free bread)
½   cup grated Parmigiano-Reggiano or Pecorino Romano

1. Preheat the broiler, adjusting the oven rack on the second shelf down from the heat source.
2. In a large skillet over medium-high heat, add 1 tablespoon of olive oil and pancetta. Cook until pancetta is crisp and add cream and garlic.
3. Crisp the pancetta and add the cream and garlic. Season salt and pepper.
4. Continue cooking until mixture has reduced to about ½ to ⅔ cups (you can eyeball this), about 7 to 9 minutes.
5. Add kale to cream and stir to coat evenly.
6. Transfer mixture to a shallow casserole dish.

7. In a medium bowl, mix together breadcrumbs, remaining 2 tablespoons of extra-virgin olive oil, salt, pepper, and cheese. Sprinkle over kale mixture in the casserole dish.
8. Place the casserole on the second shelf under broiler and cook until breadcrumbs are brown, about 5 minutes.

GRATIN CHRONICLES

Quick! What do you think of when I say the word "gratin"? Something with a bubbly, cheesy, crumbly topping? If so, you're right on. Gratin is the French term for any food that is topped with a browned crust, often using breadcrumbs, grated cheese, egg, and/or butter. French in origin, the term comes from the word grater, which means "to scrape" or "grate." Original gratins were prepared in a shallow dish and topped with some kind of crumbly mixture, before being browned in the oven or under a broiler.

PORK MADE HEALTHY

Pork has a reputation for being a fatty, unhealthy meat. And while bacon, cracklins, and high-fat sausages aren't the most health-supportive choices, pork has a lot of redeeming features. Choose a lean pork cut such as tenderloin and you've got a meal that is lower in fat than beef, high in zinc and protein, and rich in thiamin, a B-vitamin that helps your body create and use energy.

FAST FETTUCCINE WITH KALE AND SAUSAGE

MAKES 4 SERVINGS

My kids and my hubby adore Italian sausage, so they'll eat pretty much anything if it has sausage in it. This is a fun way to combine sausage and kale. If you're gluten-free (like two of my sons), use a gluten-free pasta here. (My favorite is Tinkyada brand.)

3   tablespoons olive oil
1   pound hot turkey or pork sausage, casings discarded and sausage crumbled
½   lb kale, deribbed, blanched, squeezed dry and coarsely chopped
    Salt
½   pound dry fettuccine pasta
⅔   cup chicken broth
¼   to ½ cup finely grated Pecorino Romano

1. Heat oil in a 12-inch heavy skillet over moderately high heat until hot but not smoking. Cook sausage until browned, 5 to 7 minutes, breaking up any lumps with a spoon.

2. Meanwhile, fill large pot with salted water and bring to a boil. Cook pasta in boiling water, uncovered, until al dente. Reserve 1 cup pasta-cooking water, then drain pasta in a colander. (If using gluten-free pasta, follow instructions on the bag.)

3. While the pasta cooks, add blanched kale to sausage in skillet and sauté, stirring frequently, until kale is just tender, about 5 minutes.

4. Add broth, stirring and scraping up any brown bits from bottom of skillet, then add pasta and ½ cup reserved cooking water to skillet, tossing until combined. Stir in cheese and thin with additional cooking water if desired.

ONE-POT GREEN PENNE

MAKES 6 SERVINGS

Once upon a time, when my husband and I were vegan, we ate a lot of pasta. Then I began studying nutrition and realized two things: I don't digest wheat and hubby needs occasional animal protein to be his healthiest. The result? We cut way back on pasta. That said, I still make this yummy recipe today, but to accommodate everyone in my household, I often use gluten-free pasta.

¼ cup chopped fresh basil or Italian parsley (or a blend)
Squirt of lemon juice
1 teaspoon finely grated lemon peel
2 garlic cloves, minced
1 bunch kale, deribbed and coarsely chopped
1 pound penne (you can use gluten-free if you'd like)
5 tablespoons extra-virgin olive oil, divided
½ cup coarsely chopped pitted Kalamata olives
½ cup crumbled feta cheese (about 3 ounces)
Salt and pepper to taste

OLIVE OIL: DID YOU KNOW....?

- The olive tree is native to the Mediterranean.
- Spain is the world's largest overall producer of olive oil. Italy is second.
- In Homer's *Odyssey*, the Phoenician princess Nausicaa carries a golden flask filled with olive oil. She and her maids anoint themselves with the oil after bathing in the river. In Ancient Greece and other Mediterranean countries, men and women applied olive oil to their skin and hair after bathing as a moisturizer and to protect their hair and skin from the elements.
- In Greece, women created eye shadow by mixing ground charcoal with olive oil.
- In Homer's *Iliad*, Aphrodite anoints the dead body of Hector with rose-scented olive oil. This was common in Ancient Greece, where bodies were often treated with olive oil to mask the smell of decomposition.
- Olive oil played an important role in early athletic events. Before working out or competing, Greek athletes rubbed their naked bodies with olive oil to protect themselves from the sun and to help regulate body temperature. Once their competition was over, the athletes would use a tool called a "strigil" and scrape away the oil, sweat, and dirt from their skin.
- In Rome, pregnant women applied olive oil to their skin to prevent stretch marks. Women today still do this.
- In the Bible, King Solomon uses olive oil to buy wood to build his temple.
- Christopher Columbus introduced olive oil to South and Central America in 1492.
- Olive trees were taken north from Mexico into California in the 1700s.
- Olive oil didn't become commonplace in the United States until the late 1800s and early 1900s, when Greek, Italian, and Spanish immigrants began importing it from their homelands.
- Italy exports more olive oil to the United States than to anywhere else.

1. Mix basil, lemon juice, lemon peel, and garlic in small bowl; set aside.

2. Bring large pot of salted water to boil. Add kale and cook just until tender, about 6 or 7 minutes. Using skimmer or slotted spoon, transfer greens to colander to drain.

3. Return water to boil. Add pasta and cook just until tender but still firm to bite, stirring occasionally. Drain, reserving ¾ cup pasta cooking liquid.

4. Return pasta to pot; add greens and 3 tablespoons oil and toss. Stir in olives, feta, and enough reserved pasta cooking liquid by ¼ cupfuls to moisten.

5. Stir herb-lemon mixture and remaining olive oil into the pasta and greens. Season with salt and pepper.

PORK CHOPS WITH KALE CHIP GREMOLATA

MAKES 4 SERVINGS

I first tasted gremolata in a cooking class, where I was a kitchen assistant. The instructor had given me and the other assistant some leftover cooked potatoes with the remaining tablespoons of the gremolata she had just made. I had never tasted anything so bright and sunny! What's different in this version is instead of parsley, you are using kale. The results are delicious! Use any extras to dress up sandwiches, salads, eggs, and poultry.

½ *small bunch kale, deribbed*
¾ *cup olive oil*
    Salt, to taste
    Pepper, to taste
½ *cup walnut pieces*
4 *center-cut bone-in pork chops, about ¾-inch thick (2 pounds total)*
¼ *teaspoon dried rosemary, crushed with your fingers*
1 *small clove garlic, quartered*
    Pinch crushed red pepper flakes
2 *tablespoons fresh lemon juice*
Optional: 1 teaspoon lemon zest
    Baked potato or soft polenta, for serving

1. Preheat the broiler.

2. In a large bowl, gently toss the kale leaves with two tablespoons of olive oil and ¼ teaspoon salt. Spread them in an even layer on a baking sheet

3. Place the baking sheet under the broiler, stirring greens once or twice until they are bright in color with charred edges, about 4 or 5 minutes.

4. Toss walnuts onto the baking sheet with the kale leaves and broil for another minute or two, until the walnuts are toasty but not burned. Set kale and walnuts aside to cool.

5. Sprinkle both sides of the chops with ½ teaspoon salt, ¼ teaspoon pepper, and the rosemary.

6. In a large skillet over medium heat, add 2 tablespoons of the olive oil. Add the pork chops and cook, turning once, until the meat is done. Do not over-cook. Transfer to a plate to rest for 5 minutes.

7. While the chops are cooking, add the garlic and the cooled kale and walnuts to the bowl of a food processor and pulse until chopped. Add the pepper flakes, lemon juice, optional lemon zest, ¼ teaspoon salt, and the remaining ½ cup olive oil and continue to process to make a slightly chunky pesto. Adjust the consistency as desired with up to ¼ cup water. Season to taste with salt and pepper.

8. Top each pork chop with about 2 tablespoons of the gremolata.

SPICY CHICKEN KALE STIR-FRY

MAKES 4 SERVINGS

Every cook (and non-cook) needs a good stir-fry recipe. This one is mine. I love the nutty flavor, as do my kids. I also love the healthy ingredients. Leftovers are good packed up and eaten for lunch the next day. Serve this over brown rice, quinoa, or millet.

2   tablespoons tamari (or other soy sauce)
1   teaspoon minced fresh ginger
1   clove garlic, minced
2   tablespoons dry sherry
3   teaspoons toasted sesame oil
2   teaspoons golden brown sugar
1¼ pounds skinless boneless chicken breast halves, cut crosswise into thin strips, then chopped into chunks
3   tablespoons virgin coconut oil divided
4   scallions, sliced thinly, including the light green sections
1   small jalapeno chili, seeds and veins removed, then finely chopped
1   bunch kale, deribbed, and coarsely chopped
Optional: Two tablespoons chopped cilantro leaves
Optional: ¼ cup chopped roasted salted peanuts, cashews, almonds, or walnuts

1. In a medium bowl, whisk tablespoon tamari, ginger, garlic, sherry, sesame oil, and sugar in medium bowl. Pour half of this liquid into a measuring cup or other container to reserve. Add chicken to the bowl and allow to marinade for 20 to 30 minutes.

2. Heat 2 tablespoons oil in large nonstick skillet over high heat. Add scallion and jalapeno, stirring for 30 seconds.

3. Add chicken to the skillet and stir-fry just until cooked through, about 3 minutes. Transfer chicken mixture to bowl and set aside.

4. Add 1 tablespoon oil to same skillet; heat over high heat. Add greens by large handfuls; stir just until beginning to wilt before adding more. Sauté just until tender, about 6 to 8 minutes.

5. Return chicken to skillet. Add reserved soy sauce mixture; stir until heated through, about one minute. Season with salt and pepper.

6. Transfer to serving bowl; sprinkle with optional cilantro and nuts.

SESAME: THE BACTERIA BUSTER

Sesame oil is known for both its antioxidant and antibacterial activity, which makes it a popular protective skin treatment and dietary supplement. But did you know that sesame oil is also a popular herbal cure for gingivitis and cavities? Swish 2 or more tablespoons of cold-pressed sesame oil around in the mouth for 2 or more minutes. Gargle if desired.

SIDE DISHES

CREAMED KALE

MAKES 6 SERVINGS

You're probably familiar with the original spinach version of this dish. For some people (I know you're not one of them!), creamed spinach is the only green veggie they'll eat. Do you have anyone like that in your life? If so, let me help you shake up their food world with Creamed Kale. Note: This is a pretty dairy-intensive dish, so you'll want to make this a "once in awhile" dish. You can play around with non-dairy alternatives if you'd like, but I haven't had a lot of luck with them. Just being honest.

3 pounds kale, deribbed, blanched, squeezed dry and coarsely chopped

3½ cups whole milk, or more if needed

3 tablespoons unsalted butter, plus more for the baking dish

1 medium Spanish onion, finely diced

1 small shallot, finely diced

3 cloves garlic, finely chopped

3 tablespoons all-purpose flour

Optional: ⅛ teaspoon freshly grated nutmeg

Salt, to taste

Pepper, to taste

1. Preheat the oven to 350°F.

2. Butter a 10-inch square baking dish.

3. Pour the milk into a medium saucepan and bring to a simmer over low heat.

4. Melt the butter in a medium saucepan over medium-high heat. Add the onion and shallot and cook until soft, about 5 minutes. Add the garlic and cook for 30 seconds.

5. Whisk in the flour and cook until smooth and light blonde in color, about 1 minute.

6. Slowly whisk in the warm milk, raise the heat to high, and cook, whisking constantly, until thickened and the flour taste has cooked out, about 5 minutes. If the mixture becomes too thick, add a little more milk.

7. Strain the sauce over the kale. Add the optional nutmeg, season with salt and pepper, and mix gently to combine. Scrape the mixture into the baking dish and bake in the oven until light golden brown on top and just warmed through, about 15 minutes.

GREEN POLENTA

MAKES 6 SERVINGS

Here's another green recipe. Literally. Hey if you're going to eat healthfully, why not have a little fun? Fortunately, this easy recipe is also delicious. Your kids will love it. Try it with poultry, meats, or vegetable ragouts.

2   *tablespoons extra virgin olive oil*
½   *onion, diced*
3   *cloves garlic, minced*
1   *bunch kale, deribbed and coarsely chopped*
    Salt, to taste
    Pepper, to taste
5   *cups chicken broth*
2½   *cups heavy cream*
1½   *cups stone-ground corn meal*
6   *tablespoons butter*
4   *tablespoons grated Parmesan*

1. In a large sauté pan, heat the olive oil over medium heat. Add the onions and sauté until translucent, about 3 minutes.

2. Add the garlic and kale, season with salt and pepper to taste, and cook until wilted. Set aside to cool.

3. In another large pot, bring 5 cups of broth and 2 cups heavy cream to a boil over medium heat. Whisk in the corn meal and stir constantly until the polenta is creamy, about 20 minutes. If the mixture becomes too thick, add a little water.

4. When the kale mixture has cooled, add it to the bowl of a food processor. Process until mixture is a smooth, velvety, green puree. If the mixture seems thick and chunky, add a bit of water or broth and process again.

5. Stir butter into the cooked polenta and season with salt and pepper, to taste. Fold in the kale and the Parmesan.

FRIED PORK RICE WITH KALE

MAKES 1 TO 2 SERVINGS

Do you have your local Chinese food takeout place on speed dial? It's time to take your culinary power back and learn how to make fried rice yourself. It's easy. I promise. And fun! Use cold, leftover rice for this. Freshly-cooked rice will not give you the right results. If you don't have pork tenderloin, use a leftover pork chop or chicken meat. Or leave out the animal protein altogether.

2   *tablespoons sesame oil*
2   *garlic cloves, minced*
1   *tablespoon finely minced fresh ginger*
1   *small onion, halved lengthwise and thinly sliced crosswise*
1   *carrot, cut into ⅛-inch-thick matchsticks*
¾   *cup steamed or cooked kale, squeezed dry and finely chopped*
½   *cup red bell pepper, cut into thin, short strips*
1½ *cups chilled cooked rice such as short grain brown rice*
½   *to ¾ cup roast pork tenderloin, cut crosswise into ⅓-inch-thick slices and slices cut into ⅓-inch-wide strips*
1   *tablespoon rice wine vinegar*
1   *tablespoon tamari or other soy sauce*
1   *teaspoon brown sugar or honey*
2   *scallions, thinly sliced*
Optional: 1 teaspoon minced fresh jalapeno or Serrano chili
Optional: 2 tablespoons chopped fresh cilantro
Optional: 1 large egg, lightly beaten (optional)

1. Heat oil in a wok or a deep 12-inch heavy nonstick skillet over moderately high heat until hot but not smoking. Add garlic and ginger and stir-fry until golden, about 1 minute.
2. Add onion and stir-fry until lightly browned, about 2 minutes.
3. Add carrot, kale, and red pepper and stir-fry 2 minutes.
4. Add rice and pork and stir-fry 1 minute.
5. In a small bowl, whisk together rice vinegar, tamari, honey, and chili until honey is dissolved.
6. Add soy mixture to wok, then add scallions and 1 tablespoon optional cilantro and stir-fry for one minute.
7. Add optional beaten egg and stir-fry until egg is set, about 1 minute.
8. Serve sprinkled with remaining tablespoon cilantro.

SODIUM AND SOY SAUCE

Soy sauce is used as a salty flavoring and condiment in several Asian countries. It is delicious stuff! But keep in mind that soy sauce is high in sodium. A single tablespoon of the stuff can contain up to 1,000 mg of sodium. Current dietary guidelines recommend that you get no more than 2,300 mg a day, with a healthier daily sodium intake being 1,500 mg or less. (Just to put all this sodium talk in context: Most American adults ingest 3,266 mg per day in convenience food—that's not even counting table salt that's added to food.)

GREEN POTATO PUREE

MAKES 8 SERVINGS

This is bright green. Yes it is. So bright, that people may think it is creamed spinach. It's actually better (in my opinion): A velvety, hearty puree that pairs beautifully with poultry and red meat, and makes a fun bed to sit fish atop. Thin leftovers with a bit of chicken broth for a lovely soup.

2   *pounds kale, deribbed, coarsely chopped*
1½   *pounds large boiling potatoes, peeled and*
      cut into half-inch cubes
2   *cups heavy cream*
      Salt, to taste
      Pepper, to taste

1. Fill a large pot with salted water and place, uncovered over a high flame. When the water begins to boil, add kale, cooking it until tender, about 7 minutes.

> ### KALE TRIVIA
>
> In nineteenth century Scotland "kail" was used as a generic term for "dinner" and all kitchens featured a "kail-pot" for cooking.

2. Quickly drain kale and run cold water over the greens to stop the cooking process. Set wet, cooled greens aside.

3. While kale cooks, place a heavy medium saucepan over medium heat, adding potatoes, cream, salt, and pepper. Simmer, covered, stirring occasionally, until tender, 15 to 20 minutes.

4. Add the kale to the bowl of a food processor, processing until absolutely smooth.

5. Add potatoes, and pulse until smooth.

6. Serve immediately, or transfer to a large heavy saucepan and heat through before serving.

THE POTATO EATERS: DID YOU KNOW...?

- The average American eats 137.9 pounds of potatoes each year.
- 50.7 pounds of the potatoes consumed each year are fresh.
- 55.3 pounds of the potatoes consumed each year are frozen potato products, such as French fries, hash browns, etc.
- 16.9 pounds of the potatoes consumed each year are as potato chips.
- 13 pounds of the potatoes consumed each year are dehydrated potato products, such as boxed potato flakes, au gratin mixes, and so on.
- 2 pounds of the potatoes consumed each year are canned potatoes, found in soup and other canned products.

HEARTY WINTER SALAD

MAKES 4 SERVINGS

This is truly a cold-weather salad. Heavy, hearty, rib-sticking—it's also rich in nutrients and tastes wonderful.

2 pounds Yukon Gold potatoes, cut into 1-inch pieces
⅓ cup extra virgin olive oil
4 garlic cloves (3 thinly sliced and 1 left whole)
¼ cup well-stirred tahini
2 tablespoons water
3 tablespoons fresh lemon juice
1 bunch kale, deribbed and leaves cut in a chiffonade
Salt, to taste
Pepper, to taste

1. Preheat oven to 450°F with a rack in upper third.
2. In a large bowl, mix potatoes with oil and ½ teaspoon each of salt and pepper. Tossing until potatoes are coated. Transfer potatoes to a baking pan, spreading them in an even layer. Place in oven and roast, for about 12 minutes, stirring once.
3. Stir in sliced garlic and roast 12 minutes more.
4. In the bowl of a food processor purée tahini, water, lemon juice, fourth (whole) garlic clove, and ½ teaspoon salt in a blender until smooth, about 1 minute. Add a bit of water if sauce is too thick.
5. Toss kale with hot potatoes and any garlic and oil remaining in pan, then toss with tahini sauce and salt and pepper to taste.

KALE CASSEROLE

MAKES 6 SERVINGS

I was raised on casseroles. They were at every church event I ever attended, every family reunion, and every single dinner I ever ate at home. (My mother, who didn't know how to cook, would open a can of condensed cream of mushroom soup and dump it into a Pyrex casserole dish, then add a 1 cup of canned or frozen veggies, 1 cup of leftover meat (or a can of tuna), 1 cup of leftover Minute Rice or noodles, then top the thing with a handful of saltine crackers she'd put in a plastic bag and crushed with the bottom of a drinking glass.) I was well into adulthood before I could even get near another casserole, but with a bit of perspective, I realize that casseroles are good things: Easy, economical, nourishing, and fast. This one, which contains no cream of mushroom soup, is also vegetarian and dressy enough for a holiday table.

FOR VEGETABLES

2   tablespoons olive oil
2   medium onions, halved lengthwise and thinly sliced lengthwise
1   pound cabbage, cored and cut crosswise into ⅓-inch-thick slices (4 cups)
1   pound kale, stems and center ribs removed and leaves coarsely chopped (12 cups)
½   pound carrots, cut into ¼-inch-thick matchsticks
½   cup water
2   tablespoons soy sauce
½   teaspoon salt

FOR TOPPING

1½ cups fine fresh or dried bread crumbs, preferably whole wheat
7   ounces firm tofu
1   ounce finely grated Parmigiano-Reggiano (½ cup)
⅓   cup olive oil
2   teaspoons dried basil, crumbled

1½ teaspoons dried oregano, crumbled
1   teaspoon paprika
1   garlic clove, chopped
¼   teaspoon salt

1. Put oven rack in middle position and preheat oven to 350°F.

2. Heat oil in a deep 12- to 14-inch heavy skillet over moderately high heat until hot but not smoking, then sauté onion, stirring occasionally, until softened and beginning to brown, about 5 minutes. Reduce heat to moderate and add cabbage, kale, carrots, water, soy sauce, and salt. (Skillet will be full, but volume will reduce as vegetables steam.) Cook, covered, stirring occasionally, until vegetables are just tender, 10 to 15 minutes. Transfer to a 13- by 9-inch glass baking dish.

3. Make topping: Pulse all topping ingredients together in a food processor until combined well. Alternatively, mash ingredients together in a large bowl with a potato masher. Sprinkle tofu mixture over vegetables in baking dish and bake, uncovered, until topping is golden brown and vegetables are heated through, 15 to 20 minutes.

THE STORY BEHIND THE WORD

In the United States, the word "casserole" is synonymous with church suppers, potlucks, and starchy, feed-lots-of-people dishes. The actual word, casserole, however, comes not from a food, but from a cooking vessel. Casserole is from the French word for "saucepan," a large, deep dish used both in the oven and as a serving vessel.

KALE MEAT PIES

MAKES 8 SERVINGS

I like meat pies. I don't care if they are from Jamaica, Australia, England or wherever. This tasty spin features our favorite green veggie, kale!

2½ cups all-purpose flour (spooned and leveled), plus more for rolling
1 cup (2 sticks) unsalted butter, cut into small pieces
1½ teaspoons fine salt
½ cup ice water
1 tablespoon extra-virgin olive oil
10 ounces (about 1½ links) sweet Italian sausage, casings removed
1 medium onion, diced medium
1 tart apple, such as Granny Smith, peeled and diced medium
1 bunch kale (¾ pound), tough stems and ribs removed, leaves coarsely chopped
¼ cup golden raisins
  Coarse salt and ground pepper
  Heavy cream, for brushing

1. In a food processor, pulse flour, butter, and salt until mixture resembles coarse meal, with a few pea-size pieces of butter remaining. With machine running, sprinkle with ¼ cup ice water; pulse just until dough holds together when squeezed (if necessary, add up to ¼ cup more water, 1 tablespoon at a time); do not overmix. Form dough into a disk, wrap tightly in plastic, and refrigerate 30 minutes (or up to overnight).

2. Meanwhile, in a large skillet, heat oil over medium-high. Add sausage and cook, breaking up meat with a wooden spoon, until browned, about 5 minutes.

3. Add onion and cook until translucent, about 6 minutes. Add apple, kale, and raisins and cook until kale is almost tender, about 5 minutes. Remove from heat; season with salt and pepper.

4. Preheat oven to 400°F. Line two baking sheets with parchment paper. On a lightly floured surface, roll out dough to an ⅛-inch thickness. With a large round cookie cutter or small bowl, cut out eight 6- to 7-inch rounds (reroll scraps if necessary).

5. Place ½ cup kale mixture in center of each round and fold over filling to form half-moons. With a fork, press edges firmly to seal. Place pies on baking sheets and brush with cream.

6. Cut a small vent in each pie and bake until golden brown and crisp, 25 to 30 minutes, rotating sheets halfway through. Let cool slightly on a wire rack. Serve warm or at room temperature.

KALE RICE

MAKES 2 SERVINGS

This is easy, fast, and yummy—the perfect side dish for serving alongside any type of animal protein, or veggie ragout, stew or bean dish. Everyone needs to know how to make this!

1   cup water or chicken broth
    Salt, to taste
    Pepper, to taste
½   cup long-grain brown rice (use basmati rice
    if you'd like)
2   small garlic cloves, minced
1   tablespoon olive oil
1   (14-ounce) can diced tomatoes, liquid reserved
    for another use
2   cups kale, deribbed, chopped finely

1. In a small heavy saucepan bring 1 cup water to a boil. Add the rice and salt to taste, then immediately cover the pot and turn the flame to low.

2. Cook the rice over low heat for 25 minutes, or until the liquid is absorbed and the rice is tender.

3. In a heavy skillet cook the garlic in the oil over moderately low heat, stirring, until it is soft.

4. Add the tomatoes and the kale to the skillet and cook the mixture, stirring occasionally, for 5 minutes, or until the kale is tender.

5. Dump the finished rice into a large bowl, fluff with fork, and add the kale mixture. Add salt and pepper, to taste. Mix gently until ingredients are combined.

RICE: DID YOU KNOW… ?

- Rice is the main dietary staple for more than half of the world's population.
- Rice has been cultivated for over 5,000 years.
- Arkansas is the largest producer of rice in the U.S. accounting for about 46% of U.S. rice production. California is the second largest rice producing state, growing about 17.7% of the U.S. rice crop on more than 500,000 acres.
- The U.S. exports about half of its rice crop, mostly to Mexico, Central America, Northeast Asia, the Caribbean, and the Middle East.
- September is National Rice Month.
- The first rice grown in the United States most likely came from Madagascar. It was planted in the Carolinas in the late 1680s.
- September is National Rice Month.
- It takes between 2,000 to 5,000 tons of water to produce a ton of rice.
- The major rice-producing states are Arkansas, California, Louisiana, Texas, Mississippi, and Missouri. Almost half of the U.S. rice crop is exported to over 100 countries.
- Rice is grown on every continent except Antarctica.
- Rice, millet, and sorghum are thought to be the first crops ever cultivated.
- Americans eat a little more than 24 pounds of rice per person each year. Asians eat as much as 300 pounds per person each year, while in the United Arab Emirates it is about 450 pounds, and in France about 10 pounds.

POTATO KALE CAKES

MAKES 12 SERVINGS

Unlike latkes, which are made with grated potatoes, these use mashed potatoes (yes, you can use leftovers!). The result is super elegant, super delicious, and pretty easy, too.

OPTIONAL SAUCE

½ cup mayonnaise
1 tablespoon extra-virgin olive oil
2 garlic cloves, minced
1 tablespoon tomato paste
⅛ teaspoon chipotle powder (use more if you can take the heat)
    Salt, to taste
    Pepper, to taste

POTATO CAKE

1½ pounds russet potatoes, peeled, cut into 1-inch cubes
¼ cup whole milk
2 tablespoons (¼ stick) unsalted butter
    Salt, to taste
3½ tablespoons extra-virgin olive oil, divided
1 cup onion, minced
1 large garlic clove, minced
½ pound kale, deribbed, coarsely chopped
Optional: ½ teaspoon lemon zest

SAUCE DIRECTIONS

1. Whisk all ingredients in medium bowl. Can be made 1 day ahead. Cover and chill.

POTATO CAKE DIRECTIONS

1. Cook potatoes in large saucepan of boiling salted water until tender, about 25 minutes. Drain; return potatoes to same saucepan.

2. Add milk and butter. Mash potatoes until smooth. Season with ½ teaspoon coarse salt and ½ teaspoon pepper.

3. Transfer 3 cups mashed potatoes to large bowl and cool (reserve remaining potatoes for another use).

4. Heat 1½ tablespoons oil in large deep skillet over medium heat. Add onion and garlic. Sauté until onion softens, about 5 minutes.

5. Increase heat to medium-high. Add kale and cook until kale softens, about 7 minutes.

6. Add kale mixture, ½ teaspoon salt, and ½ teaspoon pepper to potatoes and thoroughly combine. Allow to sit for 45 minutes or more until mixture is thoroughly cool.

7. When the potato-kale mixture is cool, shape it by patting ¼-cup portions into patties about ½-inch thick. Keep shaping until all potato-kale mixture has been formed into patties.

8. Heat 2 tablespoons oil in large nonstick skillet over medium-high heat. Add patties and cook, without moving (you want a crust to form!), until they are brown and crispy on bottom, about 4 minutes.

9. Carefully turn cakes over. Cook until brown on bottom, about 3 minutes more. Transfer to plates. Top each cake with dollop of optional sauce, salsa, or other condiment.

POTLIKER KALE

MAKES 2 SERVINGS

These are Southern-style greens, inspired by those long-simmered greens that are revered in the U.S. south. These have a decidedly shorter cooking time and a fresher taste, but use the same porky, puckery vinegar flavoring. And yes, of course you can omit the bacon—use a couple tablespoons of butter or your favorite oil, instead, and know that you'll have a completely different recipe.

1   *large bunch of kale, deribbed and chopped coarsely*
2   *bacon slices, chopped*
     Salt, to taste
     Pepper, to taste
2   *teaspoons cider vinegar, or to taste*

1. In a large heavy saucepan of boiling salted water boil kale for 5 minutes and drain well in colander.

2. In large skillet, cook bacon over moderate heat, stirring, until crisp.

3. Add kale to bacon and sauté over moderately high heat, stirring, until heated through.

4. Toss kale with vinegar and season with salt and pepper.

CHAPTER 8

DESSERTS & OTHER SWEETS

One of the wonderful benefits of eating lots of kale is improved hearing (it's the omega-3 fatty acids, magnesium, and vitamins A, C, and E—all of which have been shown to protect and improve hearing). In fact, my own hearing has become so good that I can hear you right now, as you read this chapter: "Kale in desserts?" you ask, incredulously. "That's just wrong!"

Perhaps, but it's also super healthy, super easy, and (yes!) super tasty! Sneaking a bit of kale into a sweet is an easy way to increase its nutrient profile and deliver a dose of nourishing kale to a picky kid (or adult); it's also terrific for gardeners who would feel terrible wasting even a leaf of their precious kale crop.

So go ahead and call me crazy, but do me a favor and try one of the recipes in this chapter. I have a feeling they'll make a "kale dessert convert" out of you. Just one bit of advice before you start: Baked goods should be allowed to completely cool to room temperature before serving. If they are the least bit warm, you will taste the kale.

BLUEBERRY KALE POPS
MAKES 4 TO 6 SERVINGS

Popsicles are a great place to slip in kale. The trick, however, is accompanying kale with dark, bold-tasting fruit. No kid wants a popsicle that tastes like frozen greens! That's why this fruity, refreshing recipe uses blueberries, kale, and grape juice, but feel free to experiment. The combinations are—quite literally—endless.

THE BEGINNING OF THE POPSICLE

- The first popsicle was invented in 1905 by an 11-year-old boy named Frank Epperson, who called his invention the Epsicle Ice Pop.
- Epperson invented the treat after leaving a cup of soda with a straw outdoors during the winter. It froze—and Epperson had himself a frozen treat.
- It took Epperson more than 18 years to finally patent his invention. By that time, his own children had taken to calling the treats "popsicles." The new name stuck.
- In 1925, Epperson sold the rights to his popsicle to the John Lowe food company of New York.
- The first commercial popsicles had birch sticks. Today, most sticks are still made of birch.

1 cup frozen blueberries
1 cup baby kale leaves (mature kale is just too "kaley" for this)
2 cups organic purple grape juice

1. In a food processor or high-power blender (such as a VitaMix or BlendTec), blend all ingredients until perfectly liquefied.
2. Pour into ice pop molds or ice cube molds.
3. Freeze until solid.

CHOCOLATE SURPRISE GRANOLA CLUSTERS

MAKES ABOUT 9 CUPS

You guessed it! The "surprise" in this recipe is kale. It's a delicious surprise at that, in an "I can't even taste the kale" kind of way. This is fun to pack in the kids' school lunches to add a touch of sweetness and makes a great "just because" kind of snack. Do not tell anyone

---

WALNUT LORE

Walnuts are filled with good things—protein, omega-3 fatty acids, vitamin E, and manganese. They benefit the cardiovascular system, the immune system, the skin, and the nervous system. But did you know that only 5.5 percent of American adults eat walnuts at any point in a year? Here are some more fun walnut facts:

- Due to their high polyunsaturated fat content, walnuts are extremely perishable and should be stored in the refrigerator or freezer.
- In the 4th century CE, the Romans introduce walnuts to many European countries, where they have been grown since.
- Walnut oil was once used as lamp oil.
- A 1-ounce serving of walnuts is about 7 shelled walnuts, or 14 walnut halves.
- Walnuts are part of the tree nut family, which includes Brazil nuts, cashews, hazelnuts, macadamia nuts, pecans, pine nuts, and pistachios.
- China is the largest commercial producer of walnuts in the world, with about 360,000 metric tons produced per year.
- The U.S. is the second largest commercial producer of walnuts, with about 294,000 metric tons of production.
- In the U.S., 90 percent of all walnuts are grown in Northern California, most notably, the Sacramento and San Joaquin valleys.
- Turkey, Iran, the Ukraine and Romania are next highest world walnut producers.
- The walnuts grown commercially in the U.S. are known as "English walnuts" because they were first brought to this country on British mercantile ships.
- Black walnuts are native to the U.S.

there is kale in it and they will always ask for seconds (and thirds).

5   dates, pitted and soaked for at least 10 minutes
1   apple or pear, chopped
1   large banana , sliced
2   tablespoons lemon juice
1   tablespoon virgin coconut oil
2   tablespoons cocoa powder
½   teaspoon almond or vanilla extract
4   large leaves of kale, washed, dried, and deribbed
2½ cups old fashioned rolled oats
½   cup unsweetened coconut flakes
½   cup ground oats (you can whir rolled oats in a coffee grinder)
¼   cup milled chia seed (you can whir whole chia seed in a coffee grinder)
½   cup raw sunflower seeds
½   cup walnuts, chopped

1. Preheat the oven to 275°F.

2. In the bowl of a food processor, combine the dates, apple, banana, and lemon juice. Pulse into a smooth puree.

3. Add the coconut oil, cocoa powder, and vanilla. Pulse until incorporated.

4. Add the kale and pulse again until completely incorporated. No kale should be visible.

5. In a large bowl, stir together the rest of the ingredients (oats through walnuts) until well combined. Pour the kale puree over the dry ingredients and stir until evenly coated.

6. Divide the mixture between two or three baking sheets lined with parchment paper and spread evenly over the sheets.

7. Bake for 25 minutes, stir, and bake for another 15 to 20 minutes. Allow to cool completely before transferring to an airtight container and storing in the refrigerator.

COCOA-DUSTED KALE CHIPS
MAKES 2-TO RESERVE SERVINGS

This is another fun, easy and chocolate way to enjoy kale chips. Kids loving helping with this recipe. For a spicy kick, add a sprinkle of chipotle pepper to the cocoa powder.

1   bunch kale, deribbed, washed and perfectly dry
1   teaspoon virgin coconut oil
1   teaspoon agave syrup
2   teaspoons cocoa powder
    Dash salt

1. Preheat an oven to 350°F.

2. Line a non-insulated cookie sheet with parchment paper.

3. In a large bowl, whisk oil and agave until thoroughly combined

4. Add kale to bowl and toss leaves to coat.

5. Sprinkle on cocoa powder and salt, tossing leaves to coat.

6. Arrange kale leaves on one or more baking sheets, so no leaves are touching. Bake for 5 minutes. Turn leaves and continuing baking 10 or more minutes until the edges brown but are not burnt.

A NUTTY KALE IDEA

Add a bit of protein to your dessert kale chips with nuts. In a food processor or coffee grinder, pulse one small handful of your favorite nuts, one or two teaspoons of sugar, and your favorite spices into a powder. Be careful not to grind the nuts into nut-butter though! Sprinkle these on the kale leaves while tossing them with oil. Arranged nut-coated leaves on a baking sheet, and bake per your recipe. Yum, yum, yum!

DEEP CHOCOLATE-CLOAKED KALE CHIPS

MAKES 2 TO 4 SERVINGS

This unusual recipe is a favorite of true chocoholics. I first tasted it at a party, then again a week later at another party. Knowing a good thing when I taste it, I had to include it here for you to try.

1   *large bunch of kale leaves, deribbed, washed and thoroughly dried*
¼   *cup dark chocolate (preferably 70%), melted*
1   *tsp. virgin coconut oil*
¼   *tsp. sea salt*
Optional: Dash of cinnamon, allspice, or chipotle powder

1. Preheat an oven to 350°F.
2. Line a non-insulated cookie sheet with parchment paper.

3. Place kale leaves in a large bowl and drizzle with oil. Toss leaves to coat.
4. Spread kale evenly onto baking sheet so no leaves are touching
5. Bake for 5 minutes. Turn leaves and continue baking 10 or more minutes until the edges brown but are not burnt
6. Remove from oven. Drizzle with melted dark chocolate. Sprinkle with salt and optional spice.

DESSERT CHIPS (KALE-STYLE)

Dress up your sweet kale chips by dusting them with any of these fun additions:
• Ground coconut flakes
• Cinnamon, ginger, allspice, cloves, nutmeg, start anise, cardamom, or a combination of these. A touch of sugar is optional.
• Finely-milled almond meal or other pulverized nuts
• Powdered sugar
• Dried lemon, lime, or orange zest, alone or mixed with powdered sugar

GREEN GODDESS PUDDING

MAKES 2 SERVINGS

This fun recipe is a real kid-pleaser—it's silky, sweet, and chocolate. But a word of very sage advice, from a mom who knows: Do not make this in front of your kids. If they see what's in it, they won't eat it. Which would be unfortunate, as it's packed with omega-3 fatty acids, healthy fats, and all kinds of antioxidants, vitamins, minerals, and fiber.

2 ripe avocados (you want avocados that are soft to the touch)
½ cup almond, coconut or rice milk
4 tablespoons cocoa powder (you can use raw cacao powder if you have it)
¼ cup agave or mild-tasting honey
¼ cup pureed baby kale (use baby kale for its mild flavor)
1 teaspoon vanilla extract
½ teaspoon salt
Optional: chopped nuts and/or saved dark chocolate for garnish

1. Add the avocado pulp, milk, cocoa, honey, kale, vanilla, and salt to the bowl of a food processor. Or use a high-power blender such as a VitaMix. Process until ingredients are well blended and the mixture is silky smooth.
2. Ladle into individual pudding cups. If not eating immediate, cover tightly with food wrap and keep in the refrigerator.

KALED-UP BOXED MIX BROWNIES

MAKES 4 TO 8 SERVINGS

This is one of those fun "sneaky" recipes that make the rounds of mommy blogs and parenting magazines. It's a fun, delicious way to slide a few tablespoons of high-impact veggies into resistant kids (and kid-like adults). Because it uses a boxed mix, this is fast and easy.

1 box brownie mix (you can use a gluten-free mix if you'd like)
¼ cup water
½ cup virgin coconut oil
2 eggs
1 large carrot, steamed until tender (or you can use a ¼ cup canned pumpkin puree)
8 kale leaves, deribbed and steamed until tender
Optional: ½ cup chopped nuts, cacao nibs, and/or chocolate chips

A NUTTY TOPPER

Sometimes you want to dress up desserts with a cloud of something creamy. A dollop of something rich. Some kind of cream. But for those of us watching our diet, traditional whipped cream may not be the smartest way to top things off. A great alternative to dairy creams is cashew cream. To make it, you'll need two cups of raw cashews. Yes, they must be raw. Place them in the bowl of a high-power blender, such as VitaMix. Or you can use a food processor . Add just enough water to cover the nuts and process on a high speed for several minutes until the mixture becomes pale and creamy. Use to top puddings, pies, cake, or sundaes. Store any leftover cream in a tightly covered container for up to two days in the refrigerator.

1. Pre-heat over to 350°F.

2. Lightly grease an 8- by 8-inch baking pan.

3. Place carrot and kale place the vegetables in a food processor or high-power blender (such as a VitaMix) and puree until perfectly smooth.

4. To the food processor, add water, oil and eggs. Puree until smooth.

5. Add brownie mix to the food processor. Being careful not to overmix, pulse a few times until the batter is blended.

6. If using, add the nuts and/or chocolate chips and pulse twice to blend.

UNDERCOVER KALE COOKIES

MAKES ABOUT 2 DOZEN COOKIES

Sometimes silence really is the best policy. Especially when it comes to giving your kids veggies. If they must have cookies, why not slide in a nourishing range of vitamins, minerals, antioxidants, and omega-3s?

½   *cup pureed baby kale*

¼   *cup unsweetened applesauce*

⅓   *cup virgin coconut oil*

3   *eggs*

¾   *cup sugar*

¾   *cup packed brown sugar*

2   *teaspoons vanilla extract*

2⅔ *cups all-purpose flour or whole wheat pastry flour (you can use a mix)*

½   *cup cocoa*

1   *teaspoon baking soda*

½   *teaspoon salt*

Optional: Dash cinnamon

Optional: ½ to ¾ cup nuts, chocolate chips, or raisins

1. Preheat oven to 350°F.

2. Prepare two baking sheets with parchment or foil.

3. In a large mixing bowl, combine kale puree, applesauce, oil, and eggs. Beat in sugars and vanilla.

4. In a separate mixing bowl, whisk together

flour, cocoa, baking soda, salt, and cinnamon, if using.

5. While mixing, gradually add dry ingredients to kale-applesauce mixture, being careful not to overmix

6. Add in any optional ingredients, stirring just to combine.

7. Cover cookie dough and refrigerate for 2 hours or until slightly firm.

8. Drop dough by rounded teaspoonfuls 2 inches apart onto greased baking sheets. Bake for 8 to 10 minutes, or until edges are browned and cookies are firm.

MAKE YOUR OWN APPLESAUCE

Need applesauce in a pinch? It's quick to make at home. Here's how:

- Take 1 apple. (You can use more if you'd like; you can even use pears. One medium apple will yield about 1 cup of applesauce.)
- Peel apple
- Slice or chop into any size pieces you'd like.
- Place apple into a small saucepan and add 2 or 3 tablespoons of water.
- Cook on medium-low heat until apple breaks down. (Add more water if the pot looks dry; you don't want the apples to scorch.)
- Puree cooked apple and liquid in a food processor or blender until silky smooth.

KALED-UP CHOCOLATE BROWNIES (from scratch)

MAKES 6 TO 10 SERVINGS

Here's another kale-and-carrot brownie recipe, this one from scratch. If someone in your family has trouble with wheat, you can easily use gluten-free oat flour.

3 ounces bittersweet chocolate or chocolate chips

¾ cup carrot or pumpkin puree

¼ cup kale puree

½ cup packed dark brown sugar

¼ cup cocoa powder (unsweetened)

2 tablespoons virgin coconut oil

2 teaspoons vanilla extract

2 large egg whites (or, you can use 1 large whole egg)

¾ cup all-purpose flour (or, you can use the same amount of gluten-free oat flour)

½ teaspoon baking powder

½ teaspoon salt

Optional: ½ cup chopped nuts, cacao nibs and/or chocolate chips

1. Preheat the oven to 350°F.

2. Lightly grease an 8- by 8-inch baking pan.

3. Melt the chocolate over a very low heat or in the microwave 30 seconds at a time.

4. In a large bowl, combine the melted chocolate, carrot puree, kale puree, sugar, cocoa powder, coconut oil, and vanilla in a large bowl. Beat until light and creamy.

5. Whisk in egg whites.

6. In a separate bowl, whisk together flour, baking powder, and salt.

7. Gently fold the dry ingredients into the chocolate mixture, stirring gently just until combined.

8. If using, gently add the nuts and/or chocolate, stirring two or three times only.

9. Pour the batter into prepared pan and bake for 35 to 40 minutes.

10. Cool completely before serving.

COCONUT PRODUCTS DEMYSTIFIED

As people become more and more savvy to coconut's many health benefits, more and more ways to enjoy this superfood appear on health food store shelves. Here is what is currently available:

- Coconut oil is the nutritious oil extracted from fresh coconut meat. Rich in medium-chain fatty acids and phytonutrients, the oil's high smoke point makes it fantastic for cooking. It's also great used as a flavoring and as a hair and skin moisturizer. When buying coconut oil, look for virgin coconut oil, which is obtained through cold-pressing instead of chemical extraction.

- Coconut flour is the finely ground, dried coconut that is left over after extracting coconut oil. Low-carbohydrate, high-fiber, and gluten-free, coconut flour is a darling in the world of wheat-free baking.

- Coconut water is the clear liquid found inside young, green coconuts. Much touted for its amazing ability to replace electrolytes, coconut water is the natural alternative to chemical-laden sports drinks.

- Coconut milk is the meat of the nut blended with water to make a creamy, dairy-like liquid. Once upon a time, all coconut milk came in cans. Now, however, many brands offer cartons of coconut milk in the refrigerated dairy section of your local supermarket or health food store.

- Dried coconut milk is coconut milk that has been dried to a powder, much like dried milk powder. To reconstitute it, simply add milk. It's a handy, shelf-stable ingredient that can be sprinkled directly into soups and curries.

- Coconut cream is what many people call the thickened, creamy looking mixture that sits at the top of a can of coconut milk.

- Cream of coconut goes by many names, including creamed coconut, coconut butter, coconut paste, coconut concentrate and more. This luxurious product is literally a block or jar of thick, shortening-like coconut made from pulverized coconut flesh, oil and all.
- Dried coconut milk is coconut milk that has been dried to a powder, much like dried milk powder. To reconstitute it, simply add milk. It's a handy, shelf-stable ingredient that can be sprinkled directly into soups and curries.
- Desiccated coconut is a baker's favorite! Dried, unsweetened coconut is fine ground for use in cookies, cakes, breads, and other recipes. Don't confuse it with the "sweetened flaked coconut" on store shelves.
- Coconut flakes or chips are related to desiccated coconut, only with bigger flakes.
- Coconut nectar is a low glycemic sweetener made from the sap of coconut trees. Though it does not have a coconuty flavor, it is rich in amino acids, minerals, and vitamins. Use wherever you would use honey or maple syrup.
- Coconut vinegar is similar to apple cider vinegar, except made with coconut water. It is rich in electrolytes and enzymes.
- Coconut aminos are a blend of 17 amino acids, which are harvested from coconut trees and mixed with mineral-rich sea salt. The dark liquid is used as a replacement for soy sauce.
- Coconut yogurt is simply yogurt made with fermented coconut milk instead of fermented cow, sheep, or goat milk. It is a terrific choice for anyone allergic to dairy products.
- Coconut kefir, like its cousin, coconut yogurt, is nothing more than a fermented "yogurt" drink made with coconut milk instead of dairy milk.

VEGAN COCOA-KALE CUPCAKES

MAKES 12 CUPCAKES

This recipe is based on the famous Wacky Cake recipe that was popular during World War II, a time when eggs and dairy products were scarce. Because it contains no animal ingredients, it is still used heavily in vegan circles. This version goes a step further, adding in a gentle dose of good-for-you kale. If you'd like to use it as a cake, bake it in prepared a 8- by 8-inch or 9- by 9-inch pan.

1½ cups all-purpose flour (you can substitute gluten-free all-purpose flour)
¼ cup cocoa
1 cup white sugar
½ teaspoon salt
1 teaspoon baking soda
1 tablespoon white distilled vinegar
⅓ cup virgin coconut oil
1 teaspoon vanilla extract
1 cup cool coffee or water
¼ cup pureed cooked kale

1. Preheat oven to 350°F.
2. Line muffin tin with cupcake liners.
3. In a large bowl, whisk together flour, baking soda, salt, cocoa, and sugar.
4. In a separate bowl, mix together vinegar, oil, vanilla, coffee, and kale.
5. Pour liquid ingredients into dry ingredients and stir just to bend.
6. Fill each muffin tin ¾ full.
7. Bake for 15 minutes or until toothpick inserted comes out clean.
8. Allow to cool in pan for 5 to 10 minutes before removing.

DRESS UP THOSE CUPCAKES

Need to give cupcakes a more formal look or quickly turn muffins into cupcakes? The trick is in the topping. Try one of these ideas:

- Dust with powdered sugar. Go as light or heavy as you'd like.
- Sprinkle vegetable-colored sprinkles (available in specialty stores and health food markets) on to cupcakes when they're partially cooked. Just open up the oven, sprinkle a bit on each cake, close up the oven, and allow the cupcakes to finish baking.
- Frost with whipped cream, drizzle with melted chocolate, or make a simple "mom's" glaze by thinning a cup or two of powdered sugar with coconut milk (or another milk), juice, or water and drizzling on cooled cupcakes.
- Make a powdered sugar buttercream by whipping together one stick of butter, a 1-pound box of powdered sugar, and a splash of vanilla or almond extract. Add 1 or 2 tablespoons of your favorite non-dairy or dairy milk for a smoother consistency.
- Follow the above directions and add 2 tablespoons cocoa powder for chocolate frosting.
- Make a nutbutter frosting with a stick of butter, 1 cup of powdered sugar, 1 teaspoon almond or vanilla extract, ½ cup creamy nutbutter of choice, and a tablespoon or two of your milk of choice. Beat together until smooth.

VEGAN JUICER-PULP MUFFIN

MAKES 12 MINI-MUFFINS

While I don't have conclusive data to back this up, a lot of kale lovers juice regularly. At least I've noticed that my friends who have juicers (and use them regularly—an important distinction), all love kale. So for all of you juicing, kale-loving powerhouses out there, I dedicate this fun cupcake. Dust with powdered sugar or frosting if you'd like.

½   *cup juicer pulp (any combination of kale beet/carrot/ginger/pineapple/pear/orange; avoid pulp with any onion-family pulp or anything bitter, such as dandelion)*

¼   *cup agave syrup*

¼   *cup virgin coconut oil*

¼   *cup unsweetened applesauce or pearsauce*

1½ *cup unbleached flour or gluten-free flour (such as Bob's Red Mill all-purpose gluten-free)*

1   *teaspoon vanilla extract*

1   *teaspoon baking soda*

½   *teaspoon sea salt*

½   *to 1 teaspoon cinnamon, ginger, allspice, or a mixture of these*

Optional: ½ cup chopped dark chocolate or chocolate chips

Optional: ½ cup chopped nuts of choice

1. Pre-heat the oven to 350°F. Lightly grease a mini muffin pan or line with paper muffin cups.

2. In a large bowl, add the juicer pulp, making sure to remove any large pieces.

3. To the juicer pulp, add the agave, coconut oil, applesauce, and vanilla. Stir to combine.

4. In a separate bowl, whisk together flour, baking soda, salt, and chosen spice. Add the optional chocolate and/or nuts and whisk again.

5. Add dry ingredients to pulp mixture. Mix gently with a silicone spatula or wooden spoon until just combined. (The batter will be thick.)

6. Transfer the batter to the mini muffin pan and bake for 10 to 12 minutes. A knife inserted in the center should come out clean when they're done.

7. Allow to cool for 10 minutes before removing from the pan. When cool, dust with powdered sugar or decorate with your favorite frosting.

WHAT TO DO WITH THE PULP?

More and more people than ever are discovering the joys of juicing. Creating and drinking home-pressed juice is not only fun, it is one of the healthiest things you can do for your body. But what to do with all that pulp? Most of us toss it into the compost heap, but you'll be glad to know that it's perfectly usable. Here are some ideas that'll use up between ¼ and ½ cup of fruit or veggie pulp:

- Puree it into creamy soups.
- Add it to marinara and other pasta sauces. To ensure a smooth, kid-friendly finish, give the sauce whir in a blender before serving.
- Add to a blender-made smoothie.
- Use as a filler for meatloaf, meatballs, shepherd's and cottage pie, and other ground meat recipes.
- Add to crab cakes, veggie burgers, potato pancakes, and similar foods.
- Tuck into baked goods, including muffins, tea breads, and cakes.

WICKED KALE CUPCAKES

MAKES 24 CUPCAKES

This is a traditional, Devils Food-style cupcake, which can also be baked in two 8-inch or 9-inch pans … should you have a hankering for a luscious layer cake. If you're out of kale, you can use spinach puree or even beet puree.

2   cups sugar
1¾ cups flour
¾   cup cocoa
1½ teaspoons baking powder
1½ teaspoons baking soda
2   eggs
1   cup dairy or non-dairy milk of choice
¼   cup virgin coconut oil
¼   cup pureed kale
1   cup boiling coffee or water

1. Heat oven to 350°F.
2. Line cupcake pans with paper liners (or grease and flour 2 cake pans).
3. In a large bowl, whisk together sugar, flour, cocoa, baking powder, and baking soda.
4. In the bowl of an electric mixer on medium speed, beat together eggs, milk, oil, and kale for 2 minutes. Stir in boiling coffee or water.
5. Add dry ingredients to the liquid ingredients and beat for a minute, until combined. The batter will be very thin; don't worry, all is well!
6. Pour batter into muffin cups, filling each ¾ full.
7. Bake 20 to 25 minutes or until a wooden toothpick inserted in the center comes out clean.

WHAT THE DEVIL?

Devil's Food cakes begin appearing in the United States in the early 1900s. These were chocolate cakes that featured a thin, coffee-infused batter with a measure of shredded beets (think of a carrot cake, only made with beets and chocolate). The beets not only added body and moisture to the cake, they infused it with its devilish crimson hue. The name Devil's Food was originally a play on the white Angel's Food cakes that appeared a few years earlier.

CHAPTER 9

KALE-GROWING GUIDE

Kale is easy to grow and fun to harvest. Plus, nothing tastes like salad that's been made with greens harvested just minutes before. There are all kinds of fun varieties to try, and growing your own food is one of the most environmentally friendly things you can do for the planet. And it's an easy challenge for all you do-it-yourself types.

Ready to give it a go? Good! Let's head out to the garden!

WHAT KALE LIKES

Not too rich, not too sandy. Not too wet, not too dry. Not too fine, not too rocky. Not to hot, not too shady. Kale likes things just so!

Choose a spot that gets between two and six hours of direct sun a day. Kale may not like heat, but it does like light. Kale also prefers loamy, well-drained, and moist (not too soggy, not too dry) soil. If this is your first time planting kale, deeply prepare the soil, mixing in compost or manure. Some people add some limestone to the soil, saying it encourages lusher growth.

Lightweight, sandy soils and heavy clay soils will impact the health and the flavor of kale,

though kale may still grow in these soils. (For you gardeners out there who like to use gardening terms, go for a soil pH of 5.5 to 6.8.)

KALE LIKES THINGS COOL

There are some veggies out there, such as tomatoes and peppers, who just adore the heat of summer. Kale is not one of these! It appreciates cool temperatures, moderate sun, a frost or two to make the leaves taste sweeter. Temperatures from 20 to 65°F are best, and a few freezing or below-zero temperature days are just fine.

When growing kale, think cool and bright. If you've got mild summers that won't scorch heat-sensitive kale, go ahead and plant your seeds in the spring; they'll grow over the summer for a fall harvest. You'll have kale just in time for Halloween and Thanksgiving! If your area has intense summers and gentle winters, aim for an autumn planting. The kale can grow through the winter for a spring harvest.

HOW MUCH TO GROW

One seed packet will give you enough kale to feed a family of four to six people.

PURCHASE THE SEEDS

Check out any reputable garden center, plant seller, seed catalog or online seed store and you'll find dozens of different varieties of kale, each more gorgeous and intriguing than the next.

Most of us have favorite types. Some of us love the curly "Scotch-style" kales, others enjoy the red "Russian-style" leaves. While others still like the unfrilled, narrow, "Tuscan" varieties. My advice: Head to a store or a site, check out what's available, matching interesting-looking varieties with your needs and climate. Choose one or more suitable varieties and experiment. Playing with different varieties of a plant is what makes gardening so creative and fun. Much more fun than heading to the supermarket and buying the lone kale variety sitting in the produce department.

PREPARE THE SITE

One of the most important things you can do when planting anything, kale included, is prepare the soil. Start by removing weeds, which can later choke and kill your young

---

ARE YOU IN THE ZONE?

For help on choosing planting times, it helps to know what agricultural zone you're in. In the United States—and in most other countries—the government's agricultural department separates the country into planting zones. Each zone represents a micro-climate which works best for a number of specific plants. In the United States, zones 5 through 9 are particularly kale-friendly. For more information on USDA plant hardiness zones, visit: **www.planthardiness.ars.usda.gov/**.

KALE COMPANIONS

Companion planting is the practice of using plants' natural preferences to create a healthier garden that needs less human and chemical intervention. It works by planting situating certain plants near other plants which can help each other. Many companion vegetables, herbs, and fruits help to deter pests, which helps to decrease the amount of pesticides and effort it takes to keep your garden pest-free. Companion planting frequently also increases the yields of the plants so you get more food from the same space.

Kale's best garden buddies are beets, celery, cucumbers, dill, garlic, hyssop, lettuce, mint, nasturtium, onions, potatoes, rosemary, sage, spinach, and Swiss chard. Plan on planting these in rows next to each other or even alternating plants within a row. If you can, keep kale away from its least favorite companions, which are beans, strawberries, and tomatoes.

KALE IN A CONTAINER

Maybe you don't have access to a single patch of dirt. Or maybe you just don't want to fuss with tilling, sowing, and thinning. Fortunately for you, kale grows beautifully outdoors in pots. (It doesn't do so well indoors in pots—it grows spindly and pale.) Follow the same directions as you would for growing kale in the garden, with these adjustments:

- Choose a pot that's at least 8-inches deep and 8-inches wide. Go larger if you want larger plants.
- Because kale likes cooler temperatures, opt for early spring or autumn planting.
- Fill the pot ²/₃ of the way up with soil, then top it off with rich compost mixed with a small amount of organic fertilizer. Check your fertilizer for mixing instructions.
- Plant one or two kale seeds in the center of the pot, about a ¹/₂-inch deep.
- Place the pot somewhere where the soil temperature is at least 45°F and no more than 65°F—75°F is ideal. This is called the germination period and if you'd like, you can move the pot or pots into a greenhouse or even indoors next to a window.
- In five to eight days, you'll see the plants break through the soil. Move the pots, weather permitting, outdoors to a spot that gets no warmer than 75°F. Kale doesn't like hot temperatures.
- Water a few times a week. You want soil to be slightly moist. Not parched and not wet.

CAN I EAT IT?

A popular winter flour in the East—New Yorkers will recognize it from outdoor flower beds—ornamental kale is, indeed, edible. It has a mellower flavor and tender texture than garden kale. Ornamental kale was first cultivated commercially during the 1980s in California. Oftentimes referred to as salad savoy, its leaves may either be pale or deep green, white, or purple, and its stalks coalesce to form a loosely knit head.

kale plants. Remember to remove weeds from the roots so they won't regrow.

Next, break up the soil with a rake or hoe, diminishing large clods of earth. Work in a manure-enriched compost, leaf mold, peat moss or a mixture of these. For you soil testers out there, kale's favorite pH is about 6.5, so if your soil is acidic you can add crushed calcium limestone or shell limestone to sweeten it.

KALE: PREVENTING DISEASE

Kale is a hardy plant, one that doesn't need a lot of special attention. That said, kale can succumb to one of several diseases or pests. To ensure that doesn't happen, follow these preventative measures:

- Inspect plants a few times a week. If you notice a problem, you can address it immediately.
- Water the soil rather than the plant. Wet plants are more susceptible to diseases than dry ones.
- Also, avoid splashing soil onto the plants when you water.
- Clean your tools thoroughly before moving from one part of the garden to another or keep separate sets of tools in different parts of the garden.
- If you're walking or working in an infested or sick part of the garden, do not visit your kale plants until you've washed your hands, changed your clothes, and cleaned the dirt off your shoes. Bits of soil or pests can travel from one part of the garden to another on your hands, clothing, or your shoes.
- Introduce ladybugs and other beneficial insects that are adept at wiping out aphid infestations.

USING SEEDLINGS

As you immerse yourself in the world of gardening, you'll hear the words "seedlings" and "transplants" bandied about. Here's what these terms refer to: Instead of planting seeds directly into the ground, you first plant them in small pots, allow them to germinate and begin growing in a warm, safe place. You then transplant the young plant directly into the ground.

It sounds like a lot of extra work, doesn't it? But there's a reason you may want to use seedlings: It allows you to get a jump on the growing season. By starting plants indoors, you can get right to the business of growing. Once the weather has warmed up a bit and soil temperatures become toasty enough for plants to thrive, you can plug your seedlings directly into the ground. (Try not to look smugly at those gardeners who will be just starting to directly sow their seeds in the ground.)

PLANT THE SEEDS

You've got your seeds, the soil is prepared, the ground is warming—it's time to get planting! Sow kale seeds in rows for easy harvest. Bury seeds ¼- to ½-inch deep, 1 inch apart, and make sure rows are spaced at least 18 inches apart from each other. Kale germinates easily in coolish or barely warm soil temperatures with even moisture.

THIN THE SEEDLINGS

Thinning is the act of removing plants. I know, it sounds counterintuitive, doesn't it? But it's an important way to ensure each kale plant has the space it needs, and the access to water and sun it needs, to grow to its full potential. To thin kale seedlings, wait until the young plants have three true leaves. This may be between two-and-a-half to four weeks. Remove the weakest-looking of the plants, leaving the strongest seedlings about 8 inches to a full foot apart. Don't toss the removed seedlings! You can add them to salads or stir-fries, replant them in a pot or a different part of the garden, or give them to a friend or family member to plant in their garden.

CULTIVATE THE KALE

Kale isn't fussy, but it does like to stay moist. So the nicest thing you can do is to keep your kale watered. Not overwatered, not soggy, not soaked. Just lightly moist. Moisture, along with cooler temperatures, is the secret to sweet, crisp kale leaves—they get bitter when exposed to above 85°F temperatures or allowed to dry out.

To further support your kale, remove yellowing leaves whenever you see them, make sure there is earth packed around the lower stems, and think about feeding kale with a scattering of compost or manure or fish emulsion at least once during the growing period. While kale plants do love nippy temperatures, if it's winter, consider covering your plants with mulch or hay to keep them productive.

HARVEST THE KALE

For most regular, non-dwarf kale varieties, harvest happens about two months after planting. Or when they reach 15 to 20 cm in length. Once the plant reaches maturity, you can simply chop the plant off at the base of the stalk. I like to wait after the first frost before harvesting—the leaves are so much more sweet and tasty.

But you have another fun option—a bit of a kale-growing secret: Kale can be treated as a cut-and-come-again plant, meaning you can continually cut small leaves for salad or other dishes as needed these leaves will replace themselves. Use a sharp knife or shears and clip leaves at the stalk. You can continue to clip and come back, clip and come back until the plant puts out flowers, usually in the warmer months.

Coconut

STEPHANIE PEDERSEN

CONTENTS

INTRODUCTION

As a young girl I lived in Australia, a place where coconuts are everywhere, even though they are not native to Australia and are not grown commercially there. In fact, they grow only sparsely along Oz's northern coast . . . and yet, Australians eat coconuts in large quantities. Yes, Aussies are coconut lovers. Go Down Under and you'll find the famous Anzac biscuits, coconut shortbread, lamingtons (small squares of cake dipped in chocolate and coated with coconut), coconut sponge, baked coconut pudding, Cherry Ripe chocolate bars (with cherries and coconut), and my favorite, Europe Apricot & Coconut bars, as well as other coconut-heavy sweets.

For me, as I was growing up, coconut was a delectable, sweet food that I associated with good times and treats. I didn't used to think of it as an ingredient that could be eaten in a wide range of dishes. And I certainly didn't grow up with the idea that coconut was good for you.

I was a child in the 1970s and '80s, a time of margarine, aspartame, and no-fat diets. Most people in Australia, the United States, and Europe (the cultures my family and I lived in) had never heard of coconut water, and we certainly didn't cook with coconut oil. The only dried coconut we ever saw was coated with sweetener and packaged in a blue plastic bag. And the idea of cooking with flour that wasn't made from wheat seemed unthinkable. In other words, it was a different time. In fact, I didn't see an actual, mature coconut until I was in my late teens, when my dad brought one home after winning it as a gag gift at work. It was only when I became an adult, and began regularly traveling to the West Indies, that I laid eyes upon a green coconut for the first time.

I don't think my coconut experience—or lack thereof—was uncommon.

My mother got her nutrition information from women's magazines, which told her that saturated fats were the enemy—so out went red meat and butter. Tropical oils were shunned, too; nutrition experts from that time told us coconut oil was the most dangerous fat possible. Thus, entire generations grew up without coconut oil and ate foods made with *more acceptable* hydrogenated vegetable shortening and margarine instead.

The first time I was exposed to thinking about alternative fats was in my twenties, when I was working in New York City as a kitchen assistant at the Natural Gourmet Institute, the renowned whole foods cooking school, where revolutionary natural food chefs such as Peter Brearley, Myra Kornfeld Elliott Prag, and Diane Carlson taught. My job was twofold: to help cooking instructors get ready for class by prepping ingredients, and to ensure that their classes ran smoothly by performing the backstage work (everything from fetching ingredients for the instructor to washing dishes).

One particular day, during an introductory lesson on whole food ingredients, instructor Diane Carlson mentioned that studies were beginning to show that coconut oil and other coconut products had powerful healing properties and were not harmful to the heart, as many people believed at the time. She passed around a few handouts on heart disease rates in Southeast Asian and West Indian countries, where coconut oil, coconut milk, and coconut meat were consumed in large quantities, as opposed to Canada and the United States, where consumption of hydrogenated vegetable shortening and margarine were the norm. The studies showed that Southeast Asian and West Indian heart disease rates were low compared to those of the Western world.

This was new.

Wanting to get every drop of wisdom we could get on coconut oil, we kitchen assistants leapt into action: One of us took frantic notes while the rest of us continued chopping, stirring, and washing dishes.

After the class was over and we'd cleaned the kitchen, we raced to a copy shop to photocopy our notes. We had a quest: find out everything we could about coconut oil.

We searched the cooking school's library shelves and pored over back issues of every healing and natural food magazine we could find. A few of us hit the public library. These were the early days of the Internet, so hopping online, as all of us did, and searching for "Coconut Oil," led us straight to a bunch of alternative health websites that were so zealous, we couldn't be sure where enthusiasm wore off and accuracy began.

What I was looking for was reassurance— proof, even—that I was not going to doom myself to a life of heart disease by regularly consuming coconut. Finally, I felt that I'd read enough; I was convinced that the product was not health threatening, and I was ready to take the plunge. Unfortunately, finding coconut oil proved to be more challenging than unearthing reliable research.

One of my friends brought back an unmarked jar of coconut oil from a trip to Barbados. She had no idea if it was cold-pressed or if the coconut that was used to make the oil was organic, but at last we had some! We split the oil among the three of us and took it home.

The first thing I did with the coconut oil was make a vegetable curry, which I finished off with a cup of coconut milk. I figured if coconut oil was good for me, coconut milk must be, too! I had been using extra-virgin olive oil for everything prior to this; the coconut oil made the dish taste so much more authentic. It was absolutely delicious.

I used the oil every day, until it ran out, to bake, roast veggies, and make salad dressings. I even used it to make popcorn and rubbed it into my hair and skin, like many of my friends from "coconut countries" did. I had found a new love. I adored the well-rounded, nutty, buttery flavor that coconut oil brought to everything I cooked, and was in awe of all the protein, fiber, calcium, iron, magnesium, manganese, potassium, zinc, vitamin C, B-complex vitamins, phytonutrients, fatty acids, amino acids, electrolytes, and antimicrobial elements this nourishing food contains.

In those early days at the Natural Gourmet Institute, my experimentation with coconut showed me that it is indeed a powerful and delicious everyday ingredient. I began by using a range of coconut products, including coconut milk, dried coconut, and fresh green and mature brown coconuts. I tried coconut water for the first time, and started to make my own coconut milk and dry my own shredded coconut. Later, when the gluten-free movement started and coconut flour became available, I jumped at the chance to play with another coconut ingredient. And when I discovered coconut nectar and coconut sugar, I pulled out my muffin tins and began to experiment. But experimentation didn't stop there; when I stumbled upon coconut vinegar and coconut aminos, out came the blender, allowing me to whip up a flurry of marinades, sauces, and dressings.

Today I enjoy coconut, in one form or another, at almost every meal. I use coconut water to make ice cubes and rely on coconut milk to replace dairy in just about every single recipe I make. I have been known to sneak coconut oil into my dog's food to treat his itchy skin, and have even used coconut butter, whipped with coconut nectar, to make an impromptu frosting for cupcakes. Even as I write this introduction, I have one hand on my keyboard and the other in a bowl of popcorn popped in coconut oil.

Along the way, I've learned a few wonderful things firsthand:

- Coconut oil, coconut meat, coconut flour, and coconut milk have reduced my cravings for sweets, probably by improving insulin secretion and utilization of blood glucose. The healthy fat in coconut has been shown to slow elevations in blood sugar and reduce hypoglycemic cravings.

- Coconut nectar and coconut sugar boast a low glycemic index, which leaves my kids happy, without the "sugar hyperactivity" they exhibit directly after eating anything made with cane sugar. Plus, there is no grouchy "post-sugar crash" with coconut sweeteners. For me, this alone makes coconut a miracle ingredient.

- Coconut improves immune system function. Before I added coconut to my oldest son's diet, he was getting sick from a virus almost every month. After adding two or three servings of coconut oil, coconut flour, and coconut milk to his everyday diet, he started catching only one or two colds a year, thanks to the antioxidant content of coconut.

- The antioxidant effects of coconut can help protect your skin from cellular damage from ultraviolet light, while the medium chain fatty acids in coconut help strengthen connective tissue—the results of which can be beautiful-looking skin.

- A naturopath friend mentioned that the medium chain fatty acids in coconut could help increase my metabolism and improve thyroid function while strengthening my sluggish adrenal gland function. A year after incorporating tablespoons of coconut oil into my diet each day, plus coconut water, coconut milk, and coconut flour most days, my adrenal gland function returned to normal.

- The electrolytes in coconut water help hydrate my husband on his runs in a more natural way than chemical-heavy sports drinks.

- Coconut flour and coconut meat contain generous amounts of fiber, which fills the tummy, leaving me so satisfied I'm not interested in after-meal snacking.

Although I have not suffered from a heart condition, high cholesterol, cancer, or a neurological disease, my research has uncovered several studies that suggest that coconut's many nutrients help prevent and heal these conditions. One—the 2003 study performed by a team out of the School of Dietetics and Human Nutrition, McGill University in Quebec—found that overweight women who consumed a diet rich in medium chain fatty acids (the primary ingredient in coconut oil) enjoyed lowered cholesterol levels than those who received the majority of their fat from beef. (I come from a family of beef-eaters, so this study was of great interest to me!) A team at the same research site, after reviewing human and animal studies on coconut oil, and the medium chain fatty acids it contains, concluded that fats, such as coconut oil, that are rich in medium chain fatty acids may result in faster satiety and facilitate weight control when included in the diet as a replacement for fats containing long chain fatty acids—the fatty acids in animal and hydrogenated fats. Coconut is indeed a "superfood," and a popular one at that. Check out any raw food, Paleo, or gluten-free blog; vegan restaurant; vegetarian magazine; or alternative health website, and you'll find anecdotal proof that coconut is the darling of the health set.

I have my own unofficial proof that coconut is one of the health world's most popular power foods: When I began writing *Coconut*, I quizzed my nutritionist and natural health friends on the foods they eat every single day (at least once, if not two or three times a day) to stay healthy. Coconut was the only food that all 226 of them ate daily in some form or another. Furthermore, each September I host the Superfood Superheroes Summit, an online education event, during which I spend a week interviewing superfood authors and other experts. Last year when I asked each health pro to share a recipe, the only superfood ingredient that every single expert's recipe included was coconut. That's pretty telling, right?

No matter how you crack it, coconut tastes amazing, is easy to find, and is wonderful for use in a staggering array of delicious recipes, from smoothies and juices to main dishes and little dishes, to baked goods and desserts—complete with the lovely bonus of health benefits that will keep you and your family as healthy and vibrant as possible. Taste, versatility, and health benefits—how many ingredients do you know that offer as many desirable qualities?

Throughout this book, you'll find plenty of tips on choosing, using, and storing your precious coconut ingredients, as well as tricks to help you make your own coconut staples. (Anyone want to know how to make Coconut Cream Dessert Topping or homemade coconut milk?) I've tried to keep the recipes as healthy as possible, which in my world means whole food ingredients, a minimum of dairy and wheat, and lots of plant food. If applicable, substitutions and alternative options are noted within the recipe, along with details about any unusual steps or storage advice.

It's a great time for coconut, and if you are ready to dive in and experience the wonders of coconut yourself, it's all here.

With love and coconut bliss to all of you,
Stephanie Pedersen, MS, CHHC, AADP
Holistic Nutritionist

CHAPTER 1

GETTING FRIENDLY WITH COCONUT

Hello coconut lovers! I am so excited to share one of my favorite superfoods with you, as well as welcome all of you healthy folks who have heard that coconut is a great way to boost your health and make sure your family gets the nutrition they need to be their best. And friendly greetings to those of you who are not coconut fans, but are here because you love someone who loves coconut, or because your doctor or nutritionist told you that you need to eat more coconut.

Coconut comes in many different forms, including coconut water, fresh coconut meat, dried coconut meat, coconut oil, coconut milk, coconut flour, coconut sweeteners, coconut vinegar, and more. I hope you'll try them all. You may be like me and love every single one of these, or you may prize one ingredient above the rest. While coconut flour has different benefits than coconut water, which in turn, has a different nutrient profile than coconut oil, all coconut foods are worthy additions to your daily diet.

That's what I tell my clients: Try for at least one coconut product every day. Each coconut product has a different host of nutrients. If you can enjoy at least one coconut product every day, you'll end each week in a powerful, healthful place.

COCONUT'S ANCIENT ORIGINS

One of the earliest descriptions of the coconut palm was written in about 545 CE, in *Topographia Christiana*, a work by Cosmas, who made several trips to India and was famous for his maps of the world.

Still, the origins of the coconut remain a mystery: Scientists have used art, fossils, genetics, and travel records to figure out where the coconut first appeared.

Odoardo Beccari, a renowned palm specialist during the late 1800s and early 1900s, suggested that the coconut is of Southeast Pacific origin. Strengthening his argument is the fact that there are more varieties of coconut palms in the Eastern Hemisphere than in the Americas. However, no conclusive evidence exists, so for now, we'll have to be content with coconut's great taste, versatility, and health benefits.

As you've probably already noticed, coconut is absolutely everywhere! Coconut oil, which was, at one time, relegated to skin care, has been a hot food for decades now, as more and more families of autistic children and Alzheimer's patients have touted its ability to help normalize brain and nervous system function. At the same time, cardiologists and others who are concerned with heart health have found coconut to be effective in helping heal cardiovascular disorders, while IBS (irritable bowel syndrome) sufferers and individuals with other digestive disorders have found coconut oil to be helpful in healing their damaged large intestine.

Coconut water, the fastest-growing beverage in the world, first appeared in US supermarkets in 2004. The popularity of this refreshing drink is borne out by these statistics from the data resource company Euromonitor: Sales of the highest-selling brands in the United States—Vita Coco, ZICO, and O.N.E., which control the vast majority of the American coconut water market—have skyrocketed by nearly 600 percent since 2009, and 2,759 percent since 2007.

Coconut milk is now available in convenient cartons right next to dairy milk, and has become a favorite of vegans and others who "don't do" dairy. In the United Kingdom, sales of nondairy alternatives (including coconut milk) have risen by 40 percent in the last three years—with similar numbers in the United States. Coconut flour, too, has grown in popularity, thanks to the rising number of gluten-free consumers and individuals who follow the Paleo diet, which eschews grains and grain-based flours in favor of high-fiber, high-protein, low-carbohydrate whole foods that nourish the body without causing bloat and inflammation.

The high reputation of low glycemic coconut sugar and coconut nectar, as alternatives to other sugars, has arrived hot on the heels of data released by the American Diabetes Association that shows nearly twenty-six million children and adults in the United States have diabetes and seventy-nine million Americans have prediabetes. These individuals must find ways to eat that don't cause dangerous fluctuations in their blood sugar—their lives literally depend upon it.

If you've been motivated to find products like apple cider vinegar—with its alkalizing, anti-inflammatory powers—to help you feel energetic and craving-free, you'll soon discover that coconut vinegar has the same superpowers. And, as more people become aware of the dangers of overusing soy, coconut aminos has become the go-to replacement for soy sauce and Bragg Liquid Aminos.

Last, there are coconut specialty products like coconut cream and coconut butter—even actual fresh young coconuts and mature coconuts—which add nutrient-dense luxury to even the most pious diet.

No matter which coconut product you try, one of the best, foolproof ways to be sure you and your loved ones enjoy a daily serving of coconut is to start with the best-quality coconut products you can find. The first step in doing that is to "buy smart."

Whether you are shopping for coconut milk or coconut vinegar, the fewer ingredients on the label the better. Like many other natural products, coconut milk, coconut flour, coconut water, and myriad other coconut products are often meddled with and altered with the addition of water, sweeteners, unnecessary flavorings, chemical preservatives, emulsifiers, stabilizers, anticaking agents, colorants, and more. None of these additives are necessary. Look for pure products in their most natural state and you will always do well.

CHAPTER 2

COCONUT: THE EVERYDAY POWERHOUSE

I call coconut an "everyday food" because it comes in so many forms and offers such a wide range of nutrients, so it's easy—and smart—for you to enjoy daily. In my household, we eat coconut in one form or another at just about every meal and snack. This gives us a generous helping of the nutrients we need to stay healthy and keeps the adults in the household looking and feeling young, vibrant, and slim, while keeping all of our immune, cardiovascular, and nervous systems strong and efficient.

Fortunately, coconut comes in oils, sweeteners, sauces, flours, and more, making it a cinch to add coconut to our diet. Coconut is also easy to use and lends itself effortlessly to everything from popcorn to salad dressings to smoothies to dinner entrées.

This chapter is dedicated to giving you an idea of the wide range of coconut products that are available, and featured in the recipe section of the book. Here, you'll learn more about the nutritional profile and health benefits of each product, where it comes from, and how it's produced. I'll also suggest tips and tricks for using each ingredient successfully. Enjoy!

GREEN COCONUT

Up until recently, young, green coconuts were a rarity in the non-coconut-growing world. It was the brown, mature fruit that most of us associated with the word "coconut." Thanks to the raw food and Paleo movements, green coconuts are a common sight in juice joints, health food stores, and supermarkets everywhere. Green coconuts are large and heavy and can be eaten raw: Just hack away the green coating, split it open, drain off the water (don't throw it away, though!), and scoop out the young, gelatinous fruit. Young coconut flesh is slightly sweet and refreshing with a subtle richness, and best of all, it offers a wide range of nutrients.

GREEN COCONUT: NUTRITION PROFILE PER SERVING (1 CUP)

CALORIES: 283

FIBER: A serving of fresh coconut provides 7.2 g of fiber, helping promote digestive health and helping you feel full so you eat less. Fiber has been found to lower the risk of certain cancers, such as colorectal cancer and other gastrointestinal cancers.

PROTEIN: At 2.66 g of coconut per serving, green coconut has a respectable amount of protein, the macronutrient responsible for helping your body build and repair itself.

MEDIUM CHAIN FATTY ACIDS: Like other coconut products, young coconut flesh contains medium chain fatty acids. MCFAs, as these are also known, have shown promise in reducing abdominal obesity and diminishing fat storage.

LAURIC ACID: Coconut flesh is also rich in lauric acid, which is known for its bacteria- and virus-killing properties. Lauric acid is also found in breast milk, helping boost newborns' immunity and protecting them against infections.

POTASSIUM: This mineral is crucial to body functions. One cup of green coconut flesh provides 285 mg of the recommended dietary allowance of about 4,700 mg.

RDAS, USDA, AND YOU

In the United States, you often read about RDAs—recommended dietary allowances. Most nutrients are assigned an RDA by the United States Department of Agriculture (USDA). This assigned number represents the ideal average daily intake of the nutrient. You'll find this number referred to as "RDA," "recommended dietary allowance," or "daily requirement." The three terms are used interchangeably throughout this book.

PHOSPHORUS: Phosphorus is a mineral that makes up 1 percent of the body's total weight, and it is present in every cell of the body—particularly in bones and teeth. Adults need about 700 mg a day. A serving of young coconut provides 90 mg.

CALCIUM: In addition to its well-known role as bone-and-teeth-builder, calcium helps the body's muscles move and enables nerves to carry messages between the brain and other parts of the body. According to the USDA, an adult should get around 1,000 mg per day. Young coconut provides 11 mg per serving.

MAGNESIUM: Magnesium is needed for more than three hundred biochemical reactions in the body. It helps maintain normal nerve and muscle function, supports a healthy immune system, keeps the heartbeat steady,

NUTRIENTS: HOW MUCH DO YOU NEED?

Name a nutrient—any nutrient—and chances are good that different people, of different ages and life stages, and of different genders, need different amounts of it. This is why the United States Department of Agriculture has created nutritional guidelines for most nutrients in the form of RDA (recommended dietary allowance) or AI (adequate intake). Here is a list of nutrients found in coconut products, along with the USDA's intake suggestions. Note: The USDA breaks down recommended dietary allowances into very narrow groups, as well as offering suggestions for larger, more general groups, some of which we share with you here.

FIBER
men, over the age of 18: **38 g**
women, over the age of 18: **25 g**
pregnant women: **28 mg**

PROTEIN
men, over the age of 18: **56 g**
women, over the age of 18: **26 g**
pregnant women: **71 g**

VITAMIN A
men, over the age of 18: **900 IUs**
women, over the age of 18: **700 IUs**
pregnant women: **770 IUs**

VITAMIN B6
men, over the age of 18: **1.3 mg**
women, over the age of 18: **1.3 mg**
pregnant women: **1.9 mg**

VITAMIN C
men, over the age of 18: **90 mg**
women, over the age of 18: **75 mg**
pregnant women: **85 mg**

VITAMIN E
men, over the age of 18: **15 mg**
women, over the age of 18: **15 mg**
pregnant women: **15 mg**

VITAMIN K
men, over the age of 18: **120 g**
women, over the age of 18: **90 g**
pregnant women: **90 g**

FOLATE
men, over the age of 18: **400 g**
women, over the age of 18: **400 g**
pregnant women: **600 g**

THIAMINE
men, over the age of 18: **1.2 mg**
women, over the age of 18: **1.1 mg**
pregnant women: **1.4 mg**

RIBOFLAVIN
men, over the age of 18: **1.3 mg**
women, over the age of 18: **1.1 mg**
pregnant women: **1.4 mg**

NIACIN
men, over the age of 18: **16 mg**
women, over the age of 18: **14 mg**
pregnant women: **18 mg**

CALCIUM
men, over the age of 18: **1,000 mg**
women, over the age of 18: **1,000 mg**
pregnant women: **1,000 mg**

IRON
men, over the age of 18: **8 mg**
women, over the age of 18: **18 mg**
pregnant women: **27 mg**

MAGNESIUM
men, over the age of 18: **400 mg**
women, over the age of 18: **310 mg**
pregnant women: **350 mg**

PHOSPHORUS
men, over the age of 18: **700 mg**
women, over the age of 18: **700 mg**
pregnant women: **700 mg**

POTASSIUM
men, over the age of 18: **4.7 g**
women, over the age of 18: **4.7 g**
pregnant women: **4.7 g**

ZINC
men, over the age of 18: **11 mg**
women, over the age of 18: **8 mg**
pregnant women: **11 mg**

SELENIUM
men, over the age of 18: **55 mcg**
women, over the age of 18: **55 mcg**
pregnant women: **60 mcg**

and helps bones remain strong. Adult women should get around 310 mg of magnesium daily (men should get 400 mg); one serving of young coconut flesh will supply 6 percent of the RDA for this important mineral.

IRON: In addition to its role in red blood cell production, iron is necessary for growth, development, normal cellular functioning, and synthesis of some hormones and connective tissue. Young coconut provides 1.94 mg of the USDA recommended dietary allowance of 8 mg per day for men and 18 mg for women.

MANGANESE: Manganese is an essential nutrient involved in many chemical interactions in the body, including processing cholesterol, carbohydrates, and protein. It may also be involved in bone formation. While no recommended dietary allowance of manganese has been established by the USDA, or any other organization, 1 to 2 mg is considered an adequate daily dosage. Young coconut contains 1.2 mg of manganese per serving.

ZINC: Young coconut provides 0.88 mg of zinc per serving; the recommended dietary allowance is 8 mg for women and 11 mg for men. Zinc plays a role in immune function, protein synthesis, wound healing, DNA synthesis, and cell division.

COPPER: Low copper intake has been associated with high cholesterol and cardiovascular disease in some individuals. While the USDA has not yet determined a daily recommended dietary allowance, it considers 2 mg an adequate daily goal for adults. Young coconut provides 0.348 mg per serving.

SELENIUM: This trace element is necessary for several critical body functions, including reproduction, thyroid hormone metabolism, DNA synthesis, and protection from oxidative damage and infection. The USDA suggests that adults consume 55 mcg daily. Young coconut provides 8.1 mcg per 8-ounce serving.

THIAMINE: Also known as vitamin B1, thiamine helps the body's cells change carbohydrates into energy. Small amounts of thiamine are found in most foods, including young coconut, which contains 0.1 mg of the recommended dietary allowance of 1.1 mg for women and 1.2 mg for men.

HEALTH BENEFITS OF GREEN COCONUT

While there are no specific studies on young green coconut, it has a long history of being used to help strengthen the sick and elderly and supply babies in coconut-producing countries with a healthy "first food." Green coconut has also been used to improve the health and appearance of skin and hair.

CHOOSING, USING, AND KEEPING GREEN COCONUT

When you are buying whole young coconuts, avoid cracks, mold, wet spots, and discoloration. When you pick up a coconut, it should feel heavy and actually sound as if it is filled with water. While the mature, brown coconuts can be kept at room temperature, green coconuts should be refrigerated and used within five days.

To open a green coconut, use a heavy chef's knife or (even better) a cleaver. Set the coconut on a flat surface and make four deep, straight cuts, each about two inches from the coconut's pointy top. Pry the top off and pour out the water.

Caution: If you open a coconut and discover that the water is pink or smells sour, discard it. It has gone bad.

For recipes in this book that call for fresh coconut, use young green coconuts from your local supermarket. Unfortunately, there is no surefire way to tell how old they are, so you may end up tossing a few. It happens to me, too!

STEPHANIE'S FAVORITE WAY TO USE GREEN COCONUT: Blended into a tropical fruit smoothie.

GREEN COCONUTS: DID YOU KNOW . . . ?

- The flesh of the young coconut has more fiber than the same amount of apple.
- Peak months for fresh coconuts are October through December.
- It takes twelve to thirteen months for a coconut to mature fully.
- Coconuts grow in groups containing five to twelve fruits.
- A coconut palm produces about 100 to 120 coconuts a year.
- More than twenty billion coconuts are produced each year.
- The only two states in the United States where coconuts can grow are Hawaii and Florida—and only the southern part of Florida, at that.
- A coconut will not ripen after being picked.
- Falling coconuts kill 150 people every year, 10 times the number of people killed by sharks.
- The coconut is the largest seed in the world.
- The scientific name for the coconut palm is *Cocos nucifera*.

COCONUT WATER

Coconuts contain a large quantity of "water," filled with potassium, vitamins, and minerals. This health-supportive fluid has nourished humans for millennia. Coconut water has only recently become big business, however, and it is now popular with fitness buffs, endurance athletes, and advocates of raw food and the Paleo diet. Since coconut water first appeared in supermarkets in 2004, its popularity has not stopped climbing. According to Convenience Store News, sales increased by $400 million in the United States in 2011 alone.

While I don't personally drink huge amounts of coconut water (my husband and two of my sons adore it!), I do use it as an ingredient in coolers and smoothies. I also give it to my kids when they're down with a stomach bug, and I appreciate how it makes me feel "normal" after an intense workout or even the morning after I've celebrated a bit too enthusiastically. (Coconut water really is the best hangover remedy I've come across—not that I've had to use it too often!)

COCONUT WATER: NUTRITION PROFILE PER SERVING (1 CUP)

CALORIES: 46

FIBER: One serving of coconut water provides 3 g of fiber to help keep your digestive tract healthy, lower blood cholesterol, and help prevent colorectal cancer.

WHAT'S THE DIFFERENCE?

- **COCONUT WATER:** Coconut water is the clear liquid inside green coconuts. It's this liquid that you get when you buy coconut water in various kinds of packaging. Brown, mature coconuts often have a bit of watery liquid as well, but it often has a sour taste and isn't used as a beverage.

- **COCONUT MILK:** This is the liquid that comes from the grated meat of a brown coconut.

- **COCONUT FLESH:** "Flesh" is most often used to describe the almost gelatinous innards of green coconuts.

- **COCONUT MEAT:** "Meat" is what most culinary types call the creamy white innards of a brown coconut. Firm and rich, this is what many people think of when they think of coconuts. You may occasionally hear someone refer to this part of a brown coconut as "flesh," but "meat" is more commonly used.

PROTEIN: Protein is considered a macronutrient, which means that your body needs it in large amounts every day to perform everything from nutrient transport to cell repair. Coconut water provides 1.78 g of protein.

AMINO ACIDS: Coconut water contains small amounts of eighteen amino acids, which are the building blocks of protein. When digested, amino acids help the body create solid matter, including skin, eyes, heart, intestines, bones, and muscle.

ENZYMES: Coconut water contains enzymes, proteins that allow certain chemical reactions to take place much more quickly than they would on their own.

VITAMIN C: This is a water-soluble nutrient that acts as an antioxidant, helping protect cells from the damage caused by free radicals, the compounds formed when our bodies convert the food we eat into energy. A serving of coconut water provides 5.8 mg of a vitamin C.

CALCIUM: This mineral is necessary to maintain strong bones and healthy communication between the brain and various parts of the body. From a serving of coconut water, you'll get 58 mg of the mineral.

COPPER: Dietary copper is helpful in the production of red blood cells and assists with your sense of taste. While the USDA has not yet determined a daily recommended dietary allowance, it considers 2 mg an adequate daily goal for adults. A serving of coconut water provides about 96 mcg of copper.

IRON: While not overly abundant in iron, a serving of coconut water will give your body about 0.94 mg of the daily requirement for this mineral. Iron is necessary for cell growth, normal cellular functioning, and synthesis of some hormones and connective tissue.

MANGANESE: You'll get 0.3 mg of manganese, a mineral that helps you metabolize both fat and protein, from coconut water. Manganese also supports both the immune and nervous systems and promotes stable blood sugar levels.

MAGNESIUM: One serving of coconut water delivers about 60 mg of your daily requirement of magnesium, a mineral responsible for many biochemical functions in the body, including regulating the heart's rhythm and supporting the function of nerve cells. Magnesium is a major electrolyte that helps maintain proper fluid levels in the body and regulate muscle function.

SELENIUM: You'll get 60 mg of in each serving of coconut water. This nutrient plays critical roles in reproduction, thyroid hormone metabolism, DNA synthesis, and protection from oxidative damage and infection.

SODIUM: A mineral that is also an electrolyte, sodium helps maintain proper fluid levels in the body and regulate muscle function. There are 252 mg of sodium in a cup of coconut water.

PHOSPHORUS: Responsible for creating some of the energy that you use every day, phosphorus also assists your body in synthesizing proteins, fats, and carbohydrates, and regulates the fluid levels in your body. You'll get 48 mg with each serving of coconut water.

POTASSIUM: You'll get a whopping 600 mg of potassium in a serving of coconut water. This essential mineral, a major electrolyte, helps maintain proper fluid levels in the body and regulate muscle function. It also plays an important role in nerve function and blood pressure.

ZINC: Found in cells throughout the body, zinc helps the immune system fight off invading bacteria and viruses. The body also needs zinc to make proteins and DNA, the genetic material in all cells. A serving of coconut water provides 0.2 mg of the mineral.

HEALTH BENEFITS OF COCONUT WATER

DIABETES PREVENTION: In the December 8, 2011, issue of the *Journal of Ethnopharmacology*, a study conducted by the Department of Pharmaceutical Technology at Jadavpur University in Kolkata, India, showed that diabetic animals that had been fed an extract of coconut water showed a significant reduction in fasting blood glucose levels compared with a diabetic control group. Other studies have shown similar results, leading to the hypothesis that coconut water might be an antidiabetic.

ALZHEIMER'S DISEASE: A study conducted in late 2010 by a research team from Prince of Songkla University in Hat Yai, Thailand, found that daily consumption of coconut water can help prevent the onset of Alzheimer's disease in menopausal women. Using menopausal rats, researchers studied brain abnormalities associated with Alzheimer's. After giving the rats coconut water, these abnormalities lessened considerably. Preliminary studies on young coconut juice (YCJ) have reported the presence of estrogen-like components.

HYPERTENSION: A 2005 study by a team from the University of the West Indies in St. Augustine, Trinidad, selected twenty-eight individuals with hypertension and divided them into three groups. Each group was assigned a specific drink; included were bottled drinking water, coconut water, and mauby fruit juice. The drinks were consumed daily for two weeks. At the end of the study, the group that received coconut water experienced a 71 percent decrease in systolic blood pressure and a 29 percent decrease in diastolic blood pressure.

HYDRATION: Several studies have pitted coconut water against commercially available sports drinks. For some people, coconut water seems to be a healthier alternative to these chemical-laden drinks. If you're one of them, you'll be interested in a study that was published in the *Journal of the International Society of Sports Nutrition*, January 18, 2012. Following a sixty-minute bout of dehydrating treadmill exercise, twelve exercise-trained men received bottled water, pure coconut water, coconut water from concentrate, or a carbohydrate-electrolyte sports drink on four occasions, separated by at least five days, in a random order. Hydration status (body mass, fluid retention, plasma osmolality, urine specific gravity) and performance (treadmill time to exhaustion; assessed after rehydration) were determined during the recovery period.

No differences were noted between coconut water, coconut water from concentrate, or the sports drink on any occasion. It was determined that all three beverages were capable of promoting rehydration and supporting subsequent exercise. That said, coconut water contains significantly less sodium than a leading commercial Gatorade-type sports drink. If sodium is a health concern for you, you'll find a way to create a special coconut water–based sports drink on page 235.

CHOOSING, USING, AND KEEPING COCONUT WATER

When purchasing packaged coconut water, look at the list of ingredients. If it contains sweeteners, flavorings, and/or other additives, pass it by. You want pure, unadulterated coconut water. Always refrigerate any container of coconut water that you've opened and use it within one or two days—or freeze it for longer storage.

Caution: You'll definitely know when coconut water is spoiled—it has a sour taste and smell.

STEPHANIE'S FAVORITE WAY TO USE COCONUT WATER: To make ice cubes.

COCONUT WATER: DID YOU KNOW . . . ?

- Ten years ago, the first-ever patent granted to a UN agency was awarded to the Food and Agriculture Organization (FAO) to bottle coconut water in a way that preserves its nutrients.
- Coconut water contains the same five electrolytes found in human blood. (Gatorade has only two of these electrolytes.)
- The three top-selling coconut water brands in the United States are ZICO (owned by Coca-Cola), O.N.E. (owned by Pepsi), and Vita Coco (which counts pop singer Madonna as a primary investor).
- Each coconut may contain about 200 to 1,000 mL of water depending on cultivar type and size.
- The water from coconuts that are five months old or younger tastes bitter and is low in nutrients.
- Coconut water needs to be kept out of sunlight. UV light causes coconut water to oxidize and lose nutrients.
- Coconut water is used as a supplement to breast milk in many coconut-growing countries.
- Coconut water in recipes: In the recipes in this book, I use coconut water from fresh green coconuts, or from one of several brands of no-additive, unflavored coconut water.

MATURE COCONUT

Round, brown, and rough, with three eyes on top: That's how most of us picture coconuts. The meat of a mature coconut is white, firm, and rich—different in texture from the flesh of green coconuts, with a different nutritional profile. When removed from the shell, coconut meat can be grated or chopped and used as an ingredient—raw, cooked, baked, or frozen—in too many recipes to count, for every conceivable meal, including snacks, desserts, smoothies, juices, and treats of all kinds. Undeniably, coconut is one of nature's most versatile (and delicious) ingredients. It is an ancient staple that has nourished civilizations for thousands of years.

MATURE COCONUT: NUTRITION PROFILE PER SERVING (1 CUP)

CALORIES: 283

FIBER: A 1-cup serving of coconut meat provides 7 g of fiber, a nutrient that helps with digestion by adding bulk to the stool, which in turn, helps move food through the digestive tract while "cleaning" the interior wall of the large intestine. Fiber has been shown to help with weight loss by creating a feeling of fullness, which discourages overeating.

PROTEIN: Proteins are the body's building blocks. All of our organs, including the skin, muscles, hair, and nails are built from proteins. The immune system, digestive system, and blood all rely on proteins to work correctly. You'll get 3 g of protein from a serving of coconut meat.

MEDIUM CHAIN FATTY ACIDS: Coconut is rich in medium chain fatty acids, which are broken down much faster than long chain fatty acids, so they provide energy, but do not contribute to high cholesterol, the way long chain fatty acids do. According to several studies, MCFAs can help lower bad cholesterol levels and increase good cholesterol levels.

LAURIC ACID: A monoglyceride compound, lauric acid boasts antiviral, antimicrobial, antiprotozoal, and antifungal properties. Researchers in the Philippines have even begun studies to prove the effectiveness of lauric acid against HIV/AIDS because of its strong antiviral properties. A 1-cup serving of coconut will give you 32 g of lauric acid. While there is no recommended dietary allowance for this powerful nutrient, some researchers suggest a minimum of 10 to 20 g per day.

VITAMIN C: Vitamin C is a powerful antioxidant that can help prevent and lessen the duration of viral illnesses, stimulate collagen production for fast wound healing, and help prevent a variety of diseases, from cancer to cataracts. A cup of coconut meat will provide a modest 2.8 g of the vitamin.

VITAMIN E: Another antioxidant, vitamin E helps keep the brain healthy and protects cells from the damage caused by free radicals. A serving of coconut meat provides 0.2 mg of the nutrient.

FOLATE: Also known as vitamin B9 or folic acid, folate helps the body make new cells. A serving of coconut meat provides 20.8 mcg.

NIACIN: Also known as vitamin B3, niacin is used in the body to release energy from carbohydrates and repair DNA. A serving of coconut meat provides 0.4 mg.

PANTOTHENIC ACID: Known as vitamin B5, pantothenic acid is essential to a wide range of chemical reactions in the body that sustain life. A serving of coconut meat will give you 2 percent of the USDA's recommended dietary allowance.

RIBOFLAVIN: Also known as vitamin B2, and formerly known as vitamin G, riboflavin is essential for metabolic energy production. You'll get 0.1 mg.

THIAMINE: Also known as vitamin B1, thiamine helps enhance brain function and keep the digestive tract healthy. You'll get 0.1 mg of the recommended dietary allowance from a cup of coconut meat.

SELENIUM: This mineral is essential in cell metabolism and is a powerful antioxidant that helps keep the immune system strong. A serving of coconut meat provides 8.1 mcg of the nutrient.

CALCIUM: This mineral is necessary to maintain strong bones and healthy communication between the brain and various parts of the body. You'll get 11.2 mg of calcium from a serving of coconut meat.

IRON: While not overly rich in iron, a serving of coconut will give your body 1.9 mg for this mineral. Iron is necessary for growth, development, normal cellular functioning, and synthesis of some hormones and connective tissue.

MAGNESIUM: Magnesium is required for the proper growth and maintenance of bones. It is also needed for the correct functioning of nerves, muscles, and many other parts of the body. A serving of coconut meat provides 25.6 mg.

MANGANESE: You'll get 1.2 mg of manganese, a mineral that helps you metabolize both fat and protein. Manganese also supports both the immune and nervous systems and promotes stable blood sugar levels.

PHOSPHORUS: After calcium, phosphorus is the second most abundant mineral in the body. It helps create strong bones and teeth. A serving of coconut meat will provide 90.4 mg of the mineral.

POTASSIUM: Potassium is essential for fluid balance within your cells. It is also necessary for proper heart function and muscle growth. A serving of coconut meat will provide 285 mg of potassium.

ZINC: Found in cells throughout the body, zinc helps the immune system fight off invading bacteria and viruses. The body also needs zinc to make proteins and DNA, the genetic material in all cells. A serving of coconut meat provides 0.9 mg of zinc.

COPPER: Some of the few functions of dietary copper are to help in the production of red blood cells and to assist with your sense of taste. A serving of coconut meat will provide 0.3 mg of the mineral.

HEALTH BENEFITS OF MATURE COCONUT

BETTER CARDIOVASCULAR HEALTH: Before 1991, coconut was the primary dietary staple in Sri Lanka. The average Sri Lankan ate 132 coconuts per year. Heart attacks and heart disease were rare. In fact, they were so rare that in 1978 the United Nations reported that Sri Lanka had the lowest death rate from ischemic heart disease than any other country in the world. And yet, after an aggressive health campaign in the early 1990s that discouraged coconut-eating (due to a misguided theory that fat in coconut leads to heart disease), coconut consumption dropped to about 90 per person. With the drop in coconut consumption, hospital admission rates for heart attacks increased by about 120 percent for women and 137 percent for men.

A study published in the January 2012 issue of *Asia Pacific Journal of Clinical Nutrition* showed that Filipino women who consumed coconut had healthier blood lipid profiles, a major determinant of heart disease, than those who didn't.

LOWER CHOLESTEROL LEVELS: In a study performed by the Food and Nutrition Research Institute, in Bicutan, Taguig, in the Philippines, twenty-one test subjects with moderately elevated blood cholesterol who ate dried coconut flakes daily for fourteen weeks lowered their serum triglycerides and LDL cholesterol levels by up to 6.3 percent.

REDUCTION OF PARASITES AND OTHER PATHOGENS: The medium chain fatty acids and lauric acid in coconut have long been credited, in coconut-eating cultures, for their impact on reducing parasites and bacterial, fungal, and viral infections. In 2010, researchers from Heinrich Heine University in Düsseldorf, Germany, found that coconut also works to keep sheep parasite-free. Sheep with gastrointestinal nematodes and cestodes were given feed containing 60 g of coconut. After eight days, the worm stages disappeared from the feces; the sheep were still clear of the parasites at both nine and twenty days after the end of the study.

REDUCTION OF STROKE AND HEART DISEASE RISK: In a study published in the March 1993 issue of the *Journal of Internal Medicine,* a team of researchers from the Primary Health Care Centre in Sjöbo, Sweden, set out to study incidence of stroke in the coconut-eating population on the island of Kitava in Papua New Guinea. The population, which practices a subsistence lifestyle that is uninfluenced by Western dietary habits, relies on found tubers, fruit, fish, and coconut as dietary staples, with coconut making up the largest portion of the inhabitants' diets. Of the total population, 1,816 subjects were estimated to be older than three years of age, and 125 were estimated to be sixty to ninety-six years old. The frequencies of spontaneous sudden death, exertion-related chest pain, hemiparesis, aphasia, and sudden imbalance were assessed through semistructured interviews of 213 adults aged twenty to ninety-six. Resting electrocardiograms (ECGs) were recorded in 119 males and 52 females. No case corresponding to stroke, sudden death, or angina pectoris was described by the interviewed subjects. Stroke and heart disease were absent in this population, even in the older adults. In Western cultures, stroke and heart disease occur in an average of more than 11.3 percent of the overall, adult population.

CHOOSING, USING, AND KEEPING MATURE COCONUT

Frozen mature coconut that has been shredded is available in some Southeast Asian and Indo-Pak groceries and has recently appeared in mainstream supermarkets (look for the Birds Eye brand) When a recipe calls for raw mature coconut meat, I prefer to do the old-fashioned thing and crack open a coconut myself.

Here's the kind of long, but very easy, way to open a mature coconut:

1. Peel away as much of the hairy fiber as you can.

2. While it is not necessary to drain the coconut before cracking, it does make things easier. To drain, insert a clean drill bit, long nail, or thin screwdriver into the softest of the three eyes on the top of the coconut. Pour any liquid into a bowl, and use immediately for cooking or making smoothies. (Discard after 24 hours; it sours quickly.)

3. To make opening easier, either freeze the coconut for a half hour before cracking or heat in a 200°F oven for 15 minutes. This is an optional step, but it will make the coconut easier to open.

4. Find the coconut's eyes. If the coconut were a globe, the eyes would be the North Pole. Look for the equator of the coconut. That's where you're going to want to tap.

5. Place the coconut in a plastic bag, if you wish, and use a hammer to tap around the equator.

6. Once the coconut cracks, pry it open and see if you can separate the white coconut meat from the shell. In many cases, you will be able to lift the meat out in large pieces.

7. With a vegetable peeler, remove any brown husk that might be stuck to the coconut meat.

MATURE COCONUTS: DID YOU KNOW . . . ?

- The husks of mature coconuts are used in gas masks. During World War I, the United States developed a type of steam-activated coconut carbon—obtained by burning coconut husks—to use in gas masks. Masks using coconut carbon were superior at filtering noxious substances. This technology is still used today.

- Coconut-fired carbon (made from mature coconut husks) is used to clean up radiation. In fact, coconut-fired carbon was recently used to help remove radiation from the damaged Fukushima nuclear plant.

- Monkeys harvest coconuts. Not only are palm trees dangerous for humans to climb but also, it is difficult to pick a ten-pound coconut from the top of a coconut tree while holding on for dear life. That's why many coconut farmers use trained monkeys to harvest their coconuts.

- The Philippines is the world's top producer of coconuts.

- The coconut palm is also known as "the tree of life" because there are more than one hundred products that can be made from coconut palms and their fruit.

- In Southeast Asia, it is said that "he who plants a coconut tree plants food and drink, vessels and clothing, a habitation for himself, and a heritage for his children."

- The coconut may reach more than one hundred feet and has a lifetime of about seventy-five to one hundred years.

- It takes four or five years for a coconut palm to begin producing coconuts.

8. Refrigerate and use the coconut meat within a day or two, or freeze for longer storage.

Caution: Avoid coconuts that are cracked, moldy, or weepy at the eyes. If you open a mature coconut and the meat, or any liquid, has a yellowy tint, it's spoiled—toss it and try again with a new coconut.

(Note that a mature coconut may not contain any liquid, but if it does, it should be clear and slightly milky.) If you're not going to use it immediately, refrigerate or even freeze the unopened coconut for up to five days.

STEPHANIE'S FAVORITE WAY TO USE MATURE COCONUT: Eaten as-is, straight from a freshly opened coconut.

COCONUT OIL

Coconut oil comes from the meat of mature coconuts and has been used by humans since coconuts first appeared. In coconut-producing countries, coconut oil is used as a cooking oil, food, medicine, and cosmetic; it is even used in industry. Today, most of the coconut oil we consume comes from fruit grown in coconut groves, or plantations, in Southeast Asia.

COCONUT OIL: NUTRITION PROFILE PER SERVING (1 TABLESPOON)

CALORIES: 117

MEDIUM CHAIN FATTY ACIDS: About two-thirds of coconut oil is made up of medium chain fatty acids, known in the health world as MCFAs. In fact, coconut oil is nature's richest source of medium chain fatty acids,

WHAT ABOUT COCONUT OIL'S UNSTUDIED BENEFITS?

There is anecdotal evidence and centuries of traditional healing wisdom that say coconut oil heals digestive disorders and soothes inflamed tissue of the large colon, helps strengthen the immune system, improves liver function, helps normalize nervous system function in children with autism and individuals with brain injuries, stabilizes blood sugar levels, helps improve bone health and lower the risk of cavities, and strengthens hair and nails. However, no research-based studies have been performed to prove any of these claims. That said, I personally believe that coconut oil can do all of these things. If you suffer from one of these conditions, why not ask your health-care provider what he or she knows about using coconut to help?

which help the body better absorb and use other nutrients, boast powerful immune-system benefits, increase metabolism for faster healing and weight loss, and assist in healing a range of health conditions from IBS to candida to cardiovascular conditions to dementia.

LAURIC ACID: Making up almost 50 percent of the fatty acids in coconut oil, lauric acid is known for its ability to kill a wide range of potent pathogens, including bacteria (such as staph), fungi (such as the yeast *Candida albicans*), and viruses. It also may help repair neuron and nerve function in the brain for those with Alzheimer's or brain injury or for individuals on the autistic spectrum.

CAPRYLIC ACID: Another fatty acid present in smaller amounts, caprylic acid is also antimicrobial. Together with lauric acid in coconut oil, caprylic acid helps increase levels of HDL cholesterol (the good cholesterol). It also helps kill bacteria, fungi (including yeast), and viruses in the body.

PALMITIC ACID: This fatty acid has antioxidant properties and has been shown, in animal studies, to help prevent atherosclerosis—better known as hardening, or narrowing, of the arteries.

PHENOLIC COMPOUNDS: The phenolic compounds found in coconut oil have antioxidant properties, and help promote healthy aging by minimizing DNA damage caused by free radicals.

HEALTH BENEFITS OF COCONUT OIL

IMPROVEMENT OF BLOOD CHOLESTEROL LEVELS: Research done with both humans and rats shows that coconut oil may reduce the risk of heart disease by having favorable effects on total cholesterol, LDL cholesterol, and HDL cholesterol. Researchers at Universidade Federal de Alagoas in Brazil found that in forty women, coconut oil reduced total and LDL cholesterol to a greater degree than soybean oil, while increasing HDL to a greater degree than soybean oil. Rat studies performed at the University of Kerala, in India, have shown that coconut oil reduces triglycerides and total and LDL cholesterol, increases HDL, and improves blood coagulation factors and antioxidant status. Research at the two universities in the Netherlands, Maastricht University and Wageningen University, came upon the same conclusions.

MEMORY IMPROVEMENT: In a study published in the March 2014 issue of *Neurobiology of Aging*, consumption of medium chain triglycerides (MCTs) led to an immediate improvement in brain function in patients with milder forms of Alzheimer's. Two more studies—one published in the August 2009 issue of *Nutrition & Metabolism*, and the other published in *Journal of the American Society*

MONO, MEDIUM, SATURATED—WHAT?

There are two kinds of fats found in nature: unsaturated and saturated. Unsaturated fat is typically liquid at room temperature. It's found most often in plant foods, from avocado to nuts and seeds.

Saturated fat is solid at room temperature. It is found mostly in animal foods, such as milk, cheese, and meat, and unfortunately, it can raise blood levels. A healthy diet has less than 10 percent of daily calories from saturated fat. Here, however, is where things get confusing: Coconut oil just happens to be a saturated fat, and yet it doesn't have the cholesterol-raising power of saturated fats from animal products. In fact, coconut oil—even though it is a saturated fat—can help lower harmful cholesterol.

How? The secret is in the length of the chain. Fats of all kinds are made up of fatty acids. These fatty acids are chains of carbon and hydrogen atoms. Fats with short chains are called short chain fatty acids, or SCFAs. These are found in large quantities in dairy products.

Fats with long chain fatty acids are known as LCFAs and are found most often in the skin and organs and muscle tissues of animals. Probably 98 to 100 percent of all the fats we eat consist of LCT.

Fats with medium chain fatty acids are called MCFAs. Coconut oil is one of the only foods around that is composed mostly of medium chain fatty acids, though they also exist in palm kernel oil. MCFAs are more easily digested and used by the body than long chain fatty acids; also they help the body metabolize other nutrients more efficiently, as well as use them for energy more readily.

Just to confuse you a bit further: Sometimes you'll see these chains referred to as SCT, LCT, or MCT. The "T" stands for "triglyceride," a molecule made up mostly of fatty acids.

for Experimental NeuroTherapeutics July 2008 issue—found that the fatty acids in coconut oil can increase energy to the brain cells of Alzheimer's patients and relieve symptoms.

IMPROVED METABOLISM AND BURNING OF CALORIES: The medium chain triglycerides in coconut oil have been shown to increase twenty-four-hour energy expenditure by as much as 5 percent, potentially leading to significant weight loss over the long term. A 1996 study performed by the University of Geneva in Switzerland found that consuming about 15 to 30 g of MCTs per day increased twenty-four-hour energy expenditure by 5 percent, totaling about 120 calories per day. Research performed at the University of Naples Federico II in Italy, in 1991, concluded that calorie burning was increased in research subjects of any size after consuming medium chain fatty acids.

KILLING OF PATHOGENS: In clinical research and studies performed by a wide range of universities, the lauric acid and other fatty acids in coconut oil have been found helpful in preventing infections on the skin and in the body. How? By killing harmful pathogens on and in the body, including those caused by bacteria, fungi (such as yeasts), and viruses. Among these are staph and candida.

FIGHTS VIRAL CONDITIONS: According to a study led by Dr. Gilda Sapphire Erguiza, a pediatric pulmonologist at the Philippine Children's Medical Center in Quezon City, children with pneumonia who were treated with antibiotics and coconut oil benefited more than those taking the antibiotics alone.

REDUCTION OF APPETITE TO HELP WEIGHT LOSS: Several studies have found that medium chain fatty acids (MCFAs)—like the ones in coconut oil—have been found to reduce appetite, which may help with weight loss and weight maintenance. A 1996 study by researchers at the Rowett Institute of Nutrition and Health in Aberdeen, Scotland, found that men who ate the most MCFAs consumed 256 fewer calories per day, on average, than their counterparts eating a typical Western diet. A 1998 study at Institut Européen des Sciences in Dijon, France, discovered that men who ate the most MCFAs at breakfast ate significantly fewer calories at lunch.

REDUCTION OF BELLY FAT: Coconut oil appears to be especially effective in reducing fat in the abdominal cavity and around organs. This is the most dangerous fat of all and is highly associated with many modern-day diseases. Research conducted by the Universidade Federal de Alagoas in Brazil in 2009 on forty women with abdominal obesity found that supplementing their diet with 30 mL (1 ounce) of coconut oil per day led to a significant reduction in both body mass index (BMI) and waist circumference in twelve weeks. A 2011 study performed by Universiti Sains Malaysia on twenty obese males discovered a reduction in waist circumference of 2.86 cm (1.1 inches) after four weeks of ingesting 30 mL (1 ounce) of coconut oil per day.

HEALING AND PROTECTION OF SKIN: Researchers at Makati Medical Center in Makati City, Philippines, found that coconut oil was superior to mineral oil–based moisturizers in healing rough, dry, itchy skin. Researchers at the University of Belgrade in Serbia recently found that in test subjects, coconut oil applied topically blocked 20 percent of the sun's ultraviolet rays.

CHOOSING, USING, AND KEEPING COCONUT OIL

USE COLD-PRESSED VIRGIN COCONUT OIL:
While there are many ways of extracting this oil—from using chemicals to heat—the most traditional method is cold-pressing. This involves literally pressing the oil from the coconut using physical force (sometimes the coconut meat is soaked in water before being pressed, called "wet-milled"). Cold-pressing preserves all of coconut oil's nutrient profile. The term "virgin" (or the infrequently used "extra-virgin"—the two names mean the same thing in the coconut oil industry) refers to how many times the coconut meat has been pressed. This terminology was originally created for olive oil, but is commonly used in the coconut oil world as well. Virgin coconut oil comes from the first pressing. This is what you want.

WHAT ABOUT ORGANIC? Pesticides are sometimes used on nonorganic coconut palms. Not all coconut growers can afford to apply for organic certification. And not all coconut growers are interested in applying for organic certification. A 2008 study published in *Extensions du domaine de l'analyse* (vol. 17, no. 2) by researchers from the Netherlands looked at pesticide residue percentages from 2003 to 2007 in coconut oil from the Philippines. They found no pesticide residue. I personally am more concerned if the oil is cold-pressed and virgin than I am with the organic label. However, organic, cold-pressed, virgin coconut oil does exist!

PREPARING FOOD WITH COCONUT OIL:
Coconut oil is a fine choice for baking, popping corn, or sautéing. It's equally good enjoyed in a room temperature salad dressing or a frozen dessert.

STORING COCONUT OIL IS EASY: Place it in the fridge if you want it to be solid. Place it in a cupboard if you like it to be more liquid. To extend its shelf life, I personally would not keep it near an oven or stove, but I know people who do and haven't experienced any rancid oil. Because of its high antioxidant content, coconut oil takes years to go rancid. Use your coconut oil up within two or three years and you should be fine.

Caution: I cannot tell a lie: Coconut oil is a high-calorie food. As noted in the nutrition profile provided earlier, 1 tablespoon has 117 calories. I give my very skinny sons several tablespoons a day. I limit myself to 1 tablespoon on most days. Some days I go a bit crazy and have 1 ½ tablespoons.

COCONUT OIL IN RECIPES: I used a variety of brands of coconut oil in the recipes in this book. When I call for "liquid coconut oil," I do not mean coconut oil that has been treated with chemicals or chemically altered to keep it liquid. I mean plain old cold-pressed virgin coconut oil that has sat in a place long enough for it to become liquid. When I call for semisolid oil, I mean the same oil, placed in the fridge for a while to harden it up a bit. Easy, safe, healthy.

STEPHANIE'S FAVORITE WAYS TO USE COCONUT OIL: To make popcorn, or to make a fast face scrub by mixing coconut oil with an equal amount of sugar.

COCONUT BUTTER

Coconut butter is a lovely, luxurious way to enjoy the meat of the mature coconut. It is simply dried coconut that has been pulverized into a creamy spread—sometimes with a bit of coconut oil, but usually not. Try making your own by tossing a handful of dried unsweetened coconut into your food processor and pulsing until it becomes a paste. This wonderful food can be whipped with sweetener and used as frosting, thinned with coconut milk and coconut nectar for a dessert sauce, spread on bread and waffles, and stirred into sauces or anything else you want to do with it.

COCONUT BUTTER: NUTRITION PROFILE PER SERVING (1 TABLESPOON)

CALORIES: 100

FIBER: A serving of coconut butter offers 2 g of fiber to help promote weight loss by creating a feeling of fullness, while encouraging efficient digestion as well. Fiber has also been found to lower the risk of certain cancers, such as colorectal cancer and other gastrointestinal cancers.

PROTEIN: With 2 g of protein per tablespoon, coconut butter is an easy way to increase the protein in your diet. Protein is the macronutrient responsible for helping your body build and repair itself.

AMINO ACIDS: Amino acids make up protein in food. When digested, they help the body create solid matter, including skin, eyes, heart, intestines, bones, and muscle. Depending upon which nutrition scientist you ask, there are between twenty and twenty-two amino acids. Of those, eight to ten are considered essential, meaning you must get these from your diet, as your body can't synthesize them from other materials.

MEDIUM CHAIN FATTY ACIDS: Like other coconut products, coconut butter boasts large amounts of medium chain fatty acids. MCFAs have shown promise in regulating blood sugar, helping brain function, reducing abdominal obesity, and diminishing fat storage.

LAURIC ACID: Coconut butter contains lauric acid, which is known for its bacteria- and virus-killing properties. It is the same acid that is found in breast milk and helps boost newborns' immunity, protecting them against infections.

IRON: While not overly rich in iron, a serving of coconut butter will give your body about 0.4 mg for this mineral. Iron is necessary for growth, development, normal cellular functioning, and synthesis of some hormones and connective tissue.

MANGANESE: One serving of coconut butter offers 0.4 mg of manganese, a mineral that the body needs to process cholesterol, carbohydrates, and protein.

HEALTH BENEFITS OF COCONUT BUTTER

Because coconut butter is made from dried coconut meat, any of the studies on dried coconut apply to coconut butter. One of these, undertaken in 2004 by a team from the Food and Nutrition Research Institute in Bicutan, Taguig, in the Philippines, found that after fourteen weeks of eating dried flaked coconut daily, twenty-one adult men and women with moderately high blood cholesterol levels reduced their LDL cholesterol and serum triglycerides by an average of 20 percent.

CHOOSING, USING, AND KEEPING COCONUT BUTTER

Look for coconut butter that contains whole coconut only, or whole coconut and coconut oil. Avoid any brands that contain sweeteners or additives. Once you bring it home, it will stay soft and spreadable if kept at room temperature, where it should be fine for up to a year. For longer storage, stash in your fridge and soften it up by allowing it to come to room temperature before using.

Caution: As coconut products get more popular and more companies rush to get in on the action, new ways are created to sell coconut. You can even find coconut butter flavored with chocolate. Yes, it sounds yummy, doesn't it? But this isn't a healthful product. If you want to get it and call it dessert, be my guest, but don't be deceived: Sweetened coconut butter ("even" with chocolate) is not a health food.

COCONUT BUTTER IN RECIPES: All of the recipes in this book that include coconut butter were tested using thick, homemade coconut butter and Nutiva brand Coconut Manna coconut butter.

STEPHANIE'S FAVORITE WAY TO USE COCONUT BUTTER: As a spread for toast and waffles.

COCONUT MILK

Coconut milk is a delicious, milky beverage that is created when mature coconut meat (either dried or not) is ground together with water and then allowed to sit for a bit to develop its flavor. Afterward, the solids are strained away. Coconut milk is an essential ingredient in Pacific Island and Southeast Asian cooking. In the Western world, coconut milk was relegated to a dessert ingredient until the last five or six years. Now it is commonly used as a dairy-free milk for people who need to remove dairy products from their diet, and for children who are on the autistic spectrum and who are thought to react to the casein in dairy milk.

Canned coconut milk is still the most popular option around. But there are other excellent options, including frozen coconut milk, coconut milk beverage boxes and cartons (these are typically thinned with water and treated with various emulsifiers, flavorings, and stabilizers), and dried coconut milk that can be mixed with water. According to research presented at the United Nations Conference on Trade and Development, coconut milk accounts for 30 percent of coconut products sold worldwide.

COCONUT MILK: NUTRITION PROFILE PER SERVING (¼ CUP)

CALORIES: 100

MEDIUM CHAIN FATTY ACIDS: Unlike long chain fatty acids, MCFAs are easily and quickly metabolized into energy in the liver. It is believed that because MCFAs are used more quickly by the body than other types of fatty acids, they are less likely to be stored as fat.

LAURIC ACID: Antiviral and antibacterial, lauric acid destroys a wide variety of disease-causing organisms. It may also reduce cholesterol and triglyceride levels, which lowers heart disease and risk of stroke.

FIBER: One serving of coconut milk provides 1.6 g of fiber to help keep your digestive tract healthy.

PROTEIN: Protein is considered a macronutrient, which means that your body needs it in large amounts every day to perform everything from nutrient transport to cell repair. Coconut milk provides just under 2 g per serving.

IRON: The mineral iron is a part of all cells and does many things in our bodies such as delivering oxygen to our blood. One serving of coconut milk provides 1.875 mg of iron.

VITAMIN C: Vitamin C is a water-soluble nutrient that acts as an antioxidant in the body, helping to protect cells from the damage caused by free radicals, the compounds formed when our bodies convert the food we eat into energy. A quarter-cup serving of coconut milk provides 2 percent of the daily requirement.

VITAMIN E: Vitamin E is a fat-soluble nutrient that also acts as an antioxidant, helping protect cells from the damage caused by free radicals.

NIACIN: A serving of coconut milk provides .456 mg of vitamin B3, also known as niacin. Niacin helps reduce atherosclerosis, or hardening of the arteries. For people who have already had a heart attack, niacin seems to lower the risk of a second one. It also helps lower the risk of Alzheimer's disease, cataracts, osteoarthritis, and type 1 diabetes.

FOLATE: Folate is a B vitamin that is naturally present in many foods. (In case you ever wondered, folate and folic acid are forms of the same B vitamin. Folate occurs naturally in food, and folic acid is the synthetic form of this vitamin.) The body needs folate to make DNA and other genetic material. Folate is also needed for the body's cells to divide. A serving of coconut milk provides 8 percent of the daily requirement.

SELENIUM: You'll get 3.72 mcg of selenium in each serving of coconut milk. This nutrient plays critical roles in reproduction, thyroid hormone metabolism, DNA synthesis, and protection from oxidative damage and infection.

POTASSIUM: You'll get 158 mg of potassium in one serving of coconut milk. This essential mineral is a major electrolyte found in the human body. In addition, it plays an important role in electrolyte regulation, nerve function, muscle control, and blood pressure.

PHOSPHORUS: Phosphorus is responsible for creating some of the energy that you use every day. It also assists your body in synthesizing proteins, fats, and carbohydrates and regulates the fluid levels in your body. You'll get 60 mg with each serving of coconut milk.

MAGNESIUM: One serving of coconut milk delivers about 25 mg of magnesium, a mineral responsible for many biochemical functions in the body, including regulating the heart's rhythm and supporting the function of nerve cells.

HEALTH BENEFITS
OF COCONUT MILK

REVS UP YOUR METABOLISM: Two small studies, one conducted in Italy with eight men, and one in Switzerland with twelve men, showed that individuals who ate meals that contained about 30 g of medium chain fatty acids had a roughly 5 percent higher metabolic rate compared to those who ate long chain fatty acids. One cup of coconut milk has around 34 g of MFCAs.

BURNS MORE CALORIES: Researchers from McGill University in Canada published the results of their MCFA study in the *American Journal of Clinical Nutrition* in 1999. Twelve women were fed meals enriched with either MCFAs from butter and coconut oil or LCFAs from beef fat. After fourteen days, the women who ate the MCFA-rich food were burning about 33 more calories per minute than the women who had eaten the LCFA meals.

SPEEDS WEIGHT LOSS: In a sixteen-week study published in the *American Journal of Clinical Nutrition* in 2008, researchers fed forty men and women meals that contained the same number of calories, but contained either long chain fatty acids or medium chain fatty acids, the type of fat found in coconut. Those who ate the MCFA-rich meals lost an average of 6.6 pounds, whereas those who ate the LCFA-laden meals lost 3.3 pounds.

CHOOSING, USING, AND
KEEPING COCONUT MILK

Be careful to check the "use by" date, and look for any damage—dents, for example—in cans of coconut milk. Once opened, transfer the contents to a resealable container and refrigerate. Use the milk within a few days. The high oil content in coconut milk can make it turn rancid if it is not stored under proper conditions.

Caution: If you are concerned with bisphenol A (BPA)—a chemical used in the lining of certain canned foods—you may want to look for coconut milk in BPA-free cans or aseptic boxes. BPA can leach into foods that are acidic (such as tomato products) or fatty (such as coconut milk). BPA has been linked to cancer, asthma, diabetes, and impaired neurological development. It has also been shown to impact the body's natural response to estrogen, leading to a wide variety of hormonal imbalances.

COCONUT MILK IN RECIPES: In recipes where coconut milk is called for, I use canned regular coconut milk (not "lite"), and preferably without a stabilizer such as guar gum. (If "lite" is all you can find, go ahead and use it.) Coconut milk in boxes and cartons has added water, thickeners, colorants, preservatives, emulsifiers, and other ingredients that aren't good for you, and that can change the character of the recipe. There are a few recipes in the book, however, where it is fine to use coconut milk from a box or carton. (These are all clearly marked.)

STEPHANIE'S FAVORITE WAY TO USE COCONUT MILK: I use coconut milk daily as a replacement for dairy milk. I can't think of a way that I don't use it!

COCONUT CREAM

Coconut cream is very similar to coconut milk but contains less water. The difference is mainly consistency. Coconut cream has a thicker, more paste-like consistency, while coconut milk is generally a liquid. Commercial coconut milks and creams are generally sold in cans, although some are sold in boxes and Tetra Paks. The main ingredient in these products is water. If the fat content is 17 percent, it is called "coconut milk." If the fat content is 24 percent, it is called "coconut cream."

COCONUT CREAM: NUTRITION PROFILE PER SERVING (1 TABLESPOON)

CALORIES: Around 50

PROTEIN: With a very modest 1 g of protein per serving, coconut cream provides some of the macronutrient responsible for helping your body build and repair itself.

MEDIUM CHAIN FATTY ACIDS: Coconut products, including coconut cream, are among the world's most concentrated sources of medium chain fatty acids, which help the body better absorb and use other nutrients. Coconut creams boast powerful immune-system benefits while increasing metabolism for faster healing and weight loss, and they help heal a range of health conditions from IBS and candida to cardiovascular conditions and dementia.

LAURIC ACID: Lauric acid makes up almost 50 percent of the fatty acids in coconut products, including coconut cream. It is known for its ability to kill a wide range of potent pathogens, including bacteria (such as staph), fungi (such as the yeast *Candida albicans*), and viruses.

IRON: The body must have iron to help it create red blood cells. Coconut cream contains just a tiny bit of the recommended 8 mg.

COCONUT CREAM VS. CREAM OF COCONUT

Coconut cream is a very thick, paste-like cream—a concentrate, in essence, where most of the water has been removed. To make coconut cream, the first step is to chill coconut milk and then skim off the rich layer of cream that forms on top.

Cream of coconut is a canned, sweetened product, typically found in the same aisle as premade drink mixes and drink syrups. I think of it as the coconut-based version of condensed sweetened milk. Most brands of cream of coconut have a photo of a piña colada or other frozen drink on the front of the can. Cream of coconut is coconut cream that has been cooked with corn syrup or sugar, and it is a popular ingredient in sweet coconut-flavored "tropical" mixed drinks.

HEALTH BENEFITS OF COCONUT CREAM

ANTIULCER: While there have been no dedicated studies using coconut cream, there have been plenty involving coconut milk, a product with almost identical—though more diluted—ingredients than coconut cream. One surprising study involved a large group of rats with ulcers. Split into three subgroups, one group was given 40 mg of the ulcer-treating medication indomethacin each day. Another was fed 2 mL of coconut milk every day. And the last group received 2 mL of coconut water each day. The group given medication and the group given coconut milk experienced a 54 percent reduction in ulcers. The coconut water group experienced a 39 percent reduction. If you suffer from ulcers or are prone to them, coconut cream and coconut milk may be helpful additions to your daily diet.

CHOOSING, USING, AND KEEPING COCONUT CREAM

treat coconut cream just as you would coconut milk: Store it in a cupboard or pantry until you open it and refrigerate any unused portion. Use the remainder within two days of opening the container. Freeze coconut cream for longer storage.

Caution: Avoid buying cream of coconut, a heavily sweetened, processed, syrupy, coconut milk product.

COCONUT CREAM IN RECIPES: In recipes where coconut cream is called for, I use both Native Forest and Trader Joe's brands interchangeably. Trader Joe's brand is richer, but both work well.

STEPHANIE'S FAVORITE WAY TO USE COCONUT CREAM: To make whipped cream to top berry desserts.

COCONUT FLOUR

Coconut flour is today's darling in the culinary world. The gluten-free crowd loves it for the way it adds moisture to typically dry wheat-free baked goods. Paleo eaters adore its low-carb, high-protein profile. Healthy types love how easy it is to add brain-gut-immune-system-healing medium chain fatty acids and lauric acid to foods by using coconut flour, and the rest of us just love the taste.

For those of you who are not familiar with coconut flour, it is a delicious by-product of coconut oil and coconut milk: To make coconut oil, coconut is dry-pressed using heat to help extract the oil. Or, it is soaked in water and then pressed for its oil. The remaining pulp is then dried and ground into flour. This is what is meant when people say that coconut flour has been defatted. I encourage you to read more about coconut flour and then give it a try! In this book, there are loads of recipes with coconut flour just waiting for you to enjoy them!

COCONUT FLOUR: NUTRITION PROFILE PER SERVING (2 TABLESPOONS)

CALORIES: 120

MEDIUM CHAIN FATTY ACIDS: Unlike long chain fatty acids, MCFAs are easily and quickly metabolized into energy in the liver. It is believed that they are less likely to be stored as fat because they are used more quickly by the body than other types of fatty acids.

LAURIC ACID: Antiviral and antibacterial, lauric acid destroys a wide variety of disease-causing organisms. It may also reduce cholesterol and triglyceride levels, thereby lowering heart disease and risk of stroke.

FIBER: One serving of coconut flour provides 11 g of fiber to help maintain a healthy digestive tract.

PROTEIN: Protein is considered a macronutrient, which means that your body needs it in large amounts every day to perform everything from nutrient transport to cell repair. Two tablespoons of coconut flour provides 2 g.

IRON: The mineral iron is a part of all cells and does many things in our bodies, including delivering oxygen to blood. Two tablespoons of coconut flour provides about 5 g.

SODIUM: A mineral that is also an electrolyte, sodium helps maintain proper fluid levels in the body and regulates muscle function. You'll get 56 g per serving of coconut flour.

COCONUT FLOUR: DID YOU KNOW . . . ?

- Coconut flour has about 1 g of healthy fat per tablespoon.

- Coconut flour has about 2.5 g of fiber per tablespoon.

- Coconut flour absorbs huge amounts of water, which can help keep foods soft and chewy. Even if you bake with traditional wheat flours, using a couple of tablespoons of coconut flour helps tenderize pie dough and shortbread and helps keep baked goods fresh. If you'd like to try using coconut flour to improve the keeping quality of most mainstream recipes, swap in 10 to 15 percent coconut flour for any wheat-based flours.

- Because coconut flour has been defatted, it's leaner than other nut flours. It cannot be used as a substitute for any type of nut meal or nut-based flour, however.

- Coconut flour has about 61 percent fiber in its makeup compared to 27 percent in wheat flour.

HEALTH BENEFITS OF COCONUT FLOUR

HELPS REDUCE RISK OF SKIN CANCER: A 1997 study performed by a team at Annamalai University in Annamalai Nagar, India, found that when rats with skin cancers were fed coconut flour, they had fewer lesions, tumors, and cancerous cells than rats that were fed red chili pepper.

LOWERS BLOOD CHOLESTEROL: A study published in the August 1998 issue of the *Indian Journal of Experimental Biology* followed rats that were fed a diet of hemicellulose fiber–rich coconut flour and another group fed a fiber-free diet. (Note: Rather than just long straight chains like cellulose fiber, hemicellulose may have side chains and branches. Both types of fiber are found in fruits, veggies, and legumes.) The rats that ate the hemicellulose-coconut diet showed decreased concentration of total cholesterol and increased HDL cholesterol (the healthy kind), while the fiber-free group showed no change.

CHOOSING, USING, AND KEEPING COCONUT FLOUR

Coconut flour absorbs large amounts of liquid. When baking with it, opt for recipes that have been developed for coconut flour, or substitute no more than 10 percent to 15 percent of the flour in a standard recipe with coconut flour. Because it is often clumpy, vigorously whisk coconut flour before using it to get the lumps out. Coconut flour does not go rancid quickly, but if you're like me, it takes a while to use up a whole bag of the stuff. To keep it fresh, store it in an airtight container in the freezer.

Caution: Coconut flour should smell and taste mild and rich, and have a very subtle coconut flavor. If it tastes rancid or off, toss it.

COCONUT FLOUR IN RECIPES: All of the recipes in this book that use coconut flour were tested using several brands. Note: Calories and nutrient contents differ—sometimes greatly—between brands.

STEPHANIE'S FAVORITE WAY TO USE COCONUT FLOUR: I love adding a few tablespoons of coconut flour to non–coconut flour recipes to create extra moistness and increase the longevity of baked goods.

DRIED COCONUT

Dried flaked coconut, often called desiccated coconut, is a worldwide favorite. It is a whole food, made by drying the meat of mature coconuts. It's typically sold in flakes of different widths, from a wide flake to the finest of flakes (called macaroon coconut). While you may be familiar with the sweetened, slightly sticky "Angel Flake" coconut found in the baking aisle of most supermarkets, make an effort to search out unadulterated dried coconut. It's delicious, easy to cook with, and nutritious. In fact, it has a similar nutritional profile to coconut meat.

DRIED COCONUT: NUTRITION PROFILE PER SERVING (2 TABLESPOONS)

CALORIES: 185

FIBER: A serving of dried coconut provides 8 g of fiber, a nutrient that helps with digestion by adding bulk to the stool, which helps move food through the digestive tract and "clean" the interior wall of the large intestine. Fiber can help with weight loss by creating a feeling of fullness, which discourages overeating.

PROTEIN: Proteins are the body's building blocks. All of our organs, including the skin, muscles, hair, and nails, are built from proteins. The immune system, digestive system, and blood all rely on proteins to work correctly. You'll get 2 g from a serving of dried coconut.

MEDIUM CHAIN FATTY ACIDS: Dried coconut is rich in medium chain fatty acids, which are broken down much faster than long chain fatty acids, so they provide energy but do not contribute to high cholesterol, as long chain fatty acids do. According to several studies, MCFAs can help lower bad cholesterol levels and increase good cholesterol levels.

LAURIC ACID: Dried coconut is rich in lauric acid, a monoglyceride compound that exhibits antiviral, antimicrobial, antiprotozoal, and antifungal properties. Because of its strong antiviral properties, studies have begun in the Philippines attempting to prove the effectiveness of lauric acid against HIV/AIDS.

VITAMIN B6: The body uses vitamin B6 for more than one hundred enzyme reactions involved in metabolism. B6 is also involved in brain development and immune function in utero and during infancy. A serving of dried coconut will give you 4 percent of the recommended dietary allowance.

VITAMIN C: Vitamin C is a powerful antioxidant that can stimulate collagen production for fast wound healing, help prevent and lessen the duration of viral illnesses, and help prevent a variety of other diseases, from cancer to cataracts. A serving of dried coconut will give you 0.1 mg.

VITAMIN E: Another antioxidant, vitamin E helps keep the brain healthy. It also protects cells from the damage caused by free radicals. A serving of dried coconut provides 1 percent of the recommended dietary allowance.

FOLATE: Also known as vitamin B9 or folic acid, folate helps the body make new cells. A serving of dried coconut provides 2.5 mcg of the recommended dietary allowance.

PANTOTHENIC ACID: Known as vitamin B5, pantothenic acid is essential to a wide range of chemical reactions in the body that sustain life. A serving of dried coconut provides 0.2 mg.

RIBOFLAVIN: Also known as vitamin B2, and formerly known as vitamin G, riboflavin is essential for metabolic energy production. You'll get 0.1 mg of the recommended dietary allowance from a serving of dried coconut.

CALCIUM: This mineral is necessary to maintain strong bones and healthy communication between the brain and various parts of the body. You'll get 7.38 mg of calcium.

COPPER: Dietary copper plays a small role in the production of red blood cells and assists with your sense of taste. A serving of dried coconut provides 0.2 mg.

IRON: While not overly rich in iron, a serving of dried coconut gives the body 0.9 g. This mineral is necessary for growth, development, normal cellular functioning, and synthesis of some hormones and connective tissue.

MAGNESIUM: Magnesium is required for the proper growth and maintenance of bones. It is also required for the proper function of nerves, muscles, and many other parts of the body. A serving of dried coconut provides 25.2 mg of the recommended dietary allowance.

MANGANESE: From one serving of dried coconut, you'll get 0.8 mg of manganese, a mineral that helps you metabolize both fat and protein. Manganese also supports both the immune and nervous systems and promotes stable blood sugar levels.

PHOSPHORUS: The body uses phosphorus to create strong bones—in fact, 85 percent of the phosphorus in the human body is found in the bones. A serving of dried coconut will provide 57.7 mg of the recommended dietary allowance.

POTASSIUM: Potassium is essential for fluid balance within your cells. It is also necessary for proper heart function and muscle growth. A serving of dried coconut provides 152 mg of the mineral.

SELENIUM: This mineral is essential in cell metabolism and is a powerful antioxidant that helps keep the immune system strong. A serving of dried coconut provides 5.2 mcg.

ZINC: Found in cells throughout the body, zinc helps the immune system fight off invading bacteria and viruses. The body also needs zinc to make proteins and DNA, the genetic material in all cells. A serving of dried coconut provides 0.6 mg.

HEALTH BENEFITS OF DRIED COCONUT

LOWERS RISK OF COLON CANCER: An animal study performed in 2014 by a team from Annamalai University in Annamalai Nagar, India, found that eating dried coconut for thirty weeks "significantly decreased the incidence and number of tumors as well as the activity of cancerous cells" in thirty rats with colon cancer.

LOWERS BLOOD CHOLESTEROL: After reviewing all available research, a team at the University of Kerala, in Thiruvananthapuram, Kerala, India, concluded that eating dried coconut with coconut oil reduced serum total and LDL cholesterol in humans with high cholesterol better than coconut oil alone. This was also found in separate research performed on rats.

CHOOSING, USING, AND KEEPING DRIED COCONUT

Dried coconut is fun to use. You'll find it in a regular medium-size shred, as well as in a finely shredded version, sometimes called macaroon coconut. I've even seen ultrawide shreds, which are a fun, chewy addition to granola and trail mix. The only thing I'd ask you to watch for is the ingredient list on packaging: Make sure you're buying a product without sweeteners and chemical preservatives. You can keep dried coconut on a dark, dry, cool shelf, but it will last longer in the refrigerator or freezer.

Caution: To avoid rancidity, store dried coconut in the freezer or fridge and use it within a year.

DRIED COCONUT IN RECIPES: All recipes in this book that use dried coconut were tested using a variety of brands of unsweetened shredded dried coconut.

STEPHANIE'S FAVORITE WAY TO USE DRIED COCONUT: As a breading for fish and poultry.

COCONUT YOGURT

Once upon a time, all yogurt was made of cow, sheep, or goat milk, and you either ate it or you didn't. If you didn't digest lactose or if casein caused neurological problems or if you just didn't like the foggy way you felt after eating dairy, then you avoided it. Today things are different. People who choose not to consume dairy have plenty of great options, including yogurt made with coconut milk. Several companies make coconut yogurt and call it either "coconut milk yogurt" or "cultured coconut milk." It is available unsweetened, unflavored, and "Greek style." You can also make your own by fermenting coconut milk with yogurt starter.

COCONUT YOGURT (UNFLAVORED, UNSWEETENED): NUTRITION PROFILE PER SERVING (4-OUNCE CONTAINER)

CALORIES: 80

FIBER: A serving of unflavored regular coconut yogurt contains 3 g of fiber, which promotes normal digestion, helps remove toxins from the body, and creates a feeling of fullness, which helps prevent overeating.

PROBIOTICS: The normal human digestive tract contains about four hundred types of probiotic bacteria that reduce the growth of harmful bacteria and promote a healthy digestive system. Fermented foods are rich in these helpful probiotics. Coconut yogurt—like its dairy counterpart—is no exception and can help reduce infections in the digestive tract, prevent (or recover from) diarrhea, and control inflammation.

MEDIUM CHAIN FATTY ACIDS: Medium chain fatty acids help the body absorb and use other nutrients. In addition, they boast powerful immune-system benefits, increase metabolism for faster healing and weight loss, and assist in healing a range of health conditions from IBS to candida to cardiovascular conditions to dementia.

CALCIUM: Because coconut milk contains only a small amount of calcium—and in order to compete with dairy yogurt—most commercial brands of coconut yogurt are fortified with calcium. Thus, a 4-ounce container of fortified regular, unflavored coconut yogurt provides about 250 mg of calcium, a mineral needed to maintain strong bones and carry out many other important functions. Almost all calcium is stored in bones and teeth, where it supports structure and hardness. The body also needs calcium for muscles to move and for nerves to carry messages between the brain and every other part of the body.

VITAMIN B12: Although coconut milk does not contain vitamin B12, most commercially available coconut yogurt is enriched with the vitamin. Thus, a 4-ounce container of unflavored coconut yogurt contains 1.5 mcg of vitamin B12. This nutrient is needed to keep the body's nerve and blood cells healthy and helps make DNA, the genetic material in all cells.

MAGNESIUM: Coconut milk—and by extension, coconut yogurt—is a magnesium-rich food. A serving of coconut yogurt provides about 80 mg of magnesium, a mineral needed for many processes in the body, including regulating muscle and nerve function, blood sugar levels, and blood pressure, as well as making protein, bone, and DNA.

IRON: A serving of coconut yogurt offers 0.75 mg of iron, a mineral used by the body to create red blood cells.

HEALTH BENEFITS OF COCONUT YOGURT

WEIGHT CONTROL: Much of the fat in coconut yogurt is in the form of medium chain fatty acids, which can help control weight, according to a joint study in 2001 by a team from the Division of Healthcare Science Research Laboratory in Kanagawa, Japan; Kagawa Nutrition University in Saitama, Japan; and the Institute of

---

YOGURT DEFINED

The word "yogurt" is derived from Turkish *yoğurt*, and is related to the Turkish verb *yoğurmak*, which means to be curdled, coagulated, or thickened.

Environmental Science for Human Life, in Tokyo. In a twelve-week, double-blind study using seventy-eight men and women, both groups were fed the same diet each day, but only one of the groups was given long chain fatty acids daily. The other was given medium chain fatty acids. It was found that the group that consumed medium chain fatty acids saw a decrease in blood cholesterol, and in body fat and weight, with an increase in metabolism.

CHOOSING, USING, AND KEEPING COCONUT YOGURT

Coconut yogurt is available in the dairy case at health food stores, and even the most mainstream supermarkets, right next to traditional dairy yogurt. Flavored and unflavored coconut yogurt is available in both regular and thick Greek styles. Store coconut yogurt in the fridge, as you would dairy yogurt, and use it before the expiration date. Coconut yogurt can be used as a direct substitute in recipes that call for dairy yogurt, or you can whisk it with a bit of sweetener to make a quick dessert sauce.

Caution: I am not a fan of flavored yogurts. Most of them provide more sugar in one sitting than you need, from 13 to 24 g! This is especially harmful to anyone who has blood sugar issues or suffers from sugar-induced cravings. If you're going to use coconut milk yogurt, keep it healthy by sticking to the unflavored varieties and dress it up with your own fruit, nuts, and other add-ins.

COCONUT YOGURT IN RECIPES: All recipes in this book that use coconut yogurt were tested using commercially available unflavored regular coconut yogurt.

STEPHANIE'S FAVORITE WAYS TO USE COCONUT YOGURT: In baked goods and other recipes that call for dairy yogurt.

COCONUT KEFIR

Kefir dates back many centuries to the shepherds of the Caucasus Mountains, who carried milk stored in leather pouches, where it would ferment into fizzy, sour yogurt. These days, confusingly enough, coconut kefir can be one of two things: a fermented coconut milk drink or a fermented coconut water drink. You will see both in markets and online.

COCONUT KEFIR: NUTRITION PROFILE PER SERVING (1 CUP)

CALORIES: 70 in a serving of coconut milk kefir; around 10 in a serving of coconut water kefir.

> ### KEFIR DEFINED
>
> The word "kefir" is said to have originated from the Turkish word *keif*, which means "good feeling."

PROBIOTICS: The normal human digestive tract contains about four hundred types of probiotic bacteria that reduce the growth of harmful bacteria and promote a healthy digestive system. Fermented foods are rich in these helpful probiotics. Coconut kefir is no exception and contains large amounts of probiotics. It is also believed to help reduce infections in the digestive tract, prevent (or recover from) diarrhea, and control inflammation.

ENZYMES: As a raw food, coconut kefir contains enzymes—proteins that allow certain chemical reactions to take place much faster than they would on their own.

HEALTH BENEFITS OF COCONUT KEFIR

INTESTINAL HEALTH: While no formal studies have been performed on either coconut milk kefir or coconut water kefir, there are numerous studies and abundant anecdotal evidence that promote the health benefits of fermented products such as coconut kefir. Probiotic-rich fermented foods help heal a damaged large intestine, normalize bowel movements, help with digestion, and encourage the body to better assimilate nutrients.

CHOOSING, USING, AND KEEPING COCONUT KEFIR

The probiotics in kefir are perishable and especially sensitive to warmth. Drink coconut kefir as soon as you open the container or refrigerate it for up to five days (or until the expiration date).

Caution: Kefir is a healthy beverage as is. There is no need to load it up with sugar! If you do, you'll have converted a healthy food into a sugary soft drink. Resist, resist, resist!!!

COCONUT KEFIR IN RECIPES: Every recipe in this book that uses coconut milk kefir or coconut water kefir was tested using homemade milk kefir, Inner-Eco brand coconut water kefir (1 tablespoon diluted in a cup of water), and Tonix brand coconut water kefir.

STEPHANIE'S FAVORITE WAY TO USE COCONUT KEFIR: Coconut water kefir as a summer cooler mixed with fresh-pressed fruit juice and coconut water ice cubes.

COCONUT NECTAR

Unlike maple syrup, coconut syrup—better known as "nectar"—doesn't come from bark (since coconut palms don't have bark). Coconut syrup is secreted by the coconut palm's blossom stems—largish stems that connect the blossom to the fronds. The same sap is used to make coconut sugar, coconut vinegar, and coconut aminos!

Coconut nectar is considered a raw food—one that is rich in enzymes and amino acids. It contains trace amounts of vitamin C, potassium, phosphorus, magnesium, calcium, zinc, iron, and copper, and also provides small amounts of antioxidant phytonutrients, such as polyphenols, flavonoids, and anthocyanidin.

The mild taste of coconut nectar makes it a favorite with bakers and children, while nutritionists love its low glycemic index ranking of 35. The glycemic index scale measures foods according to the effect they have on blood. It starts at 0 and goes

VARIETIES OF COCONUT NECTAR

Coconut nectar can vary in color from dark blond to rich brown, depending upon the year's rainfall, time of year when the coconut palm is tapped, and even the heat and fuel source used to reduce the nectar.

to 100. Foods that rate between 0 and 49 have a low glycemic index, foods between 50 and 70 have a moderate glycemic index, and foods that rate over 70 have a high glycemic index. A 2-tablespoon serving of agave nectar, for example, has a glycemic index of 30, placing it in the category of low glycemic foods.

COCONUT NECTAR: NUTRITION PROFILE PER SERVING (1 TABLESPOON)

CALORIES: 55

AMINO ACIDS: Coconut nectar contains amino acids, which make up protein in food. When digested, they help the body create solid matter, including skin, eyes, heart, intestines, bones, and muscle. Depending upon which nutrition scientist you ask, there are between twenty and twenty-two amino acids. Of those, eight to ten are considered essential, meaning you must get these from your diet, since your body can't synthesize them from other materials.

ENZYMES: As a raw food, coconut nectar is rich in enzymes, the proteins that allow certain chemical reactions to take place much more quickly than those reactions would occur on their own.

PHOSPHORUS: Coconut nectar provides trace amounts of phosphorus, a mineral important for bone growth, kidney function, and cell growth.

POTASSIUM: Coconut nectar provides trace amounts of potassium, which helps reduce hypertension, regulate blood pressure, and control cholesterol levels and weight.

CALCIUM: Coconut nectar provides trace amounts of calcium, a mineral vital for strong bones and teeth, as well as for muscle growth.

MAGNESIUM: Coconut nectar provides trace amounts of magnesium, which is essential for metabolism.

CHLORIDE: Coconut nectar provides trace amounts of chloride, which corrects the pressure of body fluids and balances the nervous system.

SULFUR: Coconut nectar provides trace amounts of sulfur, which is important for healthy hair, skin, and nails, and also helps maintain oxygen balance for proper brain function.

BORON: Coconut nectar provides trace amounts of boron, which is essential for healthy bone and joint function, and enhances the body's ability to absorb calcium and magnesium.

ZINC: Coconut nectar provides trace amounts of zinc, which is called the "nutrient of intelligence," because it is necessary for mental development.

MANGANESE: Coconut nectar provides trace amounts of manganese, which has antioxidant, free-radical-fighting properties. Manganese is important for proper food digestion and normal bone development.

IRON: Coconut nectar provides trace amounts of iron, which the body uses to make blood. Iron is necessary for normal mental development in infants and children. It also helps the immune system run efficiently.

COPPER: Coconut nectar provides trace amounts of copper, which helps with energy production, as well as melanin production in the skin.

PHYTOCHEMICALS: Coconut nectar contains trace amounts of plant chemicals that are powerful antioxidants and help repair and protect cells from free-radical damage. The phytochemicals in coconut nectar include flavonoids (which also have strong anti-inflammatory powers).

HEALTH BENEFITS OF COCONUT NECTAR

LOW GLYCEMIC SWEETENER: Although there have been no formal studies on coconut nectar, its low glycemic status could make it an option, as a sweetener, for individuals with diabetes, prediabetes, and other blood sugar disorders. Anecdotal evidence from coconut-producing countries claims it helps keep the immune system strong, wards off colds and other viral illnesses, and can be used on the skin to treat and prevent breakouts. Talk to your health-care provider about replacing your current sweetener with coconut nectar.

CHOOSING, USING, AND KEEPING COCONUT NECTAR

Coconut nectar can be kept on a dark shelf in your cupboard for a year or more. (I've kept coconut nectar for two and a half years with no problem.) Look for recipes that have been developed, specifically, with coconut nectar in mind, or find recipes that currently use another liquid sweetener and swap in coconut nectar. Coconut nectar can be used in a 1:1 ratio for honey, maple syrup, brown rice syrup, barley malt, and even agave nectar.

Caution: Coconut nectar may seem healthier than cane sugar or other liquid sweeteners, but it is still a sweetener. Go easy on it, and remember that your body doesn't need excess sweeteners, no matter what they are made of.

COCONUT NECTAR IN RECIPES: All recipes in this book that use coconut nectar were tested using Coconut Secret brand coconut nectar.

STEPHANIE'S FAVORITE WAY TO USE COCONUT NECTAR: My kids love to use it as a syrup over pancakes or as a sweetener for oatmeal and other hot cereals.

COCONUT SUGAR

Coconut sugar should be considered a "healthier food" rather than a health food per se because, let's face it, no one needs to consume a lot of sweeteners, no matter what they are made of. Coconut sugar is produced by boiling and then dehydrating the sap of the coconut palm. It contains trace amounts of vitamin C, potassium, phosphorus, magnesium, calcium, zinc, iron, and copper, and also supplies small amounts of antioxidant phytonutrients, such as polyphenols, flavonoids, and anthocyanidin.

In 2014, the United Nations' Food and Agriculture Organization named coconut sugar the world's most sustainable sweetener. Coconut palms use minimal amounts of water, especially compared to sugar cane production, and a single coconut palm can continue to produce sap for about twenty years.

Nutritionists love coconut sugar because it ranks low on the glycemic index (a list that measures the effects of carbohydrates on blood sugar). Foods listed high on the glycemic index cause your blood sugar to spike. Fast spikes in blood sugar can also cause your insulin levels to soar in a short period, and this can have serious consequences for diabetics. Coconut sugar ranks just 35 on this index, while regular table sugar (from sugar cane) ranks between 60 and 75.

COCONUT SUGAR: NUTRITION PROFILE PER SERVING (1 TEASPOON)

CALORIES: 20

PHOSPHORUS: Coconut sugar provides trace amounts of phosphorus, a mineral important for bone growth, kidney function, and cell growth.

POTASSIUM: Coconut sugar provides trace amounts of potassium, which helps reduce hypertension, regulate blood sugar, and control cholesterol levels and weight.

CALCIUM: Coconut sugar provides trace amounts of calcium, a mineral vital for strong bones and teeth, as well as muscle growth.

MAGNESIUM: Coconut sugar provides trace amounts of magnesium, which is essential for metabolism and nerve health (including helping motor nerves carry messages by electrical impulse between the brain and muscles). Magnesium also stimulates the brain (memory).

CHLORIDE: Coconut sugar provides trace amounts of chloride, which corrects the pressure of body fluids, and balances the nervous system.

SULFUR: Coconut sugar provides trace amounts of sulfur, which is important for healthy hair, skin, and nails, and also helps maintain oxygen balance for proper brain function.

BORON: Coconut sugar provides trace amounts of boron, which is essential for healthy bone and joint function, and enhances the body's ability to absorb calcium and magnesium.

ZINC: Coconut sugar provides trace amounts of zinc, which is called the "nutrient of intelligence," because it is necessary for mental development.

MANGANESE: Coconut sugar provides trace amounts of manganese, which has antioxidant, free-radical-fighting properties. Manganese is important for proper food digestion and for normal bone growth.

IRON: Coconut sugar provides trace amounts of iron, which the body uses to make blood; iron also helps with mental development and the immune system.

COPPER: Coconut sugar provides trace amounts of copper, which helps with energy production, as well as melanin production in the skin.

HEALTH BENEFITS OF COCONUT SUGAR?

LOW GLYCEMIC SWEETENER: Although there have been no formal studies on coconut sugar, its low glycemic status could make it an option, as a sweetener, for individuals with diabetes, prediabetes, and other blood sugar disorders. Check with your doctor to see if coconut sugar may be an appropriate sweetener for you.

CHOOSING, USING, AND KEEPING COCONUT SUGAR

Coconut sugar can be substituted equally for regular (white) cane sugar. Some brands of coconut sugar are especially coarse. If you prefer a finer grain, just process coconut sugar in a coffee grinder or food processor until it comes closer to the consistency of regular cane sugar.

Caution: In Thailand and other Southeast Asian countries, the term "palm sugar" is commonly used to describe coconut sugar or sugar derived from the sugar palm. Brands that come from these areas may market coconut palm sugar or palm sugar as coconut sugar. When you are shopping, always look for "coconut sugar" on the label (and in the ingredients list).

COCONUT SUGAR IN RECIPES: Regular coconut sugar has been used for the coconut sugar in these recipes.

STEPHANIE'S FAVORITE WAY TO USE COCONUT SUGAR: To replace half or all the cane sugar when making baked goods.

> ### BY ANY OTHER NAME . . .
> Coconut sugar is also known as coconut crystals, coco sap sugar, coconut palm sugar, and coco sugar.

COCONUT VINEGAR

Mild-tasting coconut vinegar is made from sap that has been tapped from the thick stem that attaches coconut blossoms to the coconut fronds. This sap, known as "tuba," is then aged for eight months to a year. It is a raw food.

COCONUT VINEGAR: NUTRITION PROFILE PER SERVING (1 TABLESPOON)

CALORIES: 0

POTASSIUM: While the level of potassium in coconut vinegar hasn't been studied, the same sap used to make the vinegar contains 192 mg per tablespoon. It's thought that coconut vinegar's potassium levels are similar. Potassium is the most important positively charged ion present in the cells of the body. It helps maintain the health of the heart, brain, kidneys, muscle tissues, and other organs of the body. It also plays a key role in the functioning of heart muscle and the contraction of voluntary and involuntary muscles.

AMINO ACIDS: Coconut vinegar contains nine essential amino acids, as well as eight nonessential amino acids. For those of you who are not familiar with amino acids, they make up protein in food, and when digested, they help the body create solid matter, including skin, eyes, heart, intestines, bones,

and muscle. Depending upon which nutrition scientist you ask, there are between twenty and twenty-two amino acids. Of those, eight to ten are considered essential, meaning you must get these from your diet, as your body can't synthesize them from other materials. Again, this depends upon which nutrition scientist you ask. Some experts believe there are eight essential amino acids, some believe there are nine, and others believe there are ten. Coconut has nine of these that many nutritionists consider essential.

ENZYMES: Coconut vinegar is rich in enzymes, the proteins that allow certain chemical reactions to take place much more quickly than those reactions would occur on their own.

PROBIOTICS: The normal human digestive tract contains about four hundred types of probiotic bacteria, which reduce the growth of harmful bacteria and promote a healthy digestive system. Fermented foods are rich in these helpful probiotics. Coconut vinegar is no exception, because it contains a large amount of probiotics, and is said to help reduce infections in the digestive tract, prevent (or recover from) diarrhea, and control inflammation.

PREBIOTICS: Coconut cider vinegar also contains prebiotics, plant fiber that beneficially nourishes good bacteria that are already present in the large bowel or colon. The body itself does not digest this fiber; instead, the fiber acts as a fertilizer to promote the growth of many of the good bacteria in the gut.

HEALTH BENEFITS OF COCONUT VINEGAR

BLOOD SUGAR STABILIZER: In 2006, a team of researchers out of Arizona State University in Mesa, Arizona, examined the scientific evidence for medicinal uses of coconut and other types of vinegar, focusing particularly on recent investigations supporting vinegar's role as an antiglycemic agent. It was determined that many recent scientific investigations have documented that vinegar does, indeed, stabilize blood sugar. It was also found that vinegar creates a feeling of satiety, which can help with weight control.

CHOOSING, USING, AND KEEPING COCONUT VINEGAR

Look for a bottle that contains "the mother," a clump of cellulose and other natural material that helps with fermentation.

Coconut vinegar can keep for extended periods if it is stored on a shelf in a dark, cool place. I have a bottle that is two years old and as fresh as it was when I first opened it. Coconut vinegar can be used in any recipe that calls for apple cider vinegar, and it shares the same alkalinizing health benefits (i.e., it helps strengthen the immune system, wards off cravings, and provides quick energy). I enjoy using chilled coconut vinegar as a toner, during the summer, to remove dirt and grime from my skin.

Caution: Avoid coconut vinegar made from the liquid found in mature coconuts, sometimes called "coconut water vinegar." This "vinegar," a by-product of the coconut oil industry, is made by taking the liquid in brown coconuts and mixing it with a "vinegar starter," and then allowing the mixture to ferment for two to four weeks. It has little nutritional value. You want the traditional vinegar made from the sap of the coconut palm.

COCONUT VINEGAR IN RECIPES: For all recipes that call for coconut vinegar in this book, I use Coconut Secret brand vinegar, which is derived from coconut sap.

STEPHANIE'S FAVORITE WAY TO USE COCONUT VINEGAR: Whisked with coconut oil and a bit of salt (and maybe some herbs) as a salad dressing.

COCONUT AMINOS

Coconut aminos, as a product, is not as well known as coconut oil, coconut milk, coconut water, and coconut flour, so don't worry if you haven't heard of this dark, rich, salty sauce. Made in small batches from the fermented sap of the coconut palm blossoms and mineral-rich sea salt from the Philippines, coconut aminos is used for flavoring, marinating, and dressing food. Think of coconut aminos as soy sauce without the soy.

Small batches ensure that coconut aminos is a raw, enzymatically alive product. It boasts seventeen amino acids and some B vitamins. (Amino acids are the building blocks of proteins in our bodies.) Coconut aminos contains 65 percent less sodium than soy sauce.

Coconut aminos is also a great substitute for Bragg Liquid Aminos, which has the same ingredients as soy sauce, but isn't fermented and contains sixteen amino acids that are not present in soy sauce. If you have issues with soy, you'll have them with Bragg Liquid Aminos.

COCONUT AMINOS: NUTRITION PROFILE PER SERVING (1 TABLESPOON)

CALORIES: 5

POTASSIUM: Rich in potassium, coconut aminos has a nearly identical nutrient profile to coconut vinegar. Potassium is the most important positively charged ion present in the cells of the body. It helps maintain the health of the heart, brain, kidneys, muscle tissues, and other organs of the body, and it plays a key role in the contraction of voluntary and involuntary muscles.

AMINO ACIDS: Coconut aminos contains nine essential amino acids, as well as eight nonessential amino acids. For those of you who are not familiar with amino acids, they make up protein in food; when digested, they help the body create solid matter, including skin, eyes, heart, intestines, bones, and muscle. Depending upon which nutrition scientist you ask, there are between twenty and twenty-two amino acids. Of those, eight nine or ten are considered essential, meaning you must get these from your diet, as your body can't synthesize them from other materials. Again, this depends upon which nutrition scientist you ask. Some experts believe there are eight essential amino acids, some believe there are nine, and others believe there are ten. Coconut has nine of these that many nutritionists consider essential.

ENZYMES: Coconut aminos is rich in enzymes, the proteins that allow certain chemical reactions to take place much more quickly than the reactions would occur on their own.

PROBIOTICS: The normal human digestive tract contains about four hundred types of probiotic bacteria, which reduce the growth of harmful bacteria and promote a healthy digestive system. Fermented foods are rich in these helpful probiotics. Coconut aminos is no exception, because it contains large amounts of probiotics, and is said to help reduce infections in the digestive tract, prevent (or recover from) diarrhea, and control inflammation.

HEALTH BENEFITS OF COCONUT AMINOS

LARGE INTESTINE HELPER: Although there have been no formal studies of coconut aminos, anecdotal evidence suggests that this product helps promote a healthy probiotic balance in the large intestine, thanks to its high probiotic content.

CHOOSING, USING, AND KEEPING COCONUT AMINOS

Coconut aminos is available in glass bottles. If you store it in a dark, cool place, it can keep for a couple of years. Coconut aminos can be used, in a 1:1 ratio, as a substitution for shoyu, tamari-style soy sauces, and Braggs Liquid Aminos (a non-fermented soy product).

Caution: When choosing coconut aminos, look for products made from the fermented sap of the coconut tree. Avoid products based on coconut water, and ones that have been artificially colored and flavored.

COCONUT AMINOS IN RECIPES: For every recipe in this book that calls for coconut aminos, I've used Coconut Secret, a brand that is derived from coconut sap.

STEPHANIE'S FAVORITE WAY TO USE COCONUT AMINOS: As a poultry or pork marinade—whisked with orange juice and flavored with fresh ginger and garlic.

CHAPTER 3

DRINK YOUR COCONUT

Mention "coconut," and one of the first things that jumps to mind is coconut water, the almost-clear liquid of young coconuts. With sales increasing by about 42 percent between 2012 and 2013 alone, coconut water is one of today's fastest-growing "health drinks." But coconut water isn't the only coconut beverage to enjoy. Coconut milk—whether homemade, from can, or from a box or carton—is a delicious option for cooking, drinking straight, or making fun flavored drinks like the ones featured here!

You can also use coconut oil, coconut nectar, and coconut crystals to create yummy cocktails, as well as hot and cold drinks that the entire family will enjoy. (Shhh . . . they're also good for you!)

Indeed almost all of coconut's various products lend themselves beautifully to drinks of all kinds, from refreshing electrolyte-filled coconut water–based beverages to creamy blender drinks to hot and frothy coffee house–style treats.

HOMEMADE COCONUT WATER

MAKES 1 TO 2 SERVINGS

While purchasing a Tetra Pack or aseptic box of coconut water is much easier than cracking open a coconut, doing it yourself lets you enjoy an ultra-fresh, clean taste that you just can't get from a packaged product.

So for the intrepid among you, here are instructions for extracting your own coconut water. Have fun!

All you need is 1 young green coconut.

1. Place the coconut on an even, sturdy surface. Using your sharpest, heaviest non-serrated knife, cut through the coconut, about 2 or 3 inches from the top, as you would a jack-o'-lantern. Tip: Cutting a square opening instead of a circle will make it easier for you to extract the juice.

2. Check the color of the coconut flesh. It should be white. If it is pink or tan or grayish or any other color, it may be going bad.

3. Using a spoon, scrape away any flesh that could be in the way of the opening.

4. Take a peek at the coconut water (also known as coconut juice; the terms are used interchangeably). It should be clear or slightly milky with no sour smell or taste. If it is an off-color or tastes sour, the coconut water has gone bad.

5. Drink the juice straight from the coconut with a straw, or pour it into glasses. Drink immediately, or mix in a squirt of lemon juice to keep the coconut water fresh in your fridge for up to 48 hours. Any unused coconut water can be frozen into ice cubes for use in cooking or for chilling drinks.

6. Using a long metal spoon, scoop out the soft flesh. This can be added to smoothies, puddings, blended with fruit and poured into ice pop molds, or eaten straight from the coconut.

HOMEMADE COCONUT MILK I (MADE WITH A WHOLE COCONUT)

MAKES 2 TO 4 SERVINGS, DEPENDING UPON THE SIZE OF THE COCONUT

Making your own coconut milk can be economical and fun, especially if you're looking for an activity to do with your kids that's just a little bit different. And, if you are wary of food or drinks from cans, since some cans are coated with an industrial chemical called bisphenol A (BPA), making your own coconut milk is an easy healthy option.

What many people feel makes BPA harmful is this: It is thought to be an endocrine disrupter, which means it interferes with the production, secretion, and function of natural hormones in a way that is hazardous to your health, possibly leaving individuals susceptible to heart disease, asthma, liver-enzyme abnormalities, type 2 diabetes, reproductive disorders, erectile dysfunction, and breast cancer, as well as reducing the efficacy of chemotherapy treatment.

There's another reason why it's best to stay away from commercially packaged coconut milk: Some brands contain thickeners, gums, or chemical preservatives that your body would be better off without.

1   *mature coconut*

   Room temperature water

1. Find the "eyes" of the coconut. Identify the softest eye. Using a corkscrew, pierce the surface and drill into the eye. Once you've burrowed through the shell and reached the interior of the coconut, remove the corkscrew. You can also use the hammer method to find the eye, described in Chapter 2.

2. Pour any liquid the mature coconut may contain into a container. Set aside to use in a smoothie. (It is not as fresh-tasting or as nutritious as coconut water from a green coconut, but it is drinkable.)

3. For this next step, you'll need a standard screwdriver and hammer. Both clean, please! Position the screwdriver over the top of the coconut, and hit it with the hammer, in order to put a crack in the coconut. Pry open the crack to open the coconut completely into two or more sections.

4. Using a spoon, scrape out the white coconut meat. It will be firm. Collect it in a bowl.

5. Put a few chunks of coconut meat into a blender. Add water until the coconut is barely covered. Process on the highest power setting until the coconut meat is liquefied, and then pour it into a container.

6. Working in batches, continue processing the coconut meat until all of it has been liquefied.

7. If you like, pour the blended coconut milk through a fine sieve or cheesecloth to remove any solids. (You can use the solids in baked goods, curries, and smoothies.)

8. Store the coconut milk in an airtight container for up to 5 days in the fridge. You can freeze any unused milk in an airtight container for up to 3 months.

HOMEMADE COCONUT MILK II (MADE WITH DRIED COCONUT)

MAKES 2 OR MORE 1-CUP SERVINGS

This is the easy-breezy homemade coconut milk recipe—no coconut opening required! And, because you can choose the amounts of ingredients you want to use, you can also control the amount of coconut milk you can make in one go.

1 cup or more high-quality, unsweetened shredded dried (also known as shredded or dried) coconut

1 cup or more near-boiling water (use 1 cup of water for every cup of dried coconut)

1. Place the unsweetened shredded dried coconut in a blender. Add 1 cup near-boiling water for every cup of coconut you use.

2. Process the mixture until it is liquefied, then pour it into a container.

3. Allow the coconut milk to cool to room temperature and strain it through a fine sieve or cheesecloth to remove any solids. (You can use the solids in baked goods, curries, and smoothies.)

4. Store the coconut milk in an airtight container for up to 5 days in the fridge. You can freeze any unused milk in an airtight container for up to 3 months.

MOCHA COCONUT COFFEE

MAKES ABOUT 3 SERVINGS

For those of you who love blended, sweet coffee drinks, here is a version that is healthier than the commercial stuff. Yum!

- 1 *cup freshly brewed strong coffee (you can use decaf, if desired)*
- 1 *15-ounce can coconut milk (or 2 cups coconut milk from aseptic box, or refrigerated carton)*
- 2 *tablespoons organic cocoa powder*
- 2 *to 3 tablespoons coconut sugar (or sweetener of choice)*

  Optional: ¼ teaspoon vanilla extract

1. In a medium pot over medium heat, whisk together the coffee and coconut milk.

2. Whisk in the cocoa powder. Continue to whisk until no lumps remain.

3. Whisk in coconut sugar and, if desired, vanilla. Continue to whisk until sugar has dissolved.

4. Remove from heat, and enjoy.

PUMPKIN COCONUT CHAI LATTE

MAKES 2 SERVINGS

I adore pumpkin. I also love how easy it is to sneak into all kinds of foods, from nut butters to baked goods to smoothies to sauces to hot drinks. At one time, pumpkin puree was the only veggie my oldest son would eat. (Well, he wasn't actually aware that he was eating it. . . .) Anyway, you'll love this pumpkin chai!

- ¾ *cup water*
- 3 *chai-flavored tea bags*
- ¼ *cup pumpkin puree*
- 2 *cups coconut milk (homemade or from can, aseptic box, or refrigerated carton)*
- 1 *teaspoon vanilla extract*
- ½ *to 2 tablespoons coconut sugar (or raw sugar, such as Sucanat)*

1. Heat water in a medium saucepan until boiling.

2. Immediately add tea bags, cover pot, and turn off heat.

3. Allow tea bags to steep for 6 minutes.

4. Remove tea bags and squeeze all liquid into the pot.

5. Turn heat on, to low, and whisk in pumpkin puree, coconut milk, vanilla extract, and sugar, until smooth. Add more water if you want a thinner drink.

- One cup of cubed pumpkin has only 30 calories but 197 percent of an adult's daily requirement of vitamin A.

- Pumpkin also contains vitamins C, B2, B3, B6, and K, as well as manganese, potassium, and magnesium.

- A 1-cup serving of pumpkin contains about 22 percent of an adult's daily requirement of fiber.

- Pumpkin and other winter squash are high in antioxidants and anti-inflammatory compounds that are helpful in cancer prevention and cancer treatment.

- One cup of baked pumpkin (or other winter squash) provides about 340 mg of omega-3 fatty acids in the form of alpha-linolenic acid (ALA).

- Winter squash, such as pumpkin, helps improve blood sugar and insulin regulation, making it an important food for anyone with a blood sugar condition such as prediabetes, hypoglycemia, and type 2 diabetes.

- Pumpkin boasts the ability to block the formation of cholesterol in our cells by inhibiting an enzyme called HMG-CoA reductase. This ability, along with pumpkin's unique antioxidant and anti-inflammatory properties, makes it an important part of a heart-healthy diet.

COCONUT COCOA

MAKES 4 SERVINGS

You'd be much better off health-wise drinking a green drink than hot cocoa. But sometimes life calls for cocoa. When it does, this delicious drink is a much better option than any old dried-chocolate-and-chemical-ridden powdered mix.

1 cup canned coconut milk (do not use "lite")

2 cups almond milk or 2 cups additional coconut milk

½ to 1 teaspoon vanilla extract (or a splash of bourbon or rum, for adults)

2 tablespoons organic cocoa powder

4 ounces high-quality raw organic dark chocolate

1. Pour coconut milk, 2 cups almond milk or the additional 2 cups of coconut milk, plus vanilla extract, and cocoa powder into a medium-size pot over low heat.

2. Whisk to incorporate.

3. As the coconut milk mixture is warming, roughly chop up the dark chocolate.

4. Turn the heat up to medium-low and add the chopped dark chocolate. Whisk until melted and combined.

5. Remove from heat, and enjoy.

6. Leftovers can be stored in the fridge and warmed over low heat.

COOLERS

COCONUT COOLER

MAKES 1 SERVING

Simple and refreshing—this is everything a cooler should be.

- ¼ cup coconut milk (homemade or from can, aseptic box, or refrigerated carton)
- ¼ cup lime juice
- 1 or 2 coconut water ice cubes or regular ice cubes
- ½ cup sparkling water

1. In a cocktail shaker, Mason jar, or other type of container with a lid, shake coconut milk and lime juice until well combined.

2. Place ice cubes in a glass and pour in coconut milk–lime juice mixture.

3. Top off glass with sparkling water.

HONEYDEW-COCONUT WATER

MAKES ABOUT 2 SERVINGS

I adore the soft, sweet, honeysuckle flavor of honeydew. Pairing it with refreshing coconut water makes for a cooling summer drink.

Coconut Simple Syrup:
- 1 cup water or coconut water
- ⅓ cup coconut sugar

Cooler:
- 4 cups honeydew melon, cubed (about 2 pounds whole honeydew melon)
- 1 cup coconut water
- 1 tablespoon coconut simple syrup
- 1 to 2 tablespoons fresh lime juice from 1 lime
- 4 coconut water ice cubes or regular ice cubes

1. To make the coconut simple syrup, combine water and coconut sugar in a small saucepan. Bring to boil, stirring frequently, then reduce heat and simmer for 10 minutes. Remove from heat and let cool to room temperature. Syrup keeps 2 months in a sealed container in the refrigerator.

2. Put the honeydew, coconut water, 1 tablespoon of the simple syrup, and lime juice in a blender and pulse a few times until melon is just broken down into a puree.

3. Add the ice cubes and pulse, just until ice is crushed and blended.

NOTE: To easily make ice pops, pour the mixture into ice-pop molds and freeze.

CITRUS ZINGER

MAKES 2 SERVINGS

Refreshing, with the bright tartness of lemons and oranges and the spicy kick of cayenne, this is a real pick-me-up.

> *Juice from 3 large juicy lemons*
>
> *Juice from 3 large juicy oranges (preferably juice oranges)*
>
> ½ *cup coconut water*
>
> ⅛ *teaspoon cayenne pepper*
>
> 1 *teaspoon coconut nectar*

1. Add all ingredients to a blender. Pulse until cayenne and coconut nectar are distributed.

NATURAL HARD-CORE SPORTS DRINK

MAKES 4 SERVINGS

You know all those reports that claim coconut water can be used interchangeably with electrolyte-replacing drinks, such as Gatorade? Well, it's not quite true. While coconut water is an amazingly healthful beverage—and it's great for gentle to moderate exercise (such as walking or an easy softball game)—it doesn't contain the sodium or glucose necessary to replace what's lost during a hard-core, sweaty workout. But if you're someone who loves the idea of a more natural sports drink—one without a neon blue, green, or orange color—I have good news: Coconut water can easily be mixed with a few other ingredients to make the perfect athletic drink.

> 3½ *cups coconut water (or regular water)*
>
> ½ *cup orange juice*
>
> 2½ *tablespoons coconut sugar*
>
> ¼ *teaspoon salt*
>
> ⅛ *teaspoon baking soda*

1. Place all ingredients in a blender and process until blended, or add to a covered container and shake until coconut sugar, salt, and baking soda are dissolved and blended.

2. Store leftovers in a tightly covered container in the fridge for up to a week.

SMOOTHIES & OTHER BLENDER DRINKS

ANOTHER GREEN SMOOTHIE

MAKES 2 SERVINGS

I call this "another" green smoothie because the health food world is overflowing with green drink recipes. This one is coconut-based, making it healthful and yummy. Feel free to play with the ingredients. You can replace the banana with mango, omit the fruit, use other greens instead of the spinach, and so on.

1   *medium ripe banana*

1   *cup fresh (or canned, or frozen) pineapple*

3   *large handfuls fresh spinach (washed)*

1   *cup plain coconut yogurt or coconut kefir*

6   *ounces coconut water (or regular water)*
    Optional: 1 tablespoon coconut oil

1. Place all ingredients in a blender. Process until smooth.

BREAKFAST POWER SMOOTHIE

MAKES 1 TO 2 SERVINGS

This protein-packed drink is easy for breakfast, but I like it as an afternoon pick-me-up when my energy is dragging. It's so much better for your body than a double latte and chocolate chip cookie!

1   *cup frozen strawberries (or other berries)*

1   *cup coconut water*

1   *tablespoon creamy roasted almond butter*
    Optional: 1 tablespoon coconut sugar

1   *scoop vegan protein powder of choice (such as brown rice protein powder)*

1   *tablespoon chia seeds*

3   *ice cubes*

1. Combine berries, coconut water, almond butter, and if desired, coconut sugar in a blender. Process until smooth.

2. Blend in protein powder and chia seeds.

3. Blend in ice cubes until smooth.

CANDY BAR SMOOTHIE

MAKES 2 SERVINGS

Okay, so there's not really a candy bar in this smoothie, but it sure tastes like one. Try it. Doesn't it remind you of a Mounds or Bounty bar? The difference is, this treat is actually good for you. It's filled with potassium, minerals, and antioxidants.

2   *cups coconut milk (homemade or from can, aseptic box, or refrigerated carton)*

1   *tablespoon coconut oil*

¼   *cup unsweetened shredded dried coconut*

1   *tablespoon raw cacao powder*

2   *pitted Medjool dates*

3   *to 5 ice cubes*

1. Place all of the ingredients, except the ice, in a blender and process until completely smooth.

2. Add ice cubes and pulse until the mixture is slushy or completely smooth, as desired.

CHOCO-COCO-MACADAMIA SHAKE

MAKES 2 SERVINGS

While it's true that this shake is healthy, it is a rich treat and should probably go into the dessert camp. Enjoy it as a healthful alternative to candy, ice cream, cookies, or other sugary sweets. It is filled with fiber, protein, fatty acids, phytonutrients, vitamins, and minerals—plus chocolate (in the antioxidant-rich form of cacao)!

1½ *cups coconut water or coconut milk (homemade or from can, aseptic box, or refrigerated carton)*

¼   *avocado*

1   *fresh or frozen banana*

10 *macadamia nuts*

½   *cup unsweetened shredded dried coconut*
    Dash of cinnamon

1   *or 2 teaspoons coconut sugar*

1   *or 2 tablespoons cacao powder or cacao nibs*

1   *tablespoon coconut oil*

1. Place all ingredients in a blender. Process until smooth.

COCO-DREAMSICLE SMOOTHIE

MAKES 2 SERVINGS

When I was a kid, Orange Julius drinks were hugely popular. I loved—still love—the orange-vanilla flavor. This updated version features our beloved coconut.

- 2 *oranges*
- 1 *cup unsweetened coconut milk (homemade or from can, aseptic box, or refrigerated carton)*
- 1 *teaspoon vanilla extract*
- 1 *tablespoon coconut oil*
- 3 *to 4 ice cubes*

1. Segment the oranges (this process is also referred to as "supreming"). To do this, for each orange, slice away the top and bottom. Then take a knife and, starting at the top, slice off the pith and peel. Go all the way around until all of the peel is gone. To remove the orange sections, cut in between the membranes to divide the flesh into its natural segments.

2. Put the coconut milk, orange pieces, vanilla, and coconut oil in a blender and process until smooth.

3. Add ice and pulse until almost smooth.

NUTTY ORANGE SHAKE

MAKES 2 SERVINGS

This shake is loaded with beta-carotene and fiber from carrots and papaya (or mango). The citrus juices add potassium and vitamin C, and the nuts add protein. This is a terrific way for those veggie-phobes in your life to get their produce.

- ¼ *cup chopped pistachios, almonds, or skinless hazelnuts*
- 1 *cup diced ripe papaya or mango*
- 1 *small carrot, peeled and chopped*
- ⅔ *cup freshly squeezed orange juice*
- 1 *cup coconut milk (homemade or from can, aseptic box, or refrigerated carton)*
- 1 *tablespoon lime juice*
- 2 *teaspoons coconut sugar*
- 3 *or 4 ice cubes*

1. Place all of the ingredients, except the ice, in a blender and process at high speed until completely smooth.

2. Add ice cubes and pulse until the mixture is slushy or completely smooth, as desired.

COCO-PECAN SHAKE

MAKES 2 SERVINGS

Ooo . . . this is luscious. And protein-filled. It also has plenty of fiber. And did I mention how nutty and delicious it is?

1   cup coconut water

1   cup coconut milk (homemade or from can, aseptic box, or refrigerated carton)

½   cup pecan pieces

1   tablespoon chia seeds

1   banana or small, ripe peeled pear

1   teaspoon coconut nectar

1   teaspoon pure vanilla extract
    Pinch of sea salt

1. Place all ingredients in a blender. Process until smooth.

COCO PINEAPPLE PEPITA SMOOTHIE

MAKES 2 SERVINGS

This is another wonderfully unique, healthful smoothie, packed with protein, minerals, antioxidants, omega-3 fatty acids, and all the health benefits of coconut. It truly is a meal (or, at the very least, a hearty snack) in a glass.

2   cups fresh or frozen pineapple chunks

½   cup freshly squeezed orange juice

2   tablespoons raw pepitas (green, hulled pumpkin seeds)

1   slice ginger, peeled

1   teaspoon coconut sugar

1   tablespoon fresh lime juice

1   cup coconut milk (homemade or from can, aseptic box, or refrigerated carton)

3   or 4 ice cubes

1. Place all of the ingredients, except the ice, in a blender and process at high speed until completely smooth.

2. Add ice cubes and pulse until the mixture is slushy or completely smooth, as desired.

CREAMY AVOCADO SHAKE

MAKES 2 SERVINGS

This shake is creamy and dairy-like, making it ideal for anyone who is trying to cut out dairy, but who misses the silkiness of milk.

½   avocado

½   cup coconut milk (homemade or from can, aseptic box, or refrigerated carton)

½   cup coconut water

¼   cup plain coconut yogurt or kefir

½   fresh or frozen banana

2   tablespoons coconut butter or dried unsweetened coconut

2   ice cubes

Optional: ½ teaspoon vanilla extract

1. Place all ingredients in a blender. Process until smooth.

GREEN COCONUT VANILLA NUT SMOOTHIE

MAKES 2 SERVINGS

You just can't go wrong combining macadamia nuts and coconut! This smoothie is filled with healthy fat. Plus, it's a great way to use the pulp from all those green coconuts you may be cracking open for their water!

 1 *cup coconut water*

 ½ *cup packed young coconut pulp (or ¼ cup unsweetened shredded dried coconut)*

 ⅓ *cup macadamia nuts*

 ½ *teaspoon pure vanilla extract*

 ½ *tablespoon coconut nectar*

1. Place all ingredients in a blender and process until smooth and creamy.

KEY LIME–COCONUT FRAPPE

MAKES 2 SERVINGS

All three of my sons and I have January birthdays. Because we each enjoy key lime pie on our special days, January is dubbed "Lime Pie Month" in our household. Is it any wonder that this is one of our favorite blender drinks?

 1 *cup coconut milk (homemade or from can, aseptic box, or refrigerated carton)*

 ¼ *teaspoon grated lime rind*
     Juice from 1 lime or two key limes

 1 *tablespoon coconut nectar or sugar*

 1 *tablespoon coconut oil*

 ¼ *cup unsweetened shredded dried coconut*

 3 *ice cubes*

1. Place first 6 ingredients in a blender; process until smooth.

2. Add ice cubes and pulse until smooth.

OUTRAGEOUS MORNING SMOOTHIE

MAKES 2 SERVINGS

This superfood-packed smoothie is a great way to give your body a lot of good stuff at once. Have one of these for breakfast and you'll be able to work well past lunchtime without snacking! You'll need a powerful blender for this one.

1   *large handful roughly chopped kale, spinach, or collards, or a combination of these greens*

1   *cup frozen mango chunks*

1   *cup coconut water*

2   *tablespoons almond butter*

1   *tablespoon chia seeds*

   Optional: squirt of lemon or lime

1. Place all ingredients in a blender and process until completely uniform in color and all the bits of green are pulverized. Serve immediately.

TROPICAL FRUIT SLUSHY

MAKES 2 SERVINGS

I prefer this tangy smoothie as an afternoon treat or even a dessert. Once you've tried it, it will become a favorite!

1   *cup fresh or frozen pineapple chunks (or a combination of pineapple and mango chunks)*

1   *cup coconut milk (homemade or from can, aseptic box, or refrigerated carton)*

1   *teaspoon finely chopped ginger*

3   *or 4 ice cubes*

1. Place the first 3 ingredients in a blender and process until smooth.

2. Add ice cubes and blend on high speed until slushy.

CHAPTER 4

BREAKFAST: START YOUR DAY WITH COCONUT

Coconut is a natural breakfast food. It marries so well—in all of its forms—with so many of the foods typically enjoyed in the morning. Plus, it provides a range of nutrients that help start the day powerfully. The antioxidant levels in coconut help slow or stop damage to healthy tissues, as well as strengthen the immune system. Coconut also has protein for sustained energy, fiber for a feeling of fullness and steady blood sugar levels, and healthy fats to keep your brain running efficiently and your heart healthy. In this chapter, I share some of my favorite ways to enjoy coconut for breakfast. If you want to start your day off even more healthily, enjoy a green drink with breakfast, as I do. (Check out Chapter 3 for great coconut-based beverages.)

CEREAL HOT & COLD

COCONUT PORRIDGE

MAKES 1 SERVING

Based on coconut, high-protein nuts, and chia, this porridge is a favorite of Paleo eaters, who appreciate its omega-3 fatty acids, fiber, and other nutrients. You can dress up this cereal—hot or cold—with chopped nuts, seeds, or fruit. If you want a thicker porridge, just add a little more chia.

²/₃ *cup coconut milk (homemade or from can, aseptic box, or refrigerated carton)*

1 *tablespoon chia seeds*

¼ *cup unsweetened shredded dried coconut*

   Pinch of salt

2 *tablespoons almond meal (or ground cashews, walnuts, pecans, or other nuts)*

1 *tablespoon coconut sugar or nectar, or to taste*

   Optional: splash of vanilla or almond extract

1. In a small saucepan, over medium-low heat, add milk and whisk in chia seeds. Cook for 1 or 2 minutes.

2. Whisk in remaining ingredients and turn heat to medium-high. Cook until porridge reaches desired thickness.

OPPOSITE: **Coconut Granola, page 244**

COCONUT GRANOLA

MAKES 5 CUPS

Coconut granola is not super sweet, but it is dense in protein, fiber, omega-3 fatty acids, heart-and-brain-healthy fats, and antioxidants, making it a great way to start the day, especially if you enjoy it with fresh fruit. Berries are particularly nice—and don't forget the coconut yogurt if you want to make a pretty breakfast parfait that tastes like dessert.

NOTE: A serving is about ⅓ cup, although most people (including me) tend to eat much more at one sitting.

> *Coconut oil for greasing the pan*

¼ *cup nut butter (almond, peanut, cashew, sunflower, or other nut)*

⅓ *cup coconut oil, melted*

⅓ *to ½ cup coconut sugar*

½ *teaspoon salt*

½ *teaspoon cinnamon*

2½ *cups old-fashioned or steel-cut oats*

1½ *cups quinoa flakes (or an additional cup of oats)*

1 *cup unsweetened shredded dried coconut*

¼ *cup chia seeds*

1 *cup almonds, or other nuts, chopped*

1 *cup sunflower seeds (or other nuts or seeds, chopped)*

1. Preheat oven to 300°F.

2. Lightly grease 2 or 3 baking sheets with a very small amount of coconut oil.

3. In a large saucepan over medium heat, whisk together the nut butter, coconut oil, coconut sugar, salt, and cinnamon until mixture is combined and smooth.

4. Turn off heat and stir in oats, quinoa flakes, shredded coconut, and chia seeds, completely coating oats in the nut butter–coconut oil mixture.

5. Stir in almonds and sunflower seeds until coated.

6. Scrape mixture onto cookie sheets in a thin, single layer, being careful not to crowd granola on top of each other. (Note: If you like chunky granola like I do, pinch pieces together into chunks.)

7. Place baking sheet on middle shelf of oven and bake for 10 minutes.

8. Stir and bake for another 8 to 10 minutes until granola is golden brown. Do not overbake granola—it will continue to cook after you remove it from the oven, so you want it to be a bit sticky when you take it out.

9. Allow granola to completely cool and firm up (about an hour) before eating or storing in airtight canisters in a cool, dry place.

10. For a pretty presentation, serve the granola layered with coconut yogurt and fresh berries.

BAKED BANANA OATMEAL

MAKES 4 SERVINGS

Baked oatmeal is a fun make-ahead dish for brunch and great for feeding a crowd (go ahead and double the recipe, if you're so inclined). This version is especially delicious and especially nutritious, thanks to the vitamins from the fruit, protein from the walnuts, and all the goodies that coconut provides. But feel free to play: Use a different nut. Experiment with different fruit. Throw in a handful of raisins. Add more sweetener. Try almond extract in place of the vanilla. You get the picture.

Coconut oil for greasing the pan

2   *cups chopped fresh fruit of choice (such as bananas, apples, or peaches)*

2   *cups old-fashioned or steel-cut oats (not instant)*

1   *teaspoon cinnamon*

¹⁄₂   *teaspoon allspice*

¹⁄₂   *teaspoon salt*

1   *teaspoon baking powder*

¹⁄₂   *cup chopped walnuts*

1   *egg*

2   *cups coconut milk (homemade or from can, aseptic box, or refrigerated carton)*

¹⁄₄   *cup coconut nectar*

1   *teaspoon vanilla*

2   *tablespoons unsweetened shredded dried coconut*

1. Preheat oven to 375°F.

2. Grease an 8-by-8-inch baking dish with coconut oil.

3. Evenly layer the bottom of the baking dish with fruit.

4. In a medium bowl, whisk together oats with cinnamon, allspice, salt, baking powder, and chopped walnuts.

5. In a separate bowl, whisk together the egg, coconut milk, coconut nectar, and vanilla.

6. Spoon oat mixture over the fruit.

7. Carefully pour the liquid mixture over the oats. Gently tilt the pan to ensure liquid evenly covers dry ingredients.

8. Scatter shredded coconut across the top.

9. Bake for 40 minutes or until the top is golden and the oatmeal is firm to the touch.

10. Allow to cool slightly before slicing.

CREAMY MILLET PORRIDGE

MAKES 2 SERVINGS

I love millet, a seed that is high in minerals, fiber, protein, and antioxidants. This recipe is a fun, different take on hot cereal, with millet playing the leading role.

⅔ cup uncooked millet

1 tablespoon unrefined coconut oil

1 ½ cups unsweetened coconut milk (homemade or from can, aseptic box, or refrigerated carton)

1 cup coconut water or plain water, preferably at room temperature

½ cup chopped nuts or sunflower seeds

Sweetener of choice

1. Place millet in a food processor, blender, or even a clean coffee grinder and pulse 2 or 3 times until the millet is coarsely ground. Don't overdo this—you don't want flour!

2. Warm coconut oil in a small saucepan over medium heat.

3. Add pulsed millet to the saucepan and sauté for 2 to 4 minutes, or until lightly toasted.

4. Slowly add coconut milk and water, and stir.

5. Bring millet to a gentle simmer and, stirring occasionally, cook until mixture is porridge-like.

6. Ladle into serving bowls and top with chopped nuts and sweetener.

EASY "COCONUTTY" PORRIDGE

Do you want to know the easiest way to add coconut to your hot cereal? Simply replace water with an equal measure of coconut milk or coconut water, and substitute butter or the oil you usually use with coconut oil or coconut butter. If you use sweetener, switch to coconut sugar or nectar. And for a fun texture, add a flurry of shredded coconut. Easy-peasy!

TOASTED COCONUT AMARANTH PORRIDGE

MAKES 2 SERVINGS

Are you familiar with amaranth? It's a Mexican seed that contains 26 g of protein and 13 g of fiber per cup! The same amount also provides large percentages of the daily recommended allowances of magnesium (119 percent), iron (81 percent), vitamin B6 (55 percent), and calcium (30 percent). There is a downside to amaranth, though: It is slightly bitter—but can easily be made tasty with a little coconut! This recipe passes the picky kid test with flying colors.

1 ½ cups water

½ cup uncooked amaranth

Pinch of salt

1 teaspoon coconut oil

½ cup coconut milk (homemade or from can, aseptic box, or refrigerated carton)

¼ cup unsweetened shredded dried coconut

¼ cup chopped walnuts, pecans, or almonds

   Optional: coconut sugar, coconut nectar, or
   other sweetener, to taste

1. In a small saucepan with a tight-fitting lid, bring water to a boil. Add the amaranth and salt, reduce heat, and cover, simmering for 20 minutes, or until the water is absorbed.

2. Remove from heat and stir in the coconut oil, coconut milk, shredded coconut and chopped nuts.

3. Serve immediately with optional sweetener.

BERRY GOOD!
RED BERRY SAUCE

MAKES ABOUT 1 CUP

Looking for something yummy to spoon on your oatmeal, pancakes, or anything else? Enjoy this fresh-tasting recipe for homemade sauce.

1½ cups frozen strawberries,
   raspberries, or a mix

3   tablespoons coconut nectar

   Squirt of lemon or lime juice

1½ tablespoons chia seeds

1. In a medium saucepan over medium heat, combine the frozen berries and coconut nectar. Cover and simmer, stirring frequently.

2. Cook about 5 minutes, or until berries are soft and beginning to break down.

3. Remove from heat and add lemon juice.

4. Lightly mash the berries with a fork or potato masher to desired chunkiness.

5. Stir in chia seeds and transfer mixture to an airtight container. Allow to firm up in refrigerator 3 hours or overnight before using.

DECADENT BREAKFAST QUINOA

MAKES 2 SERVINGS

Oh, quinoa! How I do love thee! I love your 24 g of protein and 12 g of fiber per cup. I love your high mineral content. I love that you contain nine of the essential amino acids (which cannot be made by the body and therefore must come from food), thereby making you a complete protein. I love your delicate crunch and your versatility and how energized I feel after I eat you. And I love you in this yummy breakfast recipe. Yes I do.

Coconut oil for greasing pan

- ½ cup water
- ½ cup canned coconut milk
- 2 tablespoons sweet potato or pumpkin puree
- ¼ cup uncooked quinoa
- 1 tablespoon coconut nectar or maple syrup
- 2 teaspoons coconut oil
- ¼ teaspoon vanilla extract
- ½ teaspoon ground cinnamon
- ¼ teaspoon ground ginger
- ¼ teaspoon allspice
- 1 tablespoon coconut oil, melted
- 1 tablespoon maple syrup
- 1½ tablespoons finely ground almond flour
- ¼ cup pecans, chopped

WHY QUINOA NEEDS TO BE RINSED BEFORE COOKING

Rinsing removes saponin, which is quinoa's natural coating. This coating can have a bitter or soapy taste. The easiest way to remove it is to dump the uncooked quinoa into a fine-mesh strainer and let cold water run over it for a minute or two. Allow the grain to drip-dry and continue with your recipe. If you don't have a fine-mesh strainer, try the following: Place uncooked quinoa in the bottom of a large mixing bowl, cover it with cold water—by an inch or two—and then give the mix a vigorous stir. Allow the bowl of quinoa and water to sit untouched while you do the laundry, make phone calls, or help a kid with his or her piano practice or homework (maybe about 10 minutes or more, if you'd like). Then come back, pour off the water, dump the soggy quinoa into a skillet, and let the excess water cook off over low heat. Then continue with the recipe.

1. Preheat oven to 350°F.

2. Lightly grease a small (4-cup) casserole dish or baking dish.

3. In a small bowl, whisk together water, coconut milk, pumpkin, quinoa, maple syrup, 2 teaspoons coconut oil, vanilla, cinnamon, ginger, and allspice, until thoroughly combined. Pour into prepared dish.

4. Cover with foil or lid and bake for 45 minutes.

5. While the quinoa bakes, make topping: Add the melted coconut oil, maple syrup, almond flour, and pecans to a bowl. Stir to combine.

6. Remove baked quinoa from oven, take off cover, sprinkle with topping, and return to oven, uncovered, to bake for another 10 minutes, or until browned.

7. Allow to cool slightly before serving.

FROM THE GRIDDLE

COCONUT FLOUR PANCAKES

MAKES 2 SERVINGS

This no-grain pancake is a Paleo favorite. You won't feel sluggish or bloated after eating these beauties! These protein-rich pancakes make for a fun weekend breakfast when paired with veggie juice and maybe a salad or some fruit.

- 4   *eggs*
- 1   *cup coconut milk (homemade or from can, aseptic box, or refrigerated carton)*
- 1   *tablespoon coconut water or plain water (more if batter looks too thick)*
- 1   *teaspoon vanilla extract*
- 1   *tablespoon coconut nectar*
- ½   *cup coconut flour*
- 1   *teaspoon baking soda*
- ¼   *teaspoon salt*
- 2   *tablespoons unsweetened shredded dried coconut*
- 1   *or 2 teaspoons coconut oil for the skillet*

1. In a small bowl, beat eggs until frothy.

2. Mix in coconut milk, water, vanilla, and coconut nectar. Set aside.

3. In a large bowl, whisk together coconut flour, baking soda, and salt until thoroughly combined and no lumps remain. Stir in shredded coconut.

4. Add egg–coconut milk mixture to dry ingredients and stir until well blended.

5. Add a teaspoon of coconut oil to a skillet over medium heat. Ladle in about 2 tablespoons of batter per pancake, spreading a bit with the back of a spoon if necessary.

6. Cook 2 or 3 minutes on each side, or until pancake begins to brown.

7. Serve immediately with your favorite toppings.

COCONUT WAFFLES

MAKES 3 SERVINGS

These showcase coconut in four forms to help improve the health of your brain, heart, and immune system.

⅓ cup sweetened or unsweetened dried shredded coconut

4 tablespoons coconut oil

6 large eggs

3 tablespoons coconut nectar

1 teaspoon vanilla extract

2 tablespoons pumpkin, sweet potato, banana, apple, or pear puree

⅓ cup coconut flour

¼ teaspoon salt

½ teaspoon cinnamon

½ teaspoon baking soda

1. Place a rack in the center of the oven and preheat to 350°F.

2. Place coconut on a baking sheet and toast in the oven for about 4 minutes. Keep an eye on the coconut, as it browns and burns quickly.

3. Remove toasted coconut from the oven and set aside.

4. In a medium bowl, whisk together coconut oil, eggs, coconut nectar, vanilla extract, and the puree. Whisk until well incorporated.

5. In a small bowl, whisk together the coconut flour, salt, cinnamon, and baking soda. Continue whisking until all lumps are gone.

6. Whisk the dry ingredients from the small bowl into the wet ingredients.

7. Stir in the toasted, shredded coconut. Allow mixture to sit for 5 minutes while you plug in and preheat the waffle iron.

8. Bake waffles according to the manufacturer's directions for using your waffle iron.

9. To keep finished waffles from getting cold, cover and keep them in a warm oven until serving time.

10. Freeze leftovers and reheat them in a toaster.

TROPICAL TOPPER

PINEAPPLE COCONUT SYRUP

MAKES 3½ CUPS

1 cup coconut water or plain water
½ cup coconut sugar
3 cups chopped fresh or frozen pineapple
Squirt of lemon or lime juice

1. Whisk together the first 3 ingredients in a saucepan over medium heat.

2. Bring to a boil. Let boil for 5 to 7 minutes until liquid has been reduced and pineapple is soft.

3. Puree ingredients with a squirt of lemon juice in a blender until smooth.

4. Use immediately or let the syrup cool and then store in an airtight container in the refrigerator.

COCONUT SYRUP

MAKES 1½ CUPS

1 15-ounce can coconut milk
½ cup coconut sugar
Dash of vanilla or almond extract or lemon juice

1. Whisk together all ingredients in a saucepan over medium heat.

2. Cook, stirring constantly, just until mixture comes to a boil.

3. Quickly reduce the heat to medium and let simmer for 15 to 20 minutes until mixture thickens into a syrup, being very, very careful not to let it cook at a full boil.

4. Use immediately or let the syrup cool and then store in an airtight container in the refrigerator.

COCONUT FRENCH TOAST

MAKES 6 SERVINGS

The nutritionist in me encourages you to pair this sweet, rich dish with a green drink and maybe a side of protein.

- *4 large eggs*
- *2 tablespoons coconut nectar*
- *½ cup coconut milk (homemade or from can, aseptic box, or refrigerated carton)*
- *¼ cup orange juice*
- *4 to 6 slices whole grain, gluten-free, spelt, or wheat bread*
- *1 to 2 tablespoons coconut oil*
- *Optional toppings, including coconut nectar, applesauce, maple syrup, fruit, nut butter, etc.*

1. Whisk together the eggs, coconut nectar, coconut milk, and orange juice in a shallow pan or baking dish until well blended.

2. Add the bread slices and let them soak in the mixture for 1 minute on each side, or until bread is saturated.

3. Heat coconut oil in one or two griddles or frying pans over medium heat.

4. Add bread slices, cooking for 2 or 3 minutes per side, or until golden and crispy.

5. Serve with optional toppings, as desired.

EGGS

QUICHE

MAKES 6 SERVINGS

Quiche is a fantastic make-ahead, feed-a-crowd dish for breakfast, brunch, lunch, or even dinner. Instead of all the fatty, artery-clogging heavy cream and cheese so many quiches contain, this one relies on coconut for its rich, creamy texture. This is yet another recipe you can play with and customize to suit your own taste. Please experiment with the veggies, herbs, spices, and even the crust (or be bold and try it without the crust!).

- *1 cup canned coconut milk (do not use "lite")*
- *4 large eggs*
- *1 teaspoon dry mustard powder*
- *1 tablespoon liquid coconut oil*
- *3 cups chopped vegetables (leeks, sweet bell peppers, zucchini, asparagus, mushrooms, broccoli, spinach, kale, etc.)*
- *¼ teaspoon salt*
- *¼ teaspoon pepper*
- *1 8- or 9-inch whole grain, regular, or gluten-free piecrust, unbaked and in a pie pan*
- *1 tablespoon minced chives, tarragon, minced green onion tops, or parsley*

1. Preheat oven to 350°F.

2. Whisk together coconut milk, eggs, and mustard powder. Set aside.

3. Add coconut oil to a large skillet. Sauté vegetables over medium heat until just softened, about 3 to 5 minutes. (Or simply open the fridge and pull out 3 cups of cooked veggies from last night's dinner.) Season with salt and pepper.

4. Put sautéed vegetables into unbaked piecrust. Add egg mixture and sprinkle with chives and tarragon.

5. Bake quiche for 45 minutes or until done. A knife inserted in center of filling should come out clean.

FRITTATA

MAKES 4 SERVINGS

Frittatas are a great make-ahead option for egg lovers who want an easy way to sneak more veggies into their diet. Play around with this recipe—try spinach or another green instead of the kale, or throw in a sautéed zucchini or last night's chopped vegetables. Use a shallot instead of the onion. But keep the coconut! You want all of its heart-healthy and brain-boosting benefits!

8 *large eggs*

½ *cup canned coconut milk*

  Salt and pepper, to taste

1 *tablespoon coconut oil*

⅓ *cup chopped onion*

½ *cup chopped red pepper*

2 *cups chopped baby kale*

1. Preheat oven to 350°F.

2. In a medium bowl, whisk together the eggs and coconut milk. Add salt and pepper. Set aside.

3. In a medium-size ovenproof skillet, heat coconut oil over medium heat. Add onion and red pepper and sauté for 3 minutes, until onion is translucent.

4. Add kale and cook until it wilts, about 3 minutes.

5. Add eggs to vegetables in the skillet. Cook for about 4 minutes until the bottom and edges of the frittata start to set.

6. Put frittata in the oven and cook for about 10 minutes, until the frittata is cooked all the way through.

7. Slice and serve.

OMELET

MAKES 1 OR 2 SERVINGS

From a health standpoint, omelets are a great way to gussy up any blend of veggies—just use them as a filling! Here, coconut lends healthful lauric acid and medium chain fatty acids to the mix. You provide the herbs and veggies.

- 3 large eggs
- ⅔ cup canned coconut milk
- ¼ cup chopped cooked vegetables of choice (this is a great way to deliciously use up last night's leftover veggie sauté)
- 1 to 3 tablespoons herbs of choice

  Optional: ½ tablespoon unsweetened shredded dried coconut

  Salt and pepper, to taste
- 2 teaspoons coconut oil

1. Whisk eggs together in a bowl and add coconut milk, veggies, herbs, optional shredded coconut, salt, and black pepper.

2. Warm coconut oil in small skillet over medium heat. When warm, pour in egg mixture and swirl to coat the bottom of the pan. Stir once or twice and then stop! You want to allow the omelet to set.

3. Flip after cooking omelet 2 to 3 minutes and cook for another minute or two until eggs are cooked all the way through.

SUPER EASY BREAKFAST CASSEROLE

MAKES 8 SERVINGS

This easy make-ahead meal is a great way to slip a bit of coconut into your day, so think about it for your next brunch. I wouldn't make it your entire meal, though—I suggest adding a green salad or a veggie juice.

- 1 tablespoon liquid coconut oil
- 10 slices of whole grain bread (regular or gluten-free) or leftover rolls
- 1 cup chopped banana, apple, pear, berries, or other fruit
- ¼ cup unsweetened shredded dried coconut
- 3 cups coconut milk (homemade or from can, aseptic box, or refrigerated carton)
- 7 eggs
- 1 to 2 teaspoons vanilla

1. Preheat oven to 350°F.

2. Lightly grease a 9-by-13-inch baking dish with a bit of the coconut oil and set aside the remaining oil to use in the recipe.

3. Tear the bread into bite-size pieces and arrange evenly in the bottom of the baking dish.

4. Scatter the fruit, distributing it evenly over the bread.

5. Sprinkle the shredded coconut, distributing it evenly, over the fruit.

6. In a medium bowl, whisk together the coconut milk, eggs, vanilla, and reserved coconut oil until thoroughly combined. Pour the milk mixture over the ingredients in the baking dish, covering all pieces.

7. Bake for 35 to 40 minutes, keeping an eye on the top of the casserole. Cover it with foil if it starts to burn.

8. Remove casserole from oven when puffy and firm.

9. Allow to cool for 15 minutes before serving.

BREAKFAST BAKED GOODS

OATMEAL BANANA BREAKFAST BARS

MAKES 9 BARS

If you love bars, do something nice for yourself and your family: Make your own. This coconut-rich version is a great starter recipe.

  Coconut oil for greasing the pan
2 cups old-fashioned oats (or 1 cup oats and 1 cup flaked quinoa)
1 cup unsweetened shredded dried coconut
¼ cup chia seeds
½ cup chopped walnuts, pecans, almonds, or other nuts
½ cup finely chopped dried fruit (apricots, peaches, tart cherries, etc.)
½ cup sunflower seeds
½ teaspoon salt
¾ cup mashed banana (or very thick applesauce or pear sauce)
1 egg
½ cup coconut sugar
3 tablespoons liquid coconut oil
  Splash of vanilla or almond extract

1. Preheat oven to 375°F.

2. Grease an 8-inch square baking pan.

3. In a large bowl, stir together oats, shredded coconut, chia, walnuts, dried fruit, sunflower seeds, and salt. Set aside.

4. In a medium bowl, mix together mashed banana, egg, coconut sugar, coconut oil, and either vanilla or almond extract until smooth and thoroughly combined.

5. Add banana mixture to oats and stir until evenly incorporated.

6. Scrape mixture into prepared pan and smooth the surface.

7. Bake until bars are golden brown, about 25 minutes.

8. Allow to cool before cutting into 9 bars.

SIMPLE COCONUT FLOUR MUFFINS

MAKES ABOUT 12 STANDARD MUFFINS OR 24 MINI MUFFINS

This is a grain-free muffin recipe. It is an awesome way to pack protein, fiber, and the healing benefits of coconut into a tasty package. That said, baking with coconut flour is a bit different than baking with wheat-based flour or even a gluten-free all-purpose flour. For one thing, coconut flour typically needs a lot of eggs to create the finished product, which might be a little denser than you're used to. But this recipe yields a delicious muffin—and it's versatile, too: Feel free to experiment with the sweetener, add different nuts or seeds (even a tablespoon of chia!), or introduce a ½ cup of dried fruit or chopped fresh fruit and whatever spices you'd like. Balance this with some veggie juice and a side of protein and your day is off to a great start!

¾ cup coconut flour

   Optional: ¼ cup unsweetened shredded dried coconut

½ teaspoon baking soda

   Large pinch of salt

6 eggs

½ cup liquid coconut oil

½ cup coconut nectar

½ to 1 teaspoon vanilla or almond extract, or a dash of cinnamon

1. Preheat oven to 350°F.

2. In a small bowl, whisk together coconut flour, optional shredded coconut, baking soda, and salt. Set aside.

3. In a medium bowl, whisk together eggs, coconut oil, coconut nectar, and vanilla.

4. Add liquid ingredients to the dry ingredients and mix until thoroughly combined. Allow batter to sit for 5 minutes (this allows the coconut flour and shredded coconut to absorb the liquid fully) while you prepare the muffin tins.

5. Prepare 12 standard or 24 mini-muffin cups by lightly greasing with coconut oil or lining with paper muffin liners.

6. Scrape batter into prepared muffin pan, filling each cup about ⅔ of the way.

7. Bake for about 25 minutes, or until muffins become golden and are firm to the touch.

8. Allow muffins to cool for 15 minutes before removing from them from pan.

BRUNCH CAKE

SERVES 12

Try as I might, I can't condone eating cake for breakfast—at least not on a regular basis. So for my family, this is a special-occasion breakfast food (think Christmas, New Year's, etc.). And it's always balanced with veggie juice, protein, and maybe a fruit salad for the kids and a green "brunch salad" for the adults. But as far as breakfast cakes go, this is pretty healthy.

NOTE: If you're gluten-free, use an all-purpose gluten-free flour blend instead of whole wheat pastry flour.

Streusel

2 tablespoons whole wheat pastry flour

½ cup unsweetened shredded dried coconut

¼ cup coconut sugar processed in a coffee grinder or food processor to make it fine

2 tablespoons solid (or semisolid) coconut oil

½ teaspoon ground cinnamon

¼ teaspoon ground cardamom

¼ teaspoon ground ginger

Cake

Coconut oil for greasing the pan

2 cups whole wheat pastry flour

¼ cup coconut sugar, processed in a coffee grinder or food processor to make it fine

2 teaspoons baking powder

½ teaspoon baking soda

¼ teaspoon salt

Optional: pinch of cinnamon, cardamom, and/or ginger

1 cup canned coconut milk (not "lite")

1 teaspoon vanilla extract or almond extract

2 eggs

2 cups fresh or frozen berries or chopped fruit, divided

½ cup sliced almonds or another sliced or chopped nut

1. Preheat oven to 350°F.

2. Lightly grease a 9-inch round cake pan with coconut oil. Set aside.

3. Make streusel: Put 2 tablespoons whole wheat pastry flour, shredded coconut, ¼ cup coconut sugar, solid coconut oil, cinnamon, cardamom, and ginger in a medium bowl and cut together with a fork until well combined and mixture is in large clumps. Set streusel aside.

4. Make cake: Whisk together 2 cups whole wheat pastry flour, ¼ cup coconut sugar, baking powder, baking soda, salt, and optional spices in a large bowl until thoroughly combined. Set aside.

5. In a medium bowl, whisk together coconut milk, vanilla, and eggs, then pour into bowl with dry ingredients and stir until combined. Gently fold in 1 cup of the fruit.

6. Spoon batter into prepared pan. Sprinkle streusel over the top.

7. Scatter the remaining 1 cup of fruit over the streusel and top with the almonds.

8. Bake until a toothpick inserted in center of cake comes out clean, 30 to 40 minutes.

9. Allow cake to cool before removing from pan and transferring to a plate.

CHAPTER 5

COCONUT FOR LUNCH

I believe lunch is essential to a productive, happy afternoon. Your body needs the fuel a midday meal provides to keep you sharp, efficient, and feeling great all day and into the night. And yet, so often, we choose lunch foods not for their health benefits but for their convenience. Here's a fact: What you eat at lunch plays an important role in staying healthy, so let's get used to looking at lunch as a time to replenish nutrient stores and do something to help yourself look and feel great. Fortunately, you can have good nutrition without much fuss. It just takes a bit of planning and a few easy, delicious, nourishing recipes, like the ones in this chapter. This is where I share some of my favorite midday ways to enjoy coconut, with an emphasis on portable, easy-pack foods for those of you who take your lunch to work or school.

CHILIES, SOUPS, AND STEWS

SPICED POTAGE

MAKES 6 SERVINGS

I love lentils because they contain potassium, calcium, zinc, niacin, and vitamin K—along with exceptionally large amounts of dietary fiber, lean protein, folate, and iron. Together, all of these help keep your energy high and your body's systems working at their best. Add coconut's brain-boosting lauric acid, nutritious veggies, and immune-system-strengthening spices, and wow, you have a great lunchtime dish. Love veggies? Add the leftovers from last night's dinner. You could even reduce the liquid in this recipe to only 3 cups, and make a delicious bean salad to enjoy either all on its own or as a topping for grains and greens.

- 2 tablespoons liquid coconut oil
- 1 medium yellow onion, chopped (1½ cups)
- 1 celery stalk, chopped
- 1 medium carrot, peeled and chopped
- 1 garlic clove, minced
- ½ teaspoon ground ginger
- ½ teaspoon ground turmeric
- ¼ teaspoon ground allspice
- 3 tablespoons tomato paste
- 5 cups vegetable or chicken broth or water, or a mixture

OPPOSITE: **Roasted Sweet Potato, Quinoa, and Arugula Salad, page 269**

1   cup dried French green lentils or regular brown lentils

   Pinch of salt

3   teaspoons lime juice

   Optional: pepper and additional salt, to taste

1. In a large sauté pan over medium heat, warm coconut oil. Add onion, celery, and carrot and sauté until softened, about 7 or 8 minutes.

2. Stir in garlic, and cook another minute.

3. Stir in ginger, turmeric, and allspice, and sauté 30 seconds.

4. Stir in tomato paste and sauté 30 seconds. Add 1 cup of the broth to pan, and scrape up any caramelized vegetables.

5. Add lentils and 4 cups of broth. Bring to a boil, then reduce heat to medium-low and cover.

6. Simmer 30 minutes.

7. Add pinch of salt and simmer uncovered for 10 additional minutes, or until lentils are tender (but not mushy!).

8. Stir in lime juice, and season with salt and pepper, if desired.

RED LENTIL CURRY STEW

MAKES 4 SERVINGS

The spices used in curries contain polyphenols that can help protect the body against cancer, diabetes, and heart disease, as well as help reduce blood glucose levels.

2   tablespoons liquid coconut oil

2   garlic cloves, minced

1   tablespoon minced fresh ginger

2   teaspoons mild Madras curry powder (use more if desired)

1   teaspoon ground turmeric

2   cups canned coconut milk

2   cups vegetable or chicken broth or water (or more if you want a thin soup)

1½ cups dried red lentils

2   cups frozen green peas or frozen mixed vegetables (use small-size veggies)

½   cup chopped cashews

¼   cup unsweetened shredded dried coconut

   Salt and pepper, to taste

1   tablespoon cilantro, chopped

1. Heat oil in large skillet over medium heat, and sauté garlic and ginger about 30 seconds, or until fragrant.

2. Stir in curry powder and turmeric and sauté for another 30 seconds.

3. Add coconut milk, broth (or water), and red lentils. Reduce heat to medium-low, and cook 15 minutes more, or until lentils are softened.

4. Stir in frozen peas, cashews, and coconut, and cook 3 more minutes.

5. Remove from heat. Stir in salt, pepper, and cilantro, and serve.

COCOA CHILI

MAKES 8 SERVINGS

I just love chili. Any kind. Not being a native Texan, I don't need to worry about the bean vs. no-bean, meat vs. vegetarian, red vs. white vs. green arguments that seem to arise when people talk about chili. I can just enjoy whatever is put in front of me. I especially like this recipe, which has a slightly smoky taste, thanks to the cocoa and allspice. It features a trio of pinto, kidney, and black beans, all rich in protein and fiber. But feel free to use the same measure of just one of these beans, or try another bean altogether. This chili is nothing if not flexible.

- 1 tablespoon liquid coconut oil
- 2 cups diced onion
- 1 cup celery, diced
- ½ cup diced jicama or chayote
- ½ cup red, orange, or yellow bell peppers, diced
- 6 medium garlic cloves, minced
- ½ teaspoon salt
  Freshly ground black pepper, to taste
- 2 tablespoons mild chili powder blend
- ½ teaspoon cinnamon
- ⅛ teaspoon allspice
- 3 tablespoons Dutch-processed cocoa powder
- 2 28-ounce cans diced tomatoes with liquid
- 1 14-ounce can black beans, rinsed and drained
- 1 14-ounce can kidney beans, rinsed and drained
- 1 14-ounce can pinto beans, rinsed and drained
- 1 14-ounce can coconut milk
- ½ cup unsweetened shredded dried coconut
- 1 cup frozen corn kernels

1. In a large soup pot over medium heat, add coconut oil, onion, celery, jicama or chayote, bell pepper, garlic, salt, pepper, chili powder, cinnamon, and allspice and stir to combine. Cover and cook until onions start to soften, about 7 to 9 minutes, stirring occasionally.

2. Add cocoa and stir for 1 to 2 minutes.

3. Add tomatoes, beans, coconut milk, and shredded coconut, and stir to combine. Increase heat to bring to a boil. Once boiling, reduce heat to low and cover, simmering for 20 to 25 minutes, stirring occasionally.

4. Stir in corn kernels, and cook another 5 minutes to heat through.

COCONUT CHICKEN CHILI

MAKES 4 SERVINGS

Okay, so this chili is completely untraditional. It's white. It's made with chicken. And it contains coconut, ginger, nut butter, and basil. It is delicious, filling, and loaded with protein, fiber, and nutrients that support your brain health and immune system. It also gives you a steady drip of energy so that you can make it through the day beautifully. I think you'll like it!

1   *tablespoon liquid coconut oil*

12 *ounces skinless, boneless chicken breast halves, chopped*

1   *large onion, chopped*

1½ *teaspoons chili powder*

1½ *teaspoons ground ginger*

½   *teaspoon salt*

½   *teaspoon black pepper*

¼   *teaspoon ground cayenne pepper*

1   *tablespoon coconut flour*

1   *14-ounce can coconut milk*

1   *tablespoon peanut butter or other nut butter*

1   *cup water or broth*

1   *15-ounce can cannellini beans, rinsed and drained*

3   *medium carrots, shredded*

1   *stalk celery, sliced*

1   *medium green onion, sliced*

5   *garlic cloves, minced*

2   *tablespoons chopped fresh basil*

1. Heat coconut oil in large saucepan over medium heat. Add chicken, onion, chili powder, ginger, salt, black pepper, and cayenne pepper and cook 6 to 8 minutes or until chicken is no longer pink.

2. Stir in coconut flour and cook 1 more minute.

3. Stir in coconut milk, peanut butter, and water. Bring to a boil, stirring occasionally.

4. Stir in beans, carrots, celery, green onion, garlic, and basil. Return to boiling; reduce heat. Simmer, covered, 10 minutes.

GINGER MILLET WITH VEGGIES

MAKES 4 SERVINGS

Millet is another one of my favorites. This ancient grain nourished centuries of Africans, Asians, and Europeans. Today, most people know it best as a component of birdseed. Fortunately, a growing number of healthy eaters are falling in love with this superfood, both for its nutty flavor and its impressive nutritional profile. Millet boasts protein and fiber, as well as large amounts of magnesium, iron, calcium, phosphorus, and potassium. It contains B-complex vitamins, vitamin E, and amino acids. In this recipe, it's complemented by our superfood friend, coconut, the powerful cruciferous superstar, cabbage, beans, and sunflower seeds.

1   *cup millet*

2   *to 3 tablespoons minced fresh ginger*

1   *teaspoon salt, divided*

3   *cups water or broth*

3   *tablespoons sesame oil*

3   *tablespoons coconut vinegar or apple cider vinegar*

1   *15-ounce can black beans, drained and rinsed*

2   *tablespoons liquid coconut oil*

1   *carrot, finely diced*

3   *radishes, finely diced*

½   *cup snow peas or sugar snap peas, chopped*

½   *cup shredded red cabbage*

3   *scallions, thinly sliced*

   Salt, to taste

   Freshly ground black pepper, to taste

¼   *cup sunflower seeds or walnuts or another seed or nut*

1. Place millet and ginger in a small saucepan. Add ½ teaspoon salt and the water. Bring to a boil, stir once, then reduce heat and simmer, covered, for 25 minutes.

2. As the millet cooks, whisk together sesame oil, vinegar, and remaining ½ teaspoon salt in a large bowl. Set aside.

3. Check millet. When it is done, remove from heat and allow to rest for 10 minutes.

4. Fluff with a fork and add beans. Set aside.

5. Warm coconut oil in a large sauté pan. Flash-sauté carrots, radishes, snow peas, cabbage, and scallions until firm-tender. Season with salt and pepper.

6. Spoon sautéed veggies into the bowl with the vinaigrette and stir to coat ingredients.

7. Stir in millet-bean mixture and sunflower seeds and continue stirring to coat.

BLACK RICE SALAD WITH MANGO AND PEANUTS

MAKES 4 SERVINGS

If you're not familiar with black rice, let me introduce you: Known also as "forbidden rice," this wonderful, nutty grain features a black bran coating, which gives it outrageously high levels of protein, fiber, and antioxidants, including vitamin E and anthocyanin (which gives the rice its black hue). It is so high in phytonutrients that a study done by Louisiana State University Agricultural Center found that it was more antioxidant-dense than blueberries, one of the darlings of the superfood world. Now that you know a bit about this powerhouse, give this delicious recipe a try! Black rice travels beautifully, making it the perfect lunch food.

¾ cup orange juice

¼ cup fresh lime juice

2 tablespoons liquid coconut oil

1 tablespoon coconut aminos or natural soy sauce

Salt, to taste

3½ cups water

2 cups black rice

½ red, orange, or yellow pepper, seeded and diced

2 stalks celery, cut into small dice

1 cup fresh cilantro leaves, chopped

1 cup finely chopped red onion

½ cup unsalted, dry-roasted peanuts

6 scallions, thinly sliced

1 small firm-ripe mango or avocado, cut into small dice

1 jalapeño pepper, seeded and minced

1. In a large bowl, whisk together orange juice, lime juice, coconut oil, coconut aminos, and a pinch of salt. Whisk to blend. Set aside.

2. In a medium saucepan, heat water to boiling. Season lightly with salt and pour in black rice. Cover, reduce heat to low, and simmer until all liquid is absorbed and rice is tender, about 25 minutes.

3. Remove pan from heat and let stand, covered, for 15 minutes.

4. As rice stands, add red pepper, celery, cilantro, red onion, peanuts, scallions, mango or avocado, and jalapeño to the large bowl containing dressing. Stir to coat ingredients.

5. Add black rice, stirring gently until coated.

6. Allow to sit for 30 or more minutes for flavors to blend.

GRAIN OR BEAN SALAD BLUEPRINT

MAKES 2 SERVINGS

Grain salads and bean salads are easy to make, versatile, economical, healthy, and delicious. This blueprint allows you to create your own grain salads and bean salads using what you currently have in your pantry, refrigerator, freezer, and garden. Have fun!

¼ cup (or more) vinaigrette or favorite salad dressing (homemade or store-bought)

1 tablespoon (or more) favorite herb or mix of herbs

1 garlic clove, minced

¼ cup onion, scallions, or shallots

Pinch of salt and pepper

4 cups cooked beans or grain of choice

1 cup chopped cooked or raw vegetables

Optional: 1 cup animal or plant protein of choice

Optional: ¼ cup (or more) nuts or seeds, for crunch

1. In a large bowl, whisk together salad dressing, herbs, garlic, onion, salt, and pepper.

2. Add in all other ingredients, stirring gently until well coated.

3. Adjust salt and pepper to taste.

4. Allow to sit for 30 or more minutes so flavors can blend.

MEXICALI QUINOA PILAF

MAKE 2 SERVINGS

Every ingredient in this one-dish meal
contributes a large number of nutrients.
Make this pilaf once a week, take it to
work, and you will feel energized and alert,
while doing wonderful things for your
cardiovascular system, nervous system,
immune system, and other parts of your body.
Feel free to play around with the recipe. Try
adding a cup of chopped leftover veggies, use
a different type of legume or herb, or add in
something else that isn't in the ingredient list.

- 2 *tablespoons coconut oil*
- 2 *garlic cloves, minced*
- ½ *cup diced red, orange,
   or yellow bell peppers*
- ¼ *teaspoon cayenne powder*
- ¼ *teaspoon chili powder*
- 3 *or more scallions, chopped*
- 15 *ounces black beans, rinsed and drained*
- 1 *14-ounce can coconut milk*
- ½ *cup chopped pepitas (green, hulled
   pumpkin seeds) or sunflower seeds*
- ¼ *teaspoon salt*
- ¼ *cup chopped cilantro*
- 3 *cups cooked quinoa*

1. Preheat oven to 350°F.

2. Add the coconut oil to a large skillet

WHAT ARE ANTHOCYANINS?

Anthocyanins are antioxidants that have
been found to help fight heart disease,
diabetes, and Alzheimer's, and are currently
being studied for their role in helping fight
cancer. Dark blue, red, and purple foods,
such as blueberries, acai berries, and black
rice are loaded with anthocyanins.

over medium heat, and sauté garlic, peppers,
cayenne powder, chili powder, and scallions
until just tender, about 5 minutes. Remove
from heat and set aside.

3. In a casserole dish, stir together black
beans, coconut milk, pepitas, and salt.

4. Stir in the sautéed ingredients, cilantro,
and quinoa.

5. Bake for 30 minutes, or until top is golden.

QUINOA BOWL

MAKES 2 SERVINGS

Wow, does quinoa contain a lot of
protein: 24 g per 1-cup serving! Quinoa
also contains generous amounts of fiber,
magnesium, manganese, iron, vitamins B2
and B6, lysine, and phytochemicals that help
the brain, heart, and immune system. This
delicious dish pairs quinoa with coconut, for
a portable, nourishing midday nosh.

1 tablespoon liquid coconut oil

¼ cup finely diced carrot

¼ cup diced celery

¼ cup diced onion

1 teaspoon grated fresh ginger

½ teaspoon minced garlic

10 peeled and deveined shrimp
(or 1 cup of cubed chicken or beans)

4 cups cooked quinoa

3 tablespoons unsweetened shredded dried coconut

½ tablespoon lime juice
Optional: cilantro for garnish

1. Warm coconut oil in a large sauté pan over medium heat. Add carrot, celery, and onion and sauté until tender.

2. Add ginger and garlic and cook for just about a minute.

3. Add shrimp and cook until done, being careful not to overcook.

4. Remove from heat and stir in quinoa, shredded coconut, and lime juice. Sprinkle with cilantro, if desired.

CHICKPEA COCONUT SALAD

MAKES 4 SERVINGS

This yummy chickpea salad is filled with protein, fiber, and antioxidants—the perfect dish to fuel yourself. You can change things up by adding a cup of chopped, cooked veggies; a tablespoon or more of another chopped herb; a handful of nuts or seeds; or even some dried fruit. I like a cup of this salad on top of a bed of arugula or any other salad green.

1 tablespoon lemon juice

1 tablespoon liquid coconut oil

⅓ cup chopped fresh cilantro

½ teaspoon salt
Pinch of pepper

1 15-ounce can chickpeas, rinsed and drained

⅓ cup freshly grated coconut
(or unsweetened shredded dried coconut)

1 teaspoon chopped green chili peppers

1. In a large bowl, whisk together lemon juice, coconut oil, cilantro, salt, and pepper.

2. Add remaining ingredients and gently stir to coat.

3. Allow to sit for at least 30 minutes for flavors to blend.

LUNCH SALADS

CHOPPED SUPERFOOD SALAD

MAKES 6 SERVINGS

This delicious, chopped salad is a bit different—it's almost a slaw—and contains pectin-rich apple, coconut, cilantro, and other good things that will help boost your energy and good health. You'll like this one! If you leave out the protein, it also makes a great side dish for burgers, hot dogs, or anything barbecued.

2 to 3 tablespoons lemon juice

1 tablespoon liquid coconut oil

½ teaspoon pepper

1 teaspoon salt

4 cups green cabbage, shredded, and diced into small bits

1 crisp apple or Asian pear, cored and diced

½ cup walnuts, chopped

2 cups chicken, turkey, pork, or favorite bean

½ cup fresh cilantro, chopped

½ cup unsweetened shredded dried coconut

1. In a large bowl, whisk together lemon juice, coconut oil, pepper, and salt.

2. Add remaining ingredients and gently stir to coat.

3. Allow to sit for at least 30 minutes for flavors to blend.

KALE AND COCONUT CHICKEN SALAD

MAKES 2 SERVINGS

Where would a superfood cookbook—even one on coconut—be without at least one kale recipe? Kale is a member of the Cruciferae family, known for its high antioxidant content, omega-3 fatty acids, protein, and fiber. Here, it teams up with coconut and chicken (or use another animal protein or substitute a cup of legumes), making it a wonderful choice for lunch or a light supper.

¼ cup liquid coconut oil

1 teaspoon sesame oil (dark sesame oil has the best flavor)

2 tablespoons coconut aminos or natural soy sauce

Dash of salt and pepper

5 cups baby kale

1 cup unsweetened shredded dried coconut

1 cup chicken, cooked and shredded (or substitute 1 cup white beans)

1. In a large bowl, whisk together coconut oil, sesame oil, coconut aminos, salt, and pepper.

2. Add remaining ingredients and gently stir to coat.

3. Allow to sit for at least 30 minutes for flavors to blend.

CHOPPED AVOCADO COCONUT SALAD

MAKES 2 SERVINGS

This recipe is chock-full of nutrient-dense avocado, coconut, fresh herbs, protein, and bold flavor. This is a portable salad, but if you decide to take it to work with you, consider packing the dressing on the side so that the salad stays fresh.

1   *large Hass avocado, halved, pitted*

1½ *tablespoons fresh lime juice*

1½ *teaspoons Asian chili-garlic sauce, such as sriracha*

3   *tablespoons liquid coconut oil*

Salt and pepper, to taste

2   *cups diced turkey, chicken, fish, beef, pork, or other animal protein, or a favorite bean*

1   *cup diced peeled jicama*

1   *cup diced red onion*

1   *large red bell pepper, diced*

¼   *cup unsweetened shredded dried coconut*

¼   *cup chopped peanuts or cashews*

¼   *cup chopped fresh cilantro*

7   *cups chopped Romaine lettuce*

Salad dressing of choice

1. Scoop avocado flesh into food processor or blender. Add lime juice, chili-garlic sauce, and coconut oil, and process until smooth. Season generously with salt and pepper.

2. In a large bowl, toss together remaining ingredients.

3. If you are eating right away, pour dressing over salad and toss, toss, toss, until all ingredients are coated in dressing. If you are taking the salad to work, pack dressing separately and dress salad right before eating.

ROASTED SWEET POTATO, QUINOA, AND ARUGULA SALAD

MAKES 4 SERVINGS

Oh my, this is a stunning salad, in an upscale, gourmet, truly yummy kind of way. It's so good for you, too. Sweet potatoes are packed with beta-carotene, arugula contains lutein and zeaxanthin (antioxidants thought to help prevent cancer), and quinoa is the protein-perfect grain-seed that leaves you feeling so energized. Do try this one!

1   *large sweet potato or beet, peeled and diced (about 2 cups)*

4   *to 5 tablespoons liquid coconut oil, divided*

½   *teaspoon ground cinnamon*

Salt, to taste

1   *tablespoon freshly squeezed lemon juice*

Pepper, to taste

3   *cups baby arugula leaves, roughly chopped*

1½ *cups cooked quinoa*

1. Preheat oven to 425°F.

2. Prepare a baking sheet with foil or parchment paper.

3. Toss together the sweet potatoes, 2 tablespoons coconut oil, and cinnamon on prepared baking sheet with a pinch of salt.

4. Roast the sweet potatoes until softened and a little bit browned, about 20 minutes.

5. As the sweet potatoes cook, whisk together the remaining coconut oil, lemon juice, salt, and pepper, in a large bowl.

6. When the sweet potatoes are done, allow them to cool slightly on the baking sheet.

7. Add arugula and sweet potato to the dressing and gently toss to coat.

8. Add quinoa and gently combine again, to coat.

SANDWICHES & WRAPS

MUSHROOM-BEAN BURGERS

MAKES 4 SERVINGS

Mushrooms are popular in the health world as immune-system aids. Here, they are used to give delicious bean burgers a meaty, toothsome texture. And there's lots of protein and fiber here! Leave out the coconut aminos if you don't have any, but its soy sauce–like flavor is nice here.

4 tablespoons liquid coconut oil, divided

1 onion, diced

1 clove garlic, minced

¾ cup diced fresh mushrooms
    Optional: 1 teaspoon coconut aminos

1 15-ounce can pinto beans, or another bean

¼ cup unsweetened shredded dried coconut

1 tablespoon fresh parsley or chives, minced
    Salt and pepper, to taste

2 tablespoons coconut oil

1. Sauté onion and garlic in 2 tablespoons coconut oil for 3 to 5 minutes, until onion is soft. Add mushrooms and coconut aminos, and cook for another 5 minutes, until mushrooms are cooked. Set aside.

2. In a large bowl, mash the beans until slightly chunky.

3. Stir in the coconut, parsley, salt, and pepper until thoroughly combined.

4. Add the mushroom mixture to the beans. Stir until well combined. Allow to sit for 5 minutes or more. (You can cover bowl and come back to mixture later in the day if you'd like.)

5. Shape the mixture into patties. Heat about 2 tablespoons of coconut oil and cook each patty until the veggie burgers are done, about 5 minutes on each side.

BETTER TUNA SALAD

MAKES 2 SERVINGS

A lot of my clients love tuna salad. To create a healthier version, I ask them to replace the mayo with a bit of coconut milk and add lots of veggies. This tuna salad can be eaten on top of salad greens, made into a sandwich or wrap, or packed into a container and used as a dip to enjoy with gluten-free seed crackers, veggie strips, or apple slices. For something different, use salmon or another fish instead of tuna.

- 2 to 3 tablespoons canned coconut milk, depending upon how moist you like your tuna salad
- 1 teaspoon apple cider vinegar
- 1 to 2 teaspoons curry powder
  Salt and pepper, to taste
  Optional: 1 tablespoon cilantro, parsley, or chives (or a mixture of all three), chopped fine
- 1 2.5- to 3-ounce can or pouch of tuna (or salmon)
  Optional: 1 scallion, chopped fine
  Optional: ½ celery stalk, chopped fine
  Optional: 1 small carrot, shredded
  Optional: ¼ red pepper, chopped fine
  Optional: 2 tablespoons sunflower seeds or chopped cashews

1. In a large bowl, whisk together coconut milk, vinegar, curry powder, salt, pepper, and if desired, herbs. Adjust spices to taste.

2. Stir in tuna until just coated. (Leave chunky.)

3. Stir in remaining ingredients until just coated.

BLACK BEAN BURGERS

MAKES 4 SERVINGS

Black beans are loaded with antioxidants, which you can tell from their deep color. They also have plenty of fiber and protein. Garlic, pepper, spices, veggies, and coconut add even more antioxidants, making this burger a delicious way to help your immune system stay strong. Other beans will work beautifully in this recipe, as well.

- 2 tablespoons liquid coconut oil, or as needed
- 1 small onion, diced
- 2 cloves garlic, minced
- 1 jalapeño pepper, seeded and minced
- ½ red bell pepper, diced
- 1 cup fresh or frozen corn kernels
- 1 15-ounce can black beans, drained
- ⅓ cup gluten-free, whole wheat, or regular bread crumbs
- ¼ cup unsweetened shredded dried coconut
- 3 teaspoons chili powder blend
- 1 teaspoon ground cumin
- ½ teaspoon salt
  Pinch of black pepper
- ½ cup gluten-free or all-purpose flour, or as needed

1. Heat 1 tablespoon of the coconut oil in a skillet over medium heat. Add onion, garlic, and jalapeño pepper, stirring occasionally until onion is translucent, 8 to 10 minutes.

2. Add red pepper and corn and sauté another 3 or 4 minutes, until red pepper is tender. Remove from heat and set aside.

3. In a large bowl, mash black beans until chunky.

4. Stir in vegetable mixture, bread crumbs, coconut, chili powder, cumin, salt, and black pepper. Allow to sit for 5 minutes or longer. (You can cover bowl and come back to mixture later in the day if you'd like.)

5. Divide mixture into 4 patties and coat both sides of each patty with flour.

6. Heat 1 tablespoon coconut oil in a skillet over medium heat; cook patties until browned, about 7 to 8 minutes on each side.

COCONUT CURRY CHICKEN WRAPS

MAKES 4 SERVINGS

This yummy wrap goes heavy on the veggies for a nutrient-rich lunch. Feel free to leave out an ingredient or substitute any veggies or nuts you'd like. You can even use a different animal protein if you'd prefer (turkey, pork, and beef work well). Buy green curry paste in most well-stocked supermarkets.

½ cup canned coconut milk

1 tablespoon Thai green curry paste

1 teaspoon lime or lemon juice

Pinch of salt

Pinch of pepper

2 tablespoons chopped fresh cilantro

1¼ cups shredded cooked chicken

¼ cup shredded carrot

¼ cup very thinly sliced red pepper

2 tablespoons thinly sliced green onion

2 tablespoons chopped roasted peanuts or cashews

4 8-inch tortillas or wraps

1 cup shredded lettuce or cabbage

¼ cup unsweetened shredded dried coconut

1. In a medium bowl, whisk together coconut milk, curry paste, lime juice, salt, and pepper until smooth.

2. Stir in cilantro, chicken, carrot, red pepper, green onion, and peanuts and toss to coat.

3. Arrange tortillas in a single layer on a flat surface. Place ¼ of chicken mixture down the center of each tortilla.

4. Top with lettuce and a sprinkle of shredded coconut.

5. Roll up tortillas burrito-style and tuck in the ends snugly.

6. If desired, halve each wrap crosswise. Serve immediately or wrap tightly in plastic wrap and refrigerate until ready to eat.

MAKE YOUR OWN WRAP

Did you know you can make your own wraps using healthy coconut? It's actually easy. Give these two a go. I think you'll like them.

SIMPLE COCONUT WRAP

MAKES 1 OR 2 SERVINGS

3 egg whites

½ tablespoon coconut flour

Pinch of salt

Optional: herbs, spices, or extracts to flavor the wraps

Small amount of liquid coconut oil

1. Place all ingredients except the coconut oil in a food processor or high-power blender (such as a Vitamix or Blendtec). Process until ingredients form a smooth batter.

2. Coat a large skillet with a very thin layer of coconut oil. Heat over medium heat.

3. When skillet is completely heated, pour mixture into skillet and swirl to spread evenly over entire surface of pan. Cover pan.

4. Let wrap cook for 1 or 2 minutes; it may puff up, which is fine.

5. Uncover pan and, using a large pancake turner, flip the wrap.

6. Cook another 30 seconds and slide onto plate or other flat surface.

PALEO TORTILLAS

MAKES 3 SERVINGS

2 eggs

1 teaspoon liquid coconut oil

1 tablespoon water or unflavored coconut water

¼ cup arrowroot powder

1 teaspoon coconut flour

Dash of salt

Optional: herbs, spices, or extracts to flavor the wraps

1. In a medium bowl, whisk the eggs.

2. Whisk in the coconut oil and water.

3. Add arrowroot powder, coconut flour, salt, and optional flavorings. Stir well to combine.

4. In a small skillet over medium heat, pour in about ⅓ of the batter and immediately roll it around to evenly coat the bottom. Cook about 1 minute, or until tortilla begins to pull away from the pan's edges.

5. Flip and cook another minute, or until done.

6. Use immediately or cool and store in a plastic bag or airtight container.

CHAPTER 6

SMALL BITES: COCONUT APPETIZERS AND SNACKS

Sometimes you just want a little something—a snack or something fancy before a dinner party so you can show off your ingenious culinary skills. Then there are the times when your kids come home from school or soccer practice absolutely famished, and you want something yummy and healthy to offer them.

Instead of something out of a bag, think coconut. Yes, coconut! Coconut is so versatile that it lends itself to a wide variety of appetizers, sandwiches, dips, and more. Get creative. Try the recipes in this section and then start improvising. I'm sure you'll come up with all kinds of delicious coconut munchies.

CHIPS, CRISPS, AND CRACKERS

COCONUT SEED CRACKERS

MAKES 20 TO 25 CRACKERS

If you're handy with a rolling pin, this nutritious recipe is great fun to make with kids! Try serving these crackers with one of the dips or spreads from this section.

½ cup almond flour

½ cup macadamia nuts

1 tablespoon coconut flour

¼ cup pumpkin seeds

2 tablespoons sunflower seeds

2 tablespoons sesame seeds

2 tablespoons hemp seeds

1 tablespoon chia seeds

1 tablespoon unsweetened shredded dried coconut

½ teaspoon salt

1 tablespoon coconut oil

¼ cup coconut water or regular water

1. Pulse almond flour, macadamias, and coconut flour in a food processor until thoroughly ground.

2. Pulse in seeds, dried coconut, and salt until almost fully ground (leave a little texture for crunch).

3. Pulse in oil, then coconut water, until dough forms a ball.

OPPOSITE: **Coconut Chips using a Mature Coconut, page 277**

4. Tightly wrap dough in plastic wrap or put in an airtight container and place in the refrigerator for 30 minutes or longer.

5. Preheat oven to 300°F.

6. Remove dough from refrigerator and roll out between 2 pieces of wax paper or parchment paper. Roll dough to ¼-inch thickness, or thinner if you prefer.

7. Using a sharp knife or a pizza cutter, cut dough into 2-inch squares.

8. Gently place crackers on a baking sheet (or sheets) lined with parchment paper or foil.

9. Bake for 20 to 25 minutes. Do not overcook; crackers should be golden around the edges. (They will firm up as they cool.)

10. Allow crackers to cool thoroughly before removing them from the pan.

GOLDEN RICE CRISPS

MAKES 4 APPETIZER SERVINGS

Since rice flour varies in texture, depending upon the manufacturer, go ahead and use what is convenient for you. Silky, finely milled rice flour will produce thin crisps. Slightly coarser, grittier flour makes thicker crisps. They are all delicious! Just one word of warning: Avoid sweet or glutinous rice flour—it is a different animal!

½ cup brown or white rice flour (if using finely milled rice flour, use 1½ to 2 tablespoons less water)

¼ cup cornstarch

½ teaspoon ground dried turmeric

1 cup coconut water or regular water

¼ cup canned coconut milk

2 tablespoons thinly sliced green onion, including tops

1 tablespoon coconut oil

1. Preheat oven to 350°F.

2. In a bowl, mix rice flour, cornstarch, and turmeric. Add coconut water and coconut milk, and whisk to blend. Stir in green onion.

3. Set a 12-inch nonstick frying pan (about 10 inches across bottom) over high heat. When pan is hot, add 1 teaspoon oil and tilt to coat bottom.

4. Pour ½ cup batter into pan all at once and tilt pan to cover entire bottom evenly.

5. Cook until crisp is browned and crunchy on the bottom, 3 to 5 minutes.

6. Using a wide spatula, so the crisp doesn't break, transfer to a large baking sheet. Repeat in order to make 2 more crisps, being careful to avoid stacking crisps on top of each other.

7. Transfer baking sheet (or sheets) to oven and bake until crisps are completely crisp, about 8 to 12 minutes. Transfer to racks to cool.

8. Break off pieces of the crisps and dip them into one of the relishes, salsas, or chutneys in this chapter.

NOTE: Crisps can be made up to 1 day ahead and stored in an airtight container in a cool place. To re-crisp, heat, uncovered, in a 350°F oven until crisp again, about 5 minutes.

COCONUT CHIPS USING A MATURE COCONUT

MAKES 4 SERVINGS

You can buy a small pouch of coconut chips at the supermarket for $4.99, or you can make your own.

NOTE: Dogs love these chips, so guard them well if you happen to be a pet owner who doesn't want to share.

1 mature coconut
 Coarse salt

1. Preheat oven to 350°F.

2. Test each of the three eyes at stem end of coconut to see which two are the softest. Then use a clean ice pick (or a screwdriver or large nail) and a clean hammer to pierce two of the eyes. Or pierce soft eyes with a corkscrew.

3. Strain the coconut water through a fine sieve into a bowl; reserve it for other uses (there are plenty of ideas in this book!).

4. Place coconut on a rimmed baking sheet; bake for 30 minutes, or until coconut shell begins to crack. Set aside until cool enough to handle.

5. Wrap coconut in a clean kitchen towel. Holding coconut with one hand, hit it with a hammer in the same place several times to crack the outer shell and split the coconut into several large pieces.

6. Separate coconut flesh from shell, and use a vegetable peeler to remove the dark outer skin, if desired. Rinse coconut in a colander, then spread in a single layer on a kitchen towel to dry.

7. Divide coconut strips between 2 rimmed baking sheets in a single layer. Season with salt.

8. Bake until toasted, about 10 minutes.

DIPS & SPREADS

AVOCADO-COCONUT DIP

MAKES ABOUT 1½ CUPS

I think of this dip as "coconut-kissed" guacamole. It is filled with healthy fats from both the avocado and the coconut cream, making it a nourishing (and delicious) superfood dip.

- *3 tablespoons coconut cream or coconut milk, at room temperature*
- *1 tablespoon fresh lemon or lime juice*
- *1 ripe avocado*
- *Salt, to taste*
- *Black pepper, to taste*

1. In a small bowl, thoroughly mix coconut cream and lemon juice.

2. In a separate bowl, mash avocado until smooth.

3. Mix avocado into coconut-lemon mixture and season to taste with salt and pepper.

COCONUT CHUTNEY

MAKES ABOUT 1 CUP

I love chutney as a spread on sandwiches, a relish for pork, a dip with veggie slices or crackers, and a burger topping, as well as mixed into grains. This lovely chutney recipe features our beloved coconut.

- *1 cup unsweetened shredded dried or fresh-grated coconut*
- *3 tablespoons dry-roasted cashews or peanuts (or a combination)*
- *1 teaspoon grated fresh ginger (use a box grater or microplane grater)*
- *2 fresh small mild serrano or jalapeño chilies, roughly chopped*
- *¼ cup chopped cilantro leaves*
- *1 teaspoon salt*
- *¼ teaspoon coconut sugar*
  - *Optional: ½ teaspoon coconut vinegar or apple cider vinegar (if you like a tangy chutney)*
- *⅓ cup coconut water or water*
- *1 tablespoon liquid coconut oil*
- *1 teaspoon black mustard seeds*

1. Put coconut, cashews, ginger, chilies, cilantro, salt, coconut sugar, and if desired, vinegar in a blender or food processor. Process, adding coconut water a little at a time, until paste has a smooth consistency. Transfer to a small mixing bowl and set aside.

2. Heat coconut oil in a small skillet over medium heat. Add mustard seeds and cook just until they begin to pop. Remove pan from heat and stir the seeds and oil into the chutney.

3. Serve immediately or store for up to a week in the refrigerator in a covered container.

SWEET POTATO & HEMP SEED DIP

MAKES ABOUT 4 CUPS

This high-yield recipe is both delicious and versatile—you can use it as a lighter alternative to hummus, as a lovely sandwich spread, or as a fun topping for burritos and tacos. Plus, it is a great way to get concentrated doses of phytonutrients; vitamins A, C, and E; healthy fats; fiber; and protein.

- 4 cups sweet potato, peeled and cubed
- 4 cups cauliflower florets
- 1 tablespoon liquid coconut oil
- 1 medium white onion, chopped
- 5 cloves garlic
- ½ to 1 teaspoon chipotle chili powder
- 2 teaspoons cumin powder
- 4 tablespoons lime juice (from about two limes)
- ¼ cup coconut yogurt
- ¼ cup unsweetened shredded dried coconut
  Salt, to taste
  Ground black pepper, to taste
- ⅓ cup hempseed
- ¼ to ⅓ cup cilantro, chopped

1. Bring a large pot of salted water to a boil. Place the cubed sweet potatoes and cauliflower florets in the pot. Cover and cook the vegetables until they have completely softened, about 15 to 20 minutes.

2. Drain the cooked vegetables in a colander and allow to cool slightly.

3. While the vegetables are cooling, heat the coconut oil in a skillet on medium-high heat. Sauté the chopped onion for 4 to 5 minutes, until golden brown. Then, add garlic and continue to sauté for 30 to 40 seconds. Remove from heat and transfer to a food processor.

4. Add the cooked vegetables, chipotle powder, cumin powder, lime juice, coconut yogurt, shredded coconut, salt, and pepper to the food processor. Process until almost smooth (scraping the sides of the processor may be necessary).

5. Add the hempseed and pulse until completely mixed. Taste and adjust seasonings, if required.

6. Garnish the dip with chopped cilantro.

FRESH COCONUT RELISH

MAKES 1⅓ CUPS

This is a souped-up, cucumber-free, purely coconut version of that Indian favorite: raita. It is super-healthful, and so delicious and different that you'll have people clamoring for the recipe. This relish also gives you something to make with fresh coconut meat. (Use meat from a brown, or mature, coconut for this recipe. The flesh of a young green coconut is too gelatinous to work well here.)

1   cup packed fresh grated coconut from a mature coconut

½   cup plain (unsweetened) coconut yogurt
    Optional: 2 tablespoons finely chopped cilantro leaves

2   small mild green chilies, such as a mild jalapeño

½   teaspoon salt

2   tablespoons hot water

4   tablespoons liquid coconut oil

1   teaspoon black mustard seeds

1. Put coconut, yogurt, cilantro (if desired), chilies, salt, and hot water into a food processor or blender and process until finely pureed. Scrape into a medium-size mixing bowl.

2. Heat the coconut oil over medium-high heat in a small frying pan. When it is very hot, carefully add the black mustard seeds. (The seeds may sizzle, so keep a lid handy.)

3. When the seeds stop spluttering and turn gray, immediately pour the oil and seeds over the coconut puree. Mix thoroughly, adjust salt to taste, and serve.

NOTE: This relish may be prepared in advance and refrigerated for up to 2 days. Remove from refrigerator at least 15 minutes before serving.

GREEN COCONUT PULP CHUTNEY

MAKES ALMOST 1 CUP

Have you just purchased a young coconut for the water? Are you now wondering what to do with the pulp? Here's a scrumptious idea: Make chutney! This spicy relish can be used as a condiment for Indian food, on burgers and sandwiches, as a dip, as a spread, and more.

½   teaspoon cumin seeds

½   teaspoon black mustard seeds

1   cup loosely packed cilantro

¼   cup onion, chopped

½   cup fresh coconut pulp from a young (green) coconut

1   ½-inch piece of ginger, roughly chopped

2   serrano or mild jalapeño chilies

5   tablespoons lemon juice
    Salt, to taste

1. In a heavy pan over medium heat, toast the cumin and mustard seeds by stirring them or shaking the pan to keep them from burning. When they have slightly darkened in color and smell fragrant, remove from heat and allow to cool.

2. Put the cool cumin and mustard seeds in a clean coffee grinder, spice grinder, or blender and pulse until seeds are pulverized.

3. Add pulverized spices and all other ingredients to a food processor or blender and process until smooth. If needed, add water to thin the chutney.

4. Serve immediately or store for up to a week in the refrigerator in a covered container

ISLAND SALSA

MAKES 2 ½ CUPS

This particular recipe is one of the most unusual and delicious in my collection, thanks to the coconut and peanuts. It is also rich in enzymes, high in vitamins C and A, and contains plenty of protein and fiber. Enjoy with tortilla chips or any of the crackers in this chapter. It also works beautifully as a topping for fish, poultry, or pork.

1 ½ cups chopped fresh or canned pineapple (if canned, drain and save juice)

1 cup chopped mango

¼ cup peanuts or cashews (roasted or raw, salted or unsalted), chopped

¼ cup unsweetened shredded dried coconut

1 cup pineapple juice (or orange juice or a mixture)

¼ cup canned coconut milk (not "lite")

½ small red bell pepper, diced

¼ cup red onion, diced

2 tablespoons fresh cilantro, chopped

½ teaspoon grated lime zest

2 tablespoons fresh lime juice

1 teaspoon coconut sugar
    Salt, to taste

¼ teaspoon ground ginger

¼ teaspoon ground red or black pepper

1. Stir together pineapple, mango, peanuts, and coconut.

2. In a separate bowl, stir together the rest of the ingredients. Add to pineapple mixture, and toss to coat.

3. Chill 30 minutes.

COCONUT KETTLE CORN

MAKES APPROXIMATELY 16 CUPS

I like homemade, cooked-in-coconut-oil popcorn. It provides fiber, it's low in calories, and it's economical. (All of which are important to me.) When my family wants a little sweetness, I make kettle corn. Try it. It's easy!

- ½ *cup liquid coconut oil*
- ½ *cup popcorn kernels*
- ¼ *cup coconut sugar*
- 1 *teaspoon salt*

1. In a medium stockpot or large saucepan, heat coconut oil over medium heat. Add 2 or 3 kernels. When kernels pop, add remaining popcorn kernels and sugar, cover pot, and shake continuously.

2. Once popping slows down, remove from heat. Let kernels finish popping, then pour into a bowl and toss with salt before serving. Serve immediately.

INDIAN SPICED COCO-NUTS

MAKES 2 CUPS

You can easily pack snack-size portions into small bags and tuck them into a purse or lunch box, or you can serve them at your next party—they're that good!

- 1 *cup unsalted peanuts or cashews (preferably unroasted)*
- 1 *cup pecans or walnuts, roughly chopped*
- ¼ *cup unsweetened shredded dried coconut*
- 2 *tablespoons liquid coconut oil*
- 2 *teaspoons ground cumin*
- 2 *teaspoons ground coriander*
- 2 *teaspoons garam masala curry powder*
  Salt, to taste

1. Preheat oven to 250°F.

2. Line a baking sheet with parchment paper.

3. In a medium bowl, mix the nuts, shredded coconut, coconut oil, cumin, coriander, garam masala, and salt and pour onto the prepared baking sheet.

4. Bake 20 minutes. Open oven and stir nuts.

5. Bake another 20 minutes, or until nuts are golden. Do not let nuts burn.

6. Remove nuts from oven and allow to cool on the baking sheet.

7. Store in an airtight container at room temperature for up to 2 weeks.

ROASTED COCONUT CHICKPEAS

MAKES 4 SERVINGS

Roasted chickpeas are an easy-to-make, protein-rich, fiber-filled, outrageously healthy snack. Most are flavored with salt and spices. This recipe is sweet, though you could omit the sugar, increase the salt by a couple of pinches, and add your favorite savory spices.

1   15-ounce can chickpeas, rinsed and drained

1   tablespoon liquid coconut oil

1   tablespoon coconut sugar

½   teaspoon salt

1   teaspoon ground cinnamon or ½ teaspoon allspice

    Optional: pinch of black pepper

1. Preheat oven to 450°F.

2. Thoroughly dry chickpeas with paper towels. If necessary, aim a blow-dryer, set to "low cool," on the chickpeas to help get rid of any excess moisture. The beans need to be dry.

3. Place chickpeas in a single layer on 1 or 2 baking trays. Roast for 15 minutes.

4. Remove from the oven and, while still warm, toss in a large bowl with coconut oil, coconut sugar, salt, spice, and if desired, pepper, making sure all beans are fully coated.

5. Return chickpeas to the baking trays and oven. Roast for an additional 15 to 20 minutes until crunchy and golden.

SMALL BITES

SATAY SAUCE

MAKES 1 CUP

This easy sauce is just as good with meat as it is with vegetables. Use it with the satay in this chapter. Any leftover sauce tastes great over noodles, stirred into grains, or used as a vegetable topper.

2   teaspoons red curry paste (Thai Kitchen is one brand commonly found in supermarkets)

1½   cups canned coconut milk

½   cup natural peanut butter

    Optional: 1 teaspoon tamarind paste

    Salt, to taste

¼   cup finely chopped fresh cilantro leaves

1. Heat red curry paste and coconut milk in a wok or heavy saucepan over medium-low heat, stirring for 1 minute.

2. Add peanut butter, tamarind paste (if desired), and salt. Lower heat; simmer 10 minutes, stirring constantly.

3. Remove from heat and add cilantro.

4. Serve with beef, chicken, and other satays or roast meats, or enjoy as a sauce for noodles or veggies.

CHICKPEA CAKES

MAKES 4 SERVINGS

These falafel-like treats are rich in protein and filled with healthy fiber, making them a terrific meatless snack. Serve them with your favorite sauce, salsa, chutney, or relish—any of the ones in this chapter would be fantastic.

- 1 *cup dried chickpeas*
- 3 *tablespoons coconut oil*
- ½ *cup chopped onion*
- ½ *cup chopped celery*
- 2 *tablespoons chopped fresh Italian parsley*
- 1 *teaspoon sea salt*
- 1 *teaspoon ground cumin*
- ⅓ *cup gluten-free all-purpose baking flour (or whole wheat pastry or spelt flour)*
- 1 *cup finely shredded unsweetened dried coconut*
- 2 *tablespoons coconut oil*

1. Put the dried chickpeas in a bowl and add water to cover by about 3 inches. Soak overnight. Drain and rinse.

2. In a sauté pan, heat the 3 tablespoons of coconut oil over medium heat. Add the onion and the celery and sauté until softened, about 5 minutes.

3. Put the chickpeas, parsley, salt, and cumin into a food processor, and pulse until ground.

4. Add the gluten-free flour and pulse a few more times to mix. Don't overprocess: You want a very chunky mixture. Add a tablespoon or more of water if the mixture seems too dry and is not sticking together.

5. Transfer mixture to a large bowl and fold in sautéed onion and celery. With your hands, fold the mixture into patties.

6. Dredge each patty in the unsweetened shredded dried coconut to coat the entire patty.

7. Line a baking sheet with a silicone baking mat or foil. Place patties on the baking sheet and refrigerate for 30 minutes to firm them up.

8. Heat the 2 tablespoons of the coconut oil in a sauté pan. Add a few of the chickpea patties and fry until golden brown, about 4 minutes per side. (Alternately, you can bake the patties in a 350°F oven for 10 minutes per side.) Transfer cooked chickpea cakes to a platter lined with paper towels.

9. Repeat with remaining chickpea cakes.

COCONUT LETTUCE TACOS

MAKES 4 SERVINGS

This unusual "taco" appetizer is easy, different, and addictive. As an assistant, I learned a version of this recipe years ago from a cooking teacher. You'll have fun with it, too!

Coconut Filling:

1   tablespoon coconut oil, melted
    Salt, to taste
1   teaspoon coconut nectar
½   teaspoon smoked paprika
¼   teaspoon ground chipotle
¾   cup unsweetened large coconut shreds

Coconut Dressing:

⅓   cup fresh lemon or lime juice
½   cup canned coconut milk
⅔   cup hempseed
4   cloves garlic
1   teaspoon black peppercorns
1   teaspoon salt
⅓   cup coconut oil

Taco Wraps:

8   butter lettuce leaves
    Optional: 1 cup leftover shredded chicken, flaked cooked fish, or chopped cooked shrimp
    Optional: 1 or more avocados, diced
    Optional: 1 or more tomatoes, diced

1. To make the coconut filling, combine the melted coconut oil, salt, coconut nectar, paprika, and chipotle in a medium bowl and mix well. Add coconut flakes and toss well to evenly coat.

2. For the coconut dressing: Combine lemon juice, coconut milk, hempseed, garlic, peppercorns, and salt in a high-speed blender and blend until smooth. While the blender is running, add the ⅓ cup coconut oil and blend. Add water to thin the dressing, if necessary.

3. To assemble tacos, lay lettuce leaves on a flat surface or plate. Top each lettuce leaf with a tablespoon of coconut dressing. If desired, add a thin layer of chicken and/or a layer of avocado and tomato.

4. Divide the spicy coconut filling among the lettuce leaves, place on individual plates or a platter, and serve.

CURRIED QUINOA CARROT CAKES

MAKES 4 SERVINGS

These gluten-free quinoa and carrot "cakes" are a modern take on traditional flavors from India. Try them by themselves, tucked into wraps or pita bread, placed atop salad, or as vegetarian burgers.

- 1 cup uncooked quinoa (rinsed and well drained)
- 2 cups water or mixture of canned coconut milk and water
- ½ teaspoon salt, plus more for seasoning to taste
- ⅓ cup coconut flour
- 1¼ tablespoons mild curry powder
- 1 teaspoon chili powder
- 2 cloves garlic, minced
- 1½ cups carrots, grated (I use the carrot pulp from my juicer after making carrot juice)
- 2 eggs, beaten
- ½ cup cilantro, finely chopped
  Ground black pepper, to taste
- 2 to 4 tablespoons coconut oil (for shallow frying)

1. Add the rinsed quinoa, water (or water–coconut milk mixture), and ½ teaspoon salt to a medium-size pot. Cover and bring to a boil. Turn the heat down to a simmer, cover, and cook for 15 minutes.

2. Fluff cooked quinoa with a fork, then transfer to a shallow plate or platter for faster cooling. Let cool for 5 minutes.

3. While the quinoa is cooling, whisk together coconut flour, curry powder, and chili powder in a large bowl.

4. Stir into the coconut flour mixture the cooled quinoa, along with minced garlic, grated carrots, eggs, cilantro, and salt and pepper to taste. Mix well by hand until everything is evenly distributed and there are no lumps of coconut flour remaining.

5. With your hands, shape the mixture into 2-inch-wide patties and lay them on a lightly greased plate or baking sheet.

6. Heat the coconut oil in a large skillet over medium-high heat. Once the oil is hot, gently add 3 or 4 patties, being careful not to crowd the pan.

7. Fry patties on medium heat for 2 to 4 minutes until golden brown. Then turn the cakes and cook on the other side for 2 to 4 minutes. Transfer to a plate lined with a paper towel.

8. Repeat with remaining patties.

SATAY

MAKES 6 SERVINGS

When my two older children were born, my husband and I ate a lot of Mexican, Indian, and West Indian (especially Jamaican, Trinidadian, and Bajan) foods. There came a time when we realized we needed to expand the kids' palates a bit, so we ventured into Southeast Asian cooking. Satay was the first Thai dish we served the boys. They loved it! Try serving it with Island Salsa (see page 281) or Satay Sauce (see page 283). I think you'll love it, too.

1   *pound chicken breast, London broil, top round beef, or lamb*

⅔ *cup canned coconut milk*

1   *piece (1 inch) fresh ginger, peeled and grated*

2   *tablespoons green curry paste (Thai Kitchen is a brand commonly found in supermarkets)*

1   *tablespoon coconut aminos or natural soy sauce*

2   *tablespoons coconut oil*
    Lime wedges, for serving

1. Slice the meat into ⅛-inch-thick strips.

2. In a large bowl combine the coconut milk, ginger, green curry paste, and coconut aminos.

3. Add the chicken (or beef or lamb) and toss to coat. Cover and chill for 3 hours.

4. Meanwhile, in a bowl of water, soak 24 wooden skewers for 30 minutes.

5. Thread 1 strip of the meat onto each skewer, weaving in and out at 1-inch intervals.

6. Preheat a barbecue grill to high heat or place a grill pan over medium-high heat. Rub the meat lightly with coconut oil and grill, turning once until no longer pink, about 45 seconds per side. Serve with lime wedges.

YUMMY THINGS TO DO WITH GINGER

- Spice things up by grating a bit of ginger into your next pot of millet, rice, quinoa, or other grain. This is especially delicious served with curries and stir-fry dishes.

- Make ginger lemonade by simply combining freshly grated ginger, lemon juice, cane juice or honey, and water.

- Perk up bottled salad dressing or a simple homemade vinaigrette with grated ginger.

- Add dry powdered or grated fresh ginger to pureed sweet potatoes. A squirt of lemon juice is a yummy addition.

- Add zing to your next fruit salad with some grated ginger.

- Dress up sautéed veggies by tossing in ½ teaspoon of minced fresh ginger.

BAKED COCONUT SHRIMP

MAKES 6 SERVINGS

My younger son, Anders, loves shrimp. He also adores coconut. Being an adventurous eater, he is always looking for new ways to enjoy both foods. This recipe is one of his favorites. We love it with a fruity salsa, but it's also great with chutney, peanut sauce, or a habanero-based hot sauce.

2 *large eggs*

⅓ *cup all-purpose gluten-free or regular flour*

1½ *teaspoons paprika*

½ *teaspoon garlic powder*

1¼ *cups unsweetened dried shredded coconut*

¾ *teaspoon salt*

1 *pound raw shrimp (21 to 25 per pound)*

1. Lightly grease a baking sheet. Set aside.

2. In a small bowl, beat eggs.

3. In another bowl, whisk together flour, paprika, and garlic powder.

4. In a third bowl, combine coconut and salt.

5. Peel shrimp, leaving the tails on. Butterfly the shrimp by cutting halfway through the back, and stopping at the tail, so the shrimp will stand tail up.

6. Grabbing a shrimp by the tail, dredge it in the flour mixture. Dip it in the egg. Then coat the shrimp with coconut, leaving the tail uncoated. Stand the shrimp tail up on the prepared baking sheet. Discard any unused dipping mixtures.

BUYING SHRIMP

- Shrimp is usually sold by the pound. A "21 to 25 count" means there will be 21 to 25 shrimp in a pound.

- In the shrimp world, sizes, such as "large" and "extra large," are not standardized, so to get the amount you want, order by the count per pound.

- Both wild-caught and farm-raised shrimp can potentially damage the surrounding ecosystems when not managed properly. Buy shrimp that have been raised or caught with sound environmental practices. Look for fresh or frozen shrimp certified by an independent agency, such as the Marine Stewardship Council.

- If you can't find certified shrimp, choose wild-caught shrimp from North America. It is more likely to have been sustainably caught than shrimp harvested in Asia.

Coconut Granola, page 244

TOP: Coconut Chips Using a Mature Coconut, page 277, and Avocado-Coconut Dip, page 278
BOTTOM: Coconut Lettuce Tacos, page 285

TOP: Satay, page 287, with Island Salsa, page 281 BOTTOM: Braised Coconut Spinach & Chickpeas with Lemon, page 306

Spicy Thai Steamed Mussells, page 306

TOP: Black Rice Salad with Mango and Peanuts, page 264 BOTTOM: Roasted Sweet Potato, Quinoa, and Arugula Salad, page 269

TOP: Chocoloate Coconut Cupcakes, page 319 BOTTOM: Coconut Flour Pancakes, page 249, with Red Berry Sauce, page 247

Another Green Smoothie, page 236

Berry Macaroon Tart, page 336

7. Bake the shrimp until cooked through and the coating is starting to brown, 10 to 12 minutes. Serve the shrimp with your favorite relish or salsa, such as Island Salsa on page 281.

CRISPY COCONUT CHICKEN BITES

MAKES 4 SERVINGS

This healthy version of the ever-popular chicken nugget features coconut milk, coconut flour, and shredded coconut, giving you a triple dose of coconut's goodness. Serve with any of the chutneys, relishes, dips, and salsas presented in this chapter.

1   pound chicken breasts, cut into chunks

3   eggs

¼   cup canned coconut milk

¾   cup coconut flour

¾   cup unsweetened shredded dried coconut

¼   teaspoon salt

¼   teaspoon fresh ground black pepper

   Coconut oil for frying

1. Cut chicken breasts into "fingers," strips, or large chunks. Set aside.

2. In a medium bowl, beat the eggs.

3. Whisk coconut milk into the eggs.

4. In a separate shallow bowl, mix the coconut flour, shredded coconut, salt, and pepper. Stir until well combined and all lumps are gone.

5. While the oil is heating, start preparing the chicken: Dredge a piece of chicken in the coconut flour mix. Then, dredge it in the egg mixture, and then dredge it in the coconut flour once again. Repeat with the next piece of chicken.

6. Rest dredged chicken pieces on a platter, plate, or baking sheet as you finish preparing remaining chicken.

7. In a large frying pan, over medium heat, add ¼ to ½ inch coconut oil, enough to cover the bottom of the pan.

8. Reduce heat to medium-low and add a few pieces of chicken, being careful not to crowd the pan.

9. Fry chicken pieces on one side until golden brown, then gently turn over and cook until the other side is golden brown.

10. Set cooked chicken on a plate or platter that has been lined with paper towels.

11. Repeat with remaining chicken pieces.

CHAPTER 7

COCONUT FOR DINNER

Once upon a time, dinner was really more like supper—a light meal eaten in the evening to tide you over until morning. Today, dinner is a big deal. It's when people leave their stressful work and school day behind, return home, and decompress. You know how humans use food to self-soothe? Well, dinner is often the time when we do this and eat large volumes of starchy, fatty, comforting food. In this chapter, I am going to challenge you to rethink dinner as a time to do something wonderful for yourself. The meals in this chapter are on the lighter side—I am not a fan of big dinners—and they contain coconut in its many forms, as well as other superfoods. To your health!

SALADS

DINNER SALAD BLUEPRINT

MAKES 2 SERVINGS

This is a recipe that can be played with in an infinite number of ways, so feel free to experiment and create something different at each meal!

  3 *tablespoons coconut vinegar*

  3 *tablespoons coconut aminos*

  1½ *tablespoons liquid coconut oil*

      Optional: 1 teaspoon coconut sugar

      Optional: 1 teaspoon mustard of choice

      Salt and pepper, to taste

  8 *to 9 cups salad greens of choice*

  1 *cup chopped vegetable or mix of vegetables of choice*

  2 *to 3 cups protein (chopped chicken, beef, fish, shrimp, beans, lentils, etc.)*

      Optional: ½ cup chopped nuts or seeds

      Optional: ¼ cup chopped fresh herbs

1. In a large bowl, whisk together coconut vinegar, coconut aminos, coconut oil, coconut sugar (if desired), mustard (if desired), and salt and pepper.

2. Add to the bowl salad greens, chopped vegetables, protein, and if you choose to do so, nuts and/or herbs. Toss until all ingredients are coated with dressing. Serve immediately.

OPPOSITE: **Simple Tomato Soup, page 301**

STARTER SOUPS

BEET COCONUT SOUP

MAKES 4 SERVINGS

I am a beet lover. I don't think you can be a Danish-American health writer who grew up in Australia without loving beets. If you are any of these things, you'll know what I mean.

- 1 tablespoon liquid coconut oil
- 1 large onion, diced
- 3 cloves garlic, finely chopped
- 1 tablespoon finely chopped ginger
- 3 large red beets, peeled and cut into ¼-inch pieces
- 5 cups vegetable stock, divided
- 1 14-ounce can coconut milk
- ½ teaspoon salt
- ¼ teaspoon freshly ground black pepper
  Optional: chopped chives, dill, or parsley, for garnish

1. In a large pot, heat oil over medium heat. Sauté onion for 5 minutes.

2. Add garlic and ginger. Cook, stirring often, for 5 minutes.

3. Add beets and 4 cups of the stock. Bring to a boil, then reduce heat and simmer until beets are fork-tender, about 20 minutes.

4. With an immersion or regular blender, and working in batches, puree soup, adding remaining 1 cup stock, as needed, to reach desired consistency.

5. Stir in coconut milk, salt, and pepper.

6. Garnish with herbs, if desired.

CHILLED MELON, CUCUMBER, AND COCONUT MILK SOUP

SERVES 4 TO 6

This unusual raw soup reminds me a bit of the koldskål (a cold Danish buttermilk soup) I grew up with—though it's much more fresh-tasting and light, thanks to the honeydew and cucumber. This would make a great starter for a vegetarian meal, or work nicely with seafood or poultry.

- 1 small honeydew melon, peeled, seeded, and cut into large chunks
- 1 medium cucumber, peeled, seeded, and cut into chunks
- ¾ cup canned coconut milk
- ¼ cup unsweetened shredded dried coconut
  Squirt of lemon or lime juice

1. Add all ingredients to a blender and process until absolutely smooth.

2. Transfer to an airtight container and refrigerate for 3 hours or overnight, until completely chilled.

COLD-OR-NOT CARROT COCONUT SOUP

MAKES ABOUT 6½ CUPS

This refreshing soup can be eaten chilled, at room temperature, or warm. I prefer it warm, but it is so delicious and healthy (it contains tons of beta-carotene for great skin and eyesight) that I'll take it however I can get it.

- 2   *tablespoons liquid coconut oil*
- 1   *shallot, finely chopped*
- 1   *small onion, chopped*
- 1   *tablespoon finely grated peeled fresh gingerroot*
- 1   *tablespoon mild curry powder*
- 4   *cups chopped carrots*
- 2½ *cups broth*
  Salt and pepper, to taste
- 1   *to 1½ cups canned coconut milk*
- 1   *tablespoon fresh lime juice, plus additional to taste*
  Water for thinning soup
  Optional: chopped scallions or herb of choice, for garnish

1. In a large heavy saucepan, heat coconut oil over medium heat. Add shallot, onion, gingerroot, and curry powder and cook until shallot and onion are tender.

2. Add carrots, broth, and salt and pepper, and simmer until carrots are very tender, about 20 minutes.

3. With an immersion or regular blender, and working in batches, puree soup with coconut milk and lime juice until very smooth.

4. Adjust salt and pepper, if needed, and thin with water if necessary.

5. If serving warm, allow to cool to just above room temperature and ladle into soup bowls. Serve garnished with chopped scallions or herbs, if desired.

6. If serving soup cold, transfer soup to an airtight container and place in the refrigerator. This soup actually tastes best the second day, so I usually make it the day before and stash it in the fridge so I can garnish and serve it the next day.

SIMPLE TOMATO SOUP

MAKES 6 SERVINGS

My mother couldn't cook, so most of the food we ate growing up came out of boxes, bags, and cans. Campbell's tomato soup was one of our favorites. Now that my palate is a bit more sophisticated (emphasis on "a bit"), I prefer my tomato soup homemade. If you don't like a lot spice, you can remove some or all of the ones included in this recipe, and you'll still get a beautiful bowl of soup, one that strengthens the immune system, thanks to the lycopene and vitamin C in the tomatoes, plus the antioxidant power in the spices.

4 tablespoons liquid coconut oil

2 medium yellow onions, chopped

1 teaspoon salt

3 teaspoons curry powder

1 teaspoon ground coriander

1 teaspoon ground cumin

½ teaspoon red chili pepper flakes

2 28-ounce cans whole tomatoes

4 cups chicken or vegetable broth

1 14-ounce can coconut milk

Optional: black pepper, to taste

1. Add coconut oil to a large pot over medium heat. Add the onions and salt, and cook, stirring occasionally, until the onions are very soft, about 10 minutes.

2. Stir in the curry powder, coriander, cumin, and chili flakes, and cook, stirring constantly, about 30 seconds, or until spices are fragrant.

3. Add tomatoes, broth, and coconut milk and allow soup to simmer on low heat for 20 minutes.

4. With an immersion or regular blender, and working in batches (returning each blended batch to the warm soup pot), puree soup with coconut milk until very smooth.

5. Adjust seasonings and, if desired, add black pepper.

MAIN DISHES

SLOW COOKER COCONUT BEEF ROAST

MAKES 4 TO 6 SERVINGS

The slow cooker is an easy way to ensure there is always healthy food at home for you and your family to enjoy.

4 cups chicken, beef, or vegetable broth (or a mixture)

2 large onions, chopped

7 garlic cloves, minced

2 cups sliced mushrooms

1 cup chopped red pepper

½ cup sliced celery

Salt and pepper, to taste

½ teaspoon sweet paprika

½ cup canned coconut milk (do not use "lite")

2-pound beef rump roast

1. Add broth, onion, garlic, mushrooms, red pepper, celery, salt and pepper, paprika, and coconut milk to a slow cooker. Stir once.

2. Nestle roast among other ingredients.

3. Put lid on slow cooker and turn on low setting for 6 to 8 hours, or on high for 4 to 6 hours.

CRISP COCONUT CHICKEN

MAKES 2 SERVINGS

This recipe uses shredded coconut instead of bread crumbs—a brilliant and delicious use of coconut! Try this dish with one or two vegetable sides for a light, nourishing dinner.

- 1½ cups chopped roasted red pepper (either homemade or from a jar)
- ½ teaspoon fresh lemon juice
- ¾ teaspoon coconut sugar, divided
  Pinch of cayenne
- 3 tablespoons liquid coconut oil, divided
  Salt and pepper, to taste
- 1 teaspoon garlic paste (made by mashing together one medium garlic clove with ¼ teaspoon salt)
- 1 tablespoon Dijon-style mustard
- 1 whole large, skinless, boneless chicken breast (about 10 ounces), halved
- ½ cup gluten-free or regular all-purpose flour
  Egg wash, made by whisking 1 large egg with 1 teaspoon coconut milk or water
- 1 cup unsweetened shredded dried coconut

1. Preheat oven to 375°F.

2. In a blender, puree the roasted red pepper with the lemon juice, ½ teaspoon of the coconut sugar, cayenne, 1 tablespoon of the coconut oil, and salt and black pepper until smooth. Set aside.

3. In a small bowl, whisk together the garlic paste and mustard.

4. Spread the garlic mixture onto both sides of the chicken. Set aside.

5. Get three shallow bowls ready. In one bowl, whisk together the flour, ¼ teaspoon coconut sugar, and a pinch each of salt and pepper. In the second bowl, place the egg wash. In the third, place the coconut.

6. Dredge the chicken in the flour, shaking off the excess.

7. Immediately dip the chicken into the egg wash, letting the excess drip off.

8. Immediately coat the chicken generously with the coconut, pressing it firmly to help the coconut adhere.

9. Add the remaining 2 tablespoons coconut oil to a skillet over medium-high heat. When warm, add the chicken.

10. Sauté chicken just until coconut is golden, about 2 minutes. Turn chicken and cook on the other side, just until coconut is golden.

11. Transfer chicken to a small baking dish and bake in the oven until cooked through, about 10 to 12 minutes.

12. Serve with red pepper sauce.

FISH BAKED IN COCONUT MILK

MAKES 4 SERVINGS

This is an incredibly versatile recipe. Use salmon, tuna, or your favorite mild white fish. It all works. You will be impressed. Feel free to play with the veggies.

- 4   *teaspoons lemon juice*
- 2   *tablespoons plus ¼ cup liquid coconut oil*
-     *Pinch of salt*
- 2   *pounds thick fish fillets or steaks, halibut, cod, or salmon*
- 2   *cups finely chopped onion*
- 2   *teaspoons minced garlic*
- 2   *teaspoons minced ginger*
- 1   *teaspoon minced green serrano or jalapeño chili pepper*
- 1   *cup chopped tomatoes (fresh or drained canned)*
- 5   *teaspoons ground coriander*
- 1   *teaspoon ground cumin*
- ¼   *teaspoon cayenne powder*
- ¼   *teaspoon ground black pepper*
- ¼   *teaspoon ground turmeric*
- 1   *teaspoon dried parsley*
- 1¼ *teaspoons salt*
- ½   *cup canned coconut milk*
- ¼   *cup chopped parsley, chives, or cilantro, for garnish*

1. Preheat oven to 350°F.

2. Lightly grease a baking dish large enough to hold fish in a single layer. Set aside.

3. Whisk together lemon juice, 2 tablespoons coconut oil, and salt in a small bowl. Set aside.

4. Cut fillets crosswise into 2-inch-wide strips. Rub fish with mixture of lemon juice and oil, place in the prepared baking dish, cover, and refrigerate for 1 hour.

5. In medium frying pan, over medium-high heat, fry onion in ¼ cup coconut oil until edges are browned.

6. Add garlic, ginger, and chili pepper, and stir over medium heat for 2 minutes.

7. Add tomatoes, coriander, cumin, cayenne powder, black pepper, turmeric, parsley, and 1¼ teaspoons salt, and fry, stirring until tomato breaks down into a chunky sauce.

8. Add coconut milk and simmer about 5 minutes until mixture becomes thick.

9. Remove fish from refrigerator, uncover, and bake for 10 minutes.

10. Remove fish from oven, pour sauce over fish, cover tightly with foil, and return to oven for 15 to 20 minutes or until fish is opaque.

11. Garnish, if desired, with chopped herbs.

COCONUT NUT PASTA

MAKES 4 SERVINGS

This yummy nut pasta is made with nut butter for protein. (If you want more protein, feel free to add a cup of beans or chopped animal protein.)

- 1 *pound any shape pasta, regular, whole grain, or gluten-free*
- 2 *tablespoons liquid coconut oil*
- 1 *carrot, cut into matchsticks*
- 1 *stalk celery, sliced*
- 1 *cup sugar snap or snow peas, sliced on a diagonal*
- ½ *onion, cut into slices*
- 1 *cup cherry tomatoes, halved*
- 2 *pinches of salt*
  Pinch of pepper
- ¾ *cup canned coconut milk*
- ½ *cup fresh or canned diced tomatoes*
- 6 *tablespoons nut butter (such as almond, cashew, peanut, sunflower or other)*
- 2 *tablespoons ginger, finely diced*
- 2 *tablespoons coconut aminos or natural soy sauce (use gluten-free soy sauce if desired)*
- 1 *teaspoon coconut sugar or nectar*
- 1 *tablespoon fresh lime or lemon juice*
- 1 *teaspoon curry powder*
- 1 *teaspoon Asian chili-garlic sauce (such as sriracha)*
- 3 *cloves garlic, minced*
  Optional: 1 tablespoon minced fresh parsley or cilantro

1. Prepare the pasta according to package directions. Set aside.

2. Heat coconut oil in a large sauté pan over medium heat and add carrot, celery, peas, onion, cherry tomatoes, and 1 pinch each of salt and pepper. Sauté for 2 to 3 minutes until veggies are just barely tender. Remove pan from heat and set aside.

3. In a small saucepot, over medium-high heat, whisk together coconut milk, diced tomatoes, nut butter, ginger, coconut aminos, coconut sugar, lime juice, curry powder, chili-garlic sauce, garlic, minced herbs (if desired), and pinch of salt. Allow sauce to simmer for 2 to 3 minutes, whisking until smooth.

4. Turn off heat and add pasta and sauce to the veggies in the sauté pan. Gently toss all ingredients together. Adjust seasonings and toss to coat.

SPICY THAI STEAMED MUSSELS

MAKES 6 SERVINGS

Mussels were the first nonvegetarian food I learned to make in cooking school. I couldn't believe how well they turned out. So if you've never prepared them before, give this recipe a try. You'll be pleasantly surprised. You'll also be getting an enormous amount of vitamin B12 (3 ounces of mussels contain 340 percent of the RDA for this nutrient), plus iron, calcium, magnesium, vitamins C and B6, and plenty of protein. You also get the immune system strengthening power of coconut, garlic, and curry.

5 pounds mussels (preferably cultivated)

⅓ cup lime juice

1 14-ounce can coconut milk

⅓ cup dry white wine or broth (vegetable or chicken)

1½ tablespoons Thai red curry paste

6 garlic cloves, minced

1 tablespoon Asian fish sauce

1 cup parsley or cilantro, chopped

1. Scrub mussels well and remove beards. Set aside.

2. In a large (at least 8-quart) stockpot, boil lime juice, coconut milk, wine, curry paste, garlic, and fish sauce over high heat, stirring, 2 minutes.

3. Add mussels, tossing to combine. Cook mussels, covered, stirring occasionally, until opened, about 5 to 8 minutes.

4. Discard any unopened mussels.

5. Toss herbs with mussels.

BRAISED COCONUT SPINACH & CHICKPEAS WITH LEMON

MAKES 4 SERVINGS

Tender braised greens and chickpeas create a beautiful ragout-like dish that is lovely served over pureed sweet potatoes, brown rice, millet, quinoa, polenta, potatoes, mashed cauliflower, or anything else. Your taste buds will thank you. So will your body: This dish is high in vitamins A, C, and E, as well as protein, zinc, magnesium, and fiber.

2 tablespoons liquid coconut oil

1 small yellow onion, diced

5 to 6 garlic cloves, minced

1 tablespoon grated fresh ginger

¼ to ½ teaspoon red pepper flakes

1 15-ounce can chickpeas, drained

1 pound baby spinach

1 14-ounce can coconut milk

2 tablespoons lemon juice

¼ cup tomato paste

1 teaspoon salt, or to taste

   Pepper, to taste

1. Heat the coconut oil in a large saucepan over medium-high heat. Add the onion and cook for about 5 minutes, or until it begins to brown.

2. Add the garlic, ginger, and red pepper. Cook for 3 minutes, stirring frequently.

3. Add chickpeas and cook over high heat for 2 minutes or until the chickpeas are beginning to turn golden.

4. Add spinach, in batches if needed.

5. Add coconut milk, lemon juice, tomato paste, and salt and pepper. Bring to a simmer, then turn down the heat and cook for 10 minutes, or until the chickpeas are warmed through.

6. Adjust seasoning before serving.

COCONUT MASHED POTATOES

MAKES 4 TO 6 SERVINGS

You mashed potato lovers will be thrilled to know that you can have your favorite food and get the coconut your body so deeply desires—all in this simple dish. Feel free to add 1 or 2 cups of finely chopped cooked greens to the mashies and enjoy!

2   *pounds russet or Yukon Gold potatoes*

1   *cup canned coconut milk*

   Salt and pepper, to taste

¼   *cup liquid coconut oil*

1. Add salted water to a large pot over high heat and boil potatoes until soft but not falling apart.

2. Drain potatoes in a colander and return to pot.

3. Add coconut milk and salt and pepper. Using a potato masher, mash potatoes until chunky.

4. Add coconut oil and continue mashing until smooth. Adjust seasoning.

HEARTY SIDES

COCONUT SCALLOPED POTATOES

MAKES 6 SERVINGS

Traditional scalloped potatoes really aren't that good for you. Fortunately, there is an alternative—this delicious scalloped potato recipe, which celebrates the considerable benefits of coconut milk. You will love it!

Coconut oil for greasing dish

1   *14-ounce can coconut milk*

2   *cups vegetable or chicken broth*

1½ *teaspoons salt*

½   *teaspoon dried thyme*

1   *pound russet or Yukon Gold potatoes, peeled, cut crosswise or lengthwise (depending on their size) into ¼-inch-thick slices, and submerged in a bowl of cold water to prevent browning*

6   *scallions (green tops and white bulbs), thinly sliced crosswise*

1. Preheat oven to 350°F.

2. Lightly grease a 2½- to 3-quart casserole dish with coconut oil. Set aside.

3. In a small bowl, whisk together coconut milk, broth, salt, and thyme.

4. Drain the potatoes and pat dry with a paper towel or clean dishcloth.

5. Cover the bottom of the casserole dish with a layer of potatoes, and sprinkle with ⅓ of the scallions.

6. Stir the coconut milk mixture and drizzle ⅓ of it over the potatoes and scallions.

7. Repeat the layers of potatoes, scallions, and coconut milk mixture 2 more times, ending with a layer of potatoes, scallions and coconut milk mixture.

8. Cover and bake for 30 to 45 minutes, until potatoes are just tender.

9. Remove the cover and continue to bake until the potatoes are browned, 10 to 15 minutes. Then serve.

VEGETABLE MILLET PILAF

MAKES 4 SERVINGS

Millet is actually a seed—one that is high in fiber, protein, iron, magnesium, manganese, zinc, omega-3 fatty acids, amino acids, and lignans (which protect against cancer and heart disease, and help heal digestive disorders).

1   tablespoon liquid coconut oil

1   shallot or ½ medium onion, minced

4   cloves garlic, chopped

1   cup uncooked millet

1   medium zucchini or yellow squash, diced

½   cup sliced baby bella mushrooms

1   cup vegetable or chicken broth

1   cup canned coconut milk

    Salt and pepper, to taste

1. Heat coconut oil in a medium saucepan over medium-high heat. Add the shallot and cook for 2 or 3 minutes until it begins to soften.

2. Add garlic and the millet and stir to coat. Let the millet toast for 1 or 2 minutes.

3. Add the zucchini and mushrooms and sauté for 2 to 3 minutes.

4. Add the broth and coconut milk and let the liquid come to a boil. Turn down the heat to medium-low and cover. Check every 5 minutes or so but don't stir.

5. Once all of the liquid is absorbed, take the millet off heat and allow it to sit for 5 minutes with the cover on.

6. Fluff the millet with a fork and add salt and pepper to taste.

COCONUT BROWN RICE

MAKES 6 SERVINGS

Coconut rice is one of my kids' favorite side dishes. It is full of fiber and protein, and boasts an incredible array of minerals (manganese, selenium, magnesium). Coconut Brown Rice is the perfect foil for curries, sautés, stir-fry, and other saucy dishes. It's also a great base for more elaborate dishes: Just add nuts, dried fruit, beans, or other ingredients and you've got yourself a pilaf.

2 ½ cups water

1   14-ounce can coconut milk

½   teaspoon salt

2   cups brown rice

1. In a medium saucepot, bring water, coconut milk, and salt to a boil.

2. Add rice, stir just once, reduce heat to low, and cover.

3. Simmer for about 45 minutes (without stirring even once—that's what makes rice mushy!) or until rice is cooked and grains are separated and fluffy with no liquid left in the pot. You can lift the lid once or twice while rice cooks to check on it, but quickly replace the lid.

CAULIFLOWER MASHED "POTATOES"

MAKES 6 SERVINGS

This is an absolutely delicious, as well as a sneaky, way to get high levels of vitamins C and K, manganese, and anti-inflammatory phytonutrients into your diet. And did I mention how delicious it is?

5   cups roughly chopped cauliflower

5   cloves garlic

1   cup canned coconut milk

2   tablespoons liquid coconut oil

1   teaspoon salt

1   teaspoon black pepper

    Optional: 2 tablespoons chopped chives or parsley

1. Fill a large pot with salted water and bring to a boil. Add cauliflower and garlic cloves and simmer over low heat for 8 minutes or until soft but not mushy.

2. Drain cauliflower and garlic and place in a food processor. Pulse until chunky.

3. Add coconut milk, coconut oil, and salt and pepper, and pulse until smooth.

4. Transfer to a serving dish and, if desired, garnish with chopped herbs.

VEGGIE SIDES

COCONUT MILK–BRAISED GREENS

MAKES 4 SERVINGS

Feel free to add chopped nuts, shredded dried coconut, or even raisins to the finished dish. Delicious.

- 1 *pound (about 2 bunches) collard greens, kale, or mustard greens, stems and ribs removed, roughly chopped*
- 2 *tablespoons liquid coconut oil*
- 1 *small yellow onion, thinly sliced*
- ¾ *cup canned coconut milk*
- 1 *tablespoon lemon juice*
  Salt, to taste
  Black pepper, to taste

1. Bring a large pot of salted water to a boil. Add greens and cook for 2 minutes. Drain well in a colander and set aside.

2. Heat coconut oil in a large skillet over medium heat. Add onions and cook about 5 minutes, stirring often, until onions are tender and translucent.

3. Add greens, coconut milk, and lemon juice to the skillet. Stir and allow to simmer until tender, about 7 minutes.

4. Season with salt and pepper.

SOUTHEAST ASIAN BROCCOLI

MAKES 2 SERVINGS

One of the first foods to be named a "superfood," broccoli contains high levels of vitamin K, vitamin C, vitamin B6, vitamin E, vitamin B2, vitamin A, and vitamin B1, as well as chromium, folate, fiber, pantothenic acid, manganese, choline, potassium, and a mix of cancer-fighting phytonutrients.

- 1 *tablespoon liquid coconut oil*
- 2 *heads broccoli, including the upper part of the stalk, chopped into dice-size pieces*
  Salt, to taste
- 5 *tablespoons canned coconut milk, divided*
- 2 *scallions, thinly sliced*
- 1 *large lime, zested and juiced*
- 1 *clove garlic, minced*
- 1 *small piece ginger, minced*
- ¼ *teaspoon ground coriander*
- ¼ *teaspoon ground red chili pepper*
  Optional garnish: 1 tablespoon unsweetened dried shredded coconut

1. Heat coconut oil in a large skillet over medium-high heat.

2. When the oil is hot, add the broccoli and some salt. Stir-fry the broccoli for a minute.

3. Add 2 tablespoons of the coconut milk to the broccoli and cook just until broccoli begins to get tender-crisp.

4. Remove broccoli from heat and stir in the scallions, lime zest and juice, garlic, ginger, spices, and remaining coconut milk. Adjust salt if necessary. Toss to combine.

5. Garnish with shredded dried coconut, if desired.

SHREDDED SUMMER SQUASH

MAKES 2 SERVINGS

This is how zucchini is done in the Pedersen household. (We often tuck it into burritos or pasta.)

1 *tablespoon liquid coconut oil*

1 *garlic clove, minced*

6 *small or 4 medium zucchini or yellow crookneck squash, shredded on a box grater*
   Salt and pepper, to taste

2 *tablespoons canned coconut milk*
   Optional: 1 tablespoon minced herb or herbs of choice

1. Heat coconut oil in a large skillet over medium heat. Add garlic and cook for 30 seconds.

2. Add shredded squash to skillet. Season with salt and pepper and add coconut milk. Cook for 2 to 5 minutes, until just tender and liquid has mostly evaporated.

3. Garnish with herbs, if desired.

ROASTED VEGGIES IN COCONUT OIL

MAKES 8 SERVINGS

Play with this recipe—you can use equal amounts of radish, rutabaga, fennel, burdock, kohlrabi, broccoli stems, Brussels sprouts, or anything else that strikes your fancy! No matter which veggie you roast, it will be a revelation.

4 *to 5 carrots, peeled*

2 *medium onions, peeled*

1 *acorn squash, cleaned and peeled*

1 *large sweet potato, peeled*

3 *to 4 small red potatoes*

1 *medium beet, peeled*

¼ *cup coconut oil*
   Unrefined sea salt, to taste
   Freshly ground black pepper, to taste
   Optional: 1 or more tablespoons fresh chopped herb, such as thyme

1. Preheat oven to 425°F.

2. Cut all vegetables into similarly sized pieces.

3. Place vegetables in a bowl, drizzle with coconut oil, and sprinkle with salt and pepper and optional herb. Using clean hands, toss veggies until all are coated.

4. Place vegetables in a single layer on 1 or 2 rimless baking sheets.

5. Roast for 25 to 35 minutes or until all the vegetables are tender, turning once.

CHAPTER 8

COCONUT DESSERTS AND OTHER SWEETS

A s much as it pains the nutritionist in me to admit this, coconut is the quintessential dessert ingredient. Say the word "coconut" and most people aren't even going to consider coconut water, coconut flour, or coconut oil. What they'll think of, instead, is chocolate-covered coconut candy bars, coconut cake, creamy pies, coconut shortbread, and various other sweet confections—all of which makes including a dessert chapter in this book a natural addition.

But—and this is a big "but"—unlike mainstream coconut sweets, the ones in this chapter are actually good for you. The recipes are filled with coconut in all its magnificence. Here, you'll find delectable coconut bars, coconut cakes, coconut cookies, coconut candy, and dozens of other goodies—all of which have been developed to delight your taste buds as well as nourish your body.

BARS

APRICOT COCONUT BARS

MAKES 9 BARS

As a child in Australia, one of my favorite treats was a dried apricot–coconut candy bar. It remains the closest thing to heaven I've ever tasted. I rarely get back to Oz for those bars—but this homemade version makes me just as happy. It is rich in fiber, protein, vitamins, and minerals, and it's my favorite nutrient-dense pick-me-up.

½ *cup unsalted cashews*

1 *cup dried apricots*

¾ *cup unsweetened shredded dried coconut*

⅓ *cup rolled oats*

2 *tablespoons coconut nectar or honey*

1 *tablespoon liquid coconut oil*

2 *tablespoons hempseed*

¼ *teaspoon sea salt*

1. Line an 8-by-8-inch baking pan with foil or parchment paper. Set aside.

2. In a food processor, pulse cashews just until coarsely chopped. Empty these into a small bowl and set aside.

3. Pulse apricots in a food processor until finely chopped. Add coconut, oats, coconut nectar, coconut oil, hempseed, and salt, pulsing until well combined.

4. Add chopped cashews to the mixture and pulse a couple of times until combined.

5. Firmly press mixture into prepared pan. Smooth surface.

6. Place pan in the freezer for 1 or 2 hours.

7. Using a wet knife, cut into bars.

8. Store uneaten bars in the refrigerator.

COCONUT FLOUR RECIPES: WHAT'S WITH ALL THE EGGS?

If you've ever baked with coconut flour—or even if you've ever looked up coconut recipes in your favorite healthy cookbook or online—you've probably noticed that most recipes contain a large number of eggs. There's a reason for that: Coconut flour is an absorbent flour, and one that does not bind together well. Eggs give coconut flour–based recipes a moister consistency and help these goodies stick together so they are not a dry, clumpy mess of crumbs! When baking with coconut flour, you usually want to use about 3 or more eggs (or the equivalent egg replacement) for every ½ cup of flour.

COCONUT CRISPIES
MAKES 9 BARS

I grew up eating Rice Krispies Treats made with melted margarine and marshmallows. I still love the idea of those classic sweets, but I feed my children this healthier superfood version. Keep Coconut Crispies in the freezer or fridge so they stay firm.

¼ cup organic thick (not runny) almond, cashew, peanut, sunflower, or other nut butter

¼ cup coconut oil

1½ tablespoons coconut nectar

   Pinch of salt

   Optional: 1½ teaspoons organic vanilla

   Optional: 1½ teaspoons organic cinnamon or pumpkin pie spice

2 cups brown rice cereal (you can also used puffed quinoa, millet, or barley cereal)

1 cup finely shredded unsweetened dried coconut

1. Line an 8-by-8-inch baking pan with foil.

2. In a large saucepan over low heat, melt together nut butter and coconut oil.

3. Whisk in coconut nectar, pinch of salt, and if desired, vanilla and spice. Keep stirring until mixture is smooth.

4. Add cereal and shredded coconut, stirring until thoroughly coated.

5. Firmly press mixture into prepared pan.

6. Place pan in freezer for 2 hours or overnight.

7. Using a sharp knife, slice into 9 bars.

8. Store uneaten treats in refrigerator.

BROWNIES EXTRAORDINAIRE

MAKES ABOUT 9 BROWNIES

If you are like me, you've spent years searching for the best brownie recipe. This one may be it. It has a very faint coconut taste that beautifully complements the full-on chocolaty goodness. Plus, you get the brain, heart, skin, and immune system benefits of coconut flour, coconut oil, and coconut milk. Last, these brownies are gluten- and grain-free, making them great for you if you have celiac disease or are on a Paleo diet.

½ cup coconut flour

½ cup unsweetened cocoa powder

½ teaspoon salt

½ teaspoon baking soda

   Optional: ¼ teaspoon allspice or cinnamon or pumpkin pie spice

5 large eggs

⅓ cup liquid coconut oil

¾ cup coconut nectar (or Grade B maple syrup, honey, or a blend of the two)

1 teaspoon vanilla extract

2 tablespoons canned coconut milk (do not use "lite")

1. Preheat oven to 350°F.

2. Lightly grease an 8-by-8-inch baking pan. Set aside.

3. In a large bowl, whisk together coconut flour, cocoa powder, salt, baking soda, and allspice (if desired) until thoroughly combined and clump-free. Set aside.

4. Using a stand mixer with a paddle attachment, blend together eggs, coconut oil, coconut nectar, vanilla extract, and coconut milk on a low speed. Continue until thoroughly combined.

5. Add the coconut flour mixture to the egg mixture and blend on a low speed until well combined.

6. Pour batter into prepared pan.

7. Bake for 25 minutes or until a toothpick inserted in the middle comes out clean.

8. Allow brownies to cool before cutting into bars with a wet knife.

MAKE YOUR OWN ALMOND FLOUR

If you don't have almond flour on hand—and need it for a recipe—don't panic. It's easy to make your own! Simply place whole or sliced, raw or roasted almonds in a food processor and pulse until the nuts are pulverized. Be careful not to overprocess the almonds, however—otherwise you'll end up with almond butter.

PUMPKIN PIE BARS

MAKES 9 BARS

I love pumpkin and coconut together—which is why these scrumptious bars are one of my favorites. They are rich in beta-carotene, fiber, protein, minerals, phytonutrients, and omega-3 fatty acids.

- ½ cup old-fashioned rolled oats (certified gluten-free if necessary)
- ½ cup pumpkin seeds
- ½ cup unsweetened shredded dried coconut
- ½ teaspoon cinnamon
- ⅜ teaspoon salt, divided
- ⅔ cup pitted dates, chopped (plus a few more if needed)
- 1½ cups pumpkin puree
- ⅓ cup coconut nectar or Grade B maple syrup
- ¼ cup liquid coconut oil
- 1 teaspoon vanilla
- 2 teaspoons pumpkin pie spice (or any blend of cinnamon, ginger, cloves, allspice, and/or cardamom)
- ⅛ teaspoon black pepper
- 2 tablespoons coconut flour

1. Line an 8-by-8-inch baking pan with foil or parchment paper so you'll easily be able to lift the bars out of the pan and cut them.

2. To make the crust: Place the oats, pumpkin seeds, shredded coconut, cinnamon, and ⅛ teaspoon of the salt in a food processor. Pulse just until finely ground.

3. Add ⅔ cup dates and process until well combined and sticky. The mixture may look crumbly, but it should hold together when pinched between your fingers. If necessary, add more dates to get the right consistency.

HOW TO "HEALTHY UP" A BOXED CAKE MIX

When I was growing up, most families made cakes from store-bought mixes that came in a box. These mixes may have been convenient and certainly delivered foolproof results in a jiffy, but they were—and still are—chock-full of chemical ingredients that are not so good for you. For a more nutritious alternative, head over to your local health food store and check out some of the whole-food cake mixes that are made by companies like Bob's Red Mill and Arrowhead Mills. To make these mixes even healthier, just replace the oil or melted butter that may be called for with liquid coconut oil. You can also use coconut milk to replace any liquids. These are easy, delicious ways to add omega-3 fatty acids, brain-supporting lauric acid, and cardiovascular heart-protective medium chain fatty acids to your baked goods.

4. Press the dough firmly and evenly into the baking pan. Place the pan in the freezer.

5. To make the filling: Combine the pumpkin puree, coconut nectar, coconut oil, vanilla, ¼ teaspoon salt, pumpkin pie spice, and black pepper in a food processor. Blend until smooth.

6. Add the coconut flour and blend until well combined.

7. Remove the pan from the freezer and pour the filling on top, spreading it out evenly. Cover and refrigerate for at least 6 hours or overnight.

8. Lift the bars out of the pan using the edges of the foil or parchment paper. Use a wet chef's knife to cut bars, wiping the knife clean between cuts. Serve chilled.

9. Store uneaten bars in refrigerator.

PURE COCONUT BARS

MAKES 9 BARS

This fun recipe is pure coconut—and it's filled with fats that are healthy for your brain, fiber, protein, antioxidants, and phytonutrients. Chocolate lovers may want to add ½ cup chopped dark raw chocolate to the mix—or add chopped macadamia nuts, cashews, or almonds, if you like.

> 2 *cups unsweetened shredded dried coconut*
>
> ⅓ *cup coconut nectar or Grade B maple syrup*
>
> 4 *tablespoons liquid coconut oil*
>
> 1 *teaspoon pure vanilla extract*
>
> ¼ *teaspoon salt*

1. Line an 8-by-8-inch baking pan with foil. Set aside.

2. Combine all ingredients in a food processor. Pulse until ingredients are well combined and mixture is smooth.

3. Firmly press mixture into prepared pan, smoothing the top.

4. Allow the mixture to set in the freezer for 1 hour or in the refrigerator for 3 hours before serving.

5. Cut bars with a wet knife.

CUPS AND CAKES

ALMOND-COCONUT POUND CAKE

MAKES 8 SERVINGS

Dense, flavorful, and rich with protein, vitamins, fiber, and antioxidants, this wonderful cake is a healthier, better-tasting (in my opinion!) twist on the traditional pound cake. Sometimes I dress it up even more by adding chunks of almond paste or marzipan to the batter. I've even slipped in chopped dark chocolate, though my favorite way to enjoy this recipe is just as it's written. Because this cake contains so much almond flour, it is a bit pricey to make, so save it for someone who loves almonds.

3   cups almond flour

¼   cup coconut flour

¾   teaspoon baking soda

1   teaspoon baking powder

½   teaspoon salt

½   cup liquid coconut oil

⅔   cup coconut sugar

4   large eggs

½   cup canned coconut milk

½   teaspoon almond extract

1   teaspoon vanilla extract

1. Preheat oven to 350°F.

2. Grease a mini loaf pan with a light coating of coconut oil.

3. In a large bowl, whisk together almond flour, coconut flour, baking soda, baking powder, and salt.

4. In the bowl of a stand mixer, blend together liquid coconut oil, coconut sugar, eggs, coconut milk, almond extract, and vanilla extract on a medium speed.

5. Add dry ingredients to liquid mixture 1 cup at a time, blending between additions. Blend just until smooth.

6. Scrape batter into prepared pan, smoothing the top.

7. Bake for 35 to 45 minutes, or until a cake tester inserted in the middle of the cake comes out clean.

8. Allow cake to cool for 15 minutes before slicing.

GLUTEN-FREE FUDGE CAKE

MAKES 4 SERVINGS

Rich, chocolaty, and gluten-free, this fudge cake is baked in individual portions. Coconut flour, coconut oil, and coconut sugar create a moist, nutrient-dense cake. This outrageous dessert is best tackled by more experienced bakers.

⅔ cup dark or semisweet chocolate chips
(or 4.2 ounces of chocolate)

4 tablespoons liquid coconut oil

2 large eggs

1 teaspoon vanilla extract

⅛ teaspoon salt

2 tablespoons coconut sugar

1 teaspoon coconut flour

2 teaspoons cocoa powder

1. Preheat oven to 375°F.

2. Grease and flour four 6-ounce ramekins using coconut oil and coconut flour or another gluten-free flour. Place them on a baking sheet.

3. In a double boiler or a saucepan over very low heat, melt chocolate with the coconut oil. Set aside.

4. In the bowl of a stand mixer, using the paddle attachment, beat together eggs, vanilla, salt, and coconut sugar until frothy, about 4 to 5 minutes on medium-low setting.

5. Slowly mix in melted chocolate and coconut oil.

6. Gently add in coconut flour and cocoa powder. Keep mixing until batter is smooth.

7. Pour batter evenly into ramekins.

8. Bake for 10 to 13 minutes.

CHOCOLATE COCONUT CUPCAKES

MAKES 12 CUPCAKES

Yum!!! You will love these gluten-free cupcakes! They are packed with all the goodness of coconut, including lauric acid, protein, fiber, and phytonutrients for healthy nervous system and immune system function. (Note that the batter is very thin.) If you're using purchased applesauce or pumpkin puree, check the ingredients. These are not gluten-containing foods, but you never know what some food companies add to their products!

1⅔ cups gluten-free baking flour

⅓ cup coconut flour

2 teaspoons baking soda

1 teaspoon baking powder
Pinch of salt

¾ cup cocoa

1 cup hot water or coffee

1 cup water or orange juice

4 large eggs

½ cup liquid coconut oil

½ cup applesauce, mashed banana,
or pumpkin puree

1 cup coconut sugar

1 cup canned coconut milk
Optional: gluten-free frosting or topping of choice
Optional: ¼ cup shredded dried coconut for garnish

1. Preheat oven to 350°F.

2. Lightly grease a 12-cup muffin tin with coconut oil (or use paper cupcake liners).

3. In a large bowl, whisk together the flours, baking soda, baking powder, and salt. Set aside.

4. In a second bowl, mix the cocoa with the hot water or coffee. Stir in the additional cup of water or orange juice. Set aside.

5. In the bowl of a stand mixer, cream together the eggs, coconut oil, applesauce, coconut sugar, and coconut milk.

6. To the creamed egg-applesauce mixture, add ⅓ of the flour mixture. Blend until combined, then add ⅓ of the cocoa-liquid mixture. Blend. Repeat 2 more times until everything is blended into a smooth batter.

7. Pour the batter into the prepared muffin cups until each is almost ¾ full.

8. Bake for 20 minutes, or until a toothpick in the center comes out clean.

9. If you like, frost cupcakes once they have thoroughly cooled.

10. For a dramatic presentation, scatter some shredded coconut over the frosting.

MAKING YOUR OWN SWEETENED SHREDDED COCONUT

To make a healthier version of sweetened flake coconut, put 2 cups of unsweetened shredded dried coconut in a large zip storage bag or a storage container. Add in 1 or 2 tablespoons of coconut sugar that you have pulverized into powder using a coffee grinder, food processor, or high-power blender (such as a Vitamix or Blendtec). Store in a cool location. Shake or stir well before using.

GINGER-LIME COCONUT POUND CAKE

MAKES 8 SERVINGS

This is another dense, moist pound cake. I love it made only with lime, only with ginger, and with both flavors together. Try making this pound cake all 3 ways and find your favorite! No matter how you flavor it, you're getting a hefty dose of lauric acid to help promote stable moods and brain health, and medium chain fatty acids to keep your cardiovascular system at its strongest.

Cake

1⅓ cup unbleached all-purpose flour (regular or gluten-free)

⅓ cup coconut flour

2 teaspoons baking powder

¼   teaspoon salt

½   cup coconut oil

¼   cup coconut sugar

4   large eggs

½   cup canned coconut milk (do not use "lite")

2   teaspoons vanilla extract

2   tablespoons lime zest

¼   tablespoon lime juice

1   tablespoon fresh ginger, minced or grated

¼   cup unsweetened shredded dried coconut

¼   cup crystallized ginger, chopped fine

Glaze

¼   cup coconut sugar

¼   cup lime juice

1. Preheat oven to 350°F.

2. Lightly grease a 4-by-8-inch loaf pan with coconut oil.

3. In a large bowl, whisk together both flours, baking powder, and salt. Set aside.

4. In a large bowl of a standing mixer, cream the coconut oil with ¼ cup coconut sugar. The mixture will appear crumbly.

5. Add the eggs, one at a time, beating well between each addition. The mixture will become creamy-looking.

6. To the mixer bowl, add coconut milk, vanilla, lime zest, ¼ tablespoon lime juice, and fresh ginger. Beat once more.

7. Add the flour mixture to the batter and mix only until just combined. Do not overmix.

8. Gently stir in dried coconut and crystallized ginger.

9. Pour the batter into prepared loaf pan.

10. Bake for 45 minutes, or until a toothpick inserted into the center comes out clean.

11. While the cake bakes, make the glaze: Whisk together ¼ cup coconut sugar with ¼ cup lime juice in a small saucepan over medium-low heat. Simmer until sugar is completely dissolved, about 1 minute.

12. Immediately upon removing the cake from the oven, poke holes in it using a toothpick or thin skewer. Using a pastry brush, brush glaze over the cake. Or use a spoon and smooth glaze over the top of the cake.

13. Allow cake to cool completely before slicing.

EASY COCONUT FROSTING

In a large bowl of a stand mixer, add ½ cup coconut butter, 1 teaspoon vanilla extract, and 2 tablespoons coconut nectar. (You can add 1 teaspoon of cocoa powder to make chocolate frosting.) Using a whisk attachment, beat on a high speed until blended and light and fluffy. This makes enough to frost 6 to 12 cupcakes.

DARK BARK

MAKES 4 SERVINGS

This recipe is easy, fun, and customizable.

- 1 cup coconut sugar
- 1 cup cocoa
- 1½ cups unsweetened shredded dried coconut
- 1½ cups liquid coconut oil
-    Pinch of salt
- ¼ cup coarsely or finely chopped nuts or seeds
- ¼ cup dried fruit, chopped if large

1. In a food processor, pulse coconut sugar until powdery.

2. Add cocoa and shredded coconut and pulse 2 or 3 times just to blend.

3. In a large bowl, whisk together the blended coconut-cocoa mixture with the coconut oil and salt. Mix until smooth.

4. Stir in chopped nuts and fruit.

5. Using a spatula, scrape chocolate mixture onto wax paper or a nonstick baking mat, spreading mixture to about ¼ inch in height.

6. Move wax paper or nonstick baking mat with the chocolate to the fridge and chill for 45 minutes or more.

7. Break bark into pieces (you get to choose the size).

8. Store uneaten candy in a sealed container in the refrigerator.

CANDY

APRICOT BITES

MAKES 8 PIECES

I promise that even if you don't love apricots as much as I do, you'll love this sprightly, addictive treat. The apricots are rich in beta-carotene, for a healthy immune system, eyes, and skin. There are generous amounts of fiber in the apricots and coconut, plus the coconut butter and coconut oil provide medium chain fatty acids for cardiovascular health.

- 1 cup dried apricots, divided
- ⅓ cup unsweetened shredded dried coconut
- 5 tablespoons coconut butter
- 2 tablespoons coconut oil
-    Zest of 1 lemon or lime

1. Lightly grease a mini (5½-by-3-by-2½-inch) loaf pan with coconut oil, or line the pan with wax paper. Set aside.

2. Add ½ cup of the dried apricots to the bowl of a food processor. Pulse until the apricots are chopped into medium pieces. Remove to a large bowl and set aside.

3. In the same food processor bowl, add the remaining ½ cup dried apricots and process into a creamy paste.

4. Add apricot paste and remaining ingredients to the chopped apricots. Mix together, by hand, until ingredients are thoroughly combined.

5. Scrape batter into prepared pan, smoothing the top.

6. Refrigerate for 1 hour or more until firm. Cut into small squares.

WHITE FUDGE

MAKES 12 PIECES

Did you know this fudge could, potentially, help keep colds, flu, and other viruses at bay? Well, that hasn't exactly been proven, but coconut oil and coconut butter have been proven to have antiviral, antibacterial, antifungal, and even antiparasitic healing properties. Research has also shown that coconut oil and the coconut flesh in coconut butter help support overall immune system functions. The cashews add protein and fiber to this fudge. And did I mention how delicious this dessert is?

1   cup cashews

1   cup coconut butter

½   cup cocoa butter

¼   cup coconut nectar or Grade B
     maple syrup

1   teaspoon vanilla extract

¼   teaspoon salt

1. Lightly grease a mini-muffin pan or fill the cups with muffin liners. If you have chocolate molds, you can use them instead of a mini-muffin pan. Set aside.

2. In a food processor or high-speed blender, blend cashews into a paste.

3. In a saucepan over medium heat, combine pureed cashews with remaining ingredients. Stir often until ingredients are combined and warmed through, about 5 minutes.

4. Spoon cooked fudge mixture into prepared muffin cups or molds.

5. Place the filled muffin pan or molds in the freezer for 45 minutes or in the refrigerator for 2 hours to firm up.

6. Store uneaten fudge in the refrigerator.

COCONUT PECAN CHOCOLATE TRUFFLES

MAKES 8 TRUFFLES

This tasty truffle recipe relies heavily on coconut and provides a hefty dose of fiber and protein, thanks to the nuts and seeds. I like to wear food gloves when I prepare these treats, since truffle-making is a messy business!

- 1   *cup raw pepitas*
- 1   *cup raw pecans or walnuts*
- 3   *tablespoons coconut nectar*
- 1   *teaspoon vanilla extract*
- 1   *teaspoon cinnamon*
- ¼   *teaspoon salt*
- 2   *tablespoons coconut oil*
- ¼   *cup unsweetened shredded dried coconut (preferably finely shredded)*

1. Line a baking sheet with wax paper. Set aside.

2. In the bowl of a food processor, pulse together the pepitas and pecans until they are coarsely chopped.

3. Add coconut nectar, vanilla extract, cinnamon, salt, and coconut oil, pulsing until they form a rough paste.

4. Using a tablespoon or a small cookie scoop, take a clump of the truffle paste and roll it into a smooth ball. Repeat until all the paste has been used. Place truffle balls on prepared baking sheet.

5. Place baking sheet in the refrigerator for 1 hour or until truffle balls are firm.

6. Place dried coconut in a shallow bowl or plate. Remove baking sheet from the refrigerator. Roll each truffle ball, one at a time, in the coconut until thoroughly coated. Place truffles back on prepared baking sheet.

7. Return to the refrigerator for another hour so they can re-firm after being rolled in coating.

PUMPKIN COCONUT FUDGE

MAKES 12 PIECES

Pumpkin provides beta-carotene for a healthy immune system, eyes, and skin, and coconut offers medium chain fatty acids for cardiovascular health and lauric acid for nervous system function. If you happen to have a blend of pumpkin pie spice in your cupboard, you can use 1 to 2 teaspoons of it instead of the spices listed here, and make Pumpkin Coconut Fudge a new Thanksgiving tradition.

- ¾   *cup pumpkin puree (or canned puree)*
- ¾   *cup coconut butter*
- 3   *tablespoons maple syrup or raw honey*
- 1   *teaspoon ground cinnamon*
- ¼   *teaspoon ground nutmeg*
- ¼   *teaspoon ground ginger*
- ¼   *teaspoon ground cloves*

1. Prepare a mini-muffin pan by lining it with muffin papers.

2. In a saucepan over medium heat, mix together all ingredients, stirring until thoroughly combined.

3. Pour mixture into prepared mini-muffin cups.

4. Place the pan in the refrigerator for 1 or more hours to firm up.

5. Store uneaten fudge in a covered container in the refrigerator.

NUT BUTTER FUDGE

MAKES 8 PIECES

Here is yet another coconut fudge recipe that is easy, filling, delicious, and good for you, thanks to all of the healthy coconut (great for cardiovascular, immune, and nervous systems) plus protein-packed nut butter. This recipe comes together very quickly!

½ *cup unsalted smooth almond or cashew butter*

½ *cup coconut butter*

¼ *cup coconut sugar*

¼ *cup coconut nectar, Grade B maple syrup, or honey*

1 *teaspoon vanilla extract*

¼ *teaspoon salt*

1. Lightly grease a mini (5½-by-3-by-2½-inch) loaf pan with coconut oil.

2. In a small pot set over low heat, stir together all ingredients, stirring continually until smooth and completely blended.

3. Pour mixture into prepared pan, smoothing the top with a spatula.

4. Refrigerate 2 hours or until completely firm.

5. Cut into slices to serve.

6. Store uneaten fudge in the refrigerator.

COOKIES

COCO-CHIP GLUTEN-FREE COOKIES

MAKES 12 COOKIES

Are you gluten-free? You are going to love this chocolate chip cookie recipe. It is delicious and, yep, the coconut flour and coconut oil make it health-supportive, too!

 8 *tablespoons semisolid coconut oil*

 1 *cup coconut sugar*

 1 *egg*

 1½ *teaspoons vanilla extract*

 ½ *cup coconut flour*

 ½ *cup gluten-free all-purpose flour (can be substituted with regular all-purpose flour if cookies don't need to be gluten-free)*

 ½ *teaspoon baking soda*

   Pinch of salt

 1 *cup dark chocolate chips*

1. Preheat oven to 375°F.

2. Line a baking sheet with foil or parchment.

3. In the bowl of a stand mixer, using a paddle attachment, beat together semisolid coconut oil and coconut sugar until well mixed.

4. Beat in egg and vanilla.

5. In a separate bowl, whisk together coconut flour, gluten-free all-purpose flour, baking soda, and salt.

6. Add flour mixture to the ingredients in the bowl of the mixer, and beat on low. Continue until dough is just combined.

7. Add chocolate chips and mix just until distributed.

8. Using a small ice cream scoop or a teaspoon, drop the dough onto a cookie sheet, about 2 inches apart.

9. Bake for 9 to 11 minutes on center rack until just golden.

10. Allow cookies to cool on the cookie sheet before removing.

HOW TO MAKE SEMISOLID COCONUT OIL

To make the semisolid coconut oil called for in several of this book's recipes, simply place your jar or tub of coconut oil in the refrigerator for 30 to 60 minutes. When you remove the coconut oil from the fridge, you'll find it in a soft semisolid state. To measure, spoon what you need into a measuring cup and add to your recipe.

COCONUT SUGAR COOKIES

MAKES 5 DOZEN 4-INCH COOKIES

This coconut-rich cookie is a delicious take on the standard sugar cookie. Try it the next time you want to bake holiday cookies. I like to mix things up by grating in some lemon zest.

1   *cup semisolid coconut oil*

1   *cup coconut sugar*

1   *egg*

1   *tablespoon canned coconut milk (or regular dairy whole milk)*

1   *teaspoon vanilla*

3   *cups all-purpose flour*

¾   *teaspoon baking powder*

½   *teaspoon salt*

1. In the bowl of a stand mixer, using a paddle attachment, cream together semisolid coconut oil and sugar until light and fluffy.

2. Blend in egg, milk, and vanilla until combined.

3. In a separate bowl, whisk together flour, baking powder, and salt.

4. Slowly, 1 cup at a time, add dry ingredients to the mixing bowl. Mix until just combined.

5. Place 2 large sheets of plastic wrap (each about 20 inches long) on a flat, damp surface. Divide dough between sheets of plastic. Pat each into a flat oval, about ½-inch thick.

Cover with more plastic wrap and place in the freezer until firm, about 30 minutes.

6. When ready to bake, preheat oven to 375°F.

7. Prepare baking sheet with foil or parchment.

8. Remove dough from refrigerator or freezer and, using a rolling pin, roll dough about ⅛-inch thick.

9. Cut into shapes with cookie cutters.

10. Place cookies onto prepared baking sheet about 1 inch apart.

11. Bake 8 to 10 minutes or until cookies become golden around the edges.

12. Allow cookies to cool thoroughly before decorating them with your favorite toppings—or enjoy them just as they are.

NUT BUTTER COOKIES

MAKES 12 COOKIES

This is my family's go-to cookie. It's gluten-free, super high in protein and fiber, outrageously simple to make, and very tasty. Oh, and it's flexible, too. Sometimes we add some chopped chocolate to the batter or insert a piece of chocolate into thumbprints in the dough. Sometimes I roll these versatile cookies in sugar, cinnamon sugar, finely shredded coconut, or chopped nuts. I tend to make batches of the dough ahead of time and keep it in airtight containers in the fridge for fast treats.

1 cup thick nut butter (peanut, almond, cashew, sunflower, etc.; you can also use a blend of nut butters)

1 cup coconut sugar (you can also use regular sugar or brown sugar or a blend)

1 large egg

½ teaspoon baking soda

Optional: pinch of cinnamon, allspice, or pumpkin pie spice blend

1. Preheat oven to 350°F.

2. Line a baking sheet with foil or parchment.

3. In the bowl of a stand mixer, using the paddle attachment, cream together nut butter and sugar on medium speed until light and fluffy.

4. Add in egg, baking soda, and spice, if using. Blend on low speed until just combined.

5. Cover dough and chill in the refrigerator until firm, about 30 minutes.

6. Form dough into cookies using a cookie scoop or 2 tablespoons. For a fancier look, you can shape into a ball, then press with the tines of a fork to create a classic peanut butter cookie appearance.

7. Bake for 8 to 10 minutes or until edges are golden.

8. Allow cookies to cool before removing them from baking sheet.

CARROT OATMEAL COOKIES

MAKES 18 COOKIES

I adore sneaking shredded carrots into baked goods. I literally use the pulp leftover when I juice carrots—it works beautifully. In addition to carrots, this wholesome recipe contains oats, walnuts, and coconut oil, creating a cookie filled with fiber, omega-3 fatty acids, medium chain fatty acids, and a bevy of antioxidants. It makes a great addition to any lunch box. Note that this recipe is vegan, making it perfect for those who are allergic to eggs and dairy.

1 cup whole wheat pastry flour or all-purpose flour

1 cup rolled oats

1 teaspoon baking powder

Optional: 1 teaspoon ground cinnamon or pumpkin pie spice blend

¼ teaspoon salt

⅔ cup chopped walnuts (feel free to experiment with other nuts)

1 cup finely shredded carrots

½ cup Grade B maple syrup

½ cup liquid coconut oil

1. Preheat oven to 350°F.

2. Line a baking sheet with foil or parchment paper.

3. In a large bowl, whisk together flour, oats, baking powder, cinnamon (if desired), and salt.

4. Stir in nuts and carrots. Set aside.

5. In the bowl of a stand mixer, blend together maple syrup and coconut oil until thoroughly combined.

6. Add the flour mixture to the syrup-oil mixture, blending on low, until just thoroughly combined.

7. Using a cookie scoop or 2 tablespoons, drop dough onto prepared baking sheets, leaving 1½ inches or more of space between them (this cookie spreads).

8. Bake until cookies are golden, about 12 to 15 minutes.

9. Allow cookies to cool on baking sheet before removing.

PEANUT-OAT-QUINOA COOKIES

MAKES 12 COOKIES

Here is yet another high-protein, high-fiber, nutty, yummy, not-too-sweet coconut-rich cookie! What makes this one a bit different is the quinoa flakes.

NOTE: To make these gluten-free, be sure to buy gluten-free oats and gluten-free oat bran. Gluten-free oat products are processed in dedicated, no-gluten facilities.

½ *cup oat bran*

¼ *cup old-fashioned rolled oats*

¼ *cup quinoa flakes*

¼ *cup coconut sugar*

½ *teaspoon baking powder*

¼ *teaspoon salt*

½ *teaspoon cinnamon, allspice, or pumpkin pie spice blend*

¼ *cup thick peanut butter*

1 *large egg*

¼ *cup applesauce, pear sauce, or pureed banana*

2 *tablespoons Grade B maple syrup*

1. Preheat oven to 350°F.

2. Line a baking sheet with parchment paper and set aside.

3. In a large mixing bowl, whisk together oat bran, rolled oats, quinoa flakes, coconut sugar, baking powder, salt, and spice. Set aside.

4. In the bowl of a stand mixer, blend together on a low speed peanut butter, egg, applesauce, and maple syrup.

5. Add the dry ingredients to the wet ingredients and blend until thoroughly combined.

6. Using a cookie scoop or 2 tablespoons, scoop dough onto prepared cookie sheet. If desired, flatten cookies with the back of a fork.

7. Bake until golden, 13 to 15 minutes.

8. Allow cookies to cool before removing from baking sheet.

NO-BAKE COCONUT MACAROONS

MAKES 12 MACAROONS

This no-bake recipe is perfect for those times you want something sweet that also has a bit of substance. You'll feel pleasantly full and get a nice steady drip of energy from these macaroons, thanks to the almonds and protein-packed chia. Sometimes I replace the vanilla with ¼ teaspoon of almond extract. Give it a try.

- 1   *tablespoon ground chia seeds*
- 3   *tablespoons warm water*
- 1½ *cups unsweetened shredded dried coconut*
- ½   *cup almonds*
- 10 *Medjool dates, pitted*
- 1   *tablespoon liquid coconut oil*
- 1   *teaspoon vanilla extract*

1. In a bowl, whisk together ground chia and warm water. Set aside.

2. In a food processor, pulse the coconut and almonds into a fine powder.

3. Add the dates, chia mixture, coconut oil, and vanilla. Pulse just until the mixture starts to come together.

4. Using a tablespoon, form the mixture into balls and place them on a baking sheet or plate.

5. Refrigerate for 30 minutes or more until the macaroons are firm.

VEGAN OATMEAL COOKIES

MAKES 18 COOKIES

This yummy oatmeal-coconut cookie is vegan—perfect for those of you who don't use dairy milk or eat eggs. Applesauce adds extra nutrients and gives the cookies a lovely moist texture.

- 1   *cup whole wheat pastry flour or spelt flour*
- 1   *cup old-fashioned rolled oats*
- 1½ *cups raisins (or chopped dried fruit of choice)*
- 1   *cup unsweetened shredded dried coconut*
- ½   *teaspoon baking soda*
- 1   *teaspoon ground cinnamon*
- 1   *teaspoon ground cardamom (or pumpkin pie spice or allspice)*
-     *Pinch of salt*
- ½   *cup applesauce*
- ½   *cup coconut sugar*
- ⅓   *cup coconut nectar or Grade B maple syrup*
- 1   *teaspoon vanilla extract*

1. Preheat oven to 350°F.

2. Line a baking sheet with foil or parchment.

3. In a large bowl, whisk together flour, oats, raisins, shredded coconut, baking soda, cinnamon, cardamom, and salt.

4. In a separate bowl, stir together applesauce, coconut sugar, coconut nectar, and vanilla.

5. Slowly add the dry ingredients to the wet, stirring until ingredients are thoroughly combined.

6. Make cookies using a cookie scoop or 2 tablespoons, placing each on prepared cookie sheet.

7. Bake for 15 minutes or until cookies are golden.

8. Allow cookies to cool before removing them from baking sheet.

CHOCOLATE-COCONUT BANANAS

MAKES 12 PIECES

Two of my sons love bananas. They love them even more if they are accompanied by chocolate (and coconut), hence this homemade version of chocolate-covered bananas.

NOTE: You'll need 12 ice-pop sticks or bamboo skewers to make these treats.

> ¼ *cup unsweetened shredded dried coconut*
>
> 4 *large ripe bananas, peeled, and cut into thirds crosswise*
>
> ¾ *cup semisweet or bittersweet chocolate chips, melted in a double boiler, slightly cooled*

1. Line a baking sheet with parchment, foil, or wax paper. Set aside.

2. Spread shredded coconut onto a plate or in a shallow dish. Set aside.

3. Insert an ice-pop stick into each piece of banana.

4. Working with one piece of banana at a time, dip (or coat, if that's easier) fruit in melted chocolate; then press into shredded coconut.

5. Place fully coated banana pieces onto prepared baking sheets and freeze overnight or until frozen.

SUPERFOOD FREEZER FUDGE

MAKES 12 PIECES

Eat this fudge and you get protein, fiber, fatty acids, antioxidants, and loads of phytonutrients. Feel free to play with the nut butter. For a fancier finish, sprinkle coarsely or finely chopped nuts, shredded coconut, or chopped chocolate over the top of the fudge before placing it in the freezer.

- 1 cup almond butter
- 4 tablespoons liquid coconut oil
- 1½ tablespoons coconut nectar or Grade B maple syrup
- 4 ounces 70 percent cacao dark chocolate, melted in a double boiler
- ¼ teaspoon salt

1. Lightly grease an 8-by-8-inch baking pan with coconut oil or line it with foil.

2. In the bowl of a stand mixer, cream almond butter, coconut oil, coconut nectar, melted chocolate, and salt.

3. Pour the mixture into the prepared pan.

4. Place the pan in the freezer overnight.

5. Remove the pan from freezer, and carefully cut fudge into 12 squares.

6. Store uneaten fudge in the freezer.

FRUITY COCONUT POPS

MAKES 12 POPS

My kids—like most kids, I suppose—love frozen treats. Ice pops are a favorite. This recipe is as flexible as you'd like it to be: Use whatever fresh or frozen fruit you have on hand. Coconut milk gives the treats protein and a host of nutrients for stronger immune systems, better brain function, and healthy hearts.

NOTE: You'll need 12 ice-pop molds and sticks to make these.

- 1 14-ounce can coconut milk (do not use "lite")
- 1 tablespoon coconut oil
- ¼ cup coconut sugar or cane sugar
- 1 cup chopped fruit of choice

1. In a high-speed blender or a food processor, process coconut milk, coconut oil, and sugar until smooth.

2. Add fruit and blend until fruit is liquefied—or, if you prefer, almost liquefied. (You may want a few small chunks of fruit in your ice pops.)

3. Pour liquid into ice pop molds and insert sticks. Set in the freezer overnight or until frozen solid.

COCONUT ICE CREAM

MAKES 6 SERVINGS

I buy ice cream on only the rarest of occasions. My kids are all semiprofessional singers, and mainstream ice cream means dairy. Which means mucus. Which means struggling through rehearsals and performances. This beautiful confection, however, is always welcome in my freezer. Made with coconut milk, it supports my children's health without any bothersome side effects. You will need an ice cream maker for this one.

2 *14-ounce cans coconut milk*

¾ *cup unsweetened shredded dried coconut*

2 *tablespoons arrowroot starch or cornstarch*

¾ *cup coconut sugar or cane sugar*

    Pinch of salt

    Optional: 1 or more teaspoons vanilla extract

    Optional add-ins: ½ to 1 cup chopped nuts, chocolate, fruit, etc.

1. In a blender or food processor, process 1 can of coconut milk with the shredded coconut and arrowroot starch. Set aside.

2. In a small saucepan, whisk together the second can of coconut milk, sugar, and salt over medium heat. Bring to a simmer.

3. Add the coconut milk mixture from the blender to the saucepan of coconut milk, sugar, and salt. Cook for 2 minutes or until slightly thickened.

4. Remove from heat and, if desired, stir in vanilla extract.

5. Allow mixture to cool in the refrigerator until thoroughly chilled, about 3 to 4 hours.

6. Using an ice cream maker, according to the manufacturer's directions, add chilled coconut mixture and any optional add-ins.

7. Freeze the mixture in ice cream maker, according to the manufacturer's instructions.

ARROWROOT POWDER

Arrowroot powder—also known as arrowroot starch—is derived from a tropical South American tuber. Like cornstarch, it is used as a thickener in recipes. The plant was given the name "arrowroot" by the native Caribbean Arawak people, because they used it to draw poison from wounds inflicted by poisoned arrows. Arrowroot was also a foundational food for the Arawak.

PINEAPPLE-COCONUT SORBET

MAKES 6 SERVINGS

I love this healthy, flavorful recipe (it's also rich in antioxidants from the coconut, ginger, and pineapple). An ice cream maker makes the smoothest sorbet, but you can use the "freezer tray method" outlined below.

- ½ cup coconut milk (canned or homemade)
- ½ cup coconut sugar or cane sugar
- 1-inch length of peeled fresh ginger, grated
- 1 whole pineapple (about 3½ pounds), peeled, cored, and cut into chunks
- 1 tablespoon lemon or lime juice

1. In a small saucepan over medium heat, whisk together coconut milk, sugar, and ginger. Bring to a simmer for 1 to 2 minutes. Remove from heat and let stand for 20 minutes.

2. Place pineapple and lemon juice in a food processor and process until absolutely smooth.

3. Add the cooled coconut milk mixture to the pineapple and process until thoroughly blended.

4. Pour mixture into ice cream maker and process according to manufacturer's directions. (Alternatively, freeze mixture in a shallow metal pan until solid, about 6 hours. Break into chunks and process in a food processor until smooth. Then pack into an airtight freezer container.)

COCONUT FUDGE ICE POPS

MAKES 8 POPS

The problem with commercial brand fudge pops is the ingredients: high fructose corn syrup, polysorbate 80, polysorbate 65? You don't need to put ingredients like those in your body. Try this healthful version instead. Not only is it tasty; it is good for you!

- 1 14-ounce can coconut milk
- ¼ cup unsweetened cocoa powder
- 3 tablespoons coconut or cane sugar
- 2 teaspoons vanilla extract
- Pinch of salt

1. Combine all ingredients in a blender and pulse a few times to blend thoroughly.

2. Pour mixture into ice-pop molds and freeze overnight.

KEY LIME SUPERFOOD POPS

MAKES 8 POPS

Now this is a fun recipe—one truly deserving of the title "superfood," thanks to its blend of avocado and coconut, both of which are known for their extremely beneficial fats, which also nourish the brain, heart, and skin. But, before you ask, no, you cannot taste the avocado. What you can taste, however, is the bright, refreshing flavor of key limes.

NOTE: You'll need 8 ice-pop molds and ice-pop sticks when making these treats.

1. *avocado, peeled and pitted*
½ *cup coconut milk (canned or fresh)*
¼ *cup coconut nectar*
¼ *cup key lime juice (you can use lemon if you'd like)*
2. *teaspoons vanilla extract*
¼ *teaspoon salt*

1. Process all ingredients in a blender until thoroughly integrated and smooth.

2. Pour mixture into ice-pop molds and freeze overnight, or until solid.

SUMMERTIME MANGO COCONUT SORBET

MAKES 6 SERVINGS

Mango is a natural sorbet ingredient—it is both sweet and tart and has a gorgeous bright color that doesn't go away, even when frozen. I like it because it is filled with fiber and vitamin A, for healthy skin and vision. It pairs beautifully with coconut in this elegant recipe. You will love this!

2. *cups of chopped mango*
1. *14-ounce can coconut milk (do not use "lite")*
3. *tablespoons lime juice*
3. *tablespoons coconut sugar*
1. *tablespoon arrowroot powder*

1. In a food processor or high-power blender (such as a Vitamix or Blendtec), puree mango until it becomes a smooth, creamy liquid.

2. Add in coconut milk, lime juice, coconut sugar, and arrowroot powder, and pulse just until ingredients are combined.

3. Pour liquid into an ice cream maker and freeze according to manufacturer's instructions.

PIES & TARTS

BERRY MACAROON TART

MAKES 8 SERVINGS

Berries and coconut—what a glorious combination! Not only does this taste like summer, but it is also filled with antioxidants and fiber from both the berries and the coconut. You will adore this! It's pretty easy to make, too.

Crust

1   cup plus 2 tablespoons spelt flour

½ cup plus 1 tablespoon dried unsweetened shredded coconut

½ cup plus 1 tablespoon regular cane or coconut sugar

    Optional: 1 teaspoon lemon or lime zest
    Pinch of salt

6 tablespoons liquid coconut oil

Filling

3   large egg whites

1½ cups dried unsweetened shredded coconut

6   tablespoons sugar

6   to 8 ounces fresh blackberries, raspberries, or other berries, or a mix

1. Preheat oven to 350°F.

2. Prepare a 9-inch tart pan by lining the bottom with parchment.

3. To make the crust: In a medium bowl, whisk together flour, coconut, sugar, zest, and salt.

4. Stir in coconut oil until combined and mixture gets clumpy.

5. Press mixture firmly into the bottom of the tart pan, working mixture up the sides of the pan as well. Use the back of a spoon or the bottom of a heavy glass to tamp down crust.

6. Place pan on a middle rack in the oven and bake for 15 minutes, or until just golden. Remove pan from oven and allow to cool.

7. To make macaroon filling: In a medium bowl, whisk egg whites until light and slightly frothy.

8. Stir in coconut and sugar. Set aside.

9. Start assembling the tart by scattering the berries over the tart crust.

10. Using a teaspoon, drop spoonfuls of the batter over berries. Do not smooth (yes, you want the macaroon batter to remain in lumps).

11. Bake for 20 minutes or until macaroon topping begins to turn golden.

12. Remove tart from oven and allow to cool before serving.

CHOCOLATE CREAM TART

MAKES 8 SERVINGS

This is basically what my six-year-old calls a "refrigerator pie." But it is so much healthier than the graham cracker crust, boxed pudding mix filling, and whipped topping from a tub that our moms and grandmothers used to make. This one actually has healthy ingredients, including walnuts (omega-3 fatty acids and protein), dates (fiber and minerals), avocado (vitamin K, and folate), and coconut (lauric acid, medium chain fatty acids, and antiviral properties).

1 cup walnuts

1 cup dates

1 ripe avocado

2 tablespoons coconut oil

2 tablespoons coconut nectar

2 tablespoons cocoa powder

1 teaspoon vanilla extract

Pinch of salt

¼ cup canned coconut milk, as needed

Optional: 1 cup Coconut Cream Dessert Topping (see page 155)

1. Lightly grease a 6-inch or 8-inch tart pan with coconut oil. Set aside.

2. To make the crust: In a food processor, pulse the walnuts into powder, then add the dates until it all begins to stick together. Press into prepared tart pan and set aside in the fridge.

3. To make the filling: In a clean food processor bowl, add avocado, coconut oil, coconut nectar, cocoa powder, vanilla, and salt. Process until all ingredients are smooth and thick. If filling mixture is too thin, add some coconut milk 1 tablespoon at a time, until you get the right consistency.

4. Remove tart pan from the fridge and fill with filling.

5. If desired, make the Coconut Cream Dessert Topping (see page 155) and spread 1 cup of it over the tart.

6. Place dessert back in the fridge until firm, about an hour.

COCONUT-BASED PIECRUSTS

NO-BAKE PIECRUST

MAKES ONE 8-INCH TART CRUST OR PIECRUST

This yummy, highly nutritious crust is great for unbaked fillings.

2 cups pitted dates

2 cups raw nuts (you can use a blend of nuts)

¼ cup unsweetened shredded dried coconut

½ teaspoon pumpkin pie spice

1. Prepare an 8-inch tart or pie pan by very lightly greasing with coconut oil. Set aside.

2. Add dates to the bowl of a food processor and pulse until coarsely chopped. Remove dates and set aside.

3. Wipe out food processor bowl.

4. To the clean food processor bowl, add raw nuts, dried coconut, and spice. Pulse a few times, just until it forms a coarse meal.

5. Add the dates to the nut-coconut mixture in the food processor. Pulse a few times until a ball forms.

6. Spread mixture into the bottom and up the sides of the prepared pie or tart pan, tamping it down to create a uniformly even crust.

7. Cover with plastic wrap and refrigerate until ready to be filled.

COCONUT-BASED PIECRUSTS

Need a coconut-based piecrust? Try one of these!

ALL-PURPOSE COCONUT-BASED PIECRUST

MAKES ONE 8-INCH PIECRUST

Use this buttery-tasting shell for baked or no-bake fillings.

2 *eggs*

1 *cup coconut flour*

½ *cup unsweetened shredded dried coconut*

1 *teaspoon coconut nectar or honey*

   Pinch of salt

¼ *cup melted butter*

2 *tablespoons liquid coconut oil*

1 *tablespoon water*

1 *egg white*

1. Preheat oven to 350°F.

2. In a large bowl, stir together the 2 eggs, coconut flour, shredded coconut, honey, and salt until thoroughly combined.

3. Add butter, coconut oil, and water. Mix dough together with a dough cutter or your hands until blended.

4. Pat dough into a pie pan, pressing dough firmly into the pan. Use the bottom of a heavy glass to help flatten dough. Set aside.

5. Beat egg white with a fork until frothy. Using a pastry brush or your fingers, very lightly brush crust with egg white.

6. Place piecrust on a center rack in the oven and bake for 12 to 14 minutes, until barely golden, unless you are using it for a refrigerated pie, in which case bake piecrust until thoroughly golden.

7. Cool thoroughly before using.

PUMPKIN COCONUT PIE

MAKES 8 SERVINGS

This is my favorite pumpkin pie—not only do I make it every year for Thanksgiving and Christmas; I make it almost weekly during the fall. It's that easy. My sons love this pie as an afternoon snack. I feel good about serving it, thanks to the high beta-carotene content, as well as the lauric acid from the coconut. If you have pumpkin pie spice blend, use 2½ teaspoons of that instead of the spices given in the ingredient list below.

NOTE: The coconut flavor is very light in this. You may not taste it at all.

- 1 *15-ounce can pumpkin puree*
- ¾ *cup canned coconut milk (do not use "lite")*
- 2 *large eggs*
- 1 *cup packed light brown sugar*
- ½ *teaspoon salt*
- 1 *teaspoon grated fresh ginger*
- 1 *teaspoon cinnamon*
- ⅛ *teaspoon freshly grated nutmeg*
    Optional: 1 teaspoon vanilla
    Optional: ½ teaspoon lemon zest
- 1 *prepared 8-inch or 9-inch pie shell*

1. Preheat oven to 400°F.

2. In the bowl of a stand mixer, combine pumpkin puree, coconut milk, eggs, brown sugar, salt, spices, and, if desired, vanilla and lemon zest. Mix until smooth and thoroughly combined.

3. Pour filling into prepared crust and bake on a middle rack for 45 to 55 minutes or until filling begins to set. (Note: Because this is a custard pie, the center should still be a bit jiggly when you remove the pie; it will firm up as it cools.)

4. Allow to cool 2 hours at room temperature or in the refrigerator before serving.

COCONUT CREAM PIE

MAKES 8 SERVINGS

This coconut cream pie is very much like a traditional coconut cream pie, except that it's made with a coconut flour crust (you can use a premade regular pie shell, if you like) and the filling features raw coconut and coconut cream topping. Coconut lovers will go wild for this!

- 1 *coconut-based piecrust (see recipes in sidebar on pages 338–339), cooled, or 1 premade 8-inch pie shell*
- 3 *egg yolks*
- 1½ *cups raw young coconut flesh*
- ½ *cup raw honey*
    Pinch of salt
- ⅓ *cup coconut water or regular water*
- 1½ *tablespoons unflavored powdered gelatin*
- ½ *cup coconut cream*

Optional garnish: 1 cup Coconut Cream Dessert Topping (see page 343)

Optional garnish: ¼ cup toasted coconut for topping (see sidebar)

1. Make piecrust according to one of the recipes on pages 338–339 if you are opting for homemade.

2. Preheat oven to 350°F.

3. In the bowl of a food processor or blender, add egg yolks, raw coconut meat, raw honey, and salt. Process until mixture is creamy and smooth.

4. Heat coconut water in a small saucepan until boiling. Remove from heat and whisk in gelatin. Allow to cool for 3 minutes.

5. Add gelatin mixture to the coconut filling in the food processor and blend until gelatin is mixed through.

6. Scrape filling into a mixing bowl and set aside.

7. In the bowl of a stand mixer, using a whisk attachment, beat coconut cream and whip until soft peaks form.

8. Gently fold cream into coconut filling.

9. Scrape pie filling into cooled crust. Cover pie and place in refrigerator for at least 3 hours to set.

10. If desired, dress with whipped coconut topping and/or toasted coconut.

HOW TO TOAST COCONUT

If you've ever toasted coconut before, you know it can go from light to burnt in an instant. Here are some tips to keep your coconut crunchy, not scorched:

1. Preheat your oven to 325°F. Your oven does not need to be a roaring inferno to toast coconut.

2. Spread coconut in a single later on a baking sheet.

3. Place baking sheet on a middle rack in the oven, and check on it at the 5-minute mark.

4. Give the coconut a stir, then check it again in 1 or 2 minutes.

5. Continue checking every minute until the coconut is uniformly golden. Don't let it get brown or it will taste bitter.

APPLE BERRY COCONUT CRISP

MAKES 4 SERVINGS

This multi-fruit crumble is flexible: Feel free to substitute pears for the apples, cranberries for the blackberries, and so on.

5   *large cooking apples, chopped*

1   *cup water, apple cider, or pear nectar*

2   *tablespoons coconut sugar*

1   *teaspoon cinnamon*

½   *teaspoon nutmeg*

¾   *cup coconut flour*

¼   *cup unsweetened shredded dried coconut*

3   *tablespoons coconut oil*

3   *tablespoons Grade B maple syrup*

    Dash of salt

1   *cup blackberries*

1. Preheat oven to 350°F.

2. Lightly grease a casserole dish or gratin pan with coconut oil. Set aside.

3. Add apples, water, coconut sugar, and spices to a saucepan and simmer over low heat for 5 to 10 minutes, until apples just begin to soften. Remove from heat.

4. In a bowl, whisk together the flour, dried coconut, coconut oil, maple syrup, and dash of salt. It should resemble a crumble mixture.

5. Add the apple mixture to the prepared pan and gently stir in berries.

6. Top fruit with crisp mixture, spreading crumbs evenly across the top.

7. Bake for 20 minutes until golden brown and bubbling.

8. Remove from oven and allow to cool slightly (about 30 minutes) before serving.

TWENTY-FIRST-CENTURY AMBROSIA

MAKES 6 SERVINGS

If you grew up in the United States, you probably know ambrosia. Mini marshmallows, a can of tangerine sections, and maybe some fruit cocktail topped off with Cool Whip and perhaps some sweetened shredded coconut. My mom would also throw in some pomegranate seeds, since they grew wild on our property. Well, I am here to tell all you healthy eaters out there that ambrosia can have a place in your life—as long as you use a healthy recipe, like this one.

½   *cup canned coconut milk (do not use "lite")*

½   *tablespoon arrowroot or cornstarch*

3   *tablespoons sugar*

¼   *teaspoon pure vanilla extract*

    Optional: 1 teaspoon tangerine or orange zest

1   *apple, cored, seeded, and cut into ¼-inch dice*

1   *tablespoon lemon juice*

½ cup roughly chopped walnuts or pecans

½ cup unsweetened shredded dried coconut

3 tangerines, peel and pith removed, roughly chopped

2 large oranges, peel and pith removed, roughly chopped

1. In a large bowl, whisk together coconut milk and arrowroot until smooth.

2. Whisk in sugar, vanilla, and if desired, zest until smooth. Set aside.

3. In another bowl, gently coat apple pieces with lemon juice to prevent browning.

4. To the coconut milk mixture, gently add chopped nuts and dried coconut.

5. Fold in apples, tangerines, and oranges until just combined.

6. Cover and chill for at least 1 hour before serving.

COCONUT BANANAS

MAKES 4 SERVINGS

This is the perfect after-school snack. It's healthy, sweet, kid-friendly, and easy to make no matter what your age. If you're looking for a fun recipe to make with the kids, try this one.

4 teaspoons cocoa powder

4 teaspoons finely shredded unsweetened dried coconut (pulse shredded coconut in the food processor for a finer texture)

2 small bananas, sliced on the bias

1. Place cocoa and coconut on separate plates. Roll each banana slice in the cocoa, shake off the excess, then dip in the coconut. Eat immediately or rest on a plate or sheet of waxed paper and place in the refrigerator until you're ready to enjoy.

COCONUT CREAM DESSERT TOPPING

Are you looking for a luscious alternative to whipped cream? Look no further! I've got one for you here, and it harnesses the health-supportive benefits of coconut!

To make the topping, take a 14-ounce can of coconut cream (do not use sweetened cream of coconut) and shake it well. Leave the can in the refrigerator overnight, then remove it and shake it well again. Empty the contents into the bowl of a stand mixer, add 1 tablespoon of vanilla extract, and spoon in 1 to 3 tablespoons of powdered sugar. Using the whisk attachment of the mixer, begin to beat the coconut cream and slowly increase the speed to medium. Beat the mixture until the coconut cream looks light and airy, about 3 to 5 minutes. Use this delicious stuff whenever you'd normally use whipped dairy cream.

SUMMER CRUMBLE

MAKES 6 SERVINGS

This is one nutrient-dense crumble! Here are all the good things you'll find inside: hempseed for fiber and protein; oats for fiber; coconut for fiber, antioxidants, and medium chain fatty acids; berries for antioxidants; and almond for protein. This delicious dessert is so healthy you can serve it for breakfast and know your family is getting the nutrients they need. Note that the recipe calls for many of the same ingredients in different measures and places, so follow the instructions carefully.

3   *cups mixed fresh berries*

2   *tablespoons lemon juice*

1   *tablespoon plus 1 teaspoon vanilla extract*

9   *tablespoons coconut sugar, divided*

1   *teaspoon coconut flour plus ¼ cup*

¼   *cup almond flour*

¼   *cup rolled oats, quick style*

2   *tablespoons unsweetened shredded coconut*

¼   *cup hempseed*

½   *teaspoon cinnamon*

½   *teaspoon ginger*

   Pinch of salt

½   *cup liquid coconut oil*

1. Preheat oven to 350°F.

2. Lightly grease a casserole or gratin dish with coconut oil. Set aside.

3. Gently toss the berries in a mixing bowl with the lemon juice, 1 tablespoon of the vanilla, 4 tablespoons of the coconut sugar, and 1 teaspoon of the coconut flour. Let stand.

4. To make the crumble: Whisk together the remaining coconut flour, almond flour, oats, shredded coconut, hempseed, remaining 5 tablespoons coconut sugar, cinnamon, ginger, and salt in a bowl.

5. In a separate small bowl, whisk together coconut oil and the remaining 1 teaspoon of vanilla. Drizzle this over the crumble mixture, using your hands or a dough cutter to combine until it takes on the appearance of coarse crumbs.

6. Place the berry mixture in the prepared baking dish. Sprinkle the crumble mixture on top.

7. Bake until the mixture is bubbling and the top is golden, about 20 to 30 minutes.

8. Allow to cool to room temperature before serving. Serve as is, or with Coconut Cream Dessert Topping (see page 343).

BROWN RICE COCONUT PUDDING

MAKES 4 SERVINGS

I learned this recipe in cooking school, but many people (including food writer Mark Bittman) offer similar versions. Yes, it's that good.

⅓ cup uncooked long-grain brown rice

2 14-ounce cans coconut milk
(do not use "lite")

½ cup coconut sugar, brown sugar, or maple sugar
Pinch of salt

1. Preheat oven to 300°F.

2. Add uncooked rice to the bowl of a food processor. Pulse 2 or 3 times, just enough to gently break apart the grains. You don't want to make meal or flour out of them!

3. Whisk together coconut milk, sugar, and salt in a large casserole dish or Dutch oven.

4. Stir in broken rice and place casserole dish in the oven, uncovered. Bake for 40 minutes. After 40 minutes, open oven and stir pudding mixture 3 times.

5. Close oven and allow the pudding to continue baking for an additional 45 minutes. Open oven and stir the pudding again, 3 times.

6. Close oven and bake for an additional 40 minutes.

7. The pudding is done when the grains are swollen and soft. It may not be completely thickened; the pudding will continue to thicken once it is removed from the oven. If the grains are even a bit al dente, leave the pudding in the oven for another 10 minutes and then check it again.

PUMPKIN COCONUT MOUSSE

MAKES 4 SERVINGS

I have studied health-supportive cooking and also have a pastry degree—two very different cooking school experiences to be sure! One of my favorite pastry school desserts was a pumpkin mousse made with whipping cream, nutmeg, and brown sugar. This recipe is my shot at making a delicious, whole food, healthy version of the original. I'd say I nailed it!

1 15-ounce can pureed pumpkin
(not the pumpkin pie mix), chilled

⅓ cup Grade B maple syrup

1 teaspoon vanilla extract

2 teaspoons cinnamon

¼ teaspoon nutmeg

¼ teaspoon ginger

¼ teaspoon cloves

⅓ cup coconut cream, chilled
(not cream of coconut)

1. In the bowl of a stand mixer, mix together pumpkin puree, maple syrup, vanilla, and spices. Beat until smooth and thoroughly blended. Remove bowl and set aside.

2. Set a clean bowl under the mixer. Add the coconut cream. Using a whisk attachment, whip coconut cream 3 or more minutes on medium speed until light and fluffy.

3. Using a large spatula, gently fold whipped coconut cream into pumpkin mixture. Chill in the fridge for 30 minutes, or longer, to allow flavors to blend.

4. Ladle into serving dishes.

COCONUT QUINOA PUDDING

MAKES 4 SERVINGS

When my kids talk about quinoa, they talk about this pudding—which is known as "breakfast quinoa" in my home because I serve it to them in the morning.

- 1 *14-ounce can coconut milk (not "lite")*
- ¾ *cup uncooked quinoa (red, white, or tricolor), rinsed and drained*
- 2 *tablespoons coconut nectar or Grade B maple syrup*
- 1 *teaspoon vanilla extract*

   Optional garnish: Chopped fruit, dried fruit, sunflower seeds, chopped nuts, shredded coconut, etc.

1. In a small saucepan over medium-high heat, bring coconut milk and quinoa to a boil.

2. Reduce heat to medium-low and stir in coconut nectar and vanilla.

3. Continue to cook, stirring occasionally, for about 30 minutes, until mixture is creamy and has a pudding-like consistency.

4. Serve warm or allow to cool in the refrigerator.

5. Garnish before serving, if desired.

CHIA PUDDING

MAKES 2 SERVINGS

Protein-rich chia provides an easy, steady supply of energy that works as well for the average person trying to get through the day as it does for an endurance athlete. This sweet and delicious chia pudding makes a lovely afternoon snack. It's also a great way to start the day: My kids sometimes have this for breakfast with a green drink.

- ⅔ *cup chia seeds*
- 2 *cups canned or fresh coconut milk*
- ½ *teaspoon pure vanilla extract*

   Optional sweetener: 1 to 3 teaspoons coconut nectar, honey, maple syrup, or other natural sweetener

   Optional topping: 2 tablespoons currants or chopped dried figs, or dates, or fresh berries, or diced cooked sweet potato

Optional topping: 2 tablespoons unsweetened coconut flakes

1. Put chia seeds, coconut milk, vanilla and, if using, optional sweetener in a 1-quart glass jar with a lid. Tighten the lid and shake well to combine thoroughly. Or stir together these ingredients in a bowl.

2. Allow the pudding to thicken for 30 minutes or more. (Or, even better, make the pudding in the evening and let it sit, covered, overnight in the fridge.)

3. Adjust liquid if necessary. Spoon the pudding into bowls and top with optional fruit and coconut, if desired.

COCONUT CREAM LIME PUDDING

MAKES 2 SERVINGS

Key lime pie is my family's absolute favorite. Looking for a way to get more skin-saving coconut into the diet of my eczema-riddled oldest child, I began playing with coconut-based lime recipes made from whole food ingredients. Here's my attempt. I love it and hope you will, too.

> *Flesh from ½ young coconut*
> 2 *tablespoons liquid coconut oil*
> 1 *to 2 tablespoons coconut nectar*
> 1 *peeled lime*
> *Pinch of salt*
> ½ *teaspoon ginger powder*
> ½ *teaspoon vanilla extract*
> ¼ *cup coconut water, if needed*

1. Using a food processor or a high-power blender (such as a Vitamix or Blendtec), blend all the ingredients except coconut water, until smooth and fluffy white.

2. Only if the mixture is too thick to blend, add coconut water 1 tablespoon at a time. Blend until incorporated.

3. Ladle pudding into dishes and chill for 30 minutes before serving.

CHIA

WAYNE COATES, PhD
with STEPHANIE PEDERSEN

CONTENTS

One day in 1984, I left my desk to go for a run. It was noon, and not only did I want some exercise, I wanted to get myself out of the office. That was the beginning of my new, healthier way of life. As the years rolled on, I began running more often and at greater distances, until in 2000 I decided—for some unknown reason—to enter the Tucson Marathon. I ran that race and loved every minute of it. From that time on, some might say, my love of running got out of hand.

Which, I suppose, is where chia comes in.

Today, I regularly run 5Ks, 10Ks, half-marathons, marathons, ultra-marathons, and even 100-mile runs. Before the longer events I tuck film canisters filled with chia seed into my running belt. During the run itself, I dump about half the contents of a canister into my mouth, and then wash it down with a swig of water.

Chia is extremely digestible and soothing to the stomach (not to mention joints!). It helps with stomach issues, slows digestion, increases overall hydration, helps maintain electrolyte balance, and improves stamina during these extended runs. During these ultra-distance runs, some of which have taken me up to 32 hours to complete, you go through terrible mood swings, when you start wondering what you are doing. I found that chia helps lessen these gloomy feelings.

I'm not the only marathoner who's in love with chia: Many runners consume chia regularly, thanks to the success of the book *Born to Run*, by extreme runner Christopher McDougall. This national bestseller follows McDougall as he seeks out the world's most elite ultra-distance runners in order to learn their secrets. His quest takes him to Mexico's brutal, isolated Copper Canyon, home of the reclusive Tarahumara Indians. MacDougall learns their techniques and the secrets that allow them to run hundreds of miles without fatigue. Although I have not run with them, I have visited the area several times and run on their trails. The scenery is great, but the running is tough!

Having run both with chia and without, I now know why athletes love it so much. Chia gives you an amazing amount of energy and increases endurance to unbelievable levels. In fact, whenever I talk to athletes who use chia, they always comment on gaining more energy in the later stages of their runs. They also mention an overall increase in energy, especially later in the day—a time when many people grow fatigued and sluggish, and rely on caffeine and sugar for quick and unhealthy pick-me-ups.

Chia came into my own life by accident, really. I first came across this tiny seed in

1991 as an agricultural engineer. I was part of a team from The University of Arizona that visited South America in order to research alternative crops that might grow well in northwestern Argentina. Working directly with the growers, we planted a number of different seeds to determine which might perform the best. One of these was the ancient Aztec food, chia.

I'll admit that when my fellow researchers and I first saw the maturing seed, our initial reaction was, "What the heck is this stuff good for?" To find out, we began analyzing the seed to determine its various nutrient compounds, such as fiber. In the field, we saw that if it had rained, the seed would form a gel and stick together. This showed us that chia seed was great both as a hydrating compound and for retaining moisture.

Researching the nutrient profile of the plant, we discovered that chia seed contains an incredible amount of omega-3 fatty acids—4 grams per 2-tablespoon serving. In fact, chia has more omega-3 fatty acids and, in particular, alpha-linolenic fatty acid—the only essential omega-3 fatty acid—than any other known plant.

This was a hugely important discovery because medical research shows that omega-3 fatty acids reduce inflammation in the body and help lower the risk of chronic diseases such as heart disease, cancer, and arthritis.

Omega-3 fatty acids are important for everyday cognitive function (such as memory and performance), as well as creating stable moods and helping to regulate behaviors. Many Americans show symptoms of omega-3 fatty acid deficiency, which include fatigue, poor memory, dry skin, heart problems, mood swings or depression, and poor circulation.

We also discovered that chia boasts impressive amounts of antioxidants, including the phytonutrients quercetin, kaempferol, myricetin, chlorogenic acid, and caffeic acid. These antioxidants have significant value to human health, helping ward off everything from cancer to common viral illnesses. But what I found really exciting about these high levels of antioxidants is that they keep chia fresh and prevent rancidity.

Unlike highly perishable flax—which has an indigestible hard coating that keeps its nutrients fresh—chia's antioxidant profile allows it to remain shelf-stable for years. No hard shell means chia can be eaten and digested fully as-is. Because chia doesn't become rancid at room temperature, you can pulverize it as much as you like ahead of time, to use at your convenience. Also, chia doesn't have the slightly fishy taste that flax tends to develop shortly after grinding. These are three more reasons why my fellow researchers and I were so excited about chia.

But still the question remained, "What do we do with this seed?" Our first thought was skincare—the high omega-3 and antioxidant content make the oil from chia great for the skin. We also began feeding the seed to chickens and cows to create eggs and dairy products high in omega-3s. Beginning in the 1990s, producers began feeding animals flax, marine algae, and even fish derivatives to increase the omega-3 fatty acid content in eggs and dairy. Unfortunately, the enhanced products were left with an off-putting, fishy flavor that arose from the oxidation of the omega-3 fatty acids in the flax.

Our own research showed that chia did just what we wanted—increase the omega-3 content without altering the natural taste of eggs and milk. The amount of omega-3 fatty acids in the yolks of eggs laid by chia-fed hens in- creased by more than 1,600 percent, while the saturated fat content decreased by 30 percent. In a limited trial, in which chia was fed to milk cows, the milk had a 20 percent increase in omega-3 fatty acid content and a reduced saturated fatty acid content.

A member of the mint family, *Salvia hispanica* L. (aka "chia") is a pretty plant, with "heads" of multiple small delicate flowers sitting atop several stalks on a single plant. As the heads ripen, you can pluck off a few seeds and chew on them. The flavor of the seeds is pleasantly nutty, a bit malty, and very easy to like. However, it wasn't until I began an in-depth study of how the Aztecs used chia that I considered consuming it regularly myself.

Circa 2600 B.C., Aztecs living in what is now Mexico and Guatemala considered chia one of their most important crops. It was offered to the gods and used in rituals. Chia was also used as currency. The seeds were used in medicine, ground into flour, and consumed by warriors and elite athletes as a superior source of energy and endurance. In fact, it was said that Aztec ultra-athletes could survive days of grueling, intensely physical activities by consuming nothing more than a tablespoon of chia every few hours.

It is well documented that Aztecs were ingenious inventors of agricultural production systems. Because of their sophistication, it was clear to us as researchers that if the Aztecs thought chia was special, it must be. We read all the ancient Aztec codices, written approximately five centuries ago, that we could find in order to learn more about chia. A growing body of research made it clear that chia is a complete food, not just protein or omega-3s. Nor is chia "just" composed of antioxidants, vitamins, minerals, amino acids, and fiber. Chia has so many qualities and health benefits, in fact, that I am in awe. I don't want to use the word "miracle" to describe this little seed, because it would make chia sound trendy and hyped-up, but the truth is, I don't have a better word for it. Chia truly is a miracle food and, as some have said, it's "the world's healthiest whole food."

If there's one thing I have learned as a competitive ultra-distance runner it is this: You are only as effective as your health allows you to be. Chia keeps me healthy so that I can be at my best each day—no matter what kind of race I'm running, or what my exercise routine is. Chia helps me stay healthy for everyday tasks, too, whether I'm in my office writing scientific papers, traveling to oversee chia trials, in the lab doing research, or working on my chia website, **www.azchia.com**.

Two decades after my first encounter with chia, I am still researching the plant, the seed, and its many benefits. As time and money permits, I am currently looking into what else chia can do, studying its extracts, leaves, oils, flowers, and more.

My hope for chia is that more and more people will become familiar with it and give it a try. Chia really can help everyone—children and older adults, athletes and couch potatoes, people with acute or chronic health conditions, and even those who are currently healthy. In fact, I believe chia can improve the health of the world.

Keep reading and see for yourself!

Dr. Wayne Coates
Professor Emeritus, The University of Arizona

CHAPTER 1

THE MIRACLE SEED

Chia. This petite nutrient-packed powerhouse has been used by humans since at least 3500 B.C., when the Aztecs relied on it to keep their civilization healthy. Pronounced *chee-ah*, the small seed is currently making a comeback among athletes, nutritionists, whole-food enthusiasts, and raw foodists, as well as people who just want an easy way to lose weight, improve athletic endurance, increase energy, prevent a wide range of illnesses, fight disease, and improve the look of their hair, skin, and nails.

Chia truly is a superfood all-star. Wrapped in a tiny package the size of a poppy seed, chia is nonetheless loaded with antioxidants, vitamins, minerals, fiber, amino acids, protein, and the omega-3 fatty acid called alpha-linolenic acid. This small seed boasts so many benefits and addresses so many health conditions that many people feel it is one of the most beneficial functional foods around.

DETAILED ANALYSIS OF CHIA'S COMPOSITION OBTAINED FROM VARIOUS SOURCES

Primary Name	Sub Name	Specific Constituent	Average Value	Maximum Value	Minimum Value	Units
Calories			460	529	356	Cal/100g
	Calories from Fat		233	309	110	Cal/100g
Total Fat			30.86	34.3	21.4	g/100g
	Saturated Fat		3.47	3.91	2.48	g/100g
	Trans Fat		0.14	0.191	0.04	g/100g
	Polyunsaturated fat		23.97	26	16.2	g/100g
	Monounsaturated fat		2.36	2.76	1.71	g/100g
Omega Fatty Acids						
	Essential					
		Omega-3 (linolenic)	18.56	21.1	12.3	g/100g
		Omega-6 (linoleic)	5.93	7.15	3.88	g/100g
	Non-essential					
		Omega-9 (oleic)	2.12	2.71	1.41	g/100g
Cholesterol						
Total Carbohydrates			40.27	54	32	g/100g
Dietary Fiber (total)			34.43	41.2	30	g/100g
	Insoluble Fiber		31.39	35.9	28	g/100g
	Soluble Fiber		3.68	5.8	1.1	g/100g

Primary Name	Sub Name	Specific Constituent	Average Value	Maximum Value	Minimum Value	Units
Protein			22.23	24.4	19.7	g/100g
Vitamins						
	Vitamin A		53.86	80	30	IU/100g
	Vitamin C (ascorbic acid)		1.61	2.9	0.5	mg/100g
	Vitamin D					
	Vitamin E		0.74	0.74	0.74	IU
	Vitamin K					
	Thiamin (Vitamin B1)		0.62	0.79	0.21	mg/100g
	Riboflavin (Vitamin B2)		0.17	0.22	0.12	mg/100g
	Niacin		8.83	11.9	5.97	mg/100g
	Vitamin B6					
	Folate (folic acid)		48.53	51.4	43.1	mcg/100g
	Vitamin B12					
	Ferulic		64	158	40	mcg/g
	Biotin					
	Gallic					
	Pantothenic acid					
Minerals						
	Calcium		569.80	616	523	mg/100g
	Iron		7.72	9.78	6.27	mg/100g
	Phosphorus		770.30	880	675	mg/100g
	Iodine					
	Magnesium		334.50	369	321	mg/100g
	Zinc		5.68	6.48	4.46	mg/100g
	Selenium		55.15	92.5	17.8	mcg/100g
	Copper		1.66	1.88	1.44	mg/100g
	Manganese		3.28	4.32	2.46	mg/100g
	Chromium		9.07	16.4	1.74	mcg/100g
	Molybdenum					
	Chloride					
	Sodium		128	272	22	mcg/g
	Potassium		653	741	596	mg/100g
Amino Acids – Essential						
	Arginine (Essential for young, not adults)		2221	2750	1950	mg/100g
	Histidine		550	629	485	mg/100g
	Isoleucine		830	1100	700	mg/100g
	Leucine		1421	1700	1210	mg/100g
	Lysine		1005	1100	849	mg/100g

Primary Name	Sub Name	Specific Constituent	Average Value	Maximum Value	Minimum Value	units
	Methionine		609	1200	400	mg/100g
	Phenylalanine		1053	1350	900	mg/100g
	Threonine		735	894	647	mg/100g
	Tryptophan		452	1600	178	mg/100g
	Valine		985	1110	857	mg/100g
Amino Acids - Nonessential						
	Alanine		1082	1300	920	mg/100g
	Asparagine					
	Aspartic acid		1751	2150	1490	mg/100g
	Cysteine		422	500	370	mg/100g
	Glutamic acid (Glutamate)		3628	4370	3140	mg/100g
	Glutamine		3650	4000	3300	mg/100g
	Glycine		977	1120	830	mg/100g
	Proline		804	893	683	mg/100g
	Serine		1087	1280	928	mg/100g
	Tyrosine		584	880	25	mg/100g
Phytonutrients						
	Flavonoids (polyphenols)					
		Quercetin	35	60	20	mcg/g
		Kaempferol	35	70	20	mcg/g
		Myricetin	51	62	41	mcg/g
	Phenolic Acids					
		Ferulic	64	158	40	mcg/g
		Gallic				
		Caffeic	290	387	132	mcg/g
		p-Coumaric	75	102	40	mcg/g
		chlorogenic	603	1174	31	mcg/g
	Catechins (Flavan-3-ols)					
		Epigllocatechin	893	1850	90	mcg/g
	TOTALS		1599	2312	1106	mcg/g
	Other Organic Acids					
		Phytic	20	27	13	
ORAC						
	ORAC - Lipophillic		3	12	0	umol TE/g
	ORAC - Hydrophyllic		63	85	31	umol TE/g
	Total ORAC		66	89	33	umol TE/g

Table courtesy azchia.com.

FOOD OR SUPPLEMENT?

The Food and Drug Administration (FDA) classifies chia as a food that is safe for human consumption. Chia is anti-allergenic, meaning allergies to it are very rare. Also, chia doesn't disrupt human hormone levels, like other so-called "superfoods," such as soy and flax, which chia is often compared to.

Indeed, one of the most common ways to benefit from chia is simply by eating it sprinkled onto salads and finished dishes, mixed into drinks and smoothies, stirred into yogurt and oatmeal, swirled into soups, and on and on. Wherever you might use chopped nuts, wheat bran, or flax, you can use chia instead. You can eat chia whole—the body utilizes the whole seed perfectly—milled or ground, or even soaked into a gel. You can opt for the more common black variety of chia (which has slightly higher antioxidant levels), rather than the white variety, which is less common.

Before going further into how chia can help you lose weight and get healthy, it may help to know more about the plant itself. Chia is a desert-growing member of the mint family, known as *Salvia hispanica* L. The seed is small, with a mild, nutty taste. Chia seed is hydrophilic, meaning it absorbs moisture (a good quality for a desert plant to have!). When a chia seed gets wet, its outer layer begins to swell into a slightly gelatinous covering. It's this quality (plus the fact that 38 percent of the seed is fiber) that allows chia to create a feeling of fullness (which, in turn, helps promote weight loss), while also controlling food cravings, balancing blood sugar levels, and soothing the digestive system.

THE HISTORY OF CHIA

There is evidence that chia seeds were first used as a food as early as 3500 B.C. Available to the Aztecs since 2600 BC, chia served as a cash crop in central Mexico between 1500 and 900 B.C. Chia seeds were eaten alone or mixed with other grains; consumed as a beverage when combined with water; ground into flour; included in medicines; pressed for oil; and used as a base for face and body paints. Aztec rulers received chia seeds as an annual tribute from conquered nations, and the seeds were offered to the gods during religious ceremonies.

According to records kept by the Aztecs and Spaniards, chia was traditionally cultivated in a region stretching from north-central Mexico to Guatemala. A second, smaller area of cultivation covered Nicaragua and southern Honduras.

The Salinan, Cahuilla, Sostanoan, Paiute, Maidu, and Kawaiisu indigenous peoples of the western United States used a different species of chia, called *Salvia columbariae*, for food and medicinal purposes.

My health counselor started me on chia. She said it would help my dry, eczema-prone skin and dry hair. She was so, so right! I eat about two tablespoons of chia seed a day—usually on salads, but also in green smoothies. The most remarkable thing that has happened since adopting this habit is my complexion has completely changed. The horizontal lines on my forehead have gone, as have the little dry skin lines on my cheeks, throat and arms.

My hair seems to be growing faster, and my hairdresser has noticed how much stronger, softer, and shinier my hair seems. Another interesting thing is my salon haircolor doesn't fade as quickly—it stays bright and vibrant much longer than it used to.

Lastly, I find chia really does curb my appetite and give me energy. I have recently lost seven pounds—really easily, in fact. I attribute this to chia.

— MARY SHEY, Manchester, NH

As you keep reading, you'll find that chia's high omega-3 fatty acid levels have also been found to help the body lose weight and keep it off, as well as guard against a range of health conditions, including heart disease, stroke, cancer, inflammatory bowel disease, and other autoimmune diseases such as lupus and rheumatoid arthritis. Omega-3 fatty acids are molecules that the body does not produce itself. They are, however, essential in helping a large number of body systems to function efficiently.

This is where chia comes in. There are three main types of omega-3 fatty acids: Alpha-linolenic acid (ALA), eicosapentaenoic acid (EPA), and docosahexaenoic acid (DHA). Alpha-linolenic acid is the only fatty acid that is essential and is the type of omaga-3 fatty acid found in chia.

CHIA COLORS

Chia seed is black, dark gray, or, less commonly, white. If you notice brown seeds in your chia, you've got one of two things: grass and weed seeds mixed in (which can have a bitter, unpleasant taste), or immature seeds (which contain fewer nutrients than mature chia). To ensure that you get the most pure, highest quality chia available, choose reputable online sellers, such as www.azchia.com.

PROTEIN POWER

Chia is loaded with protein. Protein occurs in all living cells. Hair and nails are mostly made of protein. The human body uses protein to build and repair tissues, as well as to make enzymes, hormones, and other body chemicals. Protein is an important building block of bones, muscles, cartilage, skin, and blood. Our bodies need relatively large amounts of protein and must draw on it from our diet, since protein isn't stored in the body.

What is even more important is that chia not only contains protein (a generous 21 percent of chia is comprised of this macronutrient), it contains complete protein—an

---

CHIA PET TRIVIA

Did you ever wonder how the chia pet craze got started? So did we!

- Terracotta chia planters, in the shape of various animals and people, were long a tourist item in various central and southern Mexican cities.
- Chia Pet® is the registered trademark belonging to Joseph Enterprises, Inc., of San Francisco, the manufacturers and originators of the Chia Pet.
- Joseph Pedott was a marketing professional who, upon seeing the original "chia curios" in Mexico, decided to create an American version, which he eventually named Chia Pet.
- The name Chia Pet was first used on September 8, 1977.
- The first Chia Pet wasn't actually a companion animal, but a man. *Chia Guy* was created on September 8, 1977.
- The first nationally-marketed Chia Pet was the ram, marketed and distributed in 1982.

- Among the most popular Chia Pets are bunnies, frogs, hippos, kittens, pigs, puppies, and turtles.
- Chia Pets use the same type of chia seed that is edible and healthy.
- Joseph Enterprises also makes Chia Head®, many of which feature the busts of various American presidents.
- Approximately 500,000 Chia Pets are sold annually.
- Chia Pets are only sold in stores during the winter holidays.
- Chia Pets and Chia Heads are handmade pottery items. It takes an entire year to produce enough Pets and Heads for one holiday season.
- Chia pottery was originally made in Mexico. Today the pottery components are produced in China.
- Joseph Enterprises, Inc. also holds the patent for the Smart Clapper®, whose slogan is "Clap On! Clap Off!"

unusual thing for a plant food. This means your body can fully utilize chia's protein as-is.

The secret behind chia's protein power are its building blocks, amino acids. Do you remember playing with wooden building blocks when you were a kid? Plant protein is often missing one or more blocks, which means your body needs to find the missing piece in another foods in order to build a complete tower. Chia contains all eight essential amino acids the body needs to fully utilize its protein: Isoleucine, Leucine, Lysine, Methionine, Phenylalanine, Threonine, Tryptophan, and Valine.

CHIA AND MICRONUTRIENTS

Micronutrients are health-supporting elements also known as vitamins and minerals. (Macronutrients are nutrients such as carbohydrates, fats, and protein, which the body uses in large amounts.) Micronutrients orchestrate a whole range of body functions that support every single body system. Chia is full of vitamins and minerals, which help keep the body well-nourished and energetic, so that it runs at peak efficiency, without experiencing deficiency-caused cravings—which, in turn, can lead to poor food choices and overeating:

CHIA IS A NON-GMO FOOD

If a food is labeled as GMO it means that its genetic material has been altered through genetic engineering. It sounds shocking, but according to the National Agriculture Statistics Board annual report for 2010, 93 percent of the planted area of soybeans, 93 percent of cotton, 86 percent of corn, and 95 percent of sugar beets in the United States were genetically modified varieties. Furthermore, genetically modified food plants took up 135 million hectares of cropland throughout the world (in 2010). The Grocery Manufacturers of America estimated in 2003 that 75 percent of all processed foods in the U.S. contain a genetically modified ingredient. Chia is not one of these food ingredients. The seed, which grows well, ships well, and stores well, does not need to be altered to make it easier to grow or use.

Genetically modified foods are newcomers to the world's food supply. The first altered food was created in 1994 by a subsidiary of agribusiness giant Monsanto. A tomato was modified to create a fruit called Flavr Savr that ripened without softening (greatly reducing natural spoilage and bruising during shipping and storage). While the United States and Canada do not label genetically modified foods, other governments—such as those in the European Union, Australia, Japan, and Malaysia—require food sellers to do so.

- **Calcium** serves as the structural element in bone and teeth, and assists with cellular processes.
- **Iron** is present in all cells in the human body and is important for many functions, including carrying oxygen from the lungs to the body's wide-ranging tissues.
- **Magnesium** is essential to all living cells. Over 300 enzymes require the presence of magnesium to function.
- **Zinc** helps regulate many genetic activities. It also supports blood sugar balance and metabolic rate, and helps the immune system and nervous system (including the brain) function at optimal levels.
- **Selenium** is a potent antioxidant that helps prevent oxidative stress and inflammation, and boosts immune system function as well.
- **Copper** is a mineral that helps the body utilize iron. It maintains the health of bones, connective tissues, and skin, and also helps the thyroid gland function normally.

HARVESTING CHIA

Chia can be harvested mechanically or by hand. After the chia plant flowers, it is allowed to go to seed. The seed heads, on which the flowers formed, are then removed and struck to release the tiny seeds. The seeds are then packed into sacks or other storage containers for subsequent cleaning. No heat or chemicals are used in these processes.

- **Manganese** assists your body to utilize many key nutrients, including biotin, thiamin, and Vitamin C. It maintains normal blood sugar levels, protects cells from free radical damage, and supports bone health.
- **Vitamin A** is best known for supporting healthy vision, but it is also essential for keeping the immune system working efficiently, maintaining skin tissues, and protecting fertility.

Chia has become the staple of my everyday diet for overall health and well-being. I love that it's an all-natural food—and not a supplement pill. I don't miss a day of this tremendous source of omega-3's and fiber.
—RICK ROSEMOND,
submitted online to azchia.com

WHOLE FOOD GOODNESS

Chia seed is a whole food because it contains all its original components: the bran, germ, and endosperm. Research shows that eating whole foods can help reduce the likelihood of being overweight and can lower the risk of diet-related diseases such as diabetes and heart disease.

COMMERCIAL CHIA PRODUCTION

Chia grows best on latitudes 15 degrees on either side of the equator, but can be grown up to 23 degrees on either side of the equator. As such, chia is grown commercially in many countries, including Bolivia, Argentina, Ecuador, and Australia. Currently the largest crops are grown in Bolivia and Australia, although Mexico, Nicaragua, and Guatemala also produce chia commercially.

AN ANCIENT RECIPE

Pinole—a type of gruel—was one of many dishes the Aztecs made with chia. To prepare it, the seeds were roasted, milled into flour, and then combined with corn flour and water. This porridge was eaten as-is, or shaped into cakes and cooked over an open fire.

- **Vitamin C** is a potent antioxidant which helps protect cells from free radical damage, lowers cancer risk, improves iron absorption, and strengthens the immune system.
- **Vitamin E** is another nutrient that is a potent antioxidant. In fact, some researchers think it is the most powerful of the antioxidant vitamins. Vitamin E also allows body cells to communicate effectively and work efficiently.
- **Niacin (Vitamin B3)** helps lower the body's cholesterol levels, stabilizes blood sugar, helps the body process fats, and is thought to help protect the brain against age-related cognitive decline and Alzheimer's disease.
- **Folate (Folic acid/Vitamin B9)** supports red blood cell production, helps cell production, allows nerves to function properly, and supports brain health.

Chia has done so much for me. At the insistence of my nutritionist and health coach, I've been taking one or two spoonfuls of chia a day for four months now. My nails are harder and don't split like they used to. My hair is growing faster than ever. My skin is no longer dry and flaky. My digestion is more efficient and regular. My carpal tunnel symptoms have disappeared. And I just feel so energetic and great—like a younger, healthier, peppier version of myself.

—MAURA SULLIVAN, New York, NY

PHYTONUTRIENTS

Chia is famous for its phytonutrients, plant chemicals that contain protective, disease-preventing compounds. The phytonutrients found in chia include quercetin, kaempferol, myricetin, chlorogenic acid, and caffeic acid. Their role is to protect the plant from disease, injuries, insects, drought, excessive heat, ultraviolet rays, and poisons or pollutants in the air or soil. In other words, they form part of the plant's immune system. And what they do for plants, they can do for us.

Although phytochemicals are not yet classified as nutrients, researchers have identified these plant chemicals as important guardians of good health. They help prevent disease and have been shown to ward off at least four of the leading causes of modern death in Western countries: cancer, diabetes, cardiovascular disease, and hypertension.

THE BEAUTY SEED

The Aztecs pressed chia for its oil, which they used to heal and moisturize the skin, and also used it as a base for face and body paints.

CHIA IS GLUTEN-FREE!

Unlike cereal grains such as wheat, spelt, kamut, rye, and barley, chia contains no gluten. This makes it ideal for people who have celiac disease and gluten sensitivities. When chia is milled, the high-protein "flour" (see page 416) can be used in gluten-free baking. See pages 416–417 and 466–467 for gluten-free baking ideas.

AN ANTI-ALLERGENIC FOOD

Chia is remarkably anti-allergenic, meaning that most people (even those sensitive to several other foods) have no problem consuming it. A 2003 study performed at Southampton University and King's College London, found that chia has no allergy-associated properties. Furthermore, after studying all the available research and data to date, the researchers were unable to find any verifiable cases of patients with allergies to chia seed or any other plant seed that had a botanical relationship to chia (such as sage).

CHAPTER 2

HOW TO USE CHIA TO LOSE WEIGHT

Chia is good for so many health conditions and helps so many people that it seems strange to single out weight loss as, perhaps, the greatest benefit of using chia. But let's face it, we live in a time when there are more overweight people than ever before. According to the Centers for Disease Control (CDC), 33.8 percent of Americans were obese in 2010.

The CDC, as well as most medical organizations, uses body mass index (BMI), to determine obesity rates. People with a BMI of 25 or above are considered overweight. (To calculate your own BMI, look at *Finding Your BMI*, on page 368.)

According to a team of researchers at John Hopkins University, if people keep gaining weight at the current rate, by 2015, 75 percent of U.S. adults will be overweight. The researchers examined 20 published obesity studies, as well as national surveys of national weight and behavior to come up with these predictions.

This chapter will help you learn how to use chia to support your weight loss goals and gives you a recipe for success by adding chia to whatever you are already eating, if you are already on an established weight-loss program. You'll also find delicious menus that make it easy to stick with and benefit the most from your program.

WHY EXCESS WEIGHT IS SUCH A BIG DEAL

Non-pregnant human bodies are not meant to carry excess weight. The heavier a person is, the shorter his or her lifespan, and the greater their likelihood is of developing a weight-related illness, such as diabetes, hypertension, high cholesterol, stroke, cancer, sleep apnea, varicose veins, and others.

From a personal standpoint, being overweight means experiencing regular shortness of breath, having less endurance, and finding it hard to enjoy simple pleasures such as playing with your children or grandchildren. It means not fitting through a turnstile, struggling to find appropriate clothing to wear, getting stuck in a movie theater seat or behind the wheel of a car, and even paying extra for a seat on some airlines.

Then there is the cost to society. The more overweight people a country has, the higher its health costs rise due to weight-related illnesses. According to the CDC, medical costs associated with obesity are estimated at

FINDING YOUR BMI: THE LABOR-INTENSIVE METHOD

Finding your BMI takes a bit of effort, but knowing this important number is important to your health. Fair warning: Calculating your BMI requires using the metric system. If you have a metric scale and measuring tape, you can skip all the conversions explained below.

1. Convert your body weight from pounds to kilograms by dividing your weight in pounds by 2.2. So, if you weigh 150 pounds, that translates to approximately 68 kilograms. This is the first number you'll need in order to calculate your BMI.

2. Convert your height into inches and then meters. If you are 5'4" tall, that means you are 64 inches tall. Divide 64 by 39.37 to determine your height in meters. The answer for this example would be 1.6 meters.

3. Multiply your height in meters by itself. So, that would be 1.6 x 1.6 in our example, which equals 2.56. You are almost finished!

4. Divide your weight in kilograms (Step One) by the number you determined in Step Three. In our example of a 1.6 meter-tall person who weighs 68 kilograms, you would divide 68 by 2.56, which equals approximately 26.56. This number is your BMI.

FINDING YOUR BMI: THE EASY WAY

There are many websites that will calculate your BMI, most of which will work with a variety of measuring systems. Here are a few:

- www.cdc.gov/healthyweight/assessing/bmi/adult_bmi/english_bmi_calculator/bmi_calculator.html
- www. nhlbisupport.com/bmi/
- www.webmd.com/diet/calc-bmi-plus

$147 billion yearly. The medical cost borne by third-party payers for obese Americans was $1,429 higher than those of average-weight individuals.

So that's where chia comes in. Chia is an easy-to-take product that encourages you to eat less. It does this in a few different ways.

First, it fills you up. Literally. Chia swells up to 12 times its original mass in your stomach, making you feel full. It also lowers blood sugar levels, which can eliminate or reduce cravings for unhealthy foods.

Some research has also shown that regular chia consumption helps tackle "middle fat"—the fat that literally hangs around the middle of your body.

Lastly, chia increases physical endurance by "lubricating" joints and muscles and keeping the body steadily hydrated so it can stay in action longer without uncomfortable cramps. It supplies a slow, constant drip of energy so you can keep on jogging, walking, swimming, rowing, skating, or doing whatever else you do to get fit.

SPORTS DRINK OR CHIA?

In 2011, the Department of Kinesiology at the University of Alabama compared the effects of the carbohydrate-rich drink Gatorade with a chia-infused sports drink (half chia seed, half Gatorade) on a group of highly trained athletes. Both sports drinks contained the same amount of calories but a different nutritional composition. In the experiment, all of the participants took part in a 1-hour run on a treadmill followed by a 10-K time trial on a track. The primary finding was that there was no difference in performance between the athletes who consumed either drink. In other words, the "chia sports drink" was just as effective as the straight Gatorade. There's a good chance that agua fresca (see page 409) would perform just as well, allowing athletes to reduce their intake of sugar and chemical ingredients even further, while increasing fiber, protein, antioxidants, and omega-3 fatty acids.

These are the golden rules for using chia to support your weight loss goals:

- **Ditch the junk.** If you are eating potato chips and chocolate chip cookies, chia may not help you lose weight. Choose fruit, vegetables, whole grains, and lean proteins instead.

- **Drink 8 to 12 glasses of water a day.** Chia is hydrophilic, meaning it absorbs water. Give it the water it needs to do its job.

- **Watch portion sizes.** One 3-ounce serving of animal protein (fish, poultry, or red meat) is the size of a deck of cards. Most people get much, much, more than this. A serving of fruit is generally one medium-sized piece.

- **Include plant protein in your diet.** Good sources include beans, dried peas, quinoa, amaranth, nuts (including nut butters), and chia.

- **Cut down or cut out alcohol.** Alcohol is a high-calorie beverage with a number of weight loss drawbacks that have been shown to raise blood sugar levels, leading to cravings. Alcohol can lessen judgment, which can cause you to eat more than you normally would. In fact, one study found that people typically consumed 20 percent more calories at a meal when they had drunk alcohol beforehand. There was a total caloric increase of 33 percent when the calories from the alcohol were added. Along

> *Dieting has always been difficult for me. I would just get so, so hungry! When I began taking chia to help my nails grow longer and harder, I noticed that on the days I took it, I would be less likely to eat chocolate bars and bread (my two downfalls). Since starting chia two months ago, I've lost five pounds.*
> —LAUREN DIAZ, Albany, NY

CHIA CURBS CRAVINGS

The January 2010 issue of the *European Journal of Clinical Nutrition* features a study on 11 healthy-weight men and women. For 12 weeks, test subjects consumed 0, 7, 15, or 24 grams of chia. Blood samples and appetite ratings were taken several times within two hours after consuming chia. The findings? Sugar levels were decreased in everyone who consumed chia, regardless of the dose. Appetite ratings were also significantly decreased, even at 120 minutes after consuming chia. Intriguingly, many people who eat chia regularly report that it "takes the edge" off their hunger, allowing them to be satiated with less food.

with the increase in weight you can have an increased risk to your health because of *where* you gain the weight. A study of over 3,000 people showed that consuming elevated amounts of alcohol is associated with abdominal obesity in men. Many people jokingly term this weight gain a "beer belly."

- **Limit caffeine.** Drinking the equivalent of two cups of coffee daily can set you up for high blood sugar levels, which in turn can lead to strong cravings for sugary, starchy (read: fattening) foods. How? Caffeine tells the hormones glucogen and adrenaline to release sugar stored in the liver. The result? High blood glucose.
- **Increase vegetables.** Your body deserves the rich bounty of vitamins, minerals, fiber, and phytonutrients these wonderful foods offer.
- **Cut out diet sodas.** A study by the American Diabetes Association (ADA) has found that individuals who drink diet sodas are heavier, on average, than individuals who don't. The ADA analyzed measures of height, weight, and waist circumference compared to diet soda consumption over a period of nine and a half years and found that adults who drank larger quantities of diet soda per day gained more weight and added more to their waistline than adults who don't drink diet sodas. The study shows that while diet sodas may be free of calories, they do not prevent you from gaining weight. Diet soda also contributes to diabetes, heart disease, cancer, and other chronic

conditions. A study by the American Stroke Association discovered that individuals who had one diet soda every day had a 61 percent higher risk of "cardiovascular events," such as stroke and heart attack, than those who never drink diet sodas.

• **Cut out regular sodas.** One 12-ounce can of soda has anywhere from 140 to 165 calories, plus loads of artificial ingredients your body doesn't need. It's better to drink water—with or without chia seed mixed in.

• **Ban hydrogenated fats,** also known as trans fats, from your diet. These are industrially-made fats that are used to increase shelf life in convenience and snack foods. Studies have found that trans fats harden arteries, raise cholesterol levels, and increase the risk of heart disease.

• **Go easy on fruit juice.** It has a lot of calories and is pure fruit sugar.

• **Get moving!** Go to Chapter Four (see page 393) and choose an exercise program. Plan on exercising regularly to lose weight and tone your muscles.

HOW OUR DIETS HAVE CHANGED

Back before electricity, plumbing, and perhaps even before the wheel, humans ate much differently than they do today. One of the most dramatic changes to the human diet has been the ratio between omega-6 and omega-3 essential fatty acids (EFA). Our bodies require both of these EFAs. However, our diet today consists of much more omega-6 fatty acids, which are found in grain-fed poultry and meat, and industrially-produced cooking oils, such as safflower and canola oils, as well as corn and soy products, then it did during our evolutionary period.

Historically, during the hunter and gatherer era, this balance was 1:1 or even 1:2 in favor of omega-3 fatty acids, the fatty acids that come from plant food and animals that eat wild plant food.

Today, this balance has shifted to 10:1 or even 20:1! What this means is that we consume 10 or 20 times more omega-6 fatty acids than omega-3s.

Why is this a problem? Research has shown that too high a ratio of omega-6 to omega-3 fatty acids can cause heart disease, along with a host of other illnesses. Most likely, this is because omega-6 fatty acids have inflammatory properties, while omega-3s are anti-inflammatory. With the high dose of omega-6 fatty acids that we consume, it is likely that most of us experience some sort of inflammation, the root of many health issues.

SUPPORTING POPULAR DIET PROGRAMS

If you are already on any established weight loss program—such as Weight Watchers, The Zone, The Blood Type Diet, Atkins, or Jenny Craig—chia can be just what you need to ensure success. Simply adding chia to what you are already eating can help fill you up, create a feeling of satiety—so you won't eat more than you need—and help regulate blood sugar levels, so you won't be waylaid by cravings for sugary or starchy foods. Here is a recipe for success:

PHASE ONE:

In this phase, you are easing into chia and getting your body acclimated to the extra dose of fiber chia provides. For every step listed below in Phase One, Two, and Three, you can either sprinkle chia onto your food or stir it into your food. If preferred, you could

also mix it into a small glass of water or juice and drink it. Plan on staying in this phase for two weeks before moving to Phase Two:

- **Breakfast:** ½ tablespoon whole chia seed or milled chia with breakfast.
- **Lunch:** ½ tablespoon whole chia seed or milled chia with lunch.
- **Dinner:** ½ tablespoon whole chia seed or milled chia with dinner.

BRAIN FOOD

Chia is rich in alpha-linolenic acid, the only essential omega-3 fatty acid. Also known as EFAs, these nutrients are known to make cell membranes more flexible and efficient, making nutrients more readily available and nerve transmission more efficient. This helps to improve mood, memory, and brain function.

My experience with chia has been very positive. About a year ago I started, sprinkling a large spoonful every day on my dinner salad. What I discovered is that I no longer had the desire to eat my 9:00 p.m. bowl of ice cream. My stomach was pleasantly full and I just didn't crave it like I once did. After a few months, I began adding a spoonful into my breakfast smoothie and I found that I no longer wanted my 10:30 a.m. granola bar. Just a month ago, I added a third spoonful, this one at lunch. What I've noticed is instead of craving chips or a Snickers bar at 3:00 p.m., I now am happy with a tomato or vegetable juice. These aren't huge changes, but they've added up to a 17-pound weight loss without changing what I like to eat for breakfast, lunch, and dinner.

—SARA CARAVILLE, Seattle, WA

PHASE TWO:

In this phase, your body is comfortable with chia so it's a great time to add more. You'll see an increase in benefits as well as experiencing greater satiety at mealtime. Plan on being in Phase Two for one month before moving onto Phase Three.

- **Breakfast:** ½ tablespoon whole chia seed or milled chia with breakfast.
- **Midmorning snack:** ½ tablespoon whole chia seed or milled chia with snack.
- **Lunch:** ½ tablespoon whole chia seed or milled chia with lunch.
- **Afternoon snack:** ½ tablespoon whole chia seed or milled chia with snack.
- **Dinner:** ½ tablespoon whole chia seed or milled chia with dinner.

SLIMMER AND HEALTHIER WITH CHIA

The place was the Twenty-Fourth International Symposium on Diabetes and Nutrition of the European Association for the Study of Diabetes, held in Salerno, Italy, in June 2004. What had everyone so excited? The University of Antwerp in Belgium presented research findings for its "chia study." For a full month, researchers gave healthy individuals 45 grams of chia (a bit under 4 tablespoons) every single day. The result? A reduction in blood pressure and triglycerides, plus smaller waist circumference and less abdominal fat.

PHASE THREE:

In this phase, you reach the 45 daily grams of chia that researchers have found best supports weight loss and maintenance. You'll see an increase in health benefits as well as experiencing greater satiety at mealtime. Plan on staying in Phase Three until you reach your goal weight.

- **Breakfast:** 1 tablespoon whole chia seed or milled chia with breakfast.
- **Midmorning snack:** ½ tablespoon whole chia seed or milled chia with snack.
- **Lunch:** 1 tablespoon whole chia seed or milled chia with lunch.
- **Afternoon snack:** ½ tablespoon whole chia seed or milled chia with snack.
- **Dinner:** 1 tablespoon whole chia seed or milled chia with dinner.

I've been eating chia seed every day for about a year and a half. Nine months ago, I had my cholesterol checked and it had gone down from 204 the year before to 178. I had been trying to get my cholesterol down below 200 for three years by eating well, to no avail. I bet it goes down even further when I get my blood work done again in January. I also bake with it and use it on my long-distance runs as energy. It is a wonderful endurance food for athletes.

—RENEE STEVENS,
posted online at azchia.com

HIGH FIBER FOODS

Fill up on fiber and you're less likely to fill up on fatty, sugary foods that compromise your weight loss efforts. Here are some favorites:

- **Chia:** One tablespoon has 5000 mg or 5 grams of total fiber
- **Avocado:** One medium avocado contains 11 grams of fiber.
- **Artichoke:** A medium artichoke boasts 10 grams of fiber.
- **Raspberries:** A cup of these red berries contains 8 grams of fiber.
- **Blackberries:** A cup of these "bramble fruits" contains 8 grams of fiber.
- **Lentils:** These legumes are not only rich in protein, a half-cup serving contains 8 grams of fiber.
- **Black beans:** An all-around favorite, black beans contain 7 grams of fiber per half-cup.
- **Broccoli:** A cup of this brassica-family favorite boasts 6 grams of fiber.
- **Pear:** One medium pear has 4.5 grams of fiber.
- **Apple:** Choose your favorite variety! One medium piece of this fruit provides 4 grams of fiber.
- **Almonds:** A ¼ cup serving offers up 4.25 grams of fiber.
- **Sesame seeds:** One ounce offers 4 grams of fiber.
- **Coconut flakes:** Choose 1 ounce of unsweetened coconut and you get 5 grams of fiber.

OPTIONAL ONE-WEEK MENUS

You do not need formal recipes to enjoy chia, nor do you need a menu plan to use chia as a weight loss support. All you need to do is read *The Chia Plan How-To's* on page 369, since the chia weight-loss "program" simply consists of choosing healthy foods, adding chia (as described in *Supporting Popular Diet Programs* on page 372), and exercising regularly.

If you enjoy following recipes, however, and find that they make it easier and more enjoyable to achieve your weight loss and health goals, take a look at Chapter 5: "Cooking, Eating, and Healing with Chia" on page 409 for some delicious examples.

You'll notice there are three phases. This is to get your body used to the amount of chia you'll be taking in.

In this phase, you are easing into chia and getting your body acclimated to the extra dose of fiber chia provides. Plan on staying in this phase for two weeks before moving to Phase Two:

Day One
Breakfast
Green Super Smoothie, page 410
Scrambled eggs
Cup of tea

Midmorning snack
Piece of fruit

Lunch
Lima Bean Winter Soup, page 430
Turkey sandwich with lettuce and tomato

Afternoon snack
Baby carrots and Chia Hummus, page 434

Dinner
Chia Chipotle Bean Burger, page 459
Sautéed spinach

Day Two
Breakfast
Basic Chia Protein Shake, page 411
2 links turkey sausage

Midmorning snack
Piece of fruit

Lunch
Power Wrap, pages 432–433
Cup of tomato soup

PROTEIN PACKED

Chia seeds contain about 20 percent protein, more than many other grains such as wheat and rice. Chia seeds also contain strontium, which helps our bodies assimilate protein and produce high energy.

Afternoon snack
Baby carrots or jicama slices with
 guacamole

Dinner
Chia Caesar Salad, pages 460–461
Mulligatawny Chia Soup, page 432

Day Three
Breakfast
1 cup low-sodium tomato
 juice, V8, or other vegetable juice
Chia Frittata, page 424

Midmorning snack
Raw veggie strips

Lunch
Chia Salad Sandwich, 434
Piece of fruit

Afternoon snack
1 cup air-popped popcorn

Dinner
2-ounce portion broiled salmon
½ cup brown rice
Green salad with vinaigrette

When my daughter was born last year, I was struggling with several things: Fatigue, losing the pregnancy weight, and just feeling calm. Chia seemed to help with all of these things. I started slowly, with one tablespoon, once a day, then worked up to three tablespoons—one with each meal. Even though my child is still not sleeping through the night, I have increased energy, I've lost 13 of the 20 pounds, and I have a wonderful sense of well-being. I just don't get as worked up as I used to.

—BELLA D'AGOSTINO, San Francisco, CA

Day Four

Breakfast
1 cup low-sodium tomato juice, V8, or other vegetable juice
Chia-Oat Porridge, page 426

Midmorning snack
Apple slices with peanut butter

Lunch
Chia Rice Salad, page 436
Piece of fruit

Afternoon snack
1 ounce cashews

Dinner
1 cup vegetarian chili
Corn tortillas

Day Five

Breakfast
1 cup low-sodium tomato juice, V8, or other vegetable juice
Scrambled Chia Eggs, page 424

Midmorning snack
Piece of fruit

Lunch
Fast Soup, page 429
Chia Fruit Salad, page 438

Afternoon snack
Carrot sticks with Chia Hummus, page 434

Dinner
Black bean burger
Sautéed greens

DID YOU KNOW?

Chia has eight times more of the antioxidant and anti-inflammatory omega-3 fatty acid than salmon. You would have to eat 790 grams (about 1¾ pounds) of Atlantic salmon to get the same amount of omega-3 fatty acids contained in 100 grams (about 9 tablespoons) of chia.

Day Six

Breakfast
Green Super Smoothie, page 410
Oatmeal

Midmorning snack
Piece of fruit

Lunch
Large green salad with ½ cup chicken
Carrot sticks

Afternoon snack
1 ounce mixed nuts

Dinner
Beef stew

BLOOD SUGAR STABILIZER

A 2007 study published in *Diabetes Care* followed 20 people with Type 2 diabetes. Subjects were divided into two groups: A chia group and a wheat bran group. For 12 weeks, subjects took 37 grams of either chia or wheat bran. At the end of the study, those who took chia reduced systolic blood pressure and inflammation. And while they did not lose large amounts of weight, it was shown that they had more stable blood sugar levels than the control group. One common cause of food cravings is erratic blood glucose levels. By stabilizing these levels, there is the potential to ward off cravings, a side effect many chia consumers report.

Day Seven

Breakfast
Basic Chia Protein Shake, page 411
Piece of fruit

Midmorning snack
Baby carrots

Lunch
Chicken breast sandwich with lettuce and
    tomato
Piece of fruit

Afternoon snack
Jicama slices with guacamole

Dinner
Meatloaf
Green salad with Zippy Dressing,
    page 438

In some ways I do see chia as a miracle. It helps me to be satisfied with less food, helps keep me full longer so I don't want to snack as much as I used to, and it gives me more energy to exercise. None of these are extreme, "out there" ways to lose weight, but put together they've helped me to lose 18 pounds in a little under five months without going crazy or trying too hard.

—JANET CISCO,
Las Vegas, NV

OPTIONAL ONE-WEEK MENU, PHASE TWO:

In this phase, your body is comfortable with chia so it's a great time to add more. You'll see an increase in benefits as well as experiencing greater satiety at mealtime. Plan on being in Phase Two for a month before moving onto Phase Three.

Day One
Breakfast
Green Super Smoothie, page 410
½ cup oatmeal
Cup of tea

Midmorning snack
Piece of fruit

Lunch
Lima Bean Winter Soup, page 430
Small turkey sandwich with lettuce and tomato slices

Afternoon snack
Baby carrots and hummus

Dinner
Chia Chipotle Bean Burger, page 459
Sautéed spinach

Day Two
Breakfast
Basic Chia Protein Shake, page 411
Piece of fruit

Midmorning snack
Carrot and celery sticks with peanut butter

Lunch
Power Wrap, pages 432–433
Piece of fruit

Afternoon snack
Baby carrots or jicama slices with Chia Guacamole, page 453

Dinner
Chia Caesar Salad, pages 460–461

Day Three
Breakfast
1 cup low-sodium tomato juice, V8, or other vegetable juice
Chia Frittata, page 424

Midmorning snack
Veggie strips

Lunch
Chia Salad Sandwich, page 434
Piece of fruit

Afternoon snack
1 ounce roasted pumpkin seeds

Dinner
2-ounce portion broiled salmon
Mexican Grain Pilaf, pages 435–436
Green salad with Zippy Dressing, page 438

Day Four

Breakfast

1 cup low-sodium tomato juice, V8, or other vegetable juice

Chia-Oat Porridge, page 426

Midmorning snack

Piece of fruit

Lunch

Chia Rice Salad with added ½ cup of black beans, page 436

Afternoon snack

Raw veggie strips

Dinner

Chia Vegetarian Chili, page 455

Corn tortillas

Day Five

Breakfast

1 cup low-sodium tomato juice, V8, or other vegetable juice

Scrambled Chia Eggs, page 424

Midmorning snack

Piece of fruit

Lunch

Fast Soup, page 429

Green salad with ½ cup of chicken, turkey or ham

Afternoon snack

1 ounce raw almonds

Dinner

Chia Cottage Pie, page 456

Green salad

Day Six

Breakfast

Green Super Smoothie, page 410

Scrambled eggs

Midmorning snack

Piece of fruit

Lunch

Small turkey sandwich with lettuce and tomato

Mulligatawny Chia Soup, page 432

Afternoon snack

Celery with almond butter

Dinner

Chia Quesadilla with Chia Guacamole, pages 452–453

Grilled vegetables

DYS-WHAT?

Many studies on chia have found that it helps prevent or treat dyslipidemia. This word may sound unfamiliar, but it has a very clear meaning: Abnormal cholesterol levels, typically high cholesterol (also known as high blood cholesterol level).

DR. OZ ON CHIA

"Chia Pets may have no apparent purpose, but chia seed? Now, that's something to get excited about. Chia—a harvested, unprocessed, nutty-tasting, nutrient-dense whole grain with omega-3 fatty acids—has among the highest antioxidant activity of any whole food, outdistancing even fresh blueberries. One study showed that 30 grams of chia seed taken with bread decreased the sharp blood sugar spike seen an hour after eating. Another study showed that chia lowers blood pressure and the risk of heart problems. My recommendation: two daily doses of about 20 grams (about two tablespoons) of seeds each."

— DR. MEHMET OZ, *You: Staying Young* (Free Press, 2007)

Day Seven

Breakfast
Basic Chia Protein Shake, page 411
Piece of fruit

Midmorning snack
Carrots and Chia Hummus, page 434

Lunch
Chia Faux Enchiladas, page 458

Afternoon snack
Piece of fruit

Dinner
Chia Meatloaf, page 454
Sautéed broccoli

My husband's running partner recommended he take chia last year when he was gearing up for the NYC Marathon. I watched how much healthier he looked. His hair seemed fuller, his skin looked better, he seemed more even-tempered. So I began using chia, too. I stir it into my morning yogurt or oatmeal. People have commented on how young I look. I absolutely see a change in my skin and hair, and my eyes seem brighter, too. What I wasn't expecting is to lose some weight. I lost six pounds the first month I used it. I think because it filled me up and made me feel full longer, so I wasn't as tempted to snack as much as I used to.

— RITA MINARDI, Stamford, CT

OPTIONAL ONE-WEEK MENU, PHASE THREE:

In Phase Three, you'll reach the amount of chia that researchers have found best supports weight loss and maintenance. You'll see an increase in benefits as well as greater satiety at mealtime. Plan on staying in Phase Three until you reach your goal weight.

Day One
Breakfast
Green Super Smoothie, page 410
Chia French Toast, page 423
Cup of tea

Midmorning snack
Chia Fresca, page 409
Piece of fruit

Lunch
Lima Bean Winter Soup, page 430
Nut Butter & Jelly Sandwich, page 424

Afternoon snack
Baby carrots and Chia Hummus, page 434

Dinner
Chia Chipotle Bean Burger, page 459
Sautéed spinach

Day Two
Breakfast
Basic Chia Protein Shake, page 411
Aussie-Style Broiled Tomato with Chia, page 428

Midmorning snack
Spicy Green Chocolate Shake, page 412

Lunch
Power Wrap, pages 432–433
Piece of fruit

Afternoon snack
Baby carrots or jicama slices with Chia Seed Guacamole, page 453

Dinner
Chia Caesar Salad, pages 460–461
Mulligatawny Chia Soup, page 432

Day Three
Breakfast
1 cup low-sodium tomato juice, V8, or other vegetable juice
Chia Frittata, page 424

Midmorning snack
Chia Fresca, page 409
Protein Muffin, pages 416–417

Lunch
Chia Salad Sandwich, page 434
Chia Fruit Salad, page 438

Afternoon snack
Protein Bites, pages 439–440

Dinner
2-ounce portion broiled salmon
Mexican Grain Pilaf, pages 435–436
Green salad with Zippy Dressing, page 438

Day Four

Breakfast
1 cup low-sodium tomato juice, V8,
    or other vegetable juice
Chia-Oat Porridge, page 426

Midmorning snack
Chia Fresca, page 409
Chia Seed Muffin, page 415

Lunch
Chia Rice Salad, page 436
Piece of fruit

Afternoon snack
Moroccan Carrot Salad, page 437

Dinner
Chia Vegetarian Chili, page 455
Chia Cornbread, page 417

Day Five

Breakfast
1 cup low-sodium tomato juice, V8,
    or other vegetable juice
Scrambled Chia Eggs, page 424

Midmorning snack
Chia Fresca, page 409
Piece of fruit

Lunch
Fast Soup, page 429
Chia Fruit Salad, page 438

Afternoon snack
Almond Delight, page 410

Dinner
Chia Cottage Pie, page 456
Green Salad with Chia Sunshine Sauce,
    page 438

WHAT'S AN ANTIOXIDANT?

To understand antioxidants, it's important to first understand oxidants. Oxidation is a chemical reaction that transfers electrons or hydrogen from a substance to an oxidizing agent. Oxidation reactions can produce free radicals, or oxidants. In turn, these radicals can start chain reactions. When a chain reaction occurs in a cell, it can cause damage or death to the cell. An antioxidant is a molecule capable of inhibiting the oxidation of other molecules.

The easiest place to get these protective molecules is from plant food. Chia, the black seed in particular, is a rich, powerful source of antioxidants. Bright- and dark-colored fruits and vegetables are also rich in these powerful nutrients. Eating numerous servings daily of antioxidant-heavy food is one of the most effective ways to maintain wellness.

Day Six

Breakfast
Green Super Smoothie, page 410
Chia-Oat Porridge, page 426

Midmorning snack
Chia Fresca, page 409
Piece of fruit

Lunch
Large Green Salad with ½ cup chicken
    and Chia Sunshine Sauce, page 438
One slice Pumpkin Bread, page 419

Afternoon snack
Ginger Pear Eggnog Smoothie,
    page 412

Dinner
Creamy Mushroom-Cashew Soup,
    pages 430–431

Chia Quesadilla with Chia Guacamole,
    pages 452–453

Day Seven

Breakfast
Basic Chia Protein Shake, page 411
Piece of fruit

Midmorning snack
Chia Snack Bar, page 420

Lunch
Chia Faux Enchiladas, page 458

Afternoon snack
Citrus Julius, page 411

Dinner
Chia Meatloaf, page 454
Green salad with Zippy Dressing,
    page 438

A DIETER'S BEST FRIEND

Eating fiber helps create a feeling of fullness and satiety that takes the edge off hunger, which makes it less likely you'll turn to candy bars, cookies, chips or other packaged junk food to satisfy food cravings.

Fortunately, chia is loaded with fiber, both the soluble kind (which swells in water) and the insoluble kind (which doesn't). Just one tablespoon—12 grams—of chia boasts 5,000 mg of total fiber, the same amount of fiber as in:

- 10 cups of Corn Flakes cereal
- 10 slices white sandwich bread
- 1 ¼ cups of Kellogg's All Bran cereal
- An entire large cantaloupe
- 1 ¼ cup cooked oatmeal
- 2 ½ cups cooked white rice
- 1 ½ cup cooked carrots
- 2 ½ medium bananas
- 4 cups popcorn
- About 3 medium tomatoes

CHAPTER 3

CHIA AND WEIGHT MAINTENANCE

Anyone who has lost weight can tell you that losing weight is difficult, but keeping lost weight off is even more difficult. Fortunately, chia can help with this.

The maintenance plan in this chapter is for those of you who enjoy your current weight. It's also perfect for individuals who have gone through the phases outlined in Chapter Two and Chapter Four and want to stay healthy, fit, and motivated in order to maintain their good health.

THE MAINTENANCE PHASE

In this phase, you'll continue to consume the 45 grams of chia that researchers have found best supports weight loss and maintenance. For every step below, you can sprinkle chia onto your food or stir it into your food. If preferred, you could also mix it into a small glass of water or juice and drink it. You'll see an increase in benefits as well as greater satiety at mealtime. You can use this guide with your favorite healthy foods or diet program menus (such as Weight Watchers, Jenny Craig, South Beach Diet, etc.):

• **Breakfast:** 1 tablespoon whole chia seed or milled chia.

• **Midmorning snack:** ½ tablespoon whole chia seed or milled chia.

• **Lunch:** 1 tablespoon whole chia seed or milled chia.

• **Afternoon snack:** ½ tablespoon whole chia seed or milled chia.

• **Dinner:** 1 tablespoon whole chia seed or milled chia.

My grandmother used to make us agua fresca almost every day in the summer. I never thought much about this. But when Stephanie, my health coach, suggested I begin drinking agua fresca each afternoon to help combat the 3:00 pm fatigue that would wash over me, I listened: My grandmother used to always call this a "pick me up". After consuming chia, not only did I have the stamina to get through my day, I quickly found that I had stopped wanting sweet snacks in the afternoon. Soon I felt so healthy and full of energy, that I began taking a midday walk. I'm happy to say I have I lost 11 pounds in just over two months.

—MARIA RODRIGUEZ, Mexico City, Mexico

In this phase when you've reached the amount of chia consumption that best supports weight loss and maintenance, you'll continue to see an increase in benefits as well as experiencing greater satiety at mealtime.

Day One

Breakfast
Green Super Smoothie, page 410
Chia Breakfast Polenta, page 458
Cup of tea

Midmorning snack
Chia Fresca, page 409
Piece of fruit

Lunch
Lima Bean Winter Soup, page 430
Nut Butter & Jelly Sandwich, page 424

Afternoon snack
Baby carrots and Chia Hummus, page 437

Dinner
Chia Chipotle Bean Burger, page 459
Sautéed spinach

Day Two

Breakfast
Basic Chia Protein Shake, page 411
Aussie-Style Broiled Tomato with Chia, page 428

Midmorning snack
Spicy Green Chocolate Shake, page 413

Lunch
Power Wrap, pages 432–433
Piece of fruit

Afternoon snack
Baby carrots or jicama slices with Chia Seed Guacamole, page 453

Dinner
Chia Caesar Salad, pages 460–461
Mulligatawny Chia Soup, page 432

Day Three

Breakfast
1 cup low-sodium tomato juice, V8, or other vegetable juice
Chia Frittata, page 424

Midmorning snack
Chia Fresca, page 409
Protein Muffin, pages 416–417

JOINT SOOTHER

Many people with arthritis and other joint disorders report reduced pain and inflammation after a few weeks of taking chia seeds. The high concentration of omega-3 fatty acids in chia helps to "lubricate" joints and keep them supple. Additionally, omega-3 fatty acids are converted into prostaglandins, which are known to have both pain relieving and anti-inflammatory effects.

Lunch
Chia Salad Sandwich, 434
Chia Fruit Salad, page 438

Afternoon snack
Protein Bites, pages 439–440

Dinner
2-ounce portion broiled salmon
Mexican Grain Pilaf, pages 435–436
Green salad with Zippy Dressing, page 438

Day Four
Breakfast
1 cup low-sodium tomato juice, V8,
   or other vegetable juice
Chia-Oat Porridge, page 426

Midmorning snack
Chia Fresca, page 409
Chia Seed Muffin, page 415

Lunch
Chia Rice Salad, page 436

Piece of fruit

Afternoon snack
Moroccan Carrot Salad, page 437

Dinner
Chia Vegetarian Chili, page 455
Chia Cornbread, page 417

Day Five
Breakfast
1 cup low-sodium tomato juice, V8,
   or other vegetable juice
Scrambled Chia Eggs, page 424

Midmorning snack
Chia Fresca, page 409
Piece of fruit

Lunch
Fast Soup, page 429
Chia Fruit Salad, page 438

Afternoon snack
Almond Delight, page 410

Dinner
Chia Polenta with White Beans, page 457
Green salad with Chia Sunshine Sauce, page 438

Day Six
Breakfast
Green Super Smoothie, page 410
Chia-Oat Porridge, page 426

Midmorning snack
Chia Fresca, page 409

Piece of fruit

Lunch
Large green salad with ½ cup chicken and Chia Sunshine Sauce, page 438
One slice Pumpkin Bread, page 419

Afternoon snack
Ginger Pear Eggnog Smoothie, page 412

Dinner
Creamy Mushroom-Cashew Soup, pages 430–431

SEEDS THAT ACT LIKE GRAINS

A whole-food diet rich in non-cereal grains (such as "grain-like" seeds) is one of the best ways to lose weight. It's also the best way to provide your body with the nutrients and fiber it needs to be healthy and run efficiently. Here are a few grain-like seeds that perfectly complement chia. Give them a try:

- **Amaranth:** Like chia, amaranth is a seed. Also like chia, amaranth was an Aztec favorite. And lastly, like chia, amaranth is loaded with protein (8 grams per ¼ cup), fiber (7 grams per ¼ cup), iron (20 percent of the daily requirement in a ¼ cup) and a full-range of amino acids.
- **Quinoa** is technically a seed, not a grain. Another surprise: It's related to spinach and Swiss chard. Cultivated in the Andean mountain regions of Peru, Chile, and Bolivia for over 5,000 years, quinoa is rich in minerals, fiber, protein, and amino acids, and has long been a staple food in the diet of native Americans. The Incas considered it a sacred food and referred to it as the "mother seed."
- **Millet** is a seed that is rich in magnesium, a mineral that acts as a co-factor for more than 300 enzymes, including enzymes involved in the body's use of glucose and insulin secretion.
- **Buckwheat** is related to sorrel and rhubarb. Rich in phytonutrients, such as flavonoids, as well as minerals, buckwheat's strong flavor is much prized by some and is a staple in Eastern European cooking.

Chia Quesadilla with Chia Guacamole, pages 452–453

Day Seven

Breakfast
Basic Chia Protein Shake, page 411
Piece of fruit

Midmorning snack
Chia Snack Bar, page 420

Lunch
Chia Faux Enchiladas, page 458

Afternoon snack
Citrus Julius, page 411

Dinner
Chia Meatballs, page 455
½ cup quinoa
Green salad with
    Zippy Dressing,
    page 438

DAILY MAINTENANCE WORKOUT

This workout is just as adaptable to your likes, needs, and abilities as the workouts featured in Chapter 4. Change things up and experiment with different components of the program. Be sure to give yourself several "low impact days" a week, to give your muscles a chance to regenerate.

- **Stretching:** Aim for 10 minutes of total body stretching a day. Although you can choose whatever stretches you want—from formal yoga moves to simply raising your arms over your head—be mindful of the many different muscles in the body so you can find stretches that work everything from your feet to your gluteus maximus to your shoulders to your neck.
- **Low-Impact Aerobics Three Times Per Week:** Go for 30 to 45 minutes of sustained

low-impact aerobics. This can be as simple as taking a brisk walk, getting on an exercise bike, or hitting the lap lane at your local pool. As you get stronger, try harder moves, such as going up and down stairs, walking up hills, strapping on wrist or ankle weights, or standing up as you cycle. Use your common sense, but don't be afraid to push yourself a bit.

- **High-Impact Aerobics Four Times Per Week:** Aim for 45 or more minutes of sustained high-impact aerobics. Your choice—do what you love and what works for you on a particular day. Suggestions include outdoor or indoor running, an aerobic dance or kickboxing class, or rebounding on a trampoline. Limiting high-impact aerobics to three times per week will allow your muscles and tendons to get strong gradually, which will help prevent injury. It also gives the heart and lungs time to get used to more intense exercise.

- **Strength Training:** Aim for ten minutes of *light* strength training three times a week on Low-Impact Aerobics Days only. This will give muscles a chance to recoup. This is another chance for you to choose the moves you like: Grab a pair of 2.5-pound hand weights and do bicep curls, squats, toe raises, and more. Or, hop on to a resistance machine. If you don't want to use weights, use your own body's resistance, by doing old-fashioned pushups, sit-ups, leg lifts, and anything else you may remember from high school gym class.

CHAPTER 4

THE CHIA EXERCISE, ENDURANCE, AND ENERGY PLAN

An exercise plan is an essential part of being healthy. You can eat all the chia in the world, but if you don't move your body, you won't have true health or be able to live up to your body's potential. Research backs this up:

- A 2011 study performed at the Fred Hutchinson Cancer Research Center in Seattle followed 439 sedentary postmenopausal women ages 50 to 75 who ranged from moderately overweight to obese, for an entire year. A quarter of the group did nothing, a quarter of the group exercised 45 minutes a day (moderate-to-vigorous aerobic exercise five days a week), a quarter of the group limited their calorie intake (1,200 to 2,000 calories a day, depending on starting weight, with fewer than 30 percent of the daily calories coming from fat), and a quarter of the group exercised *and* limited their calorie intake.

  The findings? The group that did nothing lost less than a pound during the study. The group that only exercised lost on average 2.4 percent of their starting weight, with an average weight loss of 4.4 pounds. The group that only dieted shed about 8.5 percent of their starting weight for an average of 15.8 pounds each. The group that both dieted and exercised did the best, shedding an average of 10.8 percent of their starting weight for an average of 19.8 pounds per person.

- In a 2006 study, University of Minnesota researchers found that for men, exercise alone could cause weight loss. Women, however, lost weight only when they decreased the number of high-fat packaged snack foods, dairy, and meat they ate by five to ten servings a week. Exercise helped speed and maintain weight loss in women, but did not work alone to help women reach their goal weights. Why? No one has yet figured this out.

- A 2006 study at the University of Westminster in London found that while dieting alone could help people lose weight it did not help a dieter to shed fat. A combination of dieting and exercise was needed to lose weight and replace fat with lean muscle. (Incidentally, a pound of fat takes up a whole lot more room than a pound of muscle, which explains why unfit people are a lot larger than fit people who weigh the same.)

GET READY TO MOVE

Human bodies were designed to move, which is why exercise makes good sense. Regular movement not only helps you shed weight faster and keep it off more successfully, it builds muscle, which helps create a leaner-looking, more fit body. And exercise has a host of health benefits, too, from lowering the risks of cancer and cardiovascular disease to boosting the immune system, squelching fatigue, aiding digestion, and creating a calmer nervous system.

If you've been adding chia to your diet—and now's the perfect time to begin experimenting with chia if you haven't yet—you may find that exercise feels easier than you expected. That's because chia actually helps the body exercise more and exercise more intensely. Here's how it works:

- Chia is hydrophilic and can absorb between nine and 12 times its weight in water. This means that chia increases body hydration, which is especially beneficial for athletes who need to remain hydrated during long races and endurance activities. Being well-hydrated means less fatigue and muscle cramping during workouts.
- The Aztecs used chia to help protect and heal joints. Chia is believed to decrease recovery time and fatigue in cardiovascular workouts by encouraging muscle tissue repair. Why? Omega-3 fatty acids and antioxidants, which are both found in chia, have been shown to reduce inflammation; hence they can help protect joints.
- Chia's moisture-retaining quality, plus its high potassium content, helps protect exercisers against electrolyte loss.

MIDDLE-AGE TRIUMPH

In 1997, Nike sponsored a 100-mile run in Colorado. Known as the Leadville Trail 100 Ultramarathon, the route is run at elevations higher than 10,000 feet. Twice, the course travels over the 12,600-foot Hope Pass. The grueling test was enough to make the youngest, fittest, best-outfitted professional marathoners blanch. Imagine what it would have felt like being a 50+ man running in sandals!

But that's just who ended up winning the race. Cirildo Chacarito, a 52-year-old Tarahumaran from a village near Chihuahua, Mexico, won the contest wearing homemade sandals fashioned of leather, used truck tires, and nails. Coming in second and fifth were his tribesmen Victoriano Churo and Manuel Luna. Chacarito completed the feat in 19 hours, 37 minutes, and 3 seconds. Instead of stopping at the aid stations lining the course, the men consumed the chia they brought from home, which they insisted helped them in their win.

THE MOVES

Before you start any fitness plan it's helpful to be familiar with four basic types of exercise in order to make the best fitness choices for yourself:

FLEXIBILITY WORK

Also known as stretching, flexibility work is essential to keeping your body supple, limber, and, yes, flexible. Have you ever noticed that one of the most common signs of aging is a shortened range of motion? In other words, humans tend to lose their flexibility as they age. Their steps get shorter. They shuffle. Their arms lose their swing. Their necks, shoulders, and backs no longer bend when and where they want them to.

Flexibility is important because it gives us range of motion, allowing us to take long, youthful strides, letting us execute all kinds of exercise and strength-building moves without harm, and reducing the likelihood of falls and injuries. Flexibility is essential if you want a body that "goes with the flow" and bounces back easily from physical exertion. Stretching can be as simple as the moves your high school track basketball or football coach taught you, or something more involved, such as yoga or Pilates.

LOW-IMPACT CARDIO

Also called low-impact aerobic exercise, low-impact cardio exercise is steady, prolonged exercise that continues longer than 20 or 30 minutes—such as swimming, walking, cross-country skiing, stair climbing, cycling, skating, rowing, or anything else that literally has a low impact on your joints.

Low-impact cardio is fantastic for anyone who needs to ease into exercise, such as the obese, anyone who has joint problems, or highly-fit individuals who want to alternate between high- and low-impact exercise a few times a week. Typically, low-impact cardio doesn't burn as many calories per minute or produce as much sweat as high impact cardio, but it is a more body-friendly option for everyone.

HIGH-IMPACT CARDIO

Also known as high-impact aerobics, high-impact cardio kicks things up a notch. Running, jumping, aerobic dance, kickboxing, jump roping, and rebounding on a mini-trampoline are all examples of high-impact cardio. Great for burning calories quickly, strengthening the lungs and heart, making you sweat, and strengthening bones, high-impact aerobic exercise is great for just about everyone, except pregnant women,

I am an experienced ultra-distance runner and have worn a heart rate monitor for years. I've stored all the data on my computer and find it interesting to see how the maximum values have dropped over the years and how the amount of high-intensity work outs have decreased as well. It is also interesting to see how many miles and hours a week I have been running, including total ascent during the runs, and ambient temperatures during the runs. I am not saying everyone needs this information, but it can be useful for you to track your progress as you improve your conditioning. Many people also use a heart rate monitor during runs to limit their speed, heart rate, and more, since this is an excellent way to ensure you don't overdo it!

—DR. WAYNE COATES

the obese, and anyone with joint problems. Aim for 30 or more minutes of sustained movement at a time.

RUNNING FOOD

In his book *Born to Run* (Knopf, 2009), Christopher MacDougal writes about the Tarahumara peoples of Copper Canyon, in the southwestern part of Mexico. These people are famous for their endurance, as well as their love of ultra-distant runs (sometimes 100 miles or more). MacDougal even found 90-year-old Tarahumaras running. One of their many secrets? Chia. The Tarahumara roast the seed, then crush it into a powder and mix it with water to make a basic "sports gel," which many consume daily, as well as right before running.

STRENGTH TRAINING

Strength training is any exercise that builds your muscles, whether it is push-ups, sit-ups, bench presses, or exercises with dumbbells, wrist weights, or kettleballs, or a fancy resistance machine. Building muscle should be an important part of your fitness strategy.

Having more muscles creates a lean, healthy-looking body that burns calories efficiently and keeps you strong, which is important if you want enough energy to get through your daily activities without becoming fatigued. Muscles enhance physical endurance—making it less likely that you'll become winded after walking up a few flights of stairs or running after your toddler—and help you get things done, from lifting a chair, to opening a tightly-sealed jar.

Before you start moving, here are the ground rules: Check in with your healthcare provider if you haven't exercised in a while. Choose the correct exercise program for your fitness level (jumping to a higher level will only cause you pain—it's best to start easy and build up to more intense workouts).

First, commit to getting some movement every single day. Every. Single. Day. Post it in your calendar if you must. Schedule it in your electronic diary. Just make sure you do it daily. This is especially important if you are trying to burn calories and shed pounds.

A 2009 study at the University of Colorado School of Medicine found that exercisers didn't actually experience "afterburn"—that much-touted (and perhaps near-mythical) revving-up of the metabolism that some fitness pros claim continues for hours after exercise. For the study, researchers recruited several groups of people, some of whom were lean endurance athletes, while others were either sedentary and lean or sedentary and obese. Each of the subjects spent several 24-hour periods in a special laboratory room called a walk-in calorimeter that measures the number of calories a person

YOUR TARGET HEART RATE

Some fitness pros and exercise buffs like to talk about target heart rate. Your *maximum* heart rate is approximately 220 minus your age. If you are 30 years old, your maximum heart rate is 190 beats per minute (BPM).

Your *target* heart rate is roughly 50 to 85 percent of your maximum heart rate. This is the level at which your heart is beating with moderate to high intensity, and sustaining a workout at this pace strengthens the heart and lung muscles. Beginners should exercise in the 50 to 60 percent target heart rate zone. Intermediate or average exercisers should aim for 60 to 70 percent. Advanced athletes can train in the 75 to 85 percent zone. To track your heart rate during exercise, you can take your pulse or use a heart rate monitor.

While finding your heart rate is fun (if you like this sort of thing), it isn't necessary for most healthy people. Simply exercise for 30 or more minutes until you are pleasantly winded.

That said, many physicians have strong opinions about target heart rates for people who are obese or pregnant, or have respiratory conditions or a cardiovascular disease (such as high blood pressure). If you fall into one of these categories, talk to your healthcare provider before beginning any new exercise regimen.

burns, followed by another 24 hour-period that included an hour-long bout of stationary bicycling. Researchers found that none of the groups, including the athletes, experienced "afterburn" or "metabolism revving."

According to findings, it seems that exercise's calorie-burning benefits happen during exercise itself. Period. This likelihood is all the more reason to get some movement in every single day.

As you'll see in a bit, the workouts described here are flexible, mix-and-match programs, designed to allow you to do what you love in order to shape up and slim down. All you have to do is choose your own blend of stretching, aerobic, and strength activities on any given day. Feel free to do try new stretches, aerobic exercises, or new strength training moves every single day.

DAILY WORKOUT LEVEL I

For people who are new exercisers, obese, injured, have pre-existing conditions, and whose healthcare providers have suggested gentle options, this may be your life fitness plan (if your healthcare provider feels it's best for you). Otherwise, plan to spend two or more months at this daily workout level before moving up to Level II. Advancing too quickly can leave you injured and burnt out.

STRETCHING

Aim for five to ten minutes of total body stretching a day. Although you can choose the stretches you want—from formal yoga moves to simply raising your arms over your head—be mindful of the many different muscles in the body so you can find stretches that work everything from your feet to your gluteus maximus to your shoulders to your neck.

WHY YOU SHOULD CONSIDER RUNNING

If you haven't tried distance running, and want to, what are you waiting for? The American College of Sports Medicine Position Statement on Exercise states that individuals who run more than 50 miles per week had significantly greater increases in HDL cholesterol (the good kind) and significantly greater decreases in body fat, triglyceride levels, and the risk of coronary heart disease than individuals who ran less than 10 miles per week. In addition, the long-distance runners had it over the short-distance runners with a nearly 50 percent reduction in hypertension and more than a 50 percent reduction in the use of medications used to lower blood pressure or cholesterol levels. Note: Many studies find the same benefits are available to those who run the more doable 25 to 35 miles per week.

> *I am busy, overworked, and always on the go. Like most everyone else today, I began taking chia at the suggestion of my nutritionist. I was telling her how tired I would get each afternoon. So tired that there were times when I would literally shut my office door, put my head down on my desk, and take a nap. I knew I had to do something about this when my boss caught me sleeping one day. Hence, the chia. I now have a bag at my desk that I sprinkle onto my lunchtime salad. It has made an enormous difference in my energy level. I even have time after work to play soccer or basketball with my son.*
>
> —JAMES PETERS, Los Angeles, CA

LOW-IMPACT AEROBICS

Try for 20 to 30 minutes of sustained low-impact aerobics. This can be as simple as taking a brisk walk or jumping on an exercise bike. As you get stronger, try harder moves, such as going up and down stairs, walking up hills, strapping on wrist or ankle weights, or standing up as you cycle. Use your common sense, but don't be afraid to push yourself a bit.

STRENGTH TRAINING

Aim for five to ten minutes of *light* strength training each day, making sure not to do the same exercise two days in a row—muscles need a break to regenerate. Since you are not using large amounts of weight or strength training for long periods of time, you can work your muscles daily without worry.

This is another chance for you to choose the moves you like: Grab a pair of 2.5-pound hand weights and do bicep curls, squats, toe raises, and more. Or hop on to a resistance machine. If you don't want to use weights, use your own body's resistance by doing old-fashioned push-ups, sit-ups, leg lifts, and anything else you may remember from high school gym class.

YOGA VS. WALKING

While yoga is terrific exercise, most types are far from aerobic. For instance, a 150-pound person will burn 150 calories in an hour of doing regular yoga, compared to 311 calories for an hour of walking at 3 mph.

DAILY WORKOUT LEVEL II

For those who are graduating from Daily Workout Level I or who are already moderately fit, Daily Workout Level II is a little more challenging, yet every bit as creative as the other workouts featured here. Plan to spend two or more months on this level before moving up to Daily Workout Level III. Advancing too quickly can leave you injured and burnt out.

COLON CANCER AND EXERCISE

Researchers from Washington University and Harvard University reviewed 52 studies, from the last 25 years, which linked exercise and the incidence of colon cancer, a cancer that is diagnosed in over 100,000 Americans each year. Their findings? Individuals who exercised the most (5 to 6 hours per week) were 24 percent less likely to develop the disease than those who exercised the least (less than 30 minutes per week).

STRETCHING

Aim for ten minutes of total body stretching. Although you can choose whatever stretches you want—from formal yoga moves to simply raising your arms over your head—be mindful of the many different muscles in the body so you can find stretches that work everything from your feet to your gluteus maximus to your shoulders to your neck.

A stretching note from Dr. Coates: Be careful here not to overdo it, since cold muscles are more easily injured than warm muscles. If you feel you are able to go for a little run or brisk walk prior to stretching, this seems to work best. Also, you should conclude your daily routine with a bit of stretching, when your muscles are warm and flexible.

LOW-IMPACT AEROBICS FOUR TIMES PER WEEK

Go for 30 to 45 minutes of sustained low-impact aerobics. This can be as simple as taking a brisk walk, getting on an exercise bike,

I've been doing 5Ks for about six months now as a fun way to get some exercise. Before going on chia, however, I could never run an entire race. I would usually start walking at the 3.5 mark, which is exactly when I'd get an achy, fatigued, I'm-going-to-fall-o no achy feeling! Chia really does help me feel alive and energetic through an entire race.

—STEVE PHILPOT, Chicago, IL

EXERCISE FACTS

- Fit people tend to sweat more and sooner than unfit people. Their bodies are more efficient at cooling.
- Exercise boosts mental acuity by increasing blood circulation to the brain and increasing serotonin in the brain, which leads to improved mental clarity and processing speed.
- With moderate exercise, most individuals will lose about one quart (4 cups) of fluid per hour. One tablespoon of chia gel (see page 421) taken before exercise can reduce the amount of fluid you lose, but be sure to drink 16 ounces of water shortly after working out to ensure that you remain properly hydrated.
- If your workout clothes smell like ammonia after a workout, you're burning a lot of protein for fuel. Ammonia is a by-product of protein metabolism. This is not a good thing, since burning protein means you may be burning your muscle tissue for energy instead of carbohydrates or body fat.
- Exercise decreases the harmful effects of stress by calming the body and increasing feel-good neurotransmitters such as serotonin and melatonin.
- To determine if your scale is correct, set a dumbbell or a weight plate on it. If the numbers don't match, try another weight and see if it's off by the same amount. Adjust your scale accordingly.
- Because exercise releases endorphins into the body, a daily workout can be just what you need to help improve energy levels all day.
- In 1982, the most expensive running shoe on the market was the Nike Air Columbia at a stratospheric $64.99.
- Daily movement helps slow degenerative joint disease by strengthening bones, muscles, and tendons.
- The average exercise life of a running shoe is about 400 miles.
- Most folks who wear their running shoes around on a regular basis usually only get around 200 running miles out of the shoes!

or hitting the lap lane at your local pool. As you get stronger, try harder moves, such as going up and down stairs, walking up hills, strapping on wrist or ankle weights, or standing up as you cycle. Use your common sense, but don't be afraid to push yourself a bit.

> *I'm the mother of twin toddler boys. With broken sleep, hormonal issues, and the physical demands of caring for young children, it's normal to be tired as a mother. I was so tired by late morning each day that I felt I couldn't safely look after my children the way I needed to. Chia has really helped maintain my energy levels, making me a safer, calmer, and more fun parent. A good thing for the entire family and no more difficult than a couple spoonfuls mixed into my morning veggie juice.*
>
> —MISSY ROBERTS, Miami

HIGH-IMPACT AEROBICS THREE TIMES PER WEEK

Aim for 20 or 30 minutes of sustained high-impact aerobics. It's your choice—do what you love and what works for you on a particular day. Suggestions include outdoor or indoor running, an aerobic dance or kickboxing class, or rebounding on a trampoline. Limiting high-impact aerobics to three times per week will allow your muscles and tendons to get strong gradually, which will help prevent injury and also give your heart and lungs time to get used to more intense exercise.

STRENGTH TRAINING

Aim for five to 10 minutes of strength training each day, making sure not to do the same exercise two days in a row—muscles need a break to regenerate. Since you are not using large weight or strength training for long periods of time, you can work your muscles daily without worry.

This is another chance for you to choose the moves you like: Grab a pair of 2.5-pound hand weights and do bicep curls, squats, toe raises, and more. Or hop on to a resistance machine. If you don't want to use weights, use your own body's resistance, by doing old-fashioned push-ups, sit-ups, leg lifts, and anything else you may remember from high school gym class.

AN EVERYDAY HABIT

The Aztecs consumed chia every single day, in unleavened bread, porridge, and drinks. They used the oil on their skin, blended it into medicine, and used it for a type of communion or sacrament in their religious ceremonies. For the Aztecs, chia was not only a superfood, it was an everyday staple. With the continual consumption of chia—as well as other nutrient-dense foods such as amaranth and dried beans—the Aztecs were famed for their vigor, strength, and physical prowess.

DAILY WORKOUT LEVEL III

For those who are graduating from Daily Workout Level II, or who are already fit, Daily Workout Level III is the most challenging. It's just as adaptable to your likes and needs and abilities as the other workouts featured here. You can stay at this level, changing things up and experimenting with different components of the program. Be sure to give yourself several "low impact days" a week, to give muscles a chance to regenerate.

STRETCHING

Aim for ten minutes of total body stretching. Although you can choose whatever stretches you want—from formal yoga moves to simply raising your arms over your head—be mindful of the many different muscles in the body so you can find stretches that work everything from your feet to your gluteus maximus to your shoulders to your neck.

LOW-IMPACT AEROBICS THREE TIMES PER WEEK

Go for 30 to 45 minutes of sustained low-impact aerobics. This can be as simple as taking a brisk walk or getting on an exercise bike or hitting the lap lane at your local pool. As you get stronger, try harder moves, such as going up and down stairs, walking up hills, strapping on wrist or ankle weights, or standing up as you cycle. Use your common sense, but don't be afraid to push yourself a bit.

I am a fitness instructor and personal trainer, who is on the go all day, six days a week. I would literally conk out every day right before having to teach my 2:00 high impact aerobics class. I dreaded this part of the day and felt I wasn't energetic enough to motivate the class. At my fiancé's suggestion (he's a weight lifter), I began taking two tablespoons of chia mixed with water each day (one with breakfast one with lunch). After about five days on chia, I noticed I got through the class with ease. Working with my late afternoon private clients was also much easier. The endurance that chia gives me is good for me, good for my business. My only regret about chia is that I didn't discover it earlier!

— SHARI CONNORS, Cincinnati, OH

HIGH-IMPACT AEROBICS FOUR TIMES PER WEEK

Aim for 45 or more minutes of sustained high-impact aerobics. It's your choice—do what you love and what works for you on a particular day. Suggestions include outdoor or indoor running, an aerobic dance or kick-boxing class, or rebounding on a trampoline. Limiting high-impact aerobics to three times per week will allow your muscles and tendons to get strong gradually, which will help prevent injury. It also gives the heart and lungs time to get used to more intense exercise.

MORE EXERCISE FACTS

- Running one mile burns approximately 30 percent more calories than walking one mile, and that formulation remains true whether you run outdoors or on a treadmill.
- The record for running a mile backward is 6:02.35, by D. Joseph James of India on August 10, 2002.
- In a study on walking and cognitive function, researchers found that women who walked 1.5 hours per week had significantly better cognitive function and less cognitive decline than women who walked less than 40 minutes per week.
- Running shoes are excellent for a regular walking program.
- When walking at a moderate pace, a 150-pound man burns 100 calories per mile; a 200-pound man burns 133 calories per mile; and a 250-pound man burns 166 calories per mile.
- Running uphill burns 28 percent more fat than cycling uphill.
- The first company to charge $100 for a pair of shoes was New Balance, who introduced the now legendary 990 in 1983.
- When a shoe "breaks down" it's usually in the midsole and not the outsole that goes first.
- Human thigh bones are stronger than concrete.
- Women in the Nurse's Health Study (72,488 female nurses) who walked three hours or more per week reduced their risk of a heart attack or other coronary event by 35 percent compared with women who did not walk.
- Want to keep your ankles strong? Do not use running shoes for lateral activities like tennis, basketball, step aerobics, racquetball, or any other sport that causes you to pivot and cut from side to side. Instead, go for a "cross-trainer" or "court shoe."
- People with flat feet are more prone to ankle sprains than those who have normal arches. If you have high arches you are even less likely to sprain your ankle than people who have regular arches.

WHAT IS ISKIATE?

If you're a runner, you may have heard of iskiate, a nutritious, whole food, homemade sports drink, based on an ancient recipe for Aztec Chia Fresca, the ingredients of which are water, chia, sweetener, and lemon or lime-juice. Some companies today sell pre-made "iskiate" powder that can be mixed with water.

Some say the term iskiate comes from the Tarahumara Indians of Mexico's Copper Canyon, near Chihuahua. Famous for their hardiness and distance running, the Tarahumara are dedicated chia eaters, believing that it provides energy and aids endurance. But word sleuths among you, beware: There is no clear history of the word, which may have come from the Tarahumara or from some other source altogether.

STRENGTH TRAINING

Aim for 10 minutes of *light* strength training three times a week on Low-Impact Aerobics days only. This will give your muscles a chance to recoup. This is another chance for you to choose the moves you like: Grab a pair of 2.5-pound hand weights and do bicep curls, squats, toe raises and more. Or, hop on to a resistance machine. If you don't want to use weights, use your own body's resistance, by doing old-fashioned pushups, sit-ups, leg lifts, and anything else you may remember from high school gym class.

I'm a casual runner, who runs about 15 to 18 miles a week. I also cycle, walk, row, play tennis, and swim. I began taking chia nine months ago, when I noticed that my running partner began to run longer distances than me without getting winded. He said he'd started blending chia into his breakfast smoothies. I tried it, too. Within one week, I no longer felt fatigued and out of breath toward the end of my runs. I really notice a difference in my endurance and lung capacity when I take chia.

—JOEL COHEN, Atlanta, GA

WHEN TO EXERCISE: IS THERE A BEST TIME?

Most people would agree that the best time to exercise is the time you are most likely to stick with it, whenever that happens to be. That said, there have been studies showing that exercising at certain times bestows certain benefits:

- While researching the effects of exercise on blood pressure, Appalachian State University researcher Sr. Scott Collier found that individuals who exercised at 7:00 a.m. experienced a 10 percent reduction in blood pressure that carried through the remainder of the day, dipping down to a 25 percent decrease by night fall. They also had longer and more beneficial sleep cycles than when they exercised at other times during the day.

- Researchers studying sleep apnea have found that mid- to late afternoon is the best time to exercise if you suffer from sleep apnea and want a good night's sleep.

- Research from Northwestern University points to late afternoon being the best time to exercise, as strength and physical stamina is at its peak during those times, which lessens chances of injury. This has something to do with body temperature: it is theorized that exercise is most productive when body temperature is at its highest, which is typically between 2:00 and 6:00 p.m.

- A 2010 study in Belgium found the best time to exercise to burn fat was in the morning, before breakfast (perhaps after a spoonful of chia?). For six weeks, 28 men were fed a diet of 50 percent fat, with 30 percent more calories than the men's normal diet. One group did no exercise, one group exercised in the morning before eating, and the last group exercised later in the day after meals. Only the group that exercised before breakfast gained almost no weight and showed no signs of insulin resistance.

CHAPTER 5

COOKING, EATING, AND HEALING WITH CHIA

Chia is perfectly at home in the kitchen. It's easy to store, easy to use, and doesn't require grinders or other special equipment. Chia is versatile: it can be used at any temperature; it has a neutral taste; and the seeds possess a pleasant, almost nutty texture.

Chia's low-key personality is just as wonderful. Chia is the ultimate supporting player, quietly lending a high-impact dose of nutrients and fiber to the foods you already enjoy. This makes it ideal for all you "sneaky chefs" out there who are trying to get healthy foods into your fussy children's diet. As you'll see here, it's very easy to tuck chia is into a wide variety of recipes. Just scoop, sprinkle, and enjoy. The recipes below are perfect for anyone who's ready to maintain a healthy weight and create massive wellness. Bon appetit!

BEVERAGES

CHIA FRESCA
SERVES ONE

This ancient beverage has been used as an endurance booster by many of people living in Central America, as well as Mexico and the American Southwest. Refreshing and filling, Chia Fresca supplies a slow, steady supply of energy. It's a favorite of many distance runners who jokingly refer to Chia Fresca as "Home-Brewed Red Bull." For a change, swap in coconut water—it's a great way to add a quick dose of electrolytes to this refreshing beverage.

1   tablespoon chia seeds
8 to 10 ounces cool water (or coconut water)
*   Juice of a half or whole lemon or lime (depending upon how tart you like things)*
*   Optional: Natural sweetener of your choice, to taste (sugar, honey, agave, brown rice syrup, Stevia, etc.)*

1. Add chia seed to a glass of water, stirring until combined. Drink immediately if desired, or set aside for up to 10 minutes to allow the seed to form a gel.
2. Add lemon or lime juice and sweetener to the chia mixture, stirring until combined.
3. Drink immediately or let stand until mixture becomes gel-like.

GREEN SUPER SMOOTHIE

SERVES ONE

Green smoothies are all the rage. They are a great way to get a bold dose of veggies, fiber, and nutrients in a healthy, convenient, low-calorie way. Here, a tablespoon of chia seed creates an even more super-charged drink. This treat is best made in a high-powered blender. A Blendtec or Vitamix brand power blender is ideal.

1   *tablespoon chia seeds*
1½ *cups pear juice, coconut water, water,*
    or a mixture
3   *romaine lettuce or kale leaves*
1   *small cucumber, peeled*
    Parsley sprigs

1. Add all ingredients to a blender and liquefy using the most powerful setting. Blend until smooth.
2. Drink immediately.

ALMOND DELIGHT

SERVES ONE

This slightly sweet, creamy drink is perfect to round out breakfast, but it also makes a great snack or a healthy dessert after dinner. The recipe is versatile—have fun customizing it by using different milks, nut butters, and even fruits.

1   *tablespoon chia seeds*
1½ *cup unsweetened almond milk*
1   *tablespoon almond butter*
Optional: a dash of almond or vanilla extract
Optional: a small amount of natural sweetener
    (such as honey, brown rice syrup, agave,
    Stevia, etc.)

1. Add all ingredients to a blender and liquefy using the most powerful setting. Blend until smooth.
2. Drink immediately.

BASIC CHIA PROTEIN SHAKE

SERVES ONE

This easy recipe is based on one by the talented Jackie Rafter, holistic nutritionist and founder of LivLong Inc, at **http://livlong.ca**. It's incredibly versatile, so feel free to add and subtract ingredients at will, and design a new creation each time you make it.

1 *tablespoon chia seeds*
1½ *cup liquid of choice (water, coconut water, juice, rice milk, etc.)*
½ *to 1 cup chopped raw vegetable of your choice (¼ cup of this can be fruit)*
1 *tablespoon coconut oil*
1 *scoop protein powder of choice (hemp, rice, whey, etc.)*
3 *or 4 ice cubes*
Optional: A dash of your favorite extract or spice (such as vanilla, cinnamon, or allspice), a tablespoon of nut butter, a half-tablespoon of cocoa, cocoa nibs, or carob, etc.
Optional: Small amount of natural sweetener (such as honey, brown rice syrup, agave, Stevia, etc.)

1. Add all ingredients to a blender and liquefy using the most powerful setting. Blend until smooth.
2. Drink immediately.

CITRUS JULIUS

SERVES ONE

Here's another delicious recipe from holistic nutritionist Jackie Rafter, who says, "If you didn't know better, you'd think someone just bought you a delicious Grapefruit Julius! It's incredibly refreshing and a wonderful liver tonic, too."

1 *tablespoon chia seeds*
1 *grapefruit, juiced*
2 *lemons or limes, juiced*
1 *cup cool water*
1 *inch piece fresh ginger root, peeled*
Optional: Dash cayenne
Optional: Stevia powder for sweetening

1. Add all ingredients to a blender and liquefy using the most powerful setting. Blend until smooth.
2. Drink immediately.

DRINK IMMEDIATELY?

As you read our recipes, you may notice the recommendation to "Drink Immediately" or "Eat Immediately." There's a good reason for this: Chia is chock-full of soluble fiber, the type of fiber that swells when it comes in contact with water. In fact, within 10 minutes of getting wet, the chia seed's outer coating begins to release soluble fiber, forming a gel that expands chia's size up to nine times.. This also makes them slightly gelatinous. Thus, if you wait too long to drink a chia seed smoothie, you may be facing a glass of gelatin-like goo! Of course it would still be delicious and nutritious, but it might perhaps be a bit challenging to sip.

GINGER PEAR EGGNOG SMOOTHIE

SERVES ONE

This festive shake is decadent and quick, making it the perfect treat for action-packed holidays. The recipe comes, once again, from Jackie Rafter. Here's her take on this delicious concoction: "This shake almost tastes like Christmas eggnog—A wonderful way to start your day or a great pick-me-up before going out on the town."

1   tablespoon chia seeds
1   large pear, peeled, cut in half, and core removed
1½ cups water
1   scoop vanilla protein powder (hemp, rice, or whey, etc.)
½   inch piece fresh ginger root, peeled
½   teaspoon cinnamon, or a mix of cinnamon, clove, and nutmeg
Optional: Stevia to sweeten
3 or 4 ice cubes

1. Add all ingredients to a blender and liquefy using the most powerful setting. Blend until smooth.
2. Drink immediately.

CHIA MYTH BUSTING

- Chia is an ancient South American food.
  False: Chia originally comes from Southern Mexico and Guatemala.
- Chia is the food of the Mayans.
  False: Though there is evidence the Mayans did obtain chia through trading, chia was the food of the Aztecs.
- Chia was used as a sacrificial plant for the gods, and mortals were not allowed to eat it.
  False: Though chia was given as gifts to gods, it was also used for trade, milled into flour, mixed into drinks, made into medicines, and pressed for oil.
- Chia grew on "hanging garden islands" of suspended mats hanging over marshy lowlands.
  True: The Aztecs learned this system of gardening from their predecessors, the Toltecs, and used it to grow chia and other crops.

SPICY GREEN CHOCOLATE SHAKE

SERVES ONE TO TWO

This delectable shake combines chocolate and veggies to create a powerful source of nutrients. "Plus, it's green, very alkalizing, full of minerals, and it's incredibly healthy," says its creator, Jackie Rafter. "If you're really brave, load up with ½ teaspoon of the cinnamon and double the raw ginger."

1   tablespoon chia seeds
2 or 3 tablespoons raw cacao powder or
    ¼ cup carob or cacao nibs
2   cups water
3   cups raw baby spinach
½   avocado, peeled
1 or 2 scoops chocolate or vanilla flavor
    protein powder (rice, hemp, or whey, etc.)
1   teaspoon ginger powder or 1-inch fresh
    ginger root, peeled
1   teaspoon cinnamon
8   ice cubes
    Stevia to taste
Optional: ¼ to ½ teaspoon spirulina or
    chlorophyll powder
Optional: 1 teaspoon lecithin powder

1. Add all ingredients to a blender and liquefy using the most powerful setting. Blend until smooth.
2. Drink immediately.

IT'S A KEEPER

Many whole foods—such as brown rice, flaxseed, and wheat germ—go rancid quickly or are prone to infestations by hungry pests. Not chia! Thanks to concentrated levels of antioxidants, chia resists spoilage, even when kept in a room temperature cupboard for two years!

FRUIT SLUSHY

SERVES ONE

This refreshing shake is a supercharged version of those fruit-flavored (neon-colored) Slurpee beverages found at quick marts throughout the United States. Quick, easy, and addictively delicious, this is a great, easy-to-make snack recipe for kids.

1   tablespoon chia seeds
1½ cup cool water, coconut water, or juice of
    choice (pear is especially nice and considerably
    lower on the glycemic index than apple, grape,
    and other juice favorites, meaning it won't
    cause a blood sugar spike after drinking)
½ to 1 cup frozen fruit of your choice (you
    can use a blend of different fruits or stick
    to one kind)

1. Add all ingredients to a blender and liquefy using the most powerful setting. Blend until smooth.
2. Drink immediately.

TROPICAL CHAMPAGNE PUNCH SMOOTHIE

SERVES 10 TO 20

This is for all of you who like to mix health and pleasure. Created by holistic nutritionist Jackie Rafter, this punch is a special-occasion treat that combines chia, fruit, and alcohol (though Rafter also loves it without the wine). It was "test-driven" on almost 50 people who would have never guessed it was as healthy as it was delicious. "Plus it's so simple and easy to make," says Rafter, who created the recipe for her mother's 75th birthday. "The chia seed is excellent not only for adding body, but also for absorbing alcohol."

3   *tablespoons chia seeds*
1   *grapefruit, juiced*
1 or 2 *oranges, juiced*
1   *inch piece of fresh ginger root, peeled*
1   *banana, peeled*
½   *a mango, peeled and chopped*
¼   *fresh pineapple, peeled and chopped*
2 to 3 *cups cool water*
    Stevia, to sweeten
1   *bottle champagne or sparkling wine*
    Generous amounts of ice

1. Add all ingredients, except wine and ice, to a blender and liquefy using the most powerful setting. Blend until smooth.
2. Pour into a punch bowl and add champagne.
3. Adjust sweetener if necessary.
4. Add ice.

HANGOVER CURE?

There are several underground reports that chia is used to prevent hangovers, or as a way to lessen the effect of a full-blown hangover. While we haven't tried this ourselves, it makes sense: Chia contains high levels of vitamins A, B complex, C, and E, as well as ferulates and many phytonutrients—all of which help the body get rid of unwanted toxins, and all of which are depleted by alcohol. Furthermore, chia is hydrating, so it can prevent and treat the dehydration caused by alcohol. To try this yourself, after a night of hitting the town, stir 1 tablespoon of chia into a glass of water before going to bed. Repeat upon waking if needed.

CHIA VS. SALBA

Anyone who has looked into chia has probably heard of Salba®. This is the trademarked name for white chia, which was originally planted and then produced in Peru. Tests have shown that white and black chia seeds have essentially the same composition, however, black seeds have higher levels of antioxidants.

BAKED TREATS

CHIA SEED MUFFINS

MAKES 12

Muffins are the quintessential grab-and-go breakfast treats, beloved of kids and adults alike. They're also a sweet snack—perfect for when you crave something sweet. These muffins are not only delicious, they're hearty and filling, thanks to the addition of chia.

1   stick butter, softened
¾ cup raw or regular sugar
2   large eggs, lightly beaten
¾ cup plain yogurt, at room temperature
1½ teaspoons vanilla
2   cups whole wheat pastry flour or unbleached all-purpose four
⅓ cup chia seeds
½ teaspoon salt
¼ teaspoon baking soda
Optional: Cinnamon sugar topping, made with 2 tablespoons sugar and ¼ teaspoon cinnamon

1. Preheat the oven to 375°F. Line a muffin tin with muffin papers or lightly grease a muffin tin.

2. In a large mixing bowl, cream the butter and sugar until light and fluffy. You can do this by hand, with a hand-held mixer, or in a stand mixer.

3. Blend in the eggs, yogurt, and vanilla.

4. In a separate bowl, combine the flour, chia seeds, salt, and baking soda.

5. Slowly add the dry ingredients to the creamed mixture and blend just until combined. Do not over mix.

6. Fill each muffin cup ⅔ full of batter.

7. Sprinkle with the cinnamon sugar, if using.

8. Bake until golden brown, 15 to 20 minutes. Allow the muffins to cool slightly before removing from the tin.

MILLED CHIA

Many of the recipes in this section call for milled chia. Though it sounds exotic, milled chia is nothing more than chia seeds that have been ground into meal so it can be used as a flour-like ingredient in baked goods.

To make your own milled chia, take as much chia as you'd like and grind it in a clean coffee mill, food processor, or high-speed blender (such as a Vitamix or Blendtec). Process the seed until it resembles sand in texture—you want a coarse flour. It keeps well, so go ahead and make extra so that you'll have milled chia handy for all your recipes.

GLUTEN-FREE CHIA MUFFINS

*MAKES 2 DOZEN REGULAR OR
4 DOZEN MINI MUFFINS*

Gluten is the protein found in wheat and wheat's cousins, including spelt, kamut, semolina, rye, and even barley. People with gluten intolerances and those with Celiac Sprue must avoid gluten. In this easy recipe, milled chia stands in for the standard wheat flour, illustrating just how simple it is to bake without wheat. **Note:** Try using your mini-muffin tins: The muffins bake up higher and lighter when made small.

1½ cups milled chia
2 teaspoons baking powder
½ teaspoon salt
1 large egg, lightly beaten
1 teaspoon vanilla
¼ cup oil or melted butter
½ cup milk (dairy, coconut, almond, rice, etc.)
¼ cup honey
Optional: 1 cup raisins, dried cranberries,
    chopped dried apricots, frozen blueberries,
    or chopped peaches

1. Preheat the oven to 350°F. Line two standard muffin tins or four mini muffin tins with muffin papers, or lightly greased muffin tins.
2. In a medium bowl, whisk together the chia, baking powder, and salt.
3. In a large bowl, mix together the egg, vanilla, oil, milk, and honey, combining thoroughly.
4. Add the dry ingredients to the liquid ingredients, then add the fruit, if using. Gently mix until just combined.
5. Fill each muffin cup ⅔ full of batter.
6. Bake in middle rack of the oven until golden brown, 20 to 25 minutes.
7. Cool in the tins for 5 minutes before removing.

BAKING WITHOUT GLUTEN

Gluten, the protein in wheat, gives baked goods structure and a soft, springy texture. If you've been told you have to give up gluten, you have options, one of them being chia. Just keep in mind that baked goods made without wheat may have either a heavier, moister texture, or a drier one, depending on the non-gluten flour you bake with.

PROTEIN MUFFINS

MAKES 12 MUFFINS

This muffin is great for anyone who needs a lot of protein—distance runners, power lifters, triathletes, pregnant women—as well as anyone who likes their muffins hearty. You can also pop them into your kids' lunch boxes or wrap up and tuck one into your bag for a mid-morning pick-up.

1 cup cooked black or white beans
⅓ cup milled chia
⅓ cup natural cocoa powder
½ cup raw or regular sugar

1 cup whole wheat pastry flour
1 teaspoon baking soda
1 teaspoon cinnamon
½ teaspoon ginger
½ teaspoon salt
1 cup shredded carrot (use about 2 medium-size carrots)
1 large egg, lightly beaten
⅓ cup virgin coconut oil, liquefied
1 teaspoon vanilla

1. Preheat oven to 350°F. Line a muffin tin with muffin papers, or lightly grease a muffin tin.
2. Puree the beans in a food processor or a high-power blender, such as a Vitamix or Blendtec. Set aside.
3. In a large bowl, whisk together the chia, cocoa, sugar, flour, baking soda, cinnamon, ginger, and salt.
4. In a separate bowl, combine the pureed beans, carrot, egg, coconut oil, and vanilla. Mix thoroughly.
5. Add the dry ingredients to the bean mixture, stirring gently until ingredients are combined.
6. Fill each muffin cup ⅔ full of batter.
7. Bake on the middle rack until a toothpick inserted in the muffins comes out clean, 15 to 20 minutes, checking often for doneness so as to not overcook.
8. Cool in the tins for 5 minutes before removing.

CHIA CORNBREAD
MAKES 6 TO 9 SERVINGS

Southern-style cornbread is the perfect accompaniment to sautéed greens, beans, chili, soups, and stews—and it makes a nourishing snack. This tasty, gluten-free version is made with fiber-rich, nutrient-dense chia.

3 tablespoons extra-virgin olive oil, virgin coconut oil, or other oil.
2 cups yellow or white cornmeal
1 teaspoon baking powder
1 tablespoon milled chia
½ teaspoon salt
1 large egg, beaten
1½ cups milk (dairy, buttermilk, rice milk, almond milk, coconut milk, etc.)

1. Preheat the oven to 375°F.
2. Pour the oil in a 9-inch cast-iron skillet or similar-sized glass baking dish and transfer to the preheating oven.
3. Whisk the cornmeal, baking powder, milled chia, and salt in a medium bowl until combined.
4. Add the egg and milk; stir until just combined.
5. Remove the pan from the oven and swirl the oil to coat the bottom and a little way up the sides. Very carefully pour the excess hot oil into the cornmeal mixture; stir until just combined.
6. Pour the batter into the hot pan. Bake until the bread is firm in the middle and lightly golden, about 20 minutes.
7. Let cool for 5 minutes before slicing. Serve warm.

CHIA & HEAT

To protect chia seeds' rich omega-3 fatty acid content, chia is best cooked at lower temperatures. Baking at 375°F and below is perfect. Sautéing or frying, however, is not. That's because these cooking methods, which cause food to reach temperatures over 375°F, damage chia's nutrient profile.

BANANA BREAD

MAKES 6 TO 9 SERVINGS

Who doesn't love banana bread? Sweet, fruity, and satisfying, this homey treat is true comfort food. Here, it is revved up with chia, making it a healthy snack option.

5   tablespoons butter (softened), plus more for greasing pan
½   cup raw or regular sugar
2   large eggs (or egg substitute equivalent), at room temperature
1½ cups all-purpose flour
1   teaspoon baking soda
1   teaspoon salt
½   teaspoon ground cinnamon
¼   teaspoon ground nutmeg
⅛   teaspoon ground cloves
1   tablespoon milled chia
1   (6 ounce) container vanilla low-fat yogurt (or coconut-based yogurt)
¾   cup mashed ripe banana (approximately 1½ bananas)
¼   teaspoon vanilla extract

Optional: ½ cup chopped walnuts or pecans

1. Preheat the oven to 350°F.
2. Grease an 8 x 4-inch loaf pan with butter.
3. In a large mixing bowl, cream the butter and sugar. You can do this with a hand-held mixer or in a stand mixer. Beat at medium speed until fluffy and well blended.
4. Add the eggs, one at a time, beating well after each addition.
5. In a separate bowl, sift together the flour, baking soda, salt, cinnamon, nutmeg, cloves, and milled chia.
6. Alternating, add half of the flour mixture, all of the yogurt, then the remaining half of the flour mixture to sugar mixture, beating well after each addition.
7. Fold in the bananas, vanilla, and nuts, if using.
8. Pour the batter into the prepared loaf pan and place on middle rack in the oven.
9. Bake until a wooden toothpick inserted into the bread's center comes out clean, 50 to 60 minutes.
10. Cool for 10 minutes in the pan on a wire rack. Remove from the pan, slice and serve.

VEGAN EGG REPLACEMENT

Vegans do not use eggs, making traditional baking a challenge. Luckily, there is chia, which makes a perfect egg replacement. For every egg, combine one tablespoon chia seed with three tablespoons water. Whisk together and allow to gel for 10 to 15 minutes before using.

PUMPKIN BREAD

MAKES 6 TO 9 SERVINGS

Warm, spicy and luscious, this scrumptious bread is an autumn staple in many homes. What sets this version apart, however, is chia, which gives the finished product a moist texture and ultra-nutritious profile.

½ *stick butter, softened, plus more for greasing pan*
1 *teaspoon Stevia powder or equivalent other sugar substitute*
1 *large egg, lightly beaten (you can use 2 egg whites for less fat)*
½ *teaspoon orange extract or vanilla extract*
1 *cup canned pumpkin*
1¼ *cups all-purpose flour*
2 *teaspoons baking powder*
¾ *teaspoon baking soda*
½ *teaspoon salt*
1 *tablespoon milled chia*
1½ *teaspoons ground cinnamon*
¾ *teaspoon ground ginger*
¼ *teaspoon ground nutmeg*
Optional: ½ cup raisins
Optional: ⅓ cup chopped pecans
Optional: 3 tablespoons apricot jam or spreadable fruit (for glazed topping)
Optional: Pecan halves or chopped pecans, for garnish

1. Preheat the oven to 350 °F.
2. Grease an 8 x 4-inch loaf pan with butter.
3. With mixer, beat the butter and Stevia until blended.
4. Add in the egg, orange extract and pumpkin.
5. In a separate bowl, sift together the flour, baking powder, baking soda, salt, milled chia, cinnamon, ginger, and nutmeg.
6. Add the dry ingredients to the egg-pumpkin mixture a little at a time, beating until combined after each addition.
7. Add the raisins and chopped pecans, if using.
8. Spread the batter evenly into the greased loaf pan and place on middle rack in the oven. Bake until a toothpick inserted in the center of the bread comes out clean, 35-40 minutes.
9. Let bread sit 5 minutes after removing from the oven. Remove the bread from the pan and let it finish cooling on wire rack.
10. If using, heat the jam or spreadable fruit until melted; brush or spoon the glaze onto the loaf. Garnish with pecans, if using.

CAKE MIX MADE BETTER

Cake mixes are not the most nutritious kitchen helpers around, but when you're in a pinch, they make getting a dozen cupcakes made for your kids' school bake sale a snap. "Healthy-up" a store-bought cake mix with chia. Simply replace half of the recommended oil with chia gel (see page 421). If you're using pre-made frosting, you can also stir in a tablespoon of chia gel before spreading it onto the cake.

CHIA SNACK BARS

MAKES 9 TO 12 SERVINGS

This recipe yields a soft, granola-like snack bar, the type you often find in supermarket cereal aisles. This one, however, contains only the best ingredients: Coconut oil, chia, oats, nuts, dates, and chocolate. Yum!

¼ cup virgin liquid coconut oil
1 tablespoon milled chia
1 cup chopped pitted Medjool dates or pitted prunes
¼ cup almond milk
1 teaspoon vanilla extract
Optional: ½ teaspoon almond extract
1½ cups rolled oats
½ cup whole wheat pastry flour
⅓ cup finely chopped nuts (use your favorite—one variety or a mix)
¾ teaspoon baking soda
½ teaspoon salt
¼ to ½ cup chopped dark chocolate or mini chocolate chips

1. Preheat the oven to 350°F.
2. Using a food processor or a high-power blender (such as a Vitamix or Blendtec) combine the coconut oil, milled chia, dates, milk, vanilla extract, and almond extract. Pulse until a smooth paste has formed, scraping the sides down as needed.
3. In a large bowl, whisk together the oats, flour, nuts, baking soda, and salt, and combine thoroughly.
4. Add the chia mixture and the chopped chocolate to the flour mixture, mixing gently until just combined.
5. Spread the mixture onto a cookie sheet in a half-inch thick layer, creating a rectangle. Mixture will not reach the sides of the baking sheet.
6. Before putting the mixture into the oven, dip a knife into cold water and cut the mixture into 4 x 2-inch bars.
7. Bake on the middle rack until golden brown and set to the touch, 12 to 15 minutes.

LOW-FAT BAKING WITH CHIA

Fat gives baked goods the moist, tender texture so prized in baking. For anyone looking to cut the fat in their favorite muffin, bread, cookie, or cake recipe, chia can help. Chia gel (see recipe, page 421) can be used tablespoon for tablespoon as a replacement for the fat or oil in your favorite recipe: If your cake recipe calls for 8 tablespoons of butter, you can replace half of those with chia gel without affecting the results. Chia also gives baked goods moisture. If "Grandma's Favorite Chocolate Chip Cookies" recipe calls for 8 tablespoons of butter, use 4 tablespoons of butter and 4 tablespoons of chia gel without altering the taste or texture of your recipe.

BREAKFAST FOODS

CHIA GEL

MAKES 1¼ CUPS

Many of the recipes in this book called for chia gel, a quick, easy staple you can whip up at home and store in your fridge. With a stash of chia gel at the ready, it's a cinch to increase the nutrient profile of your favorite foods. Add it to creamy foods, liquids, condiments, salad dressings, and even peanut butter and jelly. The gel doesn't affect flavors. What it does, however, is increase a food's vitamin and mineral levels, and add protein and omega fatty acids, while promoting weight loss by filling your stomach with fiber. Here is one way to make chia "gel."

1   cup cool water
1¾ tablespoons chia seeds

1. Pour the water into a sealable plastic or glass container. Slowly pour chia seeds into water while briskly mixing with wire whisk.
2. Wait 3 or 4 minutes then whisk again.
3. Let the mixture stand about 10 minutes before whisking again. Seal the container and store mixture in the refrigerator for up to two weeks to use as needed. Whisk before using. **Note:** Soaking in water will soften the chia seeds, but they will still be slightly crunchy.

CINNAMON-ORANGE PANCAKES

SERVES 4

Pancakes are the quintessential breakfast food, perfect for weekend mornings with the family. Not only are these eggless griddle cakes delicious and tremendously filling, they also pack a powerful wallop of nutrients and fiber. For an autumn treat, try them with a side of sautéed pears, apples, or quince.

¾ cup unbleached whole wheat pastry flour
1 cup oat flour
2 teaspoons baking powder
1 tablespoon brown sugar
1 teaspoon cinnamon
1 cup milk
¾ cup orange juice
¾ cup chia gel (see recipe, page 421)
Optional: 1 teaspoon grated orange zest
  Vegetable oil, or cooking spray, as needed

1. In a large bowl, combine the dry ingredients. Wisk until thoroughly combined.
2. In another bowl, combine all the liquid ingredients, including chia gel and the orange zest, if using.
3. Pour the liquid ingredients into the dry ingredients and stir only until moistened.
4. Lightly grease a non-stick griddle with oil or cooking spray and preheat over medium heat. Ladle ½–¾ cup of the batter onto the grill, depending on the size you like.
5. Flip the pancakes when bubbles appear on the surface. Cook until the underside is golden brown.
6. Serve with Orange-Date Syrup (recipe follows) or your favorite pancake topping.

VEGAN-FRIENDLY PROTEIN

As we all know by now, chia offers a powerful wallop of protein. What you may not know is that chia is a *complete protein*, meaning that it contains all the amino acids your body needs to utilize this macronutrient. This is great news for anyone looking for a high quality protein source, but it is particularly helpful for vegans (vegetarians who eat nothing of animal origin, including dairy products, eggs, or honey). Because many plant sources have incomplete protein, many vegans find it difficult to get the protein they need without complicated food combining. Chia can solve this dilemma.

ORANGE DATE SYRUP

MAKES 2 CUPS

This luxurious syrup not only tastes decadent, it's actually packed with nutrition thanks to all the dates, orange juice, and chia. It's also fantastic stirred into plain yogurt, as a sauce for ham, or syrup for ice cream. Enjoy!

1 cup boiling water
1 cup pitted dates
¾ cup frozen orange juice concentrate, thawed
1 cup chia gel (see recipe, page 421)

1. Pour the boiling water over the dates in a bowl and let stand for 10 minutes. Mash them with a potato masher or the back of a fork.
2. Add the orange juice concentrate.
3. Pour the date-orange juice mixture into a blender and liquefy.
4. Remove from the blender and whisk in the chia gel, mixing until thoroughly combined.
5. Store in a jar in the refrigerator, shaking well before using.

CHIA FRENCH TOAST

SERVES 2 OR 3

Chia infuses what is traditionally a low-nutrient breakfast dish with fiber, vitamins, minerals, omegas, additional protein, and more. Give this a try and you'll find yourself feeling satiated and more energetic. Kids adore this!

2 large eggs
4 teaspoons chia gel (see recipe, page 421)
4 to 6 slices of whole wheat bread, preferably day old or slightly dry
Vegetable oil or cooking spray, as needed

1. In a medium bowl, whisk the eggs until smooth.
2. Add the chia gel.
3. Dip the bread in the egg-chia mixture, coating both sides.
4. Heat a large skillet over medium heat and grease lightly with oil or cooking spray. Fry the soaked bread for 2 to 3 minutes until browned. Turn and repeat on the other side.
5. Serve with Chia Breakfast Syrup (see recipe, below) or the topping of your choice.

CHIA BREAKFAST SYRUP

MAKES ½ CUP

Your favorite breakfast syrup just got healthier! This easy recipe is great for pancakes, waffles, French toast—and even as an ice cream topper.

2 teaspoons chia gel (see recipe, page 421)
½ cup maple or fruit syrup. (This keeps indefinitely in the refrigerator in a tightly closed jar.)

1. In a large bowl, whisk the chia gel and syrup until smooth.
2. Store in a tightly closed jar for up to two weeks in the refrigerator.

CHIA SPREAD

You can make your own sweet nut butter spread that's perfect for quick sandwiches, graham-cracker treats, or topping apple slices. Here's how: combine ½ cup nut butter of your choice (almond, cashew, sunflower, sesame seed, peanut) and ¼ cup of your favorite syrup (maple, fruit, Chia Breakfast Syrup) with 1 tablespoon chia seeds. Mix thoroughly. This keeps in the refrigerator in a tightly closed jar for two weeks.

SCRAMBLED CHIA EGGS

SERVES 1 TO 2

If you typically have two eggs for breakfast, you may find yourself eating less with this recipe. That's because the chia expands in your stomach, creating a pleasant sensation of fullness while delivering an infusion of nutrients.

2 *large eggs*
1 *teaspoon chia gel (see recipe, page 421)*
   Vegetable oil or cooking spray, as needed

1. In a medium bowl, whisk the eggs until smooth.
2. Add chia gel and whisk until combined.
3. Heat a frying pan over medium-low heat and grease lightly with vegetable oil or cooking spray. Pour in the eggs and cook, stirring gently, until eggs are scrambled.

CHIA FRITTATA

SERVES 2

This easy recipe is a terrific way to finish last night's leftover cooked veggies. Use whatever you have on hand—this delicious recipe is infinitely flexible. Serve it up with a green salad for a fast, nutrient-rich supper.

3 *large eggs*
1 *teaspoon chia gel (see recipe, page 421)*
¼ to ½ cup *chopped cooked veggies*
   Vegetable oil, as needed

1. In a medium bowl, whisk the eggs until smooth.
2. Add the chia gel and whisk until combined.
3. Add the vegetables and stir until combined.
4. Heat a frying pan over medium heat and grease lightly with oil. Pour in the egg mixture and cook, without stirring, until eggs are set completely through.
5. Allow to cool in the pan slightly before sliding the frittata onto a cutting board. Cut into wedges to serve.

CHIA EGG TOPPERS

If you love your eggs with ketchup, salsa, or chili sauce, there's yet another way to work chia into your diet. Simply mix ½ cup of your favorite condiment with 1 tablespoon chia. Store it in the refrigerator in a tightly closed jar for up to two weeks.

RAW VANILLA COCONUT "YOGURT"

SERVES 1 OR 2

This luscious yogurt is ideal for those who don't eat dairy. Smooth and creamy, it's the creation of Jackie Rafter. Easy and quick to prepare, this recipe makes a delicious, filling breakfast all on its own or as an accompaniment to your favorite cold cereal.

1 to 2 tablespoons chia seeds
1 cup dried (desiccated) coconut
1 cup fresh filtered water or coconut water (more or less to your preference)
1 tablespoon raw agave, maple syrup, honey, or a shake of Stevia
1 teaspoon vanilla extract
1 teaspoon hazelnut or almond extract (optional)
   Pinch of sea salt
Optional topping: Fresh fruits or berries and honey or raw agave syrup

1. Place all the ingredients, except optional fruit topping, in a blender or food processor. Process until the yogurt is smooth and creamy.

2. Add more water or coconut if necessary to make more of a "yogurt" consistency.

3. Serve in a bowl and top with fresh fruits and/or berries. Decorate with a swirl of honey or raw agave syrup and enjoy! Store leftover yogurt in the refrigerator and simply add more water if a creamier texture is desired later on.

CHIA BREAKFAST SANDWICH

If you or your kids find it difficult to find time for a sit-down breakfast, here's an easy grab-and-go option called the Chia-Nut Butter Sandwich. Take two pieces of prepared French toast or bread of your choice (whole wheat, non-gluten, rye, etc.). Spread one slice with almond butter (or sunflower seed butter, tahini, peanut butter, or cashew butter). Sprinkle two teaspoons of chia seeds over the nut butter. Spread the remaining slice with honey, maple syrup, agave, or a low-sugar jelly and place on top of the nut butter-chia slice. Delicious and fast.

CHIA-OAT PORRIDGE

SERVES 2

Oatmeal and chia are a natural pairing, creating a wholesome, nourishing, stay-with-you breakfast that benefits the heart while helping dieters lose weight. Garnish this old-fashioned porridge with dried fruit, fresh fruit, honey, maple syrup, or anything else that strikes your fancy.

1¾ cup water
¾ cup old fashioned rolled oats (sometimes called 5-minute oats)
Dash salt
1 tablespoon chia seeds
Optional: 1 teaspoon butter or coconut oil

1. Place the water in small pot over medium high heat.

2. When the water comes to a rolling boil, add the oats, salt, and butter or coconut oil, if using. Stir once and reduce the heat to low.

3. After five minutes, remove from the heat. Stir in the chia seeds and serve immediately.

FAST CHIA BREAKFASTS

Chia is so easy to use that there is no need to whip up a special recipe to enjoy it. Simply add it to your current favorite breakfast foods. Here are some ideas:

- Sprinkle up to 1 tablespoon of chia, depending on your taste, over cold cereal or a bowl of oatmeal.
- Layer fruit, yogurt, and a sprinkle of chia seeds into a glass for a breakfast parfait.
- Add chia to your favorite pancake or waffle recipe (or mix).
- Sprinkle chia onto waffles before cooking or onto pancakes before turning.
- Add a dusting of chia seeds to an omelet before turning it out of the pan.
- Spoon scrambled eggs, salsa, black beans, and chia seeds into a tortilla before rolling to make a healthy breakfast wrap.

CHIA-QUINOA PORRIDGE

SERVES TWO

Superfood meets superfood in this powerful porridge of champions. Pronounced *keen-wah*, quinoa is a small seed that is treasured in the Andes for its high amino acid profile, protein, and high levels of magnesium and iron. When teamed up with chia, the two create one of the most nutrient-dense breakfasts around.

1½ cup water or milk (dairy, rice, almond, hemp, coconut, etc.)
1 cup quinoa, quickly rinsed in a colander
Dash salt
1 tablespoon chia seeds
Optional: 1 teaspoon butter or coconut oil

1. Place the water or milk in a small pot over medium-high heat.

2. When the water comes to a rolling boil, add the quinoa, salt, and butter or coconut oil, if using. Stir once, cover, and reduce the heat to lowest setting.

3. Check after 10 minutes. If the grain is soft, remove from the heat, stir in the chia seeds and serve immediately.

CHIANOLA

MAKES 12 CUPS

Granola is so fun and easy to make that you have no excuse not to give it a try. Think of this recipe as a canvas for your creativity. You can swap pumpkin seeds or hazelnuts for the almonds, almond extract for the vanilla, and so on. You'll notice this version is much leaner than commercially available granolas—it's also much lower in sugar. The addition of chia adds a high impact boost of nutrients, as well as filling fiber.

4 cups quick-cooking oats
½ cup oat bran
½ cup unsweetened dried (dessicated) coconut
¼ to ⅓ cup chopped almonds
    Dash salt
1 to 2 tablespoons chia seeds
¼ cup coconut milk
¼ cup virgin coconut oil
⅓ cup maple syrup
¼ cup apple juice
Optional: ½ teaspoon vanilla extract
Optional: ¼ cup chopped dried fruit

1. Preheat oven to 350°F.
2. In a large bowl, combine the dry ingredients until well blended.
3. In a small pot over medium heat, bring the coconut milk, coconut oil, maple syrup, and apple juice to a boil and cook for two minutes.
4. Remove from the heat and stir in the vanilla extract, if using. Pour the mixture into the dry ingredients, stirring thoroughly to coat.
5. Divide the mixture between two baking sheets and bake until granola is golden and fragrant, about 7 or 8 minutes.
6. Cool the granola on the pans. Stir in the dried fruit, if using.
7. Store the granola in an airtight container in a cool, dry spot.

MORE CALCIUM

Dairy products are not the only way to give your body the calcium it needs. Chia seeds are rich in this important bone-building mineral. Ounce for ounce, chia has five times more calcium than the same amount of cow's milk. Chia also contains boron, a trace element that helps transfer calcium into the bones.

AUSSIE-STYLE BROILED TOMATOES WITH CHIA

SERVES TWO

A broiled tomato half—often with a scattering of scrumptious browned crumbs—is a breakfast staple down under, served as part of a traditional Aussie breakfast of canned apricots and beans on toast. Don't have any beans in your pantry? No worries—this savory side dish is wonderful with anything, even by itself as a snack.

1 beefsteak tomato
2 tablespoons bread crumbs
1 teaspoon olive oil or melted butter
1 teaspoon chia seeds
    Dash salt and pepper

1. Preheat the broiler.
2. Slice the tomato in half cross-wise, through the middle. Place the tomato halves on a broiler-proof pan.

3. In a small bowl, combine the breadcrumbs, oil or butter, salt, and pepper. Spoon the mixture onto each tomato half.

4. Place the tomato halves under the broiler until the topping is golden and the tomato slightly softened. Remove from the oven and sprinkle the chia seeds over the tomatoes before serving.

LUNCH

FAST SOUP

SERVES ONE OR TWO

This is a "treatment" for canned soup more than it is a recipe, and it makes a fast, low-fat lunch—great to eat when you're hungry for something quick and nutritious.

1   12-ounce can soup or chili of your choice (no-additive brands such as Amy's, Health Valley, and Muir Glen are preferable)
1 or 2 tablespoons chia gel (see recipe, page 421)

1. Heat the soup in a small pot over medium-low heat, or according to directions.

2. Remove from the heat and swirl in chia gel.

LIMA BEAN WINTER SOUP

MAKES 6 TO 8 SERVINGS

Named after the capitol of Peru, lima beans are soft, buttery, and full of minerals, protein, and cholesterol-lowering fiber. Feel free to try the recipe with white navy beans or cannellini beans.

2   cups dried lima beans, soaked overnight
8   cups chicken or vegetable broth, plus more
    as needed
¼   cup extra-virgin olive oil
1   large onion, finely chopped
2   garlic cloves, minced
2   carrots, finely chopped
⅛   teaspoon cayenne pepper
1   teaspoon dried parsley
½   red bell pepper, chopped
½   green bell pepper, chopped
½   cup chia gel (see recipe, page 421)
    Salt to taste

1. Place the beans and broth in a stockpot or large saucepan over medium-high heat. Boil for 10 minutes.

2. Lower the heat and simmer until the beans are tender, about 30 minutes. Add more broth or water as needed.

3. Add the olive oil to a frying pan over medium heat and sauté the onions, garlic, carrots, cayenne, and dried parsley until the vegetables are tender, about 3 minutes.

4. Add the sautéed mixture to lima beans. Stir to combine.

5. Add the red and green peppers and chia gel to the pot and simmer the soup for 20 minutes to allow the flavors to meld.

CREAMY MUSHROOM-CASHEW SOUP

MAKES 4 TO 6 SERVINGS

Cashew milk is a vegan mainstay, prized for its creamy, rich, comforting taste. Here, cashew milk combines with mushrooms and chia to create a delectable soup. Add a green salad and a bit of protein and you have yourself a delicious, well-rounded meal!

1   cup raw cashews, washed thoroughly in
     hot water
5½   cups chicken or vegetable broth or water
1½   tablespoons dry chia seeds
1½   tablespoons butter
1   pound sliced mushrooms, mixed varieties
     if possible
2   tablespoons extra-virgin olive oil
1½   medium yellow or sweet onions (such as
     Maui, Vidalia, or Walla Walla), diced
2   celery stalks, with leaves, diced
2   cloves garlic, chopped
1   teaspoon cold-pressed toasted sesame oil
1   teaspoon tamari
1½   teaspoons dried basil
½   teaspoon salt, or to taste
⅛   teaspoon cayenne pepper, or to taste
Optional: 1 medium tomato, seeded and
     chopped, as garnish

1. In a food processor or high-power blender (such as Vitamix or Blendtec), process the cashews with the broth or water to make cashew milk.

2. Stir the chia seeds into the cashew milk and let stand for 15 minutes.

3. Melt the butter in a sauté pan over medium heat. Add half of the mushrooms and sauté for about 4 minutes.

4. Add the sautéed mushrooms to the food processor or blender with the cashew milk-chia mixture and blend until smooth.

5. Heat the olive oil in a large pot over medium heat and sauté the onions, celery and garlic until soft.

6. Stir in the sesame oil and tamari, and remaining mushrooms. Sauté until the mushrooms are just soft.

7. Add the pureed cashew-mushroom mixture to the pot and simmer the soup for 15 minutes.

8. Add the basil, salt, and cayenne pepper to taste.

9. Stir in the chopped tomato immediately before serving.

CASHEW TRIVIA

Cashews are the darlings of the snack world because they are lower in fat than other nuts, higher in protein, and addictively delicious. You know you love them, but did you know this about them?:

- Cashews are native to the coastal regions of northeastern Brazil.
- The cashew nut is actually the kidney-shaped seed that sits at the bottom of the cashew apple, a delicacy in Brazil and the Caribbean, where the fruit grows prolifically.
- Cashews are always sold shelled. Why? Because the interior of the cashew shell contains a caustic resin known as cashew balm, which is carefully removed before nuts are packaged for human consumption. This resin is used to make insecticides and varnishes.
- Cashew's scientific name is *Anacardium occidentale*.
- Cashews belong to the same family as the pistachio and mango.
- In the 16th century, Portuguese explorers took cashew trees from Brazil and introduced them to other tropical countries, including India and Africa.
- Currently, the leading commercial providers of cashews are Brazil, Mozambique, Tanzania, and Nigeria.
- Cashew wood is a precious, much-prized resource in Brazil.

MULLIGATAWNY CHIA SOUP

SERVES 6

This is one of those delicious recipes that everyone loves. It's also supremely versatile. Try adding a bit of leftover rice or some chopped chicken or lamb, and garnish with a flourish of nuts. Have fun playing with this one!

5   cups vegetable or chicken stock, plus
      more as needed (you can substitute one
      cup coconut milk for one cup of broth)
1   cup red lentils
½   teaspoon turmeric
Optional: 1 teaspoon Madras curry powder
1   medium potato, diced
5   cloves garlic, minced
1¼ inch piece fresh ginger root, peeled and
      finely grated
¼   teaspoon cayenne
1   teaspoon ground coriander
1   tablespoon lemon juice
3   tablespoons liquid virgin coconut oil
1½ cups chia gel (see recipe, page 421)
      Salt and black pepper to taste

1. In a large pot over medium heat, combine the broth, lentils, turmeric, curry powder (if using), and potato. Simmer until the lentils and potatoes are soft, 10 to 15 minutes. Add additional broth, water, or coconut milk as needed.
2. Add the garlic, ginger, cayenne, coriander, lemon juice, coconut oil, and chia gel and simmer for 10 minutes to meld flavors.
3. Add salt and black pepper as needed.

MULLIGA-WHAT?

The word mulligatawny is an anglicized version of a Tamil word meaning "pepper broth." This spicy soup became a favorite of Britains during the colonization of India in the late 18th century. As the dish migrated back to England and through the British Commonwealth, it began to mutate. Some versions omitted the original curry, others left out the coconut milk, while some recipes added cilantro, used chicken broth, instead of the original mutton broth, and even included chopped apples or nuts. In other words, this is a soup to be played with. Feel free to add or subtract to it at will!

POWER WRAP

MAKES 1

Wraps are fun to make and easy to eat. They are also supremely versatile. This protein-packed version can be updated and customized any way you like.

2   tablespoons hummus, plain or flavored
1   tablespoon chia gel (see recipe, page 421)
1   large tortilla or wrap of choice (we like
      whole grain or gluten-free versions)
Optional: A pinch of black pepper or a few
      dashes of hot sauce

1 tablespoon sunflower seeds
¼ cup shredded carrots
2 Romaine or other lettuce leaves
¼ to ½ of an avocado, thinly sliced lengthwise

1. In a small bowl, whisk together the hummus, chia gel, and pepper or hot sauce, if using.

2. Lay the wrap on a flat surface. Spread the hummus-chia mixture over the surface of the wrap, stopping about a half-inch before reaching the wrap's edges.

3. Sprinkle sunflower seeds over the hummus, leaving a two-inch margin at the bottom of the wrap. This will make rolling easier and cleaner.

4. Layer on the shredded carrots, lettuce, and avocado slices, being careful to leave a two-inch margin at the bottom of the wrap.

5. Starting at the top, roll the wrap into a tube. Squeeze the rolled wrap gently to seal.

EASY ADDITION

Almost any condiment, dip, or spread can be enhanced with the addition of chia gel (see recipe, page 421). Feel free to experiment, but if you'd like some guidance, start here:

- **Nut butter:** Add up to 1 tablespoon chia gel for every tablespoon nut butter.
- **Jam or jelly:** Add 1 teaspoon chia gel for every tablespoon jam or jelly.
- **Maple syrup or honey:** Add 1 teaspoon chia gel for every tablespoon of syrup.
- **Mayonnaise:** Add up to 1 tablespoon chia gel for every tablespoon mayo.
- **Mustard:** Add up to 1 tablespoon chia gel for every tablespoon mustard.
- **Ketchup and cocktail sauce:** Add 1 teaspoon chia gel for every tablespoon ketchup or cocktail sauce.
- **Barbecue sauce:** Add 1 teaspoon chia gel for every tablespoon barbecue sauce.
- **Guacamole:** Add ½ tablespoon chia gel for every tablespoon of guacamole.
- **Hummus and other bean dips:** Add 1 tablespoon chia gel for every tablespoon hummus.
- **Salsa:** Add 1 teaspoon chia gel for every tablespoon salsa.
- **Salad dressing:** Add 1 tablespoon chia gel for every tablespoon salad dressing.
- **Sour cream:** Add 1 tablespoon chia for every tablespoon sour cream.

CHIA HUMMUS

Looking for a quick, healthy dip for veggie sticks, rice crackers, tortilla chips, and other dippers? Place a small garlic clove, ½ cup hummus, ¼ cup salsa, and 2 tablespoons chia gel (see recipe, page 421) into a food processor. Pulse until the mixture forms a smooth paste. Use it as a dip or a great sandwich spread.

CHIA SALAD SANDWICH

MAKES ENOUGH FOR 1 OR 2 SANDWICHES

Chicken and turkey salad, egg and tuna salad—most people love these protein-rich sandwich fillings. In this version, you get to pick your favorite protein, then dress it up with high-mileage veggies, seasonings, and chia.

- *3 tablespoons low fat mayonnaise or plain yogurt*
- *1 tablespoon chia gel (see recipe, page 421)*
- *1 tablespoon mustard (yellow, Dijon, spicy brown, or any type you enjoy)*
- *1 6-ounce can tuna, salmon, or 1 cup chopped chicken, turkey, hardboiled eggs, ham, tofu, tempeh, or seitan*
- *¼ cup shredded or minced carrots*
- *¼ cup chopped red onion*
- *¼ cup chopped celery*
- *¼ cup chopped red bell pepper (fresh or jarred)*
- *1 tablespoon chopped fresh parsley, cilantro, or dill*
- *Bread slices, wrap, or crackers of your choice*
- *Optional: Romaine lettuce for garnish*

1. In a large bowl, mix the mayonnaise, chia gel, and mustard, whisking until smooth.
2. Add the tuna or protein of choice, carrots, onion, celery, red pepper, and herb of choice, mixing until combined.
3. Spoon onto the bread or wrap, topping with lettuce. Or, use to top crackers.

TUNA WITHOUT THE MERCURY?

Tuna and other large, oily sea fish are typically high in mercury. This is because these fish spend years absorbing mercury and other heavy metals that enter the oceans as pollution. Most canned tuna has at least 13 percent more mercury than the 0.5 ppm maximum declared safe by the USDA. You can lower your exposure to mercury and other heavy metals by using "light" tuna instead of "white" tuna.

CURRIED POTATO SALAD

MAKES 8 SERVINGS

Don't like mayo? Don't eat eggs? You'll love this flavorful vegan salad. Of course if you have to have your mayo, go ahead and swap it for the tofu and oil.

1   carton soft tofu
¼   cup extra-virgin olive oil
¼   cup chia gel (see recipe, page 421)
1   teaspoon Dijon mustard
1½ teaspoons mild curry powder
½   teaspoon cumin powder
½   teaspoon cayenne pepper
12 red potatoes, boiled, cooled, and cut into
    large cubes
1   red onion, chopped
½   green bell pepper, chopped
½   red bell pepper, chopped
1   Serrano chili pepper, minced
½   bunch flat leaf parsley, minced
1   cup celery, finely chopped
    Salt to taste

1. In a food processor or high-speed blender (such as Vitamix or BlendTex) process the tofu and olive oil until smooth.

2. Add the chia gel, mustard, curry powder, cumin, and cayenne, processing until smooth.

3. In a large bowl, gently combine the potatoes, onion, peppers, parsley, and celery.

4. Add dressing to potatoes, combining gently to coat, and season with salt.

5. Serve immediately or refrigerate until ready to serve.

DOES CURRY PROMOTE WEIGHT LOSS?

Depending upon whom you ask, *curry* comes from the Tamil word *kari*, which means sauce, or, it refers to curry leaves (also known as sweet neem leaves), one of the ingredients in curry powder.

Typically a mixture of turmeric, cumin, cinnamon, fennel, ginger, chili peppers, and black pepper, curry powder is touted as a weight loss aid by some weight loss gurus. Most likely it's the turmeric at work. This bright yellow spice helps lower LDL ("bad") cholesterol. But other ingredients may help pare down pounds, as well: A Dutch study found that turmeric and its "curry mates," cumin, chili, black pepper, and ginger all help to rev up the metabolism, speeding the amount of calories the body burns.

MEXICAN GRAIN PILAF
SERVES 2 TO 4

Think of this fun recipe as a guide—it was made to be customized. You can use millet, quinoa, barley, brown rice—or any cooked grain—as the base. Then mix in vegetables, pumpkin seeds, beans, and chia. This is a great lunchbox dish. If you want to really speed up prep time, buy pre-cooked frozen grain in the freezer section of your favorite grocer or health food store, then thaw and rinse what you need in hot water before serving.

1 to 2 tablespoons chia gel (see recipe, page 421)
1 tablespoon extra-virgin olive oil
1 teaspoon lime juice
½ teaspoon salt
Optional: A few shakes of Tabasco or other
    hot sauce
2 cups cooked brown rice, millet, quinoa,
    barley faro or other grain
½ cup cooked corn
½ cup cooked black beans
¼ cup chopped red onion
¼ cup chopped red bell pepper
¼ cup pepitas (green, hull-less pumpkin seeds)
½ to 1 tablespoons chopped cilantro

1. In a large bowl, whisk together the chia gel, olive oil, lime juice, salt, and hot sauce, if using.

2. Add the grain, corn, beans, onions, peppers, pepitas, and cilantro, stirring gently yet thoroughly to coat.

PUMPKIN POWER

Hull-less green pumpkin seeds—called pepitas in Spanish—are the perfect accompaniment to chia. High in vitamin E, niacin, iron, magnesium, manganese, and zinc, as well as tryptophan and oleic acid (which helps lower "bad" LDL cholesterol and raise "good" HDL cholesterol), these addictive kernels are delicious toasted in a dry skillet until they pop.

CHIA RICE SALAD
MAKES 6 SERVINGS

Rice salads are a terrific picnic food. They tuck into lunch boxes easily and make the perfect side dish, too. This fun version features classic Mediterranean flavors. Feel free to play with different veggies and herbs if you'd like.

½ cup chia gel (see recipe, page 421)
2 tablespoons extra-virgin olive oil
2 tablespoons lemon juice
1 to 2 cloves of garlic, minced
½ teaspoon salt
1 teaspoon fresh rosemary or oregano leaves,
    minced
⅛ teaspoon cayenne pepper
3 cups cooked brown rice (long grain, basmati,
    or short grain)
1 small zucchini, julienned
1 medium tomato, seeded and chopped
Optional: 2 tablespoons grated Parmesan cheese

1. In a small bowl, combine the chia gel, oil, lemon, garlic, salt, herbs, and cayenne. Whisk until well-blended. (You can also put ingredients into a tightly closed jar and shake vigorously to mix.)

2. In a large bowl, combine the rice, vegetables, and Parmesan cheese, if using.

3. Pour the dressing over the rice mixture, combining gently and thoroughly.

MOROCCAN CARROT SALAD

MAKES 4 TO 6 SERVINGS

Carrot salad is a classic side dish—fresh, cleansing, and satisfying. This version is made heartier (and healthier) with the addition of chia.

¼ cup chia gel (see recipe, page 421)

2 tablespoons extra-virgin olive oil

½ tablespoon lemon juice

3 cloves garlic, minced

1 teaspoon cumin

¼ teaspoon white or black pepper (or ⅛ teaspoon cayenne pepper)

8 carrots, grated (or use food processor with grating attachment)

Salt, to taste

Crushed red pepper to taste

Optional: White sesame seeds for garnish

1. In a large bowl, whisk together the chia gel, olive oil, lemon juice, garlic, cumin, and pepper.

2. Add the shredded carrots and gently mix to combine and evenly coat the carrots.

3. Season with salt and crushed red pepper. Garnish with white sesame seeds, if using.

CARROT LORE

Most of us grew up eating carrots—crunching raw carrot sticks or baby carrots after school, roasted carrots for dinner, shredded carrots in salad, and even downing carrot juice. Here are a few fun facts about this beloved veggie:

- Carrots are related to parsley, parsnips, anise, caraway, cumin, and dill.
- Carrots and their cousins are members of the *umbrelliferae* plant family, so called for the umbrella-like leaves and flower-clusters they produce.
- In the United States, carrot greens are not eaten, but in France and other European countries the leaves are minced into salads and soups, where their fresh, slightly bitter taste is greatly prized.
- Before the 15th century, orange carrots were nowhere to be seen; only purple, yellow, red, and white carrots were cultivated. These old varieties are making a comeback in green markets and farm stands across the country.
- One-third of all carrots consumed in the world are grown in China. Russia is the second largest producer, with the U.S. coming in third.
- California grows 80 percent of America's carrot crop, followed closely by Michigan, then Texas, illustrating that carrots have a very wide growth habitat.
- The average adult in the U.S. consumes 12 pounds of carrots a year.

CHIA FRUIT SALAD

MAKES 6 SERVINGS

Consider this recipe as a mere suggestion. Don't have apples? Use pears. Peaches aren't in season? Use strawberries. Be flexible, have fun, and enjoy.

3   *peaches, pitted and diced*
2   *apples, cored and diced*
2   *cups seedless grapes*
2   *cups fresh pineapple, diced*
2   *bananas, diced*
    Juice of ½ large lemon
2   *cups Chia Sunshine Sauce (see below)*

1. Gently combine peaches, apples, grapes, pineapple, bananas, and lemon juice in a large bowl.
2. Drizzle with Chia Sunshine Sauce, stirring gently just to coat.

CHIA SUNSHINE SAUCE

MAKES ABOUT 2 CUPS

This light, fruity sauce is fantastic on fruit salad or mesclun, or drizzled over Greek yogurt. It can also be used as a dessert sauce or dip for apple and pear slices. If you'd like tangier, slightly more acidic flavor, add a squirt of lemon or lime juice.

1   *large mango, peeled and chopped, or 1 cup frozen mango, thawed*

2   *bananas*
½   *cup chia gel (see recipe, page 421)*
2   *tablespoons maple syrup*

1. Process all the ingredients in a food processor or high-power blender (such as a Vitamix or Blendtec) until smooth and creamy.

ZIPPY SALAD DRESSING

MAKES 2 CUPS

You know that special sauce that a certain fast food chain puts on its burgers? Well, this is the healthy version. It's great with burgers of all kinds, and is delicious on green salads and potato salads. You can even drizzle it on chicken or fish.

1   *cup low-fat or regular mayonnaise*
½   *cup tomato juice*
½   *cup chia gel (see recipe, page 421)*
1   *teaspoon minced parsley*
1   *teaspoon minced chives*
¼   *teaspoon garlic salt*
¼   *teaspoon celery salt*

1. In a medium bowl, whisk all the ingredients together until smooth.
2. Use on garden salads or to dress pasta, grain, or potato salads.
3. Store tightly covered in the refrigerator for up to a week.

SNACKS

HIGH POWER CHIA CHIPS

AS MANY AS YOU WANT TO MAKE

This recipe may be worth the price of this book! Chia Chips are easy to make, easy to eat, and densely packed with an outrageous amount of protein, fiber, and nutrients. Bet you can't eat just one!

Cooking spray, or virgin coconut oil, for greasing pan
Chia gel, the amount of your choice (see recipe, page 421)
Optional: Sea salt, herb seasoning, or other flavoring

1. Preheat oven to 170°F.
2. Spray a clean baking sheet with a light coat of cooking spray or a thin layer of virgin coconut oil.
3. For each chip, spoon a teaspoon-sized amount of the chia gel onto the prepared cookie sheet, three inches apart. Transfer the pan to the oven.
4. Leave the pan in oven for 12 hours or overnight. The finished chips will resemble potato chips.
5. Optional: Sprinkle with salt and/or seasoning of your choice before serving.

PROTEIN BITES

MAKES 8 TO 10 BALLS

This powerful treat is just sweet enough to satisfy your cravings, but not so sweet that it'll send you on a roller coaster ride of sugar highs and lows. Concentrated with protein, fiber, and B-complex vitamins, a Protein Bite is the perfect snack to have, right before heading out for a run or to the gym. Kids love these, too.

1 cup nut butter (almond, cashew, sunflowerseed, sesame paste, etc.)

¼ cup pitted dates

¼ cup natural cacao powder (can use regular unsweetened cocoa or carob powder if you'd like)

3 tablespoons chia seeds

1 tablespoon virgin coconut oil

1 teaspoon cinnamon

Pinch of salt

Optional 1 tablespoon spirulina

Optional coating: 2 tablespoons chia seeds, chopped nuts, desiccated coconut, cacao nibs, chopped goji berries, etc.

MAKE YOUR OWN NUT BUTTER

If you have a food processor or a high-power blender, such as a Vitamix or Blendtec, making your own nut butter is a cinch! Simply add any quantity of raw or roasted nuts or seeds (you can even use a blend) to the machine and process until smooth. This may take up to 15 minutes, depending on the ingredients you use and your machine. Some people like to add a bit of salt or sweetener (maple syrup or honey are particularly good) or a teaspoon or more of virgin coconut oil to give the nut butter a silkier texture. Store nut butter in the refrigerator.

---

1. Place all the ingredients in a food processor or high-power blender (such as a Vitamix or Blendtec) and pulse until the mixture is smooth. Do not over-process—you do not want to liquefy the mixture.

2. Form the mixture into balls the size of a walnut. If desired, roll in chia seed, chopped nuts, desiccated coconut, cacao nibs, or anything else that appeals to you.

3. Store in the freezer.

ALEGRIA

MAKES ABOUT 6 SERVINGS

The word *alegria* means happiness in Spanish. It's also the name of an ancient popped amaranth candy popular in Mexico and Central America.

6 tablespoons amaranth

¼ cup chia seeds

¼ cup virgin coconut oil, *plus more for greasing pan*

¼ cup honey

¼ cup molasses

½ teaspoon vanilla extract

1. Pop the amaranth, one tablespoon at a time, into a very hot, dry skillet, until all the grains have popped. Transfer the popped grains to a shallow bowl before adding the next tablespoon to the skillet.

2. Toast the chia seed in the same pan, mixing the toasted chia with the popped amaranth.

Chia seeds (foreground); milled chia (right); chia gel (background)

Chia Snack Bars, page 420

Top: Chia Seed Muffins, page 415; *Bottom:* Nut Butter Chia Cookies, pages 466–467

Green Super Smoothie, page 410

Cinnamon-Orange Pancakes with Orange Date Syrup, pages 422–423

Top: Chia Frittata, page 424; *Bottom:* Chia Rice Salad, page 436

Chia Chipotle Bean Burger, page 459

Moroccan Carrot Salad, page 437

3. Lightly coat a baking sheet with coconut oil.

4. In a heavy pot with a lid, combine the coconut oil, honey, molasses, and vanilla over medium-high heat. Cook until boiling, and then reduce heat to medium. Cook, stirring constantly, until the mixture turns dark amber and thickens, about 10 minutes.

5. Remove the mixture from heat and stir in the amaranth and chia, mixing well.

6. Spoon the mixture onto the prepared pan, spreading evenly into a thin layer.

7. Allow the mixture to cool and then cut into bars.

CHIA PÂTÉ

MAKES 2 CUPS

This elegant pâté is ideal for your next holiday meal or dinner party. Spread it on crackers or good bread—or use it as a dip for veggie sticks or a spread to replace mayo on sandwiches.

1 cup raw cashews, soaked in water for
   at least an hour, then drained
½ cup chia seed
1 red bell pepper, chopped
1 medium carrot, chopped
¼ cup nutritional yeast
   Juice of 1 lemon
   2 tablespoons miso paste
   Salt to taste
Optional: Black pepper or paprika
Optional: 1 teaspoon maple syrup for sweetness

1. Place all the ingredients into the bowl of a food processor or high-power blender (such as a Vitamix or Blendtec). Pulse until smooth and transfer to a bowl.

2. Store any uneaten portion in a tightly closed container in the refrigerator.

COCONUT PRODUCTS DEMYSTIFIED

As people become more and more savvy about the many health benefits of coconut, more and more products that feature this superfood are appearing on health food-store shelves. Here is what is currently available:

- **Coconut oil** is the nutritious oil extracted from fresh coconut meat. Rich in medium-chain fatty acids and phytonutrients, the oil's high smoke point make it fantastic for cooking. It's also great used as a flavoring and as a hair and skin moisturizer. When buying coconut oil, look for virgin coconut oil, which is obtained through cold-pressing instead of chemical extraction.
- **Coconut flour** is the finely ground, dried coconut that is left over after extracting coconut oil. Low-carbohydrate, high fiber, and gluten-free, coconut flour is a darling in the world of wheat-free baking.
- **Coconut water** is the clear liquid found inside young, green coconuts. Much touted for its amazing ability to replace electrolytes, coconut water is the natural alternative to chemical-laden sports drinks.
- **Coconut milk** is the meat of the nut blended with water to make a creamy, dairy-like liquid. Once upon a time, all coconut milk came in cans. Now, however, many brands offer cartons of coconut milk in the refrigerated dairy section of your local supermarket or health food store.
- **Dried coconut milk** is coconut milk that has been dried to a powder, much like dried milk powder. To reconstitute it, simply add milk. It's a handy, shelf-stable ingredient that can be sprinkled directly into soups and curries.
- **Coconut cream** is what many people call the thickened, creamy-looking mixture that sits at the top of a can of coconut milk.
- **Cream of coconut** goes by many names, including creamed coconut, coconut butter, coconut paste, coconut concentrate, and more. This luxurious product is literally a block or jar of thick, shortening-like coconut made from pulverized coconut flesh and oil.
- **Desiccated coconut** is a baker's favorite! Dried, unsweetened coconut is finely ground for use in cookies, cakes, breads, and other recipes. Don't confuse it with the "sweetened flaked coconut" on store shelves.
- **Coconut flakes or chips** are related to desiccated unsweetened coconut, only with bigger flakes.

- **Coconut nectar** is a low-glycemic sweetener made from the sap of coconut trees. Though it does not have a coconut-y flavor, it is rich in amino acids, minerals, and vitamins. Use it wherever you would use honey or maple syrup.
- **Coconut vinegar** is similar to apple cider vinegar, except it's made with coconut water. It is rich in electrolytes and enzymes.
- **Coconut aminos** are a blend of 17 amino acids, which are harvested from coconut trees and mixed with mineral-rich sea salt. The dark liquid is used as a replacement for soy sauce.
- **Coconut yogurt** is simply yogurt made with fermented coconut milk instead of fermented cow, sheep, or goat milk. It is a terrific choice for anyone who is allergic to dairy products.
- **Coconut keefir**, like its cousin, coconut yogurt, is nothing more than a fermented "yogurt" drink made with coconut milk instead of dairy milk.

CHIA-COCONUT SPREAD

MAKES ¾ CUPS

Rich, slightly sweet, and immensely satisfying, this nutritious spread can be slathered on bread and crackers, used as a dip, spooned onto pancakes and waffles, even thinned with oil and vinegar and revamped into a salad dressing. This is one recipe you'll come back to again and again.

½ *cup creamed coconut, sometimes known as coconut cream concentrate or coconut paste, (such as Nutiva Coconut Manna, Tropicale Traditions Coconut Cream Concentrate, Let's Do Organic Creamed Coconut, or Coconut Tree's Organic Raw Coconut Crème)*

3 *tablespoons nut butter (cashew, almond, peanut, sunflower, etc.)*

3 *tablespoons chia gel (see recipe, page 421)*

2 *tablespoons virgin coconut oil*

1 *teaspoon maple syrup (or honey or agave, if desired)*

1. Place the creamed coconut, nut butter, chia gel, coconut oil, and maple syrup in the bowl of a food processor or high-power blender (such as a Vitamix or Blendtec). Pulse until smooth.

2. Store any uneaten portion in a tightly closed container in the refrigerator.

CHIA QUESADILLAS

SERVES 1 OR 2

For many kids in Mexico and the western United States, quesadillas are the quintessential afterschool snack, served hot off the griddle by doting abuelas or quickly fixed by older siblings. Quesadillas are easy to make and endlessly versatile—fill them with absolutely anything you've got in your fridge!

2   *8-inch corn, flour or multi-grain tortillas*

⅓ *cup shredded Monterey Jack or other mild cheese*

1   *tablespoon chia seeds*

Optional: up to ⅓ cup cooked beans, fresh or frozen corn kernels, or diced, cooked vegetables

Optional: Salsa, guacamole or hot sauce for garnish

1. Place one tortilla in a large frying pan and top with the cheese, chia seeds, and filling. Place the second tortilla on top to create a sandwich.

THE SEXIEST SUPERFOOD

While the lush, rich texture of avocados makes them a darling in the culinary world, they are also prized for a staggering array of health-boosting benefits. Here are just a few of the reasons you should make avocados part of your weekly diet:

- Avocados are a powerful anti-inflammatory food, boasting a range of phytosterols, carotenoids, antioxidants, omega-3 fatty acids, and polyhydroxylated fatty acids, all of which help prevent or lessen arthritis joint afflictions, cardiovascular disease, and auto-immune disease.
- Avocados help the body absorb other nutrients. For instance, one cup of fresh avocado when eaten with a salad or other food, can increase the body's absorption of carotenoids from that food between 200 to 400 percent.
- One cup of avocado supplies 30 percent of the daily recommendation of fiber.
- Avocado has been found to help prevent the occurrence of cancers of the mouth, skin, and prostate gland, probably due to its antioxidant boosting ability and it's high content of anti-inflammatory nutrients.
- One cup of avocado has over 35 percent of one's daily allowance for vitamin K, a vitamin associated with bone formation and proper blood clotting, as well as the transport of calcium through the body.
- Individuals with latex allergies should limit their avocado consumption or avoid it completely. Unfortunately, the fruit contains high amounts of chitinase enzymes, which are associated with latex allergies. Lightly cooking the food slightly deactivates these enzymes.

2. Turn on the heat to medium-low.

3. Turn the quesadilla when the cheese begins to melt and the bottom tortilla is starting to become golden, about 3 minutes.

4. Cook on the other side for about 3 minutes.

5. Allow the quesadilla to cool slightly before cutting into wedge-shaped slices.

6. Garnish with salsa, guacamole, or hot sauce, if desired.

CHIA GUACAMOLE

MAKES ¾ CUP

Full of brain-benefiting and heart-helping monounsaturated fatty acids, guacamole is an irresistible way to get the good fats your body needs to thrive. Here, chia gel makes this wonderful food even more super. Serve it with veggie sticks, tortilla chips, quesadillas, or any other side dish that strikes your fancy.

1   avocado, preferably Hass, pitted and peeled
¼ cup chia gel (see recipe, page 421)
1   tablespoon lemon or lime juice
    Salt, to taste
Optional: 1 tablespoon minced red onion or
    scallions
Optional: A dash of hot sauce

1. In a small bowl, mash the avocado, chia gel, lemon juice, salt, and (if using) onion and hot sauce, until smooth. Serve immediately.

SOFT PRETZELS

MAKES 8 PRETZELS

Making pretzels at home is one of those "great to do with kids" activities that is easy and fun for grownups, too. This tasty recipe is so simple that you'll find yourself making it again and again.

*   Vegetable oil, for greasing pans*
1   package (or 2 ¼ teaspoons) active dry yeast
1¾ cups of barely warm water
1   tablespoon sugar or honey
4   cups whole wheat flour, plus more as needed
½ cup chia seeds
1   teaspoon salt
Optional: 1 egg, beaten, for glazing
Optional: 1 tablespoon coarse kosher salt for
    coating

1. Preheat oven to 425°F. Lightly oil two baking sheets.

2. In a small bowl, combine the yeast, water, and sugar. Mix thoroughly to dissolve yeast and let stand 10 minutes.

3. In a large bowl, combine the flour, chia seeds, and salt. Whisk to combine.

4. Add the yeast mixture (which should now look bubbly) to the flour mixture, stirring with a wooden spoon until stiff. When the dough is too stiff to stir, knead until it is smooth and elastic, adding small amounts of additional flour if needed to prevent stickiness.

5. Pinch off small bits of dough the size of a walnut, and roll into ropes about ¼ to ½-inch in diameter. Fashion these ropes into pretzels or other shapes, gently positioning on baking sheet. Continue until all dough has been rolled and shaped.

6. If using the glaze, brush the tops of pretzels with egg, and then sprinkle with salt.

7. Bake until the pretzels are puffy and golden, 12 to 15 minutes.

SEED COATS

Many baked goods—from artisanal breads to New York City's beloved "everything bagels"—feature a coating of mixed seeds that provide crunch, taste, and texture. If you're a baker, consider adding chia to your mixed-seed combos—it's an easy way to boost the nutrition of anything you eat.

DINNER

CHIA MEATLOAF
SERVES 6

Everyone claims to have the best meatloaf. But is it the best tasting *and* the healthiest meatloaf? This recipe can justifiably make that claim. Chia is magical in ground meat dishes. It creates a wonderful moistness and lightness, helps cut fat, increases fiber, and adds so many powerful nutrients to every bite.

½ cup beef, chicken, or vegetable broth
1 cup cooked white beans or lentils, mashed
½ cup finely chopped onion
½ cup finely chopped celery
2 cloves garlic, minced
1 teaspoon salt, or to taste
  Black pepper, to taste
  Vegetable oil, for greasing the pan
⅓ cup chia seeds
2 large eggs, lightly beaten
1½ pounds ground beef, or a mixture of beef
  and pork, turkey, or chicken

1. In a large bowl, combine the broth, mashed beans, onions, celery, garlic, salt, and pepper. Stir until well until combined.

2. Add the chia seeds and stir. Set the mixture aside for 15 minutes.

3. Preheat the oven to 350°F. Lightly oil a 5 x 9-inch loaf pan. For a free-form loaf, use a lightly oiled baking sheet.

4. Gently stir eggs into vegetable-broth-chia mixture.

5. Add the ground meat, and gently yet thoroughly combine the ingredients.

6. Pat the mixture into the loaf pan, or form into an oblong loaf shape on the prepared baking sheet. Cover the pan or baking sheet with aluminum foil.

7. Bake until golden and bubbly, about 1½ hours. (For a golden crust, remove the foil for the last 5 to 10 minutes of baking). Cool in the loaf pan for at least 15 minutes before slicing.

CHIA MEATBALLS

Love meatballs? Here's an easy, delicious, healthy way to make them: Follow the meatloaf recipe above, adding any herbs or spices you would like to the vegetable mixture. Then shape into balls (the size is up to you) and bake them on a lightly oiled baking sheet, at 350°F, until set and golden brown, about 15 minutes. Serve with marinara sauce, sweet-and-sour sauce, or your favorite gravy.

CHIA VEGETARIAN CHILI

MAKES 4 TO 6 SERVINGS

Here's yet another easy, nutritious, versatile recipe. If you don't have black beans, use white. Have leftover meat or poultry in the fridge? Chop it up and stir it in. Want to add mushrooms? Go ahead.

¼ *cup olive oil*
2 *cups chopped onions*
1⅔ *cups coarsely chopped red bell peppers (about 2 medium)*
1 *cup corn kernels, fresh or frozen*
6 *garlic cloves, chopped*
2 *tablespoons chili powder*
2 *teaspoons dried oregano*
1½ *teaspoons ground cumin*
½ *teaspoon cayenne pepper*
1 *15-ounce can black beans, drained*
1 *15-ounce can red, pink or kidney beans, drained, reserving ½ cup liquid from the can*
1 *cup vegetable, chicken or beef broth*
1 *16-ounce can pureed tomatoes*
½ *cup chia gel (see recipe, page 421)*
Optional: 1 to 2 teaspoons lime juice
Optional: 1 tablespoon cilantro, chopped
   Salt to taste

1. Heat the oil in heavy large pot over medium-high heat.
2. Add the onions, bell peppers, corn and garlic. Sauté until the onions soften, about 10 minutes.
3. Mix in the chili powder, oregano, cumin, and cayenne. Stir for 2 minutes.
4. Mix in the beans, the reserved bean liquid, broth, and the tomatoes.
5. Bring the chili to a boil, stirring occasionally.
6. Reduce the heat to medium-low and simmer until flavors blend and chili thickens, stirring occasionally, about 15 minutes.
7. Turn off heat and stir in the chia gel, lime juice, and cilantro (if using) and salt.

BENEFITS WITH BITE

Many ancient cultures used hot seasonings. In Mexico and Central America (chia's home), chili pepper was the ingredient used most often to spice up food—and, thanks to the pepper's high vitamin C, B6, and vitamin A content—it is useful in treating a variety of health conditions, including viral and bacterial infections and even cancer. The capsaicin in chilies also helps relieve muscle pain.

CHIA COTTAGE PIE

MAKES 6 SERVINGS

Back in the 1790s, recipes for cottage pies used leftover roasted meat of any kind—primarily beef—and the pie dish was lined and topped with mashed potatoes. In the 1870s, recipes for Shepherd's Pie, which featured mutton, began to appear in cookbooks, and since then it has been used synonymously with Cottage Pie.

To make Shepherd's Pie, replace all or some of the beef in this recipe with ground or minced lamb, and switch in parsnips and sweet potatoes for the Yukon Golds and lentils.

Now you have two delicious options for making, easy, savory pies.

1   *tablespoon extra-virgin olive oil*
1   *large onion, chopped*
1   *large carrot, peeled and chopped*
2   *garlic cloves, minced*
1   *pound ground beef (or substitute half or more with lamb)*
1   *cup beef or chicken broth*
1   *tablespoon tomato paste or ketchup*
1   *cup cooked lentils*
1   *teaspoon chopped fresh or dry rosemary*
1   *tablespoon chopped Italian parsley*
1   *cup frozen peas*
½   *cup chia gel (see recipe, page 421)*

2   *pounds Yukon Gold potatoes (or use regular russet potatoes) peeled and cut into chunks*
6   *tablespoons extra-virgin olive oil, virgin coconut oil or unsalted butter*
½   *cup milk (dairy, coconut, almond, rice, hemp, etc.)*
   Salt to taste

1. Preheat the oven to 375°F.
2. Heat the oil in a large sauté pan over medium-high heat, then add the onions, carrots, garlic, and meat. Cook until browned, 8 to 10 minutes.
3. Drain the excess fat from the skillet and add the broth, tomato paste, lentils, and herbs. Simmer until the juices thicken, about 10 minutes.
4. Stir in the peas and chia gel.
5. Pour the mixture into a 1½-quart baking dish; set aside
6. Meanwhile, in a saucepan, cover the potatoes with cold water and a generous pinch of salt and bring to the boil over medium-high heat. Cook until tender, about 20 minutes; drain.
7. Mash the potatoes with the oil or butter, milk, and salt.
8. Spread the potatoes over the meat mixture, then crosshatch the top with a fork.
9. Bake until golden, 30 to 35 minutes. Let stand 10 minutes before serving.

CHIA POLENTA WITH WHITE BEANS

MAKES 4 SERVINGS

Polenta is pure comfort food. Here, it is made nutrient dense with chia and white beans. Protein, vitamins, minerals, omegas, fiber—all in one amazing-tasting dish.

2 *cups stone ground cornmeal*
2 *cups chicken, vegetable or beef broth*
1 *tablespoon extra-virgin olive oil*
  Salt to taste
½ *cup chia gel (see recipe, page 421)*
1 *15-ounce can white beans*
Optional garnish: Chopped tomato, minced basil, chopped scallion, marinara sauce, toasted pine nuts, chopped cooked chicken, etc.

1. In a large heavy pot over low heat, whisk together the cornmeal and broth, whisking continuously until mixture is completely lump-free.

2. Add the oil and salt, if using. Increase the heat to medium-high, stirring continuously until mixture comes to a rolling boil, about 10 minutes.

3. Lower the heat and cook, stirring continuously, for another five minutes.

4. Remove from the heat and stir in the chia gel.

5. In a small pan, warm white beans over medium-low heat.

6. To serve, spoon the polenta into shallow bowls or onto dinner plates. Top with ¼ cup of beans. Garnish as desired.

CHIA BREAKFAST POLENTA

For a warming breakfast, follow the recipe for Chia Polenta with White Beans on page 457, replacing the broth with your choice of milk (dairy, coconut, almond, rice, or hemp, etc.). Replace the olive oil with coconut oil, and omit the white beans. Garnish the cooked polenta with chopped pecans, sunflower seeds, pumpkin seeds or fruit, and a drizzle of maple syrup.

CHIA FAUX ENCHILADAS

MAKES 4 TO 6 SERVINGS

In truth, this fun recipe is more of a suggestion than a bona fide recipe. Combine the ingredients as desired—you'll get a delicious, nutritious dish each time you make these easy enchiladas. Have all ingredients at room temperature before starting.

1 *15-ounce can black or red beans*
¼ *cup chia gel (see recipe, page 421)*
1 *tablespoon extra-virgin olive oil or coconut oil*
1 *onion, sliced*
2 *red, yellow or green bell peppers, cut into narrow strips*
2 *cups protein (can be chopped meat, ground beef/pork/chicken/turkey/bison, tofu, or flaked fish)*
   Salt, to taste
1 to 2 *teaspoons lime juice*
1 *cup prepared enchilada or ranchero sauce, or salsa*
Optional: 2 tablespoons pepitas
Optional: 1 tablespoon cilantro, minced
6 *large flour, whole grain, or corn tortillas*

1. Warm the beans in a small pot over low heat. Stir in the chia gel.
2. Heat the oil in a large frying pan over medium-high heat. Add the onions and sauté for about two minutes.
3. Add the bell pepper slices to the pan. Sauté until slightly softened, about five minutes.
4. Turn off heat and add the protein, salt and lime. Stir until combined.
5. Place one tortilla on each place. Spoon one or two tablespoons of bean-chia mixture in the middle of each tortilla. Add two tablespoons of the vegetable-protein mixture.
6. Roll each tortilla, placing them seam-side down on the plate.
7. Top each faux enchilada with enchilada sauce or salsa. Garnish with pepitas and cilantro, if desired.

PEPITAS

Pepitas are green, meaty, addictive nuggets that are rich in minerals. Grown from a special variety of pumpkin that produces shell-less seeds, pepitas are high in zinc, manganese, magnesium, phosphorus, tryptophan, and iron. They also contain high doses of protein, vitamin K, and fiber. For a fun snack, dry toast pepitas in a clean pan until they pop, then dress them with salt and a dusting of chili powder or a splash of soy sauce.

CHIA CHIPOTLE BEAN BURGER

MAKES 4 TO 6 SERVINGS

Bean burgers make a fast, casual, and tasty meal that is high in protein and fiber, and low in fat. Go ahead and make this recipe your own: Play around with the veggies and seasonings and experiment with other types of beans—you can use kidney and cannellini beans, chickpeas, or even lentils.

1   15-ounce can black beans
¼   cup chia gel (see recipe, page 421)
2   cloves garlic, minced
¼   cup corn kernels or sautéed or cooked vegetables (alternatively, use frozen corn kernels, defrosted, or vegetables leftover from another meal)
1   teaspoon canned chipotle in adobo, minced, or 1 teaspoon dried chipotle powder
½   teaspoon salt
Optional: 1 tablespoon minced cilantro or parsley
1   tablespoon virgin coconut oil

1. In the bowl of a food processor or high-speed blender (such as a Vitamix or Blendtec), pulse the ingredients until blended. Do not over-process; you do not want to liquefy!

2. Form the mixture into patties.

3. Heat the coconut oil in a frying pan over medium heat.

4. Cook the patties until golden, about five minutes. Flip and repeat.

5. Alternate cooking method: Preheat oven to 325°F. Place the patties on a lightly oiled baking sheet and cook until golden, 12 to 15 minutes, turning halfway through cooking.

6. Serve on hamburger rolls with the condiments of your choice.

BLACK BEAUTIES

Black beans are well known in nutrition circles for their high fiber content. In fact, black beans have more fiber than the other legume powerhouses—lentils and chickpeas. The fiber in these treasures has been shown to be perfect for helping the lower digestive tract stay healthy, lowering the risk of colon cancer and helping to create efficient digestion.

CHIA CHICKEN BURGERS

MAKES 6 TO 8 SERVINGS

Ground chicken is a terrific option for anyone who is trying to lower their red meat consumption. It's also fantastic for dieters, containing approximately 50 percent less calories than ground pork or beef. In this recipe, ground chicken and chia team up to make the most tender, moist burgers you're ever likely to eat.

2 *pounds ground white meat chicken*
   (or dark meat, although it contains more
   calories and fat than white chicken meat)
2 *tablespoons chia gel (see recipe, page 421)*
1 or 2 *garlic cloves, minced*
   Salt and black pepper, to taste
Optional: 1 to 2 tablespoons minced fresh
   parsley, chives, or a mix of these, and any
   other fresh herb of your choice
1 *tablespoon extra-virgin olive oil or virgin*
   coconut oil

1. In large bowl, mix together the ground chicken, chia gel, garlic, salt, black pepper, and fresh herbs, if using, combining gently yet thoroughly.
2. Form the meat mixture into 6 to 8 patties, about ¾-inch thick.
3. Add the oil to a large frying pan over medium heat. Cook the patties on one side, until browned, 7 to 8 minutes. Turn, and continue cooking until cooked through completely, about 6 minutes more. Serve on hamburger rolls with the condiments of your choice.

GROUND CHICKEN VS. GROUND BEEF

Anyone who is watching their calories knows that ground beef is rich in calories. A 4-ounce serving of ground beef has roughly 250 calories. You can lighten your favorite recipes by swapping in ground chicken. It contains only 130 calories per 4-ounce serving.

CHIA CAESAR SALAD

MAKES 2 SERVINGS

Caesar salad is the quintessential restaurant salad, the go-to item when you want something light (yet filling), healthy, and delicious. This quick, at-home version tastes just like what you'd get at your favorite restaurant, except it doesn't contain eggs or anchovies, and we've left off the croutons to create a lower-calorie dish. Also, there's plenty of chia in this Caesar salad to raise its fiber and nutrient profile.

2 or 3 *Romaine hearts, leaves washed, dried*
   and chopped, or torn into bite-sized pieces
⅓ *cup extra-virgin olive oil*
2 *tablespoons chia gel (see recipe, page 421)*
   Juice of 1 lemon
1 *teaspoon Tabasco sauce*
1 *teaspoon Worcestershire sauce*
1 *teaspoon Dijon mustard*
1 or 2 *garlic cloves, minced*
¼ *cup Parmesan cheese, grated*
   Salt and freshly ground black pepper, to taste

1. Place the chopped romaine in a salad bowl.

2. In a blender, pulse the remaining ingredients until liquefied.

3. Toss the salad with dressing, using only enough to coat lettuce. Store the remaining dressing in a tightly closed container in the refrigerator and use within a week.

SUPER CAESER

If the stories are true, Caesar salad is the creation of Caesar Cardini, who owned restaurants in the United States and Mexico. According to his daughter Rosa, Cardini invented the famous salad in the kitchen of his San Diego restaurant on the Fourth of July, 1924, when a rush on the kitchen depleted supplies. While the original version featured plenty of croutons, it did not use anchovies. If you'd like, add white meat chicken or turkey to your salad for a well-rounded meal.

CHIA GAZPACHO

MAKES 8 SERVINGS

Homemade gazpacho is one of life's great pleasures. Many of us can't imagine summer without it. This savory recipe uses white chia seed, for thickening, instead of the more traditional bread crumbs.

1   46-ounce can or jar of tomato juice
2   cups vegetable or chicken broth
2   cups finely chopped fresh plum tomatoes
½   cup finely chopped yellow or red bell pepper
½   cup peeled, seeded finely chopped cucumber
½   cup finely chopped red or sweet onion (such as Maui, Walla Walla, or Vidalia)
¼   cup red wine vinegar
¼   cup white chia seeds
⅓   cup extra-virgin olive oil
    Juice of ½ lemon
¼   cup minced parsley, or a combination of parsley and chives
1   teaspoon fresh oregano, minced
2   cloves garlic, minced
    Salt, to taste
    Black pepper, to taste
    Hot sauce, to taste
Optional garnish: chopped parsley or chives, minced red or sweet onion, chopped olives, pepitas, or anything else that sounds delicious

1. In a large bowl, combine all the ingredients, except salt, pepper, hot sauce, and garnish. Mix thoroughly.

2. Taste and season with salt, pepper, and hot sauce.

3. Refrigerate at least 2 hours before serving. The soup will thicken as the chia seed swells.

4. Serve with optional garnish.

THE MYSTERIES OF GAZPACHO

Gazpacho, as you may already know, is a cold tomato soup with ancient roots. While many people believe that this famous soup's birthplace is Andalucia in southern Spain, its true origins are shrouded in culinary mystery. Two theories stand out: Either gazpacho is an update of an Arab bread soup that found its way to Spain and Portugal with the Moors, or it arrived with the Romans—without the tomatoes, which were added after they were brought to Europe from the New World, perhaps as early as 1521, when the Spanish explorer, Cortés, captured Tenochtítlan, now Mexico City. We may never know the original origins of gazpacho, but we do know it is one of the most nourishing and refreshing dishes around, overflowing with vitamins C and A, lycopene, phytonutrients, and fiber.

DESSERTS

BASIC CHIA PUDDING

MAKES 3 TO 4 SERVINGS

This is dessert at its easiest—just mix chia seeds with your a favorite liquid, sweeten it, allow it to stand and thicken, then serve it as-is—or with nuts, sugar, fruit, shaved chocolate, or anything else that strikes your fancy.

2 *cups almond milk (can also use coconut, rice, hemp, or dairy milk)*
¾ *cup chia seeds*
2 *tablespoons honey or maple syrup*
   Dash salt
Optional: vanilla or almond extract, to taste

1. In a large bowl, mix all the ingredients together, stirring well to combine. Allow pudding to sit for five minutes, and then stir again.

2. Give the pudding a stir every five minutes over a 30-minute period, until the pudding is thickened.

3. Pudding will be ready when the chia seeds have plumped up.

4. Refrigerator until ready to serve.

THE MARVELS OF MAPLE SYRUP

Maple syrup is the sweet sap tapped from Sugar, Black, and Red Maple trees. It is also a very healthy sweetener, because, ounce for ounce, maple syrup contains fewer calories and more minerals than honey or sugar. Look for grade B or Dark Amber grade maple syrup—it's darker and richer in taste than the lighter, less complex Grade A or Light Amber syrups. All shades of maple syrup, however, are high in manganese and zinc, two minerals that are essential for healthy immune-system function.

CACAO VS. COCOA

Cacao is made of the solids left behind after the liqueur and butter have been removed from the cacao beans. There is loud, frequent debate among foodies about the difference between cacao and cocoa powders. In truth, there is no difference, other than the spelling. If you come across the word "raw" tacked onto cacao powder, it simply means that the product has not been heated above 110°F.

CACAO-CHIA PUDDING

MAKES 2 SERVINGS

Deep and intense, this chocolaty dessert is rich in magnesium, iron, zinc, and many other powerful nutrients.

2½ cups water
1   cup raw cashews
5   chopped soft, pitted dates (soak in hot water for an hour if dates are hard)
2   tablespoons vanilla extract
*   Dash salt*
½ cup raw cacao powder (or cacao nibs or regular unsweetened natural cocoa powder)
⅓ cup chia seed

1. In a food processor or high-power blender (such as a Vitamix or Blendtec), process the water, cashews, dates, vanilla extract, and salt. Pulse until absolutely smooth.
2. Add the cacao powder and chia, and blend just until smooth.
3. Pour into dessert cups and refrigerate overnight until firm.

BERRY CLOUD PUDDING

MAKES 2 TO 4 SERVINGS

This brilliant pink dessert tastes like summer. It's a light, refreshing way to end a meal—but it also makes a special snack or a dressy brunch option. Go ahead and experiment with different fruit and flavorings.

2   cups frozen or fresh strawberries or raspberries (or a combination)
⅔ cup canned coconut milk, shaken before measuring (do not use "lite" coconut milk)
2   tablespoons milled chia seed (see recipe, page 415)
1 to 2 tablespoons honey, to taste
1   tablespoon lemon or lime juice
*   Splash vanilla, almond, or lemon extract*

1. Place all the ingredients in a high-power blender, such as a Vitamix or Blendtec and blend until combined and berry seeds have been pulverized.
2. Pour the pudding into 2 to 4 dessert cups and refrigerate about 2 hours, or until cold and set.

CHIA ICE POPS

MAKES 4 TO 6 SERVINGS

Popsicles are a great place to experiment with chia, milled chia, and chia gel. This fruity, refreshing recipe uses whole strawberries, mango chunks, and orange juice, but feel free to experiment. The combinations are—quite literally—endless.

1   *cup frozen strawberries*
1   *cup frozen mango chunks*
½ *cup orange juice*
⅓ *cup chia seeds*
¼ *cup water*

1. In a food processor or high-power blender (such as Vitamix or Blendtec), blend all the ingredients until liquefied.
2. Pour into ice pop molds or ice cube molds.
3. Freeze until solid.

INVENTING THE POPSICLE

- The first popsicle was created in 1905 by an 11-year-old boy named Frank Epperson, who called his invention the Epsicle Ice Pop.
- Epperson invented the treat after leaving a cup of soda with a straw outdoors during the winter. It froze—and Epperson had himself a frozen treat.
- It took Epperson more than 18 years to finally patent his invention. By that time, his own children had taken to calling the treats "popsicles." The new name stuck.
- In 1925, Epperson sold the rights to his popsicle to the John Lowe food company of New York.
- The first commercial popsicles had birch sticks. Today, most popsicle sticks are still made of birch.

CHIA GELATIN

MAKES ABOUT 4 SERVINGS

This textured dessert does not resemble the smooth, neon-colored, rubbery dessert you may remember from childhood. Chia gelatin is full of bumpy, nutty chia seeds, and is a deeply nourishing comfort food. For a creamier dessert, use coconut milk instead of fruit juice (or combine them).

3¾ cup fruit juice of your choice
¼ cup chia seeds
1   15-ounce container coconut milk
*   (this needs to be cold) or additional*
*   fruit juice*
4   envelopes powdered gelatin (Knox brand)

1. Mix ¾ cup of the fruit juice and the chia seeds in a small bowl. Let sit for 3 minutes and stir again. Place the bowl in the fridge for 1 to 2 hours until the mixture becomes firm.

2. In a medium saucepan or pot, heat the remaining 3 cups of fruit juice.

3. While the juice is heating, sprinkle the gelatin over the cold coconut milk in a small bowl and let it stand while the juice on the stove heats to a boil.

4. In an 8-inch x 11-inch glass baking-dish, mix the boiling juice and the coconut milk-gelatin mixture, whisking for about five minutes until there are no lumps and everything is dissolved.

5. Take the chia-juice mixture out of the fridge.

6. When the gelatin mixture has cooled down, for 10 or 15 minutes, add a tablespoon of the chia mixture to the gelatin mixture, whisking until combined. Continue adding small amounts of chia mixture to gelatin mixture, stirring after each addition, until finished.

7. Place in the refrigerator until set.

THE FACTS ABOUT GELATIN

Unflavored gelatin (a key ingredient in JELL-O®) is in fact an animal product that confers a number of excellent health benefits. In the autism community, for example, it is a popular remedy to help heal leaky gut syndrome (where the walls of the large intestine are porous), and studies have also found gelatin to be helpful in treating joint and tendon conditions.

RAW CHIA-CACAO COOKIES

MAKES ABOUT 12 SMALL COOKIES

For many of us, these cookies are the ultimate, high protein, high nutrient, completely raw cookie—nothing like the Toll House sweets of our youth. You'll love the energy you get from these yummy treats.

1 *cup pitted dates*
½ *cup raw slivered almonds*
2 *tablespoons raw cacao powder (or cacao nibs or regular unsweetened natural cocoa powder)*
⅛ *cup chia seeds*
1 *teaspoon vanilla*
¼ *cup whole raw cashews, hazelnuts, pistachios, or almonds*

1. Using a food processor or a high-power blender (such as a Vitamix or Blendtec), process the dates until a smooth paste forms.
2. Add the almonds, cacao powder, chia seeds, and vanilla. Pulse until everything is combined, but not liquefied.
3. Add the raw cashews and pulse only until the nuts are incorporated into the mix—you want chunky pieces of nut distributed throughout the cookies.
4. Roll tablespoon-sized balls of dough between your hands to make a perfectly round, smoothly-finished cookie.
5. Place the cookies on a piece of waxed paper to firm up for at least 2 hours. Store in the refrigerator or freezer.

RAW CACAO NIBS

If you're a hardcore raw food enthusiast, the thought of using anything but raw cacao may pain you. If you can't find raw cacao powder, simply use an equal amount of raw cacao nibs, and pulverize them into a soft powder.

NUT BUTTER CHIA COOKIES

MAKES 20 TO 24 COOKIES

These pretty little cakes are akin to the peanut butter cookies you grew up on—but they're loaded with protein and fiber. To make the cookies gluten free, try using gluten-free oat flour. The cookies will be a touch softer and more fragile than traditional peanut butter cookies, but they're every bit as delicious.

½ *cup virgin coconut oil*
½ *cup natural cane sugar (e.g., Sucanat) or regular granulated sugar*
½ *cup brown sugar*
½ *cup unsalted cashew butter (can also use almond butter)*
1 *large egg*
1 *teaspoon vanilla extract*
1¼ *cups oat flour or whole-wheat pastry flour*
¼ *cup ground almond meal*
3 *tablespoons chia seeds*
¾ *teaspoon baking soda*
½ *teaspoon fine grain sea salt*

1. Preheat the oven to 350°F. Prepare two baking sheets by lining with parchment paper.
2. Using a stand mixer, beat together the coconut oil, sugars, and cashew butter for about 4 or 5 minutes, or until light in color.
3. Add the egg and vanilla, beating just until completely blended.
4. In a medium bowl, whisk together the flour, almond meal, chia seeds, baking soda, and salt. Add the flour mixture to the wet ingredients, mixing just until blended.
5. Using a tablespoon or a medium-size cookie scoop, drop batter onto lined baking sheets. Press down gently on the cookies with the tines of a fork or use a glass tumbler to flatten them slightly.
6. Bake until golden brown, 12 to 15 minutes.
7. Cool for 1 to 2 minutes before removing the cookies from the pans.

MAKING YOUR OWN OAT AND ALMOND FLOUR

Although you can easily buy oat or almond flour at a specialty or health food store—they can be made just as easily at home. To make oat flour, simply whir the oats in a coffee grinder or food processor. To make almond flour, you can use raw or toasted almonds, just be sure to pulse the nuts carefully so that you don't over-process them. The texture of the flour should be sand-like.

WALNUT SPONGE CAKE
MAKES 12 SERVINGS

This elegant cake is based on a recipe by Vilma Lo Presti, which you can find in her magnificent chia cookbook, *Pastrymaking and Baking with Chia* (De Los Cuatrovientos, 2009). The directions are a bit involved, but when you really want to impress, you'll be happy you took the time to make this amazing cake!

6   large egg whites, divided
1   large egg
⅔   cup granulated sugar, divided
2½ tablespoons honey
3½ tablespoons virgin coconut oil, plus more
     for greasing pan
½   teaspoon cream of tartar
1   cup cake flour
⅔   cup whole wheat pastry flour, plus more
     for dusting pan
2   teaspoons baking powder
⅓   cup walnuts, finely chopped
5   tablespoon milled chia (see recipe, page 415)
Optional topping: Confectioner's sugar

1. Preheat oven to 325°F. Prepare an 8-inch cake pan by lightly oiling and dusting with flour. Set aside.
2. In the bowl of a standing mixer, using the whisk attachment, beat two of the egg whites and the whole egg with half the sugar and the honey until creamy.

3. With the motor on low, slowly drizzle the oil into the egg mixture. Remove the bowl and set aside.

4. Attach a fresh bowl to the mixer and beat the remaining four egg whites with the remaining sugar and the cream of tartar. Beat until the mixture forms soft, flexible peaks.

5. In a separate large bowl, sift together both flours and the baking powder.

6. With the mixer on low—or using a large spatula and working by hand, alternately fold the egg-sugar mixture and flour mixture into the whipped egg whites.

7. Gently fold in the walnuts and milled chia.

THE HEALTH BENEFITS OF WALNUTS

Walnuts are filled with good things—protein, omega-3 fatty acids, vitamin E, and manganese. Walnuts benefit the cardiovascular and immune systems, the skin, and the nervous system. Surprisingly, only 5.5 percent of American adults eat walnuts at any point during the year! Here are some more interesting facts about walnuts:

- Due to their high polyunsaturated fat content, walnuts are extremely perishable and should be stored in the refrigerator or freezer.
- In the 4th century A.D., the Romans introduced walnuts to many European countries, where they have been grown ever since.
- Walnut oil was once used as lamp oil.
- A 1-ounce serving of walnuts amounts to about 7 shelled walnuts, or 14 walnut halves.
- Walnuts are part of the tree nut family, which includes Brazil nuts, cashews, hazelnuts, macadamia nuts, pecans, pine nuts, and pistachios.
- China is the largest commercial producer of walnuts in the world, with about 360,000 metric tons produced per year.
- The United States is the second largest commercial producer of walnuts, with about 294,000 metric tons of production.
- In the United States, 90 percent of all walnuts are grown in Northern California, most notably, the Sacramento and San Joaquin valleys.
- Turkey, Iran, Ukraine, and Romania are the next highest walnut producers in the world, after California.
- The walnuts grown commercially in the U.S. are known as "English walnuts" because they were first brought to our shores on British mercantile ships.
- Black walnuts are native to the United States.

8. Pour batter into the prepared pan and place it in the oven. Bake until a toothpick inserted in the middle comes out clean, about 40 minutes.

9. Allow the cake to cool 10 minutes in the pan before inverting and cooling completely on a rack.

10. Dust with confectioner's sugar, if desired.

MOIST CARROT CAKE

MAKES 12 TO 16 SERVINGS

Carrot cakes, though popular in the United States since the 1960s, can be traced back to the carrot puddings of medieval Europe. This moist dessert is based upon a recipe created by Vilma Lo Presti. (You can find it in her magnificent chia cookbook, *Pastrymaking and Baking with Chia.*) It takes some care to prepare this delicious, moist cake, but it is so worth the effort! Omit the optional glaze and save yourself 180 calories per serving.

7 tablespoons virgin coconut oil, plus more
  for greasing pan
6 tablespoons granulated sugar
6 tablespoons packed brown sugar
1 large egg
3 large egg whites
1½ cups carrot puree, made by cooking carrots
  and mashing them or pureeing them in
  a food processor
7 tablespoons part skim ricotta cheese
1 tablespoon grated orange rind
1 cup all-purpose flour, plus more for
  dusting pan
½ cup whole wheat pastry flour
3 teaspoon baking powder
½ teaspoon cinnamon
  Dash salt
½ cup walnuts or pecans, finely chopped
⅓ cup dark seedless raisins, packed
¼ cup chia seeds

For the Glaze

1½ cups powdered sugar
6 tablespoons unsweetened cocoa powder
¼ cup dark rum

1. Preheat oven to 350°F. Lightly oil and flour a bundt pan.

2. In the bowl of a stand mixer fitted with the paddle attachment, beat the coconut oil, both sugars, and the whole egg together until creamy.

3. Add the egg whites, one by one, blending well after each addition.

4. Add carrot puree, blending thoroughly.

5. Mix in ricotta and orange rind, blending thoroughly.

6. In a separate bowl, whisk together the flours, baking powder, cinnamon, and salt.

7. Add the flour mixture to the egg-carrot mixture, mixing only until blended.

8. Gently mix in nuts, raisins, and chia, and pour the batter into the prepared pan.

CARROT TRIVIA

Who doesn't love a bit of trivia, especially when it is about food?

- The longest carrot, recorded in 1996, was 5.14 meters (16 feet 10 ½ inches).
- Carrots have the highest content of beta-carotene (vitamin A) of all vegetables.
- Carrots were first grown as a medicine, not a food.
- Anglo-Saxons included carrots as an ingredient in a medicinal drink to ward off the devil and insanity.
- The heaviest carrot on record, so far, weighed 18.985 pounds, and was harvested in 1998 by John V. R. Evans, an American farmer.
- Many people trace the modern carrot cake to Viola Schlicting, from Texas, who created the first carrot cake in the 1960s from her German carrot-nut bread recipe.
- Carrots were the first vegetable to be canned commercially.
- Holtville, California is known as "The Carrot Capital of the World."
- Researchers at the USDA found that study participants who consumed two carrots a day were able to lower their cholesterol levels by about 20 percent, due to the vegetable's soluble fiber.
- When juiced, one pound of carrots will make approximately 6 to 8 ounces of carrot juice.
- A teaspoon holds almost 2,000 carrot seeds.
- The last meal on the *Titanic* included creamed carrots in the fifth course.

9. Bake until golden and a toothpick inserted in the center of the cake comes out clean, 35 to 40 minutes.

10. Cool the cake in the pan for 10 to 15 minutes before inverting onto a wire rack to cool completely.

11. If using the glaze, whisk the ingredients together in a small bowl. Drizzle over the cake while it is still warm.

BEAUTY RECIPES

Omega-3 fatty acid is fantastic for skin, hair, and nails, making chia the ultimate beauty food. Eating chia regularly ensures you look your best, but you can also mix chia into your favorite lotions, cleansers, shampoos and conditioners to look even better. Or, be adventurous and use one of our recipes.

MOISTURIZING CHIA-AVOCADO MASK
MAKES ENOUGH FOR 1 APPLICATION

This rich mask is made for drier skin. It's ultra-moisturizing, nourishing, and firming. Use it weekly, if you'd like, and see the difference in your skin.

½ *avocado, pit removed*
1 *tablespoon milled chia seeds (see recipe, page 415)*
Optional: 1 drop of lavender essential oil

1. Scoop avocado flesh from the peel into a medium bowl.
2. Add chia seed and essential oil, if using. Mash mixture into a smooth paste.
3. Place on clean facial skin and allow to sit for 15 to 30 minutes.
4. Remove with a washcloth that has been moistened in warm water.

THE BEAUTY BOOSTER

If you're looking for a fast way to add chia seeds to your beauty routine, stir a tablespoon of milled chia or chia gel into your favorite packaged facial masque, body scrub, or hair conditioner. Allow the mixture to sit for as long as you'd like, then rinse it off. Voila!: softer skin and hair.

SQUEEZE YOUR OWN ALOE

Depending upon where you live, you may find large, single aloe leaves in the produce department of your local supermarket, health food store, or a market such as Whole Foods. If you've been relying on bottles of shelf-stable aloe vera gel from the drug store, give fresh aloe a try. Cooling, refreshing, tightening, brightening, ultra-healing, and super-nourishing, the aloe's light gel is heavenly on skin and great on hair as a light styling gel. To harvest your own, go ahead and purchase one of those leaves, looking for one that is firm and even in color. Once you bring it home, slit the leaf lengthwise and use a spoon to scoop out the clear gel.

SKIN FRESHENING MASK
MAKES ENOUGH FOR 1 APPLICATION

This light, refreshing mask is ideal for normal to oilier skin. It leaves your skin soft and glowing.

4   tablespoons raw aloe gel (from the health
    food store or squeezed from an aloe leaf)
1   tablespoon milled chia seeds (see recipe, page 415)
Optional: 1 drop of tea tree essential oil

1. Stir the ingredients together in a medium bowl.
2. Apply to clean facial skin, allowing the mixture to sit for 15 to 30 minutes.
3. Remove with a washcloth that has been moistened in warm water.

KELP FACE PACK
MAKES ENOUGH FOR 1 APPLICATION

Seaweed is a wonder for firming the skin and creating a glowing finish.

1   tablespoon powdered kelp (buy kelp at
    the health food store and whir in a coffee
    grinder)
1   tablespoon plain yogurt
1   tablespoon chia gel (see recipe, page 421)

1. Mix the ingredients in a medium bowl, stirring until combined.
2. Apply to clean facial skin, allowing the mixture to sit for 15 to 30 minutes.
3. Remove with a washcloth that has been moistened in warm water.

SEAWEED TO THE RESCUE

Seaweed is a common ingredient in high-end and health-food store skin preparations. Kelp, dulse, and wakame have similar properties to human plasma, and are also concentrated sources of many minerals (including iodine) and vitamins that leave skin nourished, soft, smooth, and radiant.

SUPER FAST FACE PACK I
MAKES ENOUGH FOR 1 APPLICATION

Speedy and nourishing, this quick recipe revives skin, giving it a vibrant look.

2 to 3 tablespoons chia gel (see recipe, page 421)

1. Apply to clean facial skin, allowing the mixture to sit for 15 to 30 minutes.
2. Remove with a washcloth that has been moistened in warm water.

SUPER FAST FACE PACK II
MAKES ENOUGH FOR 1 APPLICATION

Here's another quick and easy way to give your skin a glow.

2 tablespoons milled chia
2 tablespoons aloe gel, plain yogurt, rose water, or your favorite facial toner or facial moisturizer

1. Mix the ingredients in a medium bowl, stirring until combined.
2. Apply to clean facial skin, allowing the mixture to sit for 15 to 30 minutes.
3. Remove with a washcloth that has been moistened in warm water.

ROSE WATER

Rose water is the by-product of the rose oil used in perfume. Rose water is used as a flavoring agent in the Middle East and Southern Europe, and it is a popular skincare ingredient in America, where it is often found in astringents and toners. These products are designed to remove traces of makeup and impurities, and leave the skin looking even-pored, firm, and fresh.

ALMOND FACE SCRUB
MAKES ENOUGH FOR 1 APPLICATION

Almond scrubs are traditional treatments

JOJOBA OIL

Jojoba oil was the skincare darling of the 1970s, showing up in massage oil, facial creams, shaving preparations, nail strengtheners, and all kinds of mainstream hair products. We still love the all-day moisture just a few small drops provide … although we must share just one interesting bit of jojoba trivia: Jojoba oil isn't really an oil at all, but the wax ester (liquid wax) of the jojoba bean.

for sloughing off dead skin and impurities to create fresh, soft skin. Try this homemade version. You'll be happily surprised at how gorgeous your skin can look.

2 tablespoons coarse almond meal
1 tablespoon milled chia seeds
1 tablespoon jojoba oil (for drier skin)
  or aloe vera gel (for oilier skin)

1. Whisk the ingredients together in a medium bowl.
2. Apply to clean facial skin, scrubbing the mixture into the skin in small circles. Pay extra attention to rough areas or areas that contain congested pores.
3. Rise immediately with warm water, or allow the mixture to sit for 10 to 30 minutes before rinsing.

HIGH GLOW SCRUB

MAKES ENOUGH TO USE ON THE BODY AND FACE

This easy recipe creates a scrub that is both nourishing and invigorating.

½ cup chia gel (see recipe, page 421)
2 to 4 tablespoons kosher or Epsom salt,
*   or raw sugar crystals (such as Sucanat)*
Optional: 1 drop lavender essential oil

1. Whisk the ingredients to gether in a large bowl, using a larger amount of salt or sugar for a rougher-grained scrub.
2. In the shower, rub onto dry skin, working in small circles on the body and face.
3. Allow the mixture to sit for a few minutes if desired, or rinse immediately.

CHIA NAIL TREATMENT
MAKES ENOUGH FOR 1 APPLICATION

In this recipe, chia helps freshen, strengthen, and moisturize nails.

1   teaspoon lemon juice
1   teaspoon honey
1   tablespoon milled chia (see recipe, page 415)

1. Mix the ingredients in a medium bowl, stirring until combined.
2. Apply to fingernails, rubbing into the nails, cuticles, and surrounding skin. (May also be applied to toenails in the same way.)
3. Rinse immediately, or allow the mixture to sit for 10 minutes before removing.

PET FOODS

Animals thrive when given a nutrient-dense diet. Upgrading your pet's health is simple with chia. Just stir into food (or sprinkle onto it) and serve. More ideas below.

CANARY CRUNCH

MAKES 2½ CUPS

This fast, easy food creates energy and a bright coat of feathers. It's perfect as a main food or snack for canaries, parakeets, parrots, love birds, cockatiels, cockatoos, doves and other exotic pet birds.

2 cups commercial bird seed
½ cup chia seeds

1. Mix together the bird seed and chia, and store in a tightly covered container in a cool spot.

SHARING THE WEALTH

Canary Crunch can also be used in bird-feeders for small birds or scattered on the ground for peacocks, swans, and other water birds. Why should domesticated birds have all the nutrients?

EGGCELLENT!

You've probably seen "omega-enriched" eggs at the supermarket. Have you ever wonder how they got to be so high in these essential fatty acids? It all starts with chicken feed. In other words, whatever hens eat a lot of, ends up in their eggs. Thus, many farmers are feeding their chickens flax or chia to increase the amount of omega-3 fatty acid in eggs. If too much flax is fed the eggs will have a fishy flavor, this is not the case with chia, however.

CHICKEN FEED

MAKES ABOUT 12 CUPS

Chia is gaining attention not only for what it can do for the chicken you eat, but for the eggs that chickens lay: Feeding birds chia seed is a fast, easy, safe way to increase the omega fatty acid content of the meat and eggs.

5 pound bag of commercial chicken feed
1 pound bag of chia seeds

1. In a large container or bucket with a lid, combine the chicken feed and chia seeds.
2. Store, covered, in a cool, dry place.

RABBIT STUDIES

In 2010, the University of Turin conducted research to determine the difference between rabbits that consumed chia and those that had not. After replacing up to 15 percent of the bunnies' regular diets with chia, researchers found no change in meat texture or taste between the two groups. However, the chia-fed rabbits had meat with higher antioxidant levels, higher omega-3 and -6 fatty acids, less saturated fat, and more unsaturated lipids (a good thing; these contribute to cardiovascular health).

BUNNY CHIA DRINK

*MAKES ENOUGH FOR 1 DAY'S
WATER SUPPLY*

It's hard to get pet rabbits to eat chia—they aren't seed eaters, and chia doesn't stick well to the grasses, vegetables, and commercial food pellets that most domestic rabbits consume. This bunny drink is one way to get chia into your beloved pet.

1   *cup fresh water*
½   *teaspoon chia gel (see recipe, page 421)*

1. Add chia gel to water. Mix thoroughly to blend.
2. Place in a water bowl chia gel may clog a water sipper.

CHIA CAT FOOD

MAKES 1 SERVING

Chia helps cats' coats grow glossy and thick, brightens their eyes, and help sustain their energy levels.

1   *serving of canned food (depending on your cat, this is 1 ounce, 3 ounce, or 5 ounce)*
1   *teaspoon chia gel (see recipe, page 421)*

1. Mix chia gel with canned food until it's thoroughly mixed.
2. Serve immediately.

CHIA GRASS

If you're a cat owner, you've probably seen your cat chew on houseplants or grass. You may have even treated your pet with her very own pot of wheatgrass. Next time try chia grass. Chia Grass Cat Planters allow you to grow your own chia grass at home. Cats love nibbling on it—as do dogs, rabbits, guinea pigs, birds, horses, cows, sheep, and goats. You might want to get two!

A SPRINKLE OF CHIA GOES A LONG WAY

Most dogs love chia seeds—they will often try to eat them straight from the bag. And a quick sprinkle of about 1 teaspoon of chia over dry or canned food is a fine way to give your pooch the chia it loves. That said, most dogs (and cats) digest chia much better when it has been soaked first, hence the chia gel called for in so many of these recipes.

CHIA DOG FOOD

MAKES ENOUGH FOR 1 SERVING

As dogs get older, their coats get dull. Some animals become prone to skin conditions, and frankly, they begin to smell on the strong side. A daily dosage of chia can help keep fur gleaming, skin supple, and odors to a minimum.

*1   serving of canned food (half or more of a
     12-ounce can)*
1   tablespoon chia gel (see recipe, page 421)

1. Mix chia gel into the canned food until thoroughly mixed.
2. Serve immediately.

HORSE CHOW

MAKES ENOUGH FOR 1 SERVING

Omega fatty acids do wonderful thing to hair, skin, and nails—or hooves, in the case of horses. They also improve joint health, helping older animals and workhorses feel more comfortable.

⅔ cup alfalfa or grass pellets
⅓ cup chia seed

1. Place the pellets in a trough, on the ground, or in a feeder.
2. Pour chia seed on top.

CHIA-EQUINE GUIDELINES

Age, type, gender, daily routine—all of these play a part in determining which diet will work best for a horse. If you're a horse owner, you know what works or doesn't work for your particular animal, but here are a few easy chia guidelines:
• Try offering chia to your horse five days a week.
• Feed ⅓ cup chia (about 2 ounces) to each horse on pasture or maintenance.
• Feed ⅔ cup chia (about 4 ounces) to each horse on a dry lot or stalled with hay.
• Experiment with ⅔ cup of chia when feeding young, growing horses, pregnant horses, seniors, rehabilitating horses, or competition horses.

LIVESTOCK FEED

MAKES 1 SERVING

This nourishing recipe is great for cows, goats, and sheep—all ruminants, a word that comes from the Latin ruminare, which means "to chew over again."

¼ cup chia seeds per each goat or sheep; 1 cup chia seeds per cow
Regular serving of hay or grain or food pellets

1. Sprinkle or pour dry chia seeds directly over the food that your animals regularly eat.

SUPER MILK

Giving chia to cows, goats, and sheep chia is an easy way to enhance the milk they produce with omega fatty acids and other nutrients found in chia seeds. Whether it is consumed as milk or made into yogurt, sour cream, cheeses, or other dairy products, this enhanced milk is becoming a popular way for the food industry to meet consumer demands for enhanced dairy products.

CHAPTER 6

STAYING HEALTHY WITH CHIA

One of the reasons chia is such a wonder food is that it truly does offer something to just about everyone, whether you're young, old, or middle-aged, male or female, a couch potato or an elite athlete. Chia can help you overcome illnesses and help prevent them. It can even make your hair grow better!

In other words, chia is about much more than weight loss. This chapter lets you in on all the conditions that can be helped and even prevented with a daily dose of chia.

CANCER

Regardless of the type of cancer, the condition starts when the DNA within a single cell mutates, then replicates, creating more mutated cells. Soon these fast-moving, mutating cells begin invading healthy tissue—this is how cancer spreads. This mutation can be caused by a genetic mistake or by exposure to radiation or a carcinogen. Some cancers are slow-moving, easily caught, and easily treated. Others are stealthy and fast—by the time a person knows he or she has cancer, it is almost too late.

One or two tablespoons of chia a day can help both prevent cell mutations, as well as slow already-mutating cells, making conventional cancer therapies more successful. How? It all has to do with chia's high levels of antioxidants. These phytonutrients help supercharge and protect cells from DNA damage. They also help damaged cells repair themselves. Among the cancer-fighting antioxidants in chia are: Vitamins A, C, and E, chlorogenic and caffeic acids, myricetin, quercetin, and kaempferol flavonol, chlorogenic acid, and flavonol glycosides.

Omega-3 fatty acid also helps fight and prevent cancer. In 2007, researchers at the Universidad Nacional de Córdoba, in Córdoba, Argentina, studied the effect of this fatty acid on breast cancer tumors. The findings, which were published in the July 2007 issue of *Journal of Prostaglandins, Leukotrienes and Essential Fatty Acids*, showed that the omega-3 fatty acid in chia helped shrink existing tumors and prevent metastasizing.

CANCER FACTS

- Lung cancer is one of the most preventable types of cancer.
- There are over 100 kinds of cancer.
- Any body part can be affected by cancer.
- A third of cancers can be cured if detected early and treated adequately.
- Tobacco use is the single largest preventable cause of cancer in the world.
- More than 70 percent of the world's cancer deaths occur in middle- and low-income countries.
- 8.4 million Americans alive today either have cancer or have had it in their past.
- Once a person quits smoking, it will take him or her 10 years to replace all the precancerous cells in his or her body.
- Worldwide, the five most common types of cancer that kill women are (in the order of frequency): breast, lung, stomach, colorectal, and cervical.
- Remission is a sign that cancer cells may have already been eliminated.
- Not all cancers develop into tumors.
- When cancer cells spread to other parts of the body, it is called metastasis.
- Symptoms of cancer are: weight loss, tiredness, or exhaustion, fever, and swollen glands.
- Worldwide, the five most common cancers among men are (in order of frequency): lung, stomach, liver, colorectal, and esophagus.
- One-fifth of all cancers worldwide are caused by a chronic infection. For example, the human papillomavirus (HPV) causes cervical cancer and the hepatitis B virus (HBV) causes liver cancer.
- The most common cancers diagnosed in the Unites States are: bladder cancer, breast cancer, colon cancer, lung cancer, melanoma, kidney cancer, pancreatic cancer, leukemia, thyroid cancer, and prostate cancer.
- 90 to 95 percent of cancer cases are due to lifestyle as well as environmental factors, and the rest of the 5 percent are due to genetics.
- More than 30 percent of cancer cases could be prevented, mainly by not using tobacco, having a healthy diet, being physically active, and preventing infections that may cause cancer.

I am a breast cancer survivor, but that's not why I first went on chia. I first tried chia a couple years ago after going through chemically-induced menopause brought on by radiation and chemotherapy. I just found that I wasn't as sharp as I used to be. I felt as if my brain was constantly in a fog, my memory was fading, and I was so scattered. I assumed these were symptoms of menopause. A friend told me about chia, which she was giving her son for ADHD symptoms. I tried it and after a couple weeks, felt more focused, more quick-witted.

As for the cancer, it is two years later and it hasn't returned. I'll continue to take chia to help keep my brain and cells healthy.

— ROBIN HANDLY, Brooklyn, NY

CARDIOVASCULAR CONDITIONS

Heart disease—also known as cardiovascular disease or CVD—affects one out of every four Americans each year (about 57 million people). It encompasses several related conditions of the heart, arteries, and veins, all of which supply oxygen to life-sustaining areas of the body such as the brain, the heart itself, and other vital organs. Here's an easy way to think about it: if an organ or tissue doesn't get the oxygen it needs, it will die.

Hypertension is a form of heart disease, as is stroke, arrhythmias (irregular heartbeats), angina (chronic chest pain), coronary artery diseases (atherosclerosis or clogged arteries, caused by a narrowing of the arteries or a buildup of cholesterol and other substances), and heart attacks.

Most cardiovascular diseases are caused by lifestyle choices—and thus can also be prevented and even treated with healthier lifestyle choices. Consuming chia daily is a lifestyle choice—and a good one, if you want to ward off, lessen, or help treat heart disease.

Very few formal studies have looked at chia's heart-health benefits, although this is changing. In a 2007 study from the University of Toronto, researchers fed 21 diabetics either a supplement made from chia or grains with a similar fiber content. After three months, blood pressure in patients taking chia dropped (10 points diastolic, 5 points systolic) while the grain group's blood pressure remained steady. Furthermore, researchers found that blood-clotting factors dropped 20 percent and levels of C-reactive protein, a marker of inflammation in heart disease, fell 30 percent.

Research at Oxford University, and at the University of Sydney, in Australia, and published in 2003 in the *European Journal of*

Nutrition, found a correlation between high flavenol intake and low heart disease mortality rates. Flavenols are antioxidants found in some plant foods, and are especially high in chia.

The March 2011 issue of *Journal of Nutritional Biochemistry* highlighted an Australian study from the University of Queensland, which found that the alpha-linolenic acid in chia seeds help reduce cardiac inflammation and fibrosis (thickening of the heart valves) in rats that ate a chia-enhanced diet for eight weeks.

It's tempting to list study after study, but suffice it to say that chia is chock-full of substances that can help protect your heart against cardiovascular disease. All you need are just two tablespoons a day.

HEART DISEASE FACTS

- Coronary heart disease is the most common type of cardiovascular disease (CVD).
- More than 50 percent of heart attack sufferers wait two hours or more before seeking help.
- Brain death from cardiac arrest can be experienced in just four minutes.
- A person with a family history of heart disease is ten times more likely to have cardiovascular disease.
- A diet high in fat and carbohydrates will increase the risk of blood clotting.
- About 47 percent of sudden cardiac deaths occur outside a hospital. This suggests that many people with heart disease don't act on early warning signs.
- Risk factors for a heart attack are high cholesterol, high blood pressure, sedentary lifestyle, obesity, poor diet, diabetes, high alcohol consumption, and smoking.
- Heart disease is the leading cause of death for both men and women.
- In 2010, heart disease cost the United States $316.4 billion. This total includes the cost of health care services, medications, and lost productivity.
- Every year about 785,000 Americans have a first heart attack. An additional 470,000 Americans who have already had one or more heart attacks have another attack.
- About 82 percent of people who die of coronary heart disease are 65 or older. At older ages, women who have heart attacks are more likely than men are to die from them within a few weeks.
- Smokers' risk of developing coronary heart disease is two to four times that of nonsmokers. People who smoke a pack of cigarettes a day have more than twice the risk of heart attack than people who've never smoked.
- Exposure to other people's smoke increases the risk of heart disease even for nonsmokers.

HEART DISEASE: OTHER WAYS TO HELP YOURSELF

Consuming chia regularly is a fantastic way to keep your cardiovascular system healthy. But there are plenty of other things you can do to ensure things run smoothly:

- Lower stress. While medical researchers don't know exactly how stress increases the risk of heart disease, they do know it contributes to poor cardiovascular health. When you are under stress, it is common to experience a rise in blood pressure, poor eating habits, and reliance on alcohol and cigarettes to self-soothe. Also, the stress hormones adrenaline and cortisol, which are released when you are stressed, can increase the risk of heart attack.

- Stop drinking. Over-drinking can raise the levels of fats (triglycerides) in the blood. Alcohol can also lead to high blood pressure, higher calorie intake (which can in turn contribute to obesity), and heart failure—or, in the case of binge drinking—a stroke. A few glasses of wine a week probably won't hurt you, but try to keep your weekly intake down to five servings or less.

- Cut out cigarettes. Chemicals in tobacco can damage your heart and blood vessels, leading to narrowing of the arteries. Called atherosclerosis, the condition hinders the passage of oxygen and can ultimately lead to a heart attack. The nicotine in cigarettes is also dangerous, making your heart work harder by narrowing your blood vessels and increasing your blood pressure. Furthermore, the carbon monoxide in cigarette smoke replaces some of the oxygen in your blood. This increases your blood pressure by forcing your heart to work harder to supply your body with enough oxygen.

- Get enough sleep. Poor sleep has been linked with high blood pressure, atherosclerosis, heart failure, heart attack and stroke, diabetes, and obesity. Though it's not understood exactly how lack of sleep and CVD are connected, researchers believe inflammation may be the culprit.

- Lose weight. Most people gain weight as they age, which is natural. However, being overweight forces your heart to work harder than it should; it also increases the chance you'll have high cholesterol and high blood pressure.

- Exercise. Physical activity helps you control your weight and can reduce your chances of developing other conditions that may put a strain on your heart, such as high blood pressure, high cholesterol, and diabetes. It also reduces stress, which may be a factor in heart disease.

- Eat a heart-healthy diet. When eating a heart-healthy diet, think farm, not factory. Whole, natural foods—vegetables especially—are at the core of a heart-supportive eating plan. The American Heart Association espouses "DASH," which stands for Dietary Approaches to Stop Hypertension. This includes eating plenty of plant foods, making sure that foods are low in cholesterol, fat, and salt, and going easy on animal products.

continues>

- Surround yourself with positive people. Several studies suggest that having a strong social network may help protect against heart disease. A study by the University of Minnesota in Minneapolis, looked at nearly 15,000 men and women between 1999 and 2002, and found that those who go to church and social clubs, and have a lot of friends and relatives, have significantly lower blood pressure and other heart disease risk factors than loners.
- Get a pet. A 10-year study of more than 4,435 Americans, aged 30 to 75, by researchers at the University of Minnesota's Stroke Institute in Minneapolis, found that owning a pet could reduce your risk of a heart attack by nearly one-third. It is believed that pet ownership helps people cope with, and overcome, daily stress.

My wife and children have been taking chia for a year. My wife began taking it when she started running marathons, and as her running partner, I see how much more endurance and strength she has—especially toward the end of a run. I also see how much faster my children's nails grow and that they seem more calm and focused when taking chia regularly. You'd think I would have jumped on the chia wagon with them, but I didn't begin taking it until I was diagnosed with hypertension. My blood pressure reading was 150 over 90. I came straight home from the doctor's office and pulled out the bag of chia, taking my first taste. I committed to taking 2 tablespoons every day. Now, three months later, my blood pressure reading is 120/80 and I hope to get it down even lower in the next few months.

—DANIEL KENNEDY, Costa Mesa, CA

CHOLESTEROL

Cholesterol is on everyone's mind these days. Is yours high? Is it low? What is good cholesterol? What is bad cholesterol?

Before we get much further, let's talk about what cholesterol is. For you biochemistry buffs, cholesterol is a steroid alcohol produced by the liver. In fact, cholesterol is the most prominent steroid in the human body. This waxy substance helps the body manufacture hormones, vitamin D, and substances (such as bile), that help you digest foods. Your body makes all the cholesterol it needs.

However, bodies sometimes manufacture excess cholesterol. Or, they get additional cholesterol from animal foods. Because cholesterol cannot dissolve, your body may have more cholesterol than it can use. Trying to tidy itself up, the body shunts the unneeded cholesterol against artery walls, where it builds up, making arteries more and more narrow. Soon, oxygen-rich blood struggles to pass through these cluttered veins. (Just think of the hallways in your home. What would happen if you started stacking your unused stuff along the hallway walls. Soon, the hallways would be so cramped, you wouldn't be able to move through them.) The result is a number of cardiovascular diseases, including high blood pressure, stroke, and heart attacks.

Excess cholesterol can usually be managed with a few well-chosen lifestyle changes. The easiest is eating less animal foods, which contain cholesterol. Regular exercise boosts blood circulation, strengthens the heart muscle, and can help dislodge cholesterol buildup. Cutting out cigarettes and cutting down on alcohol (two things that also leads to cholesterol buildup) also helps.

Then there is chia, a wonder ingredient for lowering cholesterol levels. Though there have been no formal studies on the effects of chia on human cholesterol, studies in rats have shown that chia seed reduces blood fat and increases good cholesterol levels.

Furthermore, the alpha-linolenic acid in chia has been shown to reduce fat build up

My daughter was hounding me to eat chia to help lower my cholesterol but I thought she was crazy. Finally I said 'I'll show you—it won't work'. I started putting a tablespoon of chia in my orange juice every day and changed nothing else. In 60 days my cholesterol went down by 40 points. Now it is the lowest it has ever been at 150.

—PETER WIERCINSKI, submitted online to azchia.com

in arteries by lowering cholesterol levels. According to the American Heart Association, diets high in alpha-linolenic acid—the essential omega-3 fatty acid—have been associated with a 70 percent drop in coronary heart disease, compared with typical American diets that are low in this important omega-3 fatty acid.

Aim for two tablespoons of chia a day. If you are on medication, talk to your health care provider before consuming chia, just to be safe. However, there have been no known of complications or problems with chia.

> *Chia makes me feel great—full of energy and lowered my cholesterol significantly!*
> —DIANE SEARS,
> submitted online to azchia.com

GOOD CHOLESTEROL, BAD CHOLESTEROL

There are two types of cholesterol. One is called low-density lipoprotein. Think of this as "lousy cholesterol." The other type of cholesterol is called high-density lipoprotein. Think of this as good cholesterol. Whether it is lousy or good cholesterol, it cannot dissolve. Ideally, it hangs around the body only as long as it is needed to help create hormones and vitamins that assist with certain bodily processes. Once it's done what it is supposed to do, it heads to the liver, where it is passed from the body.

Lousy cholesterol, however, likes to hang out and party. It doesn't want to leave. It wants to stay and cause trouble. True, a few troublemakers in life are unavoidable. It's when you have too many that things get difficult. Enter good cholesterol. These conscientious workers do their jobs, swoop over, and strong-arm the LDL cholesterol to the liver, where they all leave the body together. If you don't have enough HDL cholesterol to help rid the body of troublemaking LDL cholesterol, you've got a problem—one that can be fixed with a combination of lifestyle interventions (diet and exercise) and possibly medication.

CHOLESTEROL FACTS

- Approximately one in every six adults—16.3 percent of the U.S. adult population—has high total cholesterol. The level defined as high total cholesterol is 240 mg/dL (milligrams per decilitre) and above.
- People with high total cholesterol have approximately twice the risk of heart disease as people with optimal levels. A desirable level is lower than 200 mg/dL.
- For adult Americans, the average level is about 200 mg/dL, which is borderline high risk.
- High blood cholesterol usually has no signs or symptoms. Thus, many people don't know that their cholesterol levels are too high.
- The American Heart Association recommends that daily dietary cholesterol intake not exceed 300 mg.
- Other names for high cholesterol are hypercholesterolemia and hyperlipidemia.
- More women than men have high cholesterol in the United States. The National Cholesterol Education Program recommends that all adults have their cholesterol levels checked once every five years.
- New Zealand has the highest per capita death rate from heart disease.
- Atherosclerosis, the clogging of arteries that can lead to heart attacks and strokes, can start before birth.
- One in five American teenagers has elevated cholesterol levels.
- Most of the cholesterol in your body is made in your liver, using saturated fat from your diet. Cholesterol also comes directly from some foods such as eggs, meats, and dairy products.

DIABETES

You've probably heard that diabetes is on the rise. You may even know that diabetes has something to do with blood sugar. But what, exactly is diabetes? And what causes it? Diabetes is considered a metabolism disorder, a glitch in the way our bodies use digested food for energy. You see, much of what we eat is broken down into a special type of fuel called glucose, a type of sugar found in the blood, and used by the body to fuel every bodily function.

The thing about glucose, however, is it cannot enter our cells alone. It needs to be escorted into cells by a special hormone called insulin.

Diabetes occurs when a person doesn't have enough insulin to escort the glucose into cells. This is called Type 1 diabetes. Or when a person consumes too much, creating more glucose than the body can handle. Or even, in some cases, when a body's cells simply ignore the insulin when it shows up with glucose. These are known as Type 2 diabetes. In all instances, the result is the same: too much glucose sitting around in the blood, unused, waiting to be utilized.

Like most illnesses, diabetes has signs. Some of the most obvious are frequent urination (when there is too much glucose—sugar—in your blood you will urinate more often in order to dilute it), urgent thirst, intense hunger, weight gain (or, in some instances, unusual weight loss), increased fatigue, irritability, blurred vision, cuts and bruises that don't heal well, an increase in skin infections, yeast infections, itchy skin, swollen gums, frequent gum infections, sexual dysfunction in men, and numbness or tingling in hands and feet.

Fortunately, all types of diabetes are treatable: Type 1, mainly by injectable insulin, plus some dietary and exercise adherence; Type 2, with exercise and a special diet, though in more severe cases insulin injections may also be required.

Chia can help both types of diabetes by slowing the rate of carbohydrates' conversion into sugar, thus helping to maintain healthy blood sugar levels. Chia gel surrounds carbohydrates during digestion, slowing their release into the blood stream and helping to moderate blood sugar levels. In a 2007 study performed at the St. Michael's Hospital in Toronto and reported in *Diabetes Care* magazine, 20 subjects with Type 2 diabetes were given 37 grams of chia seed a day (that's roughly three tablespoons) for 12 weeks. Not only did the chia help control blood sugar, it reduced the subject's risk markers for cardiovascular disease by lowering blood pressure, and reducing harmful LDL cholesterol and triglycerides, while increasing beneficial HDL cholesterol.

Further, a five-month study at the University of Litoral in Santa Fe, Argentina, found that rats that ate a high-sugar diet were less likely to suffer from insulin resistance when they consumed daily chia than control rats that were not given chia.

THE IMPORTANCE OF MANAGING DIABETES.

If you think you have diabetes, it's important to see a medical professional and create a treatment plan—hopefully one that includes chia! If diabetes is not adequately controlled you run the risk of developing complications, including erectile dysfunction, hypoglycemia, ketoacidosis, cardiovascular disease, retinal damage, chronic kidney failure, nerve damage, poor healing of wounds, gangrene on the feet, which may lead to amputation, and ultimately coma.

I have Diabetes Type 2, which developed shortly after I hit the 200-pound mark. I'm 5'5", so this is a lot of weight to carry! My doctor prescribed insulin, told me to take a daily walk, cut out junk foods and simple carbohydrates, and lose 50 pounds. I ended up working with a holistic health counselor to really make sure I did this for myself. She suggested two tablespoons of chia seeds every day. My doctor thought I was crazy when I asked him about it, but told me to go ahead.

In two month's time, I have lost 27 pounds, have so much more energy to exercise and to just get through the day, and have reduced the amount of insulin I take by about 25 percent. I now give chia to my two daughters, just to keep them well, and my husband, who has diverticulitis. Even my own father has begun taking it to help with his hypertension.

—MELINDA SHANNON, 43, Jersey City, NJ

DIGESTIVE HEALTH

Irritable bowel syndrome, diverticulitis, constipation, and other digestive ills—the symptoms differ—are caused by one thing: a poorly-functioning large intestine, usually caused by lack of fiber. These common ills are thought to affect more than one-third of adults under the age of 45, half of Americans between the ages of 46 and 80, and two-thirds of Americans over the age of 80. That's a lot of people! Not only do digestive conditions make individuals feel miserable, they compromise nutrient absorption, contribute to fatigue and sluggishness, and in severe cases, contribute to colorectal cancer.

That's because when partially digested food spends a lot of time in the large intestine, bile acid gets re-absorbed, bad bacteria grows unchecked and good bacteria is smothered, harmful toxins build-up in a crowded colon and can even be absorbed by the body.

While chia has not been researched specifically for digestive issues, fiber has. Several studies in the U.S. and the European Union

PSYLLIUM VS. CHIA

If you've been taking psyllium to get your daily dose of insoluble fiber, here's good news: You can go with chia and get not only fiber, but omega-3, antioxidants, and protein. To obtain the same amount of soluble fiber as found in a gram of psyllium, however, you need to consume approximately 20 grams of chia, which will bring to about 7.18 grams of insoluble fiber, and 1.07 grams of soluble fiber to boot.

have found that 20 to 35 grams of fiber a day keeps digestion regular and lowers risk of colorectal cancer. (The average American adult gets less than 15 grams daily.) Chia contains about 5 grams of fiber per tablespoon. Three tablespoons per day are enough to improve digestive health and comfort.

And yet the fiber in chia definitely aids in keeping the large intestine moving things along efficiently and easily. But roughage isn't the only thing at work. Chia, which is highly hydrophilic, brings moisture to the large intestine. As it moves through the colon, it "irrigates" the intestine, keeping the contents moist and malleable.

FATIGUE

Chia had many uses among the Aztecs, who were the first to document its use. One of the most important ways they used the seed was as an energy booster and endurance aid. Story after story has emerged from the Aztec codices (see page 353) on how their warriors, traveling messengers, and athletes sustained themselves on a daily spoonful of chia and a measure of water. In Christopher McDougall's book, *Born to Run*, he talks to the possible descendants of the Aztecs, native people living in Mexico's Copper Canyon. These super athletes are famous for their 100-mile (or longer) runs, fueled by nothing more than chia seed and water.

How does chia boost endurance? A few ways, probably. Chia is hydrophilic, meaning it helps the body retain moisture, guarding it against energy-sapping dehydration, as well as protecting joints from the wear and tear of intense physical activity.

The seed's high nutrient profile also helps sustain energy. With a wide range of protein, vitamins, minerals, amino acids, fatty acid, and antioxidants, chia delivers the nutrition body systems need to run efficiently at peak performance, as well as the omega-3 fatty acid needed to quickly repair itself.

I have taken chia over 3 months now and can tell you that it provides me with stable energy, appetite suppression, and better digestion. The amount of Omega-3 is so good for my clarity and focus daily as a business coach and mentor.

—JACOB ROIG,
submitted online to azchia.com

INFLAMMATORY CONDITIONS

Inflammation is a hot word in health circles these days, and with good reason. Recent research has found that inflammation at the root of a host of illnesses, and some scientists theorize that inflammation is the very thing that causes aging. Heart disease, arthritis, acne, asthma, allergies, food sensitivities and intolerances, pelvic inflammatory disease, inflammatory bowel disease, and autoimmune system diseases are just a few examples of inflammatory disease. They occur when some of the body's cells (different conditions involve different cells) are irritated by something—maybe bacteria, a virus, a chemical, or even dramatic change in temperature. The affected cells react by swelling. Blood floods the area, trying to send healing oxygen to the aggrieved cells. Plasma leaks into the area, making it swell further. All the activity may raise the temperature of the cells. In some cases, the swelling spreads to affect other parts of the body.

Soon the immune system is working overtime, either adding to the cells' angry response or trying to calm them down. This large expenditure of energy takes the body's energy away from its normal body systems, maintenance, and other functions. The result is fatigue, immune system dysfunction, in some cases a chronic condition, and even cancer in other cases.

Chia can help. Generous amounts of antioxidants help strengthen the immune system

> *I had terrible bursitis, which I chalked up to age and a lifelong love of tennis. Last year I began taking one tablespoon of chia a day to help my nails grow longer. I know, vanity! But an interesting thing happened. My bursitis lessened. I upped my dose to 3 tablespoons a day and the pain completely left. I am chia's biggest fan!*
>
> —LORNA SEHR,
> Minneapolis, MN

and prevent cells from over-reacting in the first place. The high levels of omega-3 fatty acid in chia help decrease inflammation, normalizing the affected area.

IMMUNE SYSTEM FUNCTION

Any time you get a cold, a flu, or a virus, you can blame your immune system. This fascinating body system is in charge of keeping out foreign invaders—from parasites and bacteria to toxins and microbes—that may make you sick. It's also in charge of getting you well, should an invader have snuck in and wrought havoc on your health. If the virus or bacteria is able to reproduce and start causing problems, your immune system is in charge of eliminating it. The immune system also has several other important jobs. For example, your immune system can detect cancer in early stages and eliminate it in many cases.

Comprised of the thymus, spleen, lymph system, bone marrow, white blood cells, antibodies, and hormones, this complex system responds exquisitely to antioxidants—something chia has in generous amounts. Antioxidants strengthen the immune system, allowing it to protect you and battle invaders even more quickly and aggressively. The alpha-linolenic acid in chia also fortifies the immune system.

IMMUNE SYSTEM FACTS

- The skin is a barrier that stops many germs from entering the body.
- The thymus is a gland in the chest, which turns ordinary white blood cells into special T-cells that fight harmful microbes.
- Some scientists believe that excess sugar decreases your body's immunity.
- Mucus lines your airways and lungs to protect them from smoke particles, as well as from germs. Your airways may fill up with mucus when you have a cold, as your body tries to minimize the invasion of airborne germs.
- The adenoids in the nose are one of the body's defense centers, releasing cells to fight infections.
- If you get a throat infection, the tonsils release cells to fight it.
- Did you know gum disease weakens the immune system? Flossing and brushing daily are easy ways to increase immune system function.
- Lymph glands in your groin often swell up as the body fights an infection.
- Sebaceous glands in the skin secrete an oil that is poisonous to many bacteria.
- Studies have shown that sleep, sex, laughter, calming music, and moderate exercise help fortify the immune system.
- Itching, sneezing, coughing, and vomiting are your body's most common ways of ousting unwelcome invaders.
- Small particles that get trapped in the mucous lining of your airways are pushed out by tiny hairs called cilia.
- Certain white blood cells are cytotoxic, which means that they are poisonous to invaders.
- The spleen not only destroys worn-out red blood cells, it also helps make antibodies and phagocytes.
- White blood cells called phagocytes are drawn to the site of an infection whenever there is inflammation. These cells swallow up invaders and then use an enzyme to dissolve them.

My daughter began taking chia to help calm and focus her. What I noticed, however, is that as we approached cold and flu season, she never got sick. I used to have to keep her home at least twice a year for various colds, but since starting a tablespoon of chia each day, she hasn't had a single sick day.

—TRACI WALKER, Reno, NV

BRAIN & NERVOUS SYSTEM HEALTH

The nervous system is in charge of keeping you calm, cool, and collected. But sometimes the nervous system doesn't work as well as it should. The result is depression, ADHD, anxiety, stress, and a host of other mood and behavior disorders.

Medication is an option for those suffering from severe nervous system conditions. But for many people, regular exercise, sleep, and an upgrade in nutrients is enough to put them back on course. Chia is a great help under these circumstances. Research has shown that deficiencies in omega-3 fatty acids are contributing factors in many mood disorders, depression among them. One of the most-cited studies is an eight-week trial conducted in 2010 at McGill University in Montreal. It found that omega-3 supplements helped about half the patients with major depression.

Indeed, the omega-3 fatty acids in chia have been shown by other studies, as well, to nourish the brain and help create a sense of calm and focus. Chia's minerals and B-vitamins also lend a sense of calm focus while helping the nervous system to work more efficiently. Tryptophan, also found in chia, is an amino acid that helps the brain create serotonin and melatonin, two feel-good neurotransmitters.

I didn't begin taking chia for anxiety, but found it to be a wonderful help. I started to take it because my running coach suggested it. I noticed a big difference in my knees and hips after longer runs. I also noticed I was less reactive to stress at work and in my marriage. It gave me a kind of 'go with the flow' outlook that other people have commented on. My nails look great, too!
—MELINDA KOONS, Chicago, IL

I began to give chia seed to my eight-year-old standard poodle mix, who had come down with a flaky, itchy skin condition as he aged. My vet said the omega-3s in chia would help heal his skin and give him a nicer coat. She was right. But what we didn't expect was to see a softening of his disposition. He had always been a high-strung, slightly nervous dog, but about three weeks into the chia, we noticed that things he once reacted to didn't seem to bother him as much. He's been a much more pleasant dog—to look at, and to be around.
—BOB DOOLEY, Albany, NY

SKIN, NAILS, AND HAIR HEALTH

Skin is our largest organ—and one of our most visible markers of health. Skin is our greatest detoxifying organ, helping to release harmful substances from the body. It's also an important member of the immune system, working to keep pathogens and other invaders out.

When we're healthy, our skin is smooth, clear, and bright. When something is off—maybe we're not metabolizing nutrients the way we should, aren't getting enough sleep, or are suffering from some kind of illness—our skin gets oily, flaky, spotty, bumpy, sallow, splotchy. In other words, our skin doesn't look good.

Our fingernails, toenails, hair, eyebrows and eyelashes are appendages of the skin, meaning that whatever nourishes the skin, nourishes them. One of the nutrients that skin absolutely loves, is omega-3 fatty acids. Chia is full of them, in the form of alpha-linolenic acid, which improves skin by reducing any inflammation that can be causing spots, bumps, or acne. Chia's hydrophilic qualities draw moisture to the skin and hair, making them soft and supple. Chia's minerals harden nails and encourage hair and skin cell growth. At the same time, chia's high volume of antioxidants protect skin and its appendages from the ravages of bacteria, fungi, viruses, parasites, and environmental toxins, all of which can change the way skin looks and grows.

Chia has been a tremendous help in keeping my skin inflammation under control. It is a great relief to use an all-natural food that works effectively, every day, eliminating the need for prescription steroid creams.
—LAUREN ROSEMOND,
submitted online to azchia.com

I had been eating chia for some time, but felt I could increase my intake easily by adding chia to my morning milk. It was not long until I noticed my hair was shinier and more easily managed. In fact my hair stylist made a comment on a recent visit that she noticed my hair was shinier and healthier.
—PATRICIA WIERCINSKI,
submitted online to azchia.com

HOW TO USE CHIA FOR BETTER SKIN

Whether you've got acne or wrinkles, chia can help your skin look better. The easiest way to tap into the looks-enhancing power of chia is simply by eating it. Try one or two tablespoons a day to start. If you've battling a stubborn skin condition, try three tablespoons a day. Of course, chia also can do wonders when placed on the skin. Opt for chia oil, or make your own chia skincare products (see pages 471–474 for more information).

I have been using chia for about a year now. What a difference. I am a lot more calm. I can sleep. My cholesterol and blood pressure are great! My hair and nails are growing stronger and faster. I would recommend this to anyone, especially if you are starting menopause.
—MAUREEN SILVA,
submitted online to azchia.com

SUPER
SEEDS

KIM LUTZ

CONTENTS

When I was in college and in my early twenties, I bought into all the hype about the benefits of eating low-fat processed foods and "lite" treats. I must have consumed gallons of chemicals, thinking I was doing the right thing for myself! Little did I know that these foods are actually devoid of any real nutrition. In fact, some manufacturers load up their products—cereals and crackers, for example—with processed sugars and sodium to make them palatable, and use refining processes that actually strip nutrient-rich bran and germ from whole grains, leaving behind only the starchy remainder of the grain.

To improve their image, these manufacturers frequently spray or augment heavily processed foods with a few vitamins and minerals to make the nutritional information panel on their packaging sound appealing. Without fiber, micronutrients, and phytochemicals, however, these products lack the blocks that actually help build healthy bodies.

It was not until the birth of my first child, in 2002, that I became fully aware of the noxious chemicals hidden inside seemingly healthy foods. Within months of my son's birth, it became clear that he had some serious health problems. After much testing and trial and error, we discovered that he has multiple food allergies, a world that we had to learn to navigate quickly, and one that requires a very close reading of food labels, it turns out. When you really look at the long lists of ingredients—many of which are unpronounceable and include scary chemicals—in so many "lite" and "healthy" foods, you can get a powerful shock, especially if you've been eating them on a regular basis, as I had been.

After the food label epiphany, I started really thinking about what I was buying and cooking. To keep my son safe from foods that could harm him, I needed to be careful about what I prepared for him, but I also wanted our whole family to be better nourished. This motivated me to do a lot more home cooking, using a greater variety of fruits and vegetables, whole grains, and legumes. As a result of this experimentation I started feeling better, too—better than I'd ever felt, in fact!

Some of my friends and family who were still eating more standard American foods, however, asked me how my two children could possibly thrive on such a "limited" diet, without meat and dairy products and so few processed and refined convenience foods. When we dined with other people, it seemed to them that we were eating very few things, but in reality our new whole-foods diet had introduced us to an incredible bounty of ingredients that I'd discovered in natural food stores, ethnic markets, and farmers' markets. Rather than shriveling up, my family was flourishing on our new diet.

One of the best and most enduring discoveries I made during my family's journey to healthier eating is a class of seeds that are now being referred to as "super seeds," which includes chia, quinoa, flax, hemp, and amaranth. In my kitchen, these versatile, nutritional powerhouses have found their way into just about every meal and snack of the day, including my family's morning smoothies and even some of our favorite desserts. Super seeds are not only rich in protein and fiber, they also provide a good source of vitamins, minerals, and phytochemicals, including iron, manganese, calcium, and omega-3 and omega-6 fatty acids. I'm confident that once you start experimenting with these tiny, delicious seeds, you'll find them indispensable.

Keep reading and see for yourself!
Kim Lutz

CHAPTER 1

THE POWER OF SUPER SEEDS

Super seeds are itty-bitty powerhouses that aren't just loaded with nutrients, they are popular, versatile players in the kitchen, whether you're enjoying quinoa as a side dish or tossing some flaxseed meal into a batch of breakfast muffins. Super seeds bring something nourishing and delicious to the table every day and at every meal. This chapter explores the astonishing nutrient profiles and health benefits of chia, quinoa, flax, hemp, and amaranth seeds. They all deliver dozens of vitamins and many minerals, plus fiber, antioxidants, fatty acids, amino acids, protein, and much more. Here you'll discover just how powerful these little seeds truly are.

OPPOSITE: **Hemp field**

NUTRITIONAL BENEFITS OF SUPER SEEDS

Our bodies need a range of nutrients to thrive. Luckily, super seeds provide a rich nutritional profile that can translate into vibrant health. Super seeds are wonderful sources of plant protein, which is crucial to cell health throughout the body and helps build strong muscles. Because these powerful little seeds come from plants, all of them are cholesterol-free and low in saturated fat, unlike animal-based protein sources, which have been linked to heart disease and other ailments.

Super seeds make their nutrition available to almost everyone, including people on a restricted diet. And, because they are all naturally gluten free, super seeds are not likely to cause allergic reactions.

WATER TO THE RESCUE

One of the many benefits of super seeds is their high fiber content. Dietary fiber absorbs liquid in the digestive tract and causes a slower release of the sugars found in food (even natural foods, such as grains, fruits, and seeds). While there are many benefits associated with a higher fiber diet, such as improved digestion, weight control, and more stable blood sugar, eating a higher fiber diet requires plenty of water. If you are following a high-fiber diet, be sure to drink a good amount of water (6 to 8 cups a day is a good goal) so that you are effectively flushing out your system. If you drink too little water, all that fiber can absorb the liquid in your system and cause you to feel bloated and uncomfortable.

WATER SOLUBLE B VITAMINS

Super seeds are rich in B vitamins (including, thiamine, folate, and vitamin B6). B vitamins are water soluble, meaning that our bodies take what they need from them and then excrete the rest in our urine. A great way to ensure that you are getting enough B vitamins for healthy cell function, energy, and overall good health, is to eat dishes containing super seeds, such as the recipes in this book.

CHIA

The nine essential amino acids in chia make it a high-quality source of protein. One ounce (a little less than 2 tablespoons) of chia delivers a whopping 11 grams of fiber and 4 grams of protein. It's the dietary fiber in chia that helps make it so filling. Many people are turning to chia to achieve or maintain a healthy weight. The fiber in chia keeps you feeling full and allows for a slower breakdown and absorption of food. Chia also can contribute to strong bones with healthy doses of calcium, phosphorus, and manganese.

WHAT IS OLD IS NEW

Chia, or *Salvia hispanica*, is a member of the mint family. Historically, it was grown and consumed in Mexico, where it fueled the Aztec Empire for centuries. The powerful nutrition provided by the tiny seed (protein, minerals, and fiber) supplied long-distance runners and warriors with a superb, long-lasting source of fuel, and today it remains a reliable source of energy.

* * *

THE BEAUTY OF GOO— USING SOAKED CHIA

Although chia seeds are tiny they can get stuck in your teeth, and because they absorb nine times their weight in water, they can get gooey pretty quickly. This can feel very weird! This absorptive quality is a benefit to cooking, though, because chia seeds mixed with water become gelatinous. Be sure to give chia seeds a good soak if you are using them to replace eggs. Soak them for at least 10 minutes in water, and make sure to stir the mixture so that there are no dry seeds. You can also grind chia seeds in a nut and seed grinder or a clean coffee grinder before using them. If you use chia seeds in a smoothie, be sure to blend them in well.

QUINOA

There's a reason this South American seed is at the top of so many superfood lists. One cup of cooked quinoa has 8 grams of complete protein and 5 grams of dietary fiber. Amino acids are the building blocks of protein. Essential amino acids are the amino acids that must come from our food, since our bodies are unable to produce them. Quinoa is rich in several of these essential amino acids, making it an excellent source of plant-based protein. Since quinoa is cholesterol-free and also full of fiber, it is a healthy alternative to animal-based sources of protein, including meat and cows' milk. In addition, quinoa contains more than 10 percent of the dietary recommended daily allowance for a wide range of vitamins that includes thiamin, riboflavin, vitamin B6, and folate, and it is packed with minerals such as, iron, magnesium, phosphorus, zinc, copper, and manganese

A SUPER START FOR BABY

Amaranth and quinoa porridge are wonderful first solids for babies because they are not likely to cause an allergic reaction, they cook up smooth, and are easy to sweeten naturally. Try mixing in mashed banana or sweet potato. You may end up eating more of this porridge than your baby!

* * *

THE SOFT SIDE OF QUINOA FLOUR

Quinoa flour can have a grassy taste and aroma. A little bit of it mixed into a flour blend can complement a dish, depending on the other flavors. If you're not crazy about the "grassiness" of the flavor, however, you can toast quinoa flour by spreading it on a rimmed baking sheet and heating it in a 225°F oven for 2 to 3 hours. (You don't need to stir it while it's heating.) You'll know it's done when the grassy smell is gone.

FLAX

Ground flaxseed is an excellent source of fiber (each tablespoon contains about 8 grams) as well as a good source of magnesium, phosphorus, copper, thiamin, and manganese. Also, since flax can be used to take the place of eggs, it is particularly helpful to folks who need to watch their intake of dietary cholesterol. In fact, all five super seeds are cholesterol-free. Whole flaxseed is encased in a very tough exterior, however, making it indigestible unless it is ground. Because it can pass through the digestive system intact, however, some people use whole flaxseed as a laxative. In addition, flax—and hemp seed, as well—is a very good source of plant-based omega-3 fatty acids, which play a role in protecting against inflammation and high blood pressure.

FLAXSEED VS. FLAXSEED MEAL

The nutrients in flaxseed aren't accessible in their whole form, but if you grind the seed into meal, you'll get all the benefits— protein, fiber, and minerals. If you don't want to bother with grinding your own meal, no worries: You can easily purchase ground or milled flax at your local health food store and many mainstream grocery stores. Once you buy it, make sure it is tightly sealed and keep it in the freezer to keep it from turning rancid.

* * *

FLAXSEED AND YOUR FURRY FRIEND

Flax really is good for the whole family, including your favorite canine. Add a little flaxseed meal or flaxseed oil to dog food to help give your pooch a shiny coat and a healthy digestive system. Before you add flaxseed to your pet's diet, however, be sure to ask your veterinarian if it is a good supplement for your pet.

HEMP

Hemp seed is loaded with protein. Just one ounce (3 tablespoons) of shelled hemp seeds contains more than 10 grams of protein. You can eat either whole hemp seed or shelled hemp seed. I prefer shelled, or hulled, hemp seeds (also called hemp hearts) because they are easier to eat. (Although the hull also contains nutrients, it is fibrous, crunchy, and a bit hard to chew.) Hemp seeds taste nutty and have a nutty texture, and since they are seeds, they are a great alternative to nuts for people who are nut allergic. Not only are hemp seeds loaded with protein (2 tablespoons have 10 grams of protein) they are also a good source of other important nutrients including iron, magnesium, and zinc, all of which are crucial minerals for good health.

CAN HEMP SEEDS GET YOU HIGH?

Although hemp seeds are related to marijuana, they are not considered a drug because hemp seeds, and foods made from hemp, contain at most miniscule amounts of THC, the psychoactive component of marijuana. Healthy eating might make you feel good, but it's not the same "high" as from marijuana!

* * *

LOVELY IN HEMP

There are many reasons to look to hemp as a fabric of choice when choosing your clothing. Where conventional cotton uses huge amounts of pesticides to grow, hemp grows well in almost any climate without the need for extra pesticides and herbicides. Its roots can grow several feet deep, which helps promote healthy soil by preventing run-off. Not only is hemp fiber good for the environment, it makes for a very durable cloth, so your clothes can last longer, too!

AMARANTH

This seed truly is the king of all seeds when it comes to protein. One cup of cooked amaranth contains more than 9 grams of protein. Unlike a lot of other plant-based proteins, amaranth contains all the amino acids (the building blocks of protein) that we need, making it a complete protein. Amaranth is also a good source of fiber (5.2 grams per cup), unlike animal proteins. When you consider the vitamins and minerals that are packed into this grainlike seed, you can't help but be wowed. One cup of cooked amaranth contains more than 10 percent of the RDA (recommended daily allowance) of vitamin B6, folate, calcium, iron, zinc, copper, and selenium; and it is a fantastic source of magnesium, phosphorus, and manganese. And amaranth is gluten-free.

AN EARLY AMERICAN SEED MAKES A COMEBACK

Amaranth was a thriving crop and a staple of the Aztec diet hundreds of years ago, but when the Spaniards brought Catholicism to Mexico, it was banned because Aztec people used it (along with human blood) in the sacrifices they made to their gods. Because of amaranth's impressive nutritional profile—it's a rich source of high-quality protein, amino acids, iron, potassium, calcium, and manganese—efforts by the nonprofit group Mexico Tierra de Amaranto are now under way to bring this super seed back into gardens and kitchens, and onto dinner plates once again. The group is also focused on improving working conditions for rural Mexican farmers through amaranth cultivation.

VITAMINS, MINERALS AND OTHER IMPORTANT CHEMICAL ELEMENTS IN SUPER SEEDS

VITAMIN B6   B6 is necessary for more than 100 enzyme reactions and is involved in metabolism, brain development, and immune function.

FOLATE   A form of vitamin B, Folate is necessary for cell division and DNA synthesis.

CALCIUM   Calcium contributes to strong bones, helps muscles move, sends messages through the nerves, and helps blood circulation.

ZINC   Zinc helps the immune system fight off invading bacteria and viruses; it also helps heal wounds.

COPPER   Copper helps form strong and flexible connective tissue. It also plays a critical role in cellular energy production.

SELENIUM   Selenium is important for reproduction (a deficit may contribute to male infertility), thyroid function, and protecting the body from infection.

MAGNESIUM   Magnesium contributes to bone formation.

PHOSPHORUS   Phosphorus is important for bone health, DNA and RNA formation, and for oxygen delivery to body tissues.

MANGANESE   Manganese is a component of many essential enzymes that work with bone development, metabolism, and wound healing.

THIAMINE   Also known as vitamin B_1, thiamine helps our bodies convert carbohydrates into fuel. It also contributes to a strong immune system.

IRON   Iron is essential for a healthy body. It helps metabolize protein and contributes to healthy blood.

WHOLE FOODS SAVE THE DAY

Being selective about the foods you eat—avoiding processed foods, for example—is the most direct way to stay healthy. The removal of refined and unhealthy products from your diet will help ensure that your body has all the nutrients it needs to thrive. Here, again, super seeds play a superhero role.

The traditional Standard American Diet (SAD—and that's not only an acronym!) is replete with processed foods in which the nutrients have been stripped away. They might taste good and satisfy our hunger over the short term, but they don't provide what our bodies need to thrive over the long run. This is where super seeds step in to provide whole-food alternatives to overprocessed and nutritionally stripped-down foods. Quinoa, for example, cooks quickly and easily and makes an ideal substitute for white rice. In 15 minutes you can have a fluffy base for a stir-fry or main-dish salad. If you're looking for a healthy alternative to instant (and sugar-filled) hot cereals, make a pot of amaranth, keep it in the refrigerator in a sealed container, and warm it up with fruit and nondairy milk.

Are you looking for cholesterol-free egg substitutes for recipes? Look no further than chia or ground flaxseed! Chia seeds and flaxseed form a gel when they're mixed with water, making them an excellent substitute for eggs in both savory and sweet dishes—without the cholesterol and saturated fat! Of course, with the addition of chia or ground flaxseed—to anything you eat—you are also getting beneficial fiber.

Adding whole-food ingredients such as quinoa or amaranth flour to gluten-free flour blends will increase the nutrition of your baked goods. Many commercial all-purpose gluten-free flour blends rely on white rice flour and tapioca starch. Although these grains may provide an appealing texture, they are fairly devoid of nutrients. To address the nutritional deficit, mix in some protein-, fiber- and mineral-rich super seed flour. It's easy to substitute ¼ cup of quinoa or amaranth flour for ¼ cup of all-purpose gluten-free flour mix for each cup of flour you need. You don't want to trade out more than ¼ cup per cup, though, because the flavors of these flours can be a little overpowering.

Another whole food—hemp seeds—can literally be a lifesaver for folks who have nut allergies. Just as their name implies, hemp seeds are seeds and not nuts. Therefore, they are safe to serve, in every form and preparation, to people who are allergic to nuts and peanuts. The fat and protein profile in hemp seeds is similar to nuts. They're creamy when they're blended, they bake up nice and crunchy, and even add a dash of nutty flavor. Hemp seeds can also be combined with sunflower seeds or shelled pumpkin seeds (pepitas) for another variation on nut-free crunch. In addition, hemp seeds are a good substitution for nuts in nondairy milk and nut-butter recipes.

All-purpose flour, white rice, vegetable oil, and margarine dominate the Standard American Diet. Using super seeds to make small changes can transform favorite dishes into health-promoting meals, however. The recipes in this book show you how you can use whole-grain flours, seed flours, cooked amaranth and quinoa, chia gel, and flaxseed meal to create this nutrition revolution. Instead of relying on ingredients with stripped-away nutrition, you can use these easy-to-use seeds to

WHAT'S SO GOOD ABOUT FIBER?

Chia, quinoa, flax, hemp, and amaranth are all good sources of fiber. Why is fiber so necessary? For one, we need fiber in our diet because it plays an important role in our digestive health. Fiber adds bulk to food, which slows down the rate at which food is absorbed. This process makes it easier for waste to pass through the bowels and can even help play a role in regulating blood sugar (and lowering your risk of diabetes). Also, fiber helps you feel full after eating, which makes it less likely that you'll over-eat. Need another reason? Recent studies have shown that high-fiber diets can help lower cholesterol and therefore your risk of heart disease.

* * *

HOW MUCH PROTEIN DO I REALLY NEED?

Protein-rich super seeds can play an important role in a well-rounded diet. Protein is an essential component of cell health. The amount of protein you need often depends on a combination of factors, such as your age and lifestyle; whether you exercise frequently; or if you are trying to lose weight, etc. A good rule of thumb? About 15 to 20 percent of your calories should come from protein.

pump up the vitamins, minerals, protein, and fiber in every meal.

Any vegetarian can tell you that he or she is frequently asked, "Where do you get your protein?" Super seeds provides an answer. For example, just adding amaranth to polenta turns a comforting dish into a complete meal. Here's why: Although polenta—cornmeal that is boiled into a porridge and then prepared in various ways—is tasty all on its own, the protein in cornmeal does not contain a full range of amino acids. If you add amaranth to cornmeal, however, you will get all the benefits of a complete protein. Another way to give baked goods a nutrient boost is to swap out a percentage of ordinary cooking oil with fiber-, protein-, and mineral-rich flax seed meal. Cooking oil doesn't contain any protein or fiber, but if you replace some of the oil with flaxseed meal, you'll get a more nutrient-dense dish. Your cookies or muffins will not only be healthier for you, they'll have a richer, nuttier flavor as well.

At every meal, super seeds keep you energized, and also make a great mid-afternoon snack whenever you need a little extra push to get you through the day. If you love smoothies, try adding hemp, chia, or flaxseed to the mix for a super creamy drink that also gives you a healthy dash of fiber.

As a natural thickener, chia is the perfect, whole-food choice for making delicious jellies, syrups, and puddings without using nutritionally empty starches or animal-derived gelatin. And, since chia can thicken even cold liquids, it is ideal for raw food preparations. Instead of cranking up your stove and heating up the house on a hot day, use chia to thicken sauces and gravies. You can also use flaxseed to add both thickness and a nutritional boost to savory liquids.

The recipes in this book use whole grains and unrefined sweeteners, along with a colorful array of fruits and vegetables, and of course super seeds. With this combination of nourishing, delicious ingredients, every meal can be super!

Starting with basic preparations and moving through breakfasts, soups and salads, entrees, baked goods, and desserts, this cookbook can help you to transform your meals—and your well-being.

HELP FOR KIDS WITH CELIAC DISEASE

Lara Field, MS, RD, CSP, LDN, a pediatric dietitian who works closely with children diagnosed with celiac disease, has pointed out that "amaranth is a wonderful addition to a gluten-free diet, because it is a rich source of many vitamins and minerals, including vitamin B6, folate, iron, magnesium, phosphorus, and manganese," nutrients that are typically consumed in lower quantities with a gluten-free diet. Amaranth, however, is "a fantastic replacement," she adds, for missing B vitamins and iron.

* * *

SUPER SEEDS AND THEIR ROLE IN AMERICAN HISTORY

The Constitution and the Bill of Rights were written on parchment (an animal skin that has been prepared for printing or writing). However, since most paper at the time of the writing of these documents (1787) was made of hemp or flax, it is probable that early drafts of these important documents were written on the fiber of super-seed plants!

CHAPTER 2

BASIC SUPER SEED RECIPES AND PREPARATIONS

Many ingredient lists in this book include more than one seed in order to give the recipes an extra nutritional boost. This chapter covers everything you need to know about basic super seed recipes and the simple tools you'll need to use super seeds in various forms, whether it is flour, a seed butter, or nondairy milk. You'll also discover what to keep on hand to serve, store, and reuse basic super seed preparations.

OPPOSITE: Antique glass storage jars

EASY INTRODUCTIONS

Getting started with chia, flax, hemp, quinoa, and amaranth is practically effortless. You can begin by sprinkling flaxseed meal or shelled hemp seeds onto yogurt or fruit, or tossing some quinoa or amaranth into soup as it's cooking to add texture, protein, fiber, vitamins, and minerals—all of which are abundant in these tiny, nutritional powerhouses. You'll enjoy their nutty flavor and also be surprised by how quickly you'll feel the health benefits of including super seeds in your diet.

One of the easiest and tastiest ways to make super seeds a welcome addition to the family dinner table is to gradually replace rice with quinoa or amaranth. As you'll discover, super seeds are incredibly versatile and easy to work into just about every meal, including snacks and desserts. They are a bit like a blank canvas that you can color with an infinite variety of flavors. In this book, you'll find basic recipes for chia, quinoa, flax, hemp and amaranth. You'll also learn how to make a nut-butter alternative, a nondairy milk, and an egg substitute.

USEFUL KITCHEN SUPPLIES

Having some basic kitchen utensils on hand can help you make the most of cooking with super seeds. Here are some items I always have in my kitchen:

- Blender
- Food processor
- Nut and seed grinder or coffee grinder
- Strainer or fine-mesh colander (to rinse quinoa)
- Parchment paper (for easy baking cleanup)
- Sheet pans
- Muffin tins and cake pans
- Lidded saucepan (for cooking quinoa and amaranth)
- Large baking dish/lasagna pan (9 × 13)
- Clean jars with lids (to store bulk seeds, hemp milk, seed butters, etc.)
- Freezer-safe containers to store leftovers and keep flaxseed fresh (in the freezer for up to 6 months)

GRINDING YOUR OWN SEED FLOURS

Although you can purchase quinoa and amaranth flours that are already perfectly milled and ready to use, it's easy to use a clean coffee or nut grinder to transform quinoa or amaranth into a fine flour. More often than not, you'll see this method used to grind whole flaxseed into flaxseed meal. And if you want to use chia without the tapioca-like texture of soaked chia, you can grind the seeds into flour as well—a process that will yield a smoother gel when the flour is combined with water or other liquids. However, I prefer to use chia as an egg substitute (see Chapter 3); to make puddings, smoothies, and syrups; or almost anything that can be enhanced by chia seeds' gel-like properties. Hemp seeds are tiny, making them ideal to use whole or ground into a delicious butter (see Sunflower Hemp Seed Butter later in this chapter) or soak them in water to make a milk (see Hemp Milk later in this chapter).

* * *

HOW TO USE SUPER SEED FLOUR
WITH ALL-PURPOSE FLOUR

For every cup of all-purpose flour, substitute ¼ cup of seed flour. Keep in mind that using too much of a seed flour can significantly alter the texture and flavor of the finished product. Quinoa, and to a lesser extent amaranth flour, can have a grassy flavor, which you can improve by toasting the flour in a 225°F oven for 2 to 3 hours. It's important to keep in mind that seed flours are gluten-free. Gluten is the component of wheat flour that binds molecules together. So if you are baking with quinoa or amaranth flour, you will need to combine it with a gluten-containing flour or oat flour, which has similar properties to wheat flour, but can be gluten-free. Or you can use a gluten-free binder such as xanthan gum or guar gum. Otherwise, your baked goods will not hold together.

BASIC QUINOA

MAKES 2 CUPS

Quinoa seeds have a soapy, bitter-tasting coating (to keep birds from eating them), but a thorough rinse makes it is easy to remove the strong taste. Most quinoa sold in the United States is pre-rinsed, but if you have any doubts, just put it in a strainer and rinse the quinoa until the water runs clear.

> *2 cups water or broth*
> *Pinch of salt (optional)*
> *1 cup quinoa (rinsed, if necessary)*

1. Combine water or broth, optional salt, and quinoa in a small saucepan over medium-high heat and bring to a boil.
2. Cover, reduce heat, and simmer for 15 minutes or until the liquid is absorbed and the outer coat spirals off the quinoa. (The mixture will look like a lot of little commas.)
3. Fluff with a fork before serving.

BASIC AMARANTH

MAKES 3 CUPS

Amaranth is a smaller seed than quinoa, and it has a smoother texture when it's cooked.

> *3 cups water or broth*
> *Pinch of salt (optional)*
> *1 cup amaranth*

1. Combine water or broth, optional salt, and amaranth in a small saucepan over medium-high heat and bring to a boil.
2. Cover, reduce heat, and simmer for 25 to 30 minutes, or until liquid is absorbed.
3. Fluff with a fork before serving.

QUINOA GETS ITS 15 MINUTES OF FAME

The United Nations declared 2013 the International Year of Quinoa. (It is only the second food to earn a UN international observance. The first food was rice in 2004.) According to United Nations Food and Agriculture Organization Director-General José Graziano da Silva, quinoa can play an important role in eradicating hunger, malnutrition, and poverty. The International Year of Quinoa highlighted quinoa's strong nutritional profile and its ability to grow in arid conditions and varied temperatures, such as in Africa.

POPPED AMARANTH

YIELDS ABOUT ¼ CUP

Popping increases the volume by about 3 times, and popped amaranth will look like tiny kernels of popcorn. A great way to raise the nutritional profile of your breakfast is to mix ¼ cup popped amaranth with ¾ cup crisp brown-rice cereal and serve it with nondairy milk (a combination of hemp milk and almond milk, for example)—a tasty way to add more super seed goodness to your breakfast bowl. Add some sliced strawberries, and you have a tasty, filling, and nutritious to start to the day. I like to make several batches of popped amaranth one at a time, and then store it in a sealed jar for use over the next couple of days as a topping to sprinkle over yogurt or a salad or to eat straight from the jar. Delicious.

5 teaspoons amaranth seeds

1. Heat a large saucepan over medium-high heat.

2. When a drop of water immediately balls up on the dry pan surface, add amaranth seeds and distribute them evenly over the bottom of the pan in a single layer. Cover and turn off heat. Most of the amaranth will pop, though the unpopped seeds can still be eaten and will have a nice toasty flavor and crunch.

3. Pour the popped amaranth into a bowl and serve with a drizzle of olive oil and a sprinkle of salt.

AMARANTH'S RISING PROFILE

Over the next few years, you can expect amaranth to become as popular as quinoa—they're both very old, high-protein plants with roots in South America; and like quinoa, amaranth is a nutrition force to be reckoned with. Both are rich in quality protein, minerals, and fiber, and of course they're gluten-free. Among its many selling points, in addition to amaranth's super seed status, is its versatility in the kitchen—it is an easy and delicious ingredient to add to just about anything, from salads and stews to soups and desserts. Behind the push to bring amaranth into the spotlight is the Amaranth Institute, a nonprofit organization that acts to collect and disseminate information about amaranth.

SUNFLOWER HEMP SEED BUTTER

MAKES 1 CUP

Although you can enjoy hemp seed butter on its own, I prefer mixing it with sunflower seeds to make a creamier, earthier peanut butter alternative. You can also substitute almonds, cashews, or peanuts for the sunflower seeds in this recipe. For an alternative all-seed version of this delicious butter, replace the sunflower seeds with shelled pumpkin seeds (pepitas).

1 cup raw sunflower seeds
1 cup shelled hemp seeds
  Optional: Pinch of salt, to taste
  Optional: Drizzle of neutral oil, such as canola, grapeseed, or sunflower, to taste
  Optional: Dash of natural sweetener, such as maple syrup, to taste

1. Preheat oven to 350°F.
2. Spread seeds in a thin layer on a rimmed baking sheet.
3. Bake 5 to 10 minutes, until seeds are fragrant and slightly soft but not burned.
4. When the seeds have cooled, grind them into a paste in a food processor or blender, scraping down the sides as necessary, 5 to 10 minutes, or until a smooth, buttery consistency is achieved.
5. Scoop butter into a sealed container. Keep refrigerated for up to one week.

CHOCOLATE SUNFLOWER SEED–HEMP BUTTER

MAKES APPROXIMATELY ¾ CUP

You can drizzle a little water into this decadent-tasting spread if you would like a thinner consistency. Just be sure to blend it well. You can store this seed butter in a covered container in the refrigerator for up to one week.

1 pitted Medjool date
½ cup Sunflower Seed–Hemp Butter (see recipe at left)
1 tablespoon cocoa powder
½ teaspoon vanilla
  pinch of salt

1. Blend all ingredients in a food processor or blender until smooth.

HEMP PESTO

MAKES 1 CUP

Hemp's nutty texture and delicate flavor make it an ideal addition to various pestos, including this variation on classic basil pesto.

½ cup hemp seeds
4 cups basil leaves
½ cup olive oil
4 shallot cloves, minced
1 teaspoon salt
Freshly ground black pepper

1. In a dry skillet over medium heat, toast hemp seeds for 1 to 2 minutes, until seeds are fragrant.
2. Puree all ingredients in a food processor or blender.
3. Store in a sealed container in the refrigerator for up to 3 days.

HEMP MILK

MAKES APPROXIMATELY 6 CUPS

It seems as if the nondairy milk section of the grocery store expands every week. Although it's wonderful to have the option to buy so many products, there is nothing easier than making your own hemp milk. You can use this in any recipe that calls for nondairy milk. If you want to enjoy it as a beverage, try adding a little salt, sweetener and/or vanilla. By making your own nondairy milk you have complete control over the ingredients. Instead of a bunch of stuff you don't want (preservatives, additives, gums, etc.) you'll have a tasty beverage bursting with protein, iron, and magnesium. You can also change the taste of your hemp milk by blending it with another nondairy milk, such as almond or coconut milk.

1 cup hemp seeds
5 to 6 cups water (depending on how creamy you want the milk to be)

1. Blend all ingredients together.
2. Store extra milk in a sealed container in the refrigerator for up to 3 days. Shake before using.

CHAPTER 3

BREAKFASTS

Remember your mom saying that breakfast is the most important meal of the day? Whether one meal is really that much more important than any other is open for debate, but there is no question that adding super seeds to the first meal of the day is a sure way to get off to a good start. The fiber in super seeds will make you feel full so that you don't need to snack before lunch, while the protein and nutrients in these little powerhouses will fuel your breakfast with all the energy you need to accomplish whatever you set out to do.

OPPOSITE: **Carrot Sweet Potato Yogurt Smoothie, page 529, foreground; Vibrant Yogurt Smoothie, page 533, background**

BREAKFAST PANCAKES

MAKES APPROXIMATELY 16 PANCAKES

Pancakes are a favorite weekend breakfast for my family. You can dress them up with fresh fruit (blueberries or diced strawberries are nice) or even add chocolate chips to the batter! If you make a big batch of these pancakes on Sunday, you can wrap any leftovers in foil, pop them in the fridge, and toast them for a special (yet quick) Monday morning treat.

2 tablespoons chia seeds

6 tablespoons water

½ cup amaranth flour

2 cups white whole-wheat flour

¼ cup coconut palm sugar or evaporated cane juice

2 teaspoons baking powder

2 teaspoons baking soda

¼ teaspoon salt

2½ cups Hemp Milk (page 523) or other nondairy milk

1 teaspoon vanilla extract

2 teaspoons neutral-tasting oil (canola, grapeseed, or sunflower)

1. In a large bowl, combine chia seeds and water. Set aside.

2. In a medium bowl, combine flours, sugar, baking powder, baking soda, and salt with a whisk.

3. Add nondairy milk, vanilla, and oil to chia mixture. Combine well.

4. Slowly mix dry ingredients into wet mixture. Stir until just combined.

5. Lightly oil a skillet or griddle. Heat over medium heat until a drop of water dances across the surface.

6. Pour approximately ¼ cup of the batter onto the skillet or griddle. Cook until bubbles form in the middle of the pancake.

7. Flip the pancake and cook until both sides are golden brown.

8. Repeat with remaining batter. Don't overcrowd the pan; make sure there is space around pancakes while they cook.

EVAPORATED CANE JUICE:
A SWEETENER THAT'S A LITTLE LESS REFINED

Evaporated cane juice is a sugar made from sugar cane that has been crushed and strained. The liquid is then boiled to evaporate the water, leaving sugar crystals behind. These crystals are less refined than table sugar, and retain small amounts of vitamins and minerals that were present in the sugar cane and are lost in table sugar. The more minimal processing leaves the sugar with an amber cast not present in the more refined table sugar. Organic evaporated cane juice is produced from sugar cane that is grown in accordance with the USDA Organic guidelines. Although slightly more nutrient-rich than table sugar, you should still use sparingly and look to whole foods, like fruits, vegetables, and seeds for your vitamins and minerals, and use sugars of any kind for a sweet treat.

COCONUT PALM SUGAR VS. TABLE SUGAR

Coconut palm sugar is the dehydrated nectar of the flower from the coconut palm tree. Although there is some controversy about whether it is any "better" for you than other sweeteners, the trip from tree to table doesn't involve a lot of steps. In fact, it is one of the least refined sweeteners available. There is also some evidence that coconut palm sugar might be lower on the glycemic index than other sweeteners, but the jury is still out on this point. Coconut palm sugar has more nutrients than cane sugar, but unless you are consuming a lot of sweetener, it probably won't make that much of a difference in your nutritional intake. There are other reasons to consider it, however. Using traditional harvesting methods, the coconut palm tree can produce sugar for up to 20 years, making it a relatively sustainable sweetener. If you're curious about other natural, granulated sweeteners, give date or maple sugar a try.

BLUEBERRY CHIA SYRUP

MAKES 1 CUP

This syrup can be made with any of your favorite fruits. Adding chia to the mix thickens it to a stick-to-the-pancake consistency. Although you don't need to grind chia seeds for this recipe, the syrup will be smoother if you do. (See page 519 for information on grinding chia.)

1½ cups blueberries
½ cup water
2 teaspoons chia seeds
   Optional: Natural sweetener, to taste

1. In a small saucepan, combine blueberries and water. Bring to a boil.
2. Reduce heat. Simmer blueberries until they are soft enough to mash easily with a fork or potato masher.
3. Stir in sweetener, if using, until it dissolves.
4. Turn off heat. Stir in chia seeds. Let mixture rest for at least 10 minutes.
5. Stir again before serving.

IS WHITE WHOLE WHEAT HAVING AN IDENTITY CRISIS?

The question whether white whole wheat is a whole grain or a white (refined) one can finally be put to rest. It is a whole grain. Traditional whole wheat, with its tan color and hearty flavor, comes from red wheat. White whole wheat is lighter in texture and flavor and comes from a white wheat plant. When it is ground from the whole grain, the nutrients in the outer bran are kept intact as opposed to being stripped away, which occurs when the grain is processed for white all-purpose flour.

CARROT SWEET POTATO YOGURT SMOOTHIE

MAKES ABOUT 8 CUPS

This smoothie has a lovely peachy golden color. If your blender is not particularly powerful, you can grate the carrots first in a food processor, then add them to the blender. The amounts in the ingredient list are approximate, since carrots and sweet potatoes vary in size. Depending on how thick you want your smoothie to be, you may also want to adjust the amount of nondairy milk and apple juice.

1 sweet potato, peeled and baked

3 carrots, cut into chunks

¾ cup frozen pineapple chunks

¾ cup frozen mango chunks

2 tablespoons chia seeds

1 large dollop (about ¾ cup) nondairy vanilla yogurt

¾ cup Hemp Milk (page 523) or other nondairy milk

¾ cup apple juice

1. Put all ingredients into a blender and process until all ingredients are well blended.

NATURALLY SWEET SMOOTHIES

Of course you could add sugar to your smoothies to sweeten them up a bit, but depending on the season and the types of fruit that are available, your smoothie might not need any extra sweetness at all! If you do want a little extra blast of sweetness, however, try adding some of these naturally sweet ingredients—and toss the sugar!

• dates
• applesauce
• fruit
• stevia
• maple syrup

BLUEBERRY OATMEAL

MAKES 2 SERVINGS

It's so easy to customize your oatmeal with wholesome ingredients, you might never make instant oatmeal again!

- *¼ cup shelled hemp seeds*
- *½ cup rolled oats (also called old-fashioned oats, gluten-free if necessary)*
- *½ cup blueberries*
- *Drizzle of maple syrup*
- *Hemp milk or other nondairy milk, to taste*

1. Toast hemp seeds in a dry skillet over medium heat for a minute or two, until the seeds are golden brown.

2. In a medium saucepan, bring oats and 1 cup water to a boil.

3. Reduce heat and simmer 3 to 5 minutes, or until oatmeal is desired consistency.

4. To serve, garnish cooked oatmeal with toasted hemp seeds and blueberries.

5. Drizzle a little maple syrup over the top and add a splash of nondairy milk.

DID YOU KNOW...

Blueberries are not only in the same botanical family as cranberries and lingonberries—Ericaceae (Heath family)—they are also related to azalea, rhododendron, heather, and heath (hence the family name).

MANGO PINEAPPLE SMOOTHIE

MAKES 4 SERVINGS

Chia adds creaminess and keeps the ingredients from separating in this delicious, tropical-fruit-flavored smoothie. If you don't drink all of it at once, you can store the rest in a sealed jar in the refrigerator for a day. Just give the smoothie a quick shake before you drink it. It will be a little thinner the next day, but you can always blend it with a little ice to bring it back to the milkshake consistency of the first day.

- *1 cup frozen pineapple chunks*
- *1 cup frozen mango chunks*
- *2 carrots, peeled and grated*
- *2 teaspoons chia seeds*
- *½ to 1 cup apple juice*
- *1 to 2 cups Hemp Milk (page 523) or other nondairy milk, to taste, depending on desired consistency*

1. Put all ingredients into a blender and process until well blended.

PUMPKIN PANCAKES

MAKES 12 PANCAKES

Whole-grain oat flour makes these pancakes
sweet and pillowy—they are just as delicious
with gluten-free oat flour.

½ cup pumpkin puree (or canned pumpkin)

2 tablespoons maple syrup

1 cup Hemp Milk (page 523) or
  other nondairy milk

1 tablespoon chia seeds

1½ cups (gluten-free) oat flour

½ cup flaxseed meal

2 teaspoons baking powder

2 teaspoons baking soda

¼ teaspoon salt

¼ teaspoon nutmeg

1 teaspoon cinnamon

2 teaspoons neutral-tasting oil (canola,
  grapeseed, or sunflower)

1. In a large bowl, combine pumpkin puree,
maple syrup, nondairy milk, and chia. Set
aside for 10 minutes.

2. In a medium bowl, use a whisk to
combine oat flour, flaxseed meal, baking
powder, baking soda, salt, nutmeg, and
cinnamon.

3. Add dry ingredients to the wet mixture.
Stir to combine.

4. Lightly brush a skillet or griddle with oil.
Heat skillet or griddle over medium heat
until a drop of water dances on the surface.

5. Scoop batter onto the surface of skillet.
Cook until bubbles form in the middle of
the pancake and the edges are set.

6. Flip and cook until set on the other side.

7. Repeat steps with remaining batter.

DO OATS CONTAIN GLUTEN?

Gluten, the protein found in wheat, barley, rye, and spelt, binds molecules together and creates a
nice crumb. For people who cannot eat gluten, either due to celiac disease or gluten intolerance,
all gluten-containing grains must be avoided. Oats contain a protein (avenin) that acts like gluten
but is not gluten. For many people who need to avoid gluten, oats are safe to eat *if they are certified
gluten-free.* If you avoid gluten, it is important to check with your doctor before adding oats to your
diet, because the protein in oats can also be problematic for some people. In addition, almost all oats
and oat products that are not certified may contain gluten from other grains. This contamination
can happen at any stage from field to grocery store shelf. The certification process ensures that
gluten-free oats do not contain any gluten.

QUINOA SCRAMBLE

MAKES 2 SERVINGS

You can turn this simple scramble into a feast by serving it with muffins or millet rolls (page 583) and fresh fruit.

- *1 teaspoon olive oil (or less, if you use an olive oil spray)*
- *½ cup onion, diced*
- *1 cup sweet potatoes, peeled and diced*
- *½ cup mushrooms, sliced*
- *2 cups kale, deribbed and coarsely chopped*
- *1 cup Basic Quinoa (page 520)*
- *¼ to ½ teaspoon soy sauce, gluten-free tamari or coconut aminos (see note)*

1. Heat olive oil in a large skillet over medium-high heat.

2. Add onion and sweet potatoes. Cook, stirring over medium-high heat, for 2 minutes.

3. Turn heat down to medium and add mushrooms. Sauté, stirring, for 1 minute.

4. Add kale, cooking another 2 minutes, or until kale is wilted.

5. Add quinoa and soy sauce (or tamari or coconut aminos), and stir until combined.

6. Remove from heat and serve.

NOTE: Tamari is a wheat-free soy sauce and is appropriate for people following a gluten-free diet. Coconut aminos is a soy-free sauce that has a zesty, salty flavor.

FRUIT-SWEETENED GRANOLA

MAKES 4 CUPS

As soon as you discover how easy it is to make your own granola, you may never buy packaged cereal again!

- *1 cup rolled oats (also called old-fashioned oats, gluten-free if necessary)*
- *1 cup quinoa flakes*
- *⅓ cup shelled pumpkin seeds (pepitas), finely chopped*
- *¼ cup shelled hemp seeds*
- *¼ cup apple juice*
- *¼ cup date paste (see note)*
- *2 tablespoons coconut oil, melted*
- *1 teaspoon cinnamon*
- *½ cup raisins or other dried fruit*

1. Preheat oven to 350°F.

2. Combine oats, quinoa, seeds, apple juice, date paste, coconut oil, and cinnamon.

3. On a parchment-lined baking sheet, spread mixture in a thin layer.

4. Bake 15 to 20 minutes, or until golden brown.

5. When cool, combine mixture with raisins. Enjoy!

NOTE: To make your own date paste, pit and soak 6 Medjool dates for 15 minutes or more. Drain the softened dates and puree them in a blender. You can store date paste in a sealed container in the refrigerator for up to a week, or you can freeze it for up to 3 months.

VIBRANT YOGURT SMOOTHIE

MAKES 2 SERVINGS

You can prepare the beets for this delicious, gorgeously pink smoothie ahead of time. After you've cooked a batch, simply peel, chop, and freeze the beets until you're ready to use them. Watch out for the beet juice, though—it can stain your hands, clothes, dishtowels, and even your countertops. A little extra care is completely worth it, though, since beets are loaded with nutrition. They're a rich source of vitamins A, B, and C; folate; fiber; and minerals, including calcium and magnesium.

1 beet (see note)

1 cup frozen strawberries

1 teaspoon vanilla extract

1 cup vanilla nondairy yogurt

1 cup Hemp Milk (page 523) or other nondairy milk

2 teaspoons chia seeds

1 cup apple juice

1. Wrap beet in foil and bake in a 400°F oven for 45 minutes. Let cool.

2. Remove beet skin and stem. Cut into chunks.

3. Combine all ingredients in blender. Blend until smooth.

NOTE: You can prebake beets, then refrigerate them for up to 3 days; if you cut them into chunks, they'll keep in the freezer for up to 3 months.

CH-CH-CH-CHIA
Many people first heard the word "chia" as a stuttered song in TV commercials for Chia Pets in the 1980s. These chia-covered clay figurines were wildly popular novelty gifts that originally came in the shape of rams and bulls. Today, Chia Pets are available in a wide range of shapes. And yes, those chia seeds are the same kind that will boost your health!

SUPERFOOD SMOOTHIE

MAKES 2 SERVINGS

Kale, blueberries, hemp, and chia seeds all in one tasty drink? That's getting your day off to a super start!

- *3 large kale leaves, deribbed and torn into pieces*
- *1 cup apple juice*
- *1 cup frozen mango chunks*
- *1 cup frozen blueberries*
- *1 cup Hemp Milk (page 523) or other nondairy milk*
- *2 tablespoons chia seeds*

1. In a blender, combine torn kale leaves and apple juice.
2. Blend on high until kale is completely broken down and liquefied.
3. Add remaining ingredients and blend until smooth.

SMOOTHIES MADE EASY
One way to always be ready for the next super-seed smoothie is to freeze hemp milk in ice cube trays, and then transfer the frozen cubes to a freezer-safe bag or container. When you want a smoothie, just blend some fruit with the frozen cubes and enjoy!

STRAWBERRY BREAKFAST PUDDING

MAKES 4 SERVINGS

Why not make breakfast a little more fun? Pudding for breakfast feels decadent, but with probiotic-rich yogurt, vitamin C–packed strawberries, and a protein boost from chia, this treat will power your morning.

- *2 six-ounce containers of strawberry-flavored nondairy yogurt*
- *½ cup applesauce*
- *½ cup strawberries (fresh or thawed frozen strawberries)*
- *2 tablespoons chia seeds (see note)*

1. Combine all ingredients in a blender or food processor. Blend thoroughly.
2. Divide pudding among four dessert dishes, small bowls, or coffee cups.
3. Cover and chill overnight.

NOTE: If you'd like a smoother pudding, grind the chia seeds in a clean grinder before adding them to the blender.

QUINOA BREAKFAST BURRITOS

MAKES 4 SERVINGS

Cholesterol-free quinoa stands in for eggs in this savory breakfast entree.

> 1 cup quinoa, rinsed
>
> 1 cup water
>
> 1 cup Basic Salsa (page 541), divided
>
> 4 whole-grain tortillas
>
> 1 avocado, cubed
>
> 1 large tomato, seeded and cubed
>
> ½ cup plain nondairy yogurt

1. In a small saucepan, combine quinoa, water, and ½ cup salsa. Bring to a boil.

2. Reduce heat, cover saucepan, and simmer for 15 minutes, or until germ ring spirals off the seed.

3. Heat tortillas, one at a time, in a dry skillet over high heat.

4. On a flat surface or plate, spoon about ½ cup quinoa onto each tortilla and top with a portion of avocado, tomato, salsa, and a dollop of yogurt.

5. Fold the bottom of the tortilla up, then roll it from one side to form a cylinder.

WAFFLES

MAKES 10

If you wrap these waffles individually, they'll keep in the freezer for up to a month. Then all you have to do is pop one into the toaster for a quick, warm breakfast.

> 3 tablespoons chia seeds
>
> ¾ cup water
>
> ¼ cup coconut oil, gently melted
>
> 2¼ cup Hemp Milk (page 523) or other nondairy milk
>
> 2 cups white whole-wheat flour
>
> 1 teaspoon salt
>
> 2 teaspoons baking powder

1. Combine chia seeds and water in a medium bowl and set aside for at least 10 minutes (to form gel).

2. Preheat waffle iron to medium-high.

3. Blend together chia gel, coconut oil, and hemp milk.

4. In a large bowl, whisk together flour, salt, and baking powder.

5. Mix in wet ingredients.

6. Pour ¼ cup mixture onto hot waffle iron.

7. Cook until golden brown, approximately 5 minutes.

8. Repeat with remaining batter.

COCONUT QUINOA GRANOLA

MAKES 3 CUPS

To make this granola nut-free you can use sunflower seeds, or shelled pumpkin seeds (pepitas) instead of almonds. Granolas are a great take-and-go snack that provide post-workout protein and healthy fats.

1 cup quinoa flakes
1 cup rolled oats (gluten-free if necessary)
¼ cup hulled hemp seeds
⅓ cup slivered almonds
½ cup unsweetened coconut flakes
⅛ teaspoon salt
1 teaspoon cinnamon
¼ cup apple juice
¼ cup maple syrup

1. Preheat oven to 350°F.
2. In a large bowl, stir together all ingredients.
3. Spread the mixture in a thin, even layer on a large, rimmed parchment-lined baking sheet.
4. Bake for 15 minutes, stirring once half-way through, until granola is golden brown.
5. Place baking sheet on a wire rack and let granola cool completely before storing in an airtight container for up to 1 week.

CREAM OF AMARANTH

MAKES 1 SERVING

This is a delicious hot cereal that can be made nut-free by replacing the sliced almonds with toasted or raw hemp seeds.

½ cup Basic Amaranth (page 520)
¼ cup toasted almond slices (or ¼ cup shelled hemp seeds, toasted)
¼ cup raisins
¼ teaspoon cinnamon
Hemp Milk (page 523) or other nondairy milk, warmed, to taste

1. Scoop warm, cooked amaranth into a cereal bowl.
2. Add almond slices (or toasted hemp seeds, if using) and raisins.
3. Sprinkle with cinnamon.
4. Top with warmed hemp milk, or other nondairy milk, and serve.

> ### WHAT ARE QUINOA FLAKES?
> Quinoa flakes are quinoa seeds that have been steam-rolled into flakes, giving them the appearance of rolled oats. In fact, you can substitute quinoa flakes for quick-cooking or old-fashioned rolled oats in many recipes, such as oatmeal cookies and granola. Quinoa flakes are gluten-free.

APRICOT QUINOA PORRIDGE

MAKES 2 SERVINGS

Quinoa makes a lovely hot cereal when you cook it in non-dairy milk instead of water or broth. You can also substitute fresh peaches for the dried apricots.

½ cup quinoa, rinsed
1½ cups non-dairy milk
1 tablespoon maple syrup
¼ cup chopped dried apricots

1. Combine all ingredients in a small saucepan.
2. Bring to a boil.
3. Cover and reduce heat. Simmer for 15 minutes.

SUMMER COOLER SMOOTHIE

MAKES 2 SERVINGS

If you are using mature spinach or kale for this smoothie, cut out any tough stems before blending. You can always use fresh rather than frozen fruit in this smoothie, but you might want to blend in a few ice cubes, as well.

2 cups coconut water
1 cup baby spinach or baby kale
1 cup frozen pineapple
1 cup frozen blueberries
1 tablespoon chia seeds
1 tablespoon ground flaxseed

1. Blend spinach or kale with coconut water until greens are broken down.
2. Add remaining ingredients and blend thoroughly.

WHAT IS THE DIFFERENCE BETWEEN COCONUT WATER AND COCONUT MILK?

Coconut water is a sweet-tasting transparent liquid that is collected from young coconuts. Many athletes promote drinking coconut water as a natural alternative to sports drinks because it contains potassium and sodium, which can promote rehydrating after a hard workout. Coconut milk is made from the flesh of mature coconuts. It is much higher in calories and fat than coconut water: One cup of full-fat coconut milk has 445 calories and 48 grams of fat (though light coconut milk is also available), while one cup of coconut water has 46 calories and no fat. A highly versatile ingredient, coconut milk can be used in a wide variety of cooked and raw dishes as well as baked goods and smoothies.

CHAPTER 4

SOUPS AND SALADS

S oups and salads are truly versatile—as light fare on their own or as a heartier meal when served together. And, if you want to bring a healthier, more substantial dish than the usual fatty, cholesterol-laden offering to a potluck (or to rustle up on the weekend or a busy weeknight), the recipes in this chapter will supply a tasty selection of alternatives that capitalize on the many nutritional benefits that super seeds deliver: iron, calcium, manganese, and a host of vitamins. They will fill you up, too, thanks to fiber-filled quinoa, amaranth, and hemp, but they won't weigh you down.

OPPOSITE: **Massaged Kale Salad, page 543**

LEMON BASIL QUINOA SALAD

MAKES 5 SERVINGS

Fresh lemon juice, basil, and capers give this hearty but light salad a bright Mediterranean flavor. It pairs beautifully with Pesto Veggie Burgers (page 564).

- 1 cup haricots verts (French green beans), trimmed and cut into ½-inch pieces
- 1 cup cucumbers, peeled, seeded, and cut into medium dice
- 2 cups Basic Quinoa (page 520)
- 10 cherry tomatoes, quartered
- 2 tablespoons plus 1 teaspoon capers, rinsed
- 2 tablespoons thinly sliced basil
- 1 tablespoon fresh lemon juice
- 1 tablespoon olive oil
  Salt and freshly ground black pepper

1. In a large bowl, toss all ingredients to combine.

QUINOA BLACK BEAN SALAD

SERVES 8

A quick and easy way to give quinoa, amaranth, or rice a deeper, more complex flavor is to add salsa, fresh lemon juice, soy sauce, or tamari (a gluten-free alternative to soy sauce) to the cooking water. This salad makes a terrific, light summer lunch.

- 1 cup quinoa, rinsed
- 1 cup Basic Salsa (page 541)
- 1 cup water
- 1 teaspoon salt
- 2 tomatoes, seeded and cut into small dice
- 1 cup corn kernels
- 1 avocado, cut into medium dice
- 1 15-ounce can black beans, drained and rinsed (or 1¾ cups cooked black beans)
- 1 tablespoon freshly squeezed lime juice
- 2 tablespoons cilantro, chopped

1. In a medium saucepan, combine quinoa, salsa, water, and salt. Bring to a boil. Cover, reduce heat, and simmer for 15 minutes.
2. In a large bowl, combine all ingredients. Serve chilled or at room temperature.

BASIC SALSA

MAKES 1½ CUPS

Why not make your own salsa and add the flavors and heat you like, instead of buying the premade commercial stuff? You can dress up this basic recipe by adding minced chipotle peppers for a smoky flavor, or ramp up the heat with jalapeño or serrano peppers.

3 medium tomatoes

½ medium red bell pepper, cut into small dice

¼ medium red onion, cut into small dice

1 jalapeño, seeded and minced

1 tablespoon apple cider vinegar

1 garlic clove, minced

¼ teaspoon salt

1. In a food processor, break down tomatoes (no need to remove seeds) into a chunky paste.

2. Add remaining ingredients, and pulse just until combined.

NOTE: Salsa will keep in a sealed container in the refrigerator for up to a week.

BLUEBERRY QUINOA SALAD

MAKES 2 SERVINGS

Any fruit spread or preserve will add natural sweetness to the dressing for this refreshing quinoa salad. Pair it with warm Whole-Grain Millet Rolls (page 583) for a light summer meal.

THE DRESSING

1 tablespoon all-fruit blueberry spread
2 teaspoons balsamic vinegar

1. In a small bowl, whisk together blueberry spread and vinegar.

THE SALAD

Mixed lettuces
3 to 4 basil leaves, thinly sliced
½ cup Basic Quinoa (page 520)
¼ to ½ cup fresh blueberries
Corn cut from one cob (cooked or raw)
3 tablespoons toasted shelled pumpkin seeds (pepitas) (see note)

1. In a large bowl, combine lettuces, basil leaves, quinoa, fresh blueberries, corn kernels, and pumpkin seeds.
2. Toss salad with dressing and serve.

NOTE: To toast pumpkin seeds (pepitas), heat for 1 to 2 minutes in a dry skillet over medium heat.

MASSAGED KALE SALAD

MAKES 2 SERVINGS

You can add any vegetables or fruits that you like to make this basic kale salad more complex. There is nothing basic, however, about kale's superfood nutrition profile, and its chewy, earthy taste makes it an exciting alternative to ordinary salad greens. This salad pairs beautifully with lasagna and makes a great meal to serve when you have company—it's easy to pull together so that you can spend more time with your guests.

> *4 cups raw kale, center ribs and stems removed, and torn into 1- to 2-inch pieces (or use 4 cups baby kale)*
> *Juice of ½ lemon*
> *3 tablespoons shelled hemp seeds*
> *1 medium tomato, chopped*
> *½ ripe avocado, cut into medium dice*
> *Salt and freshly ground black pepper, to taste*

1. In a large bowl, combine kale and lemon juice.

2. Massage the kale with your bare hands for several minutes, until the leaves are much more tender. (If you're using baby kale, you can massage the leaves just enough to coat with lemon juice, as they are already tender.)

3. Set aside for 1 hour or longer.

4. In a dry skillet, toast hemp seeds over medium heat for 1 minute.

5. Toss together all ingredients and serve.

THE MANY KINDS OF KALE

Although there is a wide range of kale varieties, three types—curly kale, Tuscan kale, and lacinato kale (also known as dinosaur kale)—are probably the most readily available at your local supermarket. You might find more exotic, heirloom varieties, such as red Russian kale, at your local farmers' market or roadside farm stand. No matter which variety you choose, your body will thank you for serving up this nutrient powerhouse: Kale is a rich source of fiber; vitamins K, A, and C; minerals such as iron, calcium, and potassium; and loads of phytonutrients.

KALE CHIPS

MAKES APPROXIMATELY 1½ CUPS

Kale chips don't qualify as a salad, but they are a convenient way to eat your greens. Combined with hemp seeds, which you can grind yourself, kale takes on a pleasing, nutty flavor and extra nutrition in this recipe. Because of their portability, kale chips are an ideal snack to throw into a picnic basket or lunch bag to ward off afternoon munchies—the healthy way.

¼ cup hemp seeds, ground

2 tablespoons nutritional yeast

1 teaspoon kosher salt

2 teaspoons smoked paprika

   Olive oil spray

4 cups kale leaves, torn and deribbed

1. Preheat oven to 150°F or the lowest setting your oven will allow (see note).
2. In a small bowl, combine hemp seeds, nutritional yeast, salt, and paprika.
3. In a large bowl, lightly coat kale with olive oil spray (or drizzle with oil and toss).
4. Toss kale with seasonings.
5. Spread kale in a single layer on a parchment-lined baking sheet. Bake for 1 hour or until kale is crunchy but not burned, shaking halfway through the baking time.

NOTE: The long baking time at a low temperature is an easy way to achieve the desired level of dehydration without actually burning the chips and leaving your kitchen with a strong sulfurous smell.

GOLDEN CORN SOUP

MAKES 8 SERVINGS

Using an immersion blender in your soup pot makes this recipe one of the easiest comfort foods you can whip up. For an even silkier texture, puree it in batches in a standard blender. This soup's golden color brings a ray of sunshine (and vitamins A and C) into even the rainiest day! You can dress up this pretty soup with a simple garnish, such as a sprig or two of fresh thyme.

4 cups corn kernels, divided

2 carrots, peeled and cut into medium dice (approximately 1 cup)

1 small sweet potato, peeled and cut into medium dice (approximately 1 cup)

1 small or ½ large yellow bell pepper, cut into medium dice (approximately 1 cup)

1 onion, cut into medium dice (approx. 1 cup)

1 cup dry amaranth

8 cups water

1 teaspoon salt

1 teaspoon dried thyme or a few fresh thyme sprigs

1. In a large soup pot, combine 2 cups of corn with the balance of ingredients.
2. Bring to a boil.
3. Reduce heat and simmer for 45 minutes.
4. Blend mixture to a creamy consistency.
5. Add in remaining corn and reheat.

VARIETIES OF AMARANTH

Amaranth's vibrant colors and hardy disposition make it an excellent addition to home gardens, and it can be planted for decoration or eating. Varieties have either blonde or black seeds. Blonde seeds are preferred in cooked dishes, however, because black seeds can make for gritty eating. Some amaranth varieties have wonderfully evocative names like Elephant Head, Love Lies Bleeding, and Golden Giant.

QUINOA NOODLE SOUP

MAKES 6 SERVINGS

When you need a comforting bowl of soup to help you feel better if you have a cold or have had a bad day, this hearty soup fits the bill. (My son takes it to school for lunch in a thermos several times a week, cold or no cold!) The quinoa provides protein, the herby broth adds a feel-good hominess, and the vegetables lend vitamins and color.

¼ cup nutritional yeast

½ teaspoon dried parsley

½ teaspoon garlic pepper

½ teaspoon salt

½ teaspoon dried thyme

¼ teaspoon dried sage

6 cups water

1 bay leaf

1 medium onion, diced

3 carrots, peeled and thinly sliced

3 celery stalks, tops removed, and finely chopped

2 cups Basic Quinoa (page 520)

1 cup cooked small whole-grain noodles

1. In a small bowl, whisk together nutritional yeast, parsley, garlic pepper, salt, thyme, and sage.

2. In a soup pot, combine water, spice mixture, bay leaf, and vegetables. Bring to a boil, reduce heat and simmer for 20 to 25 minutes, or until vegetables are soft.

3. Add quinoa and noodles, and heat through.

4. Serve piping hot and garnish with a sprinkle of any fresh herbs you have on hand.

ALTERNATIVES TO CONVENTIONAL PASTAS

These days, there are many so many delicious alternatives to white-flour pastas, you could have a different one every day of the week. They're easy to find at the grocery store, too. Need a gluten-free option? Try quinoa-corn or brown rice pasta. Want a whole-grain wheat-based choice? Not a problem. Whole-wheat and spelt varieties are available. You can even use a vegetable peeler to make your own "pasta" by slicing thin ribbons from carrots or zucchini.

QUINOA LENTIL SOUP

MAKES APPROXIMATELY 10 SERVINGS

This filling, smoky-flavored soup is loaded with fiber and protein from both the lentils and the quinoa. If you are using thick carrots, cut them in half lengthwise before slicing them. Paired with a green salad, this makes a delicious and nutritious light supper or lunch.

- 1   tablespoon olive oil
- 2   carrots, peeled and thinly sliced
- 1   onion, cut into small dice
- 3   cloves of garlic, minced
- 1   teaspoon ground cumin
- 1   teaspoon smoked paprika
- 1   15-ounce can tomato sauce or crushed tomatoes
- 1   cup dried red lentils, picked over and rinsed
- 1   cup quinoa, rinsed
- 8   cups water
- 2   teaspoons salt

1. In a soup pot, heat olive oil over medium heat.

2. Add carrots and onion. Cook for 2 minutes, or until onion is softened.

3. Add garlic and cook for 1 more minute.

4. Add cumin and smoked paprika. Stir to distribute.

5. Add remaining ingredients. Bring to a boil.

6. Reduce heat to low, cover, and simmer 25 to 30 minutes, or until quinoa is cooked and lentils are soft.

ARE NUTRITIONAL YEAST AND BAKING YEAST THE SAME?

Nutritional yeast is a common ingredient in dairy-free cooking, because it has a savory, almost cheesy, flavor. It is a single-celled organism (*Saccharomyces Cerevisiae*) that is grown on molasses and then de-activated through drying. It is a good source of many nutrients, including many B vitamins – B_6, folate, and often B_{12} (which needs to be added to vegans' diets). It also is a good source of fiber, protein and zinc. Because nutritional yeast is deactivated, it won't help raise your bread dough, which relies on live yeast.

BLACK BEAN AND SWEET POTATO CHILI

MAKES 6 SERVINGS

This easy-to-prepare chili can warm up the coldest night. It's delicious served alongside a warm wedge of freshly baked Amaranth Cornbread (page 582). The tomatoes are also an excellent source of lycopene, an antioxidant that has been associated with prostate health—so serve it up with gusto the next time the guys come over to watch a game—or at any time, since this hearty chili is ideal for a quick, healthy meal.

  1 tablespoon olive oil

  3 medium onions, cut into medium dice (approximately 3 cups)

  3 medium garlic cloves, minced

  1 jalapeño pepper, ribs and seeds removed, minced

  1 medium sweet potato, peeled and cut into medium dice

  ¼ cup plus 2 tablespoons chili powder

  1 teaspoon ground cumin

  1 teaspoon dried oregano

  ½ teaspoon salt

  1 28-ounce can crushed tomatoes (3 cups)

  1 15-ounce can black beans, drained and rinsed (or 1¾ cups cooked black beans)

  1 cup Basic Quinoa (page 520)

1. In a large pot, heat olive oil over medium-high heat.

2. Add onions, garlic, jalapeño pepper, and sweet potato. Sauté approximately 5 minutes, or until vegetables are soft.

3. Add remaining ingredients, and bring to a boil.

4. Reduce heat and simmer for 20 to 25 minutes, or until heated through.

5. Serve with a warm wedge of Amaranth Cornbread.

TACO SALAD

MAKES 4 SERVINGS

For this salad, I use canned mild chilies, because it suits my children's palate, but you can add more heat by substituting hotter canned peppers or dicing up a fresh jalapeno pepper.

  2 cups vegetable broth

  2 tablespoons taco seasoning (see recipe on page 553)

  1 cup quinoa, rinsed and drained

  1 tablespoon olive oil

  1 cup chopped onion

  2 cups fresh, diced tomatoes

  1 cup chopped mild chilies, drained

  3 cups mixed lettuces

  1 medium red onion, chopped

  1 cup corn (either raw, cut from the cob, or defrosted frozen corn)

  ½ cup black olives, sliced

  ¼ cup fresh cilantro, chopped

  2 avocados, peeled and cut in ¾-inch chunks

  1 cup broken tortilla chips

  1 cup Basic Salsa (see recipe on page 541)

1. In a small saucepan, bring vegetable broth, taco seasoning, and quinoa to a boil. Reduce heat, cover, and simmer for 15 minutes or until liquid is absorbed and the seeds look like little commas.

2. In a medium skillet, heat the olive oil over medium-high heat. Add onion, one cup diced tomato, and chilies. Sauté until soft. Add prepared quinoa to vegetables. Stir to combine.

3. In a large bowl, combine lettuces, remaining tomato, red onion, corn, black olives, and cilantro. Toss to mix. Divide lettuce mixture into four bowls or plates. Top with quinoa mixture. Add avocado. Top with tortilla chips and salsa to taste.

CHAPTER 5

ENTREES

The entrees in this chapter will not only satisfy your soul as you sit down to a family dinner or a holiday feast, they will also provide a good portion of the day's nutrition. With their broad nutrient profiles, chia, quinoa, flax, hemp, and amaranth contribute to dishes that are satisfying, nourishing, and delectable. With their rich load of plant-based protein and all nine essential amino acids, amaranth and quinoa elevate simple dishes like potato cakes and polenta, and fillings for stuffed avocados and squash, from supporting roles to the stars of well-rounded meals

OPPOSITE: **Pesto Veggie Burger with Lemon Basil Quinoa Salad, page 564**

TACO-SEASONED QUINOA-STUFFED AVOCADOS

MAKES 2 SERVINGS

At first it might seem odd to heat fresh, ripe avocados, but once you do, you'll be hooked: Just a little warming gives avocados' delicate flesh a super creamy, smooth consistency—perfect for this taco-flavored dish. If you don't want to use commercial taco seasoning, try my recipe below. I think you'll like it. And don't forget the tortilla chips for a nice, accompanying crunch!

- 1 teaspoon neutral-tasting oil (canola, grapeseed, or sunflower)
- ¼ cup small-diced onion
- ½ cup diced tomatoes (fresh or canned)
- 1 tablespoon commercial taco seasoning (If using unsalted taco seasoning, add ½ teaspoon salt) or Kim's Basic Taco Seasoning (opposite)
- 1 cup Basic Quinoa (page 520)
- 1 ripe avocado
- 2 lime wedges

1. Preheat oven to 350°F.

2. In a medium skillet, heat oil over medium heat.

3. Add onion, tomatoes, and taco seasoning. Cook 2 to 3 minutes, or until onions are soft.

4. Add quinoa, stirring to combine. Remove from heat.

5. Halve avocado and remove pit. Scoop out avocado flesh with a spoon, leaving a ¼-inch border.

6. Chop flesh. Gently mix with filling.

7. Spoon half of the filling into the peel of an avocado half. Repeat with remaining filling.

8. Bake, filling-side up, for 10 to 12 minutes.

9. Remove from heat. Drizzle with fresh lime juice before serving.

KIM'S BASIC TACO SEASONING

MAKES APPROXIMATELY 1 CUP

It's easy to rustle up a batch of your own taco seasoning to have on hand whenever a recipe calls for it. The nice thing about making your own spice blends is that you can adjust the flavorings to suit your taste.

½ cup chili powder

¼ cup onion powder

⅛ cup cumin

1 tablespoon garlic powder

1 tablespoon paprika

1 tablespoon sea salt

1 tablespoon oregano

Optional: ½ teaspoon cayenne pepper

1. Put all ingredients in a jar or container with a tight-fitting lid. Shake well to combine. Store, well sealed, in the pantry for up to 3 months (not that it will last that long!).

AMARANTH-STUFFED ACORN SQUASH

MAKES 2 SERVINGS

This recipe for stuffed acorn squash makes a festive, meat-free main dish that tastes so good you won't want to wait long to make it again. Serve the stuffed squash with a bright green salad (or any additional veggies that are in season), along with a fresh batch of warm Amaranth Biscuits (page 584) to round out the meal. Feel free to replace the almonds with shelled pumpkin seeds (pepitas), if you want to avoid using nuts.

1 acorn squash

1 tablespoon olive oil

½ cup diced onion (approximately ½ onion)

2 tablespoons diced, dried, unsulphured apricots

¼ teaspoon smoked paprika

¼ teaspoon ground cinnamon

½ teaspoon salt

2 tablespoons chopped raw almonds or shelled pumpkin seeds

1 cup Basic Amaranth (page 520)

TO PREPARE THE SQUASH

1. Preheat oven to 350°F.

2. Cut squash in half lengthwise. Scoop out seeds.

3. Lay squash facedown in a rimmed baking dish or pan.

4. Add water until it's halfway up the sides of the squash.

5. Bake for 1 hour. Remove from oven without turning off the heat.

TO MAKE THE STUFFING

1. Heat olive oil in a large skillet over medium heat.

2. Add onion and cook for 2 minutes, or until onions are soft but not brown.

3. Add apricots, paprika, cinnamon, and salt. Cook for 1 to 2 minutes.

4. Add almonds or pumpkin seeds, and stir to combine. Cook for another 2 minutes.

5. Remove mixture from heat and stir in amaranth. (If using amaranth that has been refrigerated, combine over heat for another 1 to 2 minutes.)

TO FINISH THE DISH

1. Scoop half of the filling into one of the squash halves.

2. Repeat with the other half of the squash.

3. Bake filling side up for 10 minutes.

4. Remove from oven and serve.

POTATO SCALLION PATTIES

MAKES 8 PATTIES

These crispy little fritters make a delicious light entree with a fresh green salad or roasted vegetables—they're also a great way to reuse leftover mashed potatoes.

> 3 *medium baking potatoes, peeled and cubed*
>
> 1 *cup Basic Amaranth (page 520)*
>
> 4 *scallions, white and light green parts, thinly sliced*
>
> 2 *teaspoons salt*
> *Freshly ground black pepper*
> *Olive oil spray*

1. In a large saucepan, cover potatoes with water and bring to a boil over medium heat.

2. Cook until potatoes are easily pierced with a fork.

3. Drain potatoes and place in a large bowl. Mash with a fork or a potato masher.

4. Add amaranth, scallions, and salt and pepper to potatoes. Mix well.

5. Lightly oil a skillet and heat until hot but not smoking.

6. Scoop out ¼ cup of potato mixture. Gently shape the mixture into a patty. Repeat with remaining mixture.

7. Sauté—in small batches so that they are not crowded in the skillet—for approximately 4 minutes per side, or until golden brown.

8. Keep patties warm in a 200–250 degree oven until all of them have been sautéed.

CAULIFLOWER HEMP CREAM LASAGNA

MAKES 6 SERVINGS

This lasagna is really satisfying. Depending on the texture you prefer, use a smooth tomato sauce for a silky lasagna or a chunky, vegetable-filled sauce for a heartier version. Gluten-free pasta can also be used, but what really makes this lasagna special is the cauliflower-hemp cream. Try pairing it with Massaged Kale Salad (page 543) for a complete meal.

- 3 cups pasta sauce of your choice
- 8 sheets of cooked whole-grain (or gluten-free) lasagna noodles (unless you are using "no-boil" pasta)
- 1 recipe Cauliflower Hemp Cream (recipe follows)

1. Preheat oven to 375°F.
2. Coat the bottom of a 9 × 13-inch baking dish with sauce.
3. Layer lasagna noodles on top of sauce, cover with cream, and repeat. Finish with sauce.
4. Bake, uncovered, for 40 minutes.
5. Remove from oven. Let stand 10 to 15 minutes before serving.

CAULIFLOWER HEMP CREAM

MAKES 4 CUPS

- 1 head cauliflower, stem discarded, chopped
- 2 tablespoons olive oil
- 1½ teaspoons kosher salt, divided
- 4 cloves garlic, peeled and smashed
- ½ teaspoon freshly ground black pepper
- 2 tablespoons nutritional yeast
- ½ teaspoon dry mustard
- 1 cup Hemp Milk (page 523)

1. Preheat oven to 425°F.
2. Toss together cauliflower, olive oil, 1 teaspoon salt, and garlic, then spread cauliflower on an ungreased baking sheet or a baking sheet lined with parchment paper.
3. Bake 20 minutes, or until cauliflower is tender.
4. Puree cauliflower with remaining ingredients, including remaining salt.

NOTE: You can use this savory cream as a topping for steamed vegetables and baked potatoes, or toss it with your favorite pasta. Store any extra cauliflower cream in a sealed container in the refrigerator for up to 3 days.

AMARANTH POLENTA WITH SAUTÉED MUSHROOMS

MAKES 6 SERVINGS

Polenta is a true comfort food that can easily be converted into a complete, protein-rich meal by adding amaranth and hemp milk to the cornmeal. Sautéed Mushrooms (recipe follows) beautifully complement the creamy texture of the polenta, but feel free to experiment with other toppings such as pasta sauce, sautéed greens, or anything else you can think of.

AMARANTH POLENTA

    3 cups Hemp Milk (page 523)
    ½ teaspoon salt
    ½ cup amaranth flour
    ½ cup medium- or coarsely ground cornmeal
    1 cup water
    ¼ teaspoon freshly ground black pepper

1. Bring hemp milk and salt to a boil.
2. Whisk in amaranth, cornmeal, and pepper; reduce heat to a simmer.
3. Add water. Stir to thoroughly combine.
4. Cook for 30 to 45 minutes, stirring the mixture regularly until it is very thick.
5. Keep polenta warm until ready to serve.

SAUTÉED MUSHROOMS

    2 tablespoons olive oil
    1 teaspoon dried oregano
    1 teaspoon dried thyme
    ¼ cup diced onion
    8 ounces cremini mushrooms, sliced
        (approximately 3 cups)
    1 medium tomato, diced (approximately
        1 cup)
    ½ teaspoon salt
    ¼ teaspoon freshly ground black pepper
    2 tablespoons fresh basil leaves, thinly sliced

1. In a large skillet over medium heat, heat oil and sauté oregano and thyme till the herbs give off their aromas.
2. Add onions, then sauté 2 to 3 minutes, or until onions are soft.
3. Add mushrooms, tomato, and salt and pepper. Cook, stirring over medium heat for 2 to 3 minutes, or until mushrooms are soft.
4. Transfer mushroom mixture to a serving bowl.
5. Dress each portion of warm polenta with a generous scoop of sautéed mushrooms and garnish with basil. Serve in warm bowls and enjoy.

BARBECUE BEANS

SERVES 4

This recipe gives you the slow-cooked flavor and texture of baked beans without the wait. Pureed sweet potato adds creaminess and sweet flavor, while a mere two tablespoons of chia transform the sauce into syrupy goodness. For a complete meal, serve these awesome beans with a thick slice of warm Whole-Grain Spelt and Amaranth Loaf (page 580) or a Whole-Grain Millet Roll (page 583) fresh from the oven. Don't forget the green salad!

- *1 tablespoon olive oil*
- *1 cup onion, cut in small dice*
- *½ cup pureed sweet potato*
- *2 tablespoons chia seeds*
- *½ cup barbecue sauce*
- *1 15-ounce can canellini beans, drained and rinsed*

1. In a sauté pan, heat oil over medium heat.
2. Add onion. Cook until soft.
3. Add remaining ingredients and cook until heated through.
4. Let beans rest for at least 15 minutes and stir before serving.

WHITE CHIA VS. BLACK CHIA

Chia seeds—white and black—are multipurpose stars in the kitchen with a very subtle flavor. There is no significant nutritional difference between white and black chia, although white seeds are more rare than black seeds and cost a bit more because of their rarity. Black or white, chia seeds have been touted as one of the most nutrient-dense foods available today, and they are used in myriad ways—to boost energy, assist in weight loss, and help regulate blood sugar. For the recipes in this book, there is no need to go out of your way to buy one color chia seed or the other—they'll turn out just fine no matter which chia seed you use.

EASY BARBECUE SAUCE

MAKES 1 CUP

This barbecue sauce is smoky-sweet, with just the right amount of heat. You can play with the flavor by experimenting with strawberry or even blueberry jelly or preserves instead of using grape jelly or preserves.

- *½ chipotle pepper in adobo sauce, minced*
- *1 15-ounce can tomato sauce*
- *2 tablespoons all-fruit grape jelly or preserves*
- *2 tablespoons apple cider vinegar*

1. In a small saucepan over medium heat, combine all ingredients and bring to a boil.

2. Reduce heat and simmer uncovered for 30 minutes. The sauce should be thick and reduced by about half.

3. Use immediately or store in the refrigerator in a tight-lidded container for up to 1 week.

CHAI-SPICED SWEET POTATO

SERVES 1

Sweet potatoes are excellent sources of Vitamins A and C. They are loaded with fiber and, surprisingly, they are not overly high in calories, despite their sweetness and rich texture. One large sweet potato averages only about 160 calories, making this unusual spiced tea–inflected recipe a filling, flavorful lunch that won't expand your waistline.

- *1 baked sweet potato*
- *1 to 3 tablespoons brewed spiced tea, such as chai*
- *2 to 4 tablespoons shelled hemp seeds*
- *salt to taste*

1. Scoop flesh from sweet potato and mash with a fork.

2. Gradually stir a little tea into the mashed sweet potato, until you have achieved the texture you desire.

3. In a dry skillet, toast hemp seeds over medium heat for 30 seconds or so, until fragrant but not burned.

4. Sprinkle hemp seeds and salt over the warm, mashed sweet potato and enjoy.

VEGGIE "MEATBALLS"

MAKES 40 BALLS

Commercial, frozen veggie meatballs can be filled with processed ingredients, but if you make your own, you can control what goes into the mix. You can also change up the flavor according to your preferences. Different spices, for example, can provide a different flavor profile altogether. Enjoy them in a sandwich, served with pasta, or all on their own! They are *so* good.

- *2 cups Rich Soup Base (opposite), vegetable broth, or water*
- *½ teaspoon salt*
- *1 cup kasha (roasted buckwheat)*
- *¼ cup flaxseed meal*
- *½ cup water*
- *8 ounces button or cremini mushrooms*
- *6 sundried tomato halves, softened in hot water*
- *2 tablespoons olive oil, divided*
- *1 15-ounce can garbanzo beans, drained and rinsed (or 1¾ cups cooked)*
- *1 large or 2 small cloves garlic, smashed*
- *1 teaspoon dried rosemary*
- *1 teaspoon dried oregano*
- *1 teaspoon dried thyme*
- *Freshly ground black pepper*

1. In a small saucepan, bring soup base (or broth or water) and salt to a boil.

2. Add kasha, reduce heat, cover, and simmer for 10 minutes, or until liquid is absorbed. Set aside.

3. In a small bowl, thoroughly mix together flaxseed meal and water. Set aside.

4. In a food processor, finely chop mushrooms and drained tomatoes.

5. Heat 2 teaspoons of olive oil in a skillet. Add mushrooms and tomatoes. Cook until liquid released from the mushrooms has cooked down.

6. While mushrooms are cooking, blend chickpeas and garlic into a paste.

7. In a large bowl, mix all components together, adding the herbs and freshly ground black pepper.

8. Chill mixture in the refrigerator for 30 minutes.

9. Preheat oven to 375°F.

10. Prep two baking sheets with remaining olive oil.

11. Roll meatball mixture into 1½-inch balls and place meatballs on prepared baking sheets.

12. Bake for 30 minutes, or until browned.

13. Let the meatballs stand for a few minutes before serving, since they will be fragile when first removed from the oven.

14. Serve in warm sauce or gravy.

RICH SOUP BASE

YIELD = 6–7 CUPS

Instead of using vegetable broth in your recipes, consider using a rich homemade soup base that will increase the fiber and nutrients in your food. It's easy to do: Just prepare a basic vegetable soup and put it through the blender to get a rich broth or base for recipes such as Veggie "Meatballs" (opposite). You can cook up a big pot, either on the stove or in a slow cooker, and freeze it in 1- or 2-cup portions to use whenever you need a soup starter, a liquid for macaroni and cheese, or to enrich another sauce. I stay away from starchy vegetables, such as potatoes and corn, because they will make the soup base too creamy for some uses. You can make as much of this soup base as you like, depending on the size of your soup pot and the quantity of vegetables you use.

4 cups carrots, onions, garlic, kale (or any other combination of veggies,
*   depending on what you have on hand)*

Water

Salt and freshly ground black pepper, to taste

1. Wash and roughly chop all vegetables.

2. Put vegetables in a stockpot and cover with water. (Tops of vegetables should be covered with at least 3 inches of water.)

3. Bring to a boil, cover stockpot, and reduce heat. Simmer for 30 to 40 minutes, or until vegetables are tender.

4. Transfer mixture, in batches, to a blender and blend thoroughly.

DECONSTRUCTED BROCCOLI SOUP CASSEROLE

MAKES 6 SERVINGS

In this recipe, I've combined two things that my family loves—broccoli cheese soup and casseroles. Cashew Hemp "Cheese" Sauce (opposite) gives this dish its rich, satisfying texture. For a nut-free version, substitute Cauliflower Hemp Cream (page 556).

- *1 teaspoon olive oil*
- *3 cups thinly sliced baking potatoes (russet, red, or gold)*
- *¼ teaspoon salt, divided*
- *½ cup diced onions*
- *3 cups broccoli, chopped in small pieces*
- *¼ teaspoon salt, divided*
- *1½ cups Cashew Hemp "Cheese" Sauce or nut-free Cauliflower Hemp Cream.*

1. Preheat oven to 375°F.

2. Spread olive oil over the bottom of a 9 × 13-inch baking pan.

3. Cover the bottom of the pan with a single layer of potatoes.

4. Sprinkle potatoes with ⅛ teaspoon salt.

5. Spoon half of the onions then half of the broccoli over the potatoes.

6. Pour half of the cheese sauce over the onions and broccoli.

7. Repeat with remaining ingredients.

8. Bake for 45 minutes, or until potatoes are cooked through and there is bubbling around the edges.

SUMMERY (SUPER SEED) LINEN

When the temperature rises, linen dresses and slacks appear in the pages of clothing catalogues and shop windows. Why? Because linen, a fabric made from flax, keeps you feeling cool even as things are heating up.

CASHEW HEMP "CHEESE" SAUCE

MAKES 1½ CUPS

You can toss whole-grain pasta, quinoa, or vegetables with this nutrient-rich, cheesy sauce, or use it as the base for a comforting entrée, such as Deconstructed Broccoli Soup Casserole (opposite).

1 cup raw unsalted cashews, soaked for 4 to 6 hours or overnight and drained and rinsed

¼ cup hemp seeds

2 tablespoons apple cider vinegar

1 teaspoon salt

2 tablespoons nutritional yeast

½ teaspoon smoked paprika

1 cup unsweetened Hemp Milk (page 523) or other nondairy milk

1. In a blender, process all ingredients until smooth.

2. Pour mixture into a small saucepan.

3. Cook over medium heat, stirring occasionally, 5 to 8 minutes, or until gently bubbling.

4. Remove from heat, toss with pasta, grain, or veggies of your choice, and serve. Yum.

5. You can add extra hemp milk to thin to desired consistency.

NUTTY SANDWICH SPREAD

MAKES 1½ CUPS

This savory sandwich spread is equally satisfying spread on a crusty roll, smeared into a fresh lettuce wrap, or served as a dip with an array of crunchy vegetables.

1 cup cashews, soaked for at least 4 hours in fresh water, then drained

½ cup hemp seed

½ teaspoon salt

½ tablespoon prepared Dijon mustard

4 sundried tomato halves, cut into small dice

1. Blend all ingredients in a food processor until smooth.

2. Transfer the mixture to a small saucepan and cook over medium heat for 5 minutes, stirring to keep mixture from burning.

3. Cool and store spread in a covered container in the refrigerator for up to 1 week.

PESTO VEGGIE BURGERS

MAKES 4 PATTIES

To give these hearty veggie burgers a bolder flavor, feel free to add more pesto to the mix. The burgers are delicious on a seeded bun with a slice of red onion and a couple of crisp leaves of lettuce. Lemon Basil Quinoa Salad (page 540) makes a perfect partner.

1 tablespoon flaxseed meal

3 tablespoons water

1 tablespoon olive oil

1 tablespoon minced shallots

1 cup cremini mushrooms, cut into small dice

1 15-ounce can cannellini beans, drained and rinsed

1 tablespoon Hemp Pesto (page 523)

½ cup quinoa flakes

Salt and freshly ground black pepper, to taste

Olive oil spray

1. In a small bowl, combine flaxseed meal and water. Set aside.

2. In a medium skillet, heat olive oil over medium heat.

3. Add shallots and mushrooms and cook for 2 to 3 minutes, or until vegetables are softened.

4. In a large bowl, combine flaxseed meal and cannellini beans. Mash with a potato masher.

5. Add the mushroom mixture, hemp pesto, quinoa flakes, and salt and pepper to the bowl, mixing together.

6. Shape mixture into 4 patties.

7. Spray a medium skillet with olive oil.

8. Over medium heat, cook patties, 4 to 5 minutes per side, until they are warm all the way through.

Super seeds, clockwise from left: flaxseed, chia, hemp, quinoa, roasted flaxseed, amaranth, red quinoa

Foreground: Carrot Sweet Potato Yogurt Smoothie, page 529; Background: Vibrant Yogurt Smoothie, page 533

Massaged Kale Salad, page 543

TOP: Lemon Basil Quinoa Salad, page 540; BOTTOM: Golden Corn Soup, page 545

TOP: Amaranth-Stuffed Acorn Squash, page 554; BOTTOM: Hemp Seed Hummus, page 574

Pesto Veggie Burger, page 564, with Lemon Basil Quinoa Salad, page 540

Granola Cookies, page 607; Bottom, left: Whole-Grain Spelt and Amaranth Loaf, page 580; right: Amaranth Cornbread, page 582

Blueberry Coffee Cake, page 588

ENCHILADA CASSEROLE

MAKES 4 GENEROUS SERVINGS

If you're craving tacos instead of a casserole, simply prepare the filling for these enchiladas and scoop it into either crunchy or soft tortillas. Then lay out a spread of toppings—shredded lettuce or cabbage, chopped tomatoes, onions, guacamole (or sliced avocado), and extra salsa—and enjoy the feast! (To keep this dish gluten-free, use gluten-free taco shells or tortillas.)

- 1 15-ounce can crushed tomatoes
- 2 tablespoons commercial taco seasoning or Kim's Basic Taco Seasoning (page 553)
- 1 15-ounce can black beans, rinsed (or 1½ cups cooked black beans)
- 1½ cups Basic Amaranth (page 520)
- 1 cup diced red bell pepper
- 1 cup corn kernels
- 1½ cups prepared salsa or Basic Salsa (page 541)
- 8 10-inch tortillas (whole-grain or gluten-free)

1. Preheat oven to 375°F.

2. In a large bowl, combine tomatoes with taco seasoning.

3. Add beans, amaranth, red pepper, and corn. Stir to combine.

4. Spoon ½ cup salsa onto bottom of a 9 × 13-inch baking pan or casserole dish.

5. Place one tortilla on a plate. Spoon ⅛ of the mixture onto the left side of the tortilla, leaving a 1- to 2-inch margin. Roll the tortilla and filling into a tube and place rolled tortilla into dish.

6. Continue with remaining tortillas, laying them next to each other until they tightly fill the pan.

7. Spread remaining salsa over enchiladas.

8. Bake for 35 to 40 minutes. There will be bubbling around the edges of the pan when it's done.

A TIME AND MONEY SAVER

You can save money by buying ingredients—cashews and almonds, for example—from bulk bins at your local grocery or health food store, and also save time by soaking them overnight and then freezing the soaked (and drained) nuts until you need them. All you have to do is thaw them and you're ready to cook!

HEMP SEED HUMMUS

MAKES 1½ CUPS

Hemp seeds do double duty in this recipe. First, they take the place of the traditional ingredient in hummus, tahini (some people are allergic to sesame seeds). Second, they bring crucial phytonutrients, including zinc and magnesium, to this tasty, satisfyingly textured dip. It makes a great snack, served with crudités such as baby carrots, cucumber slices, celery sticks, and strips of crunchy bell peppers. In addition to making superb sandwiches, hummus is also a salad's best friend. Try adding a healthy dollop on top of your green salad and you will have a flavorful, filling meal.

1¾ cups cooked garbanzo beans (or one 15-ounce can, drained and rinsed)

2 tablespoons hemp seeds

2 tablespoons lemon juice

¼ teaspoon ground cumin

½ teaspoon salt

3 tablespoons olive oil

1 clove garlic, minced

2 tablespoons water

1. Blend all ingredients together in a food processor or blender until smooth.

PINEAPPLE FRIED QUINOA

MAKES 4 SIDE-DISH SERVINGS
OR 2 MAIN-DISH SERVINGS

This spicy-sweet one-dish meal featuring fiber- and protein-rich quinoa comes together quickly. Delicious!

- 3 tablespoons soy sauce, gluten-free tamari or coconut aminos
- ¼ cup fresh orange juice
- ¼ teaspoon sriracha hot sauce
- 2 teaspoons neutral-tasting oil (canola, grapeseed, or sunflower)
- 2 cloves garlic, minced
- 2 carrots, peeled, halved, and thinly sliced
- 1 cup sliced mushrooms (button, cremini, or shitake)
- 1 cup diced pineapple, fresh or thawed
- 2½ cups broccoli florets and peeled, chopped stems
- 2 cups Basic Quinoa (page 520)

1. In a small bowl, combine soy sauce or tamari or coconut aminos, orange juice, and sriracha. Set aside.

2. In a large skillet, heat oil over medium-high heat.

3. Add garlic, carrots, and mushrooms. Cook, stirring, for 2 minutes.

4. Add pineapple and broccoli. Cook for another 2 minutes, or until broccoli is bright green.

5. Add sauce to the mixture in the skillet and combine.

6. Add quinoa and cook until the mixture is warmed through. Serve immediately.

HEMP TOFU LASAGNA

SERVES 4

Blending hemp tofu with non-dairy milk makes a delicious alternative to ricotta cheese. If you don't have lasagna noodles on hand, you can layer almost any other form of cooked pasta with layers of sauce and filling; it tastes just as good.

> *1 8-ounce package of hemp tofu*
>
> *1 cup hemp or other non-dairy milk*
>
> *¼ cup basil leaves*
>
> *2 cups spinach leaves, tough stems removed*
>
> *4 artichoke hearts*
>
> *2 tablespoons nutritional yeast*
>
> *1 tablespoon garlic pepper*
>
> *2 cups pasta sauce*
>
> *10–12 whole grain lasagna noodles (no-boil or prepared)*
>
> *¼ cup vegan mozzarella cheese shreds (optional)*

1. Preheat oven to 375.

2. In a food processor, thoroughly blend together tofu and non-dairy milk.

3. Add basil, spinach, artichoke hearts, nutritional yeast, and garlic pepper. Process until smooth.

4. Spread ⅓ of the pasta sauce in the bottom of a lasagna pan or 9 × 13 baking dish.

5. Lay noodles on top of sauce in a single layer.

6. Spread half of the tofu mixture on top of the noodles.

7. Layer sauce, noodles, and tofu on top of that.

8. Top with remaining noodles and sauce.

9. Sprinkle with cheese if, using.

10. Bake for 40 minutes or until bubbly.

HEMP TOFU—A DELICIOUS SOY-FREE ALTERNATIVE

Even if you can't have soy, you can still enjoy tofu. Tempt Living Foods is marketing a hemp-based tofu in the United States. Not only is tofu a tasty addition to stir-fries and Asian soups, it can also be crumbled and blended with other ingredients to create luscious lasagnas, savory bread puddings, and quiches.

QUICK AND CHUNKY PASTA SAUCE

SERVES 4

   1 tablespoon olive oil
   1 large clove garlic (or 2 small cloves)
   1 teaspoon dried basil
   1 teaspoon dried oregano
   ½ teaspoon dried thyme
   1 28-ounce can diced tomatoes, drained
     salt and pepper to taste

1. In a medium saucepan, heat olive oil over medium heat.

2. Smash and mince garlic, add to olive oil.

3. Cook for 30 seconds, add dried spices and stir. Cook for another 30 seconds or so.

4. Add drained tomatoes, stir to combine, and simmer for 10 minutes (or longer, if you have time).

MIDDLE EASTERN-INSPIRED LENTILS AND QUINOA

MAKES 6 SERVINGS

I serve this dish with a green salad for a quick, but satisfying weeknight dinner.

   1 cup quinoa, rinsed
4¼ cups vegetable broth
   1 cup brown lentils, rinsed and picked over
   ½ teaspoon cumin
   1 teaspoon salt
   2 tablespoons olive oil
   1 cup chopped onion
   1 cup chopped carrot
     freshly ground black pepper, to taste

1. In a large saucepan, combine quinoa, vegetable broth, lentils, cumin, and salt.

2. Bring to a boil. Reduce heat, cover pan, and simmer on low heat for 30 minutes, or until lentils are tender.

3. While the quinoa is cooking, heat olive oil over high heat.

4. Fry the onion and carrots until golden brown.

5. Fluff quinoa and lentils; serve on a platter topped with onions and freshly ground pepper.

CHAPTER 6

BAKED GOODS

The recipes in this chapter celebrate a range of delicious treats from muffins, rolls, and breads to decadent breakfast cakes that capitalize on the unique flavors, textures, and aromas of super seeds such as flaxseed and chia, combined with the richness of fresh produce such as pumpkin and zucchini, and market-fresh berries, apples, and pears. You'll even find super seed and chocolate combos that will quickly motivate you to tie on your apron and warm up the oven. You'll be surprised by how easy it is (and how great it tastes) to bake with super seed flours such as amaranth and flaxseed meal, along with whole-grain spelt, millet, and whole-wheat or gluten-free oat flour. Give it a shot and be prepared to change the way you bake!

OPPOSITE: **Blueberry Coffee Cake, page 588**

WHOLE-GRAIN SPELT AND AMARANTH LOAF

MAKES ONE STANDARD BREAD LOAF

This whole-grain loaf bakes up golden and aromatic. Sliced, it is ideal for toasty sandwiches.

1½ cups warm water
1½ teaspoons active dry yeast
1½ teaspoons salt
2 cups whole-grain spelt
1¼ cups amaranth flour

1. In a large bowl, combine water and yeast.
2. Add remaining ingredients and stir to thoroughly combine.
3. Cover the bowl and set it in a warm spot for 1½ to 2 hours, or until the dough has doubled in size.
4. Preheat oven to 425°F.
5. Lightly oil a standard bread pan.
6. Scoop dough into the prepared pan, lightly smoothing the top with damp hands.
7. Bake for 35 minutes. You'll know the bread is done when it's golden brown and, when you remove the loaf from the pan, the bottom sounds hollow when you tap it with your knuckles.
8. Remove the bread from the oven and turn out the loaf onto a rack or a clean kitchen towel. Allow to cool before slicing.

THE EASY WAY
TO MAKE YOUR OWN FLOUR

Buying a good-quality nut or spice grinder can pay for itself many times over if you use seed flours and nut butters as much as I do. For example, you can purchase a bag of rolled oats or buy them in bulk and easily grind up all the oat flour you need for a batch of muffins or cookies. If you need amaranth flour and have only whole amaranth on hand, your nut grinder can step in beautifully to supply what you need. If you don't have a spice or nut grinder, you can use your electric coffee grinder. To keep it clean between uses, just grind up a piece of plain bread. What could be easier?

* * *

FEAR OF KNEADING

If you've been reluctant to bake your own bread because kneading and working with yeast sounds tricky, spelt flour was made for you! Spelt truly is a wonder grain, not the least because it requires *no* kneading to bake beautifully. It contains a broad spectrum of vitamins, such as B2 and nutrients, including complex carbs, fiber, minerals, amino acids, and a lot more. To bake with spelt flour, all you need to do is mix it in with the other ingredients in your recipe, let the dough rise, and then either shape it into rolls or scoop the dough into a loaf pan and bake it. The air pockets that form during the first rise will give your bread a lovely texture—without any hassles.

AMARANTH CORNBREAD

MAKES 9 SERVINGS

This delicious quick bread, the perfect accompaniment to chili, beautifully pairs amaranth and corn while supplying plenty of protein, fiber, and phytonutrients, too.

¾ *cup cornmeal*

½ *cup amaranth flour*

¾ *cup white whole-wheat flour*

½ *teaspoon evaporated cane juice or coconut palm sugar*

2¼ *teaspoons baking powder, divided*

1 *teaspoon baking soda*

½ *teaspoon salt*

¼ *cup applesauce*

3 *tablespoons neutral-tasting oil (canola, grapeseed, or sunflower)*

1 *cup Hemp Milk (page 523) or other nondairy milk*

1. Preheat oven to 400°F.

2. In a medium bowl, combine cornmeal, flours, sweetener, 2 teaspoons baking powder, baking soda, and salt with a whisk.

3. In a large bowl, combine applesauce with ¼ teaspoon baking powder.

4. Add oil and nondairy milk to applesauce mixture.

5. Mix dry ingredients into wet ingredients.

6. Pour the mixture into an 8-inch-square baking pan that has been coated with oil or lined with parchment paper.

7. Bake for 20 minutes, or until a toothpick inserted in the middle of the bread comes out clean. Cut into squares and serve.

WHOLE-GRAIN MILLET ROLLS

MAKES 8

When you serve these homey rolls with a good bowl of soup, you'll enjoy a warm and soul-satisfying meal. Millet, a tiny, ancient grain, is a good source of manganese, phosphorus, and magnesium.

  1½ *cups warm water*
  1 *package rapid rise yeast*
  2 *teaspoons salt*
  1 *tablespoon maple syrup*
  2 *cups whole-grain spelt flour*
  ½ *cup flaxseed meal*
  ¼ *cup millet*
  1 *tablespoon olive oil*

1. In a large bowl, combine water, yeast, salt, and maple syrup. Let the mixture sit for 10 minutes.

2. Mix in spelt, flaxseed meal, and millet.

3. Coat the dough with olive oil.

4. Place the dough in a large bowl and cover it.

5. Keep the bowl in a warm place for 1½ hours or until dough has doubled.

6. Preheat oven to 425°F.

7. Lightly shape dough into dinner rolls.

8. Place the rolls on a parchment paper–covered baking pan.

9. Bake 15 to 18 minutes. Rolls are done when they sound hollow when tapped on the bottom.

10. Place on a cooling rack.

IS SPELT A FORM OF WHEAT?

If you're confused about spelt's family tree, there's a reason why! Although spelt is an ancient grain, it is in the wheat family, and it contains gluten, similar to wheat. If spelt isn't as well known or as widely used as wheat, there's a reason for that, too. Spelt simply has not had the same history of hybridization and cross-breeding that modern wheat has enjoyed, despite the fact that spelt has been grown for hundreds of years in Europe, and possibly thousands of years before that in the Middle East. Some people claim that spelt is easier to digest than wheat, but if you have celiac disease or a wheat allergy, avoid spelt.

AMARANTH BISCUITS

MAKES 8

When you slice these biscuits in half length-wise, they make a great sandwich roll, and, because they are made with cooked amaranth and nondairy yogurt, instead of butter, margarine, or shortening, they are not loaded with saturated fat and cholesterol. Turn these biscuits into a satisfying sandwich by spreading with Hemp Seed Hummus (page 574) and adding some tomato and cucumber slices.

1 cup white whole-wheat flour
1 teaspoon baking powder
½ teaspoon baking soda
¼ teaspoon salt
½ cup Basic Amaranth (page 520)
1 cup plain nondairy yogurt

1. Preheat oven to 425°F.
2. In a large bowl, whisk together flour, baking powder, baking soda, and salt.
3. Mix in amaranth and yogurt. Stir to combine.
4. Spoon batter onto a baking sheet lined with parchment paper.
5. Bake for 12 to 15 minutes, or until golden brown.
6. Remove from oven and place biscuits on a cooling rack.

DOES EVERYTHING HAVE TO BE "ORGANIC"?

When you're trying to eat healthier, one of the factors to consider is whether you should always buy organic produce or whether it's okay to buy conventionally grown produce. Eating fruits and vegetables is a key component to a healthy diet, but pesticide residue can be a problem. How do you know which veggies and fruit should always be bought organic and which are okay to eat without that designation? Luckily, the Environmental Working Group (EWG) examines the pesticide residues on a wide range of produce and publishes an annual guide to what should always be purchased organic, "The Dirty Dozen," and what can be bought conventional, "The Clean Fifteen." To find out which is which, visit www.ewg.org.

ZUCCHINI BREAD
OR MUFFINS

MAKES 2 LOAVES OR 18 MUFFINS

This is a versatile recipe that yields sweet treats that can travel from the breakfast table to the dessert plate by adding a cup of chocolate chips to the batter.

- *3 tablespoons chia seeds*
- *½ cup plus 1 tablespoon water*
- *3 cups white whole-wheat, spelt, or (gluten-free) oat flour*
- *1 teaspoon baking soda*
- *1 teaspoon baking powder*
- *1 teaspoon salt*
- *1 teaspoon ground cinnamon*
- *¼ cup coconut oil, gently melted*
- *1 cup coconut palm sugar or evaporated cane juice*
- *½ cup flaxseed meal*
- *1 tablespoon vanilla extract*
- *¾ cup Hemp Milk (page 523) or other nondairy milk*
- *2 medium zucchini, grated*

1. Preheat oven to 350°F.

2. Lightly oil loaf pans or muffin pans (or line muffin pan with papers).

3. In a large bowl, combine chia and water (to form gel). Set aside.

4. In a medium bowl, combine flour, baking soda, baking powder, salt, and cinnamon with a whisk.

5. In the large bowl, combine the chia gel with sugar, coconut oil, coconut palm sugar, or evaporated cane juice, flaxseed meal, vanilla, and nondairy milk.

6. Slowly mix dry ingredients into wet ingredients. Stir to combine.

7. Mix zucchini into the batter.

8. Divide the mixture among the pans.

9. For loaves, bake 1 hour; for muffins bake 25 to 30 minutes. Bread is done when a toothpick inserted into the center of the loaf or a muffin comes out clean.

10. Remove pans from the oven and turn out onto a cooling rack.

CRUNCHY TOPPED APPLE COFFEE CAKE

MAKES 8 TO 10 SERVINGS

Toasted pepitas and hemp seeds give this delicious brunch treat a protein-rich—and nut-free—crunch.

- 1 tablespoon chia seeds
- ¼ cup water
- ¼ cup shelled pumpkin seeds (pepitas)
- ¼ cup hemp seeds
- ¼ cup plus 2 tablespoons coconut palm sugar, divided
- ¾ teaspoon salt, divided
- ½ cup olive oil
- ¼ cup maple syrup
- ½ cup Hemp Milk (page 523) or other nondairy milk
- 2 cups white whole-wheat, spelt, or (gluten-free) oat flour
- ½ teaspoon baking soda
- ½ teaspoon baking powder
- ½ teaspoon ground cinnamon
- ¼ teaspoon ground nutmeg
- 2 medium apples, peeled and cut into ½-inch dice (approximately 1½ cups)

1. Preheat oven to 350°F.

2. Lightly oil an 8-inch-square baking pan.

3. Combine chia seeds and water in a small bowl (to form a gel). Set aside.

4. Lightly toast pepitas in a dry skillet for approximately 1 minute, or until lightly golden.

5. Using a food processor, pulse together pepitas, hemp seeds, 2 tablespoons coconut palm sugar, and ¼ teaspoon salt.

6. In a large bowl, mix together olive oil, remaining sugar, and maple syrup.

7. Mix in the chia seed mixture and nondairy milk.

8. In a separate bowl, combine flour, ½ teaspoon salt, baking soda, baking powder, cinnamon, and nutmeg using a whisk.

9. Mix dry ingredients into wet ingredients, half at a time, until well incorporated.

10. Mix in apples.

11. Pour batter into prepared pan. Smooth top with a damp spatula.

12. Spread pepita mixture over top.

13. Bake for 30 minutes, or until a toothpick inserted into the center comes out clean.

STRAWBERRY CHOCOLATE CHUNK MINI MUFFINS

MAKES 24 MINI MUFFINS
OR 12 STANDARD MUFFINS

You can make these muffins even when strawberries are not in season by chopping frozen strawberries in a food processor or letting them thaw before chopping them by hand.

- 2 cups white whole-wheat, spelt, or (gluten-free) oat flour
- 1½ teaspoons baking powder, divided
- ½ teaspoon salt
- ½ cup applesauce
- ½ cup flaxseed meal
- ¼ cup coconut oil, melted, or canola oil
- ¾ cup coconut palm sugar or evaporated cane juice
- ½ teaspoon vanilla extract
- ¼ cup Hemp Milk (page 523) or nondairy milk
- 2 cups chopped strawberries
- ½ cup chocolate chunks or chocolate chips

1. Preheat oven to 350°F.

2. Lightly oil a mini muffin (or standard muffin) pan or line with muffin papers.

3. In a medium bowl, combine flour, 1 teaspoon baking powder, and salt with a whisk.

4. In a large bowl, combine applesauce with ½ teaspoon baking powder.

5. Add flaxseed meal, oil, sugar, vanilla, and nondairy milk to the applesauce. Stir well to combine.

6. Add strawberries to wet ingredients and mix well.

7. Slowly mix dry ingredients into wet ingredients, being careful not to overmix.

8. Mix in chocolate chunks or chips.

9. Spoon batter into prepared muffin pans.

10. Bake approximately 25 to 30 minutes, or until a toothpick inserted in the middle of a muffin comes out clean. (If your muffin pan makes very small muffins—more than 24—reduce baking time accordingly.)

BLUEBERRY COFFEE CAKE

MAKES 8 SERVINGS

Inspired by a traditional Italian almond corn-meal coffee cake, this version, with fresh (or frozen) blueberries, is elevated to "super coffee cake" with the addition of hemp seeds and hemp milk. This cake is truly delicious.

- 1 cup white whole-wheat flour, spelt flour, or (gluten-free) oat flour
- 1 cup cornmeal, plus extra for dusting the pan
- ½ teaspoon salt
- 1½ teaspoons ground cinnamon, divided
- 2 teaspoons baking powder
- ¾ cup plus two teaspoons granulated sweetener (coconut palm sugar or evaporated cane juice), divided
- 1 cup Hemp Milk (page 523) (or other nondairy milk)
- ¼ cup applesauce
- 1 teaspoon vanilla extract
- 1 teaspoon almond extract (or omit for a nut-free cake)
- 1 cup blueberries (fresh or frozen)
- 1 tablespoon plus 1 teaspoon slivered almonds (or shelled pumpkin seeds, pepitas, for a nut-free cake)
- 1 tablespoon plus 1 teaspoon hulled hemp seeds

1. Preheat oven to 375°F.

2. Grease a 9-inch-round cake pan with coconut oil and dust with cornmeal. Set aside.

3. In a medium bowl, whisk together flour, cornmeal, salt, 1 teaspoon cinnamon, baking powder, and ¾ cup sweetener.

4. In a large bowl, combine hemp milk, apple-sauce, vanilla, and almond extract, if using.

5. Slowly mix dry ingredients into wet ingredients. Stir to combine.

6. Add blueberries.

7. Pour batter into prepared cake pan.

8. In a small bowl, combine almonds or pepitas, hemp seeds, 2 teaspoons sweetener, and ½ teaspoon cinnamon.

9. Sprinkle nut-and-seed mixture over the top of the cake batter.

10. Bake 25 to 30 minutes, or until a tooth-pick inserted in the center of the cake comes out clean.

11. Let cake cool on a cooling rack for 10 minutes, then turn out onto a plate and flip right side up. Serve warm.

LEMON AMARANTH MUFFINS

MAKES 12

Rosemary pairs with lemon and olive oil to give these muffins a sophisticated taste, while the addition of cooked amaranth provides a tender crumb (it also helps reduce the overall fat—another bonus).

- ¼ cup olive oil
- 1 sprig fresh rosemary or 1 teaspoon dried rosemary
- 1 cup white whole-wheat, spelt, or (gluten-free) oat flour
- ½ teaspoon salt
- 1½ teaspoons baking powder, divided
- ½ cup applesauce
- 1 cup Basic Amaranth (page 520)
- 2 tablespoons fresh lemon juice
- 1 teaspoon lemon rind
- ¾ cup granulated sweetener (evaporated cane juice or coconut palm sugar)

1. Preheat oven to 350°F.

2. Lightly oil a standard muffin pan or line with paper liners.

3. In a small saucepan over medium heat, warm olive oil with rosemary for 2 to 3 minutes, or until fragrant. Discard the rosemary and set aside the oil to cool.

4. In a medium bowl, whisk together flour, salt, and 1 teaspoon baking powder.

5. In a large bowl, combine applesauce with ½ teaspoon baking powder.

6. Add olive oil, amaranth, lemon juice, lemon rind, and sweetener to applesauce mixture. Stir to combine.

7. Slowly mix dry ingredients into wet ingredients.

8. Divide batter evenly among muffin cups.

9. Bake for 25 to 30 minutes, or until a toothpick inserted in the center of a muffin comes out clean.

PICK YOUR BERRY MUFFINS

MAKES 12

These muffins are a fantastic vehicle for any berry that's in season, but they're just as delicious as an out-of-season treat, if you use frozen fruit. Either option works beautifully in this recipe.

> ½ cup amaranth flour
>
> 1½ cups white whole-wheat, spelt, or (gluten-free) oat flour
>
> 1½ teaspoons baking powder, divided
>
> ½ teaspoon salt
>
> ½ cup applesauce
>
> ½ cup flaxseed meal
>
> ½ teaspoon vanilla extract
>
> 1 tablespoon apple cider vinegar
>
> 1 cup maple syrup
>
> ¼ cup coconut oil (gently melted)
>
> 1½ cups berries (blueberries, raspberries, strawberry slices, blackberries, or a mix)

1. Preheat oven to 350°F.

2. Lightly oil a standard muffin pan or line with muffin papers.

3. In a medium bowl, whisk together flours, 1 teaspoon baking powder, and salt.

4. In a large bowl, combine applesauce with ½ teaspoon baking powder.

5. Add flaxseed meal, vanilla, vinegar, maple syrup, and coconut oil to the applesauce mixture. Stir to combine. Add dry mixture and stir again to combine.

6. Gently fold berries into batter.

7. Divide batter evenly among muffin cups.

8. Bake for 24 to 30 minutes, or until a toothpick inserted into the center of a muffin comes out clean.

CRUNCHY TOPPED PEAR MUFFINS

MAKES 12

If you don't have any pears on hand, you can substitute apples in this muffin recipe. You'll see why it's a family favorite.

- 2 cups white whole-wheat, spelt, or (gluten-free) oat flour
- 1 teaspoon baking powder
- ½ teaspoon salt
- 1½ teaspoons cinnamon, divided
- ½ cup applesauce
- 1 tablespoon apple cider vinegar
- ½ cup flaxseed meal
- ¼ cup neutral-tasting oil (canola, grapeseed, or sunflower)
- ¾ cup granulated sweetener (evaporated cane juice or coconut palm sugar)
- ¼ cup Hemp Milk (page 523) or other nondairy milk
- 2 Bartlett or Anjou pears, diced (approximately 1½ cups)
- ¼ cup hulled hemp seeds
- ½ cup rolled oats

1. Preheat oven to 350°F.

2. Lightly oil a standard muffin pan or line with muffin papers.

3. In a medium bowl, whisk together flour, baking powder, salt, and 1 teaspoon cinnamon.

4. In a large bowl, combine applesauce, vinegar, flaxseed meal, oil, sweetener, and hemp milk. Stir to thoroughly combine.

5. Slowly mix dry ingredients into wet.

6. Stir in diced pears.

7. Evenly divide batter among muffin cups.

8. In a small bowl, combine hemp seeds, oats, and ½ teaspoon cinnamon.

9. Evenly top each muffin with seed mixture.

10. Bake 25 to 30 minutes, or until a toothpick inserted in the center of a muffin comes out clean.

BLUEBERRY SCONES

MAKES 8

These scones are really delicious when served
with Blackberry Chia Jam.

- *1½ cups white whole-wheat or spelt flour*
- *¼ cup flaxseed meal*
- *2 teaspoons baking powder*
- *½ teaspoon salt*
- *2 tablespoons coconut palm sugar or evaporated cane juice*
- *2 tablespoons cold coconut oil*
- *⅔ cup coconut milk (full fat or light)*
- *½ cup blueberries*

1. Preheat oven to 450.

2. In a medium bowl, whisk together flour, flaxseed, baking powder, salt, and sugar.

3. Blend in coconut oil with a pastry cutter or two forks.

4. Stir in coconut milk until just blended in.

5. Stir in blueberries.

6. Shape dough into a flattened disk, approximately six inches across.

7. Place on parchment covered baking sheet.

8. Cut disk into 8 wedges and separate them on the pan.

9. Bake 12 to 14 minutes until puffed and golden.

GLUTEN-FREE SCONES

Recipes for gluten-free scones usually call for oat flour, but in my opinion the moisture in this flour just doesn't yield the right texture for scones. If you'd like to convert the scones in this book to gluten-free, I suggest using an all-purpose gluten-free flour that contains some starch (potato, tapioca, etc.) and add 1 teaspoon xanthan gum to the dry ingredients. Although it is not a whole-grain alternative, this substitution will nevertheless yield scones that have just the right texture and flavor.

BLACKBERRY CHIA JAM

MAKES APPROXIMATELY 1 CUP

- *1 cup blackberries, fresh or thawed*
- *2 tablespoons apple juice*
- *1–2 teaspoons maple syrup*
- *2 tablespoons chia seed*

1. Blend well, but keep some texture.

2. Refrigerate for at least 1 hour.

PUMPKIN SCONES TWO WAYS

MAKES 8

At our house, you can never have enough chocolate. These pumpkin scones are delicious when they're studded with chocolate chips or drizzled with a simple glaze. You can also serve them alongside a bowl of soup, without any sweet-flavored additions. There are so many ways to enjoy them!

½ cup amaranth flour

1½ cups white whole-wheat or spelt flour

1 tablespoon baking powder

¾ teaspoon cinnamon

½ teaspoon allspice

3 tablespoons coconut palm sugar (or evaporated cane juice, but the coconut palm sugar really adds depth here)

½ teaspoon salt

¼ cup firm coconut oil (see note)

1 cup pumpkin puree (not pumpkin pie filling)

Optional: ½ cup chocolate chips

1. Preheat oven to 425°F.

2. In a large bowl, combine flours, baking powder, cinnamon, allspice, sugar, and salt with a whisk.

3. Mix oil into dry ingredients using a pastry cutter or two knives.

4. Thoroughly mix pumpkin into dry ingredients. Mix in chocolate chips if using. (It is easiest to use your hands.)

5. Shape the dough into a disk and cut into 8 triangles.

6. Place triangles on parchment covered baking sheet.

7. Bake for 12 to 15 minutes, or until golden brown and firm to the touch.

GLAZE

2 tablespoons coconut palm sugar or evaporated cane juice

1 teaspoon nondairy milk

1. Thoroughly mix all ingredients.

2. Drizzle on cooled scones.

NOTE: If it's warm in your kitchen and your coconut oil has melted, pop ¼ cup of it in the refrigerator until it firms up.

CHAPTER 7

DESSERTS

Sweet treats can be "super," too, whether you're making a plate of brownies for a bake sale, a fruit crisp for a holiday meal, or a frosty treat on a hot day. When you incorporate powerful ingredients like super seeds into the treats you love, you can nourish the body as well as satisfy the soul. And, since super seeds are loaded with good fiber, they can help fill you up so you don't overindulge at treat time, while the protein, vitamins, and minerals they supply actually add to your overall daily nutrition, rather than loading on empty calories, like so many traditional desserts do. Just because you are powering up your desserts, it doesn't mean you have to sacrifice flavor, as you'll soon discover, once you start rustling up some of the yummy offerings in this chapter. Enjoy!

OPPOSITE: **Strawberry Rhubarb Crisp, page 596**

595

STRAWBERRY RHUBARB CRISP

MAKES 6 SERVINGS

In the springtime, farmers' markets are loaded with beautiful, pinkish green stalks of rhubarb. The tartness of this hardy plant marries beautifully with the sun-kissed sweetness of late spring strawberries. This recipe calls for apple juice as a sweetener, which helps bring down the amount of sugar that is used in traditional rhubarb desserts.

- *1 cup apple juice*
- *1 tablespoon chia seeds*
- *1 cup rhubarb, thinly sliced (⅛ to ¼ inches thick)*
- *2 cups quartered strawberries*
- *¼ cup coconut oil*
- *½ cup coconut palm sugar or evaporated cane juice*
- *⅛ teaspoon salt*
- *1 teaspoon vanilla extract*
- *½ cup quinoa flakes*
- *¼ cup hemp seeds*

1. Preheat oven to 425°F.

2. Combine apple juice and chia seeds, and let sit for 10 minutes.

3. In a small saucepan, combine apple juice mixture, rhubarb, and strawberries. Bring to a boil.

4. Reduce heat and simmer 10 to 15 minutes, or until rhubarb is soft.

5. In a medium bowl, combine remaining ingredients to make batter.

6. Pour fruit mixture into an 8-inch-square baking pan.

7. Dollop the batter on top of the fruit, using the back of a spoon or damp hands to spread it evenly over the surface.

8. Bake for 40 minutes, or until top is set and lightly browned. Serve with a scoop of vanilla nondairy ice cream.

COCONUT OIL COULD SAVE YOUR SKIN

Coconut oil is not only a superb ingredient for cooking, it is an excellent natural moisturizer. Just rub a little on a patch of rough skin and watch what happens. Some research also indicates that coconut oil may have antimicrobial properties that can help protect skin from infection. Keep coconut oil in a cool place to keep it from liquefying.

* * *

THE BENEFITS OF USING COCONUT OIL

Coconut oil is a great nondairy butter replacement—perfect for baking because it can be substituted 1-for-1 in most recipes that call for butter or oil. Its light coconut flavor enriches all kinds of sweet treats, and it behaves similarly to butter and margarine: At cooler temperatures it is a solid, and in warmer temperatures, it melts into a fat-rich liquid. Also, coconut oil is a whole food, unlike commercial margarine, which is one of the most chemically processed and altered foods on the market. Coconut oil is rich in medium-chain fatty acids, which, research is beginning to indicate, might play a role in lowering blood cholesterol.

SUNFLOWER SEED–HEMP BUTTER SCONES

8 SCONES

If you don't want chocolate in your scone at breakfast, you can substitute raisins or dried cherries for the chocolate chips.

1½ cups white whole-wheat or spelt flour

¼ cup flaxseed meal

2 teaspoons baking powder

½ teaspoon salt

2 tablespoons coconut palm sugar or evaporated cane juice

2 tablespoons sunflower seed–hemp butter (see page 522)

⅔ cups non-dairy milk

6 tablespoons chocolate chips

1. Preheat oven to 450.

2. In a medium bowl, combine flour, flaxseed, baking powder, salt, and sugar with a whisk.

3. Mix sunflower seed–hemp butter into the flour.

4. Add non-dairy milk, and mix thoroughly.

5. Mix in chocolate chips.

6. Form dough into a disk, approximately 6 inches across.

7. Place on a parchment-covered baking sheet.

8. Cut into 8 wedges and separate them on the pan.

9. Bake 12 to 14 minutes or until puffed and golden.

GOING GREEN WITH SUNFLOWER SEED BUTTER

Sunflower seed butter is a phenomenal substitute for peanut butter or almond butter, if you need your food to be nut- or peanut-free. You can find it in many grocery and health food stores, or you can buy it online. You can also make your own. All you have to do is spread raw, shelled sunflower seeds on a baking sheet and lightly toast them in a 350°F degree oven. After 10 minutes, or until they are thoroughly toasted. With a food processor or high-speed blender, process the warm sunflower seeds until smooth. Add a dash of salt and a drizzle of neutral-tasting oil (canola, grapeseed, or sunflower) until the mixture is smooth.

Here's a wacky detail about baking with sunflower seed butter: It turns green in baked goods when combined with baking soda (or any other alkaline substance). Your cake or cookies will taste delicious, but they'll be teal-colored!

CHOCOLATE CHIP NUT BUTTER SNACK CAKE

MAKES 18 SERVINGS

I am a huge fan of what I call a "snack cake." This is a cake that doesn't need to be frosted or decorated, and you don't need a special occasion to make it. Just cut it up into chunks and eat it with your fingers! These no-frills cakes make any day feel a little fancy. This one is a favorite at our house.

  2 tablespoons flaxseed meal

  ¼ cup water

  2 cups white whole-wheat, spelt, or (gluten-free) oat flour

  ½ teaspoon salt

  1 teaspoon baking soda

  1 cup Basic Amaranth (page 521)

  1 cup maple syrup

  ½ cup almond butter or other nut or seed butter

  1 cup chocolate chips

1. Preheat oven to 375°F.

2. Lightly oil a 9 × 13-inch baking pan.

3. In a large bowl, whisk together flaxseed meal and water. Set aside.

4. In a medium bowl, whisk together flour, salt, and baking soda.

5. To the flaxseed mixture, add the amaranth, maple syrup, and nut butter and stir to thoroughly combine.

6. Mix dry ingredients into wet ingredients, half at a time.

7. Stir in chocolate chips.

8. Spread batter into prepared pan. It will be sticky, so use a damp spatula or your damp hands to spread the batter.

9. Bake 25 minutes, or until a toothpick inserted into the middle of the cake comes out clean.

STRAWBERRY NECTARINE COBBLER

MAKES 9 SERVINGS

If you're craving a taste of summer in the wintertime, use thawed frozen strawberries in this recipe. Can't find nectarines? No problem! You can substitute peach slices for the nectarines. To keep the mix from getting too watery, thaw the frozen fruit and drain off any excess liquid. This cobbler is delicious all on its own or with a scoop of ice cream, sorbet, or nondairy yogurt.

- ¾ cup white whole-wheat flour, spelt, or (gluten-free) oat flour
- ¼ cup flaxseed meal
- ½ teaspoon baking powder
- ¼ teaspoon baking soda
- ¼ teaspoon salt
- ¼ cup plus 2 teaspoons coconut palm sugar or evaporated cane juice, divided
- ¼ cup applesauce
- 3 tablespoons coconut oil
- 2 cups nectarine slices
- 2 cups strawberry slices

1. Preheat oven to 375°F.

2. In a medium bowl, combine flour, flaxseed meal, baking powder, baking soda, salt, and ¼ cup sugar with a whisk.

3. Mix the applesauce and coconut oil into the flour mixture.

4. In an 8-inch-square baking pan, toss the fruit with 2 teaspoons sugar.

5. Pour batter on top of fruit.

6. Bake 25 to 30 minutes, or until batter is set and fruit is bubbly.

CHOCOLATE CHIP ICE CREAM

MAKES 6 SERVINGS

Chia's natural thickening properties lend creaminess to this ice cream. If you don't have an ice cream maker, you can pour the mixture into ice-pop molds and enjoy a creamy frozen popsicle.

- *2 tablespoons chia seeds, ground*
- *2 15-ounce cans coconut milk (either light or regular)*
- *½ cup maple syrup*
- *1 vanilla bean*
- *1 cup chocolate chips*

1. In a medium bowl, combine chia seeds, coconut milk, and maple syrup.

2. Using a sharp knife, cut the vanilla bean lengthwise. Scrape the center of the bean with a knife or spoon and add it to the mixture.

3. Stir, cover, and chill for at least 1 hour.

4. Freeze ice cream according to ice cream maker's directions.

5. Add chocolate chips in the last couple minutes of mixing the ice cream.

DEVILISHLY GOOD CHOCOLATE CAKE

MAKES 9 SERVINGS

Using parchment paper is the key to getting this moist cake from pan to plate. Otherwise, the chocolate chips that sink to the bottom of the batter will stick to the pan. You can enjoy the cake warm or at room temperature. For an extra treat, serve it with a scoop of Chocolate Chip Ice Cream (page 601) or drizzle some Strawberry Chia Syrup (follow Blueberry Chia Syrup on page 528 and substitute strawberries) over the cake when it's warm. Delicious.

1 cup whole-grain spelt flour

½ cup flaxseed meal

½ cup cocoa powder

1 teaspoon baking soda

½ teaspoon salt

1 cup maple syrup

½ cup olive oil

1 cup brewed coffee (decaffeinated is fine)

2 teaspoons vanilla extract

2 tablespoons apple cider vinegar

½ cup chocolate chips

1. Preheat oven to 375°F.

2. Line the bottom of an 8-inch-square baking pan with parchment paper. Lightly oil the parchment and sides of the pan.

3. In a large bowl, combine flour, flaxseed meal, cocoa powder, baking soda, and salt with a whisk.

4. In a small bowl, combine syrup, olive oil, coffee, and vanilla.

5. Pour liquid ingredients into dry ingredients, and stir to thoroughly combine.

6. Add vinegar, and stir to distribute.

7. Stir in chocolate chips.

8. Spread batter in prepared pan.

9. Bake for 35 minutes, or until center is set.

10. Remove pan from oven and cool for 10 minutes in the pan.

11. Turn cake onto a cooling rack.

CHOCOLATE CHIP COOKIES

MAKES 4 DOZEN

The whole-grain flour and flaxseed meal in these chocolate chip cookies makes them cholesterol-free, and a good source of iron.

2½ cups white whole-wheat, spelt, or (gluten-free) oat flour

½ cup flaxseed meal

1 teaspoon salt

1 teaspoon baking soda

½ cup applesauce

½ teaspoon baking powder

¾ cup neutral-tasting oil (canola, grapeseed, or sunflower)

1½ cups coconut palm sugar or evaporated cane juice

1 tablespoon vanilla extract

1¼ cups chocolate chips

1. Preheat oven to 375°F.

2. In a medium bowl, combine flour, flaxseed meal, salt, and baking soda using a whisk.

3. In a large bowl, combine applesauce with baking powder.

4. Add oil, sugar, and vanilla to applesauce mixture. Mix well.

5. Stir dry ingredients into wet ingredients.

6. Add chocolate chips and stir to combine.

7. Line baking sheets with parchment paper.

8. Drop batter by rounded tablespoon onto ungreased baking sheets.

9. Bake 10 to 12 minutes, or until set.

10. Let cookies cool on baking sheets for a few minutes before removing to cooling racks.

COCOA COOKIE BATTER POWER BITES

MAKES 30

These power bites are perfect for a post-workout pick-me-up. Because they are smaller than a prepackaged nutrition bar, you can eat as many of them as you like. Form the balls all at once, and then store them in a sealed container in the refrigerator for a day or two. You can cut the recipe in half if you don't need so many.

- 1 cup pitted Medjool dates
- ½ cup water
- ¼ cup cocoa powder
- 1 tablespoon coconut oil
- ¼ cup nondairy milk
- ½ teaspoon vanilla extract
- ¼ teaspoon salt
- ¼ cup nut butter (sunflower seed butter, sunflower seed hemp butter, almond butter, peanut butter, etc.)
- 1½ cups quinoa flakes

1. In a food processor or blender, puree dates and water together.

2. In a small saucepan, combine date paste and cocoa powder. Heat while stirring for 2 to 3 minutes.

3. In a large bowl, combine date mixture with coconut oil, nondairy milk, vanilla, salt, and nut butter.

4. Mix in quinoa flakes to thoroughly combine.

5. Cover and chill mixture for at least one hour.

6. Roll mixture into 1-inch balls.

7. Refrigerate until ready to eat.

NATURE'S CANDY

Wonderfully sweet dates are a prominent feature of Middle Eastern cuisine. This isn't too surprising, given that dates, the fruit of the date palm, grow in desert conditions. In the United States, most dates are grown in parts of Arizona and California, where conditions are ideal for their cultivation. Although there are many varieties of dates grown worldwide, only two varieties, Deglet Noor and Medjool, are readily available in the United States. For making date paste, Medjool dates work especially well, since their flesh is plumper than other varieties.

HEMP CHOCOLATE CHIP COOKIE BATTER POWER BITES

MAKES 30

The texture of these power bites is as soft as cookie batter. I like to use mini chocolate chips in this recipe to really spread around the chocolate love.

  1 cup pitted Medjool dates

  ½ cup water

  ¼ cup hemp seeds

  1 tablespoon coconut oil

  ¼ cup nondairy milk

  ½ teaspoon vanilla extract

  ¼ teaspoon salt

  ¼ cup nut butter (sunflower seed, almond, or peanut)

  1½ cups quinoa flakes

  ½ cup chocolate chips

1. In a food processor or blender, puree dates with water.

2. In a large bowl, combine date paste, hemp seeds, coconut oil, nondairy milk, vanilla, salt, and nut butter.

3. Mix in quinoa flakes thoroughly.

4. Mix in chocolate chips.

5. Cover and chill mixture for at least 1 hour.

6. Roll mixture into 1-inch balls.

7. Refrigerate until ready to eat.

CHOCOLATE BROWNIES

MAKES 9 SERVINGS

A mere two tablespoons of chia in this recipe acts as a fiber-rich, cholesterol-free egg substitute, while a couple of tablespoons of coffee do double duty to bring out a rich chocolate flavor. If you don't have any brewed coffee around, don't worry, you can always use water—the brownies will be very tasty. They're my go-to treat when I need to bring a little something special to a friend's house.

- 6 *tablespoons water*
- 2 *tablespoons ground chia seeds*
- ¾ *cup coconut palm sugar or evaporated cane juice*
- ¼ *cup plus 2 tablespoons neutral-tasting oil (canola, grapeseed, or sunflower)*
- 2 *tablespoons brewed coffee*
- 1 *12-ounce bag of chocolate chips*
- 1½ *teaspoons vanilla extract*
- 1 *cup white whole-wheat, spelt, or (gluten-free) oat flour*
- ¼ *cup flaxseed meal*
- ½ *teaspoon baking soda*
- ½ *teaspoon salt*

1. Preheat oven to 375°F.

2. In a small bowl, combine water and chia seeds. Let the mixture sit for 15 minutes. Stir to thoroughly mix.

3. In a small saucepan, combine sugar, oil, and coffee. Cook over medium heat until hot but not boiling.

4. Stir half the chocolate chips and the vanilla into the sugar mixture. Stir until the chips are melted. Set aside.

5. In a separate bowl, combine the flour, flaxseed meal, baking soda, and salt.

6. Scrape the chocolate mixture into a large bowl.

7. Stir the chia seed mixture into the chocolate mixture.

8. Slowly mix dry ingredients into wet ingredients. Combine thoroughly.

9. Mix remaining chocolate chips into the batter.

10. Line an 8-inch-square baking pan with parchment paper, long enough to hang over the sides.

11. Pour batter into the parchment paper–lined baking pan. Bake for 30 minutes, or until center is set.

12. Remove pan from the oven and cool in the pan on a cooling rack. Cut into squares when completely cool. Serve with fresh fruit for a lovely dessert.

GRANOLA COOKIES

MAKES 36

These cookies pack all the goodness of super seed–loaded granola into a crunchy cookie that tastes great, travels well, and will quickly become your go-to lunch box and picnic cookie. Enjoy them with a tall glass of iced tea on a hot day or a warm cup of cocoa whenever you feel a chill setting in.

- *1 cup (gluten-free) oat flour, white whole-wheat flour, or spelt flour*
- *½ teaspoon baking soda*
- *½ teaspoon salt*
- *2 cups Fruit-Sweetened Granola (page 532) or Coconut Quinoa Granola (page 536)*
- *¼ cup applesauce*
- *¼ teaspoon baking powder*
- *½ cup coconut palm sugar or evaporated cane juice*
- *¼ cup coconut oil, melted*
- *½ cup chocolate chips or dried fruit*

1. Preheat oven to 350°F.

2. Line cookie sheets with parchment paper.

3. In a medium bowl, whisk together flour, baking soda, and salt.

4. Mix in granola. Set aside.

5. In a large bowl, combine applesauce and baking powder.

6. Mix in sugar and coconut oil.

7. Stir granola mixture into wet ingredients, half at a time.

8. Mix in chocolate chips or dried fruit.

9. Drop tablespoon-size dollops of batter onto cookie sheets.

10. Bake 10 to 12 minutes, or until golden brown.

11. Let the cookies firm up for a minute or two before moving them to a cooling rack to cool completely.

CHOCOLATE ICE POPS

MAKES 4

Avocado is the secret ingredient that makes these ice pops extra-creamy, and it also gives them a punch of healthy fat, fiber, magnesium, and vitamin C. Yum. These luscious ice pops are healthy and delicious at the same time.

1½ cups Hemp Milk (page 523)

⅛ teaspoon salt

½ ripe avocado (Use the other half right away or squeeze with lemon juice to prevent it from browning.)

3 tablespoons cocoa powder

2 tablespoons maple syrup

2 tablespoons brewed coffee (decaffeinated is fine)

1. Blend all ingredients.

2. Pour the mixture into ice-pop molds (see note).

3. Freeze until solid.

NOTE: You can pick up BPA-free ice-pop molds almost anywhere. They come in adorable shapes and colors, and they're not expensive. Best of all, they give you what you need to have a yummy frozen treat that's both sweet and also loaded with fruits and veggies—not to mention super seeds! BPA stands for bisphenol A, an industrial chemical that is found in polycarbonate plastics. Research has shown that BPA can seep into food or beverages from containers that are made with BPA, a concern, since exposure to BPA has been linked, in some studies, to serious health conditions.

SUNSHINE ICE POPS

MAKES 4 SERVINGS

Chia seeds thicken the mixture in these ice pops, making them creamier and a little less icy than the usual frozen treat.

½ cup orange juice, either fresh or from concentrate

½ cup coconut milk

1 cup mango chunks, fresh or frozen

2 teaspoons chia seeds

1. Blend all ingredients thoroughly.

2. Let mixture sit for 15 minutes, then pour into ice-pop molds.

3. Freeze until solid.

MAKE-IT-YOURSELF
FRESH PUMPKIN PUREE

MAKES APPROXIMATELY 2 CUPS

When the autumn rolls around, my family and I eat a lot of pumpkin goodies. We go through a lot of pumpkin puree, and, as convenient as the canned product is, I've found that making my own pumpkin puree raises the flavor factor by more than a few notches! I love to bake a pumpkin on a cool day, and then transform it into a spectacular treat (such as Pumpkin Pancakes on page 531). Here's the recipe I use. It's super simple.

1 medium pie pumpkin (about 2 to 4 pounds), such as Sugar Pumpkin

1. Preheat oven to 400°F.

2. Wash the outside of the pumpkin.

3. Pierce the pumpkin with a sharp knife in several places.

4. Bake for 45 to 60 minutes. The pumpkin is done when a sharp knife can easily pierce the exterior.

5. When it is cool enough to handle, cut the pumpkin in half.

6. Scoop out and discard the seeds (pepitas) or save them to roast for a snack later.

7. Scoop the flesh into a bowl.

8. Mash with a potato masher.

9. If you're not using the puree right away, store it in a tightly sealed container in the refrigerator for up to three days, or in the freezer for up to 3 months.

PEAR-PUMPKIN CRISP

MAKES 9 SERVINGS

I sometimes serve this crisp as a special break-fast. Thanks to pumpkin, pears, and quinoa flakes, this recipe is packed with iron, fiber, vitamins A and C, and protein—all of which makes me feel a lot less guilty about letting my family indulge a little! And did I mention how delicious it is? For an extra treat, serve this crisp with a dollop of vanilla-flavored coconut-milk yogurt.

1 cup pureed pumpkin (canned pumpkin is fine, but not canned pumpkin pie filling) such as Make-It-Yourself Fresh Pumpkin Puree (page 609)

½ teaspoon ground cinnamon

¼ teaspoon allspice

6 pears, such as Bartlett, peeled and thinly sliced (approximately 6 cups)

1½ cups quinoa flakes

¾ teaspoon salt

¾ cup maple syrup

1. Preheat oven to 400°F.

2. Lightly oil a large 9 × 13-inch baking pan.

3. In a large bowl, combine pumpkin with cinnamon and allspice.

4. Add pear slices and toss to cover with pumpkin mixture, then spread in baking pan.

5. In a small bowl, combine quinoa flakes with salt.

6. Add maple syrup and stir to combine.

7. Spread on top of fruit mixture.

8. Bake 35 minutes, or until the crisp is lightly golden on top.

NOT EVERY SEED IS A SUPER SEED

A little healthy skepticism about some seeds is not a bad thing. Apple seeds and apricot kernels, for example, contain small amounts of cyanide. Although you would have to eat a lot of apple seeds to get poisoned, it can be dangerous for children to eat apricot kernels. As a general policy, stick with the super seeds you know.

INDIVIDUAL PUMPKIN PIE PUDDINGS

MAKES 4 SERVINGS

This pudding is wonderfully creamy and smooth—the ultimate comfort food. For the topping, you can use the recipe for granola, below, or either of the recipes on page 532 or page 536.

PUDDING

½ cup coconut milk

2 tablespoons chia seeds

1 15-ounce can pumpkin puree or 1¾ cups Make-It-Yourself Fresh Pumpkin Puree (page 609)

1 teaspoon ground cinnamon

½ teaspoon allspice

GRANOLA

½ cup shelled hemp seeds

1½ cups gluten-free oats

1 teaspoon ground cinnamon

1 tablespoon plus 1 teaspoon canola oil

1 teaspoon vanilla extract

¼ cup maple syrup

TO MAKE THE PUDDING

1. In a medium bowl, thoroughly combine all pudding ingredients.

2. Chill in refrigerator for at least 8 hours.

3. To serve, scoop pudding into individual serving dishes and top with granola.

TO MAKE THE GRANOLA

1. Preheat oven to 350°F.

2. Line a baking sheet with parchment paper or a Silpat mat (see note).

3. In a large bowl, combine all granola ingredients.

4. Spread granola on baking sheet. Bake 15 to 20 minutes, or until golden brown, and let cool.

5. Serve with pudding or store in an airtight container and enjoy within 1 week.

NOTE: Silpat is a brand of nonstick baking mat that never needs to be greased and can be used instead of parchment paper.

APPLE CRISP

MAKES 6 SERVINGS

Although apple crisps are delicious served hot with melty vanilla ice cream for dessert, one of our favorite ways to enjoy them is with a generous drizzle of vanilla nondairy yogurt—especially if we're having it for breakfast.

APPLE MIXTURE
  6 medium-size apples, such as Granny Smith or Pink Lady, peeled, cored, and sliced
  ¾ cup coconut palm sugar
  1 teaspoon vanilla extract

TOPPING
  ½ cup gluten-free oat flour
  ¼ cup hemp seeds
  ¼ cup rolled gluten-free oats
  2 tablespoons neutral-tasting oil (canola, grapeseed, or sunflower)

1. Preheat oven to 400°F.
2. In a large bowl, combine apple slices with sugar and vanilla. Stir to mix well.
3. In a small bowl combine flour, hemp seeds, oats, and oil into a crumbly mixture for the topping.
4. Spread apple mixture into the bottom of a 1½- to 2-quart baking dish.
5. Crumble topping over apples.
6. Bake 40 minutes, or until the top is crispy and the juices are bubbly.

CHOCOLATE SUNFLOWER SEED BUTTER CHIA PUDDING

MAKES 4 SERVINGS

Cool, smooth chia puddings require no cooking, making them the perfect dessert choice for hot summer days. If you want an even smoother pudding, try using ground chia seeds.

  1 16-ounce container vanilla-flavored coconut-milk yogurt
  2 tablespoons sunflower seed butter
  2 tablespoons cocoa powder
  2 tablespoons chia seeds

1. Blend all ingredients together.
2. Spoon mixture into glasses.
3. Refrigerate for at least 1 hour and serve.

CRISPY RICE AND SEED CHOCOLATES

MAKES 12 LARGE CANDIES OR
24 SMALL CANDIES

Homemade chocolates are easy to make and can be customized for any occasion. Festive muffin or candy papers can be used in any standard or mini-muffin pan to make these delicious super-seed chocolates. Wrapped in a cellophane bag and tied with a colorful ribbon, they make a special gift.

1 cup chocolate chips
¼ cup popped amaranth (see page 521)
¼ cup sunflower seeds
½ cup crisp brown rice cereal

1. Line a standard muffin pan or mini muffin pan with muffin papers.

2. Heat chocolate chips over medium-low flame, stirring constantly until almost completely melted. Remove from heat and continue stirring until chocolate is completely melted.

3. Stir popped amaranth, sunflower seeds, and rice cereal into melted chocolate.

4. Use a tablespoon to fill a large muffin papers or a teaspoon to fill small muffin papers. Smooth mixture to fill paper cups evenly.

5. Refrigerate candies for at least 1½ hours.

INDEX